Cybersecurity Law

Cybersecurity Law

Second Edition

Jeff Kosseff

Registered Office
John Wiley & Sons, Inc., 111 River Street, Hoboken, NJ 07030, USA

Editorial Office
111 River Street, Hoboken, NJ 07030, USA

For details of our global editorial offices, customer services, and more information about Wiley products visit us at www.wiley.com.

Wiley also publishes its books in a variety of electronic formats and by print-on-demand. Some content that appears in standard print versions of this book may not be available in other formats.

Library of Congress Cataloging-in-Publication Data:

Names: Kosseff, Jeff, 1978- author.
Title: Cybersecurity law / Jeff Kosseff.
Description: Second edition. | Hoboken : Wiley, 2020. | Includes index.
Identifiers: LCCN 2019024454 (print) | LCCN 2019024455 (ebook) | ISBN
   9781119517207 (hardback) | ISBN 9781119517290 (adobe pdf) | ISBN
   9781119517320 (epub)
Subjects: LCSH: Data protection–Law and legislation–United States. |
   Computer security–Law and legislation–United States.
Classification: LCC KF1263.C65 K67 2020 (print) | LCC KF1263.C65 (ebook)
   | DDC 343.7309/99–dc23
LC record available at https://lccn.loc.gov/2019024454
LC ebook record available at https://lccn.loc.gov/2019024455

Cover image: © spainter_vfx/Shutterstock
Cover Design: Wiley

Set in 10/12pt Warnock Pro by SPi Global, Chennai, India

Printed in the United States of America

SKY10027842_062821

This book is dedicated to my two biggest supporters, my wife, Crystal Zeh, and my daughter, Julia Kosseff.

Contents

About the Author

Jeff Kosseff is an Assistant Professor of Cybersecurity Law in the Cyber Science Department at United States Naval Academy in Annapolis, Maryland. He has practiced cybersecurity and privacy law, and clerked for Judge Milan D. Smith, Jr. of the U.S. Court of Appeals for the Ninth Circuit and for Judge Leonie M. Brinkema of the U.S. District Court for the Eastern District of Virginia. Mr. Kosseff is a graduate of Georgetown University Law Center and the University of Michigan. Before becoming a lawyer, he was a journalist for *The Oregonian* and was a finalist for the Pulitzer Prize for national reporting.

Acknowledgment and Disclaimers

First and foremost, I'd like to thank my colleagues at the United States Naval Academy, and the hundreds of midshipmen whom I have taught in the Academy's cyber operations major. My daily discussions and debates with them have shaped how I think about the emerging field of cybersecurity law, and working with them every day is an inspiration.

Thanks to Wiley for seeing the need for a book that examines the many areas of the law that are related to the evolving world of cybersecurity.

I'd also like to thank the many people who have provided feedback, particularly as I have substantially revised the second edition of the book. They include Marc Blitz, Matt Bodman, Amit Elazari Bar On, Ashden Fein, Eric Goldman, Ido Kilovaty, Kurt Sanger, and Armin Tadayon. Special thanks to Brooke Graves for outstanding editing. Thanks to Liz Seif for excellent proofreading.

Any views expressed in this book are only my own, and do not represent the Naval Academy, Department of Navy, or Department of Defense. In this book, I present legal conclusions and facts as stated in judicial opinions and other court documents. By doing so, I am not necessarily endorsing those conclusions or factual claims.

This book is intended as a textbook and casebook for classes at the undergraduate, graduate, and law school levels, as well as a desk reference. However, due to the rapidly changing nature of cybersecurity law, this is not a substitute for legal advice or research on the current state of the law.

Foreword to the Second Edition (2019)

In the two years since the publication of the first edition of this book in early 2017, much has changed in the world of cybersecurity law. Legislators at the state, federal, and international levels enacted sweeping new laws to address cybersecurity. Courts issued significant new opinions in just about every area covered by the first edition. The U.S. government reorganized its civilian cybersecurity efforts amid unprecedented challenges.

I wrote the second edition to incorporate these new developments, and to make this book even more useful both in the classroom and in the workplace. Before I provide an overview of the changes to particular content, I'd like to highlight three significant additions to the book:

First, the book adds Appendix F, which includes 15 edited court opinions that cover the range of legal issues discussed in the text. I've been pleased to observe the number of professors in undergraduate, graduate, and law school programs who have assigned the book as a primary text. Some professors— particularly at the law school level—incorporate the case method into their teaching, in which their students learn about the legal rules by reading important statutes and court opinions and discussing them in class. Although the appendices to the first edition contained the text of some of the leading cybersecurity-related statutes, the first edition did not include the text of court opinions. Appendix F provides edited opinions that cover FTC data security authority, private data breach litigation, shareholder derivative data breach litigation, the Computer Fraud and Abuse Act, and the Fourth Amendment. By combining these edited cases with the narrative text, I hope that the book will be useful as both a traditional textbook and a casebook. The edited court opinions also will be useful to those using the book as a treatise, as it provides a more detailed look at some of the cases discussed in the main text.

Second, the new edition adds Chapter 11, which covers some aspects of the international law of cyberwarfare. As we have seen in the past few years, many cybersecurity threats have originated from state actors in other nations. This requires us to examine, under international law, what options a target country has to defend itself.

Third, Wiley offers a new, instructor-only website, which has suggested questions for class discussion, and model exam questions.

In addition to these three significant structural additions, the second edition adds new sections and substantively updates existing sections to incorporate the many new developments in cybersecurity law in the past few years. Among some of the additions and changes:

- **Chapter 1** adds new FTC data security enforcement actions, and the outcome of the LabMD litigation that challenged the FTC's data security enforcement authority. It also updates FTC guidance on data security practices, and new state data security laws. Since the first edition, Alabama, New Mexico, and South Dakota became the last of the 50 states to adopt data breach notification laws, and many states expanded their breach notice requirements. The new edition adds and updates the breach notification statute, and Appendix B summarizes all of these notification laws.
- **Chapter 2** incorporates many new court rulings on Article III standing in private data breach litigation, common claims in data breach lawsuits, and the attorney-client privilege in cybersecurity litigation.
- **Chapter 3** includes a new section on the New York Department of Financial Service's recently enacted cybersecurity regulations, which are among the most rigorous in the United States and affect a wide range of companies. It also adds sections on South Carolina's new cybersecurity requirements for insurance companies, and California's new Internet of Things cybersecurity law.
- **Chapter 4** discusses cybersecurity guidance for publicly traded companies that the Securities and Exchange Commission released in 2018, as well as the SEC's settlement with Yahoo over a massive data breach.
- **Chapter 5** adds a number of new Computer Fraud and Abuse Act cases, including the Ninth Circuit's second ruling in the landmark *United States v. Nosal*. It also includes new sections on bug bounty/vulnerability disclosure programs and the Budapest Convention on Cybercrime.
- **Chapter 6** describes the Department of Homeland Security's reorganization of its cybersecurity program, as well as the allocation of cybersecurity duties among federal departments under Presidential Policy Directive 41. It includes a new section about the November 2017 announcement of the federal government's vulnerability equities process.
- **Chapter 7** updates developments in Fourth Amendment caselaw, most notably the Supreme Court's 2018 opinion in *Carpenter v. United States*. The chapter also includes a new section on cases in which criminal suspects or defendants have claimed a Fifth Amendment self-incrimination privilege to challenge orders requiring them to assist law enforcement with accessing encrypted devices and computers. It also describes the Clarifying Lawful Overseas Use of Data (CLOUD) Act, which sets new rules for extraterritorial enforcement of Stored Communications Act orders.

- **Chapter 8** updates the cybersecurity requirements for federal government contractors, most notably the recently enacted regulations for the security of controlled unclassified information.
- **Chapter 9** examines the California Consumer Privacy Act, an extensive series of data protection rules enacted in 2018 and effective in 2020.
- **Chapter 10** expands the discussion of the European Union's General Data Protection Regulation, and examines China's new comprehensive cybersecurity law.

Introduction to First Edition

In recent years, cybersecurity has become not only a rapidly growing industry, but an increasingly vital consideration for nearly every company and government agency in the United States. A data breach can lead to high-stakes lawsuits, significant business disruptions, intellectual property theft, and national security vulnerabilities. Just ask any executive from Sony, Target, Home Depot, or the scores of other companies that experienced costly data breaches or the top officials at the U.S. Office of Personnel Management, which suffered a breach that exposed millions of federal workers' highly confidential security clearance applications. In short, it is abundantly clear that companies, governments, and individuals need to do more to improve cybersecurity.

Many articles and books have been written about the technical steps that are necessary to improve cybersecurity. However, there is much less material available about the legal rules that require—and, in some cases, restrict—specific cybersecurity measures. Legal obligations and restrictions should be considered at the outset of any cybersecurity strategy, just as a company would consider reputational harm and budgetary issues. Failure to comply with the law could lead to significant financial harms, negative publicity, and, in some cases, criminal charges.

Unfortunately, the United States does not have a single "cybersecurity law" that can easily apply to all circumstances. Rather, the United States has a patchwork of hundreds of state and federal statutes, regulations, binding guidelines, and court-created rules regarding data security, privacy, and other issues commonly considered to fall under the umbrella of "cybersecurity." On top of that, if U.S. companies have customers or employees in other countries, they must consider the privacy and data security laws and regulations of those nations.

This book aims to synthesize the cybersecurity laws that are most likely to affect U.S. corporate and government operations. The book is intended for a wide range of audiences that seek to learn more about cybersecurity law: undergraduate, graduate, and law school students; technology professionals; corporate executives; and lawyers. For lawyers who use this book as a reference treatise, this book contains detailed footnotes to the primary source materials, such as statutes and case citations. However, this book is not intended only for those with law degrees; it is written with the intent of being a guide for lawyers and nonlawyers alike. Similarly, in addition to being a desk reference, this book can be used as a primary or supplemental text in a cybersecurity law class.

The book focuses on the cybersecurity obligations of U.S. companies, but because cyberspace involves global private and public infrastructure, the book does not focus only on U.S. legal obligations of private companies. The book examines the efforts of the public sector and private sector to work together on cybersecurity, as well as the limits on government cyber operations under the U.S. Constitution and various statutes. Moreover, the book discusses some of the foreign cybersecurity laws that U.S. companies are most likely to encounter.

At the outset, it is important to define the term "cybersecurity law." Unlike more established legal fields, such as copyright, contracts, and torts, cybersecurity law is relatively new and not clearly defined. Indeed, some people think of cybersecurity law as consisting only of data security requirements for companies that are designed to reduce the likelihood of data breaches. Others think of cybersecurity law as anti-hacking laws. And to some, cybersecurity law is a subset of privacy law.

To all of those suggestions, I say "yes." Cybersecurity encompasses all of those subjects and more. The U.S. Department of Homeland Security's National Initiative for Cybersecurity Careers and Studies defines cybersecurity as "[t]he activity or process, ability or capability, or state whereby information and communications systems and the information contained therein are protected from and/or defended against damage, unauthorized use or modification, or exploitation." This definition is a good—and largely complete—starting point for the purposes of this book. The DHS definition captures the "CIA Triad"—confidentiality, integrity, and availability—that typically is associated with cybersecurity. Under this definition, we should be concerned with data security laws, data breach litigation, and anti-hacking laws. However, I have two additions to the DHS definition. First, it is impossible to fully evaluate cybersecurity without understanding the limits on the government's ability to conduct electronic surveillances. Accordingly, the Fourth Amendment to the U.S. Constitution and statutes that restrict government surveillance must be considered as part of an examination of cybersecurity law. Second, cybersecurity law is heavily intertwined with privacy law, which restricts the ability of companies and governments to collect, use, and disclose individuals' personal information.

To simplify, this book categorizes cybersecurity law as consisting of six broad areas of law:

- Private sector data security laws
- Anti-hacking laws

- Public–private cybersecurity efforts
- Government surveillance laws
- Cybersecurity requirements for government contractors
- Privacy law

Private Sector Data Security Laws (Chapters 1–4)

Among the most complex—and rapidly changing—areas of cybersecurity are the many requirements that apply to U.S. companies' handling of customers' and employees' personal data. A number of state and federal laws require companies to implement specific data security safeguards, and if a company faces a data breach, it may be required to notify customers, regulators, and credit bureaus. Breaches also could expose companies to costly regulatory actions and class action lawsuits.

Chapter 1 provides an overview of the state and federal laws that generally apply to data security and data breaches. Unlike other nations, the United States does not have a general law that imposes specific privacy and data security requirements on all companies. The closest analogue in the United States is Section 5 of the Federal Trade Commission Act, which prohibits unfair and deceptive trade practices. Chapter 1 examines dozens of complaints that the Federal Trade Commission has filed under this statute arising from allegedly inadequate data security. The chapter next examines the laws in nearly every state that require companies to notify regulators, customers, and credit bureaus of data breaches in certain circumstances. Finally, the chapter examines the dozen state laws that impose specific data security requirements for personal information.

Chapter 2 examines the various types of private class action lawsuits that companies could face after they experience data breaches. First, the chapter examines a concept known as Article III standing, which is among the most significant barriers to plaintiffs' lawsuits arising from data breaches. In short, Article III standing requires that plaintiffs demonstrate that they suffered an injury-in-fact that is fairly traceable to the defendant's conduct and redressable by a lawsuit. Courts are divided as to what types of injuries a data breach plaintiff must demonstrate to have Article III standing. The chapter then reviews common legal claims that arise from data breaches, including negligence, misrepresentation, breach of contract, invasion of privacy, unjust enrichment, and state consumer protection laws. The chapter also reviews the procedural requirements that data breach plaintiffs must satisfy to be permitted to sue on behalf of a larger class of plaintiffs. It examines whether commercial insurance coverage helps cover companies' liability in data breach lawsuits. Finally, the chapter examines how companies can reduce the likelihood that their internal cybersecurity communications and reports will be subject to discovery and used against them in litigation.

Chapter 3 examines the additional data security requirements that U.S. companies face if they handle particularly sensitive personal information. The Gramm-Leach-Bliley Act requires financial institutions to adopt specific security safeguards for customers' nonpublic financial information. The Payment Card Industry Data Security Standard contractually imposes data security safeguards for companies that handle credit and debit card information. Doctors, health insurers, and other healthcare companies and their business associates face stringent data security requirements under the Health Insurance Portability and Accountability Act. Finally, the chapter examines the cybersecurity requirements for electric utilities and nuclear licensees.

Chapter 4 provides an overview of data security requirements that affect corporations. The Securities and Exchange Commission expects publicly traded companies to disclose material risks, and in recent years, it has urged companies to be transparent about their cybersecurity vulnerabilities and explain how those vulnerabilities might affect shareholders. This chapter examines the level of disclosure that the SEC expects in publicly traded companies' public filings, and provides examples of various levels of transparency and disclosure. The chapter also examines the possibility of shareholders suing executives and directors if the company experiences a costly data breach. Next, the chapter explores the cybersecurity expectations of the Committee on Foreign Investment in the United States, which must approve any foreign investments in U.S. companies. Finally, the chapter examines how the ongoing debate over corporate export controls could make it more difficult for U.S. companies to conduct cybersecurity research.

Anti-Hacking Laws (Chapter 5)

Anti-hacking laws—notably the federal Computer Fraud and Abuse Act (CFAA)—are intended to help promote cybersecurity. However, some critics argue that these laws are outdated and not only fail to help protect private and government computers but also penalize individuals for conducting entirely legitimate activities, such as cybersecurity research.

Chapter 5 reviews the seven offenses that are prohibited by the CFAA, such as hacking computers to obtain information and damaging computers. The CFAA applies to activities that are conducted "without authorization" or "exceed[ing] authorized access," and the chapter examines how different courts have applied these rather ambiguous terms. The chapter briefly reviews state hacking laws that are based on the CFAA. The chapter then examines Section 1201 of the Digital Millennium Copyright Act, which restricts the ability of individuals to circumvent access controls that protect copyrighted material, and therefore imposes significant limits on cybersecurity vulnerability research. Finally, the chapter examines the Economic Espionage Act, a criminal law that companies increasingly see as a tool to penalize individuals that steal trade secrets. In 2016, Congress amended the Economic Espionage Act to allow companies to file civil lawsuits against hackers and others who steal trade secrets.

Public–Private Security Efforts (Chapter 6)

Cybersecurity law often is associated with punitive measures, such as FTC investigations and data breach class action lawsuits. While those considerations surely are an important component of cybersecurity law, the federal government also has taken a number of proactive steps to work with companies to improve cybersecurity throughout the public and private sectors. Such collaboration is particularly necessary and common in cybersecurity because public and private cyber infrastructure often is interconnected.

Chapter 6 provides an overview of the organization of the federal government's cybersecurity efforts, with the Department of Homeland Security taking an increasingly large and central role in the government's collaboration with the private sector. The chapter examines private–public information sharing, which likely will expand due to the Cybersecurity Act of 2015. The chapter examines the National Institute of Standards and Technology's 2014 cybersecurity framework, which many companies voluntarily adopt as the basis of their own cybersecurity plans. Finally, the chapter briefly examines the U.S. military's involvement with private sector cybersecurity, and the limits imposed by the Posse Comitatus Act.

Government Surveillance Laws (Chapter 7)

Government surveillance laws often restrict the government's ability to increase the security of cyberspace. By "security," what is meant is more than merely preventing the transmission of malware and other harmful programs. Security also encompasses government efforts to fight cybercrime, such as child pornography, terrorist recruitment, and other harmful online activities. The government—and, in some cases, the private sector—often is restricted by constitutional provisions and statutes.

Chapter 7 begins with an examination of how the Fourth Amendment's prohibition on unreasonable searches and seizures applies to electronic surveillance. The chapter then examines the Electronic Communications Privacy Act, a comprehensive statute that limits the ability of the government to obtain stored communications, use wiretaps to obtain data in transit, and obtain metadata via pen registers. The chapter further examines the government's ability to issue National Security Letters to obtain certain information regarding electronic communications, and the obligations of communications companies to assist law enforcement under the Communications Assistance for Law Enforcement Act. The chapter concludes with an examination of law enforcement's attempts, using the All Writs Act, to compel technology companies to help them access encrypted communications.

Cybersecurity Requirements for Government Contractors (Chapter 8)

Many small and large companies rely on the federal government as a significant client for a wide range of products and services. Increasingly, the federal government is expecting these companies to implement specific standards for cybersecurity.

Chapter 8 examines the key cybersecurity requirements for U.S. government contractors. First, the chapter examines the Federal Information Security Management Act (FISMA), the primary statute that governs data security for the federal government and its contractors. The chapter next provides an overview of the information security controls that the National Institute of Standards and Technology has developed for government agencies and their contractors as part of FISMA. The chapter then examines specific cybersecurity requirements for government contractors that handle classified information, controlled unclassified information, and covered defense information.

Privacy Law (Chapter 9)

Any examination of cybersecurity law would be incomplete without an overview of privacy law. Privacy law restricts the ability of companies to use, share, collect, and retain personal information. While data security laws traditionally focus on the measures that companies take to prevent unauthorized access to information, privacy laws restrict the ability of companies to voluntarily use or disclose customers' personal information. Privacy law should be considered alongside data security and other cybersecurity laws because they form a company's overall approach to handling personal information. Moreover, a company's statements about its data security in its privacy policy can lead to significant liability under various privacy laws.

Chapter 9 begins with an overview of the FTC's approach to privacy regulation. As with data security, the FTC uses Section 5 of the Federal Trade Commission Act to bring complaints against companies that violate their consumers' privacy rights or fail to meet the guarantees of their privacy policies.

The chapter then examines the privacy laws that restrict healthcare providers and insurers and financial institutions. The chapter describes the CAN-SPAM Act, which limits the ability of companies to send email marketing materials. It explores the Video Privacy Protection Act, which restricts the ability of companies to share online and offline video viewing information, and the Children's Online Privacy Protection Act, which limits the collection of information from children under 13 years old. Finally, the chapter examines state laws in California and Illinois that require website privacy policies, require the deletion of certain information provided by minors, and restrict the use of biometric information, including facial recognition.

Chapters 1 through 9 therefore focus primarily on the U.S. federal and state cybersecurity laws that bind U.S. companies. However, very few U.S. companies can operate without considering the cybersecurity requirements of other countries. If the companies have employees, customers, or business partners in other countries, they may also be bound by those countries' cybersecurity laws. And many countries—particularly those in the European Union—have enacted privacy and data security laws that are much more restrictive than those in the United States. For that reason, Chapter 10 examines the primary privacy and data security legal requirements of the five largest trading partners of the United States: the European Union, Canada, Mexico, China, and Japan.

As with all emerging areas of the law, cybersecurity law is rapidly evolving. At any time, legislatures, regulators, and courts may change some of the laws that are described in this book. Accordingly, this book is not intended to be a substitute for legal advice from qualified counsel.

Cybersecurity law is a complex, nascent, and rapidly changing field. As we continue to define and build this exciting new area of law, this book attempts to provide a reference for students, lawyers, information technology professionals, and others who are interested in helping companies and government agencies improve the security of their computers, systems, and networks.

About the Companion Website

This book is accompanied by a companion website:
www.wiley.com/go/kosseff/cybersecurity2e

The website includes materials for Instructors and Students

Instructors:

- Suggested points of discussion for the class discussion questions at the end of each chapter
- Bank of potential exam questions

Students:

- News updates
- New cybersecurity laws
- Recent cybersecurity policy developments

1

Data Security Laws and Enforcement Actions

The United States does not have a national law that explicitly prescribes specific data security standards for all industries. The only explicit *federal* data security laws apply to companies that handle specific types of data, such as financial information or health records (discussed in Chapter 3). This comes as a surprise to many, and is frustrating to businesses that want to assure customers and regulators that they comply with all legal requirements, particularly for securing customers' personal information. Likewise, consumer advocates and privacy groups criticize the federal government for failing to enact data security requirements. In recent years, members of Congress and the White House have introduced legislation to set minimum data security standards, but, as of publication of this book, Congress has not enacted any such legislation.

Despite the lack of a statute that sets minimum data security requirements, the Federal Trade Commission (FTC) aggressively polices data security. In recent years, the FTC has brought dozens of enforcement actions against companies that it believes have failed to take reasonable steps to secure the personal data of their customers. The FTC brings these actions under Section 5 of the FTC Act, a century-old law that was designed to protect consumers and competitors from unfair or deceptive business practices. Although the law does not explicitly address cybersecurity, it is one of the primary tools that the government uses to bring enforcement actions against companies that failed to take adequate steps to protect consumer information.

This chapter provides an overview of data security requirements under Section 5 of the FTC Act, as well as under state data security laws and private tort claims.

First, we examine what the FTC considers to constitute "unfair" or "deceptive" trade practices that violate Section 5. Next, we pay special attention to challenges to the FTC's cybersecurity authority. These challenges have been

Cybersecurity Law, Second Edition. Jeff Kosseff.
© 2020 John Wiley & Sons, Inc. Published 2020 by John Wiley & Sons, Inc.
Companion Website: www.wiley.com/go/kosseff/cybersecurity2e

raised by two companies, Wyndham Worldwide Resorts and LabMD, and we conclude that, for now, it is largely accepted that the FTC has some authority to bring Section 5 complaints against companies that fail to adequately secure customer data, though judges may impose some limits on this authority. We then review how the FTC has applied that reasoning to cybersecurity, both in guidance and the dozens of complaints that it has filed against companies that allegedly failed to adequately secure personal information.

After reviewing the FTC's data security guidance and enforcement actions, we review the laws of 50 states and the District of Columbia that require companies to notify individuals, regulators, and credit bureaus after certain types of personal information are disclosed in a data breach. These laws are fairly complex, and the notification requirements vary by state. Failure to comply with the requirements in each of these statutes could lead to significant regulatory penalties and, in some cases, private lawsuits.

This chapter also provides an overview of the state laws that require companies to implement reasonable data security programs and policies, and the state laws that require companies to securely dispose of personal information.

1.1 FTC Data Security

The FTC is the closest thing that the U.S. federal government has to a centralized data security regulator. Many other agencies—including the Department of Health and Human Services, Education Department, and Federal Communications Commission—have jurisdiction to regulate privacy and data security for particular sectors. However, only the FTC has the authority to regulate companies in a wide range of sectors, provided that they engage in interstate commerce.

1.1.1 Overview of Section 5 of the FTC Act

The FTC claims its data security authority under Section 5 of the Federal Trade Commission Act,[1] which declares illegal "unfair or deceptive acts or practices in or affecting commerce."[2] The statute does not explicitly mention data security.

In 1983, the FTC released a policy statement that elaborates on the elements necessary for it to bring a case against a company for violating the "deception"

---

1 For the full text of § 5, *see* app. A.
2 15 U.S.C. § 45(a)(1).

prong of Section 5. These factors are general and not unique to data security actions:

> First, there must be a representation, omission or practice that is likely to mislead the consumer. Practices that have been found misleading or deceptive in specific cases include false oral or written representations, misleading price claims, sales of hazardous or systematically defective products or services without adequate disclosures, failure to disclose information regarding pyramid sales, use of bait and switch techniques, failure to perform promised services, and failure to meet warranty obligations.
>
> Second, we examine the practice from the perspective of a consumer acting reasonably in the circumstances. If the representation or practice affects or is directed primarily to a particular group, the Commission examines reasonableness from the perspective of that group.
>
> Third, the representation, omission, or practice must be a "material" one. The basic question is whether the act or practice is likely to affect the consumer's conduct or decision with regard to a product or service. If so, the practice is material, and consumer injury is likely, because consumers are likely to have chosen differently but for the deception. In many instances, materiality, and hence injury, can be presumed from the nature of the practice. In other instances, evidence of materiality may be necessary.[3]

The FTC will bring data security-related claims against companies under the "deception" prong if they have misrepresented their security practices.[4] For instance, if a company were to state in its privacy policy that "we guarantee absolute security of your data and we promise we will never have a data breach," and that company subsequently experienced a breach, the FTC might assert that the privacy policy was deceptive.

The FTC also has increasingly claimed authority for data security enforcement actions under the "unfairness" prong of Section 5.[5] Throughout the 1960s and 1970s, the FTC was criticized for arbitrarily issuing unfairness rulings when determining whether a practice is unfair. The Commission considered:

> (1) whether the practice, without necessarily having been previously considered unlawful, offends public policy as it has been

---

3 FTC Policy Statement on Deception (Oct. 14, 1983).
4 *See, e.g.,* Complaint at 3–5, *In re* Upromise, FTC File No. 102-3116, No. C-4351, 2012 WL 1225058 (F.T.C. Mar. 27, 2012).
5 For additional history of the FTC's "unfairness" authority under Section 5, see part I.A. of *FTC v. Wyndham,* 799 F.3d 236 (3d Cir. 2015), in app. F of this book.

established by statutes, the common law, or otherwise—whether, in other words, it is within at least the penumbra of some common-law, statutory, or other established concept of unfairness; (2) whether it is immoral, unethical, oppressive, or unscrupulous; (3) whether it causes substantial injury to consumers (or competitors or other businessmen).[6]

This three-part test became known as the Cigarette Rule because the Commission articulated the rule as it was considering how to regulate cigarette advertising. Although the FTC did not frequently use this authority, the United States Supreme Court quoted it in 1972, describing the three prongs as "the factors [the FTC] considers in determining whether a practice that is neither in violation of the antitrust laws nor deceptive is nonetheless unfair."[7]

The FTC recognized the need to clarify the Cigarette Rule to focus more specifically on the injury to customers and benefits to society, rather than judgments about whether the practice "offends public policy," is immoral, or is unscrupulous. In 1980, the Commission issued the Unfairness Policy Statement, which the Commission claimed provides a "more detailed sense of both the definition and the limits of these criteria."[8] The statement articulates a three-part test for unfairness claims: (1) "the injury must be substantial," (2) "the injury must not be outweighed by any offsetting consumer or competitive benefits that the sales practice also produces," and (3) "the injury must be one which consumers could not reasonably have avoided."[9]

In 1994, Congress amended the FTC Act to codify the 1980 Unfairness Policy Statement into law, becoming Section 5(n) of the FTC Act. The statute states that "unfair" practices are those that cause or are likely to cause "substantial injury to consumers which is not reasonably avoidable by consumers themselves and not outweighed by countervailing benefits to consumers or to competition."[10] This causes the FTC (and courts) to apply the three-part test of the 1980 Unfairness Policy Statement:

First, has the trade practice caused or is likely to cause *substantial* injury to customers? In other words, a minor injury will not constitute an unfair trade practice. The FTC has stated that a substantial injury often "involves monetary harm, as when sellers coerce consumers into purchasing unwanted goods or services or when consumers buy defective goods or services on credit but are unable to assert against the creditor claims or defenses arising from the

---

6 Unfair or Deceptive Advertising and Labeling of Cigarettes in Relation to the Health Hazards of Smoking, 16 C.F.R. 408, 29 Fed. Reg. 8344 (July 2, 1964).
7 FTC v. Sperry & Hutchinson Co., 405 U.S. 233 (1972).
8 FTC Policy Statement on Unfairness, Appended to International Harvester Co., 104 F.T.C. 949, 1070 (1984) [hereinafter FTC Unfairness Policy Statement].
9 *Id.*
10 15 U.S.C. § 45(n).

transaction."[11] Emotional harm, and nothing more, likely will not constitute unfairness, according to the Commission.[12] In the cybersecurity world, this means that a company is more likely to face an FTC action if the Commission finds that a data breach led to actual consumer harm, such as identity theft. Absent such actual harm, the FTC is less likely to bring an action for a data breach.

Second, do benefits to consumers outweigh the injury?[13] The FTC states that it "will not find that a practice unfairly injures consumers unless it is injurious in its net effects."[14] The Commission states that it considers "the various costs that a remedy would entail," including:

- direct costs to the parties;
- paperwork;
- restrictions on information flows;
- reduced innovation; and
- restrictions on capital formation.

This means that if a company suffers a data breach that leads to substantial consumer injury, a company may be able to avoid an FTC action if the company can demonstrate that it would have been very difficult for the company to avoid the data breach. Note that this is a very high bar; a company cannot merely argue that cybersecurity safeguards were too expensive. The company must be able to demonstrate that either the remedy would have been impossible or the costs would have been so high that customers would have suffered even more than they did because of the data breach.

Third, the Commission considers whether consumers, exercising reasonable care, could have avoided the injury in the first place.[15] This prong reflects the FTC's market-based approach to consumer protection. The Commission states that it relies on "consumer choice—the ability of individual consumers to make their own private purchasing decisions without regulatory intervention."[16] The Commission becomes more likely to find a practice to be unfair if the consumer was unable to reasonably avoid the harm.[17] Applying this to cybersecurity, the

---

11 FTC Unfairness Policy Statement.

12 *Id.*

13 *Id.*

14 *Id.*

15 *Id.*

16 *Id.*

17 *Id.* ("[I]t has long been recognized that certain types of sales techniques may prevent consumers from effectively making their own decisions, and that corrective action may then become necessary. Most of the Commission's unfairness matters are brought under these circumstances. They are brought, not to second-guess the wisdom of particular consumer decisions, but rather to halt some form of seller behavior that unreasonably creates or takes advantage of an obstacle to the free exercise of consumer decisionmaking.").

FTC is less likely to take action against a company for a breach or other attack if customers could have taken simple steps to avoid harm. For instance, if a single customer's failure to install updates on an operating system led to a virus that deleted all of the customer's files from the hard drive, the FTC is not likely to bring an action against the maker of the operating system. In contrast, the FTC would be more likely to bring an action against a company whose internal servers were hacked, leading to disclosure of the customer's personal financial information and, subsequently, identity theft. In that circumstance, it is difficult to imagine how the customer could have reasonably avoided the harm.

The FTC has not issued binding regulations that explain how these three principles apply to cybersecurity. That has led a number of businesses, commentators, and industry groups to criticize the agency for failing to provide concrete standards.[18] After all, they argue, a company will be more hesitant to invest significant time, money, and resources in cybersecurity measures if it is not even sure whether these investments would satisfy the FTC's expectations. The FTC and its defenders, however, argue that cybersecurity is not a one-size-fits-all solution, and a company's safeguards should depend on its unique needs. For instance, a hospital likely stores vast amounts of highly confidential medical data; thus, it might be expected to take greater security precautions than a company that does not typically process or store personal information. Likewise, if a company has experienced a cybersecurity incident, it would be on notice of such vulnerabilities and expected to take reasonable steps to prevent future incidents.

1.1.2 *Wyndham*: Does the FTC Have Authority to Regulate Data Security under Section 5 of the FTC Act?

An August 2015 opinion from the U.S. Court of Appeals for the Third Circuit—arising from a cybersecurity complaint that the FTC filed against the Wyndham hotel chain—is the most important court decision to date involving the Commission's cybersecurity authority. In short, the opinion provides the most compelling authority for the Commission to use Section 5 to bring cases against companies that have failed to adequately secure personal information.

Up to this point, the FTC's regulation of privacy and data security had been a source of frustration for many companies. As discussed earlier, Congress has

---

18 *See, e.g.,* Geoffrey A. Manne & Kristian Stout, *When "Reasonable" Isn't: The FTC's Standardless Data Security Standard*, 15 J. L., Econ. & Pol'y 67, 117 (2018) ("The FTC aims to develop its data security enforcement practices as a kind of common law, and this is a laudable goal. But the procedural and substantive problems with its enforcement of data security cases to date provides the worst of both worlds: cases are brought under the opaque preferences of regulators, with the final results of such enforcement actions published to the world in allegedly binding 'precedent' that actually contains none of the necessary connections between conduct and injury sufficient to guide actors in the economy at large.").

not passed a statute that explicitly provides the FTC with the general authority to regulate cybersecurity. Instead, the FTC claims that inadequate data security may constitute an unfair or deceptive trade practice under Section 5 of the FTC Act, which Congress initially passed more than a century ago.

Although some commentators have long questioned the FTC's cybersecurity authority, it typically has been widely accepted. In the vast majority of cases, if the FTC threatens to file a lawsuit against a company arising from allegedly inadequate cybersecurity, the company agrees to a consent order. Although the terms vary by company, the orders generally require companies to develop comprehensive information security programs, obtain periodic independent assessments of their information security, and provide the FTC with broad oversight and access into the company's programs for up to 20 years. Failure to adhere to the order can result in significant fines. Despite the potential for draconian penalties, companies generally do not risk the adverse publicity and costs of challenging the FTC's findings in court, and instead agree to a consent order.

Wyndham Worldwide Corporation, a hotel chain, decided to be among the first companies to mount a serious challenge to the FTC's cybersecurity enforcement authority.[19] In 2008 and 2009, hackers stole hundreds of thousands of Wyndham customers' financial information and charged more than $10 million to consumer accounts.[20] After investigating the breaches, the FTC claimed that Wyndham failed to take numerous steps to safeguard customer information, leading to the compromises. Patent among the failures that the FTC cited were:

- storing credit card data in clear text;
- allowing simple passwords for the systems that store the sensitive data;
- failure to use firewalls and other "readily available security measures";
- failure to adequately oversee the cybersecurity of hotels that connect to Wyndham's central servers;
- allowing vendors to have unnecessarily broad access to Wyndham servers; and
- failure to take "reasonable measures" for security investigations or incident response.[21]

Altogether, the FTC alleged that these failures constituted unfair trade practices that violated Section 5 of the FTC Act. Rather than agree to a consent order, Wyndham allowed the FTC to file a lawsuit against the company in federal court. Wyndham moved to dismiss the lawsuit, arguing, among other things, that Section 5 does not provide the FTC with the authority to bring cybersecurity-related actions against companies.[22] The gravamen of Wyndham's

---

19 FTC v. Wyndham Worldwide Corp., 799 F.3d 236 (3d Cir. 2015).
20 *Id.* at 240.
21 *Id.* at 240–41.
22 *Id.* at 242.

argument was that Congress has addressed data security in industry-specific statutes for healthcare, banking, and credit reporting, and therefore, if Congress had intended to provide the FTC with the authority to regulate data security for all businesses, it would have explicitly granted the Commission such power. The district court disagreed and denied the motion to dismiss, holding that "the FTC's unfairness authority over data security can coexist with the existing data-security regulatory scheme."[23] Soon after the ruling, the district court granted Wyndham's request for the U.S. Court of Appeals for the Third Circuit to review its ruling. This was particularly significant because, until that point, no federal appellate court had ever ruled whether the FTC has the authority to bring cybersecurity-related actions.

After hearing oral argument, the Third Circuit, in August 2015, issued a 47-page opinion in which it upheld the district court and ruled that the "unfairness" prong of Section 5 provides the Commission with the authority to regulate data security. Although the court's ruling is only binding in the Third Circuit—Delaware, New Jersey, Pennsylvania, and the U.S. Virgin Islands—it was widely seen as an affirmation of the FTC's jurisdiction over cybersecurity.

Relying on dictionary definitions, Wyndham argued that "unfair" conditions only exist if they are "not equitable" or are "marked by injustice, partiality, or deception."[24] The Third Circuit declined to rule whether such traits are necessary to demonstrate unfairness; it concluded that a company "does not act equitably when it publishes a privacy policy to attract customers who are concerned about data privacy, fails to make good on that promise by investing inadequate resources in cybersecurity, exposes its unsuspecting customers to substantial financial injury, and retains the profits of their business."[25]

Wyndham also argued that a business "does not treat its customers in an 'unfair' manner when the business *itself is* victimized by criminals."[26] The Third Circuit rejected this argument, concluding that the fact "that a company's conduct was not *the most* proximate cause of an injury does not immunize liability from foreseeable harms."[27] The Court noted that Wyndham did not argue that the breaches were unforeseeable, a stance that the Court believed "would be particularly implausible as to the second and third attacks."[28]

The Third Circuit also gave little weight to Wyndham's argument that allowing the lawsuit to proceed would effectively provide the FTC with unlimited authority under the unfairness prong. Wyndham argued that such a result would mean that the Commission could use Section 5 to "regulate the locks on hotel

---

23 FTC v. Wyndham Worldwide Corp., 10 F. Supp. 3d 602, 613 (D.N.J. 2014).
24 FTC v. Wyndham Worldwide Corp., 799 F.3d 236, 245 (3d Cir. 2015).
25 *Id.*
26 *Id.* at 246.
27 *Id.*
28 *Id.*

room doors, ... to require every store in the land to post an armed guard at the door, and to sue supermarkets that are sloppy about sweeping up banana peels."[29] The Court dismissed this argument as "alarmist," noting that "were Wyndham a supermarket, leaving so many banana peels all over the place that 619,000 customers fall hardly suggests it should be immune" from a Section 5 action.[30]

Like the district court, the Third Circuit disagreed with Wyndham's argument that Congress's passage of data security laws for banking, credit reporting, and other specific sectors demonstrates that the FTC does not have general authority over cybersecurity. The FTC noted that many of these laws focus on the *collection* of data, and do not conflict with regulation of the data *security*.[31]

In addition to arguing that the FTC lacked the statutory authority to bring general data security enforcement actions, Wyndham also asserted that the FTC's action violates the Due Process Clause of the U.S. Constitution because it failed "to provide a person of ordinary intelligence fair notice of what is prohibited, or is so standardless that it authorizes or encourages seriously discriminatory enforcement."[32] As the Third Circuit accurately summarized, Wyndham's position is that "the FTC has not yet declared that cybersecurity practices can be unfair; there is no relevant FTC rule, adjudication or document that merits deference; and the FTC is asking the federal courts to interpret [Section 5 of the FTC Act] in the first instance to decide whether it prohibits the alleged conduct here."[33]

The Third Circuit concluded that Wyndham was only entitled to "fair notice that its conduct could fall within the meaning of the statute," and it was not entitled "to know with ascertainable certainty the FTC's interpretation of what cybersecurity practices are required" by Section 5 of the FTC Act.[34] The Third Circuit concluded that Wyndham had such notice, as the Commission, for years, had filed complaints arising from similar data security practices.[35]

Rather than asking all the judges on the Third Circuit to review the opinion *en banc*, or request the United States Supreme Court to hear the case, in December 2015 Wyndham settled the charges with the FTC. Wyndham agreed to implement a companywide data security program, undergo extensive payment card security audits, and take other precautions.[36] The order is in place for 20 years, as is standard for FTC data security settlements.

---

29 *Id.* at 246–47.
30 *Id.* at 247.
31 *Id.* at 248.
32 *Id.* at 249, quoting FCC v. Fox Television Stations, 132 S. Ct. 2307, 2317 (2012).
33 *Id.* at 253.
34 *Id.* at 255.
35 *Id.* at 257–58.
36 Press Release, Federal Trade Commission, Wyndham Settles FTC Charges It Unfairly Placed Consumers' Payment Card Information at Risk (Dec. 9, 2015).

Although the *Wyndham* case has settled—and likely will not reappear unless the Commission alleges that Wyndham has violated its consent order—the impact of this case cannot be understated. Even though the ruling is only binding in the Third Circuit, it is the only federal appellate court ruling to consider whether the FTC has general data security enforcement authority. The ruling was a significant boost to the FTC's position that Section 5 allows it to regulate cybersecurity.

The ruling also led opponents to bolster their criticisms of the FTC. While there is little dispute that private sector cybersecurity needs government support *and* regulation, a number of critics question whether an agency tasked with antitrust and consumer protection is the best equipped to carry out that mission.[37] Unless the Supreme Court overrules the Third Circuit's ruling, it is likely that the FTC's role as the de facto regulator of private sector data security will become more entrenched.

1.1.3 LabMD: What Constitutes "Unfair" Data Security?

In the only other significant challenge to the FTC's cybersecurity enforcement authority, LabMD, a medical testing laboratory, convinced an FTC administrative law judge to rule that the Commission's lawyers had failed to demonstrate that the company's allegedly inadequate data security safeguards had caused or were likely to cause substantial injury to the company's consumers. However, in July 2016, the full Federal Trade Commission reversed the judge's ruling, in a significant victory for data security regulators. A federal appellate court in 2018 overturned the FTC's order, finding that it failed to articulate clear standards for compliance.

In the LabMD case, the FTC's complaint focused on two data security incidents at the company. The first incident arose from a report by a third party that a LabMD insurance aging report containing personal information of more than 9,000 patients had been made public on a peer-to-peer network in 2008.[38] In the second incident, in 2012, documents containing personal information (including names and Social Security numbers) were found in the possession of unauthorized individuals.[39]

---

37 *See, e.g.,* Paul Rosenzweig, *The FTC Takes Charge*—FTC v. Wyndham, Lawfare (Aug. 26, 2015) ("All of this means that the FTC now owns cybersecurity in the private sector. Which is an odd result. One would surely have thought that DHS (or DoD or DOJ or even the Department of Commerce) would have had a more salient role in defining standards for the private sector. But somehow, we've converted a consumer protection mandate into a cybersecurity obligation and assigned that role to an independent agency. Candidly, I don't think the FTC is up to the task—not in terms of staffing nor in terms of expertise—but we will soon see how that turns out.").

38 *In re* LabMD Inc., No. 9537 (FTC Administrative Law Judge Nov. 13, 2015), at 1–2.

39 *Id.* at 2.

The Commission alleged in its complaint that these two security incidents were due to a number of failures to take adequate safeguards, including:

- developing an information security program;
- identifying risks;
- preventing LabMD employees from unnecessarily accessing personal information;
- training employees regarding information security;
- requiring common authentication security for remote access to LabMD's network;
- maintaining and updating LabMD operating systems; and
- employing "readily available" prevention and detection measures.[40]

The FTC administrative law judge (ALJ) collected extensive evidence, and ultimately granted LabMD's motion to dismiss the complaint. The ALJ focused on Section 5(n)'s requirement that the trade practice cause or be likely to cause substantial injury to customers. The ALJ ruled that the section "is clear that finding of actual or likely substantial consumer injury, which is also not reasonably avoidable by consumers themselves and not outweighed by countervailing benefits to consumers or to competition, is a legal precondition to finding a respondent liable for unfair conduct."[41] The ALJ concluded that the preponderance of the evidence did not show that LabMD's "alleged unreasonable data security caused, or is likely to cause, substantial consumer injury."[42]

The FTC lawyers argued that even though there was not *actual* harm due to identity theft, Section 5(n) also allows actions based on "likely" harm. The ALJ, however, concluded that the failure to produce any evidence of consumer harm, "even after the passage of many years," undermined this argument.[43] After reviewing extensive Section 5 case law, the ALJ concluded that there is no known case in which "unfair conduct liability has been imposed without proof of actual harm, on the basis of predicted 'likely' harm alone."[44]

The ALJ's LabMD ruling is important to data security because it stands for the proposition that the mere threat of identity theft after a data breach is not sufficient grounds for a Section 5 claim. This ruling, if it had become binding law, could have made it significantly harder for the FTC to bring cases under Section 5.

Accordingly, consumer and privacy advocates were relieved on July 29, 2016, when the full Federal Trade Commission reversed the ALJ's dismissal of charges against LabMD. The Commission's unanimous ruling was not entirely surprising,

---

40 *Id.*
41 *Id.* at 48.
42 *Id.* at 49.
43 *Id.* at 52.
44 *Id.* at 53.

as the commissioners had long defended the Commission's authority to regulate data security under Section 5. In its opinion, the Commission wrote that a demonstration of a "significant risk" of injury is sufficient to meet Section 5's "likely to cause" requirement.[45] Exposing sensitive personal information of millions of people via peer-to-peer networking, the Commission reasoned, creates a significant risk of injury and therefore satisfies this requirement.[46] "The ALJ's reasoning comes perilously close to reading the term 'likely' out of the statute," the Commission wrote in its opinion rejecting the ALJ's ruling. "When evaluating a practice, we judge the likelihood that the practice will cause harm at the time the practice occurred, not on the basis of actual future outcomes. This is particularly true in the data security context. Consumers typically have no way of finding out that their personal information has been part of a data breach."[47] The Commission issued a cease-and-desist order requiring LabMD to adopt a data security program that is "reasonably designed to protect the security, confidentiality, and integrity of personal information collected from or about consumers."[48]

LabMD appealed to the United States Court of Appeals for the Eleventh Circuit, which in June 2018 vacated the FTC's cease-and-desist order. The Eleventh Circuit did not base its decision on whether the FTC had jurisdiction to bring data security actions under Section 5. Rather, the court concluded that the FTC's edict for a "reasonably designed" data security program was impermissibly vague. "In the case at hand, the cease and desist order contains no prohibitions," Judge Gerald Tjoflat wrote for the three-judge panel. "It does not instruct LabMD to stop committing a specific act or practice. Rather, it commands LabMD to overhaul and replace its data-security program to meet an indeterminable standard of reasonableness. This command is unenforceable."[49]

In an analysis of the Eleventh Circuit's opinion, Joseph Jerome of the Center for Democracy and Technology speculated that the decision could further weaken the FTC's ability to bring data security actions. "Moving forward, the FTC will need to provide much more detail into exactly what constitutes unacceptable data security practices," Jerome wrote. "The likely vehicle for doing this will be to look to existing industry standards as a baseline, encourage companies to be more explicit in what steps they actually take to protect information, and then use the FTC's ability to police deceptive statements as an enforcement tool."[50]

---

45 *In re* LabMD Inc., No. 9537 (Commission Opinion and Order, July 29, 2016), at 21.
46 *Id.*
47 *Id.* at 23.
48 *Id.* at 1.
49 LabMD, Inc. v. FTC, 891 F.3d 1286, 1300 (11th Cir. 2018).
50 Joseph Jerome, *Eleventh Circuit Decision for LabMD Reshapes 'Reasonable Data Security,'* Center for Democracy and Technology, https://cdt.org/blog/eleventh-circuit-decision-for-labmd-reshapes-reasonable-data-security/ (June 7, 2018).

The Eleventh Circuit's opinion was a significant setback for the FTC, which had long relied on such broadly worded orders that require companies to adopt reasonably designed data security programs. Although the decision did not undercut the FTC's jurisdiction over data security, it called into question one of the Commission's commonly used tools for enforcement.

1.1.4   FTC June 2015 Guidance on Data Security, and 2017 Updates

In the face of criticism that it did not clearly articulate the standards to which it holds companies for data security, in June 2015, the FTC released a highly publicized document, *Start with Security: A Guide for Business*.[51] The guide was not formally approved by the Commission as a regulation, and therefore it is not binding in court, as regulations would be. Instead, the booklet draws on the facts of data security-related enforcement actions that the FTC has brought against companies, and provides ten over-arching principles to help guide companies as they develop their cybersecurity programs. In 2017, the FTC published a series of blog posts, entitled "Stick with Security," that provided additional commentary on each of the ten principles.[52]

Even though the guide does not carry the force of law, it is noteworthy because the FTC rarely provides any guidance whatsoever regarding data security. Accordingly, it is important to consider the ten principles that the FTC articulated in the guide, and an analysis of how these principles might apply to businesses:

1) ***Start with security.***   The Commission urges businesses to consider security in every aspect of their operations and processes. Businesses should not collect unnecessary information, and they should dispose of information after it has served its purpose. Companies also should avoid unnecessary use of personal information. "If you don't ask for sensitive data in the first place, you won't have to take steps to protect it," the FTC wrote in the 2017 blog post expanding on this guidance. "Of course, there will be data you must maintain, but the old habit of collecting confidential information 'just because' doesn't hold water in the cyber era."
2) ***Control access to data sensibly.***   The Commission advises businesses to allow employees to access sensitive data, such as financial account numbers, only if those employees have a valid business reason to access that data. For example, a human resources manager may have a valid reason to have access to employees' payroll data. But an entry-level marketing employee probably does not have a valid reason to access the payroll

51 Federal Trade Commission, Start with Security: A Guide for Business (June 2015).
52 *See* Federal Trade Commission, Stick With Security: A Business Blog Series, https://www.ftc.gov/tips-advice/business-center/guidance/stick-security-business-blog-series.

records of all employees. The Commission also recommends that companies limit the number of employees who have administrative access to make changes to the entire system. "Are you exercising the same care with sensitive customer or employee data?" the FTC wrote in the 2017 update. "Not everyone on your staff needs unrestricted access to all confidential information you keep. The better practice is to put sensible controls in place to allow access to employees who need to do their jobs, while keeping others out."

3) ***Require secure passwords and authentication.*** A common vulnerability that leads to data breaches and other incidents is the failure of organizations to require strong passwords. Indeed, a 2018 report found that the five most common passwords were: 123456, password, 123456789, 12345678, and 12345.[53] To compound problems, people often fail to change their passwords. Forty-seven percent of passwords in 2014 were at least five years old.[54] The FTC suggests that organizations require individuals to choose complex passwords. The Commission does not specify a minimum number of characters, but it suggests prohibiting passwords that are common dictionary words. The Commission also urges organizations to prevent employees from unnecessarily exposing passwords, such as by storing them in personal email accounts. Finally, the Commission notes that hackers often guess passwords through "brute force attacks" in which automatic programs guess combinations of characters until they hit the correct passwords. The Commission said that companies can reduce the threat of brute force attacks by limiting the number of attempted log-ins. Some risk-averse companies limit the number of failed log-in attempts to five or three. After that point, the account is locked, and the user must call an administrator to reactivate access.

4) ***Store sensitive personal information securely and protect it during transmission.*** The Commission appears to recognize that certain types of sensitive personal information, such as health records, require particularly strong security measures. Although the Commission does not provide a specific definition of "sensitive" information, it strongly encourages businesses to use strong cryptography—such as hashes and Transport Layer Security/Secure Sockets Layer—on any information that they deem to be sensitive. The Commission urges companies to use industry-standard security measures, and to avoid adopting encryption methods that have not been tested (though the Commission did not point to a specific industry standard). Sensitive data should be secured throughout its life cycle, both in

---

53 *See* Sarah Rense, *The Top 25 Passwords in 2018 Are an Embarrassment to Humankind,* Esquire (Dec. 13, 2018).
54 Carly Okyle, *Password Statistics: The Bad, the Worse, and the Ugly,* Entrepreneur (June 3, 2015).

transit and at rest on a company's server. Companies should ensure that their strong encryption is properly configured, the FTC wrote in its 2017 update. "A rock climber may have top-of-the-line gear, but if he hasn't properly attached the carabiners and pulleys or if he's using them in a way the manufacturer warns against, he could be in for a disastrous descent," the FTC wrote. "In a similar vein, even when companies opt for strong encryption, they need to make sure they've configured it correctly."

5) ***Segment your network and monitor who's trying to get in and out.*** The Commission suggests that companies segregate particularly sensitive data from other parts of the network. For instance, a retail company should segment the computers that store credit card information so that the card numbers are not accessible from every computer on the network. Furthermore, the Commission urges companies to monitor access to detect unusual activity and segment networks. "Think of it like water-tight compartments on a ship," the FTC's 2017 blog post states. "Even if one portion sustains damage, water won't flood another part of the vessel. By segmenting your network, you may be able to minimize the harm of a 'leak' by isolating it to a limited part of your system."

6) ***Secure remote access to your network.*** Bring Your Own Device (BYOD) programs[55] and virtual private networks (VPNs) are increasingly popular options that enable employees to access corporate email and files on their own mobile devices. However, these devices present a number of serious cybersecurity challenges. The Commission urges businesses to ensure that these devices and computers contain adequate security measures. For instance, if an employee accesses a company's VPN via a personal computer that is infected with malware, a hacker could track all of that employee's keystrokes—including user names and passwords. Accordingly, companies would be wise to require employees to have antivirus programs and firewalls on their computers. Companies also should require that mobile devices used for BYOD be secured with sufficiently complex passwords. It is increasingly common, for example, for companies to require employees to use device passcodes that are longer than many smartphones' default minimum of four characters.[56] For VPN access, it is increasingly common—and wise—for companies to require two-factor authentication (e.g., a password and a token).

7) ***Apply sound security practices when developing new products.*** The Commission has made it crystal clear that it will not allow companies

---

55 *See* Matt Straz, *Employees Feel the Love When Companies Embrace BYOD*, Entrepreneur (June 15, 2015). ("BYOD is when a business allows employees to use personal devices at work, ranging from smartphones to tablets to laptops, or devices sanctioned by the company and supported alongside devices that are business-owned.").

56 *See 13 Best Practices for Developing Your Mobile Device Policy*, NetStandard (Aug. 6, 2013).

to avoid responsibility for cybersecurity incidents by blaming engineers or other technical employees. Indeed, the FTC expects those who design products and services to have the same understanding of security practices as lawyers and managers. The FTC requires employees at all levels of the organization—including engineers—to prioritize cybersecurity. The Commission expects companies to provide all engineers with secure coding training, and it has brought actions against companies whose engineers did not employ industry-standard coding practices. In these cases, the FTC wrote, the company "could have reduced the risk of vulnerabilities like that by adequately training its engineers in secure coding practices." Furthermore, if a platform such as IOS has default security settings, the Commission expects that app or software developers will not circumvent that security. The Commission also urges companies to test apps and software to ensure that the security measures function properly, and to regularly test software and apps for vulnerabilities. "Keeping an umbrella in your car is a prudent idea, but test it while the sun is shining," the FTC wrote in the 2017 update. "Don't wait until a torrential downpour to find out that the ribs are bent or the handle is broken."

8) ***Make sure your service providers implement reasonable security measures.*** Just as companies cannot avoid responsibility for breaches by blaming employees, they cannot shift the responsibility to service providers. The FTC warns that companies must "keep a watchful eye" on their service providers. In the age of subcontractors and sub-subcontractors, of course, this can be quite a difficult task. However, it is necessary, at minimum, to require adequate security in contractors with service providers, and to monitor their compliance with these standards. The FTC states that companies could reduce the risks of security vulnerabilities caused by subcontracts by "asking questions and following up with the service provider during the development process."

9) ***Put procedures in place to keep your security current and address vulnerabilities that may arise.*** The Commission urges companies to keep in mind that cybersecurity "isn't a one-and-done deal." If a software provider provides a patch, the FTC expects that a company will promptly install that patch. If companies receive "credible security warnings," the Commission says, they must quickly remediate those problems. For instance, independent security researchers often alert companies to vulnerabilities that they have detected. The FTC has made clear that companies cannot turn a blind eye to such warnings. The Commission suggests that companies establish a dedicated email address for security reports. "The lesson for companies committed to sticking with security is to create channels in advance to receive and send critical information about

potential vulnerabilities," the FTC wrote in its 2017 update. "Move quickly to implement appropriate security remedies."

10) **Secure paper, physical media, and devices.** Cybersecurity involves both data *and* physical security. The Commission has brought actions against companies that have failed to secure papers and other media that contain sensitive information. Moreover, the Commission expects companies to physically secure computers and devices that contain sensitive information. Likewise, the Commission has brought enforcement actions against companies whose data has been compromised because employees have lost laptops. If employees store sensitive information on laptops, it is wise to encrypt the laptops. Finally, the FTC expects that companies securely dispose of all data—whether in electronic or paper form. "Just tossing documents in the bin or clicking DELETE is unlikely to deter infobandits," the FTC wrote in 2017. "To prevent them from reconstructing discarded files, responsible companies take the prudent step of shredding, burning, or otherwise destroying documents and using tech tools that truly render electronic files unreadable."

1.1.5 FTC Data Security Expectations and the NIST Cybersecurity Framework

Chapter 6 describes the National Institute of Standards and Technology's Cybersecurity Framework, which provides companies with five broad steps to build and operate their cybersecurity programs. As described in Chapter 6, the NIST Framework has been widely hailed as an effective and common-sense way to implement cybersecurity throughout an organization.

The FTC seems to agree with the general consensus. The Commission has not adopted regulations that explicitly require companies to adopt the NIST Framework. However, use of the framework might reduce the likelihood of the FTC bringing a data security enforcement action against the company. In an August 2016 blog post, the FTC wrote that "[f]rom the perspective of the staff of the Federal Trade Commission, NIST's Cybersecurity Framework is consistent with the process-based approach that the FTC has followed since the late 1990s, the 60+ law enforcement actions the FTC has brought to date, and the agency's educational messages to companies, including its recent 'Start with Security' Guidance."

The Commission noted that because the NIST framework is flexible, "there's really no such thing as 'complying with the Framework,'" and therefore the Framework is not necessarily a safe harbor from FTC data security actions. "Instead, it's important to remember that the Framework is about risk assessment and mitigation," the FTC wrote. "In this regard, the Framework and the

FTC's approach are fully consistent: The types of things the Framework calls for organizations to evaluate are the types of things the FTC has been evaluating for years in its Section 5 enforcement to determine whether a company's data security and its processes are reasonable."[57]

To be clear, this guidance is in the form of a blog post written by an FTC staffer. It does not carry the weight of a statute or regulation, so a company cannot rely on its adoption of the NIST framework as a bulletproof defense to an investigation by the FTC or a data breach lawsuit. However, the blog post suggests that proof of adherence to the framework—complete with a comprehensive and effective written information security plan—would be strong evidence of adequate security practices.

1.1.6 Lessons from FTC Cybersecurity Complaints

With rare exceptions such as the *Wyndham* cases, the vast majority of FTC cybersecurity investigations do not result in court opinions or judgments. That is because most of these cases quietly settle, with the company agreeing to remediation measures and oversight by the FTC for up to 20 years.

The FTC's *Start with Security* guidance, described earlier, is perhaps the Commission's clearest statement about some factors that it considers when determining whether a cybersecurity measure (or lack thereof) constitutes an "unfair" or "deceptive" trade practice. However, the document is relatively short and does not even purport to cover every possible cybersecurity safeguard and vulnerability.

The complaints that the FTC has filed against companies provide the most useful guidance as to what types of cybersecurity safeguards (or lack thereof) are most likely to result in the FTC investigating a company and filing an enforcement action. (Indeed, the FTC's guidance is based on its positions in these cases.) This section is a more complete summary of the cybersecurity-related complaints that the FTC has filed in the past decade, with a focus on the incidents that the FTC alleges constitute a violation of Section 5. Keep in mind that most of these complaints resulted in a settlement agreement before the FTC even had the opportunity to litigate the claims, so there is a chance that a court would disagree with the FTC and conclude that the company had implemented adequate data security safeguards. By settling with the FTC, the companies did not admit any wrongdoing.

Although all of the complaints involve Section 5 allegations, I have categorized them into three general types of complaints: (1) security of highly sensitive personal information, (2) security of payment card information,

---

57 Andrea Arias, *The NIST Cybersecurity Framework and the FTC*, FEDERAL TRADE COMMISSION [blog post] (Aug. 31, 2016).

and (3) security violations that contradict privacy policies. The FTC also has brought a number of complaints that allege inadequate cybersecurity practices by financial institutions, in violation of the Gramm-Leach-Bliley Act; those cases are discussed in Chapter 3.

The FTC also brings Section 5 cases against companies that it believes violated customer privacy. For instance, if a company promises to keep customer personal information confidential, and proceeds to sell that data to third parties, the FTC may bring a Section 5 complaint against that company. Because the focus of this section is *security*, I have not included purely privacy-focused Section 5 cases. However, I included cases that include both privacy- *and* security-related claims.

When possible, the docket numbers for the FTC cases are included. To obtain the full case information, including FTC complaints, press releases, and consent decrees, visit www.ftc.gov and enter the docket number.

1.1.6.1 Failure to Secure Highly Sensitive Information

Unlike other jurisdictions, such as the European Union, the FTC does not have a formal definition of "sensitive" information. However, the FTC is more likely to bring a complaint against a company if that company has failed to safeguard particularly sensitive forms of information. As the following cases demonstrate, the FTC considers data to be particularly "sensitive" if it reveals a health condition or other highly personal trait, or if its unauthorized disclosure is likely to lead to identity theft (e.g., a Social Security number or full credit card number).

The FTC generally expects companies to adopt industry-standard practices for sensitive data. Among these practices are strong encryption, securing both electronic *and* physical access, routine audits, penetration testing, and other common safeguards.

1.1.6.1.1 *Use Industry-Standard Encryption for Sensitive Data*

In the Matter of Henry Schein Practice Solutions, Inc., Docket No. C-4575 (2016)   Henry Schein Practice Solutions makes software that dentists use to enter and store patient medical records. The company used an outside vendor's database engine. The engine protected the data with a proprietary algorithm that the vendor told Henry Schein provided less robust data security than more commonly used algorithms. Nonetheless, Henry Schein promoted its software as offering "new encryption capabilities that can help keep patient records safe and secure." In 2013, the U.S. Computer Emergency Readiness Team issued an alert about the data protection used in the company's software as containing a "weak obfuscation algorithm," yet for several months after that alert, the company continued to market the claim that it "encrypts" patient data. The FTC brought a complaint against Henry Schein, alleging that despite its representations, the software "used technology that was less secure than industry-standard encryption."

Key Lesson   Although NIST and the U.S. Computer Emergency Readiness Team do not regulate agencies, they are among the leading voices on encryption and data protection. Accordingly, if either of those agencies specifically criticizes a company's data security technology, there is a good chance that an FTC complaint will soon follow.

1.1.6.1.2   *Routine Audits and Penetration Testing Are Expected*

In the Matter of Reed Elsevier Inc. and Seisint Inc., **No. C-4226 (2008)**   Reed Elsevier operates LexisNexis, which provides companies with databases of information about individuals. Companies that use these verification services included landlords, debt collectors, and potential employers. Among the data in the company's databases were individuals' credit reports, driving records, and Social Security numbers. Recognizing the sensitive nature of the information, the company imposed a number of safeguards, including authentication of customers who accessed the databases, formatting requirements for the credentials that customers used for authentication, and restrictions on access to nonpublic personal information. These safeguards, however, were not strong enough to prevent a breach of these databases. Unauthorized users obtained a customer's user ID and password and accessed the sensitive information— including names, addresses, birth dates, and Social Security numbers—of more than 300,000 individuals. In some cases, the thieves used this information to open credit accounts in the individuals' names. The FTC filed a complaint against the company, alleging that the breach was caused, in part, by the company's failure to take the following precautions:

- Prohibiting customers from using "common dictionary words" as their passwords and user IDs;
- Allowing LexisNexis customers to share credentials with others;
- Failing to require users to change their passwords routinely (the FTC used every 90 days as an example);
- Failing to limit the number of unsuccessful attempts to log in before suspending access;
- Allowing customers to log into LexisNexis automatically by storing their credentials in cookies;
- Not requiring encryption of credentials or searches in transit;
- Failing to confirm a customer's identity before allowing the customer to create new credentials;
- Failing to assess the company website's vulnerability to certain common forms of attacks; and
- Failing to broadly "implement simple, low-cost, and readily available defenses to such attacks."

Key Lesson   Companies cannot assume that data is secure merely because data is password protected. Companies must regularly assess the strength of their authentication procedures and ensure that bad actors cannot bypass the authentication safeguards.

1.1.6.1.3 *Health-Related Data Requires Especially Strong Safeguards*

In the Matter of Eli Lilly & Co., **No. 012 3214 (2002)**   Eli Lilly, which manufactures the psychiatric drug Prozac, offered an email service, "Medi-Messenger," which provided customers with personal reminders regarding their medications. For instance, if a customer was due for a 30-day refill of Prozac, the Medi-Messenger site, via Prozac.com, would email a reminder to that customer. As one might imagine, the mere fact that an individual has been prescribed an antidepressant is viewed as highly sensitive information. As of June 2001, 669 customers had used Medi-Messenger.

About three months after launching Medi-Messenger, Eli Lilly decided to terminate the service. The company informed customers via a blast email. However, the email addresses of all the Medi-Messenger customers were visible in the "To" line of the email (rather than in the "BCC" line). This resulted in every recipient of the email being able to see the email addresses of the 668 other Eli Lilly customers who had registered for the Prozac medication reminder service.

The FTC alleged that Eli Lilly violated Section 5 by failing to adequately train and oversee the employee who sent out this particularly sensitive email. The Commission also argued that Eli Lilly should have reviewed the email before sending it and tested the email system to ensure that such a communication would not reveal the email addresses of the customers.

This complaint—one of the FTC's earliest data security-related enforcement actions—is instructive on two fronts. First, it demonstrates that the FTC will hold a company accountable for the actions of one employee, no matter how inept or negligent. The employer ultimately is responsible for ensuring that *every* employee safeguards customer data. Second, the complaint illustrates that the FTC does not treat all types of data the same; it considers the sensitivity. The FTC's concern was not merely that email addresses were exposed; the truly egregious violation occurred because those email addresses were associated with the fact that the individuals had been prescribed psychiatric medications. Had the program instead been a weekly reminder for customers to go grocery shopping or pay their water bills, it is unclear whether the FTC would have shown a similar level of concern.

Key Lesson   Companies that use particularly sensitive information should carefully oversee the employees who handle that information, and provide regular, comprehensive cybersecurity training. Although healthcare-related data also is subject to requirements under the Health Insurance Portability and Accountability Act (HIPAA), disclosure of particularly sensitive information also could give rise to a Section 5 complaint from the FTC.

***In the Matter of CBR Systems, Inc.,* Docket No. C-4400 (2013)** CBR collects umbilical cord blood during the delivery of babies, and banks it for potential future use. When processing orders from potential clients, CBR collects personal information including the names, addresses, Social Security numbers, credit card numbers, blood types, medical histories, and adoption histories of families. Information about nearly 300,000 individuals was backed up on four unencrypted tapes, which a CBR employee placed in a backpack to transport between two CBR facilities that were about 13 miles apart. The employee left the backup tapes, along with a CBR laptop and hard drive, in a personal vehicle that was broken into overnight. The laptop and hard drive contained unencrypted information that could enable an unauthorized user to access other personal information on the company's network.

The FTC brought a complaint against CBR, alleging that it violated the FTC Act by allowing its employee to transport unencrypted personal information in a backpack, and failing to "employ sufficient measures to prevent, detect, and investigate unauthorized access to computer networks, such as by adequately monitoring web traffic, confirming distribution of anti-virus software, employing an automated intrusion detection system, retaining certain system logs, or systematically reviewing system logs for security threats."

Key Lesson This case demonstrates that the FTC expects companies to take exceptional care when handling information such as medical histories and adoption records. The Commission also expects companies to ensure that they safeguard not only the personal information stored on their networks but also the credentials and other tools that could be used to access that information.

1.1.6.1.4   *Data Security Protection Extends to Paper Documents*
***In the Matter of CVS Caremark Corporation,* C-2459 (2009)** CVS, one of the largest pharmacy chains in the United States, improperly disposed of papers containing customers' personal information in pharmacies in 15 cities. Among the records were pharmacy labels, credit card receipts, and prescription purchase refunds. Journalists reported that CVS had disposed of these records in public dumpsters. The FTC alleged that CVS failed to implement "reasonable and appropriate measures to protect personal information against unauthorized access," and violated its own privacy policy, which stated that "nothing is more central to our operations than maintaining the privacy of your health information."

Key Lesson Discussions about "data security" typically involve information that is stored on computers. Indeed, although FTC data security enforcement typically focuses on computer data, the Commission also will bring actions against companies that fail to properly safeguard data in physical form, such as paper records and credit card receipts. Likewise, physically disposing of a computer could raise concerns with the FTC if the company has not taken proper steps to ensure that all personal information has been permanently removed from the computer before disposal.

In re PLS Financial Services, **Case 1:12-CV-08334 (E.D. Ill. 2012)** Similarly, the FTC filed a complaint in the federal court against PLS, which operated payday loan retailers in Illinois. The FTC accused the company of disposing of boxes of consumer records that included a great deal of sensitive information, including bank account numbers, wage data, applications for loans, and consumer reports. The FTC alleged that the company "failed to implement policies and procedures in key areas, including the physical security of sensitive consumer information; the proper collection, handling, and disposal of sensitive consumer information; and employee training regarding such matters."

Key Lesson The Commission's complaint focused on the failure of PLS to develop *written* policies regarding both electronic *and* physical data security. Accordingly, it is in a company's best interests to develop such policies, and to train employees to follow them. Too often, data security policies focus on electronic data and do not account for the possibility that physical records can contain highly sensitive data.

In the Matter of Rite Aid Corporation, **Docket No. C-4308 (2010)** Television stations reported that Rite Aid, a large nationwide operator of retail pharmacies, had disposed of pharmacy labels, employment applications, and other documents containing sensitive information, in public dumpsters. The FTC alleged that this data "could be misused to commit identity theft or to steal prescription medicines." The FTC attributed this incident to Rite Aid's failure to:

- implement secure disposal policies and procedures that would ensure that sensitive information is no longer readable;
- train employees on proper disposal methods;
- evaluate its data disposal procedures; and
- establish a "reasonable process" to mitigate disposal-related risks.

Key Lesson As with the *CVS* case, this case demonstrates that companies need to care not only about the data that they store in their files and on servers, but also about the data that they dispose of once it is no longer necessary for business purposes. Companies must not only discard the data, but must also ensure that it is no longer readable or capable of being reconstructed by a bad actor.

1.1.6.1.5   Business-to-Business Providers Also Are Accountable to the FTC for Security of Sensitive Data

In the Matter of Ceridian Corporation, **Docket No. C-4325 (2011)**   Ceridian provides online payroll processing services for small businesses that do not have internal payroll departments. To process employee payroll, the company must collect employees' personal information, including addresses, Social Security numbers, birth dates, and bank account numbers. The company's website promised employers that its "comprehensive security program is designed in accordance with ISO 27000 series standards, industry best practices and federal, state and local regulatory requirements." Despite these promises, hackers used an SQL injection attack—a common hacking tool—to access the personal information of more than 27,000 employees whose employers used Ceridian. The FTC determined that Ceridian had failed to take a number of "reasonable and appropriate" security steps. Among the alleged failures: storing the information in clear text, storing the information "indefinitely on its network without a business need," neglecting to test its applications and networks for SQL injection attacks, and failing to employ standard detection and prevention measures.

Key Lesson   Unlike retailers and other companies that collect personal information directly from consumers, Ceridian receives the information from a third party. This is inconsequential; the FTC will hold service providers responsible for the security of personal information that they receive from business customers.

In the Matter of Lookout Services, **Docket No. C-4326 (2011)**   Just as Ceridian is an outsourced payroll provider, Lookout Services performs outsourced employee work status verification. To perform this service, Lookout collected a great deal of sensitive information, including employee Social Security numbers and passport numbers. Lookout's advertisements to potential customers stated that this data is transmitted securely and its interface "will protect your data from interception, as well as keep the data secure from unauthorized access." Lookout's website stated that its servers "are continuously monitoring attempted network attacks on a 24 × 7 basis, using sophisticated software tools."

Despite these claimed precautions, Lookout allegedly failed to implement a number of common security safeguards, including complex passwords, mandatory password changes, and monitoring for unauthorized access. Users also were able to circumvent Lookout's authentication procedures altogether by typing a Lookout URL directly into their web browser. Such "backdoor access" is an easily preventable vulnerability. A Lookout user took advantage of this weakness and obtained access to more than 37,000 individuals' personal information. Two months later, the user guessed common passwords, such as "test," to again access the sensitive information.

Key Lesson   Even if a company has implemented significant technical data security safeguards, its failure to implement adequate authentication policies may leave it vulnerable to scrutiny by the FTC. All companies—and particularly those that store and process particularly sensitive information—should ensure that their authentication procedures are industry standard, and that only properly authenticated users have access to the data.

In the Matter of Accretive Health, Inc., **Docket No. C-4432 (2014)**   Accretive Health provides hospitals with a variety of administrative services, including bill collection, registration services, and transcription. Its employees work onsite at hospitals. In 2011, a laptop containing highly sensitive personal information about more than 23,000 patients of an Accretive client was stolen from an Accretive employee's car. The FTC complaint against Accretive alleged that the company did not take adequate steps to prevent employees from transporting personal information in an unsecure manner, and that Accretive had a duty to limit employee access to personal data to only those employees with a legitimate need for access.

Key Lesson   Even though the personal information belonged to customers of Accretive's clients—and not to Accretive's direct clients—the FTC nonetheless held Accretive fully responsible for the failure to safeguard the information. The case also is a reminder that businesses should regularly evaluate employees' access privileges, and restrict access to those with a legitimate business need for the data.

1.1.6.1.6   *Companies Are Responsible for the Data Security Practices of Their Contractors*

In the Matter of GMR Transcription Services, Inc., **Docket No. C-4482 (2014)**   GMR Transcription Services transcribes audio recordings for doctors, hospitals, and other businesses. GMR customers typically upload audio files via GMR's website. Typists transcribe the audio into a Word document, and provide the transcript to the customer either via email or GMR's website. The FTC alleged that Fedtrans, an India-based contractor for GMR, stored audio files and transcripts on an unsecure FTP application that was accessible to unauthenticated users. Indeed, the FTC alleged that a simple web search uncovered thousands of these unsecure files, and that some of them included names, medications, employment history, and medical records. The FTC complaint alleged that GMR caused this exposure by failing to require that its contractors adhere to standard data security safeguards, such as requiring Fedtrans and other service providers, in the service contracts, to implement "reasonable and appropriate security measures to protect personal information in audio and transcript files" that are stored on the contractors' networks. For instance, the FTC cited GMR's failure to require contractors to encrypt storage and transmission of audio and transcript files, and to require strong authentication measures before typists could access the data. The FTC also asserted that GMR failed to adequately oversee the contractor's data security practices through audits or requests for written security policies and procedures.

Key Lesson   Just as the FTC holds service providers responsible for how they handle the personal information of their clients' customers, the FTC also will hold companies accountable for the data security practices of their service providers. Accordingly, it is a best practice to contractually require service providers to adopt industry-standard data security measures, particularly for sensitive information. Moreover, the FTC believes that companies have a duty to regularly oversee the data security practices of their contractors, through audits and other routine reviews.

1.1.6.1.7   Make Sure that Every Employee Receives Regular Data Security Training for Processing Sensitive Data

In the Matter of Franklin's Budget Car Sales, also dba Franklin Toyota Scion, Docket No. C-4371 (2012)   Personal information of about 95,000 customers of Franklin's Budget Car Sales, a car dealership, was publicly exposed via a peer-to-peer network that a Franklin's employee had installed on his work computer. Among the information allegedly disclosed were drivers' license numbers and Social Security numbers. Peer-to-peer networks are not only the source of a great deal of intellectual property infringement (through sharing videos and music) and illegal content (e.g., child pornography), they also carry viruses and other malware that expose a computer—and the network to which it is connected—to data theft. After an investigation, the FTC criticized the company for failing to implement a number of safeguards, including employee data security training, network monitoring, and promulgation of information security policies.

Key Lesson   Employee behavior remains one of the most significant data security vulnerabilities for businesses. To avoid regulatory action after data breaches, employers must provide ongoing employee training, and reasonably monitor employees' use of information technology to ensure that the employees are not taking large risks, particularly if the employer's computers contain sensitive consumer information. In general, companies should require employees to seek advance permission before installing any programs or apps on work computers or devices.

1.1.6.1.8   Privacy Matters, Even in Data Security

In the Matter of Compete, Inc., Docket No. C-4384 (2013)   Compete, a marketing company, provided customers with a free web browser tool bar, which provided them with information about the sites that they visited. It also offered a

"Consumer Input Panel," which provided customers with the opportunity to win prizes in exchange for their product reviews. Compete's privacy policy stated that if a customer opted in, the company would collect anonymous data about that customer's web-browsing habits. The FTC alleged that this was untrue, and that the company in fact collected information about customers' online shopping, credit card numbers, web searches, and Social Security numbers. Although at first glance this appears to be a privacy issue, it also involved data security because the FTC alleged that Compete failed to adequately safeguard this data, including by sending full bank account information in clear text. The FTC alleged that Compete's failure to adequately safeguard data created "unnecessary risk to consumers' personal information."

Key Lesson   The FTC will take a particularly close look at a potential data security violation if the company had collected that data without obtaining the proper permission from consumers. Although such an act could be the basis for a separate privacy-based claim, it could increase the chances that any subsequent data breach will receive extra regulatory scrutiny.

1.1.6.1.9   *Limit the Sensitive Information Provided to Third Parties*
In the Matter of GeneLink, Inc., **Docket Nos. C-4456 and 4457 (2014)**   GeneLink provides cheek-swab kits to consumers, and collects their DNA information. After analyzing the DNA, GeneLink sells skincare products and nutritional supplements based on what the company determines to be the customers' genetic needs. The FTC filed a lengthy complaint against GeneLink, largely focusing on the company's claims in its advertising and marketing. However, the complaint also included claims arising from inadequate data security. GeneLink's privacy policy stated that it provides some personal information to third-party subcontractors and agents, which "do not have the right to use the Personal Customer Information beyond what is necessary to assist or fulfill your order" and are "contractually obligated to maintain the confidentiality and security of the Personal Customer Information[.]" The FTC claimed that GeneLink took a number of "unnecessary risks" with customers' personal information, including providing all customer information to service providers regardless of whether the providers needed that data.

Key Lesson   Even if a company reserves the right to provide third parties with access to personal information, the FTC may closely scrutinize whether the company is unnecessarily putting customers' personal information at risk of unauthorized disclosure.

1.1.6.1.10   *Children's Data Requires Special Protection*
United States v. VTech Electronics Limited, **Case No 1:18-CV-114 (N.D. Ill. 2018)**   VTech produces electronic learning products, including apps, that are directed to

children. The FTC alleges that VTech failed to adopt reasonable security protections for children's data, including:

- a comprehensive information security program;
- segmentation of the live product from the testing environment;
- an intrusion prevention and detection system;
- monitoring for unauthorized data exfiltration;
- employee security training; and
- vulnerability and penetration testing.

In 2015, a hacker accessed the live product environment through the testing environment, due to the lack of segmentation. The Justice Department, working with the FTC, filed a lawsuit against the company, which was eventually settled. The complaint, filed in Illinois federal court, focused on the company's failure to encrypt the information, despite its representations to customers that it would do so.

Key Lesson   The Children's Online Privacy Protection Act, discussed in Chapter 9, imposes limits on how a company can collect and process personal information from children under 13 years of age. However, the FTC also may view a company's failure to adequately secure this information as unfair or deceptive under Section 5 of the FTC Act.

1.1.6.2   Failure to Secure Payment Card Information

As with particularly "sensitive" information such as health records and Social Security information, the FTC pays close attention to any breaches or exposures that involve payment card information, such as full credit card numbers, expiration dates, and security codes. It is important to note that companies that process or store payment card information also must comply with the Payment Card Industry Data Security Standard (PCI DSS), an industry-run program discussed in Chapter 3 of this book. However, in addition to the PCI DSS obligations, companies risk enforcement actions from the FTC if they do not properly handle payment card data.

1.1.6.2.1   *Adhere to Security Claims about Payment Card Data*

In the Matter of Guess?, Inc., **Docket No. C-4091 (2003)**   This case, one of the FTC's earliest data security actions, arose when a hacker used an SQL injection attack on the clothing producer's ecommerce website to access customer credit card numbers. The Commission alleged that Guess? failed to adequately secure the data by storing it in clear, unencrypted, and readable text. This was contrary to the company's privacy policy, which stated that Guess? uses SSL technology, which "encrypts files allowing only Guess? to decode your information." The FTC alleged that the company failed to "detect reasonably foreseeable vulnerabilities of their website and application" and "prevent visitors to the website from exploiting such vulnerabilities and gaining access to sensitive consumer data," and therefore the claims in its privacy policy were misleading.

Key Lesson   Any claims about security of payment card information must be strictly followed. If a breach later occurs, the FTC will closely scrutinize whether a company lived up to its claims about data security.

In the Matter of Guidance Software, Inc., Docket No. C-4187 (2007)   Guidance Software provides business customers with a variety of information technology software and services, often focused on data security and breaches. As would be expected from a company in the cybersecurity field, Guidance issued a privacy policy that promised users that their sensitive information is protected and that "information is encrypted and is protected with the best encryption software in the industry—SSL." The privacy policy also claimed that the company also does "everything in our power to protect user-information off-line" and "is committed to keeping the data you provide us secure and will take reasonable precautions to protect your information from loss, misuse, or alteration." A hacker used an SQL injection attack to obtain thousands of customer credit card numbers, security codes, and expiration dates, along with other personal information. In its complaint, the FTC noted that although Guidance did, in fact, use SSL encryption during transit, it allegedly stored the payment card data in clear text. The FTC also claimed that Guidance failed to adopt standard security measures and safeguards and did not regularly monitor outside connections to its network. The Commission asserted that the company failed to "detect reasonably foreseeable web application vulnerabilities" and "prevent attackers from exploiting such vulnerabilities and obtaining unauthorized access to sensitive personal information."

Key Lesson   Companies that actively promote their cybersecurity safeguards—such as companies that sell security software and services—should be especially careful about the promises and guarantees that they provide to the public regarding payment card data.

1.1.6.2.2   *Always Encrypt Payment Card Data*
In the Matter of Genica Corporation and Compgeeks.com and Geeks.com, Docket No. C-4252 (2009)   Genica Corporation and its subsidiary, Compgeeks.com, operated a website, geeks.com, that sold computers and accessories. Its privacy policy stated that it uses "secure technology, privacy protection controls and restrictions on employee access in order to safeguard your personal information" and that it uses "state of the art technology (e.g., Secure Socket Layer, or SSL) encryption to keep customer personal information as secure as possible." In fact, the website allegedly did not encrypt data, and instead stored payment card data and other personal customer information in clear

text. During the first half of 2007, hackers launched SQL injection attacks on the website and obtained hundreds of customers' payment card data. The FTC therefore alleged that the company "did not implement reasonable and appropriate measures to protect personal information against unauthorized access."

Key Lesson   Companies that collect and store credit card information should always encrypt the data, particularly if they promise security in their privacy policies.

1.1.6.2.3   *Payment Card Data Should Be Encrypted Both in Storage and at Rest*

In the Matter of Petco Animal Supplies, Inc., **Docket No. C-4133 (2004)**   Petco, a large pet supply retailer, operates Petco.com, which sells products directly to consumers. The website's privacy policy assured customers that entering their credit card numbers "is completely safe," and that Petco.com's server "encrypts all of your information; no one except you can access it." In 2003, a hacker used an SQL injection attack to obtain complete credit card information from Petco.com's database. After investigating, the FTC determined that although the credit card data was encrypted in transit between the consumer's computer and Petco.com's server, Petco.com stored the data in unencrypted, clear text. The Commission, in its complaint, alleged that Petco "did not implement reasonable and appropriate measures to protect personal information it obtained from consumers through www.PETCO.com against unauthorized access."

Key Lesson   Although encrypting payment card information while it is in transit is a good first step, it is not sufficient to satisfy the FTC's standards. Payment card information also must be encrypted while it is stored on servers; otherwise, it could be vulnerable to relatively simple hacking.

In the Matter of Life Is Good Retail, Inc., **Docket No. C-4218 (2008)**   Life Is Good, an online apparel retailer, promised customers in its privacy policy that "[a]ll information is kept in a secure file and is used to tailor our communications with you." In 2006, a hacker used an SQL injection attack on the company's website to access thousands of payment card numbers, security codes, and expiration dates. The FTC attributed this breach to the company's storage of payment card information in clear text and its storage of the payment card information for an indefinite period of time. The Commission also alleged that the company failed to implement standard safeguards for payment card information, such as monitoring mechanisms and defensive measures.

Key Lesson   Particularly if payment card data will be stored for a long period of time, the FTC likely will expect it to be encrypted while in storage.

1.1.6.2.4 *In-Store Purchases Pose Significant Cybersecurity Risks*

In the Matter of BJ's Wholesale Club, **Docket No. C-4148 (2005)**   At the time of the FTC complaint, BJ's operated 150 warehouse wholesale stores in the United States. The retailer accepted credit cards, and used its computers to receive authorization from the issuing banks for the card purchases. BJ's usually transmitted the credit card data, obtained from the magnetic stripes on the cards, to the banks. BJ's also used wireless scanners, connected to its store computer networks, to collect information about its store inventory. In 2003 and 2004, BJ's customers' credit cards were used for numerous fraudulent purposes, causing thousands of customers to cancel and replace their credit and debit cards. The FTC alleged that BJ's inadequate security practices caused the fraudulent uses. In particular, the FTC claimed that BJ's payment card security was inadequate because it failed to:

- encrypt payment card information both in transit and at rest;
- implement authorization and security safeguards that would reduce the likelihood of anonymous access to the data;
- restrict access to the in-store wireless networks;
- implement industry-standard intrusion detection programs; and
- delete the information after there was no business need (BJ's had been storing the data for 30 days, regardless of business need).

Key Lesson   Retailers must take care to ensure that payment card data collected in stores is secure from unauthorized access. Particularly when a company operates hundreds of locations nationwide with thousands of employees, it may be difficult to control how each of those employees protects customer payment card data. However, it is clear that the FTC will hold companies accountable for in-store cybersecurity shortfalls.

In the Matter of DSW Inc., **Docket No. C-4157 (2006)**   DSW, a footwear retailer that operated nearly 200 stores nationwide, suffered a data breach. In March 2005, DSW issued a press release announcing that credit card and purchase data was compromised. The next month, DSW announced in a second press release that checking account numbers, along with driver's license information, were compromised. In total, according to the FTC, the information for more than 1.4 million payment cards and 96,000 checking accounts was accessed, resulting in fraudulent charges. The FTC asserted in its complaint that the breach was caused by DSW's failure "to provide reasonable and appropriate security for personal information collected at its stores." The data security shortfalls that the FTC identified include:

- storing payment card data in multiple files even though there was not a legitimate need to continue to retain the data;
- failing to secure its in-store wireless networks;

- failing to encrypt payment card information while it was in storage;
- allowing DSW in-store computers to connect to computers in other DSW stores and the corporate network, without adequate limits; and
- failing to install and implement sufficient intrusion detection systems.

Key Lesson   The *DSW* case illustrates the difficulty that many companies face when communicating with the public after a data breach or other security incident. Ideally, DSW would have issued only one press release that described all categories of data that had been compromised. However, such announcements involve a difficult balancing act: although data breach announcements should be thorough and complete, companies face pressure to inform the public of a data breach as quickly as possible to stem further damage.

In the Matter of The TJX Companies, Docket No. C-4227 (2008)   In 2007, nationwide retailer The TJX Companies announced what at that time was believed to be the largest data breach in U.S. history. The company, which operates the TJ Maxx and Marshalls retail chains, suffered a massive breach in which a hacker downloaded the payment card information of hundreds of thousands of customers between July 2005 and December 2006. The hacker accessed much of this data via Internet connections to TJX computers, where it was stored in clear text. Additionally, the hacker obtained some of the data while it was in transit between stores and TJX's central network. In total, TJX reported more than 45 million payment card numbers worldwide were stolen, though banks that later sued TJX argued that the number was closer to 100 million. In the year following the breach, TJX reported spending $250 million on the incident. The FTC filed a complaint against TJX, alleging that the breach was due to numerous cybersecurity shortcomings, including a failure to encrypt personal information while in transit and at rest and a lack of "readily available security measures" for wireless access to its in-store networks. The Commission also noted that TJX failed to require strong passwords for authentication to its network and "failed to use readily available security measures to limit access among computers and the internet, such as by using a firewall to isolate card authorization computers."

Key Lesson   The TJX data breach was enormous for its time and led to some of the largest private sector cybersecurity lawsuits from customers and issuing banks (discussed in more detail in Chapter 2). However, companies should keep in mind that besides private contract and tort litigation, they still could face an additional investigation and enforcement action from the FTC. In other words, private litigation and FTC actions are not mutually exclusive.

1.1.6.2.5   Minimize Duration of Storage of Payment Card Data

In the Matter of CardSystems Solutions, Inc., **Docket No. C-4168 (2006)**   CardSystems Solutions provides credit card authentication services for retailers, and in 2005 processed at least $15 billion in purchases. In short, CardSystems acts as an intermediary between the retailer and the issuing bank and communicates whether the purchase is approved or denied. A hacker used an SQL injection attack to obtain tens of millions of payment card numbers that the company had processed. The FTC alleged that this hack led to "several million dollars in fraudulent credit and debit card purchases that had been made with counterfeit cards." The Commission, in its complaint, stated that CardSystems "created unnecessary risks to the information by storing it in a vulnerable format for up to 30 days." Additionally, the FTC alleged that CardSystems failed to assess whether its website was vulnerable to SQL injection attacks, failed to require employees to authenticate access with strong passwords, and neglected to implement a number of standard security and intrusion detection procedures and technologies.

Key Lesson   Companies should *immediately* dispose of payment card data once it is no longer necessary for business purposes. CardSystems' blanket policy of retaining all payment card data for 30 days was clearly below the FTC's standards, particularly because the information was not encrypted.

1.1.6.2.6   Monitor Systems and Networks for Unauthorized Software

In the Matter of Dave & Busters, Inc., **Docket No. C-4291 (2010)**   Dave & Busters, which operates indoor entertainment centers, experienced a breach of about 130,000 customer payment card numbers. Hackers obtained this information by installing unauthorized software on the company's networks, allowing them to obtain the payment card data while it traveled from the stores to the company's credit card processing service provider. In its complaint against Dave & Busters, the FTC alleged that the company failed to adequately detect unauthorized access to its network and to monitor the third-party access to its network.

Key Lesson   As with many data breaches, the hackers in the *Dave & Busters* case relied on software that they installed on the network to export the payment card data. Companies should routinely audit their systems to ensure that unauthorized software has not been installed by a third party.

1.1.6.2.7   Apps Should Never Override Default App Store Security Settings

In the Matter of Fandango, LLC, **Docket No. C-4481 (2014)**   Fandango provides an app for smartphones that allows customers to search for movie listing information and purchase tickets with their credit cards. Fandango's privacy policy informs customers that when they purchase tickets via the iPhone app, the "information is securely stored on your device and transferred with your approval during each transaction." Apple, which provides the iOS system for the iPhone, uses application programming interfaces (APIs) that enable secure SSL connections. This reduces the likelihood that hackers will successfully intercept payment card data, a significant risk when customers use Wi-Fi connections at coffee shops, libraries, and other public locations. The default setting for iOS requires apps to use SSL certificates. Apple warned developers that if they disable this default SSL setting, they will eliminate "any benefit you might otherwise have gotten from using a secure connection. The resulting connection is no safer than sending the request via unencrypted HTTP because it provides no protection from spoofing by a fake server." The FTC alleges that Fandango overrode this default setting and did not use the iOS SSL certificates. Fandango also failed to do any security testing that would have revealed that it was not using SSL. The FTC claimed that due to this failure, "attackers could have, in connection with attacks that redirect and intercept network traffic, decrypted, monitored, or altered any of the information transmitted from or to the application, including the consumer's credit card number, security code, expiration date, billing code, email address, and password."

Key Lesson   As companies increasingly accept payment card information via apps, they should ensure that they accept all of the default app store security settings unless they have a valid reason to do otherwise.

1.1.6.3   Failure to Adhere to Security Claims

Although the FTC pays particular attention to data breaches that compromise the security of sensitive information and payment card data, it is important to keep in mind that compromises of less sensitive information also could be on the FTC's radar. This is particularly true if the company's privacy policy, advertising, or other publicly available statement claims to provide specific data security protections, and the company nonetheless falls short. In other words, the FTC expects companies to adhere to their claims about cybersecurity, and it will pursue companies that it believes have broken their promises.

Even if a company's privacy policy or marketing materials do not explicitly guarantee a specific data security safeguard, the FTC may read broad statements about security and privacy to implicitly guarantee certain precautions. For instance, if a company's marketing materials guarantee customers that "we take every step to ensure the security of your information," and the company does not deactivate employees' log-in credentials after they leave the company, the FTC could reasonably conclude that the company's promise of security was misleading.

1.1.6.3.1   *Companies Must Address Commonly Known Security Vulnerabilities*
In the Matter of MTS, Inc., d/b/a/ Tower Records/Books/Video and Tower Direct, LLC, Towerrecords.com, Docket No. C-4110 (2004) The companies operated

TowerRecords.com, which sold music, videos, and other products via the Internet. The website's privacy policy claimed to "use state-of-the-art technology to safeguard your personal information." The policy also promised that the site "takes steps to ensure that your information is treated securely and in accordance with the relevant Terms of Service and this Privacy Policy." The FTC states that in 2002, when the website operator redesigned the site's checkout functions, they created a vulnerability to enable any customer who entered an order number to view "the consumer's name, billing and shipping addresses, email address, phone number, whether the product purchased was a gift, and all Tower products purchased online." The FTC alleges that more than 5,000 consumers' purchase information was accessed, and Internet chat rooms contained discussions about this security loophole. The FTC attributes this vulnerability to the companies' failure to "implement appropriate checks and controls on the process of writing and revising Web applications, adopt and implement policies and procedures regarding security tests for its Web applications, and provide appropriate training and oversight for their employees regarding Web application vulnerabilities and security testing." The FTC stated that such "broken account and session management" security risks had been "widely known" in the technology industry for years, and therefore, the companies misled consumers when they did not "implement measures reasonable and appropriate under the circumstances to maintain and protect the privacy and confidentiality of personal information obtained from or about consumers through the Tower Web site."

Key Lesson   If a company makes a general promise to take reasonable steps to secure customer information, the FTC will expect its data security measures to anticipate commonly known vulnerabilities. A company's failure to adopt such safeguards could attract FTC scrutiny even if the company has not exposed payment card data or highly sensitive information.

1.1.6.3.2   *Ensure that Security Controls Are Sufficient to Abide by Promises about Security and Privacy*

In the Matter of Uber Technologies, Inc., **Docket No. C-4662 (2018)**   Rideshare provider Uber made a number of strongly reassuring statements about its security to customers, such as in its privacy policy: "Personal Information and Usage Information we collect is securely stored within our databases, and we use standard, industry-wide, commercially reasonable security practices such as encryption, firewalls and SSL (Secure Socket Layers) for protecting your information—such as any portions of your credit card number which we retain (we do not ourselves retain your entire credit card information) and geo-location information." Its customer service representatives also made statements such as "Your information will be stored safely and used only for purposes you've authorized. We use the most up to date technology and services to ensure that none of these are compromised." The FTC found that Uber failed to adopt reasonable security for the personal information that Uber stored on a cloud service. Among the shortcomings:

- allowing all engineers to use the same access key for data, rather than providing each engineer with a separate access key;
- failing to limit access to data based on an employee's role at Uber; and
- failing to require multifactor authentication.

After an Uber engineer's access key was posted online, the personal information of more than 100,000 individuals was accessed in 2014. This was followed by a second breach in 2016, which exposed the personal information of more than 25 million people. The FTC alleged that this inadequate data security was unfair or deceptive. Compounding the matter was the fact that Uber paid $100,000 through its bug bounty program to one of the hackers in the 2016 incident and waited about a year to report the breach.

Key Lesson   Companies must not only be transparent and accurate about their data security practices, but they are also expected to publicly acknowledge shortcomings without undue delay. In a statement accompanying the settlement with Uber, FTC Commissioner Rohit Chopra criticized Uber's "serious misconduct" in delaying reports of the 2016 incident: "Uber's business model relies on users and drivers trusting that the company will take care to protect their most sensitive information, including Social Security numbers, geolocation information, driver's license information, and proof of insurance. This case calls into question whether the company deserves that trust."

In the Matter of Twitter, Inc., **Docket No. 4316 (2011)**   Although Twitter is known for the public-facing nature of its social media platform, it also enables users to communicate privately via direct messages and collects nonpublic information such as phone numbers and IP addresses. In its privacy policy from 2007 to 2009, Twitter's privacy policy stated that it employs "administrative, physical, and electronic measures designed to protect your information from unauthorized access." The policy also stated that direct messages "are not public; only author and recipient can view direct messages" and that users can switch the status of their accounts to "protected" in order to "control who is able to follow them, and keep their updates away from the public eye." The FTC alleged that Twitter failed to enact controls that would enable them to live up to this promise. For instance, the FTC alleged that the company "granted almost all of its employees the ability to exercise administrative control of the Twitter system, including the ability to: reset a user's account password, view a user's nonpublic tweets and other nonpublic user information, and send tweets on behalf of a user. Such employees have accessed these administrative controls using administrative credentials, composed of a user name and administrative password." Moreover, the FTC alleged that Twitter failed to require complex administrative passwords, prohibit employees from storing administrative passwords in their personal email folders, disable accounts after a certain number of unsuccessful attempts, and require password changes after a specified period of days. In 2009, hackers used unsecured administrative accounts to access users' nonpublic information, reset their passwords, and send public tweets from these accounts. For instance, one hacker accessed Barack Obama's Twitter account and offered his followers the chance to win $500 in gasoline if they completed a survey. The FTC alleged that Twitter "did not use reasonable and appropriate security measures to prevent unauthorized access to nonpublic user information."

Key Lesson   A company must ensure that its administrative accounts have adequate controls to enable it to abide by all of the promises about data security that it makes in its privacy policy and other public statements. Employees should not have robust administrative accounts as default; instead, employees should have only the authorization that is necessary for them to perform their jobs.

In the Matter of Upromise, **Docket No. C-4351 (2012)**   Upromise is a membership-based service that teams with merchants and provides online deals to customers who sign up for its service. Among its services is the Upromise TurboSaver toolbar, which promotes Upromise merchant partners in customers' search results and personalizes offers to customers based on their web-browsing information. The tool collected web-browsing information, as well as the data that customers entered into web pages. The Upromise TurboSaver privacy policy stated that the toolbar would only "infrequently" collect personal information, that a Upromise filter "would remove any personally identifiable information" before the data was transmitted, and that Upromise would make "every commercially viable effort … to purge their databases of any personally identifiable information." The Upromise security statement separately promised that Upromise "automatically encrypts your sensitive information in transit from your computer to ours." The FTC alleges that Upromise did not prevent the toolbar from collecting and transmitting personal information such as PIN numbers, credit card numbers, and expiration dates. For example, assume that a customer was entering bank account information on a bank website. Even if the bank's website employed the necessary SSL encryption technology, the Upromise toolbar allegedly would transmit that data via clear text, thus defeating any security protections that the bank's website had for this sensitive information. An external security researcher in 2010 announced that this information was collected by Upromise and conveyed via clear text. In its complaint against Upromise, the FTC alleged that the company "created unnecessary risks of unauthorized access to consumer information by the Targeting Tool transmitting sensitive information from secure web pages, such as financial account numbers and security codes, in clear readable text over the Internet," and that the company "failed to use readily available, low-cost measures to assess and address the risk that the targeting tool would collect such sensitive consumer information it was not authorized to collect."

Key Lesson If a company promises to protect and encrypt information, the FTC will hold it accountable if it fails to do so. Moreover, the Upromise case is one of many in recent years in which the FTC has brought a complaint after an independent security researcher has discovered and announced a company's security vulnerability. A number of such researchers have obtained large followings on the Internet, and their findings can prompt immediate and severe regulatory action.

1.1.6.3.3   *Omissions about Key Security Flaws Also Can Be Misleading*
In the Matter of Oracle Corporation, **Docket No. C-4571 (2016)**   Oracle makes Java, the software that enables consumers to use a variety of online programs. Java has long been known for being the target of hackers, and Oracle routinely releases updates to patch vulnerabilities. Oracle typically delivered these updates to consumers via a pop-up prompt, and when the consumer installed the update, Oracle informed the consumer that "Java provides safe and secure access to the world of amazing Java content," and informed the customer that the computer would have the latest "security improvements." Unfortunately, even if the consumer installed the update, the older, vulnerable Java version remained on the consumer's computer. The FTC brought a complaint against Oracle, alleging that it should have informed customers that updating Java still left their computers vulnerable unless they removed the older Java versions. In the complaint, the FTC alleged that by "failing to inform consumers that the Java SE update process did not remove all prior iterations of the software, Oracle left some consumers vulnerable to a serious, well-known, and reasonably foreseeable security risk that attackers would target these computers through exploit kits, resulting in the theft of personal information[.]"

Key Lesson If a company is aware of a major security vulnerability that could expose consumer information, it should disclose that vulnerability—and ways to fix it.

1.1.6.3.4   *Companies Must Abide by Promises for Security-Related Consent Choices*
In the Matter of HTC America, Inc., **Docket No. C-4406 (2013)**   HTC manufactures Windows- and Android-based smartphones. The FTC's complaint against HTC focused primarily on HTC's Android-based phones. Android, which is Google's operating system, has a "permission-based security model" that requires a customer to explicitly provide a third-party application with

permission before that application can access that customer's sensitive information (e.g., geolocation information or payment card data). HTC's user manual for its Android devices stated that apps "may require access to your personal information (such as your location, contact data, and more) or access to certain functions or settings of your device" and that during installation, a screen "notifies you whether the app will require access to your personal information or access to certain functions or settings of your device. If you agree to the conditions, tap OK to begin downloading and installing your app." As the FTC concluded, this statement led consumers to believe that "through the Android permission-based security model, a user of an HTC Android-based mobile device would be notified when a third-party application required access to the user's personal information or to certain functions or settings of the user's device before the user completes installation of the third-party application." However, the FTC alleged that HTC devices contained numerous security vulnerabilities that prevented such notice and consent. For instance, HTC had circumvented the Android permission model through a number of "permission re-delegation" vulnerabilities, which occur when one app that has the ability to access sensitive information transfers that access to another app, even if the consumer has not provided consent for that second app to obtain the information. Separately, the FTC alleged that HTC allowed customers to install apps that were not downloaded through the Android app store, creating another avenue for third-party apps to circumvent the notice-and-consent process that Android requires. In its complaint against HTC, the FTC alleged that those shortcomings, along with other vulnerabilities in HTC devices, meant that "third-party applications could access a variety of sensitive information and sensitive device functionality on HTC Android-based mobile devices without notifying or obtaining consent from the user before installation."

Key Lesson   As with the *Fandango* case, the FTC takes a very aggressive stance against companies that actively disable security settings that are provided as the default by app stores or operating systems. As online life increasingly moves from the traditional web to apps, the security policies of intermediaries such as app stores will play an increasingly important role in determining whether an app or device maker's security practices are unfair under Section 5.

1.1.6.3.5   *Companies that Promise Security Must Ensure Adequate Authentication Procedures*

In the Matter of Trendnet, Inc., **Docket No. C-4426 (2014)**   Trendnet manufactures and sells a number of connected devices, including SecurView IP-connected cameras, which enable users to install cameras in their homes (e.g., in a baby's room) and view the video live on the Internet. SecurView's website allowed its users to choose whether to require a password to access the live video (because in some cases, users may want a live video to be publicly accessible). For those who did not want the video to be available to the public, Trendnet assured them that the system was secure. Indeed, SecurView's packaging contained a sticker with a padlock and the word "security." However, from April 2010 to February 2012, 20 models of Trendnet's camera allegedly did not require log-in credentials, even if users had chosen to require them. In other words, any member of the public could access *any* of the camera feeds. Indeed, the live feeds from nearly 700 Trendnet cameras appeared online, publicly displaying scenes such as babies asleep in cribs and children playing. The FTC took this breach particularly seriously, stating that it "increases the likelihood that consumers or their property will be targeted for theft or other criminal activity, increases the likelihood that consumers' personal activities and conversations or those of their families, including young children, will be observed and recorded by strangers over the Internet." The FTC asserted that consumers "had little, if any reason to know that their information was at risk, particularly those consumers who maintained login credentials for their cameras or who were merely unwitting third parties present in locations under surveillance by the cameras."

Key Lesson   The *Trendnet* case was a particularly newsworthy complaint due to the sensitive nature of the information that was disclosed. However, from a legal standpoint, perhaps the biggest lesson from the case is that if a company markets a product or service as "secure" (and, in fact, includes "secure" in the name of its product), then the FTC is far more likely to scrutinize its practices if later there is a security vulnerability.

1.1.6.3.6   *Adhere to Promises about Encryption*
In the Matter of Credit Karma, Inc., **Docket No. C-4480 (2014)**   Credit Karma provides customers with credit reports and scores via its mobile app. The company's app privacy policy stated that it used SSL "to establish a secure connection between your computer and our servers, creating a private session." Apple, which manufactures the iPhone and provides the iOS operating system, provides application programming interfaces that, by default, use encrypted SSL communications. Apple warns developers that disabling this default setting "eliminates any benefit you might otherwise have gotten from using a secure connection. The resulting connection is no safer than sending the request via unencrypted HTTP because it provides no protection from spoofing by a fake server." Credit Karma allegedly overrode those default settings and therefore did not use SSL communications. Accordingly, the FTC alleged that "attackers could, in connection with attacks that redirect and intercept network traffic, decrypt, monitor, or alter any of the information transmitted from or to the application, including Social Security numbers, dates of birth, 'out of wallet' information, and

credit report information." Moreover, the FTC alleged that hackers could "intercept a consumer's authentication credentials, allowing an attacker to log into the consumer's Credit Karma web account to access the consumer's credit score and a more complete version of the credit report." The FTC asserted that misuse of this information "can lead to identity theft, including existing and new account fraud, the compromise of personal information maintained on other online services, and related consumer harms."

Key Lesson As with the *Fandango* and *HTC* cases, here the FTC had little tolerance for a company that circumvented a mobile operating system's default security settings. Such settings are quickly becoming the de facto standard of care for mobile app security.

1.1.6.3.7 *Promises About Security Extend to Vendors' Practices*
In the Matter of Blu Products, Inc., **Docket No. C-4657 (2018)** Blu Products, which sells mobile devices, stated in its privacy policy that it has adopted "appropriate physical, electronic, and managerial security procedures to help protect the personal information that you provide us." The FTC alleged that the company failed "to adopt and implement written data security standards, policies, procedures or practices that apply to the oversight of their service providers," including a company that provided a Firmware Over the Air update for Blu and handled highly sensitive information such as text message content. The FTC noted that Blu also failed to assess the security of third-party service providers and contractually mandate minimum security safeguards.

Key Lesson A company must ensure not only that it is abiding by all of its security guarantees, but that its third-party service providers are as well. It must accomplish this through detailed contractual requirements, and mandating that the third parties provide the company with access to security audits as well as the ability to independently conduct audits.

1.1.6.3.8 *Companies Cannot Hide Vulnerable Software in Products*
In the Matter of Lenovo (United States) Inc., **Docket No. C-4636 (2018)** Computer manufacturer Lenovo preinstalled an adware program without informing consumers before they purchased the computers. The FTC alleges that the adware contained TLS vulnerabilities that "caused consumers to not receive warning messages from their browsers if they visited potentially spoofed or malicious websites with invalid digital certificates, and rendered a critical security feature of modern web browsers useless." The FTC alleged that Lenovo failed to adequately assess the adware's security protections, preventing it from discovering the "significant security vulnerabilities."

Key Lesson   If a feature of a product or service could introduce a security vulnerability, a company at minimum must disclose that risk to consumers in advance of purchase.

1.2   State Data Breach Notification Laws

At the state level, perhaps the most pervasive cybersecurity-related laws are data breach notification laws. All 50 states and the District of Columbia have enacted such laws, which require companies and government agencies to notify consumers, regulators, and credit bureaus about data breaches under specified circumstances.

A company must be aware of every state's breach notification law, even if it does not have any employees or property in that state. Each breach notification law applies to the unauthorized acquisition of information belonging to that state's residents, provided that the company conducts business in the state—a low threshold. For example, if a California company discloses the personal information of New York residents, the New York law will determine whether and how the company is required to notify consumers, regulators, and credit bureaus. As a practical matter, because companies often process data about customers and other individuals who are located across the United States, they likely are subject to all 51 breach notification laws in the United States.

Determining whether a company's breach notice obligations are triggered can be quite time-consuming because this determination requires a careful review of the facts of the data breach. Although many of the state laws have similar provisions—indeed, some contain identical phrases and requirements—there are important differences. Because of these deviations among breach notification laws, quite often a company is required to report a data breach under the laws of some states but not under the laws of others.

If companies do not properly issue data breach notifications, they face significant fines and private litigation in many states. Yet, they must fulfill these legal obligations during a chaotic period after a data breach, when they often have incomplete information about the incident. Companies must balance their legal duties to disclose with the equally compelling need to ensure that their disclosures are accurate. If a company incorrectly describes a data breach, it could face an action from a state regulator or the FTC under Section 5 (discussed in Section 1.1.1). Moreover, a company's initial breach disclosures could have a significant impact on the company's brand and public relations.

This section provides an overview of the key elements of breach notification laws. The first subsection examines the circumstances under which state laws require companies to issue data breach notifications to customers.

The second subsection outlines the required contents of the customer notifications. The third subsection examines companies' obligations to notify state regulators and credit bureaus. The fourth subsection examines the penalties and litigation that companies can face if they do not comply with the statutes.

This section discusses the most common rules under the state data breach notification statutes and also notes many of the state laws that differ from these default rules. However, many of these state laws are unique and contain particular requirements that vary considerably, so companies should always consult the current version of the states' data breach notification laws to understand the precise requirements in each state. For ease of reference, a summary of all 51 U.S. data breach notification laws, current as of early 2019, is published in Appendix B. We reiterate that even as the second edition of this book was entering the production phase in 2019, state legislatures were continuing to consider amendments to their breach notice laws. Accordingly, it is vital to always consult the current version of a breach notice law as well as a lawyer with experience in cybersecurity and breach response.

Keep in mind that certain industries that process highly sensitive data—including healthcare companies and financial institutions—*also* face breach notification requirements under federal law, discussed in Chapter 3.

1.2.1 When Consumer Notifications Are Required

After many data breaches, the state breach notification laws do not require companies to notify customers, regulators, or credit bureaus. In many cases, the information that was compromised is not covered by the state laws, and therefore notification is not required. Moreover, states do not require notification if the breached personal information was encrypted and the encryption key was not disclosed. There also are a number of exceptions that allow companies to avoid breach notifications even if unencrypted personal information was acquired without authorization, including provisions in most laws that allow companies to withhold notifications if they determine that the disclosure will not create a reasonable likelihood of harm to the customers.

Even if companies are not required to notify a state's residents of a data breach, many do so anyway. Many companies view breach notifications as a matter of good business and transparency. Moreover, if a company is required to notify residents in even one state, news of the breach may be quickly reported in the media. That would leave customers in other states wondering whether their information also was compromised, and questioning why the company did not notify them. Failure to notify also might increase a company's potential for liability in claims brought under common law and state consumer protection statutes.

1.2.1.1 Definition of Personal Information

State data breach laws apply only to unauthorized acquisition of *personal information,* a term that is defined in each statute. If a data breach only exposes data that does not fall under the statute's definition of "personal information," then a company is not required to notify customers. In many cases, data that is not classified as "personal information" still may be quite sensitive and valuable to identity thieves or other criminals, but the notification rule does not apply.

In nearly every state with a data breach law, the definition of personal information includes, at minimum, an individual's first name or initial and last name, in combination with at least *one* of the following categories of information: (1) Social Security number; (2) driver's license or state identification number; or (3) account number, credit card number, or debit card number, along with any required password or access code.

In addition to those three elements, a number of other states include elements that, combined with an individual's name, trigger a data breach requirement (the specific definitions of "personal information" for each state, as of early 2019, are summarized in Appendix B):

- Medical information
- Health insurance information
- Online account information, such as email account (including username and unencrypted password)
- Biometric data (e.g., fingerprints)
- Taxpayer identification number
- Income tax withheld
- Tribal identification number
- Any federal or state identification number
- Date of birth
- Mother's maiden name
- Employment identification number
- Passport number
- Military ID number
- Student ID number
- Digital signature

A handful of states also require notification of the unauthorized acquisition of information even if the individual's names are not disclosed. California and Florida require notification of the disclosure of a user name or email address, in combination with a password or security question and answer that would allow access to an online account. Maine and Oregon require notification of the breach of certain categories of information, without the individual's name, if the information could be used for identity theft. Texas requires notification for the disclosure of any information related to an individual's healthcare, even if it is not disclosed with the individual's name.

Many breach notification laws explicitly state that they do not cover information that is lawfully made public by the government or media.

1.2.1.2 Encrypted Data

No state data breach notification laws require notification of the breach of personal information that is encrypted. (Tennessee's law had not explicitly exempted encrypted data, but the state added such an exception in 2017.) Most of these laws do not provide technical specifics for encryption. Additionally, many of the state encryption exceptions apply only if the encryption key was not accessed.

1.2.1.3 Risk of Harm

In most states, companies can avoid notification obligations if, after investigating the breach, they determine that the incident did not create a risk of harm for individuals whose personal information was exposed. The exact wording of this exception varies by state. For example, in Michigan, companies are not required to notify individuals if they determine that "the security breach has not or is not likely to cause substantial loss or injury to, or result in identity theft" with respect to Michigan residents. Oregon's exception is a bit narrower, applying if the company "reasonably determines that the consumers whose personal information was subject to the breach of security are unlikely to suffer harm." New York's exception applies only if the company determines that the breach did not compromise the security, confidentiality, or integrity of the personal information. Florida's risk-of-harm exception only applies if the company provides to the Florida Department of Legal Affairs its written determination that the disclosure will not result in harm and retains that determination for five years.

Some data breach notification statutes do not have risk-of-harm provisions and therefore require notification regardless of whether the company concludes that the breach is likely to lead to harm to individuals. These "strict liability" jurisdictions include California, the District of Columbia, Georgia, Illinois, Maine, Massachusetts, Minnesota, Nevada, North Dakota, and Texas.

1.2.1.4 Safe Harbors and Exceptions to Notice Requirement

Most states have some additional, narrow exceptions to the breach notification rules. Commonly, if a company follows the breach notification procedures of its own information security policy, then it does not have to notify consumers pursuant to the specific requirements of the state law, as long as the timing of its notice is consistent with the state law. Additionally, many states allow regulated financial institutions and healthcare providers to notify consumers under applicable federal laws and regulations, rather than following the state breach notice provisions.

1.2.2 Notice to Individuals

The U.S. breach notification process is not one-size-fits-all. State laws differ as to the timing of the notices, the form in which they can be delivered, and the content of the notices. Failure to comply with these technical requirements can lead to liability, so companies are wise to double-check the current version of each state's breach notification law to ensure that they are providing proper notice.

1.2.2.1 Timing of Notice

Most breach notification laws require companies to notify customers as expediently as possible and without unreasonable delay, although the exact wording of that requirement varies by state (and is summarized by state in Appendix B). Although these states do not require notification within a specified number of days after discovering the breach, state regulators likely will not tolerate an unjustified delay of more than a month or two.

Some states require notice within a specified period after discovery of the breach. The shortest time frame is in Colorado and Florida, which require individual notice within 30 days of discovery of a breach. Alabama, Arizona, Ohio, Oregon, Rhode Island, Tennessee, Washington state, Wisconsin, and Vermont require notice within 45 days; Louisiana and South Dakota require notice within 60 days; and Connecticut requires notice within 90 days of discovery of a breach.

Breach notification laws allow companies to delay notification if the delay would harm an ongoing law enforcement investigation. Many of the laws also allow companies to delay notice to determine the scope of the breach, identify affected individuals, and restore the confidentiality, integrity, and availability of the company's computer systems and data.

1.2.2.2 Form of Notice

Companies also must ensure that they deliver the notice in a medium that is approved by each statute. The breach notification laws all allow for written notice that is mailed to the last known address on record for the individual. The laws also typically allow electronic notice delivered via email to the last known email address that the company has on record. Some states allow electronic notice only if email was the primary method of communication between the company and the customer. The states also generally allow electronic communication only if the company obtained valid consent to delivery of electronic notices pursuant to the federal E-SIGN Act. About half of the statutes also allow companies to deliver the notices via telephone, and a handful also allow notice to be delivered via fax machine.

Additionally, state breach notification laws allow companies to provide "substitute" notice if the company does not have sufficient contact information to deliver the other forms of notice if the total cost of notification would exceed an amount specified in the statute or if the company would be required to notify more than a certain number of people specified in the statute. Substitute notice generally consists of three elements: (1) email notice to any individuals for whom the business has an email address on file; (2) if the company has a website, conspicuous notice of the breach on the site; and (3) notice to major statewide media.

1.2.2.3 Content of Notice

Most state breach notification laws do not require a breach notice to contain specific information. A minority of states, however, require notices to individuals to contain certain statements or data. These requirements are listed in detail, by jurisdiction, in Appendix B. Among the most common requirements are:

- contact information for the company;
- a general description of the breach;
- the categories of personal information compromised in the breach;
- the date(s) of the breach;
- contact information for major credit bureaus, the state attorney general, and the Federal Trade Commission;
- advice to remain vigilant about identity theft by reviewing financial account records and credit reports; and
- information about identity theft protection services.

Some states prohibit individual notices from containing certain types of information. For instance, Illinois prohibits companies from notifying individuals of the number of Illinois residents whose data was compromised. Massachusetts also prohibits companies from disclosing the number of state residents affected, and it also bars companies from describing the nature of the breach.

1.2.3 Notice to Regulators and Consumer Reporting Agencies

If a company notifies individuals about a data breach, it also may be required to notify state regulators or the three major credit bureaus.

About half of the states (listed in Appendix B) require companies to notify state officials—typically the state attorney general—if individuals were notified. In some of those states, regulator notification is required only if the number of individuals notified exceeds a specified threshold (typically 500 or 1,000 state residents). About half of these states require the regulator notice to contain specific content, such as a general description of the breach, the number of state residents affected, and the steps that the company has taken to remediate harm. Some statutes require companies to provide regulators with samples of the notices that were sent to individuals. Some states, including California, New York, and North Carolina, provide companies with a form to complete.

Most—but not all—states also require notification of the major credit bureaus (Experian, EquiFax, and TransUnion). Typically, credit bureau notification is required only if more than 1,000 residents of the state have been notified, though some states have higher thresholds. The breach notice laws often require companies to inform the credit bureaus of the date that the notices were sent to individuals.

1.2.4 Penalties for Violating State Breach Notification Laws

Typically, state attorneys general may bring enforcement actions against companies that fail to comply with their states' data breach notification laws. Although the remedies vary by state, the officials typically can seek injunctions ordering disclosure of the breach and civil fines. In some states, individuals can bring private lawsuits seeking damages, often under state consumer protection statutes.

1.3 State Data Security Laws

As of early 2019, more than 20 states have enacted statutes that impose data security requirements on companies that own or process personal information from the states' residents. As with the data breach notification laws, the location of a company's headquarters is irrelevant to determining whether these laws apply to the company. Instead, a state's data security law will apply if a company owns or processes personal information of even one resident of that state. Because most midsize and large companies process the personal information of residents of all 50 states, companies must pay attention to the requirements of all state data security laws.

Of the data security laws, most are relatively flexible, requiring companies to implement reasonable security procedures but not specifying precisely what constitutes "reasonable." Those states include Arkansas,[58] California,[59] Colorado,[60]

---

58 ARK. CODE ANN. § 4-110-104(b) ("A person or business that acquires, owns, or licenses personal information about an Arkansas resident shall implement and maintain reasonable security procedures and practices appropriate to the nature of the information to protect the personal information from unauthorized access, destruction, use, modification, or disclosure.").
59 CAL. CIV. CODE § 1798.81.5 ("A business that owns, licenses, or maintains personal information about a California resident shall implement and maintain reasonable security procedures and practices appropriate to the nature of the information, to protect the personal information from unauthorized access, destruction, use, modification, or disclosure.").
60 COLO. REV. STAT. § 6-1-713.5 ("a covered entity that maintains, owns, or licenses personal identifying information of an individual residing in the state shall implement and maintain reasonable security procedures and practices that are appropriate to the nature of the personal identifying information and the nature and size of the business and its operations.").

Connecticut,[61] Florida,[62] Indiana,[63] Kansas,[64] Louisiana,[65] Maryland,[66] Nebraska,[67] New Mexico,[68] Texas,[69] and Utah.[70] The data security laws in Oregon, Nevada, Rhode Island, Massachusetts, and Ohio are more specific and are described in more detail later in this section. As the second edition of this book was entering the production process, Alabama and Delaware also passed data security laws.

---

61 Conn. Gen. Stat. 42-471(a) ("Any person in possession of personal information of another person shall safeguard the data, computer files and documents containing the information from misuse by third parties, and shall destroy, erase or make unreadable such data, computer files and documents prior to disposal").

62 FLA. STAT. § 501.171(2) ("Each covered entity, governmental entity, or third-party agent shall take reasonable measures to protect and secure data in electronic form containing personal information.").

63 IND. CODE § 24-4.9-3-3.5(c) ("A data base owner shall implement and maintain reasonable procedures, including taking any appropriate corrective action, to protect and safeguard from unlawful use or disclosure any personal information of Indiana residents collected or maintained by the data base owner.").

64 KAN. STAT. ANN. § 50-6, 139b ("A holder of personal information shall ... [i]mplement and maintain reasonable procedures and practices appropriate to the nature of the information, and exercise reasonable care to protect the personal information from unauthorized access, use, modification or disclosure.").

65 LA. REV. STAT. § 51:3074(B) ("Any person that conducts business in the state or that owns or licenses computerized data that includes personal information, or any agency that owns or licenses computerized data that includes personal information, shall implement and maintain reasonable security procedures and practices appropriate to the nature of the information to protect the personal information from unauthorized access, destruction, use, modification, or disclosure.").

66 MD. CODE ANN., COM. LAW § 14-3503(a) ("To protect personal information from unauthorized access, use, modification, or disclosure, a business that owns or licenses personal information of an individual residing in the State shall implement and maintain reasonable security procedures and practices that are appropriate to the nature of the personal information owned or licensed and the nature and size of the business and its operations.").

67 NEB. REV. STAT. § 87-808 ("To protect personal information from unauthorized access, acquisition, destruction, use, modification, or disclosure, an individual or a commercial entity that conducts business in Nebraska and owns, licenses, or maintains computerized data that includes personal information about a resident of Nebraska shall implement and maintain reasonable security procedures and practices that are appropriate to the nature and sensitivity of the personal information owned, licensed, or maintained and the nature and size of, and the resources available to, the business and its operations, including safeguards that protect the personal information when the individual or commercial entity disposes of the personal information.").

68 N.M. STAT. ANN. § 57-12C-4 ("A person that owns or licenses personal identifying information of a New Mexico resident shall implement and maintain reasonable security procedures and practices appropriate to the nature of the information to protect the personal identifying information from unauthorized access, destruction, use, modification or disclosure.").

69 TEX. BUS. & COM. CODE § 521.052(a) ("A business shall implement and maintain reasonable procedures, including taking any appropriate corrective action, to protect and safeguard from unlawful use or disclosure any sensitive personal information collected or maintained by the business in the regular course of business.").

70 UTAH CODE § 13-44-201(1) ("Any person who conducts business in the state and maintains personal information shall implement and maintain reasonable procedures to ... prevent unlawful use or disclosure of personal information collected or maintained in the regular course of business").

A note about statutes, laws, regulations, and government guidelines described throughout this book: When possible, we use the language directly from the original text. However, for brevity and clarity, some of these descriptions are shortened or modestly edited. Moreover, Congress and state legislatures occasionally amend data security requirements. Accordingly, before citing any of these laws in an official document, consult the primary source, which is accessible via the citation in the footnotes.

1.3.1 Oregon

Oregon's data security law, which was significantly revised in 2015, also requires companies that own or possess Oregon consumers' personal information to develop and implement reasonable safeguards.[71] However, the Oregon law provides more detail about how companies can satisfy the requirement.

Under the Oregon law, the company could satisfy the "reasonableness" requirement by developing an information security plan that contains the following safeguards:

- Administrative safeguards, such as:
    - designating a coordinator for the security program;
    - identifying "reasonably foreseeable" internal and external risks;
    - assessing existing data security safeguards;
    - offering data security training to employees;
    - overseeing the data security practices of third-party service providers; and
    - adjusting the security program when necessary.
- Technical safeguards, such as:
    - assessing software and network risks;
    - assessing risks in information processing, transmission, and storage;
    - detecting, preventing, and responding to attacks or system failures; and
    - information security testing and monitoring.
- Physical safeguards, such as:
    - risk assessment regarding the storage and disposal of physically stored data;
    - intrusion detection, prevention, and response;

---

71 OR. REV. STAT. § 646A.622(1) ("A person that owns, maintains or otherwise possesses data that includes a consumer's personal information that the person uses in the course of the person's business, vocation, occupation or volunteer activities shall develop, implement and maintain reasonable safeguards to protect the security, confidentiality and integrity of the personal information, including safeguards that protect the personal information when the person disposes of the information").

- protection against unauthorized access to physically stored data; and
- disposing of personal information after it is no longer needed.[72]

Alternatively, companies could satisfy the Oregon law by complying with the Gramm-Leach-Bliley Act (if the company is a financial institution),[73] the Health Insurance Portability and Accountability Act (if the company is subject to HIPAA),[74] or a state or federal law that provides greater protection to personal information than the Oregon state procedures.[75]

1.3.2 Rhode Island

Rhode Island's data security law (which, like Oregon's, was amended significantly in 2015) requires state agencies and firms to have "reasonable security procedures and practices."[76] The statute requires the program to be appropriate to:

- the size and scope of the organization;
- the nature of the information; and
- "the purpose for which the information was collected in order to protect the personal information from unauthorized access, use, modification, destruction, or disclosure and to preserve the confidentiality, integrity, and availability of such information."[77]

Under Rhode Island's law, companies cannot retain covered information for any time longer than "reasonably" necessary. Organizations that disclose Rhode Island residents' personal information to third parties (e.g., service providers) must require those third parties, by contract, to implement and maintain reasonable security procedures and practices.

1.3.3 Nevada

Nevada requires data collectors that maintain records containing Nevada residents' personal information to "implement and maintain reasonable security measures to protect those records from unauthorized access, acquisition, destruction, use, modification, or disclosure."[78] Companies that disclose

---

72 Or. Rev. Stat. § 646A.622(2)(d).
73 *Id.* § 646A.622(2)(b).
74 *Id.* § 646A.622(2)(c).
75 *Id.* § 646A.622(2)(a).
76 R.I. Gen. Laws § 11-49.3-2(a).
77 *Id.*
78 Nev. Rev. Stat. § 603A.210.

Nevada residents' personal information to service providers must contractually require those companies to adopt reasonable security measures.

Nevada's data security law is unique in that it requires companies to use encryption before either (1) electronically transferring Nevada residents' personal information or (2) moving any data storage device containing Nevada residents' personal information "beyond the logical or physical controls of the data collector" or third parties that fulfill this role.[79] The encryption requirements do not apply to telecommunications providers acting solely in the role of conveying communications of other persons.[80]

Nevada's statute does not provide specific technological requirements for encryption to satisfy this requirement. The statute states that the technology could be one that was adopted by a standards-setting body, such as the Federal Information Processing Standards issued by the National Institute of Standards and Technology.[81] The encryption also should use "[a]ppropriate management and safeguards of cryptographic keys to protect the integrity of the encryption" using guidelines that have been published by a standards-setting body, such as NIST.[82]

Nevada also requires data collectors that accept payment card information to comply with the Payment Card Industry Data Security Standard (PCI DSS), which is explained in Chapter 3 of this book. Although companies that accept payment card information typically must comply with PCI DSS due to contractual requirements with credit card companies, Nevada's law is unique in that it requires companies, by law, to comply.

1.3.4 Massachusetts

Massachusetts has enacted the most detailed and comprehensive general data security requirements in the United States. These requirements have quickly become de facto national standards for midsize and large businesses that have customers nationwide, as they most likely process some personal information of Massachusetts residents.

Massachusetts's data security law requires the state's Department of Consumer Affairs and Business Regulation to adopt data security regulations to safeguard Massachusetts residents' personal information. The statute requires the regulations to:

- "insure the security and confidentiality of customer information in a manner fully consistent with industry standards";

---

79 *Id.* § 603A.215.
80 *Id.* § 603A.215(4).
81 *Id.* § 603A.215(5)(b).
82 *Id.*

- "protect against anticipated threats or hazards to the security or integrity of such information"; and
- "protect against unauthorized access to or use of such information that may result in substantial harm or inconvenience to any consumer."[83]

The Massachusetts Department of Consumer Affairs issued comprehensive data security regulations[84] to comply with this mandate. The regulations (modestly edited here for clarity and brevity) require every company and person who owns or licenses personal information about a Massachusetts resident to develop a comprehensive written information security program that contains administrative, technical, and physical safeguards that are appropriate to:

- the size, scope, and type of business of the company;
- the amount of resources available to the company;
- the amount of stored data; and
- the need for security and confidentiality of both consumer and employee information.[85]

The Massachusetts regulations are unique in their specificity as to the *required* components of a written information security plan. The regulations require all information security plans to include the following:

- At least one employee who is designated to maintain the security program.
- Identifying and assessing reasonably foreseeable internal and external risks to security, confidentiality, and integrity of records that contain personal information.
- Evaluating and improving the effectiveness of the current safeguards for limiting the risks, including but not limited to
  - ongoing employee training,
  - employee compliance with information security policies and procedures, and
  - means for detecting and preventing security system failures.
- Developing records storage, access, and transportation security policies.
- Disciplinary measures for information security violations.
- Preventing terminated employees from accessing personal information.
- Overseeing service providers that have access to consumers' personal information by:
  - taking "reasonable steps" to select and retain providers that can maintain adequate security measures, and
  - contractually requiring service providers to maintain appropriate security measures.
- Reasonably restricting physical access to personal information.

---

83 Mass. Gen. Laws ch. 93H, § 2(a).
84 201 Mass. Code Regs. 17.00 *et seq.*
85 201 Mass. Code Regs. 17.03(1).

- Regular monitoring to ensure proper operation of information security program.
- Reviewing scope of security measures at least annually or whenever there is a material change in business practices.
- Documenting responsive actions after a breach.[86]

The Massachusetts regulations also require information security programs to contain the following technical security measures when feasible:

- Secure user authentication protocols, including
  - control of identifiers,
  - a "reasonably secure" method of assigning passwords and other access mechanisms,
  - control of storage of passwords,
  - restricting access to active user accounts, and
  - blocking access to log-ins after multiple unsuccessful log-in attempts.
- Secure access control measures that
  - restrict access to personal information to those who need the information to perform their jobs, and
  - assign unique identifications plus passwords that are not default credentials and are reasonably designed to maintain integrity of access controls.
- Encryption of all personal information that travels across public networks or is transmitted wirelessly or stored on laptops or portable devices.
- Reasonable monitoring for unauthorized use.
- Up-to-date firewall protection and operating system patches.
- Reasonably up-to-date malware protection and anti-virus software.
- Employee computer security training.[87]

The Massachusetts regulations are, by far, the most detailed general data security requirements in the United States. Despite the length of the regulations, they are not significantly more onerous than the general expectations that regulators long have had of companies that handle personal information. For instance, it is unlikely that the FTC would agree to allow a company to store personal information on unencrypted laptops, nor would the California Attorney General suggest that companies allow multiple employees to access personal information with a single log-in credential. The Massachusetts regulations merely spell out what is generally considered in the industry to constitute "reasonable" data security. Even if a company does not own or process personal information of Massachusetts residents, it would be well advised to use the Massachusetts regulations as guidelines for its own data security programs.

---

86 *Id.* 17.03(2).
87 *Id.* 17.04.

1.3.5 Ohio

In 2018, Ohio's legislature took a less punitive route than other states when it passed its Data Protection Act.[88] The law provides businesses with an affirmative defense to data breach tort claims if they conform to a particular data security standard.

To take advantage of this defense, a company must "create, maintain, and comply with a written cybersecurity program that contains administrative, technical, and physical safeguards for the protection of personal information."[89] That program must "reasonably conform" to one of the following protocols:

- NIST Cybersecurity Framework
- NIST Special Publication 800-171
- NIST Special Publications 800-53 and 800-53a
- FedRAMP security assessment framework
- ISO2700

Alternately, if the business is a regulated entity that is subject to the Health Insurance Portability and Accountability Act, the Gramm-Leach-Bliley Act, or the Federal Information Security Modernization Act of 2014, it may conform to the framework of that applicable law.

The cybersecurity program must: (1) "protect the security and confidentiality of the information"; (2) "protect against any anticipated threats or hazards to the security or integrity of the information"; and (3) "protect against unauthorized access to and acquisition of the information that is likely to result in a material risk of identity theft or other fraud to the individual to whom the information relates."[90] The "scale and scope" of the program must be based on the company's "size and complexity," the "nature and scope" of the company's activities," the sensitivity of the company's information, the "cost and availability of tools to improve information security and reduce vulnerabilities," and the company's available resources.[91]

If a company faces a tort claim under Ohio law arising from a data breach, and it demonstrates that it complied with the statute's guidelines for a cybersecurity program, it may present its compliance as an affirmative defense. To be sure, the statute does not provide an absolute safe harbor from data breach litigation. However, it provides companies with an incentive to reduce the likelihood that they would lose a lawsuit stemming from a data breach.

---

88 OHIO REV. CODE ANN. § 1354.01 *et seq.*
89 OHIO REV. CODE ANN. § 1354.02.
90 *Id.*
91 *Id.*

1.4   State Data Disposal Laws

Most—but not all—states require companies to take reasonable steps to dispose of records that contain personal information.[92] Although the wording of the laws varies by state, they generally require steps such as shredding or otherwise rendering the personal information unreadable or undecipherable, and preventing the information from being reconstituted. Nonetheless, most statutes do not provide much detail on the "reasonable measures" necessary to satisfy the requirements of data disposal laws.

Massachusetts provides some additional detail about the minimum standards for disposal of personal information. Paper records should be either "redacted, burned, pulverized or shredded" so that the personal information cannot be read or reconstituted, and nonpaper media (e.g., electronic media) should be "destroyed or erased so that personal information cannot practicably be read or reconstructed."[93]

Hawaii's law provides some detail about the oversight of vendors that destroy information. It states that a business can satisfy this requirement by exercising "due diligence" over records destruction contractors. Due diligence consists of:

- reviewing an independent audit of the disposal business' operations and compliance with the state data disposal law;
- obtaining information about the disposal business from several references or other reliable sources and requiring that the disposal business be certified by a recognized trade association or similar third party with a reputation for high standards of quality review; or
- reviewing and evaluating the disposal business's information security policies or procedures, or taking other appropriate measures to determine the competency and integrity of the disposal business.[94]

---

92 As of publication of this book, state data disposal laws included: ALASKA STAT. § 45.48.500(a) (Alaska); ARIZ. REV. STAT. ANN. § 44-7601 (Arizona); ARK. CODE ANN. § 4-110-104 (Arkansas); CAL. CIV. CODE § 1798.81 (California); COLO. REV. STAT. § 6-1-713 (Colorado); CONN. GEN. STAT. ANN. § 42-471(a) (Connecticut); DEL. CODE ANN. tit. 6, § 5002c (Delaware); FLA. STAT. ANN. § 501.171(8) (Florida); GA. CODE ANN. § 10-15-2 (Georgia); HAW. REV. STAT. § 487r-2 (Hawaii); 815 ILL. COMP. STAT. 530/40 (Illinois); IND. CODE ANN. § 24-4-14-8 (Indiana); KAN. STAT. ANN. § 50-7a03 (Kansas); KY. REV. STAT. ANN. § 365.725 (Kentucky); MD. STATE GOV. CODE § 10-1303 (Maryland); MASS. GEN. LAWS ANN. ch. 93i, § 2 (Massachusetts); MICH. COMP. LAWS § 445.72a (Michigan); MONT. CODE ANN. § 30-14-1703 (2017) (Montana); NEV. REV. STAT. § 603a.200 (Nevada); N.J. STAT. (unann.) § 56:8-162 (New Jersey); N.Y. GEN. BUS. LAW § 399-h (New York); N.C. GEN. STAT. § 75-64 (North Carolina); OR. REV. STAT. § 646a.622 (Oregon); R.I. GEN. LAWS § 6-52-2 (Rhode Island); S.C. CODE ANN. § 30-2-190 (South Carolina); TENN. CODE ANN. § 39-14-150(g) (Tennessee); TEX. BUS. & COM. CODE § 72.004 (Texas); UTAH CODE ANN. § 13-44-201(2) (Utah); VT. STAT. ANN. tit. 9, § 2445(b) (Vermont); WASH. REV. CODE § 19.215.020 (Washington state); WIS. STAT. § 134.97 (Wisconsin).

93 MASS. GEN. LAWS ch. 931, § 2.

94 HAW. REV. STAT. § 487R-2.

2

Cybersecurity Litigation

For good reason, businesses pay close attention to the FTC's statements about data security. After all, the FTC is, by far, the leading regulator when it comes to data security. However, businesses are just as concerned about the threat of class action litigation arising from data breaches and other cybersecurity incidents. Using centuries-old common-law claims such as negligence, misrepresentation, and breach of contract—as well as private actions available under some state consumer protection statutes—plaintiffs' lawyers are increasingly seeking large damages from companies that they argue failed to adequately safeguard customer data. Indeed, after high-profile data breaches, it is common to see plaintiffs' lawyers battle to represent the class of individuals whose data was exposed (entitling the lawyers to a rather hefty fee if they prevail).

To understand the concepts in this chapter, it is helpful to briefly review the key procedural stages of civil lawsuits. Civil litigation in U.S. federal courts begins with the filing of a complaint, in which the plaintiffs provide a short and plain statement of the facts of their lawsuit[1] and describe why the defendant's actions raised concerns under either a common-law cause of action (e.g., negligence or breach of contract) or a statute (e.g., a state consumer protection law). The defendant then has a chance to file a motion to dismiss, in which the defendant argues that even if all of the facts in the complaint were true, the plaintiff does not state a viable legal claim. Even if a defendant has a strong argument, it may not succeed on a motion to dismiss because, at that stage, the judge must accept all facts as pleaded by the plaintiff, and the defendant does not have the opportunity to present its own evidence. If a judge does not grant a motion to dismiss, the case will proceed to discovery, in which both parties will have the opportunity to request relevant information from each other and third parties through document requests, interrogatories, and depositions. After discovery, either party may file

---

1 FED. R. CIV. P. 8.

Cybersecurity Law, Second Edition. Jeff Kosseff.
© 2020 John Wiley & Sons, Inc. Published 2020 by John Wiley & Sons, Inc.
Companion Website: www.wiley.com/go/kosseff/cybersecurity2e

a motion for summary judgment, in which they present evidence gathered in discovery to the judge, and argue that, even when viewing the evidence in the light most favorable to the other party, no reasonable jury would find in favor of the opponent. In breach cases, the defendant typically moves for summary judgment. If the judge does not grant summary judgment, the case proceeds to trial. Quite often, parties in data breach cases reach a settlement after a ruling on a motion to dismiss or summary judgment motion but before trial.

Although data breach lawsuits commonly are brought by consumers, businesses that suffer breaches face other potential plaintiffs. Often, banks that provide or process credit card payments will sue retailers for failing to adhere to payment card industry data security standards.

Fortunately for companies, there are a number of legal obstacles to plaintiffs in class action lawsuits that arise after data breaches. In short, plaintiffs often have a difficult time demonstrating that they actually have suffered damage that entitles them to compensation from the company that failed to safeguard their personal data. As we demonstrate in this chapter, customers who have suffered a concrete harm such as identity theft are more likely to prevail than those who can demonstrate only that their data was stolen.

Before we begin, a few words of caution about the court opinions cited in this book (and in particular, this chapter, Chapter 5, and Chapter 7, which rely heavily on caselaw). First, cybersecurity law is a rapidly changing field, and courts are constantly developing and refining their jurisprudence in the area. The cases in this book were last updated before the second edition went into production in spring 2019. By the time you read this book, some of the holdings may have been refined or even overturned. Accordingly, you always must check the currency of the authority before relying on it—and no book is a substitute for informed legal advice from counsel. Second, many of the opinions described in this book are thousands of words long. This book attempts to excerpt the facts and holdings most relevant to the subjects in the chapter; however, you must read the full opinion to understand the complete context of the ruling. Third, by describing the facts of disputes as stated in judicial opinions and other pleadings, this book is not necessarily endorsing the veracity of any claims made in those documents.

2.1 Article III Standing

Before examining the specific types of lawsuits that companies could face for data breaches and inadequate data security, we first must consider whether the plaintiffs even have the constitutional right to sue. In many recent data breach cases, this has been among the primary barriers to private litigation.

Under Article III of the U.S. Constitution, federal courts only have jurisdiction over actual "cases" and "controversies." More than four decades ago, the United States Supreme Court stated that "[n]o principle is more fundamental to the judiciary's proper role in our system of government than the constitutional limitation of federal-court jurisdiction to actual cases or controversies."[2]

Among the most prominent requirements for demonstrating an Article III case or controversy is a concept known as "standing." As the Supreme Court has stated, the inquiry into whether a plaintiff has standing "focuses on whether the plaintiff is the proper party to bring this suit ... although that inquiry often turns on the nature and source of the claim asserted."[3]

What Is Article III Standing?

Article III standing is the constitutional ability of a plaintiff to bring a lawsuit. Plaintiffs only have Article III standing if they have suffered an injury that is traceable to the defendant and redressable by a civil lawsuit.

Do Data Breach Victims Automatically Have Article III Standing?

It depends on which judge you ask. Some judges have ruled that if your information has been breached, you have standing to sue the company that failed to protect your information because you are at greater risk of identity theft. Other judges have ruled that data breach victims only have standing if they have *actually* suffered identity theft.

For a plaintiff to demonstrate that he or she has standing, the plaintiff "must allege personal injury fairly traceable to the defendant's allegedly unlawful conduct and likely to be redressed by the requested relief."[4] In other words, the plaintiff has the burden of demonstrating three separate prongs in order to prove standing: (1) that she has suffered an injury-in-fact, (2) that the injury-in-fact is fairly traceable to the defendant's unlawful conduct, and (3) redressability.

Although courts allow plaintiffs to make general factual allegations to establish standing, their complaints still must "clearly and specifically set forth facts sufficient to satisfy" the standing requirement.[5]

2.1.1 Applicable Supreme Court Rulings on Standing

The primary barrier to establishing standing in data breach cases is the requirement that the plaintiff demonstrate that he or she suffered an actual injury. Also known as the "injury-in-fact" requirement, the plaintiff must demonstrate "an

---

2 Simon v. Eastern Ky. Welfare Rights Org., 426 U.S. 26, 37 (1976).
3 Raines v. Byrd, 521 U.S. 811, 818 (1997) (internal citations and quotation marks omitted).
4 Allen v. Wright, 468 U.S. 737, 751 (1984).
5 Whitmore v. Arkansas, 495 U.S. 149, 155 (1990).

invasion of a legally protected interest which is (a) concrete and particularized ... and (b) actual or imminent, not conjectural or hypothetical."[6] Courts have held that mere "[a]llegations of possible future injury" are not sufficient to demonstrate the injury-in-fact that is necessary to establish Article III standing.[7] A threatened injury may constitute an injury in fact, but only if it is "certainly impending."[8]

Although the Supreme Court has ruled on the injury-in-fact standing requirement many times over the years, it has not issued any decisions in data breach litigation regarding Article III standing. Therefore, we do not know with certainty whether the Supreme Court would conclude that the mere possibility of identity theft after a data breach is sufficient to establish an injury-in-fact for Article III standing. However, two recent privacy-related Supreme Court opinions shed some light on the factors that the Supreme Court likely would consider if it were to hear a data breach case.

In 2016, the Supreme Court issued its opinion in *Spokeo v. Robins*,[9] which many believed had the potential to completely change the landscape for standing in private litigation. However, the decision was fairly narrow and did not cause a major revolution in standing jurisprudence, perhaps because the Court was operating with only eight members after the death of Justice Antonin Scalia. Nevertheless, the *Spokeo* case is important because it provides some insight into the Supreme Court's overall thought process about standing in cases that do not clearly involve harm that has *already* occurred.

The case involved Spokeo, a website that provides detailed information about individuals, such as their home addresses, phone numbers, age, finances, and marital status. Spokeo is available to the general public. Plaintiff Thomas Robins alleged that an unidentified individual searched for Robins's name on Spokeo and obtained a profile that contained incorrect information about his family status, age, employment status, and education.[10] Robins filed a class action lawsuit against Spokeo, alleging that the company violated the Fair Credit Reporting Act's requirements that consumer reporting agencies "follow reasonable procedures to assure maximum possible accuracy" of such reports.[11] Spokeo moved to dismiss the lawsuit, arguing that Robins had not alleged an injury-in-fact, and the district court granted that motion. The U.S. Court of Appeals for the Ninth Circuit reversed standing the dismissal, concluding that Robins had alleged that Spokeo violated his rights under the FCRA—not merely the statutory rights of others—and that this allegation was sufficient to establish an injury-in-fact and standing.

---

6 Lujan v. Defenders of Wildlife, 504 U.S. 555, 560–61 (1992) (internal quotation marks omitted).
7 Whitmore v. Arkansas, 495 U.S. 149, 158 (1990).
8 *Id.*
9 Spokeo, Inc. v. Robins, 136 S. Ct. 1540 (2016).
10 *Id.* at 1546.
11 *Id.* at 1544.

The Supreme Court sent the case back to the Ninth Circuit for further analysis, concluding that the appellate court had not applied the proper test for standing. As discussed earlier, an injury-in-fact must be *both* (1) "concrete and particularized," *and* (2) "actual or imminent." The Supreme Court concluded that although the Ninth Circuit concluded that the alleged injury was particularized, the Ninth Circuit failed to also consider whether the alleged injury was "concrete," which the Supreme Court said is a separate inquiry from particularization. For an injury to be "concrete," the Supreme Court ruled, it "must actually exist."

In a partial victory for plaintiffs' lawyers, the Supreme Court in *Spokeo* said that "concreteness" does not necessarily require that an injury be tangible. For instance, the Court noted that violations of free speech or free exercise of religion may be sufficiently concrete to constitute injuries-in-fact. The Court also did not rule out the possibility of satisfying Article III's standing requirement with an allegation of the "risk of real harm."[12]

However, the Court in *Spokeo* indicated that there are some limits to this ruling. The Court concluded that an allegation of a "bare procedural violation," without any further indication of harm, is not sufficiently concrete to constitute an injury-in-fact.[13]

Applying these principles to the dispute between Spokeo and Robins, the Supreme Court ordered the Ninth Circuit to analyze whether the violations of Robins's FCRA rights were sufficiently concrete. The Supreme Court indicated that such analysis could result in either dismissing the lawsuit or allowing it to proceed:

> On the one hand, Congress plainly sought to curb the dissemination of false information by adopting procedures designed to decrease that risk. On the other hand, Robins cannot satisfy the demands of Article III by alleging a bare procedural violation. A violation of one of the FCRA's procedural requirements may result in no harm. For example, even if a consumer reporting agency fails to provide the required notice to a user of the agency's consumer information, that information regardless may be entirely accurate. In addition, not all inaccuracies cause harm or present any material risk of harm. An example that comes readily to mind is an incorrect zip code. It is difficult to imagine how the dissemination of an incorrect zip code, without more, could work any concrete harm.[14]

---

12 *Id. See also id.* at 1549 ("Just as the common law permitted suit in such instances, the violation of a procedural right granted by statute can be sufficient in some circumstances to constitute injury in fact. In other words, a plaintiff in such a case need not allege any additional harm beyond the one Congress has identified").

13 *Id.* at 1549.

14 *Id.*

It is not yet clear whether *Spokeo* has significantly limited the ability of data breach plaintiffs to establish Article III standing. A year after the Supreme Court issued its ruling, for instance, the Third Circuit reversed the dismissal of a putative class action lawsuit that had been filed under the FCRA and various state laws against Horizon Healthcare Services arising from the theft of two laptops that stored personal information.[15] "Although it is possible to read the Supreme Court's decision in *Spokeo* as creating a requirement that a plaintiff show a statutory violation has caused a 'material risk of harm' before he can bring suit, we do not believe that the Court so intended to change the traditional standard for the establishment of standing," the Third Circuit wrote.[16] However, the Third Circuit cautioned that it is "nevertheless clear from *Spokeo* that there are some circumstances where the mere technical violation of a procedural requirement of a statute cannot, in and of itself, constitute an injury in fact."[17] The Third Circuit noted that the Supreme Court failed to define such circumstances in its *Spokeo* opinion, and in the future "we may be required to consider the full reach of congressional power to elevate a procedural violation into an injury in fact, but this case does not strain that reach."[18]

Another fairly recent Supreme Court opinion to address standing and the injury-in-fact issue was *Clapper v. Amnesty International USA*,[19] issued in 2013. In that case, a group of attorneys, journalists, and others who often communicate with individuals located in other countries filed a lawsuit against the federal government, challenging the Foreign Intelligence Surveillance Act (FISA), which allows surveillance of non-U.S. persons "reasonably believed" to be located abroad.[20] At issue in this case was the requirement that the plaintiffs allege both an injury-in-fact and that the injury was fairly traceable to the surveillance program.

The plaintiffs did not argue that the government actually intercepted their communications; rather, they argued that (1) there is a "reasonable likelihood" that the government will obtain their communications at some point, and (2) this risk is so great that they will be forced to "take costly and burdensome measures to protect the confidentiality of their international communications[.]"[21]

The Supreme Court rejected the plaintiffs' first argument, concluding that the plaintiffs' "speculative chain of possibilities does not establish that injury based on potential future surveillance is certainly impending or is fairly

---

15 *In re* Horizon Healthcare Servs. Inc. Data Breach, 846 F.3d 625 (3d Cir. 2017).
16 *Id*. at 637.
17 *Id*. at 638.
18 *Id*.
19 Clapper v. Amnesty Int'l USA, 133 S. Ct. 1138 (2013).
20 *Id*. at 1142.
21 *Id*. at 1143.

traceable" to FISA.[22] The Court focused on the plaintiffs' failure to allege that the government had actually targeted any of them for surveillance. Instead, the Court wrote, the plaintiffs "merely speculate and make assumptions about whether their communications with their foreign contacts will be acquired[.]"[23]

Likewise, the Court rejected the plaintiffs' second argument, reasoning that "allowing respondents to bring this action based on costs they incurred in response to a speculative threat would be tantamount to accepting a repackaged version of respondents' first failed theory of standing."[24]

The Court concluded that standing simply did not exist because the plaintiffs "cannot demonstrate that the future injury they purportedly fear is certainly impending and because they cannot manufacture standing by incurring costs in anticipation of non-imminent harm."[25]

Taken together, *Spokeo* and *Clapper* demonstrate that the Supreme Court has set a high bar for plaintiffs who bring a lawsuit based on the risk of a future, intangible injury. However, the Court has not entirely ruled out the possibility of allowing such lawsuits to proceed, provided that the potential risk of harm is particularized as to the plaintiffs bringing the lawsuit, and sufficiently concrete. As Travis LeBlanc and Jon R. Knight wrote more than a year after the *Spokeo* ruling, "[c]ontrary to expectations, the trend appears to lean in favor of the class action consumer plaintiff, with four appellate courts finding standing last year, even when consumers had not suffered any actual monetary damages or been the victims of identity theft."[26] Maren J. Messing and Peter A. Nelson noted that more recent data breach and privacy standing rulings "offer somewhat mixed guidance for defendants in privacy-related class action lawsuits looking to use a standing challenge as a quick escape."[27] They concluded that courts will examine: "(1) the nature of information that was compromised, (2) whether that information has been used or could imminently be used to cause harm such as identity theft, and (3) whether any alleged statutory violation is substantive or procedural."[28]

These standing rules matter immensely for lawsuits arising from data breaches, because in many of these cases the plaintiffs are alleging that the defendants' inadequate data security left them open to *future* harm. It will not be surprising

---

22 *Id.* at 1150.

23 *Id.* at 1148–49 ("Simply put, respondents can only speculate as to how the Attorney General and the Director of National Intelligence will exercise their discretion in determining which communications to target.").

24 *Id.* at 1151.

25 *Id.* at 1155.

26 Travis LeBlanc & Jon R. Knight, *A Wake-Up Call: Data Breach Standing Is Getting Easier*, 4 Cybersecurity L. Rep. no. 1 (Jan. 17, 2018).

27 Maren J. Messing & Peter A. Nelson, *Post-*Spokeo *Standing: An Evolving Landscape*, Data Security L. Block (Sept. 6, 2016).

28 *Id.*

if the Supreme Court eventually agrees to hear a standing challenge to a data breach lawsuit. Until then, the lower federal courts are free to develop their own rules as to whether a plaintiff has standing in a data breach case.

2.1.2 Lower Court Rulings on Standing in Data Breach Cases

The lower courts of appeals are not unified in their standing requirements for data breach lawsuits. Some courts will only allow a lawsuit to proceed if the defendant has demonstrated that a breach already has led to actual harm, such as identity theft. Other courts, however, have found standing when plaintiffs concretely allege that the breach could reasonably lead to future harm.

The decisions often are difficult to reconcile, and the practical effect is that data breach class actions are more likely to be dismissed for lack of standing in some federal courts than in others.

2.1.2.1 Injury-in-Fact

The Article III standing requirement—in particular, the injury-in-fact requirement—has proved to be a significant hurdle for data breach lawsuits. In the cases in which courts have found plaintiffs to have standing, the plaintiffs have made substantial and concrete demonstrations of injury. However, the result often depends on whether the courts have taken a broad or narrow view of the types of harms that constitute an injury-in-fact.

2.1.2.1.1 Broad View of Injury-in-Fact

Two opinions in which federal appellate courts have found plaintiffs to have Article III standing to sue over data breaches—*Krottner v. Starbucks Corp* from the Ninth Circuit and *Pisciotta v. Old National Bancorp* from the Seventh Circuit—present the most useful roadmap for demonstrating injury-in-fact. However, the results in these cases depend on a court's willingness to consider the mere *risk* of harm as an injury-in-fact.

In *Krottner v. Starbucks Corp.,*[29] an unencrypted Starbucks laptop containing nearly 100,000 current and former Starbucks employees' names, addresses, and Social Security numbers was stolen. Three current and former employees filed a putative class action lawsuit against the company, in which they alleged claims of negligence and breach of implied contract. The first plaintiff claimed in the complaint that she spent a "substantial amount of time" monitoring her banking and retirement accounts because of the breach. The second plaintiff claimed that he "has spent and continues to spend substantial amounts of time checking his 401(k) and bank accounts" and "has generalized anxiety and stress regarding the

---

29 628 F.3d 1139 (9th Cir. 2010).

situation." The third plaintiff stated that within a few months of the laptop theft, he was alerted by his bank of a third party's attempt to open a bank account with his Social Security number, though the bank's response prevented him from suffering an actual financial loss. The district court dismissed the case, finding that the plaintiffs failed to demonstrate the injury necessary to establish Article III standing.

The Ninth Circuit reversed the standing dismissal, finding that the plaintiffs' complaints sufficiently alleged injury because they "have alleged a credible threat of real and immediate harm stemming from the theft of a laptop containing their unencrypted personal data." However, the court noted that "more conjectural or hypothetical" allegations of harm may not have established Article III standing: "for example, if no laptop had been stolen, and Plaintiffs had sued based on the risk that it would be stolen at some point in the future."

The *Krottner* case quickly made it easier for data breach plaintiffs to establish standing in the Ninth Circuit. For instance, in 2014, the U.S. District Court for the Southern District of California found that plaintiffs had standing to bring a class action lawsuit against Sony Computer Entertainment America, LLC, for a breach of the network that stores personal and financial information of Play Station Network customers.[30] The only injuries claimed by the named plaintiffs were the inability to access the Play Station Network while Sony was responding to the breach, and the cost of credit monitoring. Ten of the 11 named plaintiffs did not allege unauthorized charges on their financial accounts or other identity theft resulting from the breach.[31] One of the named plaintiffs alleged that he later received two unauthorized charges on his credit card, but the complaint did not state whether he was reimbursed for those charges.[32] Sony moved to dismiss the lawsuit, alleging that the plaintiffs did not allege an injury-in-fact sufficient to establish Article III standing. Applying the Ninth Circuit's standard from *Krottner,* the court held that the plaintiffs' claims that Sony collected and later wrongly disclosed their information were "sufficient to establish Article III standing at this stage in the proceedings."[33] The court held that even though the plaintiffs did not claim that a third party actually accessed their personal information, *Krottner* only requires a plausible allegation of "a 'credible threat' of impending harm based on disclosure of their Personal Information following the intrusion."[34] Notably, the court held that even though the Supreme Court appeared to tighten its standing requirement in *Clapper*—decided after *Krottner*—the *Clapper* decision did not overrule the *Krottner* framework for

---

30 *In re* Sony Gaming Networks & Customer Data Security Data Breach Litig., 996 F. Supp. 2d 942 (S.D. Cal. 2014).
31 *Id*. at 956-57.
32 *Id*. at 957.
33 *Id*. at 962.
34 *Id*.

analyzing standing in data breach cases.[35] One court, however, said that in the post-*Clapper* era, "courts have been even more emphatic in rejecting 'increased risk' as a theory of standing in data-breach cases."[36]

Indeed, the Ninth Circuit itself reaffirmed the holding of *Krottner* in another case decided after *Clapper*. In a 2018 opinion,[37] the Ninth Circuit reversed a district court's standing-related dismissal of claims against online retailer Zappos arising from a breach of customer information. Although the district court had allowed claims to proceed that were filed by plaintiffs who alleged that their identities had been stolen due to the breach, it dismissed claims from those who did not allege such losses. The district court had concluded that *Clapper* prevents such speculative claims. On appeal, the Ninth Circuit disagreed, and stated that *Krottner* remains controlling precedent in data breach cases even after *Clapper* because the two cases have important factual differences.

"Unlike in *Clapper*, the plaintiffs' alleged injury in *Krottner* did not require a speculative multi-link chain of inferences," Judge Michelle Friedland wrote for the Ninth Circuit. "The *Krottner* laptop thief had all the information he needed to open accounts or spend money in the plaintiffs' names—actions that *Krottner* collectively treats as 'identity theft.' Moreover, *Clapper*'s standing analysis was 'especially rigorous' because the case arose in a sensitive national security context involving intelligence gathering and foreign affairs, and because the plaintiffs were asking the courts to declare actions of the executive and legislative branches unconstitutional."[38]

The Ninth Circuit is not the only court to take a broad view of standing. In fact, the Seventh Circuit was among the first courts to articulate a standing theory that allowed data breach class actions to proceed. In *Pisciotta v. Old National Bancorp*,[39] two plaintiffs brought a putative class action lawsuit against a bank whose system allegedly was hacked, enabling a hacker to obtain a great deal of personal information, such as driver's license numbers and social security numbers, about thousands of customers. In their complaint, the two named plaintiffs—consumers whose data was disclosed—did not allege that the breach had directly caused either of them any actual financial loss. Instead, the complaint stated that the plaintiffs "have incurred expenses in order to prevent their confidential personal information from being used and

35 *Id*. at 961 ("Therefore, although the Supreme Court's word choice in *Clapper* differed from the Ninth Circuit's word choice in *Krottner*, stating that the harm must be 'certainly impending,' rather than 'real and immediate,' the Supreme Court's decision in *Clapper* did not set forth a new Article III framework, nor did the Supreme Court's *decision* overrule previous precedent requiring that the harm be 'real and immediate.'").

36 *In re* Science Applications Int'l Corp. (SAIC) Backup Tape Data Theft Litig., 45 F. Supp. 3d 14, 28 (D.D.C. 2014).

37 *In re* Zappos.com, 888 F.3d 1020 (9th Cir. 2018).

38 *Id*. at 1026 (internal citations omitted).

39 499 F.3d 629 (7th Cir. 2007).

will continue to incur expenses in the future."[40] They sought compensation "for all economic and emotional damages suffered as a result of the Defendants' acts which were negligent, in breach of implied contract or in breach of contract," and "[a]ny and all other legal and/or equitable relief to which Plaintiffs … are entitled, including establishing an economic monitoring procedure to insure [sic] prompt notice to Plaintiffs … of any attempt to use their confidential personal information stolen from the Defendants."[41] The district court granted the bank's motion to dismiss, concluding that the plaintiffs' complaint did not allege a cognizable injury-in-fact, and that "expenditure of money to monitor one's credit is not the result of any present injury but rather the anticipation of future injury that has not yet materialized."[42] On appeal, the Seventh Circuit upheld the dismissal of the case but, importantly, disagreed with the district court's ruling on Article III standing. The circuit court concluded that a data breach plaintiff can establish an injury-in-fact by alleging "a threat of future harm or … an act which harms the plaintiff only by increasing the risk of future harm that the plaintiff would have otherwise faced, absent the defendant's actions."[43] Courts nationwide have relied on the *Pisciotta* ruling to find that plaintiffs have standing in data breach cases.[44]

Indeed, since *Pisciotta*, the Seventh Circuit has found standing in two other large data breach class actions. In *Remijas v. Neiman Marcus Group, LLC*,[45] the Seventh Circuit allowed a lawsuit to proceed against a department store chain that experienced a breach of a system that stored payment card data. Although the plaintiffs did not allege that any identity theft or fraud had actually occurred, they claimed that the fear of future charges prompted them to take "immediate preventative measures."[46] The department store argued that the plaintiffs had not alleged an injury-in-fact and, instead, merely speculated without any actual evidence of impending harm. The Seventh Circuit rejected this claim, reasoning that the department store's customers "should not have to wait until hackers commit identity theft or credit-card fraud in order to give the class standing, because there is an 'objectively reasonable likelihood' that such an injury will

---

40 *Id.* at 632.
41 *Id.*
42 *Id.* at 632–33.
43 *Id.* at 634.
44 *See, e.g.,* Ruiz v. Gap, Inc., 622 F. Supp. 2d 908, 912 (N.D. Cal. 2009) ("The Court finds that Ruiz has standing to bring this suit. Like the plaintiffs in *Pisciotta,* Ruiz submitted an online application that required him to enter his personal information, including his social security number."); Caudle v. Towers, Perrin, Forster & Crosby, Inc., 580 F. Supp. 2d 273 (S.D.N.Y. 2008) ("[T]his Court concludes that plaintiff has alleged an adequate injury-in-fact for standing purposes. [S]tanding simply means that the plaintiff is entitled to 'walk through the courthouse door' and raise his grievance before a federal court.") (internal citations omitted).
45 794 F.3d 688 (7th Cir. 2015).
46 *Id.* at 692.

occur."[47] The next year, the Seventh Circuit extended this pro-plaintiff holding when it refused to dismiss a data breach class action lawsuit brought against P.F. Chang's, a restaurant chain.[48] The restaurant argued that there was no standing because the restaurant's customers only faced the prospect of unauthorized credit card charges—not identity theft—and therefore they had not suffered an injury-in-fact.[49] The court found this distinction unpersuasive.[50] "If P.F. Chang's wishes to present evidence that this data breach is unlike prior breaches and that the plaintiffs should have known this, it is free to do so, but this goes to the merits," the court wrote.[51]

In 2017, the U.S. Court of Appeals for the D.C. Circuit became the most recent federal appellate court to adopt a broad view of standing in data breach cases. In *Attias v. Carefirst*,[52] plaintiffs filed a putative class action lawsuit against a health insurer that suffered a breach of customers' personal information, including credit card data. Because the plaintiffs did not allege that the breach led to the theft of their identities, the district court dismissed the case. The D.C. Circuit reversed, concluding that the plaintiffs had sufficiently alleged an injury: "No long sequence of uncertain contingencies involving multiple independent actors has to occur before the plaintiffs in this case will suffer any harm; a substantial risk of harm exists already, simply by virtue of the hack and the nature of the data that the plaintiffs allege was taken."[53] The risk in this case, the court wrote, was "much more substantial" than that in the *Clapper* case.[54]

2.1.2.1.2 Narrow View of Injury-in-Fact

Other courts, however, have gone to great lengths to distinguish other data breach cases from *Krottner* and *Pisciotta* and hold that plaintiffs do not have Article III standing. For instance, the leading case for this narrower view is *Reilly v. Ceridian Corp.*,[55] in which plaintiffs filed a putative class action lawsuit against their employer's payroll processing company, Ceridian, after Ceridian experienced a data breach.[56] There was no evidence in the record as to whether the hacker actually reviewed the breached information.[57] The district court granted Ceridian's motion to dismiss for lack of standing, and the U.S. Court of Appeals for the Third Circuit affirmed the dismissal, holding that "allegations of an

---

47 *Id.* at 693 (internal citations omitted).
48 Lewert v. P.F. Chang's China Bistro, 819 F.3d 963 (7th Cir. 2016).
49 *Id.* at 967.
50 *Id.*
51 *Id.*
52 Attias v. Carefirst, Inc., 865 F.3d 620 (D.C. Cir. 2017).
53 *Id.* at 629.
54 *Id.*
55 664 F.3d 38 (3d Cir. 2011).
56 *Id.* at 40.
57 *Id.*

increased risk of identity theft resulting from a security breach are therefore insufficient to secure standing."[58] The Third Circuit reasoned that hypothetical harm—and nothing more—does not establish an injury-in-fact: "we cannot now describe how Appellants will be injured in this case without beginning our explanation with the word 'if': *if* the hacker read, copied, and understood the hacked information, and *if* the hacker attempts to use the information, and *if* he does so successfully, only then will Appellants have suffered an injury."[59] Some federal district courts have adopted similar reasoning for data breach cases and held that the mere risk of identity theft after a breach—without any additional showing of imminent or actual harm—is insufficient to establish an injury-in-fact.[60]

The Third Circuit acknowledged that the courts in *Pisciotta* and *Krottner* found that data breach victims had standing to sue, but differentiated those cases because the harm was more "imminent" and "certainly impending" than the harm alleged by the plaintiffs suing Ceridian:

> In *Pisciotta*, there was evidence that "the [hacker's] intrusion was sophisticated, intentional and malicious." ... In *Krottner*, someone attempted to open a bank account with a plaintiff's information following the physical theft of the laptop. ... Here, there is no evidence that the intrusion was intentional or malicious. Appellants have alleged no misuse, and therefore, no injury. Indeed, no identifiable taking occurred; all that is known is that a firewall was penetrated. Appellants' string of hypothetical injuries do not meet the requirement of an "actual or imminent" injury.

---

58 *Id.* at 43.

59 *Id.*

60 *See, e.g., In re* SuperValu, Inc., Customer Data Sec. Breach Litig., Court File No. 14-MD-2586 ADM/TNL (D. Minn. Mar. 7, 2018) ("the allegations about the technological ability to link information are insufficient to tip the balance from a mere possibility to a substantial risk that Plaintiffs will suffer identity theft or credit card fraud in the future."); Taylor v. Fred's, Inc., 285 F. Supp. 3d 1247, 1257 (N.D. Ala. 2018) ("Simply asserting facts that plausibly show a FACTA statutory violation is not automatically enough to trigger constitutional concreteness."); *In re* Science Applications Int'l Corp. (SAIC) Backup Tape Data Theft Litig., 45 F. Supp. 3d 14, 28 (D.D.C. 2014) ("increased risk of harm alone does not constitute an injury in fact. Nor do measures taken to prevent a future, speculative harm."); Randolph v. ING Life Ins. & Annuity Co., 486 F. Supp. 2d 1 (D.D.C. 2007) ("Plaintiffs' allegation that they have incurred or will incur costs in an attempt to protect themselves against their alleged increased risk of identity theft fails to demonstrate an injury that is sufficiently 'concrete and particularized' and 'actual or imminent.'"); Key v. DSW, Inc., 454 F. Supp. 2d 684, 690 (S.D. Ohio 2006) (dismissing data breach lawsuit for lack of standing because the plaintiff "has not alleged evidence that a third party intends to make unauthorized use of her financial information or of her identity" and that the "mere inquiry as to who would cause harm to Plaintiff, when it would occur, and how much illustrates the indefinite, and speculative nature of Plaintiff's alleged injury."); Forbes v. Wells Fargo, 420 F. Supp. 2d 1018 (D. Minn. 2006) (plaintiffs' "expenditure in time and money was not the result of any present injury, but rather the anticipation of future injury that has not materialized.").

Thus, at least according to the Third Circuit, a data breach plaintiff cannot have standing unless there has been *some* indication of potential harm, such as an attempt to open a credit account or a high level of sophistication of the hacker. The distinction seems a bit artificial, and suggests that it may be easier for data breach plaintiffs to establish standing in certain circuits (such as the Seventh and the Ninth) than other circuits (such as the Third).

The courts that have held that a data breach—and nothing more—is insufficient proof of injury-in-fact have reasoned that the mere possibility of identity theft or other harm is far too uncertain and depends on unknown variables. The U.S. District Court for the Eastern District of Missouri articulated this concern when it dismissed a lawsuit against a prescription drug benefit provider that suffered a breach:

> For plaintiff to suffer the injury and harm he alleges here, many "if's" would have to come to pass. Assuming plaintiff's allegation of security breach to be true, plaintiff alleges that he would be injured "if" his personal information was compromised, and "if" such information was obtained by an unauthorized third party, and "if" his identity was stolen as a result, and "if" the use of his stolen identity caused him harm. These multiple "if's" squarely place plaintiff's claimed injury in the realm of the hypothetical. If a party were allowed to assert such remote and speculative claims to obtain federal court jurisdiction, the Supreme Court's standing doctrine would be meaningless.[61]

Moreover, if a plaintiff sues a company for inadequate data security but a breach has not yet occurred, it is highly unlikely that the court will conclude that an injury-in-fact exists. For instance, in *Katz v. Pershing*,[62] the plaintiff sued a financial services company because she believed that the company did not implement adequate data security safeguards, and that, as the court described it, "her nonpublic personal information has been left vulnerable to prying eyes" and that therefore "authorized end-users can access and store her data at home and elsewhere, twenty-four hours a day and seven days a week, in unencrypted form; that the data, once saved by an authorized user, can potentially be accessed by hackers or other third parties; that the defendant fails adequately to monitor unauthorized access to her information; and that it employs inadequate methods for end-user authentication."[63] However, she did not allege that her information actually had been provided, even

---

61 Amburgy v. Express Scripts, Inc., 671 F. Supp. 2d 1046, 1053 (E.D. Mo. 2009).
62 672 F.3d 64 (1st Cir. 2012).
63 *Id.* at 70.

temporarily, to an unauthorized party. The First Circuit swiftly affirmed the dismissal of her lawsuit for lack of standing, concluding that "because she does not identify any incident in which her data has ever been accessed by an unauthorized person, she cannot satisfy Article III's requirement of actual or impending injury."[64]

Unlike the Ninth Circuit, some courts have concluded that *Clapper* requires them to set a high bar for injuries in data breach cases. For instance, in a 2017 Fourth Circuit opinion, *Beck v. McDonald*, plaintiffs filed a putative class action lawsuit against the Secretary of Veterans Affairs arising from the theft of a laptop that contained personal information of more than 7,400 patients.[65] Although the plaintiffs did not allege that they had experienced identity theft due to this incident, one group of the plaintiffs claimed that they suffered "embarrassment, inconvenience, unfairness, mental distress, and the threat of current and future substantial harm from identity theft and other misuse of their Personal Information," and that the possibility of identity theft required them to often review their "credit reports, bank statements, health insurance reports, and other similar information, purchas[e] credit watch services, and [shift] financial accounts."[66] The Fourth Circuit concluded that if it were to allow the suit to proceed, it would need to "engage with the same 'attenuated chain of possibilities' rejected by the Court in *Clapper*."[67] However, even this narrower view of standing may still allow some claims to proceed. The next year, in *Hutton v. National Board of Examiners in Optometry*,[68] the Fourth Circuit allowed a lawsuit to proceed because the plaintiffs alleged that a data breach resulted in unauthorized parties attempting to open credit accounts. "The Plaintiffs have been concretely injured by the data breach because the fraudsters used—and attempted to use—the Plaintiffs' personal information to open Chase Amazon Visa credit card accounts without their knowledge or approval," the court wrote. "Accordingly, there is no need to speculate on whether substantial harm will befall the Plaintiffs."[69]

Some courts are more likely to take a narrow view of the injury-in-fact requirement if the compromised data is not particularly sensitive. For instance, in a 2017 case from the Eighth Circuit, *In re SuperValu*,[70] a grocery store chain's systems were breached, leading to the theft of credit and debit card information, but in most of the plaintiffs' cases there were no actual reports of identity

---

64 *Id.* at 80.
65 Beck v. McDonald, 848 F.3d 262 (4th Cir. 2017).
66 *Id.* at 267.
67 *Id.* at 275.
68 892 F.3d 613 (4th Cir. 2018).
69 *Id.* at 622.
70 *In re* SuperValu, Inc., 870 F.3d 763 (8th Cir. 2017).

theft. The Eight Circuit concluded that these plaintiffs lacked standing, in part because "there is little to no risk that anyone will use the Card Information stolen in these data breaches to open unauthorized accounts in the plaintiffs' names, which is the type of identity theft generally considered to have a more harmful direct effect on consumers."[71]

2.1.2.2 Fairly Traceable

Even if a data breach plaintiff can demonstrate an injury-in-fact, the plaintiff also must credibly allege that the injury is "fairly traceable" to the defendant's failure to adopt adequate data security measures.

For instance, in *Resnick v. AvMed, Inc.*,[72] laptops containing patients' personal information were stolen from AvMed, a healthcare provider, exposing personal information such as Social Security numbers. Customers who later were victims of identity theft—and had credit accounts opened in their names without their authorization—sued AvMed. The company filed a motion to dismiss, and the district court dismissed the complaint, briefly stating that the complaint "fails to allege any cognizable injury."[73] On appeal, the U.S. Court of Appeals for the Eleventh Circuit disagreed, and found that plaintiffs established an injury-in-fact because they "allege that they have become victims of identity theft and have suffered monetary damages as a result."[74] The more difficult questions for the court, however, were whether this injury was "fairly traceable" to the company's actions and whether the injury was redressable through the litigation. The court concluded that a "fairly traceable" finding "requires less than a showing of 'proximate cause,'" and therefore the plaintiffs established this prong by alleging that they "became the victims of identity theft after the unencrypted laptops containing their sensitive information were stolen."[75]

2.1.2.3 Redressability

Finally, in order to demonstrate that standing exists, a plaintiff must sufficiently allege that the injury likely could be redressed by a ruling favorable to the plaintiff. As with the fairly traceable requirement, this prong is relatively easy for plaintiffs to satisfy.

In *AvMed*, the court also found that the plaintiffs satisfied the final prong, redressability, because they "allege[d] a monetary injury and an award of compensatory damages would redress that injury."[76] Accordingly, the court concluded that the plaintiffs had standing to sue AvMed for harm arising from the data breach.

---

71 *Id*. at 770–71 (internal quotation marks and citations omitted).
72 Resnick v. AvMed, Inc., 693 F.3d 1317 (11th Cir. 2012).
73 *Id*. at 1323.
74 *Id*.
75 *Id*. at 1324.
76 *Id*.

Similarly, in 2014, a federal district judge in Minnesota held that plaintiffs had standing to sue Target after the retail chain's massive 2013 data breach because they alleged "unlawful charges, restricted or blocked access to bank accounts, inability to pay other bills, and late payment charges or new card fees."[77] The *Target* court concluded that these are injuries-in-fact that are fairly traceable to Target's data security measures and redressable through the class action lawsuit.[78]

In the data breach lawsuit against P.F. Chang's,[79] the Seventh Circuit concluded that the plaintiffs had pleaded redressability because they "have some easily quantifiable financial injuries: they purchased credit monitoring services."[80] Likewise, in the 2017 *Carefirst* opinion, the D.C. Circuit observed that "[t]he fact that plaintiffs have reasonably spent money to protect themselves against a substantial risk creates the potential for them to be made whole by monetary damages."[81]

In short, Article III standing often is the largest barrier for plaintiffs in data breach cases, and the injury-in-fact requirement often is the largest sticking point of the three prongs in the standing analysis. Especially since the Supreme Court's decision in *Clapper*, courts are reluctant to allow a lawsuit to proceed merely because of the remote possibility that identity theft or another harm might occur at a later point. Many—but not all—courts will require a greater showing of harm, such as actual or imminent identity theft. However, as described earlier, the courts are somewhat split on this issue, and some courts are more likely than others to find that a plaintiff has standing.

2.2 Common Causes of Action Arising from Data Breaches

If a court concludes that a plaintiff has standing to sue over a data breach, the court then must consider the merits of the plaintiff's claims and whether the plaintiff credibly alleges the violation of any legal duties.

Private litigation arises from two types of law: common law and statutes. First, common-law claims are created by state courts through decades or centuries of legal precedent. They include negligence, breach of contract, some warranty cases, and negligent misrepresentation. Second, statutes are passed by legislatures. State consumer protection laws—which prohibit unfair and deceptive trade practices—frequently are cited as the basis for class action lawsuits after data breaches.

---

77 *In re* Target Corp. Data Sec. Breach Litig., 66 F. Supp. 3d 1154, 1159 (D. Minn. 2014).
78 *Id.* at 1159–61.
79 Lewert v. P.F. Chang's China Bistro, 819 F.3d 963 (7th Cir. 2016).
80 *Id.*
81 Attias v. Carefirst, Inc., 865 F.3d 620, 629 (D.C. Cir. 2017).

2.2.1 Negligence

A common claim in data breach-related lawsuits is negligence. This common-law claim is a frequent basis for lawsuits against companies. Customers might claim that retailers are negligent if the customers slip on freshly washed or waxed floors. Similarly, plaintiffs who are injured in car accidents may sue the other driver for negligence. In recent years, customers have also claimed that companies' inadequate data security measures are negligent.

Because negligence is a common-law tort, precise rules have developed over centuries from court rulings. Accordingly, the exact requirements for negligence vary by state (the highest courts in each state—and not federal courts—ultimately are responsible for creating common-law torts). Typically, common-law negligence requires that a plaintiff demonstrate four elements: (1) the defendant owed a "legal duty" to the plaintiff (e.g., a duty to protect the plaintiff's personal information), (2) the defendant breached that duty (e.g., by failing to adequately safeguard the plaintiff's personal data), and (3) the defendant's breach foreseeably caused (4) a "cognizable injury" to the plaintiff.[82]

Frequent Claims in Data Breach Litigation

- *Negligence.* The defendant owed the plaintiff a legal duty, breached that duty, and foreseeably caused injury to the plaintiff.
- *Negligent misrepresentation.* The defendant, in the course of business, failed to exercise reasonable care and supplied false information, causing the plaintiff to suffer pecuniary loss.
- *Breach of contract.* The defendant breached a bargained-for contract with the plaintiff.
- *Breach of implied warranty.* The defendant's product or services failed to satisfy basic expectations of fitness.
- *Invasion of privacy/publication of private facts.* The defendant published private facts that are offensive and are not of public concern.
- *Unjust enrichment.* The defendant knowingly obtained a benefit from the plaintiff in a manner that was so unfair that basic principles of equity require the defendant to pay the fair value of that benefit.
- *State consumer protection laws.* The defendant's conduct constituted unfair competition, unconscionable acts, and unfair or deceptive acts of trade or commerce.

---

82 *In re* Sony Gaming Networks & Customer Data Sec. Data Breach Litig., 996 F. Supp. 2d 942, 963 (S.D. Cal. 2014).

2.2.1.1 Legal Duty and Breach of Duty

The first two elements typically are not the subject of significant dispute in data breach litigation. Courts have often assumed that businesses have a legal duty to safeguard the personal information of their customers and employees and that a failure to meet that duty constitutes a breach. For instance, in the Sony data breach litigation, the district court held that finding a legal duty is supported not only by state law but also by "common sense":

> [B]ecause Plaintiffs allege that they provided their Personal Information to Sony as part of a commercial transaction, and that Sony failed to employ reasonable security measures to protect their Personal Information, including the utilization of industry-standard encryption, the Court finds Plaintiffs have sufficiently alleged a legal duty and a corresponding breach.[83]

If the defendant is subject to mandatory security requirements, such as an industry standard set of protocols, courts may view those requirements as a legal duty for the purposes of a negligence lawsuit. For instance, the retailer Michaels experienced a breach of the PIN code entry system for its in-store debit and credit card processing systems. Michaels allegedly had failed to comply with the payment card industry's PIN Security Requirements, which, among other things, required retailers to prevent counterfeit devices from collecting PIN numbers at the retailers' stores. The court reasoned:

> Plaintiffs allege that Michaels failed to comply with various PIN pad security requirements, which were specifically designed to minimize the risk of exposing their financial information to third parties. Because the security measures could have prevented the criminal acts committed by the skimmers, Michaels' failure to implement such measures created a condition conducive to a foreseeable intervening criminal act.[84]

As the *Michaels* case demonstrates, companies must be aware of industry best practices and suggested security standards, as those are likely to create a standard of care that could trigger liability in negligence lawsuits.

Defendant companies occasionally argue that if their computer systems were hacked by a third party, the defendant did not breach a duty of care to the plaintiffs. The gravamen of this argument is that the harm was caused by a third party, and not the defendant. Courts generally reject such an argument in

---

83 *Id.* at 966.
84 *In re* Michaels Stores Pin Pad Litig., 830 F. Supp. 2d 518, 522 (N.D. Ill. 2011).

data breach cases. Target made this argument in its attempt to persuade the court to dismiss the class action that arose out of its 2013 data breach and was brought by financial institutions. The court rejected Target's position, concluding that "[a]lthough the third-party hackers' activities caused harm, Target played a key role in allowing the harm to occur."[85] The court considered the following factors in determining whether a duty exists: "(1) the foreseeability of harm to the plaintiff, (2) the connection between the defendant's conduct and the injury suffered, (3) the moral blame attached to the defendant's conduct, (4) the policy of preventing future harm, and (5) the burden to the defendant and community of imposing a duty to exercise care with resulting liability for breach," and ultimately concluded that imposing a legal duty on Target to protect customers' personal information "will aid Minnesota's policy of punishing companies that do not secure consumers' credit- and debit-card information."[86]

2.2.1.2 Cognizable Injury

Perhaps the largest barrier to plaintiffs in negligence claims arising from data breaches is demonstrating that the breach of the legal duty caused a *cognizable injury*. That is due to a rule known as the Economic Loss Doctrine, which states that "no cause of action exists for negligence that results solely in economic damages unaccompanied by physical or property damage."[87] The Economic Loss Doctrine applies in many (but not all) state common-law negligence claims. The doctrine dates back to a 1927 opinion in which the United States Supreme Court concluded that "a tort to the person or property of one man does not make the tortfeasor liable to another merely because the injured person was under a contract with that other, unknown to the doer of the wrong."[88] As the Pennsylvania Supreme Court stated in 1985, this general rule leads to the conclusion that "negligent harm to economic advantage alone is too remote for recovery under a negligence theory."[89]

Over the past century, state courts have determined how—and if—to adopt this doctrine for common-law negligence claims. Keep in mind that the Economic Loss Doctrine can differ greatly by state, and therefore a data breach plaintiff who might have a viable claim in one state might be unsuccessful in a state that has a more defendant-friendly Economic Loss Doctrine. For instance, in the Target data breach consumer class action lawsuit, Target moved to dismiss negligence claims from consumers in 11 states, citing those states'

---

85 *In re* Target Corp. Customer Data Sec. Breach Litig., 64 F. Supp. 3d 1304, 1309 (D. Minn. 2014).
86 *Id.* at 1309–10.
87 Sovereign Bank v. BJ's Wholesale Club, 533 F.3d 162, 175 (3d Cir. 2008) (internal quotations and citation omitted).
88 Robins Dry Dock & Repair Co. v. Flint, 275 U.S. 303 (1927).
89 Aikens v. Baltimore & Ohio R.R. Co., 501 A.2d 277 (1985).

Economic Loss Doctrines.[90] After an extensive analysis of the common law in each of those states, the court concluded that the Economic Loss Doctrine required dismissal of the negligence claims from 5 of the 11 states, whereas the claims in the remaining states should not be dismissed under those states' versions of the doctrine.[91] The court noted two primary differences among the various versions of the Economic Loss Doctrine. First, some states recognize an "independent duty" exception to the doctrine, meaning that "the rule does not apply where the duty alleged is an independent duty that does not arise from commercial expectations."[92] Second, some states created an exception to the doctrine if there is a "special relationship" between the plaintiff and the defendant.[93] The *Target* opinion's state-by-state analysis of the economic loss doctrine is excerpted in Appendix F of this book.

The most stringent (and defendant-friendly) formulation of the doctrine "bars recovery unless the plaintiffs can establish that the injuries they suffered due to the defendants' negligence involved physical harm or property damage, and not solely economic loss."[94] For instance, a data breach of the payment card data at retailer BJ's Wholesale Club resulted in unauthorized charges at a number of credit unions. The credit unions, and the insurer that partially reimbursed the credit unions, sued BJ's for negligence arising from the costs of replacing the breached credit cards. The Massachusetts Supreme Judicial Court affirmed the dismissal of the negligence claims under the Economic Loss Doctrine, concluding that the credit cards were "canceled by the plaintiff credit unions for the purpose of avoiding future economic losses."[95] Other courts similarly have relied on the Economic Loss Doctrine to dismiss negligence claims filed by companies against businesses that have experienced data breaches that have led the plaintiffs to experience financial losses.[96]

The Economic Loss Doctrine also presents a barrier to customers who are suing businesses for failing to adequately safeguard their personal information. For instance, despite finding that Michaels had breached a legal duty to protect payment card PIN data, the Illinois federal judge dismissed the negligence

---

90 *In re* Target Corp. Customer Data Sec. Breach Litig., 66 F. Supp. 3d 1154, 1171 (D. Minn. 2014).

91 *Id.* at 1176 ("The economic loss rule in Alaska, California, Illinois, Iowa, and Massachusetts appears to bar Plaintiffs' negligence claims under the laws of those states. Plaintiffs' negligence claims in the remaining states may go forward.").

92 *Id.* at 1171.

93 *Id.* at 1172.

94 Cumis Ins. Soc'y, Inc. v. BJ's Wholesale Club, 455 Mass. 458, 469 (Mass. 2009).

95 *Id.* at 470.

96 *See, e.g., In re* TJX Cos. Retail Sec. Breach Litig., 564 F.3d 489, 498 (1st Cir. 2009) (affirming dismissal of negligence claim by banks against retail chain that suffered a data breach because "purely economic losses are unrecoverable in tort and strict liability actions in the absence of personal injury or property damage.").

claim filed by customers. The judge noted that "other courts dealing with data breach cases have also held that the economic loss doctrine bars the plaintiff's tort claim because the plaintiff has not suffered personal injury or property damage."[97] Similarly, in the Sony Play Station Network data breach litigation, the court relied on the Economic Loss Doctrine for its dismissal of negligence claims under California and Massachusetts laws.[98]

In some states, in contrast, the Economic Loss Doctrine is more limited. For instance, in Maine, the doctrine means that courts "do not permit tort recovery for a defective product's damage to itself."[99] A federal court in Maine, applying Maine common law, refused to dismiss a negligence claim arising from a breach of the defendant's computer system, concluding that "[t]his is not a case about a defective product that [the defendant] has sold to the customer."[100] In these states, it may be easier for a plaintiff to successfully bring a claim for negligence arising from a data breach.

The Economic Loss Doctrine does not bar claims in California if the defendant has a "special relationship" with the plaintiff.[101] In a 2018 opinion in a class action lawsuit arising from a breach of Yahoo! email account information, a federal judge concluded that a special relationship existed, and therefore the Economic Loss Doctrine did not block a negligence claim.[102] That court's analysis is instructive for other cases in California in which a special relationship applies, as it systematically applies the prevailing special relationship test to a data breach lawsuit:

> First, the contract entered into between the parties related to email services for Plaintiffs. Plaintiffs were required to turn over their PII [personally identifiable information] to Defendants and did so with the understanding that Defendants would adequately protect Plaintiffs' PII and inform Plaintiffs of breaches. ... Second, it was plainly foreseeable that Plaintiffs would suffer injury if Defendants did not adequately protect the PII. .... Third, the [complaint] asserts that hackers were able to gain access to the PII and that Defendants did not promptly notify Plaintiffs, thereby causing injury to Plaintiffs. ... Fourth, the injury was allegedly suffered exactly because Defendants provided inadequate security and knew that their system was insufficient. ... Fifth, Defendants

---

97 *In re* Michaels Stores Pin Pad Litig., 830 F. Supp. 2d 518, 530-31 (N.D. Ill. 2011).

98 *In re* Sony Gaming Networks & Customer Data Sec. Data Breach Litig., 996 F. Supp. 2d 942, 967 (S.D. Cal. 2014).

99 *In re* Hannaford Bros. Co. Customer Data Sec. Breach Litig., 613 F. Supp. 2d 108, 127 (D. Me. 2009), *aff'd in part & rev'd in part on other grounds sub nom* Anderson v. Hannaford Bros. Co., 659 F.3d 151 (1st Cir. 2011).

100 *Id.*

101 J'Aire Corp. v. Gregory, 24 Cal. 3d 799 (1979).

102 *In re* Yahoo! Customer Data Sec. Breach Litig., 313 F. Supp. 3d 1113, 1132 (N.D. Cal. 2018).

"knew their data security was inadequate" and that "they [did not] have the tools to detect and document intrusions or exfiltration of PII." ... "Defendants are morally culpable, given their repeated security breaches, wholly inadequate safeguards, and refusal to notify Plaintiffs ... of breaches or security vulnerabilities." ... Sixth, and finally, Defendants' concealment of their knowledge and failure to adequately protect Plaintiffs' PII implicates the consumer data protection concerns expressed in California statutes[.][103]

As with establishing Article III standing, plaintiffs suing for data breaches or inadequate data security have their best chances at succeeding in negligence claims if they can demonstrate *actual* harm that has occurred as a result of the defendant's poor data security. However, it still is possible to recover even if harm such as identity theft has not occurred, depending on the scope of the state's Economic Loss Doctrine and other legal rules surrounding negligence.

2.2.1.3 Causation

Even if a negligence plaintiff has demonstrated that the defendant breached a duty to safeguard the plaintiff's information and that the plaintiff suffered cognizable injury, the plaintiff still must demonstrate that the breach of duty actually and proximately *caused* the injury. In other words, the defendant must link the inadequate data security to the identity theft or other harm. Causation is not disputed nearly as frequently as the other elements of negligence in data breach lawsuits; however, it potentially could present a barrier to an otherwise successful claim.

Nevertheless, courts are willing to make reasonable assumptions if the allegations in a lawsuit lead to the likely conclusion that the breach caused harm to the plaintiffs. For example, in the *AvMed* case discussed earlier, the two plaintiffs were victims of identity theft approximately one year after an unencrypted laptop with their personal information was stolen.[104] Both plaintiffs stated that they had taken a number of steps to prevent themselves from becoming victims of identity theft, and that they had not previously experienced identity theft.[105] The court recognized that whether the breach caused the identity theft was a close call, particularly because the breach occurred approximately a year before the identity theft. The plaintiffs succeeded in convincing the Eleventh Circuit that they plausibly alleged causation because the information that was used in the identity theft was identical to the information on the stolen laptop.[106] Applying "common sense" to the allegations, the court concluded that the plaintiffs' allegations of causation "move from the realm of the possible into

---

103 *Id.*
104 Resnick v. Avmed, Inc., 693 F.3d 1317, 1322 (11th Cir. 2012).
105 *Id.* at 1326.
106 *Id.*

the plausible," and it therefore denied AvMed's motion to dismiss.[107] However, the court noted that if the complaint had contained fewer specific factual allegations, the negligence claim might have been dismissed.[108]

Causation is easier to establish when the duration between the data breach and the identity theft is shorter. For instance, in *Stollenwerk v. Tri-West Health Care Alliance*,[109] the plaintiff suffered identity theft six weeks after computers containing his personal information were stolen from defendant Tri-West's headquarters. The Ninth Circuit concluded that the plaintiff had demonstrated causation because "(1) he gave Tri-West his personal information; (2) the identity fraud incidents began six weeks after the hard drives containing Tri-West's customers' personal information were stolen; and (3) he previously had not suffered any such incidents of identity theft."[110] However, the court cautioned that plaintiffs cannot prove causation merely because two incidents occurred within weeks of each other. Here, causation also was *logically* plausible because "[a]s a matter of twenty-first century common knowledge, just as certain exposures can lead to certain diseases, the theft of a computer hard drive certainly *can* result in an attempt by a thief to access the contents for purposes of identity fraud, and such an attempt *can* succeed."[111]

2.2.2 Negligent Misrepresentation or Omission

In a claim somewhat related to general negligence, some consumers and businesses bring data breach lawsuits against companies for misrepresenting their data security practices or omitting crucial details about their failure to adequately safeguard customer data.

In many states, negligent misrepresentation claims require the same elements as general negligence claims: legal duty, breach, causation, and injury. But some states allow negligent misrepresentation claims to proceed even if the plaintiffs only allege economic losses. This makes it easier, in those states, for plaintiffs to bring claims under the tort of negligent misrepresentation than under general negligence.

For instance, a Nevada federal judge refused to dismiss negligent misrepresentation claims that customers brought against online retailer Zappos.com after a data breach. Quoting an opinion from the Nevada Supreme Court, which is the highest authority for determining the scope of Nevada common law, the federal judge reasoned that liability "is proper in cases where there is significant risk that the law would not exert significant financial pressures to avoid such negligence," and that such cases include "negligent misstatements

---

107 *Id.*
108 *Id.*
109 Stollenwerk v. Tri-West Health Care All., 254 Fed. Appx. 664 (9th Cir. 2007) (unpublished opinion).
110 *Id.* at 667.
111 *Id.*

about financial matters."[112] The court reasoned that because the customers did not have a "highly interconnected network of contracts" outlining the company's data security obligations, the customers did not have the ability to exert pressure to prevent such negligence, and therefore the tort of negligent misrepresentation should be available to them.[113]

Many state courts have adopted the definition of negligent misrepresentation from the *Restatement (Second) of Torts*, which states that negligent misrepresentation occurs under the following circumstances:

> One who, in the course of his business, profession or employment, or in any other transaction in which he has a pecuniary interest, supplies false information for the guidance of others in their business transactions, is subject to liability for pecuniary loss caused to them by their justifiable reliance upon the information, if he fails to exercise reasonable care or competence in obtaining or communicating the information.[114]

In the banks' lawsuit against TJX, negligent misrepresentation was among the claims against the retailer. The banks claimed that because TJX accepted Visa and MasterCard credit cards, the retailer had "impliedly represented that they would comply with MasterCard and Visa regulations and this was the negligent misrepresentation."[115] To determine whether this amounted to negligent misrepresentation, the U.S. Court of Appeals for the First Circuit applied Massachusetts common law, which has adopted the *Restatement* test for negligent misrepresentation. The court appeared to be highly skeptical about the banks' argument that merely accepting credit cards constitutes a representation about TJX's data security, stating that the "implication is implausible and converts the cause of action into liability for negligence—without the limitations otherwise applicable to negligence claims."[116] Although conduct "can be part of a representation," the court reasoned, "the link between the conduct and the implication is typically tight."[117] However, because the court was only considering a motion to dismiss—a stage at which all factual claims must be viewed in the light most favorable to the plaintiff—the court allowed the negligent misrepresentation claim to survive "on life support."[118]

---

112 *In re* Zappos.com, Inc. Customer Data Sec. Breach Litig., No. 3:120cv-00325-RCJ-VPC. MDI No. 2357 (D. Nev. Sept. 9, 2013).
113 *Id.*
114 RESTATEMENT (SECOND) OF TORTS § 522 (Am. L. Inst. 1977).
115 *In re* TJX Cos. Retail Sec. Breach Litig., 564 F.3d 489, 494 (1st Cir. 2009).
116 *Id.*
117 *Id.*
118 *Id.* at 495.

The financial institutions suing Target alleged that Target "failed to disclose material weaknesses in its data security systems and procedures," and therefore was liable for negligent misrepresentation by omission.[119] The district court concluded that the plaintiffs plausibly alleged that Target owed a duty to disclose because it "knew facts about its ability to repel hackers that Plaintiffs could not have known, and that Target's public representations regarding its data security practices were misleading."[120] The court also found that the plaintiffs complied with Federal Rule of Civil Procedure 9(b), which requires plaintiffs alleging fraud or mistake to "state with particularity the circumstances constituting fraud or mistake." The court concluded that the plaintiffs complied with this rule because they "have identified the omitted information, namely Target's failure to disclose that its data security systems were deficient and in particular that Target had purposely disengaged one feature of those systems that would have detected and potentially stopped the hackers at the inception of the hacking scheme."[121] However, the court ultimately found that the financial institutions' complaint fell short of properly alleging negligent misrepresentation because it did not plead that the institutions relied on Target's omissions. The court rejected the plaintiff's claims that they were not required to plead reliance, and held that although securities fraud-by-omission claims do not require such an allegation, "courts have not extended this presumption of reliance outside of the securities fraud context."[122]

2.2.3 Breach of Contract

Consumers whose information has been compromised in a data breach often present claims that the companies with which they entrusted their information breached a contract with the customer. As with torts, the precise elements of breach of contract may vary by state. For services, contract laws are set by courts under the common law; for the sale of goods, contract laws are set by the state legislature's adoption of the Uniform Commercial Code. Typically, however, a plaintiff must demonstrate (1) a contract between the plaintiff and the defendant, (2) the defendant's breach of that contract, and (3) damage caused to the plaintiff as a result of that breach.[123]

If a company enters into a contract in which it guarantees a specific level of data security, but then fails to provide that data security, and a breach exposes customers' information and leads to identity theft or other harm, the customer

---

119 *In re* Target Corp. Customer Data Sec. Breach Litig., 64 F. Supp. 3d 1304, 1310 (D. Minn. 2014).
120 *Id*. at 1311.
121 *Id*.
122 *Id*.
123 *See generally* Kaymark v. Bank of Am., NA, 783 F.3d 168, 182 (3d Cir. 2015).

would have a fairly strong claim for breach of contract. The company would have breached an express duty in the contract, and that breach would have caused damage to the plaintiff. However, breach of contract claims in data breach cases often are not so clear-cut.

Data breach plaintiffs have attempted to bring breach of contract claims against companies for promises that they have made in their privacy policies or other public statements. Such claims will fail unless the plaintiff can prove that these statements are part of the bargained-for agreement between the plaintiff and the defendant. For example, in 2016, a California district court dismissed a breach of contract claim in the class action lawsuit against Anthem, the health insurer that had experienced a large data breach. The plaintiffs alleged that Anthem had failed to adhere to a statement in its privacy notice, which stated: "We keep your oral, written and electronic [PII] safe using physical, electronic, and procedural means."[124] The court dismissed this claim, concluding that the plaintiffs' complaint failed to "allege that the privacy notices or public website statements were part of or were incorporated by reference" into the plaintiffs' contracts with Anthem.[125]

In some cases, the plaintiff alleges that a company—such as a service provider—breached an agreement with an intermediary by failing to safeguard information, and that in turn caused harm to the plaintiff. In such a case, the plaintiff must convince a court that he was a *third-party beneficiary* of this agreement. Unless a contract explicitly names a third party as a beneficiary of a contract, a court must determine whether a third party was an "intended beneficiary" of the contract's data security provisions.

A number of state courts have adopted the test for intended beneficiaries articulated in Section 302 of the *Restatement (Second) of Contracts*:

Intended and Incidental Beneficiaries

1) Unless otherwise agreed between promisor and promisee, a beneficiary of a promise is an intended beneficiary if recognition of a right to performance in the beneficiary is appropriate to effectuate the intentions of the parties and either
   a) the performance of the promise will satisfy an obligation of the promisee to pay money to the beneficiary; or
   b) the circumstances indicate that the promisee intends to give the beneficiary the benefit of the promised performance.
2) An incidental beneficiary is a beneficiary who is not an intended beneficiary.[126]

---

124 *In re* Anthem, Inc. Data Breach Litig., 162 F. Supp. 3d 953, 967 (N.D. Cal. 2016).
125 *Id.* at 980.
126 Restatement (Second) of Contracts § 302.

In 2008, the U.S. Court of Appeals for the Third Circuit applied this definition of "intended beneficiary" in a case arising from the BJ's Wholesale Club retailer data breach referenced earlier. A number of lawsuits arose out of that breach, including a lawsuit by Sovereign Bank, a credit card issuer, against BJ's and its bank, Fifth Third. Among the many claims by Sovereign was breach of contract, alleging that Fifth Third breached its agreement with Visa to ensure adequate data security. Sovereign claimed that BJ's breached this agreement, and banks whose customers' data were breached—such as Sovereign—were intended third-party beneficiaries of the agreement between Fifth Third and Visa.[127] Fifth Third argued that the contract was not intended to benefit issuing banks such as Sovereign, but instead to "benefit the Visa system as a whole."[128] The district court dismissed this claim, but the Third Circuit reversed, finding that a Visa executive's testimony that the data security requirements are intended to benefit "the members that participate in it" was sufficient to allow a "reasonable jury" to conclude that Sovereign was an intended beneficiary, and therefore could sue Fifth Third for breach of contract.[129]

Some contracts, however, clearly preclude third-party beneficiary claims. For instance, Pershing LLC, which provides an online platform for financial companies, was sued by the customer of a financial institution that used Pershing's platform. The plaintiff filed a lawsuit against Pershing, alleging that the company failed to adequately secure her personal information by using safeguards such as encryption and proper end-user authentication.[130] Among her legal claims was that Pershing breached the data confidentiality provision of an agreement between Pershing and the plaintiff's financial institution. The U.S. Court of Appeals for the First Circuit swiftly rejected this claim, noting that the agreement stated that it "'is not intended to confer any benefits on third-parties[.]'"[131] The court held that when the intent to preclude third-party beneficiaries is "unambiguously disclaimed, a suitor cannot attain third-party beneficiary status."[132]

In many data breach cases, there is not an express contract between a consumer and a company. For instance, if a customer walks into a store and purchases a product with her credit card, the customer typically does not first require the retailer to agree to adequately safeguard her credit card number and other personally identifiable information. However, in many states, it is possible to allege that a company's failure to safeguard data breaches an *implied* term of a contract.

---

127 Sovereign Bank v. B.J.'s Wholesale Club, 533 F.3d 162, 168 (3d Cir. 2008).
128 *Id.* at 169.
129 *Id.* at 172.
130 Katz v. Pershing, LLC, 672 F.3d 64, 69–70 (1st Cir. 2012).
131 *Id.* at 73.
132 *Id.*

For instance, in the *Hannaford* case, which consumers brought against a retailer after a breach of payment card information, the plaintiffs relied on Maine common law, which states that contracts can include "all such implied provisions as are indispensable to effectuate the intention of the parties and as arise from the language of the contract and circumstances under which it was made," provided that the provision is "absolutely necessary to effectuate the contract."[133] In *Hannaford*, the plaintiffs alleged that when they provided their credit cards to the grocers' cashier at the cash register, they entered into an implied contract for the grocer to protect their credit card numbers. The grocer moved to dismiss this claim, stating that such an assumption is not "absolutely necessary" to engage in the payment transaction. The district court disagreed with the grocer and refused to dismiss the claim. The judge reasoned that a jury "could reasonably find that customers would not tender cards to merchants who undertook zero obligation to protect customers' electronic data."[134] However, the judge recognized that such an implied contract is limited, because "in today's known world of sophisticated hackers, data theft, software glitches, and computer viruses, a jury could not reasonably find an implied merchant commitment against every intrusion under any circumstances whatsoever (consider, for example, an armed robber confronting the merchant's computer systems personnel at gunpoint)."[135] In short, the court held that a jury could find an implied contract for the grocer to enact *reasonable* safeguards, similar to the negligence standard. However, the court does not believe that the implied contract creates an absolute prohibition of all data breaches, because such a duty would be impossible in light of modern cyber threats. Nor did the judge agree with the plaintiff that there is an implied contract for the grocer to notify consumers of data breaches, because such notification is not "absolutely necessary" for the contract.[136] The grocer appealed the district court's refusal to dismiss the claim entirely, and the U.S. Court of Appeals for the First Circuit affirmed the district court's conclusion, stating that a jury "could reasonably conclude, therefore, that an implicit agreement to safeguard the data is necessary to effectuate the contract."[137]

In contrast, the plaintiff in the case against Pershing, described earlier, claimed that in addition to being a third-party beneficiary to an express contract between Pershing and her service provider, she had an implied contract with Pershing, under which Pershing implicitly agreed to protect her personal

---

133 *In re* Hannaford Bros. Co. Customer Data Sec. Breach Litig., 613 F. Supp. 2d 108, 118 (D. Me. 2009), *aff'd in part & rev'd in part on other grounds*, Anderson v. Hannaford Bros. Co., 659 F.3d 151 (1st Cir. 2011).
134 *Id.* at 119.
135 *Id.*
136 *Id.*
137 Anderson v. Hannaford Bros. Co., 659 F.3d 151, 159 (1st Cir. 2011).

information.[138] The First Circuit rejected this argument, holding that a contract did not exist between the plaintiff and Pershing because there was not any consideration (i.e., the plaintiff did not provide a "bargained-for benefit," nor did she suffer any "bargained-for detriment in exchange for the defendant's supported promises").[139]

Some courts may be willing to recognize an implied contract for adequate data security even if they refuse to determine that an express contract existed. For instance, in 2017, a federal judge in New York dismissed a breach of express contract claim against TransPerfect, a company whose employees' data was breached.[140] The plaintiffs claimed that their contracts to work at TransPerfect "involved a mutual exchange of consideration whereby TransPerfect entrusted Plaintiffs and Class Members with particular job duties and responsibilities in furtherance of TransPerfect's Services, in exchange for the promise of employment, with salary, benefits and secure PII."[141] The court dismissed this claim, concluding that the complaint "fails to allege any facts to support the conclusion that Defendant expressly contracted to protect employees' PII."[142] However, the judge found that the complaint raises "a strong inference of implied contract," and therefore refused to dismiss the breach of implied contract claim. "Plaintiffs allege conduct and a course of dealing that raise a strong inference of implied contract," the court wrote. "TransPerfect required and obtained the PII as part of the employment relationship, evincing an implicit promise by TransPerfect to act reasonably to keep its employees' PII safe. TransPerfect's privacy policies and security practices manual—which states that the company 'maintains robust procedures designed to carefully protect the PII with which it [is] entrusted'—further supports a finding of an implicit promise."[143] The *TransPerfect* case demonstrates that implicit contract claims arising from data breaches are possible even when express contracts do not exist.

Even in cases in which plaintiffs allege that they had a direct contract with a breached company, courts may be skeptical of such claims. For instance, in a 2017 case in the Eighth Circuit, *Kuhns v. Scottrade*,[144] a brokerage firm, Scottrade, was hacked, resulting in the unauthorized acquisition of personal information of more than 4.6 million customers. One customer, Matthew Kuhns, filed a putative class action, alleging, among

138 Katz v. Pershing, LLC, 672 F.3d 64, 69-74 (1st Cir. 2012).
139 *Id.*
140 Sackin v. TransPerfect Global, 278 F. Supp. 3d 739, 744 (S.D.N.Y. 2017).
141 *Id.* at 750.
142 *Id.*
143 *Id.*
144 Kuhns v. Scottrade, 868 F.3d 711 (8th Cir. 2017).

other things, breach of contract and breach of implied contract. He pointed to a "Privacy Policy and Security Statement" that was an addendum to the brokerage agreement that he had signed with Scottrade. That agreement stated, among other things, that the company would "maintain physical, electronic and procedural safeguards that comply with federal regulations to guard your nonpublic personal information," encrypt data, and comply with data security laws.[145] Although the Eighth Circuit concluded that Kuhns had standing to bring the contract claims, it concluded that his complaint failed to allege a breach-of-contract claim because it did not adequately allege misrepresentation, "just bare assertions that Scottrade's efforts failed to protect customer PII."[146]

Companies often include disclaimers in their terms of service and user contracts that seek to limit the ability of customers to sue for breach of contract and other causes of action arising from data breaches. For instance, after Yahoo! was sued for its data breaches, it sought to dismiss the breach-of-contract claims by pointing to the following clause in its Terms of Service:

> YOU EXPRESSLY UNDERSTAND AND AGREE THAT YAHOO! ... SHALL NOT BE LIABLE TO YOU FOR ANY PUNITIVE, INDIRECT, INCIDENTAL, SPECIAL, CONSEQUENTIAL OR EXEMPLARY DAMAGES, INCLUDING, BUT NOT LIMITED TO, DAMAGES FOR LOSS OF PROFITS, GOODWILL, USE, DATA OR OTHER INTANGIBLE LOSSES (EVEN IF YAHOO! HAS BEEN ADVISED OF THE POSSIBILITY OF SUCH DAMAGES), RESULTING FROM: ... UNAUTHORIZED ACCESS TO OR ALTERATION OF YOUR TRANSMISSIONS OR DATA ... OR ... ANY OTHER MATTER RELATING TO THE YAHOO! SERVICE.[147]

The plaintiffs argued that this limitation is "unconscionable," and therefore unenforceable by the courts. For a court to hold that a contractual provision is unconscionable, it must determine that it is unconscionable as a matter of *both* substance *and* procedure. The court concluded that this provision satisfied both prongs and was therefore unconscionable. It was procedurally unconscionable, the court wrote, because the plaintiffs alleged "that Defendants' liability limitations appear near the end of the 12-page legal Terms of Service document where the Terms of Service are contained in an adhesion contract and customers may not negotiate or modify any terms."[148]

---

145 *Id.* at 714.
146 *Id.* at 717.
147 *In re* Yahoo! Customer Data Sec. Breach Litig., 313 F. Supp. 3d 1113, 1136 (N.D. Cal. 2018).
148 *Id.* at 1137.

The provision is substantively unconscionable, the court wrote, because the plaintiffs claimed "that the limitations of liability are overly one-sided and bar any effective relief."[149]

In sum, there are three primary methods whereby a plaintiff could attempt to bring a breach of contract lawsuit arising from a data breach or poor data security. First, the plaintiff could sue for breaching an express contract between the plaintiff and a defendant in which the defendant agreed to provide a specified level of data security. This is the most likely route for success for the plaintiff, but in many recent data breach cases, such contracts did not exist. Second, the plaintiff could claim that she was the *intended* third-party beneficiary of a contract between the defendant and another party, in which the defendant agreed to provide a certain level of data security. As demonstrated in this section, it often is difficult to prove that the plaintiff was an intended third-party beneficiary of a contract. Third, the plaintiff can claim that even though there was not an express contract with the defendant, the parties had an *implied* contract in which the defendant agreed to provide a reasonable level of data security. Such claims are fact-specific and their success is difficult to predict with great certainty.

2.2.4 Breach of Implied Warranty

Consumers also have claimed that companies breached implied warranties by failing to safeguard their data. Plaintiffs bringing such claims typically argue that by selling the plaintiffs a product, the defendants provided an implied warranty that the good was fit for a particular purpose. The defendants breached that warranty, they argue, by failing to provide proper data security.

In the United States, there are two general sources of implied warranties: Article 2 of the Uniform Commercial Code, which applies to the sale of goods, and the common law (rulings by state court judges over many decades), which applies to the sale of services. Implied warranties under both the Uniform Commercial Code and the common law have arisen in data breach cases.

Most states have adopted the implied warranty provisions of Article 2 of the Uniform Commercial Code, which governs the sale of goods. Article 2 creates two implied warranties that are particularly relevant to data breach cases: warranty of merchantability and warranty of fitness for a particular purpose. Data breach plaintiffs have alleged that by failing to provide adequate security for personal information, a company breached both the implied warranties of merchantability and fitness.

---

149 *Id.*

Section 2-314 of the Uniform Commercial Code, which creates an implied warranty of merchantability, requires goods to be "merchantable," which the statute defines as:

a) pass without objection in the trade under the contract description; and

b) in the case of fungible goods, are of fair average quality within the description; and

c) are fit for the ordinary purposes for which such goods are used; and

d) run, within the variations permitted by the agreement, of even kind, quality and quantity within each unit and among all units involved; and

e) are adequately contained, packaged, and labeled as the agreement may require; and

f) conform to the promise or affirmations of fact made on the container or label if any.[150]

The implied warranty of merchantability only applies to merchants who sell "goods of that kind." In other words, a car dealer implicitly warrants the merchantability of cars that it sells, but if it sells an old desk that it had used in its office, it will not imply merchantability of the desk.

Section 2-315 of the Uniform Commercial Code (UCC), which creates an implied warranty of fitness for a particular purpose, states:

> Where the seller at the time of contracting has reason to know any particular purpose for which the goods are required and that the buyer is relying on the seller's skill or judgment to select or furnish suitable goods, there is unless excluded or modified under the next section an implied warranty that the goods shall be fit for a particular purpose.[151]

The UCC allows merchants to "disclaim" implied warranties and thereby avoid the obligations imposed by these requirements. To do so, the UCC states, the disclaimer must be "by a writing and conspicuous."[152] To disclaim implied warranties, the UCC states that it is sufficient for the written disclaimer to use expressions such as "with all faults," "as is," or "There are no warranties which extend beyond the description on the face hereof."[153]

It is vital to remember that the UCC is only a *model* for states to use as a framework for adopting their own laws governing the sale of goods. Some

---

150 UCC § 2-314 (2002).
151 UCC § 2-315 (2002).
152 UCC § 2-316 (2002).
153 *Id.*

states do not allow companies to disclaim the UCC's implied warranties. For instance, Massachusetts's version of the UCC states that any attempts to limit or exclude the implied warranties of merchantability or fitness for a particular purpose are "unenforceable."[154] This prohibition of such disclaimers makes Massachusetts a particularly attractive venue for implied warranty claims. To that end, a company must ensure that it understands all applicable warranty laws, particularly if it is a larger business with customers nationwide.

However, the UCC often does not apply to data breach lawsuits. Many data breach cases arise when customers sue online networks, banks, healthcare providers, and other companies that provide them with *services*. The UCC only applies to the sale of goods, whereas the common law (law created by centuries of court rulings) typically applies to the sale of services. Determining whether a data breach arises from a sale of goods or a sale of services can, however, be tricky.

For instance, in the Sony Play Station Network data breach class action, among the plaintiffs' many claims was breach of the implied warranty of fitness for a particular purpose under the Massachusetts UCC.[155] Because Sony had disclaimed implied warranties, the Massachusetts statute appeared to be an attractive route for the plaintiffs to bring an implied warranty claim. However, the court rejected the claim because it involved a breach of the online *services* that Sony provided via the Play Station Network. The Massachusetts version of the UCC defines "goods" as "all things ... which are movable at the time of identification to the contract for sale."[156] The court concluded that even though the online services could only be accessed by the consumer's purchase of a Play Station Network game console, the "thrust, or purpose of the contract" was to provide access to the Play Station Network, which is not a movable "thing" as defined by the UCC.[157]

Similarly, in the *Hannaford* case,[158] a lawsuit arising from the breach of payment card information at a grocery store, the plaintiffs brought a breach of implied warranty claim under Maine's version of the Uniform Commercial Code. They alleged that the retailer's acceptance of card data rendered its electronic payment processing system a "good" that it implicitly guaranteed would securely process card transactions. The court swiftly dismissed this claim, concluding that "goods" under the UCC would include the retailer's groceries but not the payment system that it uses to process card data.[159]

---

154 MASS. GEN. LAWS § 2-316A(2).

155 *In re* Sony Gaming Networks & Customer Data Sec. Data Breach Litig., 996 F. Supp. 2d 942, 983 (S.D. Cal. 2014).

156 MASS. GEN. LAWS § 2-105(1).

157 *In re* Sony Gaming Networks & Customer Data Sec. Data Breach Litig., 996 F. Supp. 2d 942, 983 (S.D. Cal. 2014).

158 *In re* Hannaford Bros. Co. Customer Data Sec. Breach Litig., 613 F. Supp. 2d 108, 127 (D. Me. 2009), *aff'd in part & rev'd in part on other grounds*, Anderson v. Hannaford Bros. Co., 659 F.3d 151 (1st Cir. 2011).

159 *Id.* at 120 ("The term 'goods' does not include the payment mechanism.").

Many states also recognize *common-law* implied warranty claims. Because these are not derived from the UCC, the warranties *do* apply to the sale of services, such as online accounts, but the common law in many states typically allows companies to use disclaimers to avoid being bound by implied warranties. However, for such disclaimers to protect a company, they must be presented prominently.

For instance, in the Sony Play Station Network case, the plaintiffs claimed that Sony breached implied warranties under the common law of Florida, Michigan, Missouri, and New York. Sony argued that these claims were invalid because it disclaimed all warranties both in the Play Station Network User Agreement and Privacy Policy. The user agreement stated:

> No warranty is given about the quality, functionality, availability or performance of Sony Online Services or any content or service offered on or through Sony Online Services. *All services and content are provided "AS IS" and "AS AVAILABLE" with all fault.* SNEA does not warrant that the service and content will be uninterrupted, error-free or without delays. In addition to the limitations of liability in merchantability, warranty of fitness for a particular purpose and warranty of non-infringement, SNEA assumes no liability for any inability to purchase, access, download or use any content, data, or service.[160]

Likewise, the Play Station Network Privacy Policy stated:

> We take reasonable measures to protect the confidentiality, security, and integrity of the personal information collected from our website visitors …. Unfortunately, there is no such thing as perfect security. As a result, although we strive to protect personally identifying information, *we cannot ensure or warrant the security of any information transmitted to us through or in connection with our websites,* that we store on our systems or that is stored on our service providers' systems.[161]

The court granted Sony's motion to dismiss, reasoning that the two documents, when considered together, sufficiently disclaim any guarantees that consumers' personal information will be secure.[162] "Read in conjunction, both documents explicitly disclaimed any and all claims arising under the implied

---

160 *In re* Sony Gaming Networks & Customer Data Sec. Data Breach Litig., 996 F. Supp. 2d 942, 981 (S.D. Cal. 2014) (emphasis added).
161 *Id.* (emphasis added).
162 *Id.* at 982.

warranty of merchantability, disclaimed any and all claims arising under the implied warranty of fitness for a particular purpose, stated in all caps that Sony Online Services would be provided 'AS IS' and 'AS AVAILABLE', and informed consumers that Sony was not warranting the security of consumer personal information transmitted to Sony via the network," the court wrote.[163] It is unclear whether one of those documents, standing alone, would have been sufficient to avoid all implied warranty lawsuits arising from the data breach. The disclaimer in the user agreement satisfies the long-standing legal rule that disclaimers of warranties should state that goods and services are provided "as is." However, the privacy policy provides a clear disclaimer that Sony does not guarantee the safety of personal information. Had this language not been in the privacy policy, the plaintiffs would have had a strong argument that a reasonable consumer would not expect the user agreement's "As Is" provision to apply to data security.

In short, implied warranty claims probably are not the strongest route for plaintiffs in data breach lawsuits. Unless a related data breach loss arises from the plaintiff's purchase of a tangible good, it is unlikely that the UCC's implied warranties will apply. Also, it remains to be seen whether state supreme courts will conclude that recognizing common-law implied warranties for data security is in the public interest. Even if a warranty does apply, many large companies easily address such risk with clear and conspicuous disclaimers.

2.2.5 Invasion of Privacy by Publication of Private Facts

In some data breach cases, plaintiffs bring a claim under the common-law tort of invasion of privacy due to publication of private facts. These claims will almost definitely fail, absent extraordinary circumstances.

Publication of private facts is one of four common-law privacy torts, and the most applicable to data breaches.[164] To state a claim for the publication of private facts, the plaintiff generally must prove "(1) the publication, (2) of private facts, (3) that are offensive, and (4) are not of public concern."[165] If plaintiffs' personal data is exposed due to a data breach, they could seek damages under this tort.

However, convincing a court to allow such a lawsuit is difficult, absent demonstration that the material was widely circulated and the defendant was somehow involved in the publication. For instance, in *Galaria v. Nationwide Mutual Insurance Co.*,[166]

---

163 *Id.*

164 The other three torts are misappropriation of the plaintiff's name or likeness (i.e., using the plaintiff's name or likeness in an advertisement without permission); intrusion upon seclusion (i.e., spying on the plaintiff in her home); and false light (i.e., disclosing information, in a highly offensive manner, that places the plaintiff in a false light).

165 Spilfogel v. Fox Broadcasting Co., 433 Fed. Appx. 724, 725 (11th Cir. 2011) (unpublished).

166 Galaria v. Nationwide Mut. Ins. Co., 998 F. Supp. 2d 646 (S.D. Ohio 2014), *rev'd* on other grounds, 663 F.3d Appx. 384 (6th Cir. 2016).

plaintiffs filed a class action lawsuit against Nationwide Mutual Insurance, after a breach at Nationwide. The plaintiffs did not allege misuse of their personal information. Among the claims in the plaintiffs' putative class action lawsuit was invasion of privacy due to publication of private facts. The district court dismissed this claim for two reasons. First, the court stated that even though the breach exposed their personally identifiable information, there was no allegation that Nationwide *disclosed* the data. Instead, the data was allegedly *stolen* from Nationwide.[167] This ruling suggests that an invasion of privacy claim will succeed only if the defendant in a breach case takes an affirmative action to disseminate information, such as posting it on a website. Second, the court held that even if Nationwide had disseminated the data, the plaintiffs did not allege "publicity" of the information. The plaintiffs would have needed to demonstrate "publicity to the public at large or to so many persons that the information is certain to become public knowledge."[168] The court found that the allegations fell far short of this standard. "While the Complaint alleges Named Plaintiffs face an increased risk the hackers will sell their PII and that it will become a matter of public knowledge, there is no allegation that that has yet occurred," the court wrote. "Moreover, if the hacker(s) sell Named Plaintiffs' PII or otherwise disseminate it into the public domain, it would not be the *Defendant* who 'publicized' Named Plaintiffs' PII."[169] The *Galaria* ruling, if followed for other similar claims after data breaches, strongly suggests that the mere fact that a breach of private information has occurred will not suffice for invasion of privacy claims. The plaintiff, at the very least, must make a sufficient claim that the hacker disseminated and publicized the private data.

2.2.6 Unjust Enrichment

Even if a plaintiff cannot establish a breach of an express or implied contract due to a data breach or inadequate data security, the plaintiff may attempt to bring a similar type of claim under the theory of "unjust enrichment."

Unjust enrichment is a theory of recovering damages "when one person has obtained a benefit from another by fraud, duress, or the taking of an undue advantage."[170] As with other common-law claims, the precise rules for unjust enrichment vary by state. The U.S. Court of Appeals for the Eleventh Circuit articulated a common framework for unjust enrichment in the AvMed data breach case.[171] Under Florida law, the court held, a plaintiff must demonstrate "(1) the plaintiff has conferred a benefit on the defendant; (2) the defendant has

---

167 *Id.* at 662.
168 *Id.*
169 *Id.* at 662–63.
170 Heldenfels Bros. v. City of Corpus Christi, 832 S.W.2d 39, 41 (Tex. 1992).
171 Resnick v. AvMed, Inc., 693 F.3d 1317 (11th Cir. 2012).

knowledge of the benefit; (3) the defendant has accepted or retained the benefit conferred; and (4) the circumstances are such that it would be inequitable for the defendant to retain the benefit without paying fair value for it."[172] Applying these factors, the Eleventh Circuit concluded that the plaintiffs alleged a viable unjust enrichment claim. The court reasoned that the plaintiffs adequately alleged that they paid premiums to the company, which AvMed should have used to cover the costs of adequate data security, and that the company failed to do so.[173]

Similarly, in the consumer class action against Target, the district court refused to dismiss the unjust enrichment claim against the retailer, reasoning that if the plaintiffs "can establish that they shopped at Target after Target knew or should have known of the breach, and that Plaintiffs would not have shopped at Target had they known about the breach, a reasonable jury could conclude that the money Plaintiffs spent at Target is money to which Target in equity and good conscience should not have received."[174] However, the court rejected the plaintiff's other unjust enrichment claim, in which they asserted that they were overcharged for their products because the goods that Target sold "included a premium for adequate data security."[175] The court found that this allegation did not support an unjust enrichment claim because Target charges the "price for the goods they buy whether the customer pays with a credit card, debit card, or cash," and the customers who paid with cash were not harmed by the data breach. This unjust enrichment claim, the Court concluded, might be more viable if Target charged a higher price to credit card customers.

Typically, unjust enrichment is not available to plaintiffs if another cause of action covers the same claim.[176] So, for example, if a plaintiff's unjust enrichment claim regarding a data breach arises primarily out of the defendant's failure to abide by the terms of a contract, then the unjust enrichment claim would not succeed.[177]

---

172 *Id.* at 1328 (quoting Della Ratta v. Della Ratta, 927 So. 2d 1055, 1059 (Fla. Dist. Ct. App. 2006)).
173 *Id.*
174 *In re* Target Corp. Data Sec. Breach Litig., 66 F. Supp. 3d 1154, 1178 (D. Minn. 2014).
175 *Id.* at 1177.
176 *See, e.g.,* Goldman v. Metropolitan Life Ins. Co., 841 N.E.2d 742, 746–47 (N.Y. 2005) ("Given that the disputed terms and conditions fall entirely within the insurance contract, there is no valid claim for unjust enrichment.").
177 *See In re* Anthem, Inc. Data Breach Litig., 162 F. Supp. 3d 953 (N.D. Cal. 2016) ("As the parties acknowledge, the viability of Plaintiffs' New York unjust enrichment claim depends largely upon the viability of Plaintiffs' breach of contract claims."); *In re* Sony Gaming Networks & Customer Data Sec. Data Breach Litig., 996 F. Supp. 2d 942, 984 (S.D. Cal. 2014) ("Under Florida, Massachusetts, Michigan, Missouri, New Hampshire, New York, Ohio, and Texas law a plaintiff may not recover for unjust enrichment where a 'valid, express contract governing the subject matter of the dispute exists.'").

2.2.7 State Consumer Protection Laws

Besides the court-created common-law claims that companies face after data breaches, state consumer protection statutes provide plaintiffs with an additional cause of action. All 50 states and the District of Columbia have enacted consumer protection laws.[178] Although the exact wording of the statutes—and courts' interpretations of them—vary by state, they generally prohibit unfair competition, unconscionable acts, and unfair or deceptive acts of trade or commerce. The state consumer protection laws are similar to Section 5 of the FTC Act, but unlike Section 5, most of the state consumer protection laws allow private plaintiffs to bring lawsuits.

State consumer protection law claims in data breach cases often allege that the defendant fraudulently misrepresented its data security practices. However, such claims typically will only succeed if the court concludes that the misrepresentations likely would deceive a reasonable person. For instance, in the Sony Play Station Network breach litigation, the plaintiffs brought claims under California consumer protection laws, alleging that Sony misrepresented the following aspects of its products and services:

- continual access to the Play Station Network was a feature of the game consoles;
- "online connectivity" was a feature of the game consoles;
- "characteristics and quality" of the security of the Sony Play Station Network; and
- Sony uses "reasonable security measures" to protect its consumers' personal information.[179]

The court ruled that the first two alleged misrepresentations were not valid grounds for a consumer protection lawsuit because a reasonable consumer would not believe that Sony promised "continued and uninterrupted access" to its online services,[180] in part because its terms of service explicitly stated that Sony "does not warrant that the service and content will be uninterrupted, error-free or without delays." However, the court concluded that the third and fourth statements provided a sufficient basis for consumer protection claims, as Sony's policies had promised "reasonable security" and "industry-standard" encryption."[181]

---

178 *See* National Consumer Law Center, Consumer Protection in the States: A 50-State Evaluation of Unfair and Deceptive Practices Laws (2018).
179 *In re* Sony Gaming Networks & Customer Data Sec. Data Breach Litig., 996 F. Supp. 2d 942, 989–90 (S.D. Cal. 2014).
180 *Id.* at 990.
181 *Id.*

Common among the obstacles to cybersecurity-related consumer protection law claims is the demonstration that the consumer suffered a financial loss. For instance, in the Sony Play Station Network litigation, the plaintiffs also brought a claim under Florida's consumer protection statute, which requires consumers to demonstrate "actual damages." Florida state courts have defined "actual damages" as the "difference in the market value of the product or service in the condition in which it was delivered and its market value in the condition in which it should have been delivered according to the contract of the parties."[182] The *Sony* plaintiffs sought to recover three costs: (1) the amount that they overpaid for their game consoles, (2) the payments for the services when they were unavailable, and (3) the value of their breached personal information. The district court dismissed this claim, concluding that none of these claims constituted "actual damages" as defined by the Florida law. The plaintiffs failed to demonstrate that they overpaid for the consoles or the services because of Sony's alleged misrepresentations about its data security, the court concluded.[183] Moreover, the court concluded that personal information "does not have an apparent monetary value" and therefore is not a proper basis for a claim of actual damages under the Florida law.[184]

However, the injury requirement is surmountable for plaintiffs, particularly during the early stages of litigation. For example, in the *Target* consumer class action arising from the 2013 data breach, the plaintiffs alleged violations of the consumer protection laws of 49 states and the District of Columbia. They claimed that Target violated these laws by failing to: implement adequate data security, disclose its inadequate data security, and notify consumers of the breach. The plaintiffs also alleged that Target violated the laws by continuing to accept credit and debit cards after it "knew or should have known of the data breach and before it purged its systems of the hackers' malware."[185] Twenty-six of the consumer protection laws require economic injury, and Target argued that the claims under those statutes therefore should be dismissed. However, the district court denied this motion, concluding that plaintiffs alleged that they accumulated costs, such as late fees, arising from the breach.[186]

State consumer protection laws are primarily designed to be enforced by state officials, such as state attorneys general, just as the FTC enforces Section 5 of the FTC Act. Accordingly, courts are hesitant to allow private lawsuits under consumer protection statutes when common-law remedies such as negligence are

---

182 Rollins, Inc. v. Heller, 454 So. 2d 580, 585 (Fla. Dist. Ct. App. 1984) (internal citations omitted).
183 *In re* Sony Gaming Networks & Customer Data Sec. Data Breach Litig., 996 F. Supp. 2d 942, 994 (S.D. Cal. 2014).
184 *Id.* (quoting Burrows v. Purchasing Power, LLC, No. l:12-cv-22800-UU, 2012 WL 9391827, at *3 (S.D. Fla. Oct. 18, 2012).
185 *In re* Target Corp. Customer Data Sec. Breach Litig., 66 F. Supp. 3d 1154, 1162 (D. Minn. 2014).
186 *Id.*

available. In the *Hannaford* grocery store data breach case, the plaintiffs brought a claim under the Maine Unfair Trade Practices Act, which provides that "[u]nfair methods of competition and unfair or deceptive acts or practices in the conduct of any trade or commerce are declared unlawful."[187] The provision of the statute creating a private right of action states that "[a]ny person who purchases or leases goods, services or property, real or personal, primarily for personal, family or household purposes and *thereby suffers any loss of money or property,* real or personal," due to the defendant's actions, may sue for damages and other relief.[188] The First Circuit affirmed the district court's dismissal of the claim under the Maine law, concluding that the substantial injury requirement, combined with the requirement that a plaintiff suffer a loss of money or property, requires a narrow reading of the Maine statute. "This narrow application of the private right of action section is consistent with the Maine legislature's choice of statutory language, which is narrower than that of other states," the court wrote.[189] Claims for breach of contract and negligence are more appropriate for the data breach for which the plaintiffs are not seeking damages for restitution, the court suggested.[190]

2.3   Class Action Certification in Data Breach Litigation

Even if plaintiffs demonstrate that they have standing *and* that they have stated a sufficient common-law or statutory claim, they usually face an additional hurdle: class certification. Most data breach complaints are filed as putative class action cases, in which the plaintiffs seek to represent all of the people who were harmed by a data breach.

This is largely a matter of economy. Assume that a breach of a retailer's payment card systems led to damages of $250 per consumer. It would make little sense for an attorney to take on the case on behalf of a single plaintiff, as the $250 that the plaintiff might eventually win in litigation would not come close to covering the costs of the attorney's time. A class action lawsuit allows the plaintiff's attorney to file a lawsuit on behalf of *all* similarly situated consumers. If the attorney sues on behalf of 100,000 customers whose data was compromised in the breach, then $25 million is at stake. Plaintiffs' attorneys who work on contingency often recover one-third of a damages award *plus* costs, so, suddenly, this case is quite lucrative for the attorney. Because of the large number of individuals often affected by data breaches, breach litigation has become an increasingly popular form of class action litigation.

---

187 Me. Rev. Stat. tit. 5, § 207.
188 Me. Rev. Stat. tit . 5, § 213(1).
189 Anderson v. Hannaford Bros. Co., 659 F.3d 151, 161 (1st Cir. 2011).
190 *Id.*

Class actions typically begin with a small group of plaintiffs—known as "class representatives"—who file a class action complaint on behalf of the entire class of affected individuals. If the judge does not grant the defendant's motion to dismiss or motion for summary judgment, the case may proceed to trial, which could lead to a verdict that is divided among all class members (minus attorney fees and costs, of course). However, if a court denies a defendant's motion to dismiss or for summary judgment, it is common for the plaintiffs and defendants to reach a settlement, avoiding trial altogether.

However, plaintiffs are not automatically entitled to receive damages—or settle—on behalf of similarly situated individuals. They first must meet a set of requirements known as "class certification." Since 2005, when Congress passed a law that makes it easier to bring class action litigation in federal courts,[191] most class action cases have been brought in federal courts, rather than state courts. To receive class certification in federal court, plaintiffs must convince the judge that they satisfy the requirements of Federal Rule of Civil Procedure 23.[192] This rule is divided into two sections: 23(a) and 23(b).

Under Rule 23(a), plaintiffs must satisfy four prerequisites before being permitted to sue on behalf of a class:

1) ***Numerosity.*** "[T]he class is so numerous that joinder of all members is impracticable."[193]
2) ***Commonality.*** "[T]here are questions of law or fact common to the class."[194]
3) ***Typicality.*** "[T]he claims or defenses of the representative parties are typical of the claims or defenses of the class."[195]
4) ***Adequacy.*** "[T]he representative parties will fairly and adequately protect the interests of the class."[196]

Perhaps the biggest barrier under Rule 23(a) is demonstrating commonality, due to a 2011 United States Supreme Court opinion. In *Wal-Mart v. Dukes*,[197] a massive employment discrimination case, the Supreme Court held that three plaintiffs

---

191 Class Action Fairness Act of 2005, Pub. L. No. 109-2, 119 Stat. 4 (codified as amended in scattered sections of 28 U.S.C.).

192 Even if a class action lawsuit is brought in state court, the procedural requirements often mirror those in Federal Rule of Civil Procedure 23. *See* Thomas E. Willging & Shannon R. Wheatman, *Attorney Choice of Forum in Class Action Litigation: What Difference Does It Make?*, 81 Notre Dame L. Rev. 591, 593 (2006) ("[T]here is little empirical evidence supporting the belief that state and federal courts differ generally in their treatment of class actions ... .").

193 Fed. R. Civ. P. 23(a)(1).

194 Fed. R. Civ. P. 23(a)(2).

195 Fed. R. Civ. P. 23(a)(3).

196 Fed. R. Civ. P. 23(a)(4).

197 Wal-Mart Stores, Inc. v. Dukes, 131 S. Ct. 2541 (2011).

did not satisfy the commonality requirement to represent a class of 1.5 million female Wal-Mart employees who allegedly were denied promotion or equal pay because of their gender. The gist of the class action lawsuit was that "that a strong and uniform 'corporate culture' permits bias against women to infect, perhaps subconsciously, the discretionary decisionmaking of each one of Wal-Mart's thousands of managers—thereby making every woman at the company the victim of one common discriminatory practice."[198] Despite the plaintiffs' statistical evidence of discrimination throughout the company, the Supreme Court held that a policy that provides discretion to local supervisors is not enough to satisfy the commonality requirement.[199] The Supreme Court noted that merely raising common questions is not sufficient: class action lawsuits must be able "to generate common *answers* apt to drive the resolution of the litigation."[200] Although an employment discrimination case is quite different from a standard data breach case, the *Wal-Mart* case is important for data security because it demonstrates the high bar that all class representatives face in establishing commonality. For instance, if a company has suffered multiple data breaches, *Wal-Mart* makes it more difficult for class representatives whose data was compromised in Breach A to sue on behalf of plaintiffs whose data was compromised in Breaches B and C unless the class representatives can demonstrate a common cause for all three of the breaches.

In addition to satisfying all four requirements of Section 23(a), the class representatives must demonstrate that their case falls into one of four categories provided in Rule 23(b). They are:

1) separate claims would possibly create "inconsistent or varying adjudications,"[201]
2) separate claims would "be dispositive of the interests of other members not parties to the individual adjudications or would substantially impair or impede their ability to protect their interest,"[202]
3) the goal is declaratory or injunctive relief,[203] or
4) "questions of law or fact common to class members predominate" and "class action is superior to other available methods."[204]

The final type of Rule 23(b) claim, known as "predominance," is a common avenue through which data breach plaintiffs seek class certification.

---

198 *Id.* at 2548.
199 *Id.* at 2556–57 ("Because respondents provide no convincing proof of a companywide discriminatory pay and promotion policy, we have concluded that they have not established the existence of any common question.").
200 *Id.* at 2551 (internal citation omitted).
201 Fed. R. Civ. P. 23(b)(1)(A).
202 Fed. R. Civ. P. 23(b)(1)(B).
203 Fed. R. Civ. P. 23(b)(2).
204 Fed. R. Civ. P. 23(b)(3).

As with other areas of data breach litigation, courts vary in their approaches to class certification. Unlike environmental litigation and other common forms of class action lawsuits that have existed for decades, data breach litigation does not have the same depth of judicial precedent, causing widely different results. Some courts easily find that plaintiffs satisfy Rules 23(a) and 23(b) for all victims of a single data breach, whereas other courts are much more skeptical of certifying data breach class action lawsuits.

To understand how courts have applied the class certification standards to data breach cases, here we provide examples of two notable class certification opinions.

In re Hannaford Bros. Co. Customer Data Security Breach Litigation, No. 2:08-MD-1954 (D. Me. Mar. 13, 2013)   In this putative class action lawsuit, described earlier, the class representatives brought seven claims arising from a large data breach of a grocery store chain. The U.S. Court of Appeals for the First Circuit upheld the district court's dismissal of five claims, but allowed the plaintiffs to proceed on claims of negligence and breach of implied contract. The case returned to the district court, which then faced the task of deciding whether to certify the class.

The district court concluded that the plaintiffs satisfied all four of the Rule 23(a) requirements:

- **Numerosity.** The court relied on data from credit card issuers which showed that thousands of cardholders whose data was compromised purchased identity theft protection, and that thousands also paid fees to replace their credit cards. The court acknowledged that it was impossible to determine whether the Hannaford breach was the "sole cause" of every cost cited by the issuers, but noted that it is permitted to draw "reasonable inferences" about numerosity. The judge noted that the case likely will result in "generous fees" for the lawyers representing the plaintiffs, and that he was concerned that "few class members will ultimately be interested in taking the time to file the paperwork necessary to obtain the very small amount of money that may be available if there is a recovery." However, the judge stated that such concerns are for Congress, "not for this individual judge applying the language of the Rule."
- **Commonality.** Although the losses suffered by the individual class members may vary, the judge determined that the plaintiff satisfied the commonality requirement because all of the claims arise from the common question of whether Hannaford caused the breach and remediation measures. He wrote: "Whether Hannaford's conduct was negligent or a contractual breach and whether it caused a data security breach that resulted in theft of customers' data and reasonably prompted customers to take mitigation measures are questions that are common among all the class members."

- **Typicality.** The judge concluded that the class representatives satisfied the typicality requirement because they "are entirely typical of the class in those respects. Two of the named plaintiffs incurred fees for card replacement; one incurred fees for prompt card replacement; and two incurred fees to purchase credit monitoring or identity theft insurance." Hannaford argued that the alleged economic harm to class members varied; for example, some purchased credit monitoring and others paid fees for new cards. Because the claims differ, they require different evidence to prove their case, and therefore fail to satisfy the typicality requirement, the company asserted. The judge acknowledged that "there is some force" to this argument, but held that the customers' mitigation steps—whether by purchasing identity theft protection or ordering a new card—was mitigation of the same alleged action (or inaction) of Hannaford.
- **Adequacy.** To satisfy the adequacy requirement, class representatives must demonstrate: (1) there is not a "potential conflict" between the representatives and class members, and (2) the lawyers are "qualified, experienced, and able to vigorously conduct the proposed litigation." Hannaford argued that the class representatives do not meet the adequacy requirement because they "have chosen to participate in class litigation rather than apply to Hannaford for refund gift cards," but the judge concluded that this is not a conflict. "Although reasonable people can certainly maintain that as a matter of policy other solutions are preferable to litigation, I do not see how that argument has a place in the class certification decision under the current Rule," the judge wrote. "A named plaintiff can represent a class only by filing a lawsuit; that is what the Federal Rules of Civil Procedure (and Rule 23 in particular) are for. Named plaintiffs are hardly adequate representatives of a class by not filing a lawsuit, because then they are not class representatives at all!"

Although the court concluded that the plaintiffs satisfied all of the requirements of Rule 23(a), the court denied class certification because the plaintiffs failed to satisfy Rule 23(b). The plaintiffs argued that their lawsuit satisfied Rule 23(b)(3), a lawsuit in which "questions of law or fact common to class members predominate over any questions affecting only individual members, and … a class action is superior to other available methods for fairly and efficiently adjudicating the controversy." Accordingly, the court considered both (1) superiority and (2) predominance. The court had little difficulty finding that the class action is superior to individual lawsuits, since "[g]iven the size of the claims, individual class members have virtually no interest in individually controlling the prosecution of separate actions[.]"

However, the judge concluded that the plaintiffs did not satisfy the predominance requirement. Although the class members' alleged injuries arose from the same data breach, the types of injuries (lost card fees, identity theft protection, etc.) varied. The plaintiffs claimed that they could find "experts who will be able to testify by statistical probability what proportion of the fees incurred are attributable to the Hannaford intrusion, as distinguished from other causes (like card loss or theft, other things in the news, marketing of services, etc.)," and that class administrators would determine how to distribute any proceeds from the case. However, the plaintiffs did not present the judge with an expert opinion about how the damages would be determined, and therefore the judge ruled that the plaintiffs cannot prove total damages, and the alternative "is a trial involving individual issues for each class member as to what happened to his/her data and account, what he/she did about it, and why."

The *Hannaford* case demonstrates a key barrier to plaintiffs in achieving class certification for data breach cases. Even if all class members are affected by the same data breach, it is quite likely that at least some class members suffered different types of damage. Before seeking class certification, the plaintiff must be able to demonstrate to the court how it can accurately determine the damages that this wide range of class members have suffered.

In re Heartland Payment Systems, Inc. Customer Data Security Breach Litigation: Consumer Track Litigation, 851 F. Supp. 2d 1040 (S.D. Tex. 2012)   Heartland, a large processor of payment card data, suffered a breach that exposed approximately 100 million customers' payment card data to hackers. Consumers nationwide filed a number of complaints against the company, and the Judicial Panel on Multidistrict Litigation consolidated the complaints into a single case in Texas federal court. As with many data breach cases, the parties reached a settlement. However, in order for the settlement to be binding on all of the approximately 100 million affected individuals, the court needed to determine whether to certify the class.

The judge concluded that the plaintiffs met all four requirements of Rule 23(a):

- **Numerosity.** In two sentences, the judge concluded that the 100 million-member nationwide class easily met the numerosity requirement.
- **Commonality.** The judge concluded that the plaintiffs satisfied the commonality requirement, even under the more stringent *Wal-Mart* standard, because there is a common factual question regarding "what actions Heartland took before, during, and after the data breach to safeguard the Consumer Plaintiffs' financial information."
- **Typicality.** The judge ruled that the plaintiffs satisfied the typicality requirement because the outcome of the claims centers on Heartland's conduct, not the characteristics of any individual class member. "Because this claim revolves around Heartland's conduct, as opposed to the characteristics of a particular class member's claim, no individualized proof will be necessary to determine Heartland's liability under the Act," the court wrote.

- **Adequacy.** The judge concluded that the plaintiffs satisfied the adequacy requirement. The plaintiffs' lawyers have "extensive experience" in class action litigation, and therefore provide adequate representation, the judge ruled, and the class representatives do not have any apparent conflicts with the proposed class members.

As in the *Hannaford* case, the *Heartland* plaintiffs asserted that their lawsuit satisfied the "predominance" and "superiority" requirements of Rule 23(b)(3). The judge ruled that the plaintiffs satisfied both requirements. The class action is superior to individual litigation, the judge ruled. The judge concluded that common questions predominate over individual issues. The judge noted that only one member of the 100 million-member proposed class objected. Even though there are some differences in the state laws at issue in the class action, the court concluded that those differences are not so large as to affect any class members' rights. The case "presents several common questions of law and fact arising from a central issue: Heartland's conduct before, during, and following the data breach, and the resulting injury to each class member from that conduct." Moreover, because the parties were seeking to settle, the judge concluded that it was unnecessary to be concerned about the manageability of a trial.

It is difficult to entirely square the results of *Hannaford* and *Heartland*. In both cases, it is likely that class members suffered different levels of harm from a breach, yet the class was certified in *Heartland* and denied in *Hannaford*. One explanation for the difference in results is that *Heartland* involved a class certification for the purposes of settlement. Therefore, the defendant was not opposing certification. In contrast, *Hannaford* involved a costly dispute that had been going on for many years, and the defendant vigorously opposed class certification.

A 2017 opinion from the Eighth Circuit in the *Target* breach case reinforces the need for district courts to conduct a thorough analysis of the Rule 23 factors before certifying a class. After the court refused to entirely dismiss the consumer class action lawsuit against Target, the plaintiffs and Target agreed to a settlement, in which Target would create a $10 million settlement fund for all class members nationwide, and pay up to an additional $6.75 million toward the plaintiffs' legal fees. After the district court issued a preliminary class certification and settlement approval, two class members challenged the certification of the class and the settlement. They argued that the settlement was insufficient compensation, and one of the class members alleged that the named plaintiffs' harms were different from his situation. Nonetheless, the district court issued a final order approving the class certification and settlement. The two class members appealed, and the Eighth Circuit agreed, instructing the district court to reconsider its class certification. Class certification, the Eighth Circuit wrote, requires a "rigorous analysis" of the Rule 23(a) factors. "Though the Supreme Court has not articulated what, specifically, a 'rigorous analysis' of class certification prerequisites entails, at a minimum the rule requires a district court to state its reasons for certification in terms specific enough for meaningful appellate review," the Eighth Circuit wrote.[205] The district court issued orders certifying the class without sufficiently addressing the concerns about certification. "The district court's certification of the settlement class does not meet this standard. In its preliminary order, the court replaces analysis of the certification prerequisites with a recitation of Rule 23 and a conclusion that certification is proper," the Eighth Circuit wrote.[206]

2.4 Insurance Coverage for Cybersecurity Incidents

When facing these large class action lawsuits—which frequently carry the potential of break-the-company damages or settlements—companies often seek coverage from their insurance providers under their commercial general liability policies. Unfortunately, such coverage is far from certain unless the company has purchased special additional cyber insurance. Even with specialized insurance, companies may not be fully covered for the many types of costs that are likely to arise after a cybersecurity incident.

Companies typically have commercial general liability insurance coverage, which covers the businesses for bodily injury, property damage, and other incidents that could cause harm to others and lead to litigation. These policies contain a number of limitations and exceptions to coverage.

Although each insurer determines the precise language of its commercial general liability policy, Insurance Services Office, Inc. offers a standard form, ISO CG, which typically is used as the starting point for insurers' policies. After data breaches, companies may seek coverage under the policy's promise to pay certain expenses related to "personal and advertising injury," which the form policy defines as including "[o]ral or written publication, in any manner, of material that violates a person's right of privacy[.]"[207]

Insurers often go to court to challenge companies' attempts to obtain coverage for data breaches under commercial general liability policies. The most common argument is that a data breach—often caused by an unknown hacker—does not constitute a "publication" by the covered company. Courts are divided on this issue.

----

205 *In re* Target Corp. Customer Data Sec. Breach, 847 F.3d 608, 612 (8th Cir. 2017).
206 *Id.*
207 Kevin DiGrazia, *Cyber Insurance, Data Security, and Blockchain in the Wake of the Equifax Breach*, 13 J. Bus. & Tech. L. 255, 261 n. 91 (2018), *quoting* Insurance Service Office Inc., Amendment of Personal and Advertising Injury Definition, CG 24 13 04.

Some courts easily conclude that any data breach constitutes a "publication" of personal information and therefore is covered under commercial general liability policies. For instance, in *Travelers Indemnity Company of America v. Portal Healthcare Solutions, LLC,* customers had filed a class action lawsuit against Portal, a healthcare company, arising from a data breach that allegedly exposed their medical records online. Portal sought coverage for the litigation from Travelers, its commercial general liability carrier. The policy required Travelers to pay money arising from Portal's "electronic publication of material that ... gives unreasonable publicity to a person's private life[.]"[208] Travelers then sued Portal, seeking a court judgment that it was not required to cover Portal's expenses for the breach. Travelers's primary argument was that the exposure does not constitute "publication." Travelers pointed to a dictionary definition of "publication" as "to place before the public (as through a mass medium)." The insurer argued that no "publication" occurred because Portal had no intent to expose the information to the public, and also because there was no allegation that a third party viewed the information. The district court ordered the insurer to cover Portal, and the Fourth Circuit affirmed.[209] The Fourth Circuit agreed with the district court's conclusion that such distinctions are irrelevant, and that the online exposure of a patient's medical records constitutes publication of material that gives "unreasonable publicity" to a person's private life.[210] "Given the eight corners of the pertinent documents, Travelers's efforts to parse alternative dictionary definitions do not absolve it of the duty to defend Portal," the Fourth Circuit wrote in an unpublished opinion.

Other courts, however, have reached opposite conclusions about similar policy language. For instance, Sony sought coverage under its commercial general liability policy for the Play Station Network breach discussed earlier in this chapter. Its policy required the insurer, Zurich American Insurance, to cover Sony's costs related to "[o]ral or written publication, in any manner, of material that violates a person's right of privacy." A New York state trial judge, ruling from the bench, indicated that he had a difficult time determining whether to require Zurich to cover Sony.[211] On the one hand, the judge stated during a court hearing that in the "electronic age," allowing exposure of data that a company had promised would be secure might constitute "publication." On the other hand, the judge ultimately concluded that the policy only covers "publication" by Sony, and because the information was acquired by outside hackers

---

208 Travelers Indem. Co. of Am. v. Portal Healthcare Sols., LLC, Case No. 1:13-cv-917 (GBL) (E.D. Va. Aug. 7, 2014).

209 Travelers Indem. Co. of Am. v. Portal Healthcare Sols., LLC, No. 14-1944 (4th Cir. Apr. 11, 2016) (unpublished).

210 *Id.*

211 Transcript of Proceedings, Feb. 21, 2014, Zurich Am. Ins. Co. v. Sony Corp., No. 651982/2011 (N.Y. Sup. Ct. 2014).

without any affirmative acts by Sony, Zurich was not required to cover Sony for the breach.[212] "The third party hackers took it. They breached the security," the judge stated. "They have gotten through all of the security levels and they were able to get access to this. That is not the same as saying Sony did this."[213]

Even if personal information is exposed due to the actions of a policy-holder, some courts still may conclude that the incident was not "publication" that triggers insurance coverage under commercial general liability policies. For instance, in *Creative Hospitality Ventures, Inc. v. United States Liability Insurance Co.*,[214] the policyholder had been sued for violating the Fair and Accurate Credit Card Transaction Act by printing more than the last five digits of consumers' credit card numbers on their receipts. The policyholder sought coverage under its insurer's commercial general liability policy. The district court denied coverage, reasoning that the receipts do not amount to "publication" under the policy. To define "publication," the court looked to a dictionary, which defined the term as "communication (as of news or information) to the public: public announcement" or "the act or process of issuing copies ... for general distribution to the public."[215] The Eleventh Circuit affirmed the district court's denial. Although the policyholder allegedly communicated the credit card information on its receipts, it did not disclose the information to the public, the Eleventh Circuit reasoned. Instead, the policyholder only provided the receipts to the customers. Therefore, the court concluded, the alleged credit card disclosures do not constitute "publication" and the insurer was not required to cover the costs of litigation.[216]

Insurance policies also contain a number of exclusions, and because cybersecurity coverage is so poorly defined, insurers often will attempt to claim that these exclusions apply after data breaches. For instance, Spec's Family Partners, a Houston-based retailer, experienced a breach of its credit card systems. Spec's credit card processor, First Data Merchant Services, was forced to reimburse the transaction costs to issuing banks. First Data then sent demand letters to Spec's, alleging that the breach was caused by the company's noncompliance with Payment Card Industry Data Security Standards, and demanding that the company create a reserve account to cover First Data's costs. First Data argued that its agreement with Spec's required Spec's to indemnify First Data. Spec's had a directors, officers, and corporate liability policy with Hanover Insurance, which

---

212 *Id.* at 76–77.

213 *Id.* at 78.

214 Creative Hospitality Ventures, Inc. v. United States Liab. Ins. Co., 444 Fed. Appx. 370 (11th Cir. Sept. 30, 2011).

215 *Id.* at 375–76.

216 *Id.* at 376.

stated that it does not apply to claims against insureds that are made "directly or indirectly based upon, arising out of, or attributable to any actual or alleged liability under a written or oral contract or agreement. However, this exclusion does not apply to your liability that would have attached in the absence of such contract or agreement." Although Hanover agreed to cover some costs, it refused to pay the costs related to a lawsuit that Spec's filed against First Data to recover money in the reserve accounts. Spec's sued Hanover for breaching the insurance policy, and the district court granted Hanover's motion to dismiss the claim, citing the exclusion for contract-related claims.[217]

Spec's appealed, and the U.S. Court of Appeals for the Fifth Circuit reversed the dismissal, concluding that the disputed claims are distinct from claims arising out of liability under the agreement with First Data. "The demand letters themselves include references to Spec's 'non-compliance' with third-party security standards and not insignificant demands for non-monetary relief, wholly separate from the Merchant Agreement," the court wrote in a June 25, 2018, opinion.[218]

Recognizing the uncertainty of coverage under commercial general liability policies, insurers are increasingly offering supplemental cybersecurity insurance policies to companies. These policies cover losses and expenses for a wide range of cyber-related incidents. Companies must carefully examine such cybersecurity-specific policies to understand the types of incidents to which they apply, as well as the incidents that are excluded from coverage. For instance, does the policy only apply to losses caused by data breaches, or would it also cover business disruption caused by ransomware? If a company is particularly reckless with its cybersecurity practices, would such behavior trigger an exemption from coverage?

Because of the unpredictability of insurance coverage for cybersecurity, many companies choose to self-insure by setting aside money to cover expenses in the event of a cyber incident.[219] Such a strategy has some significant upsides. Rather than being at the mercy of an insurance company—and perhaps paying significant attorney fees to resolve an insurance dispute—self-insurance provides a company with immediate funds to cover cybersecurity expenses. However, self-insurance is quite expensive. A company must have large cash reserves to set aside the amount required to cover breach-related costs.

---

217 Spec's Family Partners v. Hanover Ins. Co., No. 17-20263 (5th Cir. June 25, 2018).
218 *Id.*
219 *See* National Protection and Programs Directorate, U.S. Department of Homeland Security, CYBERSECURITY INSURANCE WORKSHOP READOUT REPORT (Nov. 2012), at 42 ("Another insurer cautioned that self-insurance should not be discounted as a reasonable risk management strategy. When a company decides to self-insure, he stated, it typically knows about its cyber risks, however inexactly, and sets aside funding in the event of a loss.").

> **Questions to Ask When Shopping for Cybersecurity Insurance**
>
> - What cybersecurity incidents are already covered by my commercial general liability policy?
> - Does the insurance place a cap on hourly fees for forensics experts and lawyers?
> - Does the insurance only cover data breaches, or does it cover other types of attacks, like denial of service?
> - Does the insurance cover disruption to business and reputational damage?
> - Does the insurance cover credit monitoring services for consumers?
> - Does the insurance apply to intellectual property-related risks?
> - Does the insurance cover fees from credit card companies and other business partners that result from data breaches?
> - Would it be less expensive to self-insure for cybersecurity incidents?

2.5 Protecting Cybersecurity Work Product and Communications from Discovery

As this chapter has demonstrated, businesses that experience data breaches face a number of legal claims from plaintiffs who often seek tens of millions of dollars.[220] Many of the legal claims described earlier in this chapter depend on the specific facts of a data breach, such as:

- What steps did a company take to secure the data?
- Were those steps in line with other companies in the industry?
- Did executives have any advance warning that the data security measures were inadequate?
- Were executives aware of similar incidents?
- Did the company divert money from cybersecurity to other areas of the business?
- How did executives respond when they learned of the breach?

These are just some of the many questions that are bound to arise when plaintiffs are attempting to demonstrate that a company's negligence or other violation of a legal duty caused the plaintiffs' personal information to be exposed.

Unfortunately for companies, answers to many of these questions are readily available in the email inboxes of their executives and information technology staffers, as well as in incident reports and assessments of security vulnerabilities. Indeed, companies increasingly hire cybersecurity forensics firms to prevent

---

220 Much of this section originally appeared in *The Cybersecurity Privilege*, an article by this book's author in I/S: A JOURNAL OF LAW AND POLICY FOR THE INFORMATION SOCIETY (2016).

cybersecurity incidents from occurring. Companies engage cybersecurity professionals to perform penetration tests, which "prove (or disprove) real-world attack vectors against an organization's IT assets, data, humans, and/or physical security."[221] The results of these tests can help a company reconfigure its systems, policies, and processes to guard against security threats.[222]

Companies also increasingly hire consultants for the more urgent task of remediating and mitigating harm after a security incident has taken place. Cybersecurity professionals must immediately gain full access to a network to determine the extent of the intrusion, and the necessary steps to remediate any damage and prevent further unauthorized access.[223] The cybersecurity experts and lawyers must work together to determine whether they are legally required to notify state regulators or consumers of the breach under the state notification laws described in Chapter 1. Cybersecurity professionals also collaborate with public affairs departments and consultants to publicly explain the incident in a manner that is prompt, complete, and accurate.[224]

Cybersecurity professionals wear multiple hats, including auditor, technologist, policymaker, strategist, and spokesperson. To perform such wide-ranging duties, cybersecurity professionals must have broad and unfettered access to information that a company or organization may store in a variety of media and formats, and they must be able to candidly communicate with their clients.

Unfortunately for companies, there is a strong possibility that cybersecurity professionals' reports and emails can be obtained by plaintiffs and used against the companies in litigation. In United States civil litigation, parties typically have a broad right of discovery, which allows them to obtain documents, depositions, and other relevant information from the opposing party and third parties. The law generally has a strong presumption in favor of allowing parties to conduct discovery and present evidence to courts.[225] The only way to avoid this

---

221 Eric Basu, *What Is a Penetration Test and Why Would I Need One for My Company?* Forbes (Oct. 12, 2013) ("A penetration test is designed to answer the question: 'What is the *real-world* effectiveness of my existing security controls against an active, human, skilled attacker?'").
222 *Id.*
223 Nate Lord, *Data Breach Experts Share the Most Important Next Step You Should Take After a Data Breach in 2014-15 and Beyond*, Digital Guardian (May 4, 2015) ("By bringing in an unbiased, third-party specialist, you can discover exactly what has been accessed and compromised, identify what vulnerabilities caused the data breach, and remediate so the issue doesn't happen again in the future.").
224 Natalie Burg, *Five Lessons for Every Business from Target's Data Breach*, Forbes (Jan. 17, 2014) ("[A] security crisis can very quickly turn into a crisis of trust and loyalty if swift communications and responsive customer service aren't employed—even if the fault lies with the same weak credit card security used by so many other businesses.").
225 *See* Univ. of Pa. v. EEOC, 493 U.S. 182, 189 (1990) ("We do not create and apply an evidentiary privilege unless it promotes sufficiently important interests to outweigh the need for probative evidence") (citations and internal quotation marks omitted).

presumption in favor of disclosure is to demonstrate that an evidentiary privilege applies. Courts and legislatures have created evidentiary privileges for communications and work products of certain professionals for whom confidentiality is an integral part of their jobs. For instance, the United States recognizes evidentiary privileges, to varying degrees, for attorneys, psychotherapists, clergy, and journalists. No court or legislature has created a stand-alone privilege for the work of cybersecurity professionals, owing partly to the fact that the profession is so new, and evidentiary privileges are slow to develop.[226]

Despite the lack of a stand-alone privilege for cybersecurity professionals, companies and their forensics experts still have a reasonable chance of getting at least some protection for their communications and reports. To shield this material from discovery, companies attempt to benefit from three attorney-related evidentiary privileges. To do so, companies are increasingly hiring attorneys to supervise the work of cybersecurity consultants. The three privileges are (1) the attorney-client privilege, (2) the work product doctrine, and (3) the nontestifying expert privilege. As we will see, these privileges offer only limited protection, and are not always guaranteed to prevent confidential cybersecurity information from being obtained by plaintiffs.

2.5.1 Attorney-Client Privilege

The attorney-client privilege protects from discovery communications between attorneys and clients in the course of seeking and providing legal advice.[227] The privilege is nearly absolute and allows only a few limited exceptions, such as instances in which the attorney helped the client perpetrate crime or fraud,[228] or if the client disputes the attorney's competence or job performance.[229]

This broad privilege is intended "to encourage full and frank communication between attorneys and their clients and thereby promote broader public interests in the observance of law and administration of justice."[230] The privilege

---

226 *See* Wolfle v. United States, 291 U.S. 7, 12 (1934) (evidentiary privileges are "governed by common law principles as interpreted and applied by the federal courts in the light of reason and experience.").

227 Upjohn Co. v. United States, 449 U.S. 383, 388 (1981).

228 United States v. Zolin, 491 U.S. 554, 563 (1989) ("It is the purpose of the crime-fraud exception to the attorney–client privilege to assure that the seal of secrecy between lawyer and client does not extend to communications made for the purpose of getting advice for the commission of a fraud or crime.") (citation and internal quotation marks omitted).

229 United States v. Pinson, 584 F.3d 972 (10th Cir. 2009) ("The theoretical basis for the assertion that raising an ineffective-assistance claim waives attorney–client privilege is the exception to the privilege that applies when a litigant chooses to place privileged communications directly in issue.").

230 *Upjohn,* 449 U.S. at 388.

"exists to protect not only the giving of professional advice to those who can act on it but also the giving of information to the lawyer to enable him to give sound and informed advice."[231]

Although the attorney-client privilege is absolute, it only covers certain types of communications.[232] The specific elements of the privilege vary slightly by jurisdiction, but the following Ninth Circuit summary generally is an accurate illustration of the privilege's scope of coverage:

> (1) When legal advice of any kind is sought (2) from a professional legal adviser in his or her capacity as such, (3) the communications relating to that purpose, (4) made in confidence (5) by the client, (6) are, at the client's instance, permanently protected (7) from disclosure by the client or by the legal adviser (8) unless the protection be waived.[233]

The privilege, therefore, protects communications from the client to the attorney—or from the attorney to the client—that are exchanged for the purpose of rendering legal advice. The privilege protects *communications*, and does not protect the evidence underlying the communications. For instance, suppose that a company is reviewing its server logs and discovers an apparent breach. The company's CIO immediately emails a description of the apparent breach to the company's outside counsel. Although the CIO's email to the attorney may be privileged, the server's logs would not be privileged.

Additionally, the attorney-client privilege only applies to communications that seek or provide *legal* advice. For instance, if a company's lawyers advise on *and* help implement a business transaction, only the legal advice that they provide will be privileged. Any "business advice" likely will fall outside of the scope of the privilege, though courts may disagree as to whether a specific communication is legal or business advice.[234] Applying this framework, if a company emails a cybersecurity consultant with a question about network protection and merely cc's the company's lawyer, a court may find that the communication was unrelated to *legal* advice, and therefore not protected by the attorney-client privilege.

---

231 *Id.* at 384.
232 *See generally* Mohawk Indus., Inc. v. Carpenter, 130 S. Ct. 599 (2009).
233 United States v. Martin, 278 F.3d 988, 999 (9th Cir. 2002).
234 United States v. ChevronTexaco, 241 F. Supp. 2d 1065, 1069 (N.D. Cal. 2003) ("Because the purported privileged communications involve attorneys who apparently performed the dual role of legal and business advisor, assessing whether a particular communication was made for the purpose of securing legal advice (as opposed to business advice) becomes a difficult task."); Cuno, Inc. v. Pall Corp., 121 F.R.D. 198, 204 (E.D.N.Y. 1988) ("[w]here a lawyer mixes legal and business advice the communication is not privileged 'unless the communication is designed to meet problems which can fairly be characterized as predominantly legal' ").

Moreover, if a third party receives the communication, a court may find that the attorney-client privilege does not apply in that situation.[235] However, communications may still be protected if they include nonlawyers who are assisting the lawyer in the representation. For instance, the communications of an accountant or translator working for a law firm may be protected by the privilege. As Judge Friendly wrote a half-century ago, "[w]hat is vital to the privilege is that the communication be made in confidence for the purpose of obtaining legal advice from the lawyer."[236] Similarly, the attorney-client privilege covers consultants who perform work under the supervision of attorneys, if that work is conducted as part of the attorney's representation of clients.[237]

Accordingly, if a cybersecurity professional helps an attorney provide legal advice to a client, those communications may be covered by the attorney-client privilege. However, the attorney-client privilege is of limited use for a good deal of the work that cybersecurity professionals perform. Perhaps the biggest obstacle for the purposes of cybersecurity consulting is the requirement that the communications relate to legal advice.[238] For instance, an email that describes the result of a network vulnerability test, for example, likely would not qualify as legal advice. Even if a cybersecurity professional is supervised by an attorney, there is no guarantee that the professional's communications with the attorney or client would be protected under the attorney-client privilege.

2.5.2 Work Product Doctrine

The work product doctrine is more likely to cover some cybersecurity work that is performed at the direction of attorneys, but the doctrine, unlike the attorney-client privilege, is not absolute.

The doctrine was first articulated in 1947, when the Supreme Court ruled in *Hickman v. Taylor*[239] that an attorney's notes and reports based on witness interviews could not later be discovered in litigation involving the attorney's client. Although the Court concluded that the attorney-client privilege did not protect the documents,[240] it nonetheless denied discovery, reasoning that the

---

235 *See* Cavallaro v. United States, 284 F.3d 236, 237 (1st Cir. 2002) ("The presence of third parties during an attorney–client communication is often sufficient to undermine the 'made in confidence' requirement, or to waive the privilege") (internal citations omitted).
236 United States v. Kovel, 296 F.2d 918, 922 (2d Cir. 1961).
237 *See* Fed. Trade Comm'n v. TRW, Inc., 628 F.2d 207, 212 (D.C. Cir. 1980) ("[T]he attorney-client privilege can attach to reports of third parties made at the request of the attorney or the client where the purpose of the report was to put in usable form information obtained from the client").
238 *See Kovel,* 296 F.2d at 922 ("If what is sought is not legal advice but only accounting service …, or if the advice sought is the accountant's rather than the lawyer's, no privilege exists.").
239 329 U.S. 495 (1947).
240 *Id.* at 508.

request was "an attempt to secure the production of written statements and mental impressions contained in the files and the mind of the attorney ... without any showing of necessity or any indication or claim that denial of such production would unduly prejudice the preparation of petitioner's case or cause him any hardship or injustice."[241]

The *Hickman* work product doctrine was later codified in Federal Rule of Civil Procedure 26(b)(3).[242] That rule provides that "[o]rdinarily, a party may not discover documents and tangible things that are prepared in anticipation of litigation or for trial by or for another party or its representative (including the other party's attorney, consultant, surety, indemnitor, insurer, or agent)."[243] However, the rule is not absolute: it allows discovery if "the party shows that it has substantial need for the materials to prepare its case and cannot, without undue hardship, obtain their substantial equivalent by other means[,]"[244] or if a court otherwise finds good cause to order the disclosure of relevant work product.[245] If a court orders disclosure of work product, "it must protect against disclosure of the mental impressions, conclusions, opinions, or legal theories of a party's attorney or other representative concerning the litigation."[246]

The work product doctrine covers more than just communications that are necessary for legal advice. The doctrine protects *work product* that is prepared in anticipation of litigation or trial. Moreover, Federal Rule of Civil Procedure 26 explicitly states that *consultants'* work product may be protected, provided that it is prepared in anticipation of litigation. Indeed, courts have held that the work product doctrine applies to materials prepared by environmental consultants[247] and insurance claims investigators.[248] Similarly, a cybersecurity professional's report might be protected by the work product doctrine.[249]

---

241 *Id.* at 509.
242 *See* United States v. Adlman, 134 F.3d 1194, 1197 (2d Cir. 1998) ("Rule 26(b)(3) codifies the principles articulated in *Hickman*").
243 Fed. R. Civ. P. 26(b)(3).
244 Fed. R. Civ. P. 26(b)(3)(A)(ii).
245 Fed. R. Civ. P. 26(b)(3)(A)(i).
246 Fed. R. Civ. P. 26(b)(3)(B).
247 Martin v. Bally's Park Place Hotel & Casino, 983 F.2d 1252, 1260–62 (3d Cir. 1993).
248 Carver v. Allstate Ins. Co., 94 F.R.D. 131 (S.D. Ga. 1982).
249 *See* Benjamen C. Linden et al., *Use Outside Counsel to Control Data Breach Loss,* Bloomberg BNA (Mar. 21, 2014) ("The work product doctrine may be an additional means to shield findings from a post-breach investigation during subsequent litigation. Whereas the attorney-client privilege applies only to communications, work product applies broadly to 'documents and tangible things that are prepared in anticipation of litigation or for trial by or for another party or its representative (including the other party's attorney, consultant, surety, indemnitor, insurer, or agent).' Thus, when investigative documents in the aftermath of a breach are prepared primarily in anticipation of litigation, the doctrine might protect them. However, when documents appear to be the product of a routine investigation and were not prepared primarily in anticipation of litigation, courts are much less likely to protect the work product doctrine").

However, the exceptions to the work product doctrine limit the extent of the protection that it provides to cybersecurity work. Perhaps most important is the requirement that the work product be prepared in anticipation of litigation or trial. The Second Circuit, reflecting a common approach to the doctrine, interpreted work product to have been created "in anticipation of litigation" if "in light of the nature of the document and the factual situation in the particular case, the document can fairly be said to have been prepared or obtained because of the prospect of litigation."[250] Although this approach is relatively broad and could encompass large swaths of documents, the party asserting the work product doctrine would need to demonstrate that the materials were created *because of* potential litigation. A consultant's report about the causes of a data breach likely would have a greater chance of being covered by the work product doctrine than the consultant's annual, routine assessment of a company's cybersecurity controls. The company would have a stronger argument that the consultant prepared the data breach report in response to a real threat of actual litigation. The annual, routine assessment, in contrast, is less likely to be linked to a real prospect of litigation. This creates a perverse result: companies likely receive *less* protection for taking proactive measures to *protect* their networks from attacks than they do for taking remedial measures *after* breaches have occurred.

Moreover, even if work product was prepared in anticipation of litigation, a court still can require its disclosure if the court concludes that the party requesting the materials has demonstrated a substantial need or other good cause for the discovery.[251] Routine work product is less likely to receive protection under the work product doctrine unless it is "core" or "opinion" work product related to an attorney's conclusions or impressions about particular litigation.[252] In the cybersecurity context, this means that a forensics expert's initial evaluation of a data breach most likely could be discovered in subsequent litigation if the opposing party demonstrates substantial need or good cause. In contrast, that consultant's analysis of claims in a pending complaint

---

250 *See* United States v. Adlman, 134 F.3d at 1202 (citations and internal quotation marks omitted).

251 FED. R. CIV. P. 26(b)(3)(A)(i)–(ii).

252 *In re* Cendant Corp. Secs. Litig., 343 F.3d 658 (3d Cir. 2003) ("Stated differently, Rule 26(b)(3) establishes two tiers of protection: first, work prepared in anticipation of litigation by an attorney or his agent is discoverable only upon a showing of need and hardship; second, 'core' or 'opinion' work product that encompasses the mental impressions, conclusions, opinion, or legal theories of an attorney or other representative of a party concerning the litigation is generally afforded near absolute protection from discovery.") (internal quotation marks omitted); *In re* San Juan Dupont Plaza Hotel Fire Litig., 859 F.2d 1007, 1015 (1st Cir. 1988) ("Courts typically afford ordinary work product only a qualified immunity, subject to a showing of substantial need and hardship, while requiring a hardier showing to justify the production of opinion work product.").

arising from the data breach is more likely to be protected under the work product doctrine. Again, this dichotomy results in cybersecurity professionals' work receiving less protection if it is not related to ongoing litigation.

Although the work product doctrine has a broader scope than the attorney-client privilege, the work product doctrine is not absolute. Because litigants could successfully argue that a good deal of the work performed by cybersecurity consultants falls within one of the doctrine's exceptions, companies cannot rely on the work product doctrine to prevent the compelled disclosure of cybersecurity material.

2.5.3 Nontestifying Expert Privilege

A third, narrower privilege prevents the compelled disclosure of certain nontestifying experts. Federal Rule of Civil Procedure 26(b)(4)(D) states that "a party may not, by interrogatories or depositions, discover facts known or opinions held by an expert retained or specially employed by another party in anticipation of litigation or to prepare for trial and who is not expected to be called as a witness at trial," unless the party can demonstrate "exceptional circumstances under which it is impracticable for the party to obtain facts or opinions on the same subject by other means."[253] The nontestifying expert privilege is "designed to promote fairness by precluding unreasonable access to an opposing party's diligent trial preparation."[254]

The nontestifying expert privilege is quite strong, and courts have interpreted the "exceptional circumstances" exemption as being quite limited.[255] However, it has limited value for cybersecurity investigations. As the Ninth Circuit noted in 2012, the rule "shields only against disclosure through interrogatories and depositions[.]"[256] Accordingly, the rule would not prevent the disclosure of a report prepared by a cybersecurity expert; it would only prevent that expert from being subjected to interrogatories and depositions. Moreover, like the work product doctrine, the nontestifying expert privilege only applies to anticipated litigation or trial preparation.[257] A routine cybersecurity investigation, therefore, likely would not be covered under this privilege. This privilege might however, apply to an incident assessment that a cybersecurity professional prepares to assess the merits of pending litigation.

---

253 Fed. R. Civ. P. 26(b)(4)(D).
254 Durflinger v. Artiles, 727 F.2d 888, 891 (10th Cir. 1984).
255 *In re* Shell Oil Refinery, 132 F.R.D. 437, 442 (E.D. La. 1990) ("The exceptional circumstances requirement has been interpreted by the courts to mean an inability to obtain equivalent information from other sources.").
256 Ibrahim v. Dep't of Homeland Sec., 669 F.3d 983, 999 (9th Cir. 2012).
257 Fed. R. Civ. P. 26(b)(4)(D).

	Attorney-client privilege	**Work product doctrine**	**Nontestifying expert privilege**
Type of material protected	Communications between attorneys and clients while providing legal advice	Documents and tangible things that are prepared in anticipation of litigation	Facts known or opinions held by a retained expert
Individuals to whom it applies	Attorneys and individuals who assist them (such as paralegals or consultants)	Attorney, consultant, surety, indemnitor, insurer, or agent	Expert retained in anticipation of litigation and who is not expected to be called as a witness
Scope	Absolute, with a few narrow exceptions	Qualified—may be overcome in certain circumstances	Qualified—may be overcome in exceptional circumstances

2.5.4 Genesco v. Visa

Few published opinions have directly addressed the application of the attorney-client privilege, work product doctrine, and nontestifying expert privilege to the work of cybersecurity professionals. This is not surprising; discovery disputes often are settled orally in discussions between the parties and magistrate judges; therefore, there is not a written opinion documenting many of these disputes. The first extensive written discussion of the application of these privileges to cybersecurity was in *Genesco* v. *Visa*.[258]

In that case, hackers had accessed customer payment card information that was stored on the network of Genesco, a retail chain.[259] Genesco's general counsel, Roger Sisson, retained Stroz Friedberg, a cybersecurity consulting firm.[260] Genesco's retention agreement with Stroz stated that the retention was "in anticipation of potential litigation and/or legal or regulatory proceedings."[261]

After conducting its own investigation, Visa assessed more than $13 million in fines and reimbursement assessments against two banks that processed Genesco's credit card purchases, claiming that Genesco's inadequate data security violated payment card data security standards and Visa's operating regulations.[262] Genesco, which had an indemnification agreement with the

---

258 Genesco v. Visa U.S.A., 302 F.R.D. 168 (M.D. Tenn. 2014).
259 *Id.* at 171.
260 *Id.* at 180–81.
261 *Id.* at 181.
262 *Id.* at 170.

banks, sued Visa, asserting that the assessments lacked a factual basis and violated various state laws.[263] In discovery, Visa subpoenaed Stroz for deposition testimony and its work product related to the investigation, and also requested permission to depose Sisson and that Sisson provide documents related to his investigation of the incident.[264]

The court largely denied Visa's discovery requests. The court first held that the requests for Stroz's deposition and work product are prohibited by the nontestifying expert privilege.[265] Visa argued that Stroz was a fact witness, but the court rejected this argument, concluding that "the Stroz representative would necessarily be applying his or her specialized knowledge," and that Visa had not established the "extraordinary circumstances" needed to overcome the nontestifying expert privilege.[266]

The court also held that the attorney-client privilege and the work product doctrine prevented the compelled disclosure of the requests both to Sisson and to Stroz.[267] The court held that an "[a]ttorney's factual investigations 'fall comfortably within the protection of the attorney-client privilege,'" [268] and that the privilege "extends to the Stroz firm that assisted counsel in his investigation."[269] The court also recognized that the work product doctrine "attaches to an agent's work under counsel's direction."[270] The court held that the work product doctrine applies because "Genesco's affidavits satisfy that the Stroz firm was retained in contemplation of litigation, as reflected in the express language of the retainer agreement."[271]

In 2015, Visa subpoenaed IBM for work product regarding remedial security measures that IBM performed for Genesco after the breach.[272] In a brief order, the court rejected this request, concluding that because Genesco "retained IBM to provide consulting and technical services so as to assist counsel in rendering legal advice[,]" IBM's materials are protected by the attorney-client privilege and work product doctrine.[273]

Commentators hailed the *Genesco* rulings as a demonstration that cybersecurity work could be privileged, provided that such work is conducted under the supervision of an attorney. Lawyers at one large law firm hailed the opinion

---

263 *Id.*
264 *Id.* at 181–82.
265 *Id.* at 189–90.
266 *Id.* at 190 ("To accept that characterization would effectively eviscerate and undermine the core purpose of Fed. R. Civ. P. 26(b)(4)(D).").
267 *Id.* at 195.
268 *Id.* at 190 (quoting Sandra Te v. S. Berwyn Sch. Dist. 100, 600 F.3d 612, 619 (7th Cir. 2010)).
269 *Id.*
270 *Id.*
271 *Id.* at 193.
272 Genesco, Inc. v. Visa U.S.A., 2015 U.S. Dist. LEXIS 52314 (M.D. Tenn. Mar. 24, 2015).
273 *Id.*

as "a roadmap for confidentiality protections" that "underscores legal counsel's critical role in today's digital economy where the question is not 'if' but 'when,' an organization will be breached."[274] Lawyers at another firm advised that the decision "demonstrates how important it is for you to designate experienced privacy counsel to lead cybersecurity initiatives, including determining proactive privacy and security measures, directing forensic investigations, and spearheading data breach response efforts."[275] A news article declared that, in light of the opinion, the "smart and most conservative proactive approach" to cybersecurity risk management is "to have the appropriate law firm take the lead, hire the required consultants, and have all reports, analysis, memos, plans and communications protected under the attorney–client and work product privileges."[276]

The commentators were correct, to an extent. The *Genesco* rulings extend the same protections to communications and work product of cybersecurity consultants as previous court opinions have extended to the work and communications of environmental consultants, product safety experts, and others retained and supervised by counsel for the purposes of providing legal advice or preparing for litigation. The 2015 order regarding IBM, in particular, is encouraging because IBM provided technical consulting to help remediate security flaws on Genesco's network. Although the court viewed these services as part of Genesco's legal strategy, remedial measures for a computer network could have longer lasting effects that help Genesco in the future, entirely unrelated to the Visa litigation.

That said, the *Genesco* case also illustrates the limits of the evidentiary privilege for cybersecurity work. The gravamen of Genesco's argument throughout the discovery dispute was that Stroz and IBM were merely helping Genesco challenge the Visa fees or prepare for its defense in other claims related to the breach.[277] Genesco framed its arguments as such for good reason: had it not

---

274 Aravind Swaminathan & Antony Kim, *Court Says Cyber Forensics Covered by Legal Privilege,* ORRICK (Apr. 24, 2015), *available at* https://www.orrick.com/Events-and-Publications/Pages/Court-Says-Cyber-Forensics-Covered-by-Legal-Privilege.aspx.

275 *Communications with Your Cybersecurity Consultant and Forensic Reports May Now Be Protected,* MCDONALD HOPKINS (June 11, 2015), *available at* https://mcdonaldhopkins.com/Insights/Alerts/2015/06/11/Data-Privacy-and-Cybersecurity-Communications-with-your-cybersecurity-consultant-and-forensic-reports-may-now-be-protected.

276 Denis Kleinfeld, *Your Computer Will Be Hacked, It's Just a Question of When,* NEWSMAX (May 4, 2015), *available at* http://www.newsmax.com/Finance/Kleinfeld/Cybersecurity-Hack-Passcodes-Risk/2015/05/04/id/642323/.

277 Opp. Brief of Genesco, Genesco, Inc. v. Visa U.S.A., 2015 U.S. Dist. LEXIS 52314 (M.D. Tenn. Mar. 24, 2015) ("Here, it is undisputed that IBM prepared the PCI Gap Assessment pursuant to an engagement by Genesco's General Counsel for the purpose of assisting Genesco's General Counsel in providing legal advice to Genesco regarding its *legal* obligation to be PCI DSS compliant.").

framed the IBM and Stroz work as part of a legal defense strategy, the communications and work product likely would have been discoverable, as reflected in the court's focus on the three attorney-related privileges.

2.5.5   *In re Experian Data Breach Litigation*

After the data breach of consumer reporting agency Experian, the company's law firm retained Mandiant for a breach analysis. The company stated that the report's "only purpose" was to assist its law firm in giving "legal advice to Experian regarding the attack." [278] In discovery in a subsequent putative class action lawsuit, the plaintiffs sought the report and other documents related to the Mandiant investigation.

Experian claimed that the work product doctrine barred the request, and the court agreed. According to the court, the plaintiffs' primary response to this argument was that "Experian had independent business duties to investigate any data breaches and it hired Mandiant to do exactly that after realizing that its own experts lacked sufficient resources."[279] The court acknowledged that Experian did, in fact, have a duty to investigate the breach, but "Mandiant conducted the investigation and prepared its report for [Experian's law firm] in anticipation of litigation, even if that wasn't Mandiant's only purpose."[280]

The fact that Mandiant had already done work for Experian did not alter the judge's conclusion that the work product doctrine applied, "in part because Mandiant's previous work for Experian was separate from the work it did for Experian regarding this particular data breach."[281]

The court also rejected the plaintiff's argument that an exception to the work product doctrine applies because it is "impossible to go back in time and access those live servers at the moment they were inspected," creating a "substantial hardship."[282] The court pointed to evidence that Mandiant's investigation did not rely on such live, real-time evidence, and reasoned that the plaintiffs could reconstruct the data via the discovery process. "A showing of expense or inconvenience to Plaintiffs in hiring an expert to perform the same analysis isn't sufficient to overcome the protection of the work product doctrine," the court wrote.[283]

---

278 Civil Minutes, In re Experian Data Breach Litig., Case No. SACV 15-01592 AG (C.D. Cal. May 18, 2017) at 3.
279 *Id.* at 4.
280 *Id.*
281 *Id.*
282 *Id.* at 5.
283 *Id.*

The *Experian* decision is perhaps the most defendant-friendly discovery opinion in a data breach class action lawsuit, broadly shielding forensics reports that could be highly useful to plaintiffs in litigation.

2.5.6   *In re Premera*

In October 2017, Oregon federal judge Michael Simon issued a lengthy opinion in a data breach lawsuit against Premera Blue Cross, outlining how the various privileges apply to cybersecurity documents.[284] The opinion provides further guidance on the extent of the privilege that companies might expect for cybersecurity-related communications and reports.

The *Premera* opinion examined the discoverability of three categories of documents that are relevant to cybersecurity litigation: (1) those that incorporate legal advice but were not prepared by counsel, nor were they sent to counsel; (2) those that lawyers requested to be created, but were not prepared by lawyers or sent to them; (3) documents that were created as part of a technical and public relations response to the breach.[285] (A fourth category involved Premera's assertion of a joint defense privilege with other companies.)

The first category included documents that "were drafted by persons who are not attorneys and were sent to and from persons who are not attorneys."[286] Many of the documents in this category, Simon found, were not privileged. "Premera has withheld entire drafts of documents that it was required as a business to prepare in response to the data breach," Simon wrote. "Premera prepared press releases and notices to be sent to its customers. The fact that Premera planned eventually to have an attorney review those documents or that attorneys may have provided initial guidance as to how Premera should draft internal business documents does not make every internal draft and every internal communication relating to those documents privileged and immune from discovery."[287] Some documents, such as those containing redlines from attorneys, may contain privileged information, he noted. "If underlying edited or redlined documents contain legal advice from counsel, those documents (or at least the edits or redlines) are entitled to protection," Simon wrote.[288]

The second category included documents "prepared by Premera employees and third-party vendors who are not attorneys[,]" such as "information relating to technical aspects of the breach and its mitigation, company policies, public

---

284 *In re* Premera Blue Cross Customer Data Sec. Breach Litig., 296 F. Supp. 3d 1230 (D. Or. 2017).
285 *Id.* at 1240.
286 *Id.*
287 *Id.* at 1241.
288 *Id.* at 1242.

relations and media matters, and remediation activities."[289] Outside counsel retained these third-party vendors. Because the "primary purpose" of functions such as press release drafting is not to communicate with counsel for legal advice, Simon concluded that these documents were not covered by the attorney-client privilege. "Having outside counsel hire a public relations firm is insufficient to cloak that business function with the attorney-client privilege," Simon wrote.[290] Likewise, he was skeptical that these documents were entitled to protection under the work product doctrine. "Premera has not shown that the documents were created because of litigation rather than for business reasons, or that the documents would not have been created in substantially similar form but for the prospect of litigation," he wrote.[291]

The third category of documents included a "remediation report" prepared by Mandiant. Premera initially retained Mandiant directly, but later amended the agreement so that Mandiant was supervised by outside counsel. Simon was skeptical about application of the attorney-client privilege or work product doctrine to these materials. "Premera argues that Mandiant is the equivalent of a private investigator or other investigative resource hired by an attorney to conduct an investigation on behalf of an attorney, and thus that Mandiant's work is privileged and protected as work-product," he wrote. "The flaw in Premera's argument, however, is that Mandiant was hired in 2014 to perform a scope of work for Premera, not outside counsel. That scope of work did not change after outside counsel was retained. The only thing that changed was that Mandiant was now directed to report directly to outside counsel and to label all of Mandiant's communications as 'privileged,' 'work-product,' or 'at the request of counsel.'"[292]

The *Premera* opinion demonstrates the difficulty of protecting some cybersecurity documents and communications via the attorney-client privilege and work product doctrine. It likely will be insufficient to merely copy a lawyer on cybersecurity-related emails, or to label reports as privileged. A court will conduct a searching review of the attorney's involvement in the work product or communication, as well as whether the work was performed for legal purposes.

2.5.7 *In re United Shore Financial Services*

Companies also must keep in mind that by disclosing *part* of the content of a breach investigation, they may entirely waive whatever privilege they had hoped to claim. This can be seen in a 2018 order from the U.S. Court of Appeals for the Sixth Circuit in *In re United Shore Financial Services*.

---

289 *Id.*
290 *Id.*
291 *Id.* at 1244 (internal quotation marks and citation omitted).
292 *Id.* at 1245.

In that putative class action lawsuit, the district court granted a motion to compel a data breach defendant, United Shore, to produce documents that United Shore claimed were privileged. The documents were related to a postincident investigation that United Shore had hired consulting firm Navigant to conduct. In interrogatory responses, United Shore already had disclosed the conclusions that Navigant had reached in its investigation, yet it refused to provide certain underlying documents. In light of this disclosure, and United Shore's apparent intent to rely on the investigation in its defense, the district court concluded that the litigant is "entitled to see documents related to how the investigation was conducted and what was considered during the investigation."[293]

United Shore asked the Sixth Circuit to vacate this order, and the appellate court refused. In a brief order, the Sixth Circuit reasoned that United Shore had "implicitly waived" the attorney-client privilege. "Once waived, the privilege is waived with respect to all communications involving the same subject matter," the court concluded.[294]

---

293 Leibovic v. United Shore Fin. Servs., Case No. 15-12639 (E.D. Mich. Aug. 2, 2017).
294 *In re* United Shore Fin. Servs., No. 17-2290 (6th Cir. Jan. 3, 2018).

3

Cybersecurity Requirements for Specific Industries

Chapters 1 and 2 covered the general data security obligations that all U.S. companies face under Section 5 of the FTC Act, state data security laws, and common-law torts that could lead to class action lawsuits and other litigation. These requirements apply equally to companies regardless of their industry.

In addition to these general data security requirements, companies that handle particularly sensitive information or operate in industries that carry particularly high national security risks face more stringent requirements. This chapter covers nine such prominent legal requirements for sensitive information: (1) the Gramm-Leach-Bliley Act Safeguards Rule for financial institutions, (2) the New York Department of Financial Services cybersecurity regulations, (3) the Red Flags Rule for information for certain creditors and financial institutions, (4) the Payment Card Industry Data Security Standard (PCI DSS) for credit and debit card information, (5) California's Internet of Things cybersecurity law, (6) the Health Insurance Portability and Accountability Act (HIPAA) Security Rule for certain health-related information, (7) Federal Energy Regulatory Commission guidelines for electric grid cybersecurity, (8) Nuclear Regulatory Commission cybersecurity requirements for nuclear reactor licensees, and (9) South Carolina's insurance industry cybersecurity regulations.

Keep in mind that the general cybersecurity requirements described in Chapters 1 and 2 *also* apply to these industries, unless there is an exception for companies that comply with industry-specific laws and regulations. Moreover, it is increasingly common for companies that provide highly sensitive information to certain contractors, such as law firms and accountants, to *contractually* require additional cybersecurity protections.

Cybersecurity Law, Second Edition. Jeff Kosseff.
© 2020 John Wiley & Sons, Inc. Published 2020 by John Wiley & Sons, Inc.
Companion Website: www.wiley.com/go/kosseff/cybersecurity2e

3.1 Financial Institutions: Gramm-Leach-Bliley Act Safeguards Rule

In 1999, Congress enacted the Gramm-Leach-Bliley Act (GLBA), a comprehensive overhaul of financial regulation in the United States. Many of the most controversial portions of the act, which relaxed decades-old ownership restrictions on financial institutions, are outside of the scope of this book. For the purposes of cybersecurity, the most relevant section is known as the Safeguards Rule, which requires federal regulators to adopt data security standards for the financial institutions that they regulate.

The Gramm-Leach-Bliley Act requires the agencies to adopt administrative, technical, and physical safeguards:

1) to insure the security and confidentiality of customer records and information,
2) to protect against any anticipated threats or hazards to the security or integrity of such records, and
3) to protect against unauthorized access to or use of such records or information that could result in substantial harm or inconvenience to any customer.[1]

The statute only applies to "nonpublic personal information," which it defines as personally identifiable financial information that is (1) "provided by a consumer to a financial institution," (2) "resulting from any transaction with the consumer or any service performed for the consumer," or (3) "otherwise obtained by the financial institution."[2]

A number of agencies regulate financial institutions, and they have taken slightly different approaches to developing regulations under the GLBA Safeguards Rule. The remainder of this section examines the primary regulations issued by the various agencies.

3.1.1 Interagency Guidelines

Agencies that regulate banks and related financial institutions have collaborated to develop Interagency Guidelines to implement the Safeguards Rule. The agencies that have adopted the Interagency Guidelines are the Office of the Comptroller of the Currency, the Federal Reserve Board, the Federal Deposit Insurance Corporation, and the Office of Thrift Supervision.[3]

---

1 15 U.S.C. § 6801(b).
2 15 U.S.C. § 6809(4).
3 The National Credit Union Administration, which regulates credit unions, has adopted a Safeguards Rule that is largely identical to the Interagency Guidelines. 12 C.F.R. § 248.

The Interagency Guidelines require covered institutions to implement a "comprehensive written information security program" to safeguard non-public personal information.[4] The agencies stated that financial institutions must take the following steps while developing and implementing their programs:

- *Involve the board of directors.* The board or a board committee should approve the security program and oversee its development, implementation, and maintenance.
- *Assess risk.* The institutions should conduct an "assessment of reasonably foreseeable risks" involving the security of customer information.
- *Manage and control risk.* The institutions should design their programs to control the risks by considering measures such as access controls, restrictions on physical locations where customer information is stored, encryption of information in transit and at rest, segregation of duties, background checks for employees, and system monitoring. Components of a risk control system may include:
  - *Train employees on the information security program.*
  - *Maintain regular testing of controls and systems.*
  - *Properly dispose of customer information.*
  - *Provide adequate oversight of service providers' information security measures.*
  - *Adjust information security programs as new threats arise.*
  - *Report to board of directors any "material matters" related to the information security program at least once a year.*[5]

The Interagency Guidelines further require financial institutions to maintain incident response programs for *sensitive* customer information, which the guidelines define as a customer's name, address, or phone number in combination with at least one of the following:

- Social Security number,
- driver's license number,
- account number,
- credit or debit card number, or
- personal identification number or password that permits access to a customer's account.[6]

---

4 Each participating agency has adopted a version of the Interagency Guidelines in its regulations. For ease of reference, this subsection will refer to the version of the Interagency Guidelines in the Federal Reserve's regulations, appendixes D-2 to 12 C.F.R. § 208.

5 *Id.*

6 *Id.*

Sensitive customer information includes any additional information that would enable an unauthorized user to access a customer's account (e.g., username and password).[7]

Incident response programs for sensitive information must contain procedures to:

- assess "the nature and scope of the incident";
- determine what information types have been accessed;
- notify its primary federal regulator (e.g., the Office of the Comptroller of the Currency) as soon as possible after the institution becomes aware of an incident;
- notify appropriate law enforcement authorities consistent with requirements to file Suspicious Activity Reports;
- take steps "to contain and control the incident to prevent further unauthorized access to or misuse of customer information"; and
- notify the customer as soon as possible if the institution, after investigation, determines that sensitive customer information likely was misused or that the unauthorized access likely will result in misuse or harm to individuals (the institution may delay notification if law enforcement provides a written request for a delay because notice would interfere with a law enforcement investigation).[8] Note that this requirement is similar to the state laws that take a "risk-of-harm" approach to notification requirements, as it allows financial institutions to conduct a balancing test to determine whether to issue notifications.[9]

The notices must contain a description, in general, of the data breach, the types of information that were accessed without authorization, and mitigation steps taken by the financial institution; a telephone number for further information about the breach; and a reminder to "remain vigilant" and report apparent identity theft.[10]

Although the Interagency Guidelines are comprehensive, the banking regulators have not focused on enforcement of their data security regulations as much as many other regulators, such as the Securities and Exchange Commission and the FTC.

3.1.2 Securities and Exchange Commission Regulation S-P

The Securities and Exchange Commission's Regulation S-P sets the GLBA Safeguards Rule requirements for brokers, dealers, investment companies,

---

7 *Id.*
8 *Id.*
9 *Id.*
10 *Id.*

and investment advisers that are registered with the SEC.[11] The SEC's version of the Safeguards Rule is not as detailed as the Interagency Guidelines, though the SEC has been fairly aggressive in its enforcement of the rule in recent years.

The SEC's regulations broadly require institutions to adopt written information security policies and procedures that contain administrative, technical, and physical safeguards that meet the three goals of the GLBA Safeguards Rule: ensuring security and confidentiality of customer information, protecting such information from anticipated threats or hazards, and protecting the information from unauthorized access that could substantially harm or inconvenience the customer.[12] Regulation S-P also requires institutions to properly dispose of consumer report information and take steps to protect against unauthorized access.[13]

Despite the relative lack of specificity in the SEC's version of the Safeguards Rule, the agency has indicated that cybersecurity is a high priority and that it will use the regulation to pursue institutions that do not adequately protect customer information. In September 2015, the SEC announced a settlement of an administrative proceeding with R.T. Jones Capital Equities Management, an investment adviser that experienced a data breach, compromising the personal information of approximately 100,000 people.[14] Despite the lack of reported identity theft associated with the incident, the SEC brought the administrative action because the company did not have a written information security program. In the settlement order, the SEC noted that the company failed to conduct risk assessments, use a firewall, encrypt customer information, or develop an incident response plan.[15] The no-fault settlement required the company to cease future violations of the SEC's Safeguards Rule and to pay a $75,000 penalty. In announcing the settlement, Marshall S. Sprung, Co-Chief of the SEC Enforcement Division's Asset Management Unit, warned that firms "must adopt written policies to protect their clients' private information and they need to anticipate potential cybersecurity events and have clear procedures in place rather than waiting to react once a breach occurs."[16]

---

11 17 C.F.R. § 248.30.

12 *Id.*

13 *Id.*

14 *In re* R.T. Jones Capital Equities Mgmt., Administrative Proceeding File No. 3-16827, Order Instituting Administrative and Cease-and-Desist Proceedings Pursuant to Sections 203(e) and 203(k) of the Investment Advisers Act of 1940, Making Findings, and Imposing Remedial Sanctions and a Cease-and-Desist Order.

15 *Id.*

16 Securities and Exchange Commission, *SEC Charges Investment Adviser with Failing to Adopt Proper Cybersecurity Policies and Procedures Prior to Breach* (Sept. 22, 2015) [press release].

3.1.3 FTC Safeguards Rule

The FTC regulates financial institutions that are not regulated by one of the banking agencies or the SEC. Among the types of financial institutions that the FTC regulates are consumer reporting agencies, retailers that offer credit to customers, and mortgage brokers.

Like the SEC, the FTC did not adopt an extremely detailed Safeguards Rule. Nonetheless, the FTC has been quite aggressive in its enforcement of the Safeguards Rule, partly due to the key role that customer information plays for consumer reporting agencies and other financial institutions regulated by the FTC. The FTC's Safeguards Rule, like those of the other agencies, requires financial institutions to develop, implement, and maintain a comprehensive written information security program that contains administrative, technical, and physical safeguards that meet the GLBA Safeguards Rule's three key objectives listed at the start of this chapter.

The FTC's regulations require information security programs to be carried out and protected as follows:

- Designate employees to coordinate the program.
- Identify "reasonably foreseeable internal and external risks to the security, confidentiality, and integrity of customer information."
- Based on this assessment, companies should implement safeguards and conduct regular assessments of the strength and viability of those safeguards.
- Contractually require service providers to comply with the Safeguards Rule and oversee their compliance.
- Regularly evaluate and adjust information security policies and procedures.[17]

The FTC has brought a number of enforcement actions against companies that failed to develop information security programs that meet these requirements. Often, the FTC brings cases after a financial institution has experienced a data breach. The summaries that follow are a few of the most prominent settlements of enforcement actions that the FTC has brought under the Safeguards Rule.

In the Matter of ACRAnet, Inc., **Docket No. C-4331 (2011)** Data breaches often trigger FTC scrutiny of a financial institution's compliance with the Safeguards Rule. ACRAnet assembles consumer reports for the three major consumer reporting agencies: Equifax, Experian, and TransUnion. The reports contain a great deal of sensitive and nonpublic information, such as consumers'

---

17 16 C.F.R. § 314.4.

names, addresses, Social Security numbers, birth dates, and work history. The company sells these reports to mortgage brokers and therefore is a financial institution subject to FTC's Safeguards Rule. In 2007 and 2008, hackers accessed nearly 700 consumer reports due to vulnerabilities in the networks of ACRANet's clients. After the breach, the FTC states that ACRANet did not take steps to prevent similar breaches by, for instance, requiring clients to demonstrate that their computer networks are free of security threats. The FTC asserted that ACRANet violated the Safeguards Rule by failing to:

- implement adequate customer information safeguards;
- test and monitor its information security controls;
- assess and improve its information security program; and
- develop a comprehensive information security program.

In the Matter of James B. Nutter & Co., Docket No. C-4258 (2009)   James B. Nutter & Co. makes and services residential loans and is therefore covered by the FTC Safeguards Rule. The company collects a great deal of highly sensitive information, including employment history, credit history, Social Security numbers, and driver's license numbers. It uses its website and computer network to obtain personal information from customers, store data, and otherwise conduct its lending business. An unauthorized individual managed to hack into the company's network and send spam. Although there was no evidence of theft of customer information, the FTC stated in its complaint that the hacker "could have accessed personal information without authorization." The FTC claimed that the company violated the Safeguards Rule by failing to:

- develop a comprehensive written information security program;
- identify risks to personal information;
- develop personal information risk controls;
- evaluate and adjust the information security program; and
- oversee service providers' security procedures.

In the Matter of Superior Mortgage Corporation, Docket C-4153 (2005)   The FTC brought a complaint against Superior Mortgage Corporation, a mortgage lender, for violating the Safeguards Rule. Although the complaint does not mention a specific data breach or other attack on the company's system, the complaint noted that the company's website only encrypted sensitive customer information while in transit, but not while the information was at rest. The decrypted customer information allegedly was then emailed in clear text to the company's headquarters and branch offices. The company's online privacy policy claimed that "[a]ll information submitted is handled by SSL encryption[.]" The FTC alleged that Superior Mortgage violated the Safeguards Rule by, among other things, failing to:

- conduct a security risk assessment;
- implement adequate password policies;
- encrypt sensitive customer data; and
- oversee service providers' compliance with information security requirements.

In the Matter of Goal Financial LLC, Docket No. C-4216 (2008) The FTC also expects companies to adequately oversee their employees' handling of personal information. In such a case, employees of Goal Financial, a marketer and originator of student loans, transferred more than 7,000 consumer files to third parties. Additionally, a Goal Financial employee sold hard drives that had not yet been wiped of approximately 34,000 customers' sensitive personal information. In its complaint against Goal Financial, the FTC alleged that the company violated the Safeguards Rule by failing to: identify risks, design and implement safeguards to control those risks, develop a written information security program, and require contractors to safeguard customer information.

3.2 New York Department of Financial Services Cybersecurity Regulations

In 2017, the New York Department of Financial Services (DFS) finalized cybersecurity regulations for entities that it regulates. This applies to a wide range of companies, including many that are not headquartered in New York. The regulations are among the most specific and onerous in the United States.[18]

Under these regulations, regulated companies must conduct periodic assessments[19] that consider the risks particular to the companies' cybersecurity, information system, and nonpublic information, which includes: (1) business information that could cause a "material adverse impact" to the company if disclosed; (2) individual's personal information, which is a name or other identifier in combination with a social security number, drivers' license number, financial account number, financial account password, or biometric information; or (3) certain health information.[20] Companies must use these risk assessments to develop cybersecurity programs that: (1) address risks to the security and integrity of nonpublic information; (2) use "defensive infrastructure" to protect systems and nonpublic information; (3) detect cybersecurity events, which are

---

18 Much of this subsection was originally published in a Georgetown Law Technology Review article by the author of this book in 2017. *See* Jeff Kosseff, *New York's Financial Cybersecurity Regulation: Tough, Fair, and a National Model*, 1 GEO. L. TECH. REV. 432 (2017).

19 N.Y. COMP. CODES R. & REGS. tit. 23, § 500.09.

20 N.Y. COMP. CODES R. & REGS. tit. 23, § 500.01(g).

broadly defined as acts or attempts "to gain unauthorized access to, disrupt or misuse an Information System or information stored on such Information System[;]"[21] (4) respond to cybersecurity events and reduce harm; (5) allow recovery from cybersecurity events; and (6) fulfill reporting requirements.[22]

The cybersecurity program must require monitoring and testing to regularly evaluate the program's effectiveness.[23] If a company does not continuously monitor for vulnerabilities, it must annually conduct penetration tests to determine whether the systems are accessible to hackers.[24] Companies that do not continuously monitor also must conduct biannual vulnerability assessments.[25] The companies also must develop programs to ensure the ongoing security of applications that have been developed in-house.[26] Moreover, companies must securely dispose of nonpublic information once it is no longer necessary for business purposes.[27] Cybersecurity programs also must include written incident response plans, which address the processes and goals for responding to cybersecurity events, the roles and responsibilities of decisionmakers, internal and external communications, remediation procedures, and reporting incidents.[28] Companies must notify DFS within 72 hours of determining that a cybersecurity event occurred.[29]

In addition to developing cybersecurity programs, regulated companies must develop written cybersecurity policies, approved by a senior officer or the board of directors, that address the following topics, if applicable:

- Information security;
- Data governance and classification;
- Asset inventory and device management;
- Access controls and identity management;
- Business continuity and disaster recovery planning and resources;
- Systems operations and availability concerns;
- Systems and network security;
- Systems and network monitoring;
- Systems and application development and quality assurance;
- Physical security and environmental controls;
- Customer data privacy;
- Vendor and third party service provider management;

---

21 N.Y. Comp. Codes R. & Regs. tit. 23, § 500.01(d).
22 N.Y. Comp. Codes R. & Regs. tit. 23, § 500.02.
23 N.Y. Comp. Codes R. & Regs. tit. 23, § 500.05.
24 *Id.*
25 *Id.*
26 N.Y. Comp. Codes R. & Regs. tit. 23, § 500.08.
27 N.Y. Comp. Codes R. & Regs. tit. 23, § 500.13.
28 N.Y. Comp. Codes R. & Regs. tit. 23, § 500.16.
29 N.Y. Comp. Codes R. & Regs. tit. 23, § 500.17.

- Risk assessment; and
- Incident response.[30]

The regulation also requires companies to have a chief information security officer (CISO), employed directly by the company, an affiliate, or a third-party vendor.[31] The CISO is responsible for compliance with the cybersecurity regulation and must submit a written report to the Board of Directors, at least annually, that documents the company's cybersecurity program and risks.[32] Companies also must ensure that cybersecurity personnel receive updated and sufficient training,[33] and they must ensure that third-party service providers adhere to adequate cybersecurity policies and practices.[34] Furthermore, companies should maintain "audit trails" that allow them to "reconstruct" financial transactions after cybersecurity events and help them detect and respond to potentially harmful attacks.[35] The regulation requires companies to use "effective controls" to prevent unauthorized access, and suggests that these controls may include multifactor authentication or risk-based authentication, which requires additional information at log-in if the system detects anomalies.[36]

The regulation also strongly encourages companies to encrypt nonpublic information both while the information is being transmitted across networks and while it is in storage ("at rest").[37] However, the regulation allows companies to determine whether encryption is appropriate based on their risk assessments.[38] If companies determine that encryption is infeasible, the CISO must approve alternative controls and review them at least once a year.[39]

The regulation is less onerous for small businesses, which have fewer than 10 employees in New York (including independent contractors), less than $5 million in gross annual revenues from New York over the previous three fiscal years, or less than $10 million in year-end total assets.[40] Those companies are exempted from the following requirements: having a CISO, monitoring and testing their networks, maintaining audit trails, having application security policies, training cybersecurity personnel, using multifactor authentication or encryption, and maintaining an incident response plan.[41]

---

30 N.Y. COMP. CODES R. & REGS. tit. 23, § 500.03.
31 N.Y. COMP. CODES R. & REGS. tit. 23, § 500.04.
32 Id.
33 N.Y. COMP. CODES R. & REGS. tit. 23, § 500.10.
34 N.Y. COMP. CODES R. & REGS. tit. 23, § 500.11.
35 N.Y. COMP. CODES R. & REGS. tit. 23, § 500.06.
36 N.Y. COMP. CODES R. & REGS. tit. 23, § 500.12.
37 N.Y. COMP. CODES R. & REGS. tit. 23, § 500.15.
38 Id.
39 Id.
40 N.Y. COMP. CODES R. & REGS. tit. 23, § 500.19.
41 Id.

3.3 Financial Institutions and Creditors: Red Flags Rule

In 2003, amid growing concern about identity theft, Congress passed the Fair and Accurate Credit Transaction Act of 2003. Among other provisions, the statute required banking regulators and the FTC to develop regulations that require financial institutions and creditors that offer covered accounts to develop "reasonable policies and procedures" to prevent their account holders from becoming the victims of identity theft.[42]

The Red Flags Rule only applies to companies that (1) are financial institutions or creditors *and* (2) offer "covered accounts" to individuals. To determine whether the Red Flags Rule applies, companies must analyze the definition of both terms.

What Are Examples of Red Flags?

In a supplement to the Red Flags Rule regulations, the FTC provided the following illustrative list of examples of red flags. Keep in mind that these are only examples, and there may very well be other indications of risk:

Alerts, notifications, or warnings from a consumer reporting agency

1) A fraud or active duty alert is included with a consumer report
2) A consumer reporting agency provides a notice of credit freeze in response to a request for a consumer report
3) A consumer reporting agency provides a notice of address discrepancy, as defined in § 641.1 (b) of this part [16 C.F.R. § 641.1(b)].
4) A consumer report indicates a pattern of activity that is inconsistent with the history and usual pattern of activity of an applicant or customer, such as:

    a) a recent and significant increase in the volume of inquiries,
    b) an unusual number of recently established credit relationships,
    c) a material change in the use of credit, especially with respect to recently established credit relationships, or
    d) an account that was closed for cause or identified for abuse of account privileges by a financial institution or creditor.

Suspicious documents

1) Documents provided for identification appear to have been altered or forged.
2) The photograph or physical description on the identification is not consistent with the appearance of the applicant or customer presenting the identification.

---

42 15 U.S.C. § 1681m.

3) Other information on the identification is not consistent with information provided by the person opening a new covered account or customer presenting the identification.
4) Other information on the identification is not consistent with readily accessible information that is on file with the financial institution or creditor, such as a signature card or a recent check.
5) An application appears to have been altered or forged, or gives the appearance of having been destroyed and reassembled.

Suspicious personal identifying information

1) Personal identifying information provided is inconsistent when compared against external information sources used by the financial institution or creditor. For example:
   a) the address does not match any address in the consumer report, or
   b) the Social Security Number (SSN) has not been issued, or is listed on the Social Security Administration's Death Master File.
2) Personal identifying information provided by the customer is not consistent with other personal identifying information provided by the customer. For example, there is a lack of correlation between the SSN range and date of birth.
3) Personal identifying information provided is associated with known fraudulent activity as indicated by internal or third-party sources used by the financial institution or creditor. For example:
   a) the address on an application is the same as the address provided on a fraudulent application, or
   b) the phone number on an application is the same as the number provided on a fraudulent application.
4) Personal identifying information provided is of a type commonly associated with fraudulent activity as indicated by internal or third-party sources used by the financial institution or creditor. For example:
   a) the address on an application is fictitious, a mail drop, or a prison; or
   b) the phone number is invalid, or is associated with a pager or answering service.
5) The SSN provided is the same as that submitted by other persons opening an account or other customers.
6) The address or telephone number provided is the same as or similar to the address or telephone number submitted by an unusually large number of other persons opening accounts or by other customers.
7) The person opening the covered account or the customer fails to provide all required personal identifying information on an application or in response to notification that the application is incomplete.

8) Personal identifying information provided is not consistent with personal identifying information that is on file with the financial institution or creditor.
9) For financial institutions and creditors that use challenge questions, the person opening the covered account or the customer cannot provide authenticating information beyond that which generally would be available from a wallet or consumer report.

Unusual use of, or suspicious activity related to, the covered account

1) Shortly following the notice of a change of address for a covered account, the institution or creditor receives a request for a new, additional, or replacement card or a cell phone, or for the addition of authorized users on the account.
2) A new revolving credit account is used in a manner commonly associated with known patterns of fraud. For example:
   a) the majority of available credit is used for cash advances or merchandise that is easily convertible to cash (e.g., electronics equipment or jewelry), or
   b) the customer fails to make the first payment or makes an initial payment but no subsequent payments.
3) A covered account is used in a manner that is not consistent with established patterns of activity on the account. There is, for example:
   a) nonpayment when there is no history of late or missed payments,
   b) a material increase in the use of available credit,
   c) a material change in purchasing or spending patterns,
   d) a material change in electronic fund transfer patterns in connection with a deposit account, or
   e) a material change in telephone call patterns in connection with a cellular phone account.
4) A covered account that has been inactive for a reasonably lengthy period of time is used (taking into consideration the type of account, the expected pattern of usage, and other relevant factors).
5) Mail sent to the customer is returned repeatedly as undeliverable although transactions continue to be conducted in connection with the customer's covered account.
6) The financial institution or creditor is notified that the customer is not receiving paper account statements.
7) The financial institution or creditor is notified of unauthorized charges or transactions in connection with a customer's covered account.

Source: Federal Trade Commission, Appendix A to Subpart C of 16 C.F.R. 681.

> ## How Do Companies Implement the Red Flags Rule?
>
> The regulations require the financial institution or creditor's board of directors or board committee to approve the initial Red Flags Rule program,[43] and to involve the board, a board committee, or a senior manager in the oversight, development, implementation, and administration of the program.[44] Companies are required to train their staff to implement the program[45] and to appropriately and effectively oversee service provider arrangements.[46]
>
> The FTC has stated that it expects companies to take a variety of approaches to meeting their requirements under the Red Flags Rule, and that while "some businesses and organizations may need a comprehensive program to address a high risk of identity theft, a streamlined program may be appropriate for businesses facing a low risk."[47] In other words, the Red Flags Rule is not a one-size-fits-all program, and companies should adopt their own program relative to their company's needs and risks.

3.3.1 Financial Institutions or Creditors

The FTC and banking regulators issued their first iteration of the Red Flag regulations in 2007, but the implementation of those regulations was delayed after an outcry from the business community about the lack of clarity in the regulations. Although "financial institution" is clearly defined, the regulations contained a broad definition of "creditor" that could have included professionals such as doctors and lawyers because they bill clients after performing services. Many such professionals argued that their operations do not pose a substantial risk of identity theft, and therefore they should not be required to develop comprehensive identity theft prevention programs.

Congress responded to the industry concerns in 2010 by passing the Red Flag Program Clarification Act of 2010.[48] The law defines "creditor" as a company that, in the ordinary course of business:

> i) obtains or uses consumer reports, directly or indirectly, in connection with a credit transaction;
> ii) furnishes information to consumer reporting agencies ... in connection with a credit transaction; or

---

43 16 C.F.R. § 681.1(e)(1).
44 16 C.F.R. § 681.1(e)(2).
45 16 C.F.R. § 681.1(e)(3).
46 16 C.F.R. § 681.1(e)(4).
47 Federal Trade Commission, Fighting Identity Theft with the Red Flags Rule: A How-To Guide for Business (May 2013).
48 Pub. L. No. 111-319.

iii) advances funds to or on behalf of a person, based on an obligation of the person to repay the funds or repayable from specific property pledged by or on behalf of the person.[49]

The Clarification Act explicitly states that the term "creditor" does not include an entity that "advances funds on behalf of a person for expenses incidental to a service provided by the creditor to that person."[50]

The new definition clarifies that the Red Flags Rule applies to financial institutions; companies that obtain, use, or provide information for credit reports; and companies that lend money to people, provided that the loan is for something other than the lender's own services. Accordingly, under the clarified Red Flags Rule, a doctor or lawyer does not become subject to the Red Flags Rule merely by billing a customer after providing a service.

3.3.2 Covered Accounts

Not all financial institutions and creditors are covered by the Red Flags Rule. The requirements only apply if the company offers a "covered account." The Red Flags Rule regulations define "covered accounts" as including two types of accounts:

i) [a]n account that a financial institution or creditor offers or maintains, primarily for personal, family, or household purposes, that involves or is designed to permit multiple payments or transactions, such as a credit card account, mortgage loan, automobile loan, margin account, cell phone account, utility account, checking account, or savings account; and

ii) [a]ny other account that the financial institution or creditor offers or maintains for which there is a reasonably foreseeable risk to customers or to the safety and soundness of the financial institution or creditor from identity theft, including financial, operational, compliance, reputation, or litigation risks.[51]

To determine whether an account falls within either definition, the regulations instruct the financial institution or creditor to consider the methods that the company provides to open its accounts, the methods that the company provides to access the accounts, and the company's previous experience with identity theft.[52] Keep in mind that the regulations apply as long as the financial institution or creditor has at least *one* covered account.

---

49 *Id.*
50 *Id.*
51 16 C.F.R. § 681.1(b)(3).
52 16 C.F.R. § 681.1(c).

In other words, financial institutions and creditors must conduct a balancing test to determine whether the risk of identity theft to its customers is reasonably foreseeable. They are only required to develop an identity theft prevention plan if they determine that the risk is reasonably foreseeable and, therefore, they offer covered accounts. The regulators expect the companies to periodically reassess this risk. Companies should make an honest assessment of the risk. If a company obtains highly sensitive personal information via an unencrypted Internet connection, it is difficult to conceive of how a company could find that there is not a reasonably foreseeable risk of identity theft. It is a best practice to document the reasoning behind the determination of whether a company offers a covered account.

3.3.3 Requirements for a Red Flags Identity Theft Prevention Program

The Red Flags regulations require financial institutions and creditors that offer at least one covered account to develop a *written* identity theft prevention program designed "to detect, prevent, and mitigate identity theft in connection with the opening of a covered account or any existing covered account."[53]

The written program must explain how the financial institution or creditor will accomplish four goals:

1) Identify "red flags," which the regulations define as a "pattern, practice, or specific activity that indicates the possible existence of identity theft."[54]
2) Detect the red flags that the financial institution or creditor has identified. Companies should obtain identifying information about and verify the identities of people opening covered accounts, authenticate those customers, monitor their transactions, and verify the validity of address change requests.
3) Appropriately respond to red flags that are detected to prevent and mitigate identity theft. The regulators wrote that appropriate responses may include continued monitoring of customers' accounts, contacting customers or law enforcement to inform them of red flags, modifying log-in credentials to customer accounts, or closing accounts that appear to have been compromised.[55]
4) Periodically update the red flags program to reflect changes in risk. When updating the program, the regulation states, financial institutions and creditors should consider, among other things, recent incidents of identity theft that the company has experienced, changes to identity theft mitigation practices, new types of identity theft, and changes to the company's structure or ownership that might increase the likelihood of identity theft.[56]

---

53 16 C.F.R. § 681.1(d)(1).
54 16 C.F.R. § 681.1(b)(9).
55 Appendix A to 16 C.F.R. § 681.
56 16 C.F.R. § 681.1(d)(2) and Appendix A to pt. 681.

3.4   Companies that Use Payment and Debit Cards: Payment Card Industry Data Security Standard (PCI DSS)

Companies that accept or use credit or debit cards (including, but not limited to retailers), are required to comply with the Payment Card Industry Data Security Standard (PCI DSS), an extensive set of operational and technical rules that are intended to protect payment card numbers and associated data. The goal of the rules is to reduce the chances of the data being stolen and used for identity theft.

The PCI DSS standards are adopted not by courts or legislatures but by an organization comprised of the major credit card companies (American Express, Discover Financial Services, JCB, MasterCard, and Visa).

The PCI Security Standards Council has developed detailed technical guidance for businesses of varying sizes to comply with the standards (available on its website, www.pcisecuritystandards.org). In short, PCI DSS consists of six goals and twelve requirements:

Build and maintain a secure network and systems.
Requirement 1: Install and maintain a firewall configuration to protect cardholder data.
Requirement 2: Do not use vendor-supplied defaults for system passwords and other security parameters.

Protect cardholder data.
Requirement 3: Protect stored cardholder data.
Requirement 4: Encrypt transmission of cardholder data across open, public networks.

Maintain a vulnerability management program.
Requirement 5: Protect all systems against malware and regularly update anti-virus software or programs.
Requirement 6: Develop and maintain secure systems and applications.

Implement strong access control measures.
Requirement 7: Restrict access to cardholder data by business need to know.
Requirement 8: Identify and authenticate access to system components.
Requirement 9: Restrict physical access to cardholder data.

Regularly monitor and test networks.
Requirement 10: Track and monitor all access to network resources and cardholder data.
Requirement 11: Regularly test security systems and processes.

> **Maintain an information security policy.**
> *Requirement 12: Maintain a policy that addresses information security for all personnel.*[57]

The credit card companies individually enforce these requirements by contractually imposing them on the banks, which in turn impose the requirements on the merchants and others that accept and use their credit cards. The credit card companies and banks can impose substantial fines on retailers that fail to comply with PCI DSS, but the amount of those fines is not publicly disclosed.

Additionally, two state laws refer to PCI DSS:

- Nevada requires merchants that conduct business in Nevada to comply with PCI DSS.[58]
- Washington state requires certain businesses to "take reasonable care to guard against unauthorized access" to payment card information, but exempts those businesses from liability if the information was encrypted or the business was "certified compliant with the payment card industry data security standards."[59] In 2016, Home Depot attempted to use this safe harbor to dismiss a class action filed by financial institutions after a data breach at the retailer, but the court denied the motion because the financial institutions' complaint alleged that Home Depot did not comply with PCI DSS.

Even in states that have not adopted laws that incorporate PCI DSS, the standards could help determine the general standard of care in common-law tort and contract claims. For example, in the *Hannaford* case discussed in Chapter 2, involving the breach of a grocery chain's payment card systems, the district court concluded that it is possible that retailers have an implied contract with their consumers to incorporate industry data security standards with their payment card data:

> If a consumer tenders a credit or debit card as payment, I conclude that a jury could find certain other implied terms in the grocery purchase contract: for example, that the merchant will not use the card data for other people's purchases, will not sell or give the data to others (except in completing the payment process), and will take reasonable measures to protect the information (which might

---

57 This list is provided courtesy of PCI Security Standards Council, LLC ("PCI SSC") and is protected by copyright laws. © PCI Security Standards Council, LLC. All rights reserved.
58 NEV. REV. STAT. § 603A.215(1) ("If a data collector doing business in this State accepts a payment card in connection with a sale of goods or services, the data collector shall comply with the current version of the Payment Card Industry (PCI) Data Security Standard, as adopted by the PCI Security Standards Council or its successor organization, with respect to those transactions, not later than the date for compliance set forth in the Payment Card Industry (PCI) Data Security Standard or by the PCI Security Standards Council or its successor organization.").
59 WASH. REV. CODE § 19.255.020.

include meeting industry standards), on the basis that these are implied commitments that are "absolutely necessary to effectuate the contract," and "indispensable to effectuate the intention of the parties." A jury could reasonably find that customers would not tender cards to merchants who undertook zero obligation to protect customers' electronic data. But in today's known world of sophisticated hackers, data theft, software glitches, and computer viruses, a jury could not reasonably find an implied merchant commitment against every intrusion under any circumstances whatsoever (consider, for example, an armed robber confronting the merchant's computer systems personnel at gunpoint).[60]

In short, PCI DSS has become the de facto standard of care for all companies—large and small—that accept, use, process, or store credit or debit card information. Companies are wise to keep informed about the PCI Council's latest guidance regarding PCI DSS compliance.

3.5 California Internet of Things Cybersecurity Law

In September 2018, California became the first state to impose specific cybersecurity requirements for Internet of Things (IoT) devices. Although the law does not impose terribly specific requirements, it marked a renewed focus on the security of cameras, appliances, and other devices that are connected to the Internet.

The California law applies to manufacturers of "connected devices," which it defines as "any device, or other physical object that is capable of connecting to the Internet, directly or indirectly, and that is assigned an Internet Protocol address or Bluetooth address."[61]

The law requires that manufacturers of connected devices sold in California implement a "reasonable security feature or features." These features should be "appropriate to the nature and function of the device," "appropriate to the information it may collect, contain, or transmit," and "designed to protect the device and any information contained therein from unauthorized access, destruction, use, modification, or disclosure."[62]

The law does not provide substantial guidance as to how an IoT device could satisfy these requirements. It does state, however, that a reasonable security feature exists if a "preprogrammed password is unique to each device manufactured" or

---

60 *In re* Hannaford Bros. Co. Customer Data Sec. Breach Litig., 613 F. Supp. 2d 108, 119 (D. Me. 2009), *aff'd in part & rev'd in part on other grounds,* Anderson v. Hannaford Bros. Co., 659 F.3d 151 (1st Cir. 2011).
61 CAL. CIV. CODE § 1798.91.05.
62 CAL. CIV. CODE § 1798.91.04.

the "device contains a security feature that requires a user to generate a new means of authentication before access is granted to the device for the first time."[63]

Because it is unlikely for a webcam or appliance manufacturer to avoid selling its products into California, the law likely will become a de facto nationwide requirement. The law appears to address the lack of security features that had existed on IoT devices, enabling hackers to easily spy on individuals through webcams and other devices.

3.6 Health Providers: Health Insurance Portability and Accountability Act (HIPAA) Security Rule

Certain health-related providers and companies are required to comply with an extensive series of regulations for the security of health data. Under its authority from the Health Insurance Portability and Accountability Act, the Department of Health and Human Services has promulgated regulations known as the HIPAA Security Rule.

The HIPAA Security Rule applies to two types of entities: "covered entities" and "business associates." Other companies, even if they handle health information, are not subject to HIPAA, unless required by a contract. A "covered entity" is a health plan, a healthcare clearinghouse, or a healthcare provider who transmits health information in electronic form. A "business associate" is a provider of "data transmission services" to a covered entity, a person who offers a personal health record to individuals on behalf of a covered entity, or a subcontractor that "creates, receives, maintains, or transmits protected health information on behalf of the business associate."[64] Examples of business associates include attorneys who require access to protected health information to provide services and medical transcriptionist services.

The HIPAA Security Rule only applies to "protected health information" that is collected from an individual and is created or received by a covered entity, and relates to "the past, present, or future physical or mental health or condition of an individual; the provision of health care to an individual; or the past, present, or future payment for the provision of health care to an individual."[65] Information is protected health information only if it directly identifies an individual or if there is a reasonable basis to believe that it could identify an individual.[66]

The HIPAA Security Rule requires covered entities and business associates to ensure the confidentiality, integrity, and availability of electronic protected health information and take steps to protect against reasonably anticipated

---

63 *Id.*
64 45 C.F.R. § 160.103.
65 45 C.F.R. § 160.103.
66 *Id.*

threats. [67] As with the GLBA Safeguards Rule, the HIPAA Security Rule is not a one-size-fits-all approach, instead stating that covered entities and business associates may "use any security measures that allow the covered entity or business associate to reasonably and appropriately implement the standards and implementation specification[.]"[68] The regulations instruct covered entities and business associates to consider their size, complexity, and capabilities, technical infrastructure, costs of security measures, and likelihood and magnitude of potential information security risks.[69]

Despite its flexible approach, the HIPAA Security Rule imposes a number of administrative, physical, technical, and organizational standards that covered entities and business associates must adopt. The following are the requirements from the current HIPAA regulations, located at 45 C.F.R. Part 164, modestly edited here for clarity and brevity:

Administrative safeguards.[70]

- Manage security process to "prevent, detect, contain, and correct security violations." The entity must conduct an "accurate and thorough" assessment of potential risks and vulnerabilities, implement security procedures that reduce these risks, sanction noncompliant employees, and regularly review system activity.
- Designate an information security official.
- Develop authorization procedures to reduce the likelihood of unauthorized employees accessing electronic protected health information.
- Develop clearance procedures to determine whether employees should be entrusted with access to electronic protected health information.
- Develop procedures to terminate access by former employees or employees who are no longer eligible to access the information.
- If a healthcare clearinghouse is part of a larger entity, the clearinghouse "must implement policies and procedures that protect the electronic protected health information of the clearinghouse from unauthorized access by the larger organization."
- Develop policies and procedures to allow authorized users to access electronic protected health information.
- Develop a security awareness and training program for all employees. The program should include security reminders, information about protection from malicious software, log-in monitoring, and password management. The training should be tailored to the employees' job responsibilities. For instance, executives' training might differ from training for call center employees.

---

67 45 C.F.R. § 164.306(a).
68 45 C.F.R. § 164.306(b).
69 *Id.*
70 45 C.F.R. § 164.308.

- Develop policies for security incident response and reporting.
- Develop a contingency plan for physical emergencies such as fires and other natural disasters.
- Periodically conduct technical and nontechnical evaluations of information security policies and procedures.

Physical safeguards.[71]

- Limit physical access to facilities and systems that store protected health information.
- Establish contingency operations and plans that allow restoration of lost data.
- Develop procedures and policies to physically safeguard the equipment that stores electronic protected health information.
- Develop procedures to prevent unauthorized physical access to facilities.
- Document repairs and modification to doors, locks, and other physical components that safeguard protected health information.
- Develop physical safeguards to "restrict access to authorized users" to all systems that contain electronic protected health information.
- Develop policies that restrict the physical removal and transit of devices that store electronic protected health information.

Technical safeguards.[72]

- Develop technical policies and procedures to limit access to only those who have been granted access rights. These technical safeguards include unique user identification, emergency access procedure, automatic log-off after a specified time of inactivity, and encryption and decryption of electronic protected health information.
- Develop mechanisms that routinely log activity on systems that store electronic protected health information.
- Develop policies and procedures that protect the integrity of electronic protected health information and prevent improper modifications.
- Develop procedures for verifying an individual's identity before providing that individual with access to protected health information.
- Implement technical safeguards for networks that carry electronic personal health information, with the goal of preventing unauthorized access.
- Prevent the improper modification of electronic protected health information.
- Encrypt electronic protected health information "whenever deemed appropriate." Although the HIPAA regulations do not explicitly require encryption in all circumstances, it is increasingly common for encryption to be default for sensitive information such as the health data covered by HIPAA.

---

71 45 C.F.R. § 164.310.
72 45 C.F.R. § 164.312.

Organizational requirements.[73]

- A covered entity's contract with a business associate that has access to electronic protected health information must explicitly require the business associate to comply with HIPAA's security requirements.
- The business associate contract must "ensure that any subcontractors that create, receive, maintain, or transmit electronic protected health information on behalf of the business associate" also agree to comply with HIPAA's security requirements.
- Group health plans must include, in their plan documents, a statement that the sponsor of the plan "will reasonably and appropriately safeguard electronic protected health information created, received, maintained, or transmitted to or by the plan sponsor on behalf of the group health plan."

The Department of Health and Human Services also has developed a detailed set of regulations that require covered entities to notify affected individuals and regulators about data breaches of unsecured protected health information. If business associates experience a breach, they are required to notify the covered entity within 60 days, and the covered entity is obligated to inform individuals.[74]

The breach notification requirement does not apply if all of the protected health information has been "secured" pursuant to guidance from the Department of Health and Human Services or if there is a "low probability" of compromise.[75] The department states that protected health information can be secured by an encryption method that has been validated by the National Institute of Standards and Technology, or if the media on which the protected health information has been properly destroyed (i.e., by shredding paper, film, or other hard-copy media or destroying electronic media). Redaction alone does not constitute "securing" data, according to the department.[76]

Unless law enforcement requests a delay for investigative purposes, covered entities must provide breach notifications to affected individuals without unreasonable delay and no later than 60 calendar days after first discovering the breach.[77]

HIPAA requires notices to contain many of the same elements as the notices required by the state data breach statutes discussed in Chapter 1. Keep in mind that many of the state breach notice laws contain safe harbors that allow HIPAA-covered entities to satisfy the state breach notice requirements by complying with HIPAA's notice procedures. HIPAA breach notifications must contain the following:

---

73 45 C.F.R. § 164.312.
74 45 C.F.R. § 164.410.
75 *See* DEPARTMENT OF HEALTH AND HUMAN SERVICES, GUIDANCE TO RENDER UNSECURED PROTECTED HEALTH INFORMATION UNUSABLE, UNREADABLE, OR INDECIPHERABLE TO UNAUTHORIZED INDIVIDUALS (2013).
76 *Id.*
77 45 C.F.R. § 164.404.

- A description of the breach, including the date of the breach and date of discovery of the breach.
- A description of the types of unsecured protected health information that were involved (date of birth, diagnosis, etc.). Companies should be careful to avoid the inadvertent disclosure of personally identifiable information in their descriptions of the breach and the information involved.
- Steps that the individual should take to protect from harm, such as identity theft.
- A brief description of the covered entity's investigation and mitigation following the breach.
- Contact information for more questions, including a toll-free telephone number, email address, website, or mailing address.[78]

The notification must be provided in writing to each individual's last known mailing address, or to an email address if the individual had agreed to electronic notice and had not revoked consent.[79] If the covered entity is aware that the individual is deceased, and has a mailing address for the individual's next of kin or personal representative of the affected individual, the covered entity should send the notification to that address via first-class mail.[80]

If there is not sufficient contact information to send written notifications to individuals via postal mail, covered entities may use a substitute notice process. If there is insufficient contact information for fewer than 10 individuals, then covered entities can provide an alternative form of written notice, notice by telephone, or other means. If there is insufficient or out-of-date contact information for 10 or more people, the substitute notification must (1) be a conspicuous posting on the covered entity's website for 90 days, or a conspicuous notice in major local print or broadcast media, *and* (2) include a toll-free number, active for at least 90 days, to provide individuals with more information about whether they were affected by the breach.[81]

If the covered entity determines that there is an urgent need to notify individuals, the entity may also notify the individuals by telephone and other means, in addition to written notice.[82]

If a breach involves the unsecured protected health information of more than 500 residents of a single state or jurisdiction, the covered entity must notify prominent outlets in the state or jurisdiction within 60 calendar days of discovery of the breach, and the content of the notification should be the same as in the individual notifications.[83]

---

78 45 C.F.R. § 164.404(c).
79 45 C.F.R. § 164.404(d)(1).
80 *Id.*
81 45 C.F.R. § 164.404(d)(2).
82 *Id.*
83 45 C.F.R. § 164.406.

The regulations also require notification to the Department of Health and Human Services. If the breach involves 500 or more individuals, a covered entity must inform the department at the same time that it notifies individuals.[84] If the breach involves fewer than 500 individuals, the covered entity must maintain a log of breaches and, within 60 days after the end of each calendar year, provide the department with the log of all breaches from the preceding calendar year.[85] The Department of Health and Human Services' website contains instructions for the manner in which to notify the department of both categories of breaches.[86]

On its website, the department summarized some cases without specifying the identities of the covered entities:

- A pharmacy chain's pseudoephedrine log books were visible to customers at the check-out counter. After a written analysis from the department, the chain developed policies to safeguard the logs, and trained its staff on these policies.
- A local Medicaid-funded agency sent protected health information to vendors that had not signed business associate contracts (and had therefore not agreed to comply with the Security Rule). After an investigation by the department, the agency developed procedures for disclosure of information only to its business associates and trained staff accordingly.
- A large health maintenance organization had a computer flaw that accidentally sent a customer's explanation of benefits to a family member who was not authorized to receive them. After an investigation by the department, the HMO corrected this flaw and reviewed all transactions over a six-month period for similar flaws.

3.7 Electric Transmission: Federal Energy Regulatory Commission Critical Infrastructure Protection Reliability Standards

Of the many concerns about potential cyber threats, attacks on the nation's electric grid is among the most frequently discussed. A cyberattack that causes large metropolitan areas to go dark could have devastating effects on national security and the economy.

Accordingly, the Federal Energy Regulatory Commission (FERC), which oversees the nation's bulk power system and regulates the transmission companies that connect the power grid, has increasingly focused on cybersecurity.

---

84 45 C.F.R. § 164.408.
85 *Id.*
86 *Id.*

In January 2016, FERC adopted seven critical infrastructure protection reliability standards that originated from the North American Electric Reliability Corporation, a nonprofit organization. Unlike many of the other industry-specific laws and regulations, such as GLBA and HIPAA, the FERC standards are not primarily concerned with the confidentiality of data but also with preventing any disruptions due to cyberattacks. FERC regulates the transmission companies that comprise the power grid, but does not regulate local electric utilities.

This section contains the key provisions from each of the seven standards, but companies should review the complete standards to ensure compliance.

3.7.1 CIP-003-6: Cybersecurity—Security Management Controls

At least every 15 months, regulated companies' senior managers should approve cybersecurity policies that address:

- employee training;
- electronic security perimeters, including remote access;
- cyber system physical security;
- system security management;
- incident response planning;
- incident recovery plans;
- configuration change management;
- information protection; and
- response to exceptional circumstances.

Companies should name a responsible manager for leading the implementation of the cybersecurity standards, who is permitted to delegate authority to other employees, provided that this delegation has been approved by a senior manager of the company. In practice, it is common for the responsible manager to be a chief information security officer or equivalent.

3.7.2 CIP-004-6: Personnel and Training

Regulated companies should implement quarterly training for security awareness that "reinforces cyber security practices (which may include associated physical security practices) for the [companies'] personnel who have authorized electronic or authorized unescorted physical access" to the companies' systems. These training sessions should be designed for individual jobs. For instance, a supervisor's training likely will differ from that of a line worker.

Companies should review employees' criminal history at least once every seven years, and conduct other "personnel risk assessment" programs for individuals who need access to companies' cyber systems.

In addition to training, companies should ensure that employees do not have access to cyber systems when they no longer need to have access (e.g., if they leave their jobs). Companies also should develop processes to timely revoke access to cyber systems.

3.7.3 CIP-006-6: Physical Security of Cyber Systems

This guideline requires companies to develop a comprehensive plan for the physical security of facilities that house the companies' cyber systems. These plans should include controls such as intrusion alarms and logs of physical entries. The policies should require "continuous escorted access of visitors" within the physical perimeter of the company's facilities, except under exceptional circumstances.

3.7.4 CIP-007-6: Systems Security Management

To minimize the attack surface, when technically feasible, companies should enable only the logical network accessible ports that are needed for the companies' operations. The companies also should implement a patch management process. At least once every 35 days, the companies should evaluate new security patches and take other steps to reduce the likelihood of harm from malicious code.

CIP-007-6 suggests that companies maintain audit logs of failed log-in attempts, malicious code, and other potential cybersecurity events. Companies should develop a process that alerts them to such events.

The guidelines also require companies to pay close attention to log-in credentials. Companies should inventory user accounts; change default passwords; establish standards for minimum password length; and, when possible, require authorized users to change passwords at least once every 15 months. Companies also should either impose a maximum number of failed log-in attempts, or implement a system that alerts the information security staff to unsuccessful log-in attempts.

3.7.5 CIP-009-6: Recovery Plans for Cyber Systems

CIP-009-6 provides a framework for regulated companies to create plans that enable them to respond to cyber incidents. Companies should develop recovery plans that designate specific responsibilities of responders, describe how data will be stored, and provide plans for backing up and preserving data after an incident. At least once every 15 months, companies should test recovery plans by recovering from an incident that has occurred during that time period, conducting a paper drill or tabletop exercise, or conducting an operational exercise. The companies should test the recovery plans at least once every 36 months through an "operational exercise of the recovery plans."

Within 90 days of a recovery plan test or actual recovery, companies should document "lessons learned," update the recovery plan, and notify relevant individuals of the updates.

3.7.6 CIP-010-2: Configuration Change Management and Vulnerability Assessments

Companies must develop configuration change management processes to "prevent unauthorized modifications" to cyber systems. Change management processes should include a "baseline configuration" that identifies operating systems, installed software, accessible ports, and security patches. The processes also should authorize and document any changes that fail to comply with this baseline configuration.

At least once every 35 days, companies should monitor for deviations from the baseline configuration. At least once every 15 months, they should conduct a vulnerability assessment to ensure proper implementation of cybersecurity controls. At least every 36 months, when feasible, the company should assess the vulnerabilities, based on this baseline configuration.

Companies should authorize the use of transient cyber assets (e.g., removable media), except in exceptional circumstances. The authorization should specify the users, locations, defined acceptable use, operating system, firmware, and software on the removable media. Companies must determine how to minimize threats to these transient assets. Within 35 days before use of a transient cyber asset, companies must ensure that security patches to all transient cyber assets are updated.

3.7.7 CIP-011-2: Information Protection

Companies should implement information protection programs that include procedures for securely handling information regardless of whether the data is at rest or in transit. Companies should prevent the "unauthorized retrieval" of information from their systems and ensure that information is securely disposed.

3.8 Nuclear Regulatory Commission Cybersecurity Regulations

Just as policymakers are concerned about a cyberattack threatening the electric grid, they also are deeply concerned about the prospect of a cyberattack on a U.S. nuclear power facility. Such an attack could have devastating national security implications. Accordingly, in 2009, the U.S. Nuclear Regulatory Commission (NRC) adopted a thorough cybersecurity regulation for licensees of nuclear power reactors. In 2013, the NRC created a Cybersecurity Directorate, which oversees the cybersecurity of the nuclear industry and works with FERC, the Department of Homeland Security, and others that oversee the cybersecurity of the nation's power system.

The NRC's cybersecurity rule[87] requires nuclear licensees to protect their computer and communication systems with safety-related and important-to-safety functions, security functions, emergency preparedness functions, and support systems and equipment that, if compromised, would harm safety, security, or emergency preparedness.[88] The NRC regulations require nuclear licensees to protect these systems and networks from cyberattacks that would harm the integrity or confidentiality of data or software; deny access to the systems, services, or data; and harm the operation of the systems, network, and equipment.[89] The NRC's regulations broadly require nuclear operators to develop cybersecurity programs to implement security controls that protect nuclear facilities from cyberattacks, reduce the likelihood of cyber incidents, and mitigate harm caused by cyber incidents.[90] The regulations provide a great deal of flexibility for nuclear licensees to determine how to develop and draft these plans.

To implement the cybersecurity program, the NRC regulations require licensees to ensure that nuclear licensee employees and contractors receive appropriate cybersecurity training, properly manage cybersecurity risks, incorporate cybersecurity into any considerations of modifications to cyber assets, and properly notify regulators of cybersecurity incidents.[91]

The NRC requires licensees to develop a written cybersecurity plan that implements the program. The plan must describe how the licensee will implement the program, and account for relevant site-specific conditions. The cybersecurity plan also must provide an incident response and recovery plan that describes the capability for detection and response, mitigation, correction of exploited vulnerabilities, and restoration of affected systems.[92]

3.9 South Carolina Insurance Cybersecurity Law

In 2018, South Carolina became the first state in the nation to impose specific cybersecurity requirements on people and companies who are licensed by its Department of Insurance. The law applies to any "person licensed, authorized to operate, or registered, or required to be licensed, authorized, or registered" under South Carolina's insurance laws, but does not cover "a purchasing group

---

87 10 C.F.R. § 73.54.
88 10 C.F.R. § 73.54(a)(1).
89 10 C.F.R. § 73.54(a)(2).
90 10 C.F.R. § 73.54(c).
91 10 C.F.R. § 73.54(d).
92 10 C.F.R. § 73.54(e).

or a risk retention group chartered and licensed in a state other than this State or a licensee that is acting as an assuming insurer that is domiciled in another state or jurisdiction."[93]

The law requires the licensee to maintain a "comprehensive written information security program based on the licensee's risk assessment and that contains administrative, technical, and physical safeguards for the protection of nonpublic information and the licensee's information system." The statute also imposes the following specific requirements on licensees:

1) designate one or more employees, an affiliate, or an outside vendor designated to act on behalf of the licensee as responsible for the information security program;
2) identify reasonably foreseeable internal or external threats that could result in the unauthorized access to or transmission, disclosure, misuse, alteration, or destruction of nonpublic information including the security of information systems and nonpublic information that are accessible to or held by third-party service providers;
3) assess the likelihood and potential damage of these threats, considering the sensitivity of the nonpublic information;
4) assess the sufficiency of policies, procedures, information systems, and other safeguards in place to manage these threats, taking into consideration threats in each relevant area of the licensee's operations, including:
   a) employee training and management;
   b) information systems, including network and software design, and information classification, governance, processing, storage, transmission, and disposal; and
   c) detecting, preventing, and responding to attacks, intrusions, or other systems failures; and
5) implement information safeguards to manage the threats identified in its ongoing assessment, and at least annually assess the effectiveness of the safeguards' key controls, systems, and procedures.

After conducting the risk assessment, the company must take the following steps:

1) design its information security program to mitigate the identified risks, commensurate with the size and complexity of the licensee's activities, including its use of third-party service providers, and the sensitivity of the nonpublic information

---

93 2017 S.C. Act No. 171.

used by the licensee or in the licensee's possession, custody, or control;

2) determine the appropriateness of and implement the following security measures:

a) placing access controls on information systems, including controls to authenticate and permit access only to authorized individuals to protect against the unauthorized acquisition of nonpublic information;

b) identifying and managing the data, personnel, devices, systems, and facilities that enable the organization to achieve business purposes in accordance with their relative importance to business objectives and the organization's risk strategy;

c) restricting access at physical locations containing nonpublic information to authorized individuals;

d) protecting by encryption or other appropriate means, all nonpublic information while being transmitted over an external network and all nonpublic information stored on a laptop computer or other portable computing or storage device or media;

e) adopting secure development practices for in-house developed applications used by the licensee and procedures for evaluating, assessing, and testing the security of externally developed applications used by the licensee;

f) modifying the information system in accordance with the licensee's information security program;

g) utilizing effective controls, which may include multifactor authentication procedures for an individual accessing nonpublic information;

h) regularly testing and monitoring systems and procedures to detect actual and attempted attacks on, or intrusions into, information systems;

i) including audit trails within the information security program designed to detect and respond to cybersecurity events and designed to reconstruct material financial transactions sufficient to support normal operations and obligations of the licensee;

j) implementing measures to protect against destruction, loss, or damage of nonpublic information due to environmental hazards such as fire and water damage or other catastrophes or technological failures; and

k) developing, implementing, and maintaining procedures for the secure disposal of nonpublic information in any format;

3) include cybersecurity risks in the licensee's enterprise risk management process;

4) stay informed regarding emerging threats or vulnerabilities and use reasonable security measures when sharing information relative to the character of the sharing and the type of information shared;

5) provide its personnel with cybersecurity awareness training that is updated as necessary to reflect risks identified by the licensee in the risk assessment.

The regulations also require boards of directors to oversee corporate security, and the companies to carefully evaluate the security of vendors. The companies must develop detailed incident response plans. Insurers must annually certify compliance to the state.

After South Carolina passed its cybersecurity law, Ohio and Michigan followed with their own cybersecurity laws for insurance companies.

4

Cybersecurity and Corporate Governance

As cybersecurity vulnerabilities increasingly have threatened companies' bottom lines and operational abilities, boards of directors and top executives understandably have become concerned about the protection of confidential information and ensuring uninterrupted business operations. A number of federal laws, regulations, and guidelines also require top management to ensure adequate cybersecurity, both as an ongoing part of business operations and as a prerequisite for certain corporate events, such as securities offerings, obtaining foreign investments, and exporting goods.

This chapter reviews some of the legal issues that often arise in these scenarios. First, the chapter reviews the Securities and Exchange Commission's (SEC's) expectations for cybersecurity of publicly traded companies, as well as the general fiduciary duty that companies have to shareholders, and how that applies to cybersecurity. The chapter then examines the cybersecurity expectations of the Committee on Foreign Investment in the United States (CFIUS), which reviews foreign investments in U.S. companies.

The laws and regulations discussed in this chapter affect different areas of corporate governance and in some cases are not directly related. SEC regulations require companies to be transparent to investors about cybersecurity challenges and incidents. Courts hold that companies violate a fiduciary duty when they harm shareholders by egregiously failing to protect against cyber threats. The CFIUS regulations restrict foreign investments that raise cybersecurity concerns. In all of these areas, the unique, real-time nature of cybersecurity intersects with the slower-paced world of government regulation of large corporations. In all of these instances, the rules are far from settled, creating great uncertainty for executives and boards of directors.

4.1 Securities and Exchange Commission Cybersecurity Expectations for Publicly Traded Companies

The Securities and Exchange Act of 1934, a Depression-era law intended to regulate publicly traded companies, provides the Securities and Exchange Commission with great discretion. Among its comprehensive regulations for publicly traded companies is Regulation S-K, which sets forth the requirements for regular public filings that companies must make with the SEC. Such filings include the 10-Q, a quarterly financial report; the 10-K, a more comprehensive annual financial report; and 8-Ks, which are issued at any time to inform the SEC—and investors—about any material developments. The goal of both Regulation S-K and the SEC's requirement for such filings is to increase transparency so that investors can make informed decisions.

The SEC has long required companies to make these annual filings in an effort to provide transparency to investors and potential investors. By understanding a company's finances (including its key risks), the SEC believes that investors can make more informed decisions. In a 2016 statement, then-SEC Chair Mary Jo White explained the rationale for the SEC's requirements for quarterly and annual filings:

> The SEC's disclosure regime is central to our mission to protect investors and the integrity of our capital markets. Since 1934, our disclosure requirements have been designed to foster transparency, honesty, and confidence in the markets so that investors can make informed investment and voting decisions and companies can appropriately access the capital they need. In the modern era, Regulation S-K has become the key tool for furthering these goals and is a central repository for the Commission's rules covering the business and financial information that companies must provide in their filings, including information describing a company's business, risks that the company faces, and management's discussion and analysis of a company's financial condition and results of operations.[1]

In recent years, SEC officials have recognized that cybersecurity is among the risks that require greater transparency for investors. In a 2014 speech, White said that the "SEC's formal jurisdiction over cybersecurity is directly focused on the integrity of our market systems, customer data protection, and disclosure of material information."[2] Former SEC Commissioner Luis

---

1 Statement from Chair White on Regulation S-K Concept Release, Apr. 14, 2016.
2 Opening Statement at SEC Roundtable on Cybersecurity, Chair Mary Jo White (Mar. 26, 2014).

A. Aguilar, who focused on the need for better cybersecurity among U.S. companies, encouraged companies to broadly disclose cybersecurity risks that could impact not only the company, but others. "It is possible that a cyber-attack may not have a direct material adverse impact on the company itself, but that a loss of customers' personal and financial data could have devastating effects on the lives of the company's customers and many Americans," Aguilar said. "In such cases, the right thing to do is to give these victims a heads-up so that they can protect themselves."[3]

Neither the Securities Exchange Act of 1934 nor Regulation S-K explicitly requires companies to disclose cybersecurity risks in their 10-Ks or other SEC filings. However, in October 2011, the SEC's Division of Corporation Finance issued *CF Disclosure Guidance: Topic No. 2, Cybersecurity*, a nonbinding guidance document in which it strongly encouraged companies to disclose a range of cybersecurity risks.[4] In the 2011 Guidance, the SEC noted the many potential costs and negative consequences that could arise from a cyber incident, including increased costs resulting from remediation, cybersecurity incident preparation, litigation, and reputational harm. While the SEC does acknowledge that its regulations do not explicitly require cybersecurity disclosures, it nonetheless imposes a number of disclosure requirements that obligate registrants to disclose such risks and incidents: "material information regarding cybersecurity risks and cyber incidents is required to be disclosed when necessary in order to make other required disclosures, in light of the circumstances under which they are made, not misleading."[5] In February 2018, the SEC adopted interpretive guidance that reinforced and expanded upon the 2011 Guidance.[6]

"I believe that providing the Commission's views on these matters will promote clearer and more robust disclosure by companies about cybersecurity risks and incidents, resulting in more complete information being available to investors," SEC Chairman Jay Clayton said in a press release announcing the 2018 Cybersecurity Guidance. "In particular, I urge public companies to examine their controls and procedures, with not only their securities law disclosure obligations in mind, but also reputational considerations around sales of securities by executives."[7]

---

3 Commissioner Luis A. Aguilar, Board of Directors, *Corporate Governance and Cyber-Risks: Sharpening the Focus* (June 10, 2014).
4 SECURITIES AND EXCHANGE COMMISSION, CF DISCLOSURE GUIDANCE: TOPIC NO. 2, CYBERSECURITY (Oct. 13, 2011).
5 *Id.*
6 Statement and Guidance on Public Company Cybersecurity Disclosures, Securities and Exchange Commission Release Nos. 33-10459; 34-82746 (Feb. 26, 2018) (hereinafter "2018 Cybersecurity Guidance").
7 Securities and Exchange Commission, *SEC Adopts Statement and Interpretive Guidance on Public Company Cybersecurity Disclosures* (Feb. 21, 2018) [press release].

In practice, companies typically disclose cybersecurity risks and vulnerabilities in four sections of their 10-K annual reports: (1) Risk factors; (2) Management's discussion and analysis of financial condition and results of operations (MD&A); (3) Description of business; and (4) Legal proceedings.

4.1.1   10-K Disclosures: Risk Factors

The commonly used 10-K section for cybersecurity disclosures is "Risk factors." Regulation S-K requires publicly traded companies to provide a "concise" and logically organized list of "the most significant factors that make the offering speculative or risky."[8] Regulation S-K instructs companies to explain "how the risk affects the issuer or the securities being offered," and to "[s]et forth each risk factor under a subcaption that adequately describes the risk."[9]

In the 2018 Cybersecurity Guidance, the SEC urged companies to consider the following issues in their disclosures of risk factors:

- The occurrence of prior cybersecurity incidents, including their severity and frequency;
- The probability of the occurrence and potential magnitude of cybersecurity incidents;
- The adequacy of preventative actions taken to reduce cybersecurity risks and the associated costs, including, if appropriate, discussing the limits of the company's ability to prevent or mitigate certain cybersecurity risks;
- The aspects of the company's business and operations that give rise to material cybersecurity risks and the potential costs and consequences of such risks, including industry-specific risks and third party supplier and service provider risks;
- The costs associated with maintaining cybersecurity protections, including, if applicable, insurance coverage relating to cybersecurity incidents or payments to service providers;
- The potential for reputational harm;
- Existing or pending laws and regulations that may affect the requirements to which companies are subject relating to cybersecurity and the associated costs to companies; and
- Litigation, regulatory investigation, and remediation costs associated with cybersecurity incidents.[10]

The SEC advises companies that disclosure of past or current cybersecurity incidents may be necessary to fully describe its risk factors:

---

8 17 C.F.R. § 229.503.

9 *Id.*

10 2018 Cybersecurity Guidance.

For example, if a company previously experienced a material cybersecurity incident involving denial-of-service, it likely would not be sufficient for the company to disclose that there is a risk that a denial-of-service incident may occur. Instead, the company may need to discuss the occurrence of that cybersecurity incident and its consequences as part of a broader discussion of the types of potential cybersecurity incidents that pose particular risks to the company's business and operations. Past incidents involving suppliers, customers, competitors, and others may be relevant when crafting risk factor disclosure.[11]

The SEC's Cybersecurity Guidance demonstrates the inherent conflict between the SEC's long-standing rule that companies should be transparent about risk factors, and the unfortunate reality in cybersecurity that information about vulnerabilities can quickly be used against companies by cybercriminals. Companies are still attempting to determine the necessary balance between the two demands, and thus (as will be seen later in this section) companies have developed a fairly wide range of disclosure practices.

4.1.2 10-K Disclosures: Management's Discussion and Analysis of Financial Condition and Results of Operations (MD&A)

Regulation S-K also requires 10-K filings to include a section entitled "Management's discussion and analysis of financial condition and results of operations" (MD&A), in which the company discusses its changes in its financial condition and the results of its operations.[12] Among the results that companies must describe are "any unusual or infrequent events or transactions or any significant economic changes that materially affected the amount of reported income from continuing operations[.]"[13]

In its 2018 Cybersecurity Guidance, the SEC states that "the cost of ongoing cybersecurity efforts (including enhancements to existing efforts), the costs and other consequences of cybersecurity incidents, and the risks of potential cybersecurity incidents, among other matters, could inform a company's analysis."[14] The SEC also encourages companies to consider cybersecurity-related costs, such as "loss of intellectual property, the immediate costs of the incident, as well as the costs associated with implementing preventative measures, maintaining insurance, responding to litigation and regulatory investigations,

---

11 *Id.*
12 17 C.F.R. § 229.303.
13 *Id.*
14 2018 Cybersecurity Guidance.

preparing for and complying with proposed or current legislation, engaging in remediation efforts, addressing harm to reputation, and the loss of competitive advantage that may result."[15]

Companies typically are much more likely to include information about such uncertainties in their discussions about risk factors, although the SEC has not explicitly stated which section should include information about cybersecurity. Often, companies that discuss cybersecurity threats in their MD&A section also have included similar information in the risk factors section.

4.1.3 10-K Disclosures: Description of Business

Regulation S-K requires companies to describe the "general development" of their business over the past five years.[16] In its 2018 Cybersecurity Guidance, the SEC states that "[i]f cybersecurity incidents or risks materially affect a company's products, services, relationships with customers and suppliers, or competitive conditions, the company must provide appropriate disclosure."[17] In practice, "Description of business" is a relatively rare 10-K section for cybersecurity disclosures unless the company is in the technology sector and cybersecurity is an essential part of its business.

4.1.4 10-K Disclosures: Legal Proceedings

Regulation S-K requires companies to briefly describe "any material pending legal proceedings,"[18] though companies are not required to report "ordinary routine litigation incidental to the business[.]"[19] Regulation S-K states that companies must report legal proceedings if the total claim for damages (arising out of either a single lawsuit or multiple related lawsuits) exceeds 10 percent of the company's current assets.[20] The SEC's 2018 Cybersecurity Guidance states that if a cybersecurity incident results in "material litigation," the company should "describe the litigation, including the name of the court in which the proceedings are pending, the date the proceedings are instituted, the principal parties thereto, a description of the factual basis alleged to underlie the litigation, and the relief sought."[21]

---

15 *Id.*
16 17 C.F.R. § 229.101.
17 2018 Cybersecurity Guidance.
18 17 C.F.R. § 229.103.
19 *Id.*
20 *Id.*
21 2018 Cybersecurity Guidance.

4.1.5   10-K Disclosures: Financial Statements

The SEC's 2018 Cybersecurity Guidance recognized that cybersecurity risks may affect more than just the narrative sections of 10-K disclosures. Companies may also need to incorporate cybersecurity incidents and risks in their financial statements. For instance, they may need to include the following types of items:

- Expenses related to investigation, breach notification, remediation and litigation, including the costs of legal and other professional services;
- Loss of revenue, providing customers with incentives or a loss of customer relationship assets value;
- Claims related to warranties, breach of contract, product recall/replacement, indemnification of counterparties, and insurance premium increases; and
- Diminished future cash flows, impairment of intellectual, intangible or other assets; recognition of liabilities; or increased financing costs.[22]

4.1.6   10K Disclosures: Board Oversight of Cybersecurity

The SEC expects boards of directors to provide meaningful oversight of businesses. The Commission said in 2009 that "disclosure about the board's involvement in the oversight of the risk management process should provide important information to investors about how a company perceives the role of its board and the relationship between the board and senior management in managing the material risks facing the company."[23] The SEC reasoned that the requirement "gives companies the flexibility to describe how the board administers its risk oversight function, such as through the whole board, or through a separate risk committee or the audit committee, for example."[24] In its 2018 Cybersecurity Guidance, the SEC stated that "[t]o the extent cybersecurity risks are material to a company's business, we believe this discussion should include the nature of the board's role in overseeing the management of that risk."[25]

4.1.7   Disclosing Data Breaches to Investors

The 10-K is an annual report that requires publicly traded companies to disclose significant events of the past year and forward-looking risks. However, a

---

22 2018 Cybersecurity Guidance.
23 Securities and Exchange Commission, Proxy Disclosure Enhancements, Release No. 33-9089 (Dec. 16, 2009), at 43.
24 *Id.*
25 2018 Cybersecurity Guidance.

data breach could have immediate consequences for a company's finances and, in some cases, viability. It is becoming increasingly common for companies to file an "8-K" form (known as a "current report") to notify investors soon after a data breach occurs.

In its 2011 guidance, the SEC provided little direction as to when such updates are necessary, merely stating that companies should consider whether it is necessary to file 8-K reports "to disclose the costs and other consequences of material cyber incidents."[26] The form 8-K merely states that companies may choose to file 8-Ks of "other events" that the company "deems of importance to security holders."

In many cases, investors are already well aware of high-profile data breaches due to the state data breach reporting requirements discussed in Chapter 1 of this book. Without any clear guidance on the topic from the SEC, companies have developed different approaches. Some do not disclose cyber incidents on separate 8-Ks, either mentioning the incidents in their 10-K report or determining that the incidents are not material. Some companies file 8-K reports around the same time that they disclose incidents to state regulators and consumers. Still other companies delay their notifications.

Target, for instance, publicly disclosed its large data breach on December 19, 2013. It did not immediately file an 8-K report, and it began to receive substantial criticism for not doing so. On January 30, 2014, lawyers published a commentary piece in which they questioned the lack of an 8-K, writing, "Target's securities lawyers may believe that the breach is not 'important to security holders,' or is not sufficiently material enough to the roughly $38 billion company to warrant an 8-K filing, but 70 million to 110 million affected customers is hardly immaterial, even for Target."[27] Senator Jay Rockefeller sent a letter to Target's chief executive asking why the company "appears to be ignoring SEC rules that require you to disclose to the SEC and your investors the costs and business consequences of this recent data breach."[28]

On February 26, 2014—more than two months after the initial public disclosure—Target filed an 8-K in which it disclosed the breach to investors. The filing amended the risk factors section of its 10-K, and stated, in part:

> The data breach we experienced in 2013 has resulted in government inquiries and private litigation, and if our efforts to protect the security of personal information about our guests and team members are unsuccessful, future issues may result in additional costly government enforcement actions and private litigation and our sales and reputation could suffer.

---

26 SEC, CF DISCLOSURE GUIDANCE: TOPIC No. 2, CYBERSECURITY (Oct. 13, 2011).
27 Cynthia J. Larose, *To 8-K or Not—For Target, That Is Indeed the Question*, LAW 360 (Jan. 30, 2014).
28 *Id.*

A significant disruption in our computer systems and our inability to adequately maintain and update those systems could adversely affect our operations and our ability to maintain guest confidence.

We experienced a significant data security breach in the fourth quarter of fiscal 2013 and are not yet able to determine the full extent of its impact and the impact of government investigations and private litigation on our results of operations, which could be material.[29]

The widespread criticism of Target's failure to more promptly notify investors has caused an increasing number of companies to file 8-Ks soon after they publicly report data breaches. Although the SEC has not explicitly stated that companies must do so, there always is a risk that regulators may eventually expect such reporting, as the 8-K requirements are ambiguous. Moreover, prompt disclosure of cyber incidents to shareholders weakens potential claims in shareholder derivative lawsuits, as discussed later in this section.

Some companies file 8-Ks about major data breaches in a much more expeditious manner. For instance, on September 2, 2014, Home Depot began investigating blog reports of a data breach on its systems. Home Depot soon discovered that hackers had accessed approximately 56 million payment card numbers of its retail customers from April to September 2014.[30] On September 18, 2014, Home Depot publicly announced its findings. On the same day, Home Depot filed an 8-K with the SEC, in which it stated, in part:

The investigation into a possible breach began on Tuesday morning, September 2, immediately after The Home Depot received reports from its banking partners and law enforcement that criminals may have breached its systems.

Since then, the Company's IT security team has been working around the clock with leading IT security firms, its banking partners and the Secret Service to rapidly gather facts, resolve the problem and provide information to customers.

The Company's ongoing investigation has determined the following:

Criminals used unique, custom-built malware to evade detection. The malware had not been seen previously in other attacks, according to Home Depot's security partners. The cyber-attack is estimated to have put payment card information at risk for approximately 56 million unique payment cards.

---

29 Target Corp., 8-K Filing, Feb. 26, 2014.
30 Brian Krebs, *Home Depot: 56M Cards Impacted, Malware Contained,* KREBS ON SECURITY (Sept. 18, 2014).

The malware is believed to have been present between April and September 2014.

To protect customer data until the malware was eliminated, any terminals identified with malware were taken out of service, and the Company quickly put in place other security enhancements. The hackers' method of entry has been closed off, the malware has been eliminated from the Company's systems, and the Company has rolled out enhanced encryption of payment data to all U.S. stores.

There is no evidence that debit PIN numbers were compromised or that the breach has impacted stores in Mexico or customers who shopped online at HomeDepot.com or HomeDepot.ca.

The Home Depot is offering free identity protection services, including credit monitoring, to any customer who used a payment card at a Home Depot store in 2014, from April on.[31]

Home Depot's filing is a model for prompt and responsible disclosure of a cybersecurity incident. Although the SEC does not have a threshold requirement for 8-K filings regarding data breaches, it is clear that the breach of more than 50 million customers' credit and debit card information will lead to significant legal liability (and Home Depot quickly faced multiple lawsuits). Home Depot's 8-K clearly describes what its investigation uncovered and the steps that Home Depot took to mitigate damage. Home Depot provided enough detail to paint a useful picture of the situation for investors, but it did not "over-disclose" and provide information that hackers could use to further exploit its network and systems.

To be sure, lawyers recommend that companies think carefully before disclosing to ensure that they are not exposing themselves to unnecessary legal or security risks. Companies also should be certain of the facts of the incident before disclosure. A 2016 Bloomberg law article, based on interviews with cybersecurity lawyers, concluded that companies "should focus on internal investigations and shoring up their cybersecurity before making any material disclosures to federal regulators or the public[.]"[32]

4.1.8 Yahoo Data Breach

The SEC underscored the importance of adequate cybersecurity disclosures in April 2018, when it reached a $35 million settlement with the company formerly known as Yahoo. In December 2014, Russians obtained access to hundreds of millions of Yahoo customers' email addresses, encrypted passwords, security

---

31 Home Depot, 8-K Filing (Sept. 16, 2014).
32 Daniel R. Stoller, *Less Data Breach Disclosure Is Wise, Attorneys Say*, BLOOMBERG BNA (July 5, 2016).

questions, and other personal information. Yahoo learned about the compromise within days, but failed to publicly report the breach for more than two years, when its operating business was being acquired by Verizon. "We do not second-guess good faith exercises of judgment about cyber-incident disclosure. But we have also cautioned that a company's response to such an event could be so lacking that an enforcement action would be warranted. This is clearly such a case," Steven Peikin, co-director of the SEC Enforcement Division, said in a press release.[33]

In the settlement order, the SEC detailed the material omission of the breach from Yahoo's filings over the two years: "Yahoo acted negligently in filing materially misleading periodic reports with the Commission. In particular, Yahoo knew, or should have known, that its risk factor disclosures and MD&A in its annual reports on Form 10-K for the fiscal years ended December 31, 2014 and December 31, 2015, and in its quarterly reports on Form 10-Q for the first three quarters of 2015 and the first two quarters of 2016, and its stock purchase agreement with Verizon (which was filed as an exhibit to a current report on Form 8-K), as incorporated into its Form S-8 registration statements, were materially misleading."[34]

4.1.9 Cybersecurity and Insider Trading

Insider trading on nonpublic information about a publicly traded company could constitute illegal insider trading. Federal law prohibits individuals from trading securities "on the basis of material nonpublic information about that security or issuer, in breach of a duty of trust or confidence that is owed directly, indirectly, or derivatively, to the issuer of that security or the shareholders of that issuer, or to any other person who is the source of the material nonpublic information."[35] A cybersecurity incident such as a large-scale data breach could materially affect a company's finances and share prices. Accordingly, the SEC suggests that companies consider adopting restrictions on insider trading during cybersecurity incident investigation and remediation. "Company insider trading policies and procedures that include prophylactic measures can protect against directors, officers, and other corporate insiders trading on the basis of material nonpublic information before public disclosure of the cybersecurity incident," the SEC wrote in its 2018 Cybersecurity Guidance.[36]

---

33 Securities and Exchange Commission, *Altaba, Formerly Known as Yahoo!, Charged with Failing to Disclose Massive Cybersecurity Breach; Agrees to Pay $35 Million* (Apr. 24, 2018) [press release].

34 Securities and Exchange Commission Order, In the Matter of ALTABA INC., f/d/b/a YAHOO! INC. (Apr. 24, 2018).

35 17 C.F.R. § 240.10b-5-1(a).

36 2018 Cybersecurity Guidance.

4.2 Fiduciary Duty to Shareholders and Derivative Lawsuits Arising from Data Breaches

If a data breach causes significant harm to a company, shareholders may attempt to bring a suit, known as "derivative litigation," against company officers whom they allege were responsible for the harm. The lawsuits often arise under the state laws of Delaware, where many large U.S. corporations are incorporated.

Derivative lawsuits often arise when shareholders claim that officers or directors breached their "duty" to the company by allowing harm to occur. Shareholders must meet a high hurdle before being permitted to sue on behalf of the company, as courts typically presume that directors and officers make decisions that they believe, in good faith, to be in the companies' best interests. To defeat this presumption, known as the "business judgment rule," plaintiffs must demonstrate that the board's refusal to sue was made in "bad faith" or "based on an unreasonable investigation."[37]

Delaware courts have stated that a breach of fiduciary duty can occur when the directors caused or "allowed a situation to develop and continue which exposed the corporation to enormous legal liability and that in doing so they violated a duty to be active monitors of corporate performance."[38] The Delaware Court of Chancery stated that among the harms that could be the basis of derivative suits are "regulatory sanctions, criminal or civil fines, environmental disasters, accounting restatements, misconduct by officers or employees, massive business losses, and innumerable other potential calamities."[39]

To demonstrate that a board or officers acted in bad faith, the plaintiffs must establish that the board utterly failed to meet its obligations to the corporation and shareholders. Among the scenarios that Delaware courts have concluded would constitute bad faith:

- the directors intentionally acted with a purpose that was not intended to advance the company's best interests;
- the directors intentionally violated the law; or
- the directors intentionally failed "to act in the face of a known duty to act, demonstrating a conscious disregard" for their duties.[40]

The third scenario could be the basis of a data breach-related derivative lawsuit. Shareholders could claim that the directors failed to adequately monitor a company's data security, therefore causing harm to the company.[41]

---

37 *In re* Merrill Lynch & Co., 773 F. Supp. 2d 330, 351 (S.D.N.Y. 2011).
38 *In re* Caremark Int'l Inc. Derivative Litig., 698 A.2d 959, 967 (Del.Ch. 1996).
39 La. Mun. Police v. Pyott, 46 A.3d 313, 2012 (Del. Ct. Chancery 2012).
40 *Id.*, citing *In re* Walt Disney Co. Derivative Litig., 906 A.2d 27, 67 (Del. 2006).
41 *See* Stone *ex rel.* AmSouth Bancorporation v. Ritter, 911 A.2d 362, 364, 369 (Del. 2006) ("The third of these examples describes, and is fully consistent with, the lack of good faith conduct that

There have been few published court opinions regarding derivative lawsuits arising from data breaches. In 2014, a New Jersey federal court (applying Delaware law) dismissed a lawsuit against Wyndham Worldwide Corporation officials arising from the data breach discussed in Chapter 1.[42] The court rejected two attempts by the plaintiffs to overcome the business judgment rule. First, the plaintiffs argued that the board did not act in good faith because it was represented by the same counsel in the FTC action and the shareholder demand for a lawsuit.[43] The court held that counsel's duties were not conflicting; rather, in both instances, it was responsible for acting in Wyndham's best interests.[44] Second the plaintiffs argued that the board failed to reasonably investigate the demand to bring a lawsuit. The court similarly rejected this argument, reasoning that board members had discussed the breaches at 14 board meetings between October 2008 and August 2012 and that the board's audit committee routinely discussed the breaches, and therefore, those investigations alone "would indicate that the Board had enough information when it assessed Plaintiff's claim."[45] The *Wyndham* case demonstrates the difficulty of bringing a viable shareholder derivative claim even in cases in which the company likely was not providing adequate oversight of its cybersecurity.

Similarly, after the Home Depot customer data breach, shareholders filed a derivative lawsuit in Georgia federal court against current and former officers and directors, claiming that they breached their duties of loyalty and care by failing to implement sufficient cybersecurity safeguards in light of significant threats. Because the plaintiffs did not make a demand of the Board before suing, the court held the claims to a high standard of review. As the court would describe, all of the charges in the complaint "ultimately relate to what the Defendants knew before the Breach and what they did about that knowledge."[46] Applying Delaware law, the court dismissed the entire complaint. The duty-of-loyalty claim failed because the court reasoned that the plaintiffs failed to meet the "incredibly high hurdle" of demonstrating "with particularized facts beyond a reasonable doubt that a majority of the Board faced substantial liability because it consciously failed to act in the face of a known duty to act."[47]

The court also dismissed the claims that Home Depot's directors committed waste of corporate assets. Delaware law defines "corporate waste" as "an exchange

---

the *Caremark* court held was a 'necessary condition' for director oversight liability, i.e., 'a sustained or systematic failure of the board to exercise oversight—such as an utter failure to attempt to assure a reasonable information and reporting system exists.'").

42 Palkon *ex rel.* Wyndham Worldwide Corp., Civ. Action No. 2:14-CV-01234 (SRC) (D.N.J. Oct. 20, 2014).

43 *Id.*

44 *Id.*

45 *Id.*

46 *In re* the Home Depot, Inc. Shareholder Derivative Litig., 223 F. Supp. 3d 1317, 1322 (N.D. Ga. 2016).

47 *Id.* at 1325.

that is so one sided that no business person of ordinary, sound judgment could conclude that the corporation has received adequate consideration."[48] The plaintiffs argued that the board's "insufficient reaction" to cybersecurity threats constituted corporate waste. The court rejected this argument in part because it did not stem from a transaction. "Corporate waste claims typically involve situations where there has been an exchange of corporate assets for no corporate purpose or for no consideration; in effect, waste is a gift," the court wrote.[49] Requiring the directors to exercise a particular business judgment merely based on "red flags" is not consistent with Delaware corporate law; as the court wrote: "With hindsight, it is easy to see that the Board's decision to upgrade Home Depot's security at a leisurely pace was an unfortunate one. But this decision falls squarely within the discretion of the Board and is under the protection of the business judgment rule."[50]

Although shareholders have not yet been successful in data breach-related derivative lawsuits, that very well may change as data breaches increasingly put the viability of publicly traded companies at risk. Although cybercrime and breaches were at one point a minor annoyance that resulted in some negative publicity, they now can put a company's future at risk, due to the sophistication of the attacks. Accordingly, companies should be aware of the very real possibility that, in the future, shareholders could succeed in a lawsuit against corporate officials due to a serious data breach.

4.3 Committee on Foreign Investment in the United States and Cybersecurity

Cybersecurity has also become a significant concern when foreign investors seek to invest money in U.S. companies. Policymakers worry that foreign control of U.S. technology companies could expose the United States to national security vulnerabilities.

All investments that would result in foreign controlling ownership of a U.S. business must first be reviewed by the Committee on Foreign Investment in the United States (CFIUS). CFIUS is an interagency committee that is chaired by the Secretary of Treasury, and also includes the Attorney General, Secretary of Homeland Security, Secretary of Commerce, Secretary of Defense, Secretary of State, Secretary of Energy, U.S. Trade Representative, and Director of the White House Office of Science and Technology Policy.[51]

In recent years, Congress and CFIUS have been concerned that the attempts of investors in some countries—in particular, China—to acquire U.S.

---

48 *Id.* at 1327.
49 *Id.*
50 *Id.* at 1328.
51 *See* 50 U.S.C. § 4565.

technology companies could undercut U.S. security. In a report to Congress for 2014, CFIUS wrote that it believes "there may be an effort among foreign governments or companies to acquire U.S. companies involved in research, development, or production of critical technologies for which the United States is a leading producer."[52]

Among the highest profile cybersecurity-related concerns in a CFIUS matter was Japan-based SoftBank's acquisition of a majority interest in Sprint Nextel Corporation. Congressman Mike Rogers, then-Chair of the House Intelligence Committee, raised concerns that Softbank would require Sprint to use equipment from China-based Huawei Technologies in its U.S. telecommunications network, a move that could compromise the security of U.S. communications.[53] In a report issued by Rogers's committee the previous year, his staff described its investigation of national security concerns related to Huawei and ZTE, the two largest China-based telecommunications equipment makers. The report concluded that the "risks associated with Huawei's and ZTE's provision of equipment to U.S. critical infrastructure could undermine core U.S. national-security interests."[54] The House Committee urged CFIUS to block any acquisitions involving Huawei and ZTE. To obtain CFIUS approval, Sprint and SoftBank agreed that they would not use Huawei equipment, and that the U.S. government could block certain new equipment purchases by Sprint.[55] The quick response and agreement to provide the U.S. government such leeway over the company's operations demonstrated a renewed focus on cybersecurity by CFIUS, as well as a recognition by industry that CFIUS has significant leverage in such deals.

CFIUS conducts much of its review proceedings in confidence,[56] so there is not significant guidance as to exactly what cybersecurity measures U.S. companies must take in order to satisfy CFIUS. However, in November 2008, CFIUS revised its operating regulations to require an applicant to include a copy of its cybersecurity plan, if any, "that will be used to protect

---

52 COMMITTEE ON FOREIGN INVESTMENT IN THE UNITED STATES, ANNUAL REPORT TO CONGRESS, CY 2014, at 29.
53 Elizabeth Wasserman and Todd Shields, *Softbank, Sprint Pledge Not to Use Huawei, Lawmaker Says*, BLOOMBERG TECHNOLOGY (Mar. 28, 2013).
54 HOUSE PERMANENT SELECT COMMITTEE ON INTELLIGENCE, INVESTIGATIVE REPORT ON THE U.S. NATIONAL SECURITY ISSUES POSED BY CHINESE TELECOMMUNICATIONS COMPANIES HUAWEI AND ZTE (Oct. 8, 2012).
55 Alina Selyukh & Nathan Layne, *Spring, SoftBank Reach Deal with U.S. over Security Concerns*, REUTERS (May 28, 2013).
56 Thomas C. Klanderman & Giovanna M. Cinelli, *Navigating CFIUS Review, National Security Restrictions on Foreign Ownership of U.S. Real Estate*, MORGAN LEWIS (June 18, 2018) ("Chaired by the US Treasury secretary and comprised of the heads of various federal departments and offices, CFIUS operates under the cloak of confidentiality and does not issue public decisions or otherwise publish public reports on specific investigations or findings.").

against cyber attacks on the operation, design, and development of the U.S. business' services, networks, systems, data storage, and facilities."[57] In its commentary to the 2008 regulations, CFIUS noted that this requirement applies to all companies—not just technology businesses—and that the regulations do not require a particular form of cybersecurity plan to satisfy CFIUS.[58]

In practice, companies are less likely to face cybersecurity-related obstacles with CFIUS if they provide a thorough description of their access and authorization procedures, cybersecurity safeguards, internal security organization, incident response plan, and other standard cybersecurity safeguards. Moreover, companies are more likely to face CFIUS-related cybersecurity scrutiny if they provide critical infrastructure (e.g., a cellular phone carrier or electric utility) or have a direct relationship to national security (e.g., a defense contractor).

---

57 31 C.F.R. § 800.402.
58 73 Fed. Reg. 70713 (Nov. 21, 2008).

5

Anti-Hacking Laws

U.S. legislators have passed statutes to address what they view as the increasingly big threat of computer hacking. This chapter looks at some of the laws commonly used to prosecute people who access computers, software, or data without authorization or in excess of authorization: the Computer Fraud and Abuse Act, state computer hacking laws, Section 1201 of the Digital Millennium Copyright Act, and the Economic Espionage Act. Section 2701 of the Stored Communications Act, which penalizes individuals for hacking stored communications, such as email, is discussed in Chapter 7, along with the rest of the Stored Communications Act.

Some laws discussed in this chapter provide government prosecutors with the ability to bring criminal charges against individuals who hack computers without authorization. In some cases, conviction on a single count of violation of these laws can result in a prison sentence of ten or more years, as well as severe fines. The laws also allow the victims of computer hacking to bring civil suits to recover damages from the hackers and obtain injunctions to prevent further damage.

Unfortunately, some anti-hacking laws were written before the arrival of many technologies that are now commonplace in computer networks and systems. Accordingly, in many cases there are disagreements about the reach of the laws, and what constitutes illegal "hacking" that should lead to criminal sentences and civil liability.

Some prosecutors, plaintiffs, and courts have adopted particularly broad views of these anti-hacking laws. Many of these statutes prohibit not only traditional unauthorized access but also the unauthorized use or transfer of information, or circumvention of access controls. Indeed, the laws often present barriers to cybersecurity researchers who are seeking to identify software bugs and other flaws in order to help companies improve the security of their products and services. At the same time, companies that often are the victims of hacking argue that the laws are not strong enough to deter the worst behavior. Anti-hacking legislation is particularly a concern for companies that experience widespread theft of their trade secrets and other confidential information.

Cybersecurity Law, Second Edition. Jeff Kosseff.
© 2020 John Wiley & Sons, Inc. Published 2020 by John Wiley & Sons, Inc.
Companion Website: www.wiley.com/go/kosseff/cybersecurity2e

In short, there is little agreement about the scope and reach of computer hacking laws. For that reason, many of the laws discussed in this chapter are still controversial, and a number of key political players have long called for significant amendments to the laws.

5.1 Computer Fraud and Abuse Act

The Computer Fraud and Abuse Act (CFAA) is the primary U.S. federal statute that prohibits and penalizes certain forms of computer hacking. The statute imposes both criminal and civil penalties for actions taken by an individual who either lacks authorization to access a computer or exceeds authorized access to that computer.

5.1.1 Origins of the CFAA

Congress passed the CFAA due to concerns about computers becoming increasingly networked and insecure, compromising sensitive data such as credit card numbers. The modern version of the CFAA is based on a 1986 amendment to a 1984 law, the Counterfeit Access Device and Computer Fraud and Abuse Act, which was focused primarily on hacking of financial institutions and the federal government. Rather than addressing particular types of sensitive information, Congress chose to regulate the *method* by which people access any information without proper authorization. As the 1984 House Judiciary Committee Report accompanying the initial bill noted, experts testified in committee hearings that they must protect intangible property *as well as* tangible property.[1] The Committee clearly was attempting to be forward looking, rather than addressing only the current technological issues. "The Committee believes that just reviewing present trends may not be adequate, for rapidly changing technology will leave them obsolete in another 5 or 10 years, and possibly sooner," the committee wrote.[2]

The Judiciary Committee acknowledged that computer fraud was neglected in federal and state laws because it was seen as a "white collar" crime. This neglect was a mistake, the House Report concluded, because "an attack on white collar crime can often be much more productive, economically, to this country than the more publicized emphasis on violent crime."[3] For instance,

---

1 H.R. Rep. No. 98-894 (1984), at 4 ("Experts told the Committee that we need to shift attention in our statutes from concepts such as 'tangible property' and credit and debit instruments to concepts of 'information' and 'access to information.'").
2 *Id.*
3 *Id.* at 4–5.

the Committee cited a decline in highway construction costs of between 25 and 35 percent and attributed that change to successful federal prosecutions for bid-fixing in that industry.[4] In other words, increased penalties for white collar crime will result in significant economic benefits for society by reducing white collar crime.

Congress was particularly concerned about the possibility of white collar criminals using the rapidly developing computer technology to carry out economic crimes. In 1983, the Judiciary Committee noted, personal computer sales were estimated at $1.5 billion, up from "virtually zero" in 1976.[5] The Committee heard extensive testimony that "criminal elements gained access to computers in order to perpetuate crimes," and that the criminals "possess the capability to access and control high technology processes vital to our everyday lives[.]"[6] The criminal justice system at the time was not up to speed on technology, the Committee wrote, and very well might not be effective against computer crimes.[7] The Committee was particularly concerned that a new crime, known as "hacking," did not fit easily into existing criminal laws. The Committee reasoned that the general public fails to appreciate the harm that can be caused by hacking: "People can relate to mugging a little old lady and taking her pocketbook, but the perception is that perhaps there is not something so wrong about taking information by use of a device called a computer even if it costs the economy millions now and potentially billions in the future."[8]

To address these concerns, in 1984 Congress passed the Counterfeit Access Device and Computer Fraud and Abuse Act,[9] which created felonies and misdemeanors for certain computer hacking and counterfeit access device crimes. It has been substantively amended six times since its initial passage and is now known as the Computer Fraud and Abuse Act. The statute currently criminalizes seven different categories of behavior, which are outlined in sections (a)(1) through (a)(7) of the CFAA. It is useful to think of each of these sections as a stand-alone crime because alleged hackers often are charged under multiple sections of the CFAA.

5.1.2 Access Without Authorization and Exceeding Authorized Access

The seven subsections of the CFAA primarily apply to acts that individuals commit when they use a computer either without "authorization" to access the computer or "exceeding authorized access" to the computer. Some of the CFAA

---

4 *Id.* at 5.
5 *Id.* at 8.
6 *Id.* at 9.
7 *Id.*
8 *Id.* at 12.
9 18 U.S.C. § 1030.

sections only apply if the defendant did not have authorization, and others apply either if the defendant didn't have authorization *or* if the defendant exceeded authorized access.

At the outset, it is important to understand the forms of "access" that trigger the protections of the CFAA. The CFAA does not define "access," though one court, relying on the dictionary definition of the word, stated that the transitive verb "access" means "to gain access to," and the noun "access" means "to exercise the freedom or ability to make use of something."[10] Regardless of the exact definition of the term, courts generally require the defendant to have played an active role in entering the computer and either obtaining information or causing damage. Merely *receiving* information—and nothing more—does not constitute access under the CFAA. For example, in *Role Models America, Inc. v. Jones,*[11] a school sued its former principal, alleging that he used his access to the academy's computer systems to disclose proprietary information to Nova Southeastern University, where he was completing his dissertation. The academy sued the former principal and Nova, alleging that they both violated the CFAA. The district court granted Nova's motion to dismiss, reasoning that even if the academy's allegations were true, Nova did nothing more than receive information to which the principal was not entitled. The court wrote that in the context of the CFAA, "access" is an "active verb: it means 'to gain access to,' or 'to exercise the freedom or ability to make use of something.'"[12]

Courts are more divided when asked to determine whether a defendant accessed a computer without authorization or in excess of authorization. Among the most common defenses in CFAA cases surrounds the definition of "authorization" or "exceeds authorized access." The statute does not provide an incredibly clear definition of either term. "Authorization" is not defined in the statute, and the statute defines "exceeds authorized access" as "to access a computer with authorization and to use such access to obtain or alter information in the computer that the accesser is not entitled so to obtain or alter."[13] Unfortunately, this definition does not specifically address whether specific types of access exceed authorization, leading to a great deal of uncertainty in CFAA cases. In fact, whether a user has exceeded authorized access or accessed a computer without authorization is among the most frequently litigated issues in CFAA cases.

The issue is frequently disputed in cases in which a defendant had previously been authorized to access a computer but either obtains information that the defendant was not entitled to access or uses the information in a way

---

10 Am. Online, Inc. v. Nat'l Health Care Discount, 121 F. Supp. 2d 1255, 1273 (N.D. Iowa 2000) (internal quotations and ellipses omitted).
11 Role Models Am., Inc. v. Jones, 305 F. Supp. 2d 564 (D. Md. 2004).
12 *Id.* at 566–67.
13 18 U.S.C. § 1030(e)(6).

unintended by the owner of that information. Typically, in these cases, the government or a civil plaintiff argues that the defendant exceeded authorized access, though there are some cases in which prosecutors and plaintiffs have argued that the defendant no longer had any authorization to access a computer, and therefore was acting "without authorization."[14] There is a good deal of uncertainty about whether accessing "without authorization" or "exceeding authorized access" includes actions that violate a website's terms of use or a company's internal information technology policies.

Orin Kerr, a leading expert on cybercrime, has articulated three primary theories under which CFAA claims are stated. According to his framework, "code-based" CFAA violations occur when the defendant circumvents computer software code in order to access a computer without authorization or in excess of authorized access.[15] "Contract-based" CFAA violations occur when the defendant's access is in violation of an agreement, policy, or terms of service.[16] "Norms-based" CFAA violations occur when the defendant's access is contrary to general societal expectations.[17] There is little dispute that code-based violations fall within the scope of the CFAA. However, there is great disagreement as to whether contract-based and norms-based violations are covered by the statute.

A narrow reading of the statute might lead to the conclusion that you only violate the CFAA if you commit a code-based violation. A broader reading of the statute would allow prosecutors and plaintiffs to bring CFAA cases arising not only from code-based violations but also contract-based and norms-based violations. Federal courts currently are split as to how broadly to interpret the CFAA,[18] as will be discussed in detail later in this chapter. Their interpretations of the scope of "exceeds authorized access" and "without authorization" can decide whether a CFAA civil claim or criminal prosecution moves forward. Accordingly, as of 2019, the success of a CFAA claim or prosecution often hinges on how the particular court interprets the breadth of the CFAA. Courts generally take two approaches: a narrow view and a broad view.

---

14 *See* Justice Department, Prosecuting Computer Crimes (n.d.) at 6 ("Prosecutors rarely argue that a defendant accessed a computer 'without authorization' when the defendant had some authority to access that computer. However, several civil cases have held that defendants lost their authorization to access computers when they breached a duty of loyalty to the authorizing parties, even if the authorizing parties were unaware of the breach").

15 *See* Orin Kerr, *Norms of Computer Trespass*, 116 Colum. L. Rev. 1143 (2016); Orin Kerr, *Obama's Proposed Changes to the Computer Hacking Statute: A Deep Dive*, Washington Post, Volokh Conspiracy blog (Jan. 14, 2015).

16 *Id.*

17 *Id.*

18 *See* Greg Pollaro, *Disloyal Computer Use and the Computer Fraud and Abuse Act: Narrowing the Scope*, 2010 Duke L. & Tech. Rev. [i] (2010) ("This split in authority raises questions about how broadly or narrowly the CFAA should be applied—or whether it should be applied at all—in the context of an employee's disloyal computer use.").

5.1.2.1 Narrow View of "Exceeds Authorized Access" and "Without Authorization"

The more defendant-friendly reading of the CFAA is seen in *United States v. Nosal*,[19] a 2012 decision of the United States Court of Appeals for the Ninth Circuit, sitting en banc. David Nosal, a former employee of an executive search firm, convinced his ex-coworkers (while they remained at the firm) to use their access to the firm's computer systems to provide him with confidential information, in violation of company policy. The ex-coworkers had access to this data, which Nosal allegedly planned to use to start a competing search firm. Nosal was indicted under numerous criminal laws, including section (a)(4) of the CFAA (discussed in depth later). The government charged that Nosal aided and abetted his ex-coworkers in exceeding their authorized access to the network with intent to defraud.[20]

Nosal moved to dismiss the CFAA charges, arguing that he did not violate the CFAA because neither he nor his former colleagues exceeded authorized access. According to Nosal, the CFAA only covers hackers.[21] The Ninth Circuit agreed with Nosal and adopted his restrictive reading of "exceeds authorized access." The court concluded that "[i]f Congress meant to expand the scope of criminal liability to everyone who uses a computer in violation of computer use restrictions—which may well include everyone who uses a computer—we would expect it to use language better suited to that purpose."[22] The court reasoned that the government's proposed broad interpretation of "exceeds authorized access" would enable the government to bring federal criminal charges against individuals who innocuously violated workplace computer policies. Such broad governmental discretion, the court reasoned, would lead to truly absurd results:

> Employees who call family members from their work phones will become criminals if they send an email instead. Employees can sneak in the sports section of the New York Times to read at work, but they'd better not visit ESPN.com. And sudoku enthusiasts should stick to the printed puzzles, because visiting www.dailysudoku.com from their work computers might give them more than enough time to hone their sudoku skills behind bars.
>
> The effect this broad construction of the CFAA has on workplace conduct pales by comparison with its effect on everyone else who uses a computer, smart-phone, iPad, Kindle, Nook, X-box, Blu-Ray player or any other Internet-enabled device. The Internet is a means for communicating via computers: Whenever we access

---

19 United States v. Nosal, 676 F.3d 854 (9th Cir. 2012) (en banc).
20 *Id.* at 856.
21 *Id.*
22 *Id.* at 857.

a web page, commence a download, post a message on somebody's Facebook wall, shop on Amazon, bid on eBay, publish a blog, rate a movie on IMDb, read www.NYT.com, watch YouTube and do the thousands of other things we routinely do online, we are using one computer to send commands to other computers at remote locations. Our access to those remote computers is governed by a series of private agreements and policies that most people are only dimly aware of and virtually no one reads or understands.[23]

That is not to say that the Ninth Circuit has entirely abandoned the application of the CFAA. In fact, after its decision, the government refocused its criminal charges against Nosal on a second method by which Nosal allegedly accessed the company's information after his accomplices had left the company. One of the accomplices asked to borrow the credentials of an executive assistant who remained at the company, and the executive assistant provided the accomplice with the credentials, allowing them to continue accessing the data.[24] The government charged that because the accomplices did not have the authority to access the company's network with the executive assistant's credentials, they violated the CFAA by accessing "without authorization." The key difference between this indictment and the government's previous charges against Nosal is that the first time, the accomplices still were Korn/Ferry employees and therefore had authorization; the government had charged that they *exceeded* the authorization. In the government's second attempt, it focused on the period when the accomplices no longer worked for the company and therefore were accessing the system entirely *without authorization*, as the executive assistant who provided the credentials to them did not have the authority to authorize them to access their former employer's systems. In a 2–1 decision, the Ninth Circuit agreed with the government:

> We therefore hold that Nosal, a former employee whose computer access credentials were affirmatively revoked by Korn/Ferry acted "without authorization" in violation of the CFAA when he or his former employee co-conspirators used the login credentials of a current employee to gain access to confidential computer data owned by the former employer and to circumvent Korn/Ferry's revocation of access.[25]

The panel clarified the difference between its opinion and the en banc opinion in favor of Nosal from four years earlier (known as *Nosal I*): "In *Nosal*

---

23 *Id.* at 860.
24 United States v. Nosal, 844 F.3d 1024, 1030 (9th Cir. 2016).
25 *Id.* at 1038.

I, authorization was not in doubt. The employees who accessed the Korn/Ferry computers unquestionably had authorization from the company to access the system; the question was whether they exceeded it. What *Nosal I* did not address was whether Nosal's access to Korn/Ferry computers after both Nosal and his coconspirators had terminated their employment and Korn/Ferry revoked their permission to access the computers was 'without authorization.'"[26]

In a stinging dissent, Judge Reinhardt accused the two-judge majority of making the mistake of adopting an overly broad interpretation of the CFAA, which the Ninth Circuit had rejected in its earlier decision ruling in favor of Nosal. The new opinion, he said, would lead to absurd consequences by criminalizing the common practice of password sharing:

> It is impossible to discern from the majority opinion what principle distinguishes authorization in Nosal's case from one in which a bank has clearly told customers that no one but the customer may access the customer's account, but a husband nevertheless shares his password with his wife to allow her to pay a bill. So long as the wife knows that the bank does not give her permission to access its servers in any manner, she is in the same position as Nosal and his associates.[27]

The Ninth Circuit's first *Nosal* holding is the most forceful articulation of the narrow approach to interpreting CFAA's "exceeds authorized access" provision. One commentator stated that the opinion "is a huge victory for those of us who have urged the courts to adopt a narrow construction of the CFAA."[28] Another argued that the ruling was in line with the CFAA's legislative purpose, as "Congress did not intend to criminalize ordinary breach-of-contract claims."[29]

Less than a year after the Ninth Circuit issued the first *Nosal* opinion, the U.S. Court of Appeals for the Fourth Circuit adopted the Ninth Circuit's reasoning in a civil CFAA case. In *WEC Carolina Energy Solutions LLC v. Miller,*[30] WEC, an energy services company, brought a CFAA lawsuit against Mike Miller, a former employee. WEC alleged that before leaving the company, Miller used his access to the company's computer systems to

---

26 *Id.* at 1034.
27 *Id.* at 1055 (Reinhardt, J., dissenting).
28 Orin Kerr, *Ninth Circuit Hands Down En banc Decision in* United States v. Nosal, *Adopting Narrow Interpretation of Computer Fraud and Abuse Act,* VOLOKH CONSPIRACY (Apr. 10, 2012).
29 Paul J. Larkin, Jr., United States v. Nosal: *Rebooting the Computer Fraud and Abuse Act,* 8 SETON HALL CIR. REV. 257, 277 (2012).
30 WEC Carolina Energy Sols. LLC v. Miller, 687 F.3d 199 (4th Cir. 2012).

download confidential documents, and later took a job at a WEC competitor and used the confidential information in an attempt to lure a potential customer.[31]

WEC claimed that this violated sections (a)(2), (a)(4), and (a)(5) of the CFAA because Miller used the information without authorization or in excess of authorized access. Although (a)(2) and (a)(4) apply to acts that are *either* without authorization or exceeding authorized access, (a)(5) only applies to acts that are without authorization. The Fourth Circuit observed that the "distinction between these terms is arguably minute[.]"[32] The court concluded that, based on the ordinary meaning of the terms, authorization means "that an employee is authorized to access a computer when his employer approves or sanctions his admission to that computer," and therefore "without authorization" means that the employee "gains admission to a computer without approval."[33] The court concluded that "exceeds authorized access" means that the employee "has approval to access a computer, but uses his access to obtain or alter information that falls outside the bounds of his approved access."[34] Importantly, the court reasoned that neither "without authorization" nor "exceeds authorized access" can be read to include "the improper *use* of information validly accessed."[35]

Imposing liability on individuals based on an individual's use of information—even if that person had lawful access—would lead to absurd results, the Fourth Circuit reasoned. For instance, the court stated, this interpretation "would impute liability to an employee who with commendable intentions disregards his employer's policy against downloading information to a personal computer so that he can work at home and make headway in meeting his employer's goals."[36]

The U.S. Court of Appeals for the Second Circuit adopted the *Nosal* reasoning in *United States v. Valle.*[37] In that case, Gilberto Valle, a New York City Police Department officer, was charged with crimes arising from online communications in which he discussed committing sexual violence against women he knew. Among the charges for which he was convicted was a CFAA violation because he allegedly used his access to law enforcement databases that contain home addresses, birth dates, and other information about the women who were objects of his violent fantasies.[38] Prosecutors charged that this violated

---

31 *Id.* at 202.
32 *Id.* at 204.
33 *Id.*
34 *Id.*
35 *Id.* (emphasis in original).
36 *Id.* at 206.
37 United States v. Valle, 807 F.3d 508 (2d Cir. 2015).
38 *Id.* at 512–13.

the CFAA because Valle knew of the NYPD's policy that the information was strictly limited to use for official police business.[39]

The Second Circuit held that Valle did not violate the CFAA. It relied in part on the legislative history of the 1986 amendments to the CFAA.[40] The Senate Committee Report on these amendments explained that Congress did not intend to impose liability for those "who inadvertently stumble into someone else's computer file or computer data," and that such a scenario was "particularly true in those cases where an individual is authorized to sign onto and use a particular computer, but subsequently exceeds his authorized access by mistakenly entering another computer or data file that happens to be accessible from the same terminal."[41] The court reasoned that this legislative history "consistently characterizes the evil to be remedied—computer crime—as 'trespass' into computer systems or data, and correspondingly describes 'authorization' in terms of the portion of the computer's data to which one's access rights extend."[42] The Second Circuit acknowledged that the terms "authorization" and "exceeds authorized access" are ambiguous, but ultimately decided that it is required to adopt the narrower, less punitive version under the "rule of lenity," a principle of statutory interpretation that requires courts to interpret ambiguous criminal statutes in favor of criminal defendants, based on the principle that it is the duty of Congress, and not the courts, to create laws that punish criminals.[43]

The ruling was a particularly defendant-friendly one, especially surprising in light of the gruesome nature of the charges. One commentator noted that even under the narrower *Nosal*-type interpretation of the CFAA, the Second Circuit might have been able to rule against Valle: "While the 2nd Circuit agreed with the 9th Circuit, the court could have found that Valle was on notice—Valle should have known he wasn't allowed to use the police database to feed his own fetishes. He had to have known that his conduct was not in any sense permitted by the NYPD."[44]

Under the narrow interpretation of "without authorization" and "exceeds authorized access," as articulated in *Nosal, WEC,* and *Valle,* individuals are only liable for CFAA violations if their initial *access* to the system or data was not permitted. Therefore, how the individual *used* the data is irrelevant.

---

39 *Id.* at 513.
40 *Id.* at 525.
41 *Id.,* quoting S. Rep. No. 99-432, at 2480 (1986) (internal quotation marks omitted).
42 *Valle,* 807 F.3d at 525.
43 *Id.* at 526–27.
44 Michael Rosenbloom, United States v. Valle: *The Second Circuit Agrees with the Fourth and Ninth Circuits on the Meaning of "Exceeds Authorized Access" under the CFAA,* Colum. Sci. & Tech. L. Rev. blog (Dec. 15, 2015).

5.1.2.2 Broader View of "Exceeds Authorized Access" and "Without Authorization"

Some other courts have adopted a broader reading of the CFAA, in which individuals may be liable for misusing information to which they initially had lawful access. Typically, courts that adopt the broad approach to the CFAA will hold that violations of contracts, terms of use, and other rules or agreements constitute acting either without authorization or in excess of authorization. In other words, the broader view of the CFAA allows liability not only for code-based violations but also for contract-based violations.[45]

In a 2001 civil CFAA case, *EF Cultural Travel BV v. Explorica*,[46] the U.S. Court of Appeals for the First Circuit explored the scope of the CFAA. In that case, a company, EF, brought a CFAA claim against a competitor and the competitors' employees for allegedly using an automated software program to scrape pricing information from the company's publicly available website. The employees had previously worked for EF, and had entered into a confidentiality agreement in which they agreed "not to disclose to any third party, either orally or in writing, any Confidential or Proprietary information."[47] The plaintiffs presented evidence that the former employee used his knowledge of confidential EF information to develop the scraping tool. The defendants requested that the court dismiss the lawsuit, contending that they did not "exceed" authorized access. The First Circuit rejected this argument, concluding that the defendants "would face an uphill battle trying to argue that it was not against EF's interests for appellants to use the tour codes to mine EF's pricing data."[48] This is a particularly broad interpretation of the term "exceeds authorized access" because there was not even an allegation that the scraping program violated an explicit provision of a terms of use.

Violations of terms of use and workplace policies are more common for charges of exceeding authorized access under the CFAA. For instance, in *United States v. Rodriguez*,[49] the government brought CFAA charges against Roberto Rodriguez, a former Social Security Administration customer service representative. SSA's policies prohibited its employees from obtaining information "without a business reason." Rodriguez refused to sign forms acknowledging the policy, asking a supervisor "Why give the government rope to hang

---

45 *See* Matthew Gordon, *A Hybrid Approach to Analyzing Authorization in the Computer Fraud and Abuse Act,* 21 B.U. J. Sci. & Tech. L. (2015) ("The contract-based approach has the benefit of not being as restrictive as the code-based approach. The contract-based approach provides protection even when information is not protected by a password. This is useful when the information needs to be protected from an insider who would have the password[.]").

46 EF Cultural Travel BV v. Explorica, Inc., 274 F.3d 577 (1st Cir. 2001).

47 *Id.* at 581.

48 *Id.* at 583.

49 United States v. Rodriguez, 628 F.3d 1258 (11th Cir. 2010).

me?"[50] He allegedly accessed the Social Security records of 17 individuals without a business reason and without the individuals' knowledge. Among the individuals whose records were accessed was Rodriguez's ex-wife.[51] Rodriguez was convicted of violating the CFAA, and on appeal to the U.S. Court of Appeals for the Eleventh Circuit, he argued that he did not "exceed authorized access" because his access was limited to the databases that he was permitted to access due to his job requirements.[52]

The court rejected Rodriguez's argument and held that he exceeded his authorized access by accessing the information for reasons unrelated to his job.[53] "Rodriguez exceeded his authorized access and violated the Act when he obtained personal information for a nonbusiness reason," the court wrote.[54] The court reasoned that this constituted a CFAA violation because the Social Security Administration had explicitly told him that he was not permitted to *obtain* the information for reasons that were unrelated to business purposes. In other words, the court concluded, the violation occurred not because Rodriguez *misused* the information, but because he *obtained* the information in violation of the Social Security Administration's policy.

Rodriguez also argued that he did not exceed authorized access because he did not *use* the information in a criminal manner (e.g., for identity theft). The court quickly disregarded this argument, concluding that the manner in which he *used* the information is not relevant to deciding whether he violated the CFAA; the inquiry for the court was whether he *obtained* the information in violation of the statute.[55] "That Rodriguez did not use the information to defraud anyone or gain financially is irrelevant," the court wrote.[56] The *Rodriguez* case is an example of a broad reading of the CFAA, in which the focus of the court's inquiry is not merely whether the initial access was authorized, but whether the access was used to further unauthorized activities.

Similarly, in *United States v. John,*[57] Dimetriace Eva-Lavon John, a Citigroup employee, allegedly used her credentials to provide information about corporate customers' financial accounts to her half-brother, who used the information to commit fraud.[58] John was charged and convicted on a number of counts, including violation of the CFAA. On appeal, she argued that she did not exceed authorized access because she was authorized to access and view the corporate customer account information. The U.S. Court of Appeals for the Fifth Circuit

---

50 *Id.* at 1261.
51 *Id.* at 1260.
52 *Id.* at 1263.
53 *Id.*
54 *Id.*
55 *Id.* at 1264.
56 *Id.*
57 United States v. John, 597 F.3d 263 (5th Cir. 2010).
58 *Id.* at 269.

rejected this argument, concluding that "authorized access" may include use limitations, "at least when the user knows or reasonably should know that he or she is not authorized to access a computer and information obtainable from that access in furtherance of or to perpetrate a crime."[59] For instance, the court wrote, if an employer authorizes employees "to utilize computers for any lawful purpose but not for unlawful purposes and only in furtherance of the employer's business," the company's employees would exceed authorized access if they "used that access to obtain or steal information as part of a criminal scheme."[60]

Applying this definition to the charges against John, the Fifth Circuit concluded that she clearly violated the CFAA. The court noted that Citigroup's internal policy, which was discussed at employee training sessions, explicitly barred employees from misusing confidential information. "Despite being aware of these policies," the court concluded, "John accessed account information for individuals whose accounts she did not manage, removed this highly sensitive and confidential information from Citigroup premises, and ultimately used this information to perpetrate fraud on Citigroup and its customers."[61] Key to the court's decision was evidence that John had actually been trained on the policies that prohibited such access.

In short, the broad interpretation of CFAA includes not only code-based violations, but also violations based on contract and norms.

5.1.2.3 Attempts to Find a Middle Ground

Courts nationwide have recognized the clear split between the *Nosal/WEC/Valle* narrow reading of the CFAA and the *John/Rodriguez* broad reading. Some courts, rather than selecting one definition, have attempted to distinguish the two lines of thinking and find a middle ground in which the facts of each case determine which reading of the CFAA to apply.

For instance, in 2015, the U.S. District Court for the District of Columbia reasoned that the reading of the CFAA depends in part on whether the defendant *knowingly* violated the law or an agreement. In *Roe v. Bernabei & Wachtel PLLC*,[62] the plaintiff had secretly recorded her employer allegedly sexually harassing her. She allowed a coworker to copy the video. The coworker, along with other colleagues, later sued the employer. They also allegedly provided the media with copies of the video.[63] The plaintiff sued the former coworker and their law firm for, among other things, violating various provisions of the CFAA by obtaining information in excess of authorized access.[64]

59 *Id*. at 271.
60 *Id*.
61 *Id*. at 272.
62 Roe v. Bernabei & Wachtel PLLC, 85 F. Supp. 3d 89 (D.D.C. 2015).
63 *Id*. at 94.
64 *Id*.

The defendants moved to dismiss this claim, arguing that a CFAA violation did not exist because the plaintiff had voluntarily allowed her coworker to copy the video. The judge recognized that courts have different interpretations of the term "exceeds authorized access." The judge ultimately concluded that the narrower version, as articulated by the Ninth Circuit, applied to this case, and dismissed the CFAA claims. The judge reasoned that the more expansive view, as stated in cases such as *Rodriguez,* involves "circumstances in which employees knowingly violated internal employer policies related to the use of data, either unlawfully, or in violation of their employment agreement."[65] In this case, there was no allegation of an explicit agreement or law that prohibited the defendants from copying this information; indeed, the judge reasoned that the coworker "did exactly what [the plaintiff] permitted him to do at the time he copied the video."[66] Although the court adopted the narrower interpretation of the CFAA in this case, it is possible that, had the coworkers violated an explicit agreement, the court would have sustained the CFAA claims.

As courts continue to apply both interpretations of the CFAA to a wide variety of fact patterns, it will be increasingly difficult for courts to find such a middle ground; the interpretations clearly conflict with each other. Quite simply, the federal courts are split as to whether an individual can be found guilty of violating the CFAA merely by misusing information to which the individual had proper access. Unless the United States Supreme Court eventually resolves the issue, federal courts will continue to apply different definitions of "without authorization" and "exceeds authorized access." A court's decision about which interpretation to use will inevitably affect the fate of any CFAA criminal prosecution or civil lawsuit.

5.1.3 The Seven Sections of the CFAA

Although courts exert a great deal of effort determining whether a CFAA defendant has accessed a computer without authorization or exceeded authorized access, that determination is only the beginning of their inquiry under the CFAA. Individuals only violate the CFAA if, while acting without authorization or in excess of authorization, their behavior falls into one of seven categories specified by the CFAA, such as obtaining information or damaging a computer. The box here features an overview of the seven subsections of the CFAA, and the types of behavior that courts have held constitute—and do not constitute—violations of the law. For all seven of these subsections, the CFAA imposes criminal penalties not only on the commission of these acts but also on conspiracies and attempts to commit the acts.[67]

---

65 *Id.* at 103.
66 *Id.*
67 18 U.S.C. § 1030(b).

Summary of the Seven Prohibited Acts under the Computer Fraud and Abuse Act

Here are the seven sections of the CFAA, modestly edited for brevity and clarity. The full text of the CFAA appears in Appendix D of this book.

Section (a)(1): *Hacking to commit espionage.* Knowingly accessing a computer without authorization or exceeding authorized access, and by means of such conduct having obtained classified or national security information, with reasons to believe that the information could be used to the injury of the United States or to the advantage of any foreign nation, willfully communicating or otherwise delivering the information to a person not entitled to receive it, or willfully retaining the information and failing to deliver it to the individual entitled to receive it.

Section (a)(2): *Hacking to obtain information.* Intentionally accessing a computer without authorization, or exceeding authorized access, and thereby obtaining information in a financial record of a financial institution, card issuer, or consumer reporting agency; information from any department or agency of the United States; or information from any computer that is used in or affecting interstate or foreign commerce.

Section (a)(3): *Hacking a federal government computer.* Intentionally, without authorization, accessing any nonpublic computer of a department or agency of the United States, accessing a computer that is exclusively for the use of the government of the United States, or, in the case of a computer not exclusively for government use, is used by or for the U.S. government and such conduct affects that use.

Section (a)(4): *Hacking to commit fraud.* Knowingly and with intent to defraud, accessing a protected computer without authorization, or exceeding authorized access, and by means of such conduct furthering the intended fraud and obtaining anything of value, unless the object of the fraud and the thing obtained consists only of the use of the computer and the value of the use is not more than $5,000 in any one-year period.

Section (a)(5): *Hacking to commit damage.* (A) Knowingly causing the transmission of a program, information, code, or command, and as a result of such conduct, intentionally causing damage without authorization, to a computer used in or affecting interstate or foreign commerce; (B) intentionally accessing without authorization a computer used in or affecting interstate or foreign commerce, and as a result of such conduct, recklessly causing damage; or (C) intentionally accessing without authorization a computer used in or affecting interstate or foreign commerce, and as a result of such conduct, causing damage and loss.

Section (a)(6): ***Trafficking in passwords.*** Knowingly and with intent to defraud trafficking in any password or similar information if the trafficking affects interstate or foreign commerce or the computer is used by or for the U.S. government.

Section (a)(7): ***Threats of hacking.*** With intent to extort money or other things of value, transmitting in interstate or foreign commerce any communication containing any: (A) threat to damage a computer used in or affecting interstate or foreign commerce; (B) threat to obtain information from a computer used in or affecting interstate or foreign commerce without authorization or in excess of authorization or to impair the confidentiality of information obtained from such a computer without authorization or by exceeding authorized access; or (C) demand or request for money or other thing of value in relation to damage a computer used in or affecting interstate or foreign commerce, where such damage was caused to facilitate the extortion.

5.1.3.1   CFAA Section (a)(1): Hacking to Commit Espionage

Section (a)(1) prohibits individuals from knowingly accessing a computer without authorization or exceeding authorized access, and obtaining classified or national security information, and willfully communicating, delivering, transmitting, or causing the communication, delivery, or transmission to any person who is not authorized to receive the information.[68] The statute also prohibits the willful retention of the data, and failure to deliver it to the U.S. employee who is entitled to receive it. Section (a)(1) only applies if the individual had reason to believe that the information could be used to injure the United States or to the advantage of a foreign nation.

No published court opinion interprets this subsection, largely because it is rare for prosecutions to be brought under this subsection. That likely is because the federal government typically brings espionage-related hacking prosecutions under Section 793(e) of the Espionage Act,[69] which criminalizes many forms of unauthorized access, use, and disclosure of classified information.[70]

Violations of Section (a)(1) are felonies, and violations carry prison terms of up to ten years and fines. If an individual violates Section (a)(1) after having been convicted of another CFAA violation, the prison term can be up to 20 years.

---

68 18 U.S.C. § 1030(a)(1).

69 18 U.S.C. § 791 *et seq.*

70 U.S. Justice Department, Prosecuting Computer Crimes at 15 ("Violations of this subsection are charged quite rarely. The reason for this lack of prosecution may well be the close similarities between sections 1030(a)(1) and 793(e). In situations where both statutes are applicable, prosecutors may tend towards using section 793(e), for which guidance and precedent are more prevalent.").

5.1.3.2 CFAA Section (a)(2): Hacking to Obtain Information

Section (a)(2) of the CFAA prohibits individuals from intentionally accessing computers without authorization or in excess of authorized access, and *obtaining* (1) information contained in a financial record of a financial institution, card issuer, or consumer reporting agency; (2) information from any federal government department or agency; or (3) information from any "protected computer," which the CFAA defines as a computer that is either used by a financial institution or the federal government, or is used in or affecting interstate or foreign commerce.[71]

Because it is relatively easy to demonstrate that companies' computers affect interstate or foreign commerce, Section (a)(2) is a frequent basis for CFAA criminal prosecutions and civil litigation. Indeed, the CFAA had initially only applied to computers that are used in interstate commerce, but in 2008, Congress amended the statute to include computers that affect interstate commerce because it recognized the need to "address the increasing number of computer hacking crimes that involve computers located within the same state[.]"[72] Under this incredibly broad definition of "protected computer," it is difficult to imagine any U.S. companies whose computers do not qualify as "protected computers" covered by the CFAA. Indeed, one federal court in California stated that the requirement for a "protected computer" will "always be met when an individual using a computer contacts or communicates with an Internet website."[73] Moreover, in 2001, Congress amended the CFAA to clarify that it applies to attacks on computers both inside and outside of the United States. As the U.S. Justice Department observed, this amendment "addresses situations where an attacker within the United States attacks a computer system located abroad and situations in which individuals in foreign countries route communications through the United States as they hack from one foreign country to another."[74]

The act covered by Section (a)(2)—obtaining information—is quite broad. In the Senate report accompanying the 1986 amendments to CFAA that established Section (a)(2), the legislators wrote that "obtaining information" includes

---

71 18 U.S.C. § 1030(a)(2).
72 153 Cong. Rec. S14570 (Oct. 16, 2007) (remarks of Sen. Leahy).
73 United States v. Drew, 259 F.R.D. 449, 457 (C.D. Cal. 2009), *citing* Brookfield Comms. v. West Coast Ent. Corp., 174 F.3d 1036, 1044 (9th Cir. 1999) ("The Internet is a global network of interconnected computers which allows individuals and organizations around the world to communicate and to share information with one another."); *see also* Paradigm Alliance v. Celeritas Techs., LLC, 248 F.R.D. 598, 602 (D. Kan. 2008) ("The essence of defendants' CFAA claim is that Paradigm repeatedly accessed or attempted to access Celeritas' password protected 'web-based' application after being told that access was no longer permitted. As a practical matter, a computer providing a 'web-based' application accessible through the internet would satisfy the interstate communication requirement.").
74 U.S. Justice Department, Prosecuting Computer Crimes at 5.

"mere observation of the data."[75] The legislators clarified that, for the government or a litigant to demonstrate that an individual obtained information under Section (a)(2), they need not prove that the defendant had been "physically removing the data from its original location or transcribing the data[.]"[76] In the three decades since this report, there has been little dispute that "obtaining information" under Section (a)(2) does not necessarily include the actual removal of the data. Observation of data—such as by hacking into a company's website—is sufficient to establish that the individual "obtained" the information.[77] However, there are some limits to the breadth of this definition. Merely accessing a computer without authorization or in excess of authorization—and not actually viewing or otherwise obtaining any information—will not constitute a Section (a)(2) violation.

Perhaps the most significant barrier to charges or claims under Section (a)(2) is the requirement that the act of obtaining information without authorization be intentional. Congress intentionally set this higher standard in its 1986 amendments to the CFAA. The initial 1984 version of the CFAA applied to acts that were committed "knowingly." In 1986, Congress replaced "knowingly" with "intentionally." In the report accompanying the 1986 amendments, the Senate committee members wrote that "intentional acts of unauthorized access—rather than mistaken, inadvertent, or careless ones—are precisely what the Committee intends to proscribe."[78] The Committee analyzed Supreme Court precedent that interpreted the term "knowingly," and reasoned that the "knowingly" standard could apply to acts that apply whenever the individual is "aware that the result is practically certain to follow from his conduct, whatever his desire may be as to that result."[79]

Replacing "knowingly" with "intentionally," the Committee concluded, is intended to prosecute "those whose conduct evinces a clear intent" to hack.[80] The Committee, relying on earlier interpretations of the term "intentional," stated that it "means more than one voluntarily engaged in conduct or caused a result."[81]

The limits imposed by the word "intentionally" were evident in a 2006 federal court opinion in the District of Columbia, arising from a civil action against

---

75 S. Rep. No. 99-432, at 6 (1986).
76 *Id.* at 6–7.
77 U.S. Justice Department, Prosecuting Computer Crimes at 18.
78 S. Rep. No. 99-432 at 5.
79 *Id.* at 6.
80 *Id.*
81 *Id.* ("Again, this will comport with the Senate Report on the Criminal Code, which states that intentional means more than that one voluntarily engaged in conduct or caused a result. Such conduct or the causing of the result must have been the person's conscious objective.") (internal quotation marks omitted).

IBM.[82] Butera & Andrews, a DC law firm, alleged that its servers were hacked, and the attacker's IP addresses were located at an IBM facility in North Carolina. The law firm sued IBM and the anonymous hacker—whom the firm alleged to be "a person who is employed by Defendant IBM at its Durham, North Carolina facility"—under a variety of causes of action, including a violation of Section (a)(2) of the CFAA. IBM moved to dismiss the claims, arguing that the plaintiff's complaint failed to allege that IBM "acted intentionally."[83] The district court granted IBM's motion to dismiss, agreeing that the complaint failed to allege that IBM acted with any intent. The court reasoned that the mere allegation that the hacker's IP addresses were located in IBM's facilities did not permit an inference that IBM *participated* in the alleged hacking.[84] "Far from pleading any intentional conduct on the part of IBM," the court observed, "the plaintiffs' position appears directed, at most, at establishing the likelihood that an individual employed at the IBM facility in Durham is responsible for the alleged attacks."[85] Such an allegation does not rise to the level of "intentional" hacking, the court concluded.[86]

Demonstrating intent under Section (a)(2), however, is not an insurmountable task. Indeed, courts generally have held that for the government or a civil plaintiff to establish a Section (a)(2) violation, they only need to prove that the defendant intended to obtain information by accessing a computer without authorization or exceeding authorized access. It is unnecessary to demonstrate that the defendant intended for the information to be used in any particular way.

For example, in a 2007 case, *United States v. Willis*,[87] defendant Todd A. Willis, an employee of an Oklahoma City debt collection business, had access to a proprietary database of individuals' personal information, and was prohibited from obtaining that information for personal reasons.[88] A law enforcement investigation revealed that Willis provided his drug dealer with credentials to the database, and the credentials were later used to commit identity theft.[89] Willis was charged with aiding and abetting a violation of Section (a)(2), convicted by jury, and sentenced to 41 months in prison.[90] On appeal to the U.S. Court of

---

82 Butera & Andrews v. Int'l Bus. Machines, 456 F. Supp. 2d 104 (D.D.C. 2006).

83 *Id*. at 107–8.

84 *Id*. at 110.

85 *Id*. at 111.

86 *Id*. at 112 ("The plaintiff does not allege that the complained-of attacks were committed by the John Doe defendant to 'further[] his employer's interests,' even assuming that the Doe defendant was employed by IBM. Rather, all the plaintiff alleges is that 'John Doe in his capacity as IBM employee or agent, initiated, directed, and managed all attacks[.]'") (internal citation omitted).

87 United States v. Willis, 476 F.3d 1121 (10th Cir. 2007).

88 *Id*. at 1123.

89 *Id*.

90 *Id*. at 1124.

Appeals for the Tenth Circuit, Willis argued that his conviction was invalid because he did not intend to defraud when he provided the credentials. The Tenth Circuit rejected this argument after reviewing the legislative history of the 1986 amendments to CFAA, and concluded that the government did not have an obligation to demonstrate that Willis intended to use the information in any particular way; the inquiry for the court was whether his intentional *access* and obtaining of the information violated the CFAA.[91]

Similarly, in *Thayer Corporation v. Reed*,[92] Thayer Corporation filed a civil lawsuit against its former chief financial officer, David Reed. Among the many counts in the complaint was a CFAA claim under Section (a)(2). Thayer alleged that for approximately a week after Reed's employment ceased, he forwarded Thayer human resources emails to his personal email account. Reed asserted that the email transfers were the result of a mistake by his phone provider, and that as soon as he saw that he was receiving the Thayer emails, he directed the phone company to fix the issue. The court rejected this argument, reasoning that the complaint alleged that Reed "intercepted, read, deleted and forwarded emails from Thayer's human resources director;" explained that Reed had created Thayer's password system; and alleged that Reed "knew of discussions regarding his severance package, information that only could have been obtained from the human resources manager's emails." Assuming that the allegations in the complaint were true, the court concluded, "Mr. Reed could not have unintentionally done any of these things; each requires the intent to access, intercept, and use Thayer's email system without authorization, causing harm."[93]

These cases have a consistent theme: to satisfy the "intentional" requirement of Section (a)(2), the government or civil plaintiff must establish that the defendant intentionally obtained the information through unauthorized hacking. However, they need not establish that the defendant intended to cause harm, defraud, or support the commission of another crime.

Section (a)(2) violations may be charged as felonies or misdemeanors. If a violation is charged as a misdemeanor, the defendant could be punished by a fine and up to one year in prison. A violation of Section (a)(2) may be charged as a felony, carrying a fine and up to five years in prison, if one of the following

---

91 *Id.* at 1125 ("A plain reading of the statute reveals that the requisite intent to prove a violation of § 1030(a)(2)(C) is not an intent to defraud (as it is under (a)(4)), it is the intent to obtain unauthorized access of a protected computer.... . That is, to prove a violation of (a)(2)(C), the Government must show that the defendant: (1) intentionally accessed a computer, (2) without authorization (or exceeded authorized access), (3) and thereby obtained information from any protected computer if the conduct involved an interstate or foreign communication. The government need not also prove that the defendant had the intent to defraud in obtaining the information or that the information was used to any particular ends.").
92 Thayer Corp. v. Reed, Case No. 2:10-cv-00423-JAW (D. Me. July 11, 2011).
93 *Id.*

is true: (1) the defendant committed the offense "for purposes of commercial advantage or private financial gain;" (2) "the offense was committed in furtherance of any criminal or tortious act in violation of the Constitution or laws of the United States or of any State;" or (3) the information obtained is valued at more than \$5,000. Additionally, if an individual violates Section (a)(2) after having previously been convicted of a CFAA violation, that individual can be charged with a felony punishable by a fine and up to ten years in prison.

5.1.3.3 CFAA Section (a)(3): Hacking a Federal Government Computer
Section (a)(3) prohibits individuals from intentionally accessing nonpublic federal government computers without authorization. This prohibition applies to both computers that are "exclusively for the use of the Government of the United States," and computers that are "used by or for the Government of the United States and such conduct affects that use by or for the Government of the United States."[94]

At first glance, one might wonder why Section (a)(3) is necessary, since Section (a)(2) also explicitly prohibits certain hacks of federal government computers. Section (a)(3) differs because it prohibits the mere act of intentionally *accessing* a federal government computer without authorization, regardless of whether the defendant actually obtained any information. This provision was conceived two years after the initial CFAA was enacted, when members of Congress indicated a desire to "balance its concern for Federal employees and other authorized users against the legitimate need to protect Government computers against abuse by 'outsiders.'"[95] Congress addressed this balance by amending the CFAA to create this separate prohibition on unauthorized access to federal computers. According to the Senate report accompanying the amendments, this section was drafted in response to the U.S. Justice Department's concerns about whether Section (a)(2) "covers acts of mere trespass," that is, unauthorized access, or whether it requires a further showing that the information perused was "used, modified, destroyed, or disclosed."[96] Congress stated that it intended for Section (a)(3) to create "a simple trespass offense" that applies "to persons without authorized access to Federal computers."[97] In this respect, Section (a)(3) is significantly broader than Section (a)(2).

However, Section (a)(3) also is narrower than Section (a)(2) in one important area: while Section (a)(2) applies to *both* access without authorization *and* exceeding authorized access, Section (a)(3) only applies to access without authorization. Congress intentionally excluded "exceeding authorized access"

---

94 18 U.S.C. § 1030(a)(3).
95 S. Rep. No. 99-432, at 7 (1986).
96 *Id.*
97 *Id.*

from Section (a)(3), according to the 1986 Senate report.[98] The legislators concluded that if a government employee "briefly exceeds his authorized access and peruses data belonging to the department that he is not supposed to look at," the employee should be subject to administrative sanctions, but not criminal penalties.[99]

Section (a)(3) does not apply to unauthorized access of *any* federal government computer. In 1996, Congress amended Section (a)(3) to clarify that it only applies to unauthorized access of *nonpublic* federal government computers. In the Senate report accompanying the 1996 amendment, Congress warned that despite the new restriction of Section (a)(3) to nonpublic federal government computers, "a person who is permitted to access publicly available Government computers, for example, via an agency's World Wide Web site, may still be convicted under (a)(3) for accessing without authority any nonpublic Federal Government computer."[100]

There have been few prosecutions under Section (a)(3). The U.S. Department of Justice's manual on computer crimes attributes the lack of prosecutions under Section (a)(3) to the fact that a first-time violation of Section (a)(3) is a misdemeanor, whereas a first-time violation of Section (a)(2) may be charged as a felony, with greater penalties.[101] Accordingly, if an act falls under both Section(a)(2) and Section (a)(3), prosecutors may have greater incentive to bring the charges under Section (a)(2).

If, however, an individual is charged under Section (a)(3) after having previously been convicted of a CFAA violation, the crime can be charged as a felony with a fine and up to ten years in prison.

5.1.3.4   CFAA Section (a)(4): Hacking to Commit Fraud

Section (a)(4) prohibits individuals from "knowingly and with intent to defraud" accessing a protected computer without authorization, or exceeding authorized access, and furthering the intended fraud and obtaining "anything of value." This provision does not apply if the object of the fraud and the thing obtained consist only of the use of the computer, and the value of that use is not more than $5,000 during any one-year period.[102]

Section (a)(4) is similar to the federal mail fraud and wire fraud statutes. But when Congress enacted this provision in the 1986 amendments to CFAA, it expressed a desire to ensure that fraud conducted over a computer—rather than the mails or wires—be covered explicitly under a criminal law. According to the Senate report accompanying the amendments, Congress did not believe

---

98 *Id.*
99 *Id.*
100 S. Rep. No. 104-357 (1996).
101 U.S. Department of Justice, Prosecuting Computer Crimes, at 25.
102 18 U.S.C. § 1030(a)(4).

that "a scheme or artifice to defraud should fall under the ambit of subsection (a)(4) merely because the offender signed onto a computer at some point near to the commission or execution of the fraud," calling that a "tenuous link."[103] For a prosecution under Section (a)(4), the defendant's computer use "must be more directly linked to the intended fraud."[104]

Courts generally have been willing to conclude that a wide range of types of improper access "further" the intended fraud, as required by Section (a)(4). For instance, in *United States v. Bae*,[105] the defendant, a retailer whose store sold lottery tickets, pleaded guilty to a Section (a)(4) violation. He was charged with using his lottery terminal to create more than $500,000 in tickets for himself. The tickets were redeemable for more than $296,000 and the defendant redeemed them for approximately $224,000. When calculating his sentence, the district court calculated $503,650 in losses, equal to the "market value of the tickets less the commission [the defendant] would have received from the Lottery Board had he sold those tickets." The defendant appealed the sentence, arguing that the market price does not reflect the actual cost to the lottery system, and that therefore the district court should have calculated his sentence based on the redemption value of the tickets. The U.S. Court of Appeals for the D.C. Circuit rejected this argument and affirmed his sentence, concluding that the proper measure of damage under Section (a)(4) is the "fair market value of the lottery tickets at the time" that they were illegally printed.[106] Although the opinion dealt with the narrow issue of criminal sentencing, the court's reasoning indicates a willingness to broadly attribute subsequent fraud to an initial illegal access. In other words, even if the eventual fraud is attenuated from the initial access, the defendant still may be liable under Section (a)(4).

Perhaps the largest barrier to Section(a)(4) cases is the requirement to demonstrate that the defendant obtained something "of value." Consider the prosecution of Richard Czubinski, a customer service employee at the Internal Revenue Service. The federal government brought charges against Czubinski under numerous statutes, including Section (a)(4), alleging that he used his credentials to search the tax records of a number of people for whom he had no legitimate business reason to be querying.[107] At trial, there was evidence that he only mentioned his access to the data to one acquaintance, and there was no further evidence that he had shared or otherwise used any of the information that he viewed.[108] He was convicted by a jury on 13 counts, and appealed.

---

103 S. Rep. No. 99-432, at 9 (1986).
104 *Id.*
105 United States v. Bae, 250 F.3d 774 (D.C. Cir. 2001).
106 *Id.* at 776.
107 United States v. Czubinski, 106 F.3d 1069, 1072 (1st Cir. 1997).
108 *Id.*

In 1997, the U.S. Court of Appeals for the First Circuit reversed his Section (a)(4) conviction. (At the time, Section (a)(4) required proof that the hacker obtained something of "value," but did not have a $5,000 minimum provision.) At issue in the appeal was whether the taxpayer IRS information qualified as something of "value," even though there was no evidence that Czubinski used it in any way. The court concluded that in this case, the government failed to demonstrate that the information had any "value" to Czubinski. Instead, the court reasoned, he accessed the data merely to satisfy his "idle curiosity."[109] In other words, viewing confidential information—and not doing anything with that knowledge—does not constitute obtaining a thing "of value" in violation of Section (a)(4). The mere act of accessing information on a computer without authorization or in excess of authorization more easily fits under Section (a)(2).

Section (a)(4)'s intent requirement is more specific than in other sections of the CFAA: the violation must not only be done knowingly, but it must also be done with intent to defraud. One of the few courts that has interpreted this phrase in the context of the CFAA took a fairly broad approach. In *Shurgard Storage Centers v. Safeguard Self Storage,*[110] the plaintiff, a self-storage company, alleged that one of its managers emailed confidential business information to its competitor, which later hired him. The plaintiff sued the competitor alleging a number of claims, including violation of Section (a)(4). The competitor moved to dismiss the complaint, arguing that the complaint did not adequately allege that the competitor intended to defraud the plaintiff.[111] At common law, to demonstrate that fraud occurred, a plaintiff must demonstrate nine elements, including a representation of fact that was false, and the plaintiff's reliance on this false statement. Requiring a Section (a)(4) plaintiff (or a government prosecutor) to demonstrate common-law fraud would make it exceptionally difficult to bring a case under this provision. The court rejected this reading of Section (a)(4), agreeing with the plaintiff that, in the context of Section (a)(4), "defraud" means "wronging one in his property rights by dishonest methods or schemes."[112] The court reasoned that Section (a)(4) does not require proof of common-law fraud, and only requires demonstration of a "wrongdoing."[113]

A federal judge in Iowa later adopted the broad definition of "defraud" as articulated in *Shurgard Storage Centers.* In *NCMIC Finance Corporation v. Artino,*[114] a company alleged that a former executive violated Section (a)(4)

---

109 *Id.* at 1078.
110 Shurgard Storage Ctrs. v. Safeguard Self Storage, 119 F. Supp. 2d 1121 (W.D. Wash. 2000).
111 *Id.* at 1125.
112 *Id.*
113 *Id.*
114 NCMIC Fin. Corp. v. Artino, 638 F. Supp. 2d 1042 (S.D. Iowa 2009).

when he used his access to the company's computer systems to obtain confidential customer information. The judge concluded that these actions constituted an intent to defraud for the purposes of Section (a)(4) because they harmed the plaintiff's property rights when the former executive "accessed [the company's] customer spreadsheet, e-mailed it from his work e-mail account to his personal e-mail account without authorization, and used the customer spreadsheet for his own personal gain and against [the company's] financial interests."[115]

Violations of Section (a)(4) carry penalties of up to five years in prison and a fine. If the defendant has previously been convicted of violating the CFAA, the prison term can be up to ten years.

5.1.3.5 CFAA Section (a)(5): Hacking to Damage a Computer

Section (a)(5) of the CFAA prohibits three types of behavior, all related to damaging computers through hacking: (1) knowingly causing "the transmission of a program, information, code, or command, and as a result of such conduct, intentionally causes damage without authorization, to a protected computer;" (2) "intentionally access[ing] a protected computer without authorization, and as a result of such conduct, recklessly causes damage;" or (3) "intentionally access[ing] a protected computer without authorization, and as a result of such conduct, causes damage and loss."[116]

Section (a)(5) is among the more commonly prosecuted and litigated provisions of the CFAA, as it covers a wide range of actions, including the deployment of viruses and malware, denial-of-service attacks, and deletion of data. The three subsections of (a)(5) are quite different, and therefore we will examine each separately.

5.1.3.5.1   CFAA Section (a)(5)(A): Knowing Transmission that Intentionally Damages a Computer Without Authorization

Section (a)(5)(A) requires prosecutors (or a private plaintiff) to demonstrate four general elements: that the defendant (1) knowingly caused the transmission of a program, information, code, or command; (2) and as a result of such conduct, *intentionally* caused (3) damage to a protected computer; (4) without authorization.

The first element requires a demonstration that the plaintiff knowingly caused the transmission of program, information, code, or command. The first hurdle for satisfying this element is a demonstration that a transmission occurred, though courts generally have interpreted this to cover a fairly wide range of activities. For instance, in *International Airport Centers,*

---

115 *Id*. at 1062.
116 18 U.S.C. § 1030(a)(5).

LLC v. Citrin,[117] a company filed a Section (a)(5)(A) civil claim against a former employee who allegedly deleted proprietary company data from his laptop before quitting and starting his own business.[118] The former employee also allegedly installed a secure-erasure program that ensured that the files could not be recovered.[119] The former employee argued that the claim should be dismissed because merely deleting a file does not constitute a "transmission" under the CFAA. The U.S. Court of Appeals for the Seventh Circuit agreed it might be "stretching the statute too far" to hold that merely pressing "delete"—and nothing more—constitutes "transmission." However, the court allowed the claim to proceed because the installation of the secure-erasure program did constitute "transmission."[120] The *Citrin* opinion, which has been widely cited in other CFAA cases, demonstrates that, although courts consider many types of acts to be "transmission," there are some limits to the scope of the term.

The second element requires the government or plaintiff to demonstrate that as a result of the knowing transmission, the defendant *intended* to damage a protected computer. It is important to keep in mind that this requirement is separate from the first element: not only must the government or plaintiff establish a *knowing* transmission, it also must demonstrate *intentional* damage. Although the CFAA does not define "intentional," courts generally have held that it requires a greater showing than a "knowing" act. For instance, the U.S. Court of Appeals for the Third Circuit has defined "intentionally," in the context of Section (a)(5), as "performing an act deliberately and not by accident."[121] In perhaps the most extensive discussion of the requirement to demonstrate intentional causation of damage, the U.S. Court of Appeals for the Sixth Circuit considered a civil lawsuit by a homebuilder against a labor union that organized an extensive email campaign, which the company claimed overwhelmed employee inboxes and brought business to a standstill.[122] Relying on the dictionary definition, the Sixth Circuit, in *Pulte Homes, Inc. v. Laborers' International Union of North America,* concluded that in the context of the CFAA, "intentionally" means acting "with the conscious purpose of causing damage (in a statutory sense)" to a computer system.[123] Applying that definition, the court reasoned that the union may have acted intentionally because it instructed thousands of union members to email three of the company's executives and urged union members to "fight back." The court reasoned that such

---

117 Int'l Airport Ctrs., LLC v. Citrin, 440 F.3d 418 (7th Cir. 2006).
118 *Id*. at 419.
119 *Id*.
120 *Id*.
121 United States v. Carlson, 209 Fed. Appx. 181, 185 (3d Cir., Dec. 22 2006) (unpublished).
122 Pulte Homes, Inc. v. Laborers' Int'l Union of N. Am., 648 F.3d 295 (6th Cir. 2011).
123 *Id*. at 303.

language "suggests that such a slow-down was at least one of its objectives."[124] These opinions suggest that as long as there is some credible evidence that the defendant committed the act with the purpose of causing damage, courts will conclude that the "intentional" requirement is satisfied.

However, courts must have some evidence of intent to sustain a claim under Section 5(A). In a 2016 case, a federal judge in Pennsylvania dismissed a claim against Resultly, a company that, without authorization, allegedly sublicensed participation in a marketing affiliate program run by QVC. In its lawsuit against Resultly, QVC alleged that Resultly's unauthorized participation in the program "overloaded QVC's servers by bombarding its website with search requests at rates ranging from 200-300 requests per minute up to 36,000 requests per minute" and that "[a]t one point the [Resultly] Program's crawling activity alone accounted for approximately 30% of the overall worldwide traffic being experienced by QVC."[125] The court noted that Section 5(A) requires allegations that "suggest the defendant knew his actions would cause damage and that it was his conscious desire to take those actions."[126] As the court summarized, QVC argued that it should infer Resultly's intent from QVC's claim that "Resultly disguised its web crawler as individual online users, disguised its source IP address, and sent excessive requests to overload QVC's website and network." The court found these allegations insufficient to demonstrate intent, as Resultly's incentives—having a functional QVC website—were aligned with those of QVC, as Resultly would earn commission from those sales. "Although the Court could plausibly infer from these facts that Resultly wished to disguise its identity, they do not, on their own, suggest that it was Resultly's conscious objective to cause an 'impairment to the integrity or availability of' QVC's website or servers."[127]

The third element requires the government or plaintiff to demonstrate that the defendant caused *damage* to a protected computer. The CFAA defines "damage" as "any impairment to the integrity or availability of data, a program, a system, or information."[128] A federal court in Illinois, after reviewing CFAA cases, concluded that "damage" includes "the destruction, corruption, or deletion of electronic files, the physical destruction of a hard drive, or any diminution in the completeness or usability of the data on a computer system."[129]

---

124 *Id.*

125 QVC v. Resultly, 159 F. Supp. 3d 576, 582 (E.D. Pa. 2016) (internal quotation marks and citations omitted).

126 *Id.* at 593.

127 *Id.*

128 18 U.S.C § 1030(e)(8).

129 TriTeq Lock & Sec. LLC v. Innovative Secured Solutions, LLC, Civ. Action No. 10 CV 1304, 2012 WL 394229, at *6 (N.D. Ill. Feb. 1, 2012) ("It is well established that the disclosure of trade secrets misappropriated through unauthorized computer access does not qualify as damage under the CFAA's definition of the term.") (internal quotation marks and citation omitted).

Although this is a fairly broad definition, it has some limits. For instance, in *New South Equipment Mats, LLC* v. *Keener*,[130] a federal judge in Mississippi dismissed a Section (a)(5) claim against a former employee who allegedly copied confidential business information but did not alter the data in any way, or render it inaccessible.[131] The court concluded that because the company did not allege anything more than copying the information, it could not demonstrate that the former employee "caused damage" for the purposes of the CFAA.[132] In contrast, in the *Pulte* case, the Sixth Circuit concluded that the email campaign *did* cause damage to Pulte because it disrupted the company's operations and prevented it from fully using its computer systems.[133] Although there is little binding precedent on the exact scope of "damage," these court opinions suggest that any harm to the original data or computer system, including an inability to access, likely will qualify as "damage," but merely copying data will not.

The fourth element is that the damage must have occurred without authorization. This typically does not present a significant issue in claims under Section (a)(5)(A) because the government or plaintiff must only demonstrate that the *damage*—not the access—was not authorized.[134]

5.1.3.5.2 CFAA Section (a)(5)(B): Intentional Access Without Authorization that Recklessly Causes Damage

Section (a)(5)(B) requires prosecutors to demonstrate three general elements: (1) intentional access of a protected computer; (2) without authorization; and (3) as a result of the access, recklessly causes damage. This is a very different crime from Section (a)(5)(A). In short, Section (a)(5)(B) focuses on whether the *access* was intentional and unauthorized, whereas Section (a)(5)(A) focuses on whether the *damage* was intentional and unauthorized.

The first element, intentional access of a protected computer, focuses on whether the *access* was intentional. In contrast, Section (a)(5)(A) only applies if the defendant intended to *cause damage*. In other words, the inquiry into intent under Section (a)(5)(B) is whether the defendant intentionally accessed

---

130 New South Equip. Mats, LLC v. Keener, 989 F. Supp. 2d 522 (S.D. Miss. 2013).

131 *Id*. at 524–25.

132 *Id*. at 530 ("[T]here is nothing in the complaint's factual allegations to indicate that Keener did more than copy files and transmit information. There is no allegation that he deleted files.").

133 Pulte Homes, Inc. v. Laborers' Int'l Union of N. Am., 648 F.3d 295, 301–02 (6th Cir. 2011) ("Because Pulte alleges that the transmissions diminished its ability to send and receive calls and e-mails, it accordingly alleges an impairment to the integrity or availability of its data and systems—i.e., statutory damage.").

134 *See* Shamrock Foods Co. v. Gast, 535 F. Supp. 2d 962, 967 n.1 (D. Ariz. 2008) (explaining the difference between provisions in the CFAA that "define violation in terms of accessing a protected computer without authorization" and those that are "violated by causing damage without authorization").

a protected computer. Whether the defendant intended to cause damage is irrelevant to a prosecution or civil action under Section (a)(5)(B). For instance, in the case that QVC brought against Resultly, described in the previous subsection, although the court dismissed the Section (a)(5)(A) claim because QVC failed to sufficiently allege intent to damage, the court refused to dismiss a Section (a)(5)(B) claim in the same lawsuit.[135]

The second element requires a demonstration that the intentional access was without authorization. Again, this differs from Section (a)(5)(A), which focuses on whether the *damage* was authorized. Section (a)(5)(B)'s authorized access requirement also is narrower than the access provisions of other sections of the CFAA. Other sections, such as Section (a)(2), apply to acts that are done *either* without authorization *or* exceeding authorized access, but Section (a)(5) only applies to the first category. These terms are discussed more generally in Section 5.1.2 of this chapter, but they have special significance for this provision of the CFAA because it does not apply to exceeding authorized access. One court concluded that "without authorization" only applies to people who have "no rights, limited or otherwise, to access the computer in question."[136] The Sixth Circuit in *Pulte*, which, as discussed earlier, ruled that the company had stated a viable claim under Section (a)(5)(A), dismissed the company's claim under Section (a)(5)(B).[137] The court reasoned that because the company allows the general public to contact its employees, it could not allege that the union encouraged people to access its computer systems without authorization.[138]

The third element requires the government or plaintiff to demonstrate that the intentional, unauthorized access recklessly caused damage. The definition of "damage" generally is the same as for Section (a)(5)(A), discussed earlier. The key difference is that for a claim under Section (a)(5)(B), the damage must have been caused *recklessly*. The CFAA does not define "recklessly," nor is there a significant discussion of the term in precedential CFAA cases. The Model Penal Code, which many states have adopted as the framework for their criminal laws, states that a person acts recklessly "when he consciously disregards a substantial and unjustifiable risk that the material element exists or will result from his conduct."[139] Applying this definition to Section (a)(5)(B), a person recklessly causes damage if she consciously disregards a large risk of damage created by her unauthorized, intentional access to a computer system.

135 QVC v. Resultly, 159 F. Supp. 3d 576, 595 (E.D. Pa. 2016).
136 LVRC Holdings LLC v. Brekka, 581 F.3d 1127, 1133 (9th Cir. 2009).
137 Pulte Homes, Inc. v. Laborers' Int'l Union of N. Am., 648 F.3d 295, 304 (6th Cir. 2011).
138 *Id.*
139 MODEL PENAL CODE § 2.02(2)(c). The Model Penal Code elaborates that "[t]he risk must be of such a nature and degree that, considering the nature and purpose of the actor's conduct and the circumstances known to him, its disregard involves a gross deviation from the standard of conduct that a law-abiding person would observe in the actor's situation."

Often, individuals will be found to have violated *both* Sections (a)(5)(A) and (a)(5)(B) with a single act. For instance, in the *Citrin* case described earlier, in which the Seventh Circuit concluded that the defendant violated Section (a)(5)(A) by deleting his former employers' files and installing a secure-erasure program to permanently wipe the memory, the court concluded that the defendant *also* violated Section (a)(5)(B). The court concluded that he did not have authorized access after he left the company, and that his intentional access recklessly caused damage because "he resolved to destroy files that incriminated himself and other files that were also the property of his employer, in violation of the duty of loyalty that agency law imposes on an employee."[140]

5.1.3.5.3   CFAA Section (a)(5)(C): Intentional Access Without Authorization that Causes Damage and Loss

Section (a)(5)(C) requires prosecutors to demonstrate three general elements: (1) intentional access of a protected computer; (2) without authorization; and (3) as a result of the access, causes damage and loss.

Section (a)(5)(C) is quite similar to Section (a)(5)(B), with two key differences: Section (a)(5)(C) applies even if the damage was not recklessly caused, therefore allowing it to apply to a wider range of actions. However, Section (a)(5)(C) only applies if the defendant caused both damage *and* loss, whereas Section (a)(5)(B) only requires a showing of damage. "Loss" under the CFAA is defined as "any reasonable cost to any victim, including the cost of responding to an offense, conducting a damage assessment, and restoring the data, program, system, or information to its condition prior to the offense, and any revenue lost, cost incurred, or other consequential damages incurred because of interruption of service."[141] The next subsection, which covers the requirements for misdemeanors and felony convictions under Section (a)(5), explains how courts have interpreted the definition of "loss" for the purposes of CFAA cases.

5.1.3.5.4   CFAA Section (a)(5): Requirements for Felony and Misdemeanor Cases

Any violation of Section (a)(5) can be charged as a misdemeanor, punishable by a fine and up to a year in prison. However, if prosecutors seek more than a year in prison, they must charge the defendant with a felony. Section (a)(5) only allows felony charges in certain situations.

First-Time Violations of Sections (a)(5)(A) or (a)(5)(B), without Aggravating Factors   To convict a defendant of a felony under Sections (a)(5)(A) or (a)(5)(B), if the defendant had not been convicted under the CFAA before

---

140 Int'l Airport Ctrs., LLC v. Citrin, 440 F.3d 418, 420 (7th Cir. 2006).
141 18 U.S.C. § 1030(e)(11).

committing the act, prosecutors must demonstrate that the offense caused one of the following:

- loss to one or more persons during a single year, totaling at least $5,000 in value;
- the "modification or impairment, or potential modification or impairment, of the medical examination, diagnosis, treatment, or care of at least one individual";
- "physical injury to any person";
- public health or safety threat;
- damage to a federal government computer "in furtherance of the administration of justice, national defense, or national security"; or
- damage to at least ten protected computers during a single year.[142]

If the government can establish one of these forms of harm, it can seek a fine and imprisonment of up to ten years under Section (a)(5)(A), and a fine and imprisonment of up to five years under Section (a)(5)(B). If the government cannot establish one of those forms of harm, these violations are punishable as misdemeanors, with a fine and up to a year in prison. According to the Justice Department's Computer Crime manual, felonies under Sections (a)(5)(A) and (a)(5)(B) are most often charged under the first scenario on the list: causing a loss to one or more persons of at least $5,000 over a one-year period.[143]

When courts determine whether a Section (a)(5) charge is punishable as a felony due to a loss, they must decide whether the government has adequately alleged at least $5,000 in losses. Congress's 2001 amendments that defined "loss" were modeled after an opinion issued a year earlier by the U.S. Court of Appeals for the Ninth Circuit, *United States v. Middleton*.[144] The government brought a Section (a)(5)(A) charge against Nicholas Middleton, the former employee of an Internet service provider. After leaving the ISP, he allegedly accessed an administrative account to create new accounts, change administrative passwords, modify the computer's registry, and delete the ISP's billing system and other databases.[145] The ISP stated that it devoted well over 100 hours of staff time to recovering from the damage caused by this access, and that it purchased new software. At his criminal trial, the judge denied his request to instruct the jury using his preferred definition of "damage," and he was convicted of a Section (a)(5)(A) violation.

---

142 18 U.S.C. § 1030(c)(4)(A)(i).
143 U.S. JUSTICE DEPARTMENT, PROSECUTING COMPUTER CRIMES, at 42.
144 United States v. Middleton, 231 F.3d 1207 (9th Cir. 2000). Until Congress amended the CFAA in 2008 to add a Section (a)(5)(A) misdemeanor provision, the government only had the option of charging Section (a)(5)(A) violations as a felony.
145 *Id*. at 1209.

On appeal, Middleton argued that the government had not demonstrated that he caused at least $5,000 in losses. The government had alleged that he caused approximately $10,000 in losses, and it arrived at this estimate by calculating the amount of time that each employee spent on remediation, and multiplying it by their hourly rates, and adding the nonstaff costs (such as new software).[146] Middleton asserted that this method was incorrect because at least one of the employees was paid on a fixed salary and therefore the alleged damage did not result in additional charges. The Ninth Circuit agreed with the government's calculation, and concluded that whether the employee is hourly or salaried is irrelevant; the proper question is "whether the amount of time spent by the employees and their imputed hourly rates were reasonable for the repair tasks that they performed[.]"[147] Applying that definition to Middleton's case, the Ninth Circuit concluded that the jury was reasonable to find that Middleton's actions caused at least $5,000 in losses.[148]

The 2001 amendments to the CFAA, based at least partly on *Middleton*,[149] provide more clarity by defining "loss" as "any reasonable cost to any victim, including the cost of responding to an offense, conducting a damage assessment, and restoring the data, program, system, or information to its condition prior to the offense, and any revenue lost, cost incurred, or other consequential damages incurred because of interruption of service."[150] Few published opinions in Section (a)(5) criminal cases have interpreted this definition. However, there has been some dispute about its application in CFAA civil cases, which are discussed in Section 5.1.4 of this chapter.

First-Time Violations of Section (a)(5)(C)   Unlike the two other crimes in Section (a)(5), Section (a)(5)(C) does not provide for felony charges for first-time offenders. If a defendant has not been convicted of any other CFAA crime before violating Section (a)(5)(C), the government can only charge the defendant with a misdemeanor, punishable by a fine and up to a year in prison.

Repeat Violations under Section (a)(5)   If the defendant had been convicted of a CFAA crime before violating Section (a)(5), the penalties will be higher (and, in the cases of Sections (a)(5)(A) and (a)(5)(B), do not require proof of at least $5,000 in losses or the five other scenarios described earlier). A defendant previously convicted of a CFAA crime can be sentenced to a fine and up to 20 years in prison for violations of Section (a)(5)(A) and (a)(5)(B), and a fine and up to ten years in prison for violations of Section (a)(5)(C).

---

146 *Id.* at 1214.
147 *Id.*
148 *Id.*
149 See U.S. Justice Department, Prosecuting Computer Crimes, at 44.
150 18 U.S.C. § 1030(e)(11).

Aggravating Factors   In certain cases, an individual convicted of a Section (a)(5)(A) violation can receive a greater sentence, regardless of whether it is a first-time offense or the size of the losses caused by the hacking. If the defendant attempted to cause or knowingly or recklessly caused serious bodily injury via a Section (a)(5)(A) violation, she may be sentenced to a fine or up to 20 years in prison. If the defendant attempted to cause or knowingly or recklessly caused death via a Section (a)(5)(A) violation, she can be sentenced to a fine and up to a life term in prison.

5.1.3.6   CFAA Section (a)(6): Trafficking in Passwords

Section (a)(6) of the CFAA prohibits individuals from "knowingly and with intent to defraud traffic[king] in any password or similar information through which a computer may be accessed without authorization," provided that the trafficking either affects interstate or foreign commerce, or the computer is used by or for the federal government. Because of the relatively small penalties attached to Section (a)(6), it is among the less commonly prosecuted and litigated sections of the CFAA. Congress added Section (a)(6) to the CFAA in 1986, out of concern that "so-called 'pirate bulletin boards' have sprung up around the country for the sole purpose of exchanging passwords to other people's computer systems."[151]

Section (a)(6) is intended to broadly define the term "password," and cover a wide range of information that can be used to access a computer. The Senate Judiciary Committee's report accompanying the 1986 bill clarified that the legislators not only intended to protect the single string of characters commonly thought of as a "password," but also intended to cover "longer more detailed explanations on how to access others' computers."[152]

In the rare instances in which courts have written opinions interpreting Section (a)(6), there occasionally has been a dispute about the meaning of "trafficking." Section (a)(6) defines "traffic" as "transfer, or otherwise to dispose of, to another, or obtain control of with intent to transfer or dispose of." This is a fairly broad definition of "traffic," and it does not require evidence that the defendant sold the password or information for money. However, the defendant will not be liable for *receiving* passwords. For instance, in *State Analysis v. American Financial Services,*[153] a federal judge dismissed a Section (a)(6) civil claim filed by a database provider against a company that allegedly received a password for the database from another source. The court reasoned that such behavior does not qualify as "trafficking" for the purposes of the CFAA.[154]

---

151 S.R. Rep. No. 99-612, at 13 (1986).

152 *Id.* at 13.

153 State Analysis v. Am. Fin. Servs., 621 F. Supp. 2d 309 (E.D. Va. 2009).

154 *Id.* at 317 ("The Complaint does not allege that KSE transferred, or otherwise disposed of, AFSA's passwords; rather, it alleges that KSE received them from AFSA and used them without authorization.").

Even if the defendant trafficked in passwords, Section (a)(6) only applies if the prosecutor or plaintiff can demonstrate that the defendant did so with an intent to defraud. In *AtPac, Inc. v. Aptitude Solutions, Inc.*,[155] Nevada County, California was transitioning software service providers, from AtPac to Aptitude Solutions. To make the transition easier, Nevada County created a user account for Aptitude, potentially in violation of the county's user agreement with AtPac. An email allegedly instructed the county employee to "obfuscate the login so that AtPac doesn't know that we are working in the system."[156] AtPac sued the county and Aptitude for violating, among other provisions, Section (a)(6). The district court swiftly dismissed this claim. The court noted that merely providing another person with a password is not prohibited by Section (a)(6). That provision only applies, the court noted, if the defendant intended to defraud. Although the county employee's actions might have violated AtPac's license agreement, the court reasoned, there was no evidence that the county intended to defraud AtPac. The county's actions were "not the sort of fraud Congress envisioned when it made password trafficking subject to criminal penalties," the court wrote.[157]

Moreover, Section (a)(6) applies only if the traffic password allows a computer to be accessed "without authorization." The *AtPac* court concluded that this also provided it with a reason to dismiss the lawsuit. The court determined that under the CFAA, "a person cannot access a computer 'without authorization' if the gatekeeper has given them permission to use it."[158] AtPac had already given the county permission to log in to the server. The court wrote that it "cannot conclude that Congress intended to impose criminal liability on third parties just because a computer licensee violates a license agreement."[159]

That is not to say that all Section (a)(6) claims are futile. For instance, in a 2017 opinion in *Sprint Nextel Corporation v. Simple Cell, Inc.*,[160] a federal judge in Maryland denied summary judgment dismissal of a Section (a)(6) claim that Sprint brought against a company that allegedly resold Sprint phones on the secondary market. Sprint alleged that the reseller hired an outside party to hack Sprint's systems to verify whether the phones obtained by the reseller had "clean" electronic serial numbers that would enable resale. The court allowed the claim to proceed, along with a claim under (a)(4), finding that Sprint had presented evidence that the defendant hired a third party to conduct such checks: "Summary judgment on these CFAA claims will be denied in order to allow further

---

155 AtPac, Inc. v. Aptitude Sols., Inc., 730 F. Supp. 2d 1174 (E.D. Cal. 2010).
156 *Id*. at 1177.
157 *Id*. at 1183.
158 *Id*. at 1180.
159 *Id*.at 1183.
160 Sprint Nextel Corp. v. Simple Cell Inc., 248 F. Supp. 3d 663 (D. Md. 2017).

development of the record at trial as to whether Simple Cell had an intent to defraud and whether the other elements of these two CFAA claims are met."[161]

If the defendant has not been convicted of a CFAA violation before violating Section (a)(6), the defendant can be sentenced to a fine and no more than a year in prison. If the defendant has been convicted of a CFAA violation before violating Section (a)(6), the defendant can be sentenced to a fine and up to ten years in prison.

5.1.3.7 CFAA Section (a)(7): Threatening to Damage or Obtain Information from a Computer

Section (a)(7) prohibits individuals from transmitting in interstate or foreign commerce any communication containing three types of threats or demands: (1) "threat to cause damage to a protected computer;" (2) "threat to obtain information from a protected computer without authorization or in excess of authorization or to impair the confidentiality of information obtained from a protected computer without authorization or by exceeding authorized access;" or (3) a demand or request for "money or other thing of value in relation to damage to a protected computer, where such damage was caused to facilitate the extortion."[162] Section (a)(7) only applies if the defendant was acting with intent to extort from any person any money or other thing of value.

Unlike Sections (a)(1)–(a)(5), Section (a)(7)'s applicability does not depend on whether the defendant *actually* accessed, damaged, or obtained information from a computer. Instead, Section (a)(7) applies to the defendant's *attempt* to extort money from a victim by threatening a computer crime.

Section (a)(7) addresses a similar crime that is prohibited by the Hobbs Act, a 1948 federal extortion law. That statute imposes a sentence of a fine and up to 20 years in prison on any individual who "threatens physical violence to any person or property."[163] In the 1996 Senate Report accompanying the CFAA amendments, Section (a)(7)'s authors wrote that Section (a)(7) was necessary because the term "property" in the Hobbs Act "does not clearly include the operation of a computer, the data or programs stored in a computer or its peripheral equipment, or the decoding keys to encrypted data."[164] The government likely could attempt to argue that computers, networks, and data are property under the Hobbs Act, but it wanted a more direct route to prosecute online extortionists that would present less legal uncertainty. In fact, defendants who are charged with violating Section (a)(7) are often also charged with violating the Hobbs Act.

---

161 *Id.* at 690.
162 18 U.S.C. § 1030(a)(7).
163 18 U.S.C. § 1951.
164 S. Rep. No. 104-367 (1996), at 12.

Section (a)(7) is relatively new to the CFAA. Congress added the provision in 1996, after the U.S. Justice Department reported that hackers had increasingly made threats to penetrate computer systems. In the Senate report accompanying the 1996 amendments to the CFAA, the legislators expressed a desire to "address a new and emerging problem of computer-age blackmail."[165]

In fact, Congress's motivations for amending the CFAA appear to have been quite prescient more than two decades later. As Congress explained:

> One can imagine situations in which hackers penetrate a system, encrypt a database and then demand money for the decoding key. This new provision would ensure law enforcement's ability to prosecute modern-day blackmailers, who threaten to harm or shut down computer networks unless their extortion demands are met.[166]

Sound familiar? Twenty years after Congress enacted Section (a)(7), ransomware became among the most concerning trends in cybersecurity. Theoretically, Section (a)(7) provides a very direct mechanism to bring criminal and civil actions against hackers who have used ransomware to attempt to extort money from companies and individuals. However, many of the most egregious ransomware distributors hide behind well-masked anonymity, making prosecutions and civil lawsuits quite difficult. They use Bitcoin as the payment currency, further cloaking their identities and hampering law enforcement's ability to track them.

Ransomware—and other extortion attempts—often originate from other countries. Congress contemplated this problem in 1996 when it drafted Section (a)(7), and explicitly stated that it covers threats used in both interstate *and* foreign commerce. The government used this ability to prosecute foreign extortionists in *United States v. Ivanov*.[167] Aleksey Ivanov allegedly gained unauthorized access to the computer system of a Connecticut company that processes online retailers' credit card transactions. While he was located in Russia or another former Soviet bloc country, Ivanov emailed the company to inform it that he had obtained its system administrator root passwords, threatened to destroy its database, and demanded $10,000.[168] Among the email messages that he sent was the following:

> [name redacted], now imagine please Somebody hack you network (and not notify you about this), he download Atomic

---

165 *Id.*
166 *Id.*
167 United States v. Ivanov, 175 F. Supp. 2d 367 (D. Conn. 2001).
168 *Id.* at 369.

software with more than 300 merchants, transfer money, and after this did 'rm-rf/' and after this you company be ruined. I don't want this, and because this i notify you about possible hack in you network, if you want you can hire me and im allways be check security in you network. What you think about this?[169]

Ivanov was indicted in federal court in Connecticut on eight counts, including a violation of Section (a)(7). Ivanov filed a motion to dismiss the indictment, arguing that because he was in Russia or another Soviet bloc country at the time of the alleged email threats, the CFAA and other statutes could not apply to him. The district court denied this motion for two reasons. First, it reasoned that if an individual violates a law with the intent to cause effects within the United States, then U.S. courts have jurisdiction to hear criminal cases involving that action.[170] Ivanov allegedly transmitted a threat to a company located in Connecticut, and threatened to further damage its computers, also located in Connecticut.[171] Second, the court concluded that Section (a)(7)'s explicit reference to computers used in "foreign" commerce demonstrated an intent of Congress to apply the statute extraterritorially.[172] "Congress has the power to apply its statutes extraterritorially, and in the case of 18 U.S.C. 1030, it has clearly manifested its intention to do so," the court wrote.[173]

Courts have generally required a Section (a)(7) indictment or civil claim to provide proof of an explicit threat. Merely hacking to cause damage or obtain information will not sustain a Section (a)(7) claim, even if that action violates other parts of the CFAA. In Ivanov's case, the email was clear proof of an explicit threat that violates Section (a)(7).

In other cases, however, the evidence of a threat is not as compelling. In Vaquero Energy v. Herda,[174] Vaquero Energy, an oil and gas collection and installations company, hired Jeff Herda to provide information technology support. Vaquero Energy alleges that Herda and his company changed the passwords to SCADA systems and devices without Vaquero Energy's permission.[175] Vaquero Energy claimed that it asked Herda to provide "logins and passwords to the various server, firewalls, and any other devices," but Herda provided incomplete information, and that he later stopped providing services to the company. Vaquero Energy claimed that its lack of password information left its

---

169 *Id.*
170 *Id.* at 370.
171 *Id.* at 372.
172 *Id.* at 374.
173 *Id.* at 375.
174 Vaquero Energy v. Herda, Case No. 1:15-cv-00967 JLT, 2015 U.S. Dist. LEXIS 126122 (E.D. Cal. Sept. 25, 2015).
175 *Id.* at *3.

systems vulnerable and insecure, and sued Herda under a number of statutes, including Section (a)(7) of the CFAA. The court concluded that the Section (a)(7) claim failed because Vaquero Energy did not allege that Herda made a threat or demand. Although Vaquero Energy's lawyer demanded that Herda provide the passwords, and Herda responded, the court concluded that this alleged exchange did not constitute a demand or threat made by Herda.[176] Moreover, the court found that the claim also failed because there was no allegation that Herda changed the password in order to extort money. The *Vaquero Energy* case demonstrates the need for prosecutors and civil litigants to allege a specific threat and intent to extort money.

A defendant who is convicted of a violation of Section (a)(7) faces a fine and up to five years in prison. If the defendant had been convicted of a CFAA offense before violating Section (a)(7), the defendant faces a fine and up to ten years in prison.

5.1.4 Civil Actions Under the CFAA

Although the CFAA is a criminal statute that is enforced by federal prosecutors, the statute allows certain private parties that have suffered a damage or loss due to CFAA violations to bring civil actions against the violators. Indeed, many of the CFAA cases discussed in this section involve civil litigation between two private parties. This is partly due to the nature of the acts that constitute CFAA violations: obtaining information or causing damage without proper authorization. These actions often cause significant harm to companies, which understandably seek compensation. Moreover, private CFAA claims often arise in high-stakes disputes with former employees who later work for a competitor.

CFAA lawsuits must be brought within two years of the harmful act, or the date of discovery of the damage.[177] The statute prohibits private CFAA lawsuits that arise from the negligent design or manufacture of hardware, software, or firmware.

The CFAA only allows private litigants to sue if they have suffered a "damage" or "loss." The CFAA defines "damage" as "any impairment to the integrity or availability of data, a program, a system, or information,"[178] and defines "loss" as "any reasonable cost to any victim, including the cost of responding to an offense, conducting a damage assessment, and restoring the data, program, system, or information to its condition prior to the offense, and any revenue

---

176 *Id.* at *13.
177 18 U.S.C. § 1030(g).
178 18 U.S.C. § 1030(e)(8).

lost, cost incurred, or other consequential damages incurred because of inter-ruption of service."[179]

Courts generally have applied broad definitions of these terms. For instance, in the *Shurgard Storage Centers* case, discussed in Section 5.1.3.4 of this chapter, the plaintiff alleged that its former employee's use of its com-puter systems to send trade secrets to the defendant, its competitor, caused damage under the CFAA.[180] The defendant contended that these actions did not constitute "damage" for the purpose of the required element in a Section 1030(a)(5) claim because there was not any *impairment* to data's integrity or availability, as required in the statute.[181] The court acknowledged that the term "integrity," in this context, is "ambiguous." To resolve the dispute, the court looked to the Senate report accompanying the 1996 CFAA amend-ments, which changed the definition of "damage." The Senate wrote that it intended the term "damage" to include the "theft of information by com-puter"—such as passwords—even if the original data was not altered or rendered inaccessible. Applying this broad definition of "damage" to Shurgard Storage's claims, the court concluded that even though the confi-dential business information remained intact and unharmed on the compa-ny's computers, the integrity of the data was impaired because it was stolen. The court reasoned that "the defendant allegedly infiltrated the plaintiff's computer network, albeit through different means than in the example, and collected and disseminated confidential information. In both cases no data was physically changed or erased, but in both cases an impairment of its integrity occurred."[182] Therefore, the court held that the plaintiffs had suf-ficiently alleged damage under Section (a)(5)(C) of the CFAA.[183]

In some cases, it may be easier for a plaintiff to demonstrate a "loss" than to demonstrate "damage." For instance, in 2016, RSM, an audit and consult-ing firm, filed a CFAA civil claim against former employees who, while still employed, allegedly downloaded confidential client files and provided them to a former employee who had already left the firm.[184] The court concluded that the downloading was not "damage" because RSM "has not alleged any destruction or impairment to its computer systems. Defendants allegedly copied and downloaded files, but RSM has not alleged that any data, pro-grams, systems, or files were altered by these actions."[185] However, the court concluded that because RSM had claimed that the alleged incident caused

---

179 *Id.*
180 Shurgard Storage Ctrs. v. Safeguard Self Storage, 119 F. Supp. 2d 1121 (W.D. Wash. 2000).
181 *Id.* at 1126.
182 *Id.* at 1127.
183 *Id.* at 1126–27.
184 RSM US v. Bober, No. 16 C 4297 (N.D. Ill. 2016).
185 *Id.*

the company to spend more than \$5,000 on investigations, the company stated a claim for a loss.[186]

Even if private parties have suffered a damage or loss, they may only bring CFAA lawsuits in certain circumstances. To establish the right to file a civil action, the plaintiff must allege that the CFAA violation resulted in one of the following:

I) loss to 1 or more persons during any 1-year period (and, for purposes of an investigation, prosecution, or other proceeding brought by the United States only, loss resulting from a related course of conduct affecting 1 or more other protected computers) aggregating at least \$5,000 in value;

II) the modification or impairment, or potential modification or impairment, of the medical examination, diagnosis, treatment, or care of 1 or more individuals;

III) physical injury to any person;

IV) a threat to public health or safety; [or]

V) damage affecting a computer used by or for an entity of the United States Government in furtherance of the administration of justice, national defense, or national security.[187]

If the lawsuit alleges only a loss to a person that totals at least \$5,000, the plaintiff may recover only economic damages. However, if the lawsuit alleges any of the four other types of harms arising from the CFAA violation, the plaintiff may obtain compensatory damages, injunctive relief, and other equitable relief.[188]

The statute provides a right to economic damages if the offense caused "loss to 1 or more persons during any 1-year period (and, for purposes of an investigation, prosecution, or other proceeding brought by the United States only, loss resulting from a related course of conduct affecting 1 or more other protected computers) aggregating at least \$5,000 in value."[189] For instance, in *Creative Computing v. Getloaded.com LLC*,[190] the Ninth Circuit considered a civil action under Section (a)(4) that the operator of a trucking services website, Creative Computing, filed against a competitor, Getloaded.com. Creative Computing alleged that Getloaded.com used its customers' credentials to obtain information from Creative Computing's website. Creative Computing also alleged that Getloaded.com's officers accessed Creative Computing's website code without authorization, and hired a

---

186 *Id.*

187 18 U.S.C. § 1030(g); 18 U.S.C. § 1030(c)(4)(A)(i).

188 18 U.S.C. § 1030(g).

189 18 U.S.C. § 1030(c)(4).

190 Creative Computing v. Getloaded.com LLC, 386 F.3d 930 (9th Cir. 2004).

former Creative Computing employee, who downloaded confidential information.[191] With all of this data, Creative Computing alleged, Getloaded.com attempted to replicate Creative Computing's website and business model. Getloaded.com sought to dismiss the lawsuit, arguing that the CFAA only applies if the plaintiff suffered at least $5,000 in damages from *each* instance of unauthorized access.[192] The Ninth Circuit rejected this reading of the statute, holding that the $5,000 minimum "applies to how much damage or loss there is to the victim over a one-year period, not from a particular intrusion."[193]

The Eleventh Circuit elaborated on the meaning of "loss" under the CFAA in a 2017 case, *Brown Jordan International v. Carmicle*.[194] In that case, a company brought a CFAA claim against a terminated employee who allegedly accessed coworkers' email accounts. The defendant argued that because the company did not experience an "interruption of service" from the alleged act, it did not suffer a "loss" under the CFAA. The Eleventh Circuit disagreed, reading the definition of "loss" in the CFAA to include "interruption of service" as only one type of cost. "The plain language of the statutory definition includes two separate types of loss: (1) reasonable costs incurred in connection with such activities as responding to a violation, assessing the damage done, and restoring the affected data, program system, or information to its condition prior to the violation; and (2) any revenue lost, cost incurred, or other consequential damages incurred because of interruption of service," the court wrote. "The statute is written in the disjunctive, making the first type of loss independent of an interruption of service."[195] The court held that "loss" also could include payments to an outside consultant.

Particularly in early stages of litigation, courts are reluctant to second-guess the estimated value of alleged losses. For instance, a 2018 case, *Hill v. Lynn*, involved a business, FoodTrace, that was a collaboration between the plaintiff and the defendant. After their business relationship deteriorated, the defendant allegedly deleted the code for FoodTrace from the plaintiff's GitHub account. FoodTrace reportedly was later sold for $14 million. The plaintiff sued the defendant for, among other things, violating the CFAA. He estimated that the losses caused by the GitHub code deletion were "in excess of $75,000." The defendant moved to dismiss, claiming that the plaintiff failed to adequately plead a loss. The district court denied the motion: "Although there is not much explanation for the $75,000 figure, the allegations in the complaint are enough for a plausible inference that the code was worth at least that much, and indeed much more. FoodTrace was reportedly sold for $14 million, so it is fair to infer that the code that formed the

---

191 *Id*. at 932.
192 *Id*. at 933.
193 *Id*. at 934.
194 Brown Jordan Int'l, Inc. v. Carmicle, 846 F.3d 1167 (11th Cir. 2017).
195 *Id*. at 1174.

basis of the business (and [the plaintiff's] claimed share of its value) was worth much more than the $5,000 required by the CFAA."[196]

5.1.5 Criticisms of the CFAA

Companies, government agencies, and advocacy groups have criticized the CFAA, effectively presenting many proposals to amend—and in some cases, repeal—the CFAA. Some argue that the CFAA is far too punitive in light of the relatively minor acts that it prohibits, while others argue that it does not effectively prevent some of the most pressing cybersecurity threats.

Some of the most prominent criticisms of the CFAA come from advocacy groups and some legislators, who argue that the CFAA imposes significant criminal penalties on technical violations of the CFAA that do little or no harm to people or property. Perhaps their most compelling argument comes from the case of Aaron Swartz, who as a teenager helped develop Reddit and the technology underlying RSS news feeds.[197] Throughout his teens and twenties, Swartz was an active member of the CopyLeft movement, which challenged the ability of companies to control the distribution of their materials on the Internet.[198]

In 2010, Swartz, while working at a laboratory at Harvard, accessed the Massachusetts Institute of Technology's network and, without the school's approval, downloaded millions of articles via the school's access to JSTOR, a proprietary database. In 2011, Swartz was arrested, and later indicted in federal court for 11 counts under CFAA Sections (a)(2), (a)(4), and (a)(5), as well as 2 counts of wire fraud, exposing Swartz to up to 35 years in prison.[199] In 2013, at age 26, Swartz committed suicide.[200]

A number of critics used this tragedy to highlight what they viewed as significant problems with the CFAA. Justin Peters, in *Slate*, wrote that the Swartz suicide demonstrates the "disproportionate" nature of U.S. computer crime laws, and "the laxity with which these laws have been conceived and amended—and the increasing severity of their corresponding penalties—has had serious consequences."[201] Senator Ron Wyden introduced Aaron's Law, which would make the following changes to the CFAA:

- explicitly adopt the narrower *Nosal* reading of "exceeds authorized access" and clarify that merely violating an agreement does not trigger the CFAA;

---

196 Hill v. Lynn, No. 17 C 06318 (N.D. Ill. 2018).
197 *See RSS Creator Aaron Swartz Dead at 26*, HARVARD MAGAZINE (Jan. 14, 2013).
198 *See* Larissa MacFarquhar, *Requiem for a Dream*, NEW YORKER (Mar. 3, 2013).
199 Superseding Indictment, United States v. Swartz, Crim. No. 11-CR-10260-NMG (Sept. 12, 2012).
200 *See* MacFarquhar, *supra* note 198.
201 Justin Peters, *Congress Has a Chance to Fix Its Bad 'Internet Crime' Law*, SLATE (Apr. 24, 2015).

- prevent a defendant from being liable for multiple CFAA counts arising from a single incident; and
- prevent the prosecution for a single act under both the CFAA and state hacking laws.[202]

Cybersecurity researchers also are among the most vocal critics of the CFAA.[203] They argue that the rigid requirements of many CFAA sections have a chilling effect on researchers who seek to help companies find and patch vulnerabilities in their systems and networks. Zach Lanier, a cybersecurity researcher, told the *Guardian* newspaper in 2014 that after he informed a device maker of a security vulnerability that he had discovered, he received a response from the device maker's lawyer, who claimed that Lanier had violated the CFAA. Lanier said that this threat caused him to abandon the research on this flaw. "The looming threat of CFAA as ammunition for anyone to use willy-nilly was enough," Lanier told the *Guardian*, "and had a chilling effect on our research."[204]

Cybersecurity professionals also criticize the CFAA for limiting their ability to engage in active defense of their computers and networks (also known as "hacking back").[205] Consider a company that is barraged with attacks from a specific set of IP addresses. That company's information security professionals might be tempted to counterattack, in an attempt to knock the adversary offline. Unfortunately for the company, such responses pose a very real risk of violating Section (a)(5) of the CFAA. Critics of "hacking back" assert that it is difficult to attribute the source of an attack with 100 percent certainty, and therefore the retaliatory actions could hurt innocent bystanders. For instance, Robert M. Lee, co-founder of Dragos Security LLC, said that if "organizations cannot effectively run defense programs and tackle the security basics, they cannot run an effective offensive program."[206] They argue that the CFAA correctly prohibits individuals and companies from taking the law into their own hands.

---

202 S. 1030, 114th Congress.

203 *See* Kaveh Waddell, *Aaron's Law Reintroduced as Lawmakers Wrestle over Hacking Penalties*, THE ATLANTIC (Apr. 21, 2015) ("The CFAA in its current form is harmful to computer security researchers—who hack into devices and networks to find and expose vulnerabilities—according to the Electronic Frontier Foundation, because it exposes researchers to liability and punishment at the same level as malicious hackers.").

204 Tom Brewster, U.S. Cybercrime Laws Being Used to Target Security Researchers, THE GUARDIAN (May 29, 2014).

205 *See* Nicholas Schmidle, *The Digital Vigilantes Who Hack Back*, NEW YORKER (April 30, 2018) ("But now, in the wake of enormous cyberattacks on such companies as Uber, Equifax, Yahoo, and Sony—and Russian hackers' theft of e-mails from the Democratic National Committee's server—some members of Congress are trying to pass a significant revision of the Computer Fraud and Abuse Act. The changes would permit companies, and private citizens, that are victims of cybercrimes to hack back.").

206 Taylor Armerding, *Hack the Hackers? The Debate Rages On*, CSO (May 1, 2015).

Other proposals for reform are a bit more modest, as they are intended to modernize the CFAA to current technology and challenges. For instance, in a 2017 article, Bailey McGowan proposed a CFAA amendment to clarify that the statute protects data rather than computers. "This slight tweak covers the information stored electronically and is a better descriptor at the root of the litigation," McGowan wrote. "If an employee were to walk out of the office with the intent to steal their work computer, it would be theft. If the employee were to take the information from the computer, they are only stealing data."[207]

5.1.6 CFAA and Coordinated Vulnerability Disclosure Programs

Organizations have increasingly found that input from the public can lead to valuable information about the vulnerabilities of their websites, apps, software, and hardware. Unfortunately, well-intentioned white-hat hackers might be discouraged from informing organizations of these vulnerabilities, particularly in light of the expansive view of the CFAA that some courts have taken.

To address this disincentive, a number of companies and other organizations have adopted coordinated vulnerability disclosure programs, which provide guidelines and safe harbors for outside parties to report vulnerabilities (and, in some cases, receive recognition or compensation). Most importantly, the policies may provide limited authorization for people to participate in coordinated vulnerability disclosure programs, allowing them to report vulnerabilities without risking prosecution or civil actions. Coordinated vulnerability disclosure programs that offer awards are known as "bug bounty" programs.

In a 2017 article, Amit Elazari Bar On succinctly summarized some of the key benefits a bug bounty program may provide:

> Bug Bounty Programs proactively invite security researchers from around the world to expose the company's vulnerabilities in exchange for monetary and, sometimes more importantly, reputational rewards. If adequate report mechanisms are in place, Bug Bounty Programs could serve as an additional security layer, an external monitoring system, and provide management and directors with essential information concerning cyber vulnerabilities. Indeed, bug bounty programs are moving from the realm of novelty towards becoming best practice—but they can also serve as a corporate governance best practice, by operating as an additional objective and independent report system for management. Naturally, this will require the company's senior management and board to become more involved in the program, demand timely

---

207 Bailey McGowan, *Eject the Floppy Disk: How to Modernize the Computer Fraud and Abuse Act to Meet Cybersecurity Needs*, 14 SETON HALL CIR. REV. 19, 42 (2017).

reports, and that direct communication channels will be established. This is an increased standard both in terms of resources as well as time, but in the context of million-dollar breach damages, these preventative actions are worth the price.[208]

Facebook's Responsible Disclosure Policy, as of December 2018, stated that it "will not initiate a lawsuit or law enforcement investigation" against individuals who comply with the following policies:

- You give us reasonable time to investigate and mitigate an issue you report before making public any information about the report or sharing such information with others.
- You do not interact with an individual account (which includes modifying or accessing data from the account) if the account owner has not consented to such actions.
- You make a good faith effort to avoid privacy violations and disruptions to others, including (but not limited to) unauthorized access to or destruction of data, and interruption or degradation of our services.
- You do not exploit a security issue you discover for any reason. (This includes demonstrating additional risk, such as attempted compromise of sensitive company data or probing for additional issues.)
- You do not intentionally violate any other applicable laws or regulations, including (but not limited to) laws and regulations prohibiting the unauthorized access to data.
- For the purposes of this policy, you are not authorized to access user data or company data, including (but not limited to) personally identifiable information and data relating to an identified or identifiable natural person. [209]

In July 2017, the U.S. Justice Department provided a nonbinding framework for organizations to consider while designing and implementing their formal vulnerability disclosure programs.[210] Among the factors the Justice Department recommends that organizations consider when designing the programs are:

- The networks, systems, and types of data to include in the program (including whether to include sensitive data)

---

208 Amit Elazari Bar On, *Bug Bounty Programs as a Corporate Governance "Best Practice" Mechanism*, BERKELEY TECH. L.J. [online edition] (Mar. 23, 2017).

209 Facebook, *Responsible Disclosure Policy*, available at https://www.facebook.com/whitehat.

210 U.S. JUSTICE DEPARTMENT, A FRAMEWORK FOR A VULNERABILITY DISCLOSURE PROGRAM FOR ONLINE SYSTEMS, https://www.justice.gov/criminal-ccips/page/file/983996/download (July 2017).

- Legal restrictions, including contractual restrictions, on the data
- Potentially developing "restrictions on accessing, copying, transferring, storing, using, and retaining such information"
- Designating whether the vulnerability program "should differentiate among and specify the types of vulnerabilities (and perhaps poor security practices) that may be targeted." For instance, does the program only seek information about software vulnerabilities, or does it also seek information about poor security hygiene among the organization's employees?
- "[W]hether any of the network components or data within the scope of the vulnerability disclosure program implicates third-party interests and, therefore, whether they should be excluded from the program entirely or require the organization to obtain additional authorization before including them in the program." For instance, if the organization uses a cloud provider, the contract with that cloud provider may impose restrictions on the program.[211]

The Justice Department also suggests that organizations put thought into how they will administer the program. The department suggests that organizations "[p]rovide a readily available means of reporting discovered vulnerabilities, such as by identifying an email account to which reports should be sent and a public encryption key to be used to safeguard the information. Given the value and potential for abuse of some vulnerabilities, encrypting vulnerability reports is advisable."[212] The department advises against using an individual employee's email account to receive vulnerability reports. "Instead, create an account specifically for vulnerability reports that is accessible to all personnel responsible for handling vulnerability disclosures. A common naming convention for such an account is 'security@[organization].'"[213]

The Justice Department advises that organizations describe their programs in "a vulnerability disclosure policy that accurately and unambiguously captures the organization's intent" and is free of jargon.[214]

In October 2018, the U.S. House of Representatives Energy and Commerce Committee issued a white paper that strongly endorsed the use of coordinated vulnerability disclosure (CVD) programs, and suggested that Congress consider providing "legal certainty" to participants in the programs: "The nature of our modern connected society requires collaboration, and thus—as recent years have manifestly demonstrated—CVD remains one of the most valuable, effective methods for embracing that collaboration and facing those risks."[215]

---

211 *Id.*
212 *Id.*
213 *Id.*
214 *Id.*
215 House Energy & Commerce Committee, The Criticality of Coordinated Disclosure in Modern Cybersecurity (Oct. 2018).

The Story of Megan Meier, Lori Drew, and the CFAA

Among the highest profile CFAA cases in recent years was the U.S. government's unsuccessful attempt to prosecute Lori Drew under the statute. The story of Drew's prosecution demonstrates the limits of the CFAA in the increasingly complex world of social media and always-on connectivity.

Megan Meier, a 13-year-old Missouri girl, was contacted via MySpace by an individual calling himself "Josh Evans," a 16-year-old boy who appeared to be interested in pursuing a relationship with Meier. After flirting with Meier for a few weeks, Josh Evans told her that the world would be a better place without her in it. That same day, Meier committed suicide.

Josh Evans was not a teenage boy. Rather, he was a fictional character created as a result of a collaboration by Lori Drew, Meier's adult neighbor; Drew's teenage daughter; and an employee of Drew. The suicide—and the revelation that an adult was behind a deadly prank—grabbed national attention. However, Missouri prosecutors did not have a viable state law under which to bring charges against Drew.

Federal prosecutors in California, where MySpace is headquartered, decided to take matters into their own hands. They charged Drew with violating Section (a)(2) of the CFAA, alleging that she violated MySpace's terms of service to obtain information about Meier, therefore exceeding authorized access. At trial, the jury found her not guilty of three CFAA felony counts (which required a demonstration that she violated Section (a)(2) in furtherance of the tort of intentional infliction of emotional distress), but found her guilty of a misdemeanor count under Section (a)(2), which did not require a link to the emotional distress tort.

The district court judge set aside the jury's misdemeanor conviction of Drew, concluding that it would be unconstitutionally vague to convict someone based on the violation of a website's terms of service. The court reasoned that "if any conscious breach of a website's terms of service is held to be sufficient by itself to constitute intentionally accessing a computer without authorization or in excess of authorization, the result will be that section 1030(a)(2)(C) becomes a law that affords too much discretion to the police and too little notice to citizens who wish to use the Internet." The government did not appeal this decision.

The difficulty of convicting Drew of what was indisputably a horrendous act demonstrates the difficulty of applying the 1980s-era Computer Fraud and Abuse Act to many of the emerging social issues that arise online. In recent years, victims' rights groups have proposed many laws that create new civil and criminal remedies for online harassment.

Sources: *United States v. Drew*, 259 F.R.D. 449 (C.D. Cal. 2009); Jennifer Steinhauer, *Verdict in MySpace Suicide Case*, N.Y. TIMES (Nov. 26, 2008); Kim Zetter, *Lori Drew's Daughter 'Devastated by Friend's Suicide but Doesn't Feel Responsible*, WIRED (Nov. 24, 2008); P.J. Huffstutter, *A Town Fights Back in MySpace Suicide Case*, L.A. TIMES (Nov. 22, 2007).

5.2   State Computer Hacking Laws

Most states also have similar anti-hacking laws that apply to hacking that occurs within their boundaries.[216] Some state laws predate the CFAA, and might prohibit activities that are not addressed by the CFAA. Therefore, if you are considering the legal implications of computer fraud or hacking, you must consider not only the CFAA but also state law.

To illustrate the requirements of some state computer hacking laws—and the key differences from the CFAA—it is useful to examine California Penal Code 502, one of the most prominent and commonly prosecuted state computer crime laws. California Penal Code 502 explicitly penalizes 14 types of computer-related actions. California Penal Code 502 (edited slightly here for clarity and brevity) prohibits all of the following acts, provided that they were committed knowingly:

1) Accessing and without permission altering, damaging, deleting, destroying, or otherwise using any data, computer, computer system, or computer network in order to either (a) devise or execute any scheme or artifice to defraud, deceive, or extort, or (b) wrongfully control or obtain money, property, or data.

2) Accessing and without permission taking, copying, or making use of any data from a computer, computer system, or computer network, or taking or copying any supporting documentation, whether existing or residing internal or external to a computer, computer system, or computer network.

3) Without permission using or causing to be used computer services.

4) Accessing and without permission adding, altering, damaging, deleting, or destroying any data, computer software, or computer programs that reside or exist internal or external to a computer/computer system, or computer network.

5) Without permission disrupting or causing the disruption of computer services or denies or causes the denial of computer services to an authorized user of a computer, computer system, or computer network.

6) Without permission providing or assisting in providing a means of accessing a computer, computer system, or computer network.

7) Without permission accessing or causing to be accessed any computer, computer system, or computer network.

---

216 For a complete list of the state anti-hacking laws, visit the National Conference of State Legislatures website, which contains a list of the state laws and links to the full text of the laws. The website is available at http://www.ncsl.org/research/telecommunications-and-information-technology/computer-hacking-and-unauthorized-access-laws.aspx.

8) Introducing any computer contaminant into any computer, computer system, or computer network.
9) Without permission using the Internet domain name or profile of another individual, corporation, or entity in connection with the sending of one or more electronic mail messages or posts and thereby damages or causes damage to a computer, computer data, computer system, or computer network.
10) Without permission disrupting or causing the disruption of government computer services or denying or causing the denial of government computer services to an authorized user of a government computer, computer system, or computer network.
11) Accessing and without permission adding, altering, damaging, deleting, or destroying any data, computer software, or computer programs that reside or exist internal or external to a public safety infrastructure computer system computer, computer system, or computer network.
12) Without permission disrupting or causing the disruption of public safety infrastructure or denying or causing the denial of computer services to an authorized user of a public safety infrastructure computer system computer, computer system, or computer network.
13) Without permission providing or assisting in providing a means of accessing a computer, computer system, or public safety infrastructure computer system computer, computer system, or computer network in violation of this section.
14) Introducing any computer contaminant into any public safety infrastructure computer system computer, computer system, or computer network.[217]

Like the CFAA, California Penal Code 502 provides hacking victims with the ability to sue individuals who violate this statute and cause damage or loss.[218]

The most striking difference between California Penal Code Section 502 and the CFAA is that the California law enumerates twice as many prohibited acts. However, the statutes prohibit many of the same types of actions, though the California law is more specific, in part because it has been amended six times since 2000 and more directly addresses new technological issues. For instance, sections 4, 5, 10, 11, 12, and 14 all involve damage to computers, systems, or data, and many of these acts likely could fall under the broader umbrella of CFAA Section (a)(5).

The California hacking law also covers actions that the CFAA does not explicitly address. For instance, the prohibition in section 3 of the California law—related to the use of computer services without permission—criminalizes

---

217 CAL. PENAL CODE § 502(c).
218 CAL. PENAL CODE § 502(e).

the theft of services such as email and cloud storage. The CFAA does not directly address such a crime, though in some cases it could be covered under Section (a)(2)'s prohibitions regarding obtaining information. Likewise, Section 9 of the California law explicitly prohibits hacking Internet domain names to send spam. Although the CFAA does not address spam, there is a reasonable argument that in some cases, such activities cause damage in violation of Section (a)(5) of the CFAA.

Perhaps the largest overall difference between the California law and the CFAA is the type of access required to trigger the law's prohibition. As discussed earlier, the CFAA applies to acts that are done either without authorization or exceeding authorized access. In contrast, the California hacking law applies to access that is done knowingly and "without permission."

Unfortunately, the definition of "without permission" is not entirely clear. The statute does not define the term, and the California Supreme Court—which has the final authority in interpreting California state laws—has not weighed in on the issue. However, federal judges interpreting the California statute in civil cases have reached opposite conclusions.

In a 2007 case, *Facebook, Inc. v. ConnectU*,[219] a California federal judge refused to dismiss a complaint filed by Facebook alleging that ConnectU, a Facebook competitor, violated Section 502 by accessing the email addresses of "millions" of Facebook users, in violation of Facebook's terms of use. ConnectU argued that private companies such as Facebook should not be permitted to dictate terms of service that could lead to criminal penalties. The judge rejected this argument, reasoning that "[t]he fact that private parties are free to set the conditions on which they will grant such permission does not mean that private parties are defining what is criminal and what is not."[220]

5.3 Section 1201 of the Digital Millennium Copyright Act

Since the founding of the United States, laws have provided the authors of creative works and expressions with a copyright, which gives them a limited right to control the distribution, publication, and performance of their works. The U.S. Constitution encourages such protection, providing Congress with the ability to "promote the progress of science and useful arts, by securing for limited times to authors and inventors the exclusive right to their respective writings and discoveries."[221] For more than two centuries, copyright law has been

---

219 Facebook, Inc. v. ConnectU, 489 F. Supp. 2d 1087, 1089 (N.D. Cal. 2007).
220 *Id.* at 1091.
221 U.S. Const, art. I, § 8.

an integral part of the economic framework for producing books, newspapers, music, movies, and other creative expression. U.S. copyright law provides the creators of content with certain exclusive rights to control the republication, performance, and other uses of their content for a limited duration. Over the past two decades, as content such as books, music, and videos has increasingly moved online, Congress and regulators have grappled with determining how to apply copyright law to the Internet.

Section 1201 of the Digital Millennium Copyright Act (DMCA) restricts the ability of individuals to circumvent access controls that protect copyrighted material. Unlike other provisions in U.S. copyright law, which protect the rights of copyright owners to control the distribution, performance, copying, and other use of their protected works, Section 1201 protects the technology that companies use to control access to their works. Because of this close nexus with technology, Section 1201 is deeply intertwined with cybersecurity. Like the CFAA, it restricts the ability of individuals to access digital materials. However, it also has received a great deal of criticism for making it more difficult to perform vulnerability testing and other security research on any products, software, or services that contain access controls.

5.3.1 Origins of Section 1201 of the DMCA

In 1998, Congress enacted the Digital Millennium Copyright Act, which significantly amended U.S. copyright laws to implement the World Intellectual Property Organization's (WIPO's) Copyright Treaty and, more generally, "to make digital networks safe places to disseminate and exploit copyrighted materials."[222] The law contains many important and noteworthy provisions, such as Section 512, which establishes a process by which websites and other online services may be notified of infringing content on their services, and under which they must remove that content to avoid being sued for copyright infringement. For the purposes of cybersecurity, however, the most relevant DMCA provision is Section 1201.

Section 1201 of the DMCA is intended to satisfy the WIPO Copyright Treaty's requirement regarding circumvention. In the Senate report accompanying the DMCA, legislators stated that they intended to punish the circumvention of measures that are intended to protect copyrighted works, such as passwords, if the "primary purpose" of that circumvention is to break the control. The report states that such prohibitions are analogous to "making it illegal to break into a house using a tool, the primary purpose of which is to

---

222 S. Rep. No. 105-190 (1998) at 1.

break into houses.”²²³ The House report accompanying the DMCA explained the goals of the United States and WIPO in addressing circumvention in the copyright law:

> The treaties address the problems posed by the possible circumvention of technologies, such as encryption, which will be used to protect copyrighted works in the digital environment and to secure on-line licensing systems. To comply with the treaties, the U.S. must make it unlawful to defeat technological protections used by copyright owners to protect their works. This would include preventing unauthorized access as well as the manufacture and sale of devices primarily designed to decode encrypted copyrighted material.²²⁴

5.3.2 Three Key Provisions of Section 1201 of the DMCA

Section 1201 of the DMCA has three separate provisions that each restrict certain actions regarding access controls:

- Section (a)(1) prohibits the act of **circumventing** technology that controls access to copyrighted material.
- Section (a)(2) prohibits **trafficking** in technology that facilitates circumvention of access control measures.
- Section (b)(1) prohibits **trafficking** in technology that facilitates circumvention of measures that protect against copyright infringement.

This subsection examines each of these restrictions, and how courts have interpreted them.

5.3.2.1 DMCA Section 1201(a)(1)

Section 1201(a)(1) of the DMCA is perhaps the most direct of the three sections. It prohibits individuals from circumventing “a technological measure that effectively controls access to a work” that is protected by copyright law.²²⁵

Congress included Section (a)(1) because, at the time the DMCA was passed, “the conduct of circumvention was never before made unlawful,” according to the Senate report accompanying the DMCA.²²⁶

At the outset, it is important to note that Section (a)(1) focuses solely on whether the defendant *circumvented* technology that protects access to a

---

223 *Id.* at 11.
224 H.R. Rep. No. 105-551, pt. 1 (1998), at 10.
225 17 U.S.C. § 1201(a)(1).
226 S. Rep. No. 105-190 (1998), at 12.

copyrighted work. As legislators stated when they drafted the DMCA, the types of actions prohibited by Section (a)(1) are analogous to "breaking into a locked room in order to obtain a copy of a book."[227] The legislators wrote that Section (a)(1) "establishes a general prohibition against gaining unauthorized access to a work by circumventing a technological protection measure put in place by the copyright owner where such protection measure otherwise effectively controls access to" a copyright-protected work.[228] Section (a)(1) does *not* restrict subsequent use, performance, or distribution of the copyrighted materials that are obtained via this circumvention; those activities are prohibited in other provisions of U.S. copyright law.[229]

The statute explicitly states that a technological measure "effectively controls access to a work" if the measure, "in the ordinary course of its operation, requires the application of information, or a process or a treatment, with the authority of the copyright owner, to gain access to the work."[230] Courts generally have broadly included many types of controls under this definition, and they typically do not require a high degree of technological sophistication for a control to qualify as a technological measure. For instance, in *IMS Inquiry Management Systems, LTD v. Berkshire Information Systems, Inc.*,[231] the plaintiff, which operated a magazine advertising tracking website, alleged that its competitor accessed its service without authorization and copied content, in violation of the user agreement.[232] The court concluded that the plaintiff's password protection constitutes an effective "technological measure" under Section (a)(1) because to access the plaintiff's service, "a user in the ordinary course of operation needs to enter a password, which is the application of information."[233]

The more difficult question under Section (a)(1), however, is whether the defendant *circumvented* a technological measure. Alleging that the defendant infringed the copyright of a work that is protected by a technological measure

---

227 H.R. Rep. No. 105-551, pt. 1, at 17 (1998).
228 *Id.* at 17–18.
229 *See* Universal City Studios v. Corley, 273 F.3d 429, 443 (2d Cir. 2001) ("[T]he DMCA targets the circumvention of digital walls guarding copyrighted material (and trafficking in circumvention tools), but does not concern itself with the use of those materials after circumvention has occurred."); H.R. Rep. No. 105-551, pt. 1, at 18 ("Paragraph (a)(1) does not apply to the subsequent actions of a person once he or she has obtained authorized access to a copy of a work protected under Title 17, even if such actions involve circumvention of additional forms of technological protection measures").
230 17 U.S.C. § 1201(3)(B).
231 IMS Inquiry Mgmt. Sys., LTD v. Berkshire Info. Sys., 307 F. Supp. 2d 521 (S.D.N.Y. 2004).
232 *Id.* at 523.
233 *Id.* at 531.

is not, by itself, sufficient to sustain a Section (a)(1) claim.[234] The statute defines "circumvent a technological measure" as "to descramble a scrambled work, to decrypt an encrypted work, or otherwise to avoid, bypass, remove, deactivate, or impair a technological measure, without the authority of the copyright owner."[235] In the *IMS* case, the court concluded that the plaintiff failed to allege that the defendants circumvented a technological measure.[236] The court reasoned that the plaintiff merely accused the defendant of using a "valid password" to access the site, and the defendant "is not said to have avoided or bypassed the deployed technological measure in the measure's gatekeeping capacity."[237] The court noted that unlike the CFAA, which prohibits access based on whether it is authorized and injurious, the DMCA is focused on *circumventing technology* that protects copyrighted content.[238] Similarly, a Texas federal judge in 2018 noted that many courts "have held that using the correct username and password to access a copyrighted work, even without authorization to do so, does not constitute circumvention under Section 1201(a) of the DMCA."[239] In this respect, the DMCA covers a narrower set of actions than the CFAA and other hacking laws.

Likewise, courts have made clear that Section (a)(1) violations do not occur merely because a user violates an agreement. For instance, in *Auto Inspection Services, Inc. v. Flint Auto Auction,*[240] the plaintiff, Auto Inspection Services (AIS), developed software for automobile inspections. One of its former customers, Flint Auto Auction (FAA), developed very similar software. One of the former FAA employees who helped develop the competing software testified that FAA provided him with a printout of Auto Inspection Services' software interface, and instructed him to design the software based on that interface.[241] Auto Inspection Services sued FAA for, among other things, a violation of Section (a)(1), and sought a preliminary injunction to effectively block the use of FAA's software.[242] The district court denied this request, concluding that

---

234 Dish Network, LLC v. World Cable, Inc., 893 F. Supp. 2d 452, 463 (E.D.N.Y. 2012) ("[M]erely alleging that a defendant 'accessed' a copyrighted work that is protected by a technological measure is not enough to state a claim for a violation of the DMCA. Rather, the plain language of the statute ... requires a plaintiff alleging circumvention (or trafficking) to prove that the defendant's access was unauthorized.") (internal citation and quotation marks omitted).
235 17 U.S.C. § 1201(3)(A).
236 IMS Inquiry Mgmt. Sys., LTD v. Berkshire Info. Sys., 307 F. Supp. 2d 521, 532 (S.D.N.Y. 2004).
237 *Id.*
238 *Id.*
239 Digital Drilling Data Sys. v. Petrolink Servs., Civil Action No. 4:15-CV-02172 (S.D. Tex. May 16, 2018).
240 Auto Inspection Servs. v. Flint Auto Auction, Case No. 06-15100, 2006 U.S. Dist. LEXIS 87366 (E.D. Mich. Dec. 4, 2006).
241 *Id.* at *4.
242 *Id.* at *6.

Auto Inspection Services failed to provide any evidence that "FAA circumvented a technological measure to gain access to AIS's work."[243]

Courts also require Section (a)(1) plaintiffs to allege in their complaints the *specific* technology that the defendant circumvented, and how that circumvention occurred. For instance, in *LivePerson, Inc. v. 24/7 Customer, Inc.,*[244] LivePerson, which makes real-time interaction software, filed a number of claims against 24/7 Customer, a competitor. The two companies had worked together at one point. LivePerson alleges that 24/7 Customer developed competing technology, in part by accessing LivePerson's back-end system and copying LivePerson's technology. In its complaint, LivePerson alleged that 24/7 used its access to LivePerson's systems to "observe, penetrate, and manipulate the operation of LivePerson's technology and download extensive data ... in order ... to reverse engineer and copy LivePerson's technology."[245] The court noted that LivePerson's complaint did not allege that 24/7 used reverse engineering to circumvent LivePerson's security measures, but rather that "LivePerson believes that 24/7 breached its security measures in an effort to reverse engineer and misappropriate the proprietary technology and methodologies that LivePerson pioneered," an allegation that the court concluded was not specific enough to constitute circumvention under the DMCA.[246]

Unlike the CFAA and other statutes, Section (a)(1) does not explicitly require the defendant to have acted in a specific mental state (e.g., "knowingly" or "intentionally") in order for the statute to apply to that conduct. However, courts might not allow a Section (a)(1) claim to move forward unless there is evidence that the defendant *actively* circumvented a technological measure that was designed to protect copyrighted material. If, for instance, the defendant accessed copyrighted material because the technological measure is not functioning properly, the plaintiff's claim likely will not succeed. In *Healthcare Advocates, Inc. v Harding, Earley, Follmer & Frailey,*[247] a law firm allegedly used the Internet Archive's Wayback Machine, www.archive.org, to investigate Healthcare Advocates, an organization that was suing the firm's client for trademark infringement. The Wayback Machine archives old versions of websites.[248] Healthcare Advocates used a robots.txt file on its website to prevent the Wayback Machine from archiving its old content. However, due to a malfunction with the Wayback Machine, the previous versions of the Healthcare Advocates website were available when the law firm searched for them.

---

243 *Id.* at *10.
244 LivePerson, Inc. v. 24/7 Customer, Inc., 83 F. Supp. 3d 501 (S.D.N.Y. 2015).
245 *Id.* at 510.
246 *Id.*
247 Healthcare Advocates, Inc. v Harding, Earley, Follmer & Frailey, 497 F. Supp. 2d 627 (E.D. Pa. 2007).
248 *Id.* at 631.

Healthcare Advocates sued the law firm under Section (a)(1), alleging that the firm obtained the archived websites by "hacking."[249] The district court agreed with the plaintiff that, in this context, the robots.txt file constituted a technological measure, as it was intended to prevent public access to archived screenshots of the company's website. However, the court disagreed with Healthcare Advocates—and dismissed the Section (a)(1) claim on summary judgment—because Healthcare Advocates did not provide any evidence that the law firm circumvented the measure. The court reasoned that the law firm employees had no reason to know that Healthcare Advocates used robots.txt, and therefore "[t]hey could not avoid or bypass any protective measure, because nothing stood in the way of them viewing these screenshots."[250]

Another dispute that arises in Section (a)(1) cases is whether the access control that was circumvented protects materials that are covered by U.S. copyright law. A good illustration of this inquiry can be seen in the Eighth Circuit's decision, *Davidson & Associates v. Jung*.[251] The plaintiff, a video game creator, offered a gaming website, Battle.net, which allowed users to play the games with others. To use Battle.net collaboratively, users were required to enter a "CD Key" that was included with CD-ROM games.[252] The defendants organized the bnetd project, a nonprofit project that emulated Battle.net and circumvented the need to use the actual website to play the games. To make their alternative site function with the games, they allegedly reverse-engineered the software to test the interoperability.[253] Users were able to access the plaintiff's games on bnetd without a CD Key.[254] The plaintiff sued the bnetd developers and organizers under Sections (a)(1) and (a)(2). The plaintiff alleged that the defendants violated Section (a)(1) by circumventing the CD Key requirement, which controlled access to the plaintiff's games.[255] The defendants argued that Battle.net is a "functional process" that is not protected by copyright because it does not constitute creative expression.[256] The Eighth Circuit rejected this argument and affirmed the district court's ruling that the defendants violated Section (a)(1).[257] "Here, Battle.net's control measure was not freely available," the court wrote. "Appellants could not have obtained a copy of Battle.net or made use of the literal elements of Battle.net mode without acts of reverse engineering, which allowed for a circumvention of Battle.net and Battle.net mode."[258]

---

249 *Id.* at 632.
250 *Id.* at 644.
251 Davidson & Assocs. v. Jung, 422 F.3d 630 (8th Cir. 2005).
252 *Id.* at 634–35.
253 *Id.* at 636.
254 *Id.*
255 *Id.* at 640.
256 *Id.* at 641.
257 *Id.*
258 *Id.*

Section (a)(1) cases often are not as complex as cases involving the other two subsections of the DMCA because the scope is relatively clear. As the U.S. Court of Appeals for the Second Circuit noted in 2001, Section (a)(1) differs from the other two DMCA subsections "in that it targets the use of a circumvention technology, not the trafficking in such a technology."[259] As we will see in the next subsection, the inquiry becomes much more complicated—and courts disagree more frequently—when the alleged DMCA violations arise from trafficking in circumvention technology.

5.3.2.2 DMCA Section 1201(a)(2)

Section 1201(a)(2) states that no person "shall manufacture, import, offer to the public, provide, or otherwise traffic in any technology, product, service, device, component, or part thereof" that:

a) "is primarily designed or produced for the purpose of circumventing a technological measure that effectively controls access" to a copyrighted work;
b) "has only limited commercially significant purpose or use other than to circumvent a technological measure that effectively controls access" to a copyrighted work; **or**
c) "is marketed by that person or another acting in concert with that person with that person's knowledge for use in circumventing a technological measure that effectively controls access" to a copyrighted work.[260]

In short, Section (a)(2) prohibits the *trafficking* of technology that is used to circumvent controls that protect access to copyrighted works.[261] In contrast, Section (a)(1) prohibits the actual act of circumvention of those controls. The House wrote that Section (a)(2) was "designed to protect copyright owners, and simultaneously allow the development of technology."[262] In the Senate report accompanying the DMCA, the legislators stated that Section (a)(2) would provide a cause of action against a company that manufactured a device that was designed to circumvent a control that only allowed authorized individuals to access the "plain text" of a copyrighted work.[263]

---

259 Universal City Studios v. Corley, 273 F.3d 429, 441 (2d Cir. 2001).

260 17 U.S.C. § 1201(a)(2).

261 *See* H.R. Rep. No. 105-551 Part 1, at 18 ("In order to provide meaningful protection and enforcement of the copyright owner's right to control access to his or her copyrighted work, this paragraph supplements the prohibition against the act of circumvention in paragraph (a)(1) with prohibitions on creating and making available certain technologies, products and services used, developed or advertised to defeat technological protections against unauthorized access to a work."); S. Rep. No. 105-190 (stating that the "device limitation in 1201(a)(2) enforces" 1201(a)(1)'s "new prohibition on conduct.").

262 H.R. Rep. No. 105-551 Part 1, at 18.

263 S. Rep. No. 105-190 (1998), at 12.

The primary legal dispute that arises in Section (a)(2) cases is whether the technology trafficked actually facilitates copyright infringement or other violations of rights protected by the Copyright Act. The DMCA does not directly address this issue, though Section 1201(c)(1) states that "[n]othing in this section shall affect rights, remedies, limitations, or defenses to copyright infringement, including fair use, under this title."[264] Section 1201(c)(1) might be read to merely prevent the anti-circumvention provisions from abrogating existing rights that owners and consumers have under the Copyright Act, but it also can be read to limit Section 1201's scope only to cases that involve circumvention that leads to actual copyright infringement.[265] In the House report accompanying the DMCA, legislators wrote that they included the provision "to ensure that none of the provisions in section 1201 affect the existing legal regime established in the Copyright Act and case law interpreting that statute."[266]

Courts have taken two very different approaches to interpreting the scope and reach of Section (a)(2). Some courts have taken a narrow approach, requiring a nexus between the access that is violated and the protection of copyright. Other courts, in contrast, have held that Section (a)(2) applies to technology that circumvents controls that are used to protect copyrighted content, regardless of whether that technology is *actually* used to access copyrighted content.

5.3.2.2.1 *Narrow Interpretation of Section (a)(2):* Chamberlain Group v. Skylink Technologies

The U.S. Court of Appeals for the Federal Circuit took the narrow approach to interpreting Section (a)(2) in a 2004 case, *Chamberlain Group v. Skylink Technologies*.[267] Chamberlain makes a garage door opener that uses a copyrighted "rolling code" software that "constantly changes the transmitter signal needed to open the garage door."[268] Skylink manufactures a fixed-code transmitter, Model 39, that circumvents the rolling code and enables users to open garage doors that are connected to Chamberlain's garage door openers.[269] Chamberlain argued that rolling code openers are more secure because they prevent burglars from "grabbing" the signal and using it later.

---

264 17 U.S.C. § 1201(c)(1).

265 *See* Universal City Studios v. Corley, 273 F.3d 429, 443 (2d Cir. 2001) (rejecting contention that 1201(c)(1) allows an exception for fair use, instead interpreting it as "simply clarify[ing] that the DMCA targets the *circumvention* of digital walls guarding copyrighted material (and trafficking in circumvention tools), but does not concern itself with the *use* of those materials after circumvention has occurred.").

266 H.R. Rep. No. 105-551 Part 1, at 20.

267 Chamberlain Group v. Skylink Techs., 381 F.3d 1178 (Fed. Cir. 2004).

268 *Id.* at 1183.

269 *Id.*

Chamberlain did not claim that Skylink infringed Chamberlain's copyright in the code. Instead, Chamberlain claimed that by selling a transmitter that circumvents Chamberlain's rolling code, Skylink violated Section (a)(2) by trafficking in a product that circumvents technology that protects copyrighted content.[270]

The Federal Circuit rejected Chamberlain's interpretation of Section (a)(2), concluding that for a plaintiff to state a valid Section(a)(2) claim, there must be a link between the access that is being circumvented and the *infringement* of copyrighted content. The court reasoned that Chamberlain's interpretation of the DMCA "ignores the significant differences between defendants whose accused products enable copying and those, like Skylink, whose accused products enable only legitimate uses of copyrighted software."[271] In other words, Section (a)(2) does not create a broad new property right; instead, it protects circumvention that is reasonably related to a property right that is currently provided by the Copyright Act. The court articulated this Section (a)(2) interpretation in a six-element test:

> A plaintiff alleging a violation of § 1201(a)(2) must prove: (1) ownership of a valid *copyright* on a work, (2) effectively controlled by a *technological measure,* which has been circumvented, (3) that third parties can now access (4) *without authorization,* in a manner that (5) infringes or facilitates infringing a right protected by the Copyright Act, because of a product that (6) the defendant either (i) *designed or produced* primarily for circumvention; (ii) made available despite only *limited commercial significance* other than circumvention; or (iii) *marketed* for use in circumvention of the controlling technological measure. A plaintiff incapable of establishing any one of elements (1) through (5) will have failed to prove a prima facie case. A plaintiff capable of proving elements (1) through (5) need prove only one of (6)(i), (ii), or (iii) to shift the burden back to the defendant.[272]

Although the Federal Circuit's six-part test largely relies on the wording of the statute, the Federal Circuit clearly emphasizes the need to demonstrate that the trafficked product helps circumvent access in order to violate an *existing* right under the copyright laws. Elaborating on this framework, the court concluded that it *necessarily* requires a link between the access circumvention and a violation of existing copyright law, and that Chamberlain failed to

---

270 *Id.* at 1185.
271 *Id.* at 1198.
272 *Id.* at 1203 (emphasis in original).

demonstrate such a link, and therefore failed to prove the fifth element of the six-part test:

> The DMCA does not create a new property right for copyright owners. Nor, for that matter, does it divest the public of the property rights that the Copyright Act has long granted to the public. The anticircumvention and anti-trafficking provisions of the DMCA create new grounds of liability. A copyright owner seeking to impose liability on an accused circumventor must demonstrate a reasonable relationship between the circumvention at issue and a use relating to a property right for which the Copyright Act permits the copyright owner to withhold authorization—as well as notice that authorization was withheld. A copyright owner seeking to impose liability on an accused trafficker must demonstrate that the trafficker's device enables either copyright infringement or a prohibited circumvention. Here, the District Court correctly ruled that Chamberlain pled no connection between unauthorized use of its copyrighted software and Skylink's accused transmitter. This connection is critical to sustaining a cause of action under the DMCA.[273]

Soon after the Federal Circuit issued its opinion in *Chamberlain*, courts quickly adopted its narrow interpretation of Section (a)(2). For instance, in 2005, the U.S. District Court for the Northern District of Illinois rejected a Section (a)(2) claim by the distributor of more than 3,300 copyrighted fonts against Adobe Systems, arising out of a feature on Adobe Acrobat that allowed users to select among the plaintiff's fonts when completing a PDF form.[274] The plaintiffs claimed that this feature was "only possible because Acrobat 5.0 allows the embedding bits set by Plaintiffs to be 'circumvented' in violation of the DMCA."[275] However, embedding bits do not actually prevent users from accessing the specifications for the fonts, which are available for free online.[276] The primary issue here arose from the second prong of the *Chamberlain* test: whether the embedding bits constituted a technological measure that "effectively controlled" access to the copyrighted fonts. The court concluded that the embedding bits did not satisfy this requirement, reasoning that an embedding bit "is a passive entity that does nothing by itself," and that the fonts had long been available to the public for free download. The court focused on the lack of technological restrictions placed on

---

273 *Id.* at 1204.
274 Agfa Monotype Corp. v. Adobe Sys., Inc., 404 F. Supp. 2d 1030 (N.D. Ill. 2005).
275 *Id.* at 1034.
276 *Id.* at 1031.

the fonts, reasoning that the plaintiffs' embedding bits are neither encrypted nor authenticated, and software such as Acrobat "need not enter a password or authorization sequence to obtain access to the embedding bits or the specification for the TrueType font."[277] Although the outcome of this case focused on the nature of the technological control, the overall approach was quite similar to that of *Chamberlain,* which was decided based on whether the control prevented copyright infringement. In both opinions, the court's broader inquiry was whether the technology actually protected against violation of rights provided in U.S. copyright law.

5.3.2.2.2 *Broad Interpretation of Section (a)(2):* MDY Industries, LLC v. Blizzard Entertainment

For more than five years, *Chamberlain* was viewed as the prevailing interpretation of Section (a)(2), and many district courts applied its relatively restrictive test to claims under the statute. This changed in 2010, when the U.S. Court of Appeals for the Ninth Circuit issued its opinion in *MDY Industries, LLC v. Blizzard Entertainment, Inc.*[278] That case arose from Glider, a game-playing bot that enabled World of Warcraft players to automatically win early levels of the game, allowing them to focus on the more advanced stages. The developer of Glider started a company, MDY Industries, which earned approximately $3.5 million from licensing Glider.[279]

In response to Glider, World of Warcraft's developer, Blizzard Entertainment, developed Warden, a technology designed to block the use of such bots on World of Warcraft.[280] Warden contained a "resident" component that occasionally scans a user computer's RAM while it is playing World of Warcraft to determine whether there are any activities that indicate the presence of an auto-playing bot.[281] Warden also used scan.dll, a software module, to scan a computer's RAM before allowing a connection to World of Warcraft's servers, and block connections if such bots were detected.[282] MDY responded to this feature by only allowing Glider to launch *after* scan.dll scanned the RAM for bots. MDY promoted its ability to circumvent World of Warcraft's detection systems as "additional protection from game detection software[.]"[283] Blizzard requested that MDY cease and desist, threatening to sue, and MDY responded by filing its own lawsuit, asking the

---

277 *Id.* at 1036.
278 MDY Indus., LLC v. Blizzard Entm't, 629 F.3d 928 (9th Cir. 2010).
279 *Id.* at 935–36.
280 *Id.* at 942.
281 *Id.*
282 *Id.*
283 *Id.* at 936.

court to declare that it did not violate the anti-circumvention provisions of Section 1201 of the DMCA.

Once the *Blizzard* case reached the U.S. Court of Appeals for the Ninth Circuit, the court refused to adopt the narrow interpretation of Section (a)(2) as stated in *Chamberlain*. Flatly rejecting the Federal Circuit's conclusion that Section 1201 does not create a new property right, the Ninth Circuit held that Section 1201(a) "creates a new anti-circumvention right distinct from the traditional exclusive rights of a copyright owner."[284] In short, the Ninth Circuit criticized the *Chamberlain* approach as ignoring the plain language of Section (a)(2). Although the *Chamberlain* court reasoned that its construction of the statute was more logical and sound public policy, the Ninth Circuit concluded that such considerations should not be a factor when the plain language of a statute is clear.[285]

Moreover, the Ninth Circuit noted that Section 1201(b)(1) (discussed later) already explicitly links a violation to copyright infringement.[286] Section (a)(2) applies when the defendant "circumvent[s] a technological measure," and the statute defines that term by providing two examples: "descrambling" scrambled work or "decrypting an encrypted work." The court noted that these acts "do not necessarily result in someone's reproducing, distributing, publicly performing, or publicly displaying the copyrighted work, or creating derivative works based on the copyrighted work."[287] In contrast, Section (b)(1) applies to defendants who "circumvent protection afforded by a technological measure" that "effectively protects the right of a copyright owner" under U.S. copyright law. Distinguishing between Sections (a)(2) and (b)(1) "ensures that neither section is rendered superfluous," the court wrote.[288] The court also recognized that the Senate Judiciary Report accompanying the DMCA stated that Sections (a)(2) and (b)(1) were "designed to protect two distinct rights and to target two distinct classes of devices," and that "many devices will be subject to challenge only under one of the subsections."[289]

Like the Federal Circuit, the Ninth Circuit articulated a six-element test that plaintiffs must satisfy in order to succeed on a Section (a)(2) claim. The tests differ, however, in that the Ninth Circuit does not require a *link* between the

---

284 *Id*. at 950.
285 *Id*. at 951 ("As a threshold matter, we stress that such considerations cannot trump the statute's plain text and structure.").
286 *Id*. at 950. *See also id*. at 944 ("[I]n contrast to § 1201(a), § 1201(b)(1) prohibits trafficking in technologies that circumvent technological measures that effectively protect 'a right of a copyright owner.' Section 1201(b)(l)'s prohibition is thus aimed at circumventions of measures that protect the copyright itself: it entitles copyright owners to protect their existing exclusive rights under the Copyright Act.").
287 *Id*. at 945.
288 *Id*. at 946.
289 *Id*. at 946–47, quoting S. REP. No. 105-190, at 12 (1998).

control measure and preventing copyright infringement. The Ninth Circuit stated that the plaintiff must demonstrate that the defendant:

> (1) traffics in (2) a technology or part thereof (3) that is primarily designed, produced, or marketed for, or has limited commercially significant use other than (4) circumventing a technological measure (5) that effectively controls access (6) to a copyrighted work.[290]

Applying this broader interpretation of Section (a)(2) to the World of Warcraft dispute, the Ninth Circuit considered three types of components of World of Warcraft: (1): the literal elements, which comprise "the source code stored on players' hard drives;" (2) the individual nonliteral elements, which are "the 400,000+ discrete visual and audible components of the game, such as a visual image of a monster or its audible roar;" and (3) the dynamic nonliteral elements, which it described as "real-time experience of traveling through different worlds, hearing their sounds, viewing their structures, encountering their inhabitants and monsters, and encountering other players."[291]

The Ninth Circuit concluded that under its definition of Section (a)(2), Glider does not violate Section (a)(2) with respect to the computer game's literal elements and individual nonliteral elements because "Warden does not effectively control access to these [World of Warcraft] elements."[292] The literal element, which is the computer game's code, resides on the player's hard drive, and not on the server.[293] Similarly, World of Warcraft users can access the individual nonliteral elements—such as a single sound or image—even if they do not connect to Blizzard's server.[294] Warden only blocks users from accessing the servers to play World of Warcraft online with other users; it does not prevent players from accessing the code, images, and sounds that are stored on their computers.

The Ninth Circuit, however, concluded that MDY likely violated Section(a)(2) regarding the dynamic nonliteral elements of the game, that is, the overall experience of playing the game and encountering other players.[295] The gist of the court's reasoning is that Warden controlled access to the overall display of the game online, which is protected by copyright law, and MDY trafficked in a technology—Glider—that it marketed as a means to circumvent Warden.[296]

---

290 *MDY Indus., LLC,* 629 F.3d at 953.

291 *Id.* at 942–43.

292 *Id.* at 952.

293 *Id.*

294 *Id.*

295 *Id.* at 953–54.

296 *Id.*

"For a player to connect to Blizzard's servers which provide access to WoW's dynamic non-literal elements, scan.dll must scan the player's computer RAM and confirm the absence of any bots or cheats," the court wrote. "The resident component also requires a 'process' in order for the user to continue accessing the work: the user's computer must report portions of WoW code running in RAM to the server."[297] The ruling on the dynamic nonliteral elements illustrates the significant difference between the Federal Circuit's approach to Section (a)(2) in *Chamberlain,* and the Ninth Circuit's approach in this case. If the Ninth Circuit had adopted the Federal Circuit's analytical framework for Section (a)(2), it is highly unlikely that it would have found that MDY violated the statute. Glider was not intended to help users *infringe* the copyright of World of Warcraft by copying or redistributing it; instead, Glider merely allowed users to advance through early stages of the game.

The Ninth Circuit's framework received some criticism for failing to appreciate the consequences of broader liability. For instance, one commentator wrote that the framework "is problematic because it ignores the serious policy consequences articulated by the Federal Circuit in *Chamberlain.* The Ninth Circuit brushed aside the potential antitrust or copyright misuse concerns of the Federal Circuit because they were not implicated by the facts of *MDY.*"[298] Another commentator wrote that the rulings are "completely incompatible, with the Ninth Circuit expressly rejecting the Federal Circuit's interpretation," and argued that "[t]he time is ripe for either a Supreme Court review or Congressional action to determine which court got it right."[299] As of the time that this book went to print in mid-2019, neither solution had occurred. Nor has the Ninth Circuit altered its interpretation of Section (a)(2). In a 2017 opinion, the Ninth Circuit flatly rejected a litigant's attempt to convince the court to adopt the *Chamberlain* interpretation, reasoning that "this panel is bound by *MDY.*"[300]

The fact that this broad view of Section (a)(2) was reached in the Ninth Circuit is particularly important because the Ninth Circuit covers the western United States, including California, which is home to many large technology companies that are more likely to bring anti-circumvention complaints. Unless the Ninth Circuit reverses its interpretation of Section (a)(2), or the United States Supreme Court decides to hear an anti-circumvention case and adopts the Federal Circuit's approach, the *MDY* interpretation of Section (a)(2) will remain binding precedent throughout the Ninth Circuit.

---

297 *Id.* at 954.
298 Michael Czolacz, *Decrypting DMCA Sec. 1201 in the Wake of the Ninth Circuit's Ruling in MDY Industries v. Blizzard Entertainment,* 11 Nw. J. Tech. & Intell. Prop. 441, 451 (2013).
299 Robert Arthur, *Federal Circuit v. Ninth Circuit: A Split Over the Conflicting Approaches to DMCA Section 1201,* 17 Marq. Intell. Prop. L. Rev. 265 (2013).
300 Disney Enters. v. VidAngel, 869 F.3d 848, 864 n.16 (9th Cir. 2017).

In a 2015 case in the U.S. District Court for the Central District of California, *NNG, KFT. v. AVA Enterprises, Inc.*,[301] plaintiff NNG, which makes navigation software, alleged that navigation device maker AVA violated Sections (a)(1) and (a)(2). NNG claimed that AVA installed pirated copies of NNG's software on its devices, along with software code that circumvents the authentication code that NNG uses to prevent unauthorized use of its software.[302] AVA moved to dismiss the complaint, contending that the authentication code "does not control access to the underlying software files or code," but rather simply validates whether the device is authorized to run NNG's software.[303] The authentication code only controls access to the dynamic nonliteral elements—namely, the experience of using the software. Because NNG did not allege that AVA infringed the copyright of the dynamic nonliteral elements, AVA argued, NNG could not claim a Section 1201(a) violation.[304] The district court rejected this argument, concluding that it "would be correct in other Circuits, but not here." The court recognized that because it is located in the Ninth Circuit, it is bound by the *MDY* holding that a Section 1201(a) claim does not necessarily have to be linked to an allegation of copyright infringement.[305] Applying *MDY* to the allegations in the lawsuit, the court reasoned that it is "undisputed that the technological measure in this case, the Authentication Code, effectively controls access to one element of NNG's copyrighted computer software—the dynamic non-literal elements."[306] NNG's failure to allege that AVA infringed the dynamic nonliteral elements "is of no consequence," the court concluded.[307]

The *NNG* case clearly demonstrates the huge divide among circuits in their interpretation of the scope of Section 1201(a). In the courts that adopt *Chamberlain's* ruling, Section 1201(a) protects only rights that are already provided in the copyright law, such as the ability to control the copying and distribution of copyrighted works. In the courts that adopt the *MDY* reading of the statute, Section 1201(a) creates a new right to prevent companies from distributing products that circumvent access controls. The *MDY* reading is particularly relevant to the cybersecurity profession because it creates a fairly powerful legal remedy for companies to pursue those who assist in bypassing technological controls.

---

301 NNG, KFT v. Ava Enters., Inc., Case No. 2:14-cv-00220-ODW(AJW), 2015 U.S. Dist. LEXIS 88742 (CD. Cal. July 8, 2015). ·

302 *Id.* at *3.

303 *Id.* at *4.

304 *Id.*

305 *Id.* at *10.

306 *Id.* at *11.

307 *Id.* at *13. The court did grant AVA's motion to dismiss the Section (a)(2) claim, but on different grounds. The court concluded that AVA's devices did not satisfy the statute's requirements because they are not "primarily designed to circumvent any technological measure and do not conduct the actual circumventing," rather, they "merely house the alleged pirated software to which 'access ... has already been obtained.'" *Id.*

5.3.2.3 DMCA Section 1201(b)(1)

Section (b)(1) states that no person:

> shall manufacture, import, offer to the public, provide, or other-
> wise traffic in any technology, product, service, device, compo-
> nent, or part thereof that—
>
> a) is primarily designed or produced for the purpose of circum-
>   venting protection afforded by a technological measure that
>   effectively protects a right of a copyright owner under this title
>   in a work or a portion thereof;
> b) has only limited commercially significant purpose or use other
>   than to circumvent protection afforded by a technological
>   measure that effectively protects a right of a copyright owner
>   under this title in a work or a portion thereof; or
> c) is marketed by that person or another acting in concert with
>   that person with that person's knowledge for use in circum-
>   venting protection afforded by a technological measure that
>   effectively protects a right of a copyright owner under this title
>   in a work or a portion thereof.[308]

Section (b)(1) defines "circumvent protection afforded by a technological measure" as "avoiding, bypassing, removing, deactivating, or otherwise impairing a technological measure."[309] The statute states that a technological measure "effectively protects a right of a copyright owner under this title" if the measure, "in the ordinary course of its operation, prevents, restricts, or otherwise limits the exercise of a right of a copyright owner under this title."[310]

Both Sections (a)(2) and (b)(1) prohibit trafficking in technology that circumvents technological measures. The primary difference between the two sections is that Section (a)(2) applies to technology that circumvents technological measures that control access to copyrighted works, whereas Section (b)(1) is narrower, and only applies to technology that circumvents a technological measure that *protects against violations of copyright owners' rights*—that is, copyright infringement.[311] Under the narrow *Chamberlain* interpretation of Section (a)(2), there is some degree of similarity between Sections (a)(2) and

---

308 17 U.S.C. § 1201(b)(1).

309 17 U.S.C § 1201(b)(2)(A).

310 17 U.S.C. § 1201(b)(2)(B).

311 *See* Ticketmaster LLC v. RMG Techs., Inc., 507 F. Supp. 2d 1096 (C.D. Cal. 2007) ("Sections 1201(a)(2) and 1201(b)(1) differ only in that 1201(a)(2), by its terms, makes it wrongful to traffic in devices that circumvent technological measures that *control access to protected works*, while 1201(b)(1) makes it wrongful to traffic in devices that circumvent technological measures that *protect rights of a copyright owner in a work*.") (emphasis in original).

(b)(1), as both sections require a link to copyright infringement. However, under the Ninth Circuit's more expansive view of Section (a)(2), the two sections are significantly different, with Section (a)(2) applying broadly to circumvention of technology that protects access to copyrighted works, regardless of whether the circumvention aids infringement. The Senate Commerce Committee's report accompanying the DMCA indicated its intention for Section (b)(1) to be more narrowly focused on technology that aids copyright infringement.[312] The Senate elaborated on the differences between the two sections:

> Although sections 1201(a)(2) and 1201(b) of the bill are worded similarly and employ similar tests, they are designed to protect two distinct rights and to target two distinct classes of devices. Subsection 1201(a)(2) is designed to protect access to a copyrighted work. Section 1201(b) is designed to protect the traditional copyright rights of the copyright owner. As a consequence, subsection 1201(a)(2) prohibits devices primarily designed to circumvent effective technological measures that limit access to a work. Subsection 1201(b), on the other hand, prohibits devices primarily designed to circumvent effective technological protection measures that limit the ability of the copyrighted work to be copied, or otherwise protect the copyright rights of the owner of the copyrighted work. The two sections are not interchangeable, and many devices will be subject to challenge only under one of the subsections.[313]

Indeed, in *MDY*, the Ninth Circuit concluded that even though the plaintiff had sufficiently alleged a violation of Section (a)(2) under the court's broad reading of that statute, the plaintiff did not prevail on its claim under Section (b)(1). The court reasoned that the Warden software does not protect against infringement or any other violation of copyright laws, and therefore the circumvention could not violate Section (b)(1). "[A]lthough WoW players can theoretically record game play by taking screen shots, there is no evidence that Warden detects or prevents such allegedly infringing copying," the Ninth Circuit wrote. "This is logical, because Warden was designed to reduce the

---

312 S. Rep. No. 105-190, at 29 ("Subsection (b) applies to those technological measures employed by a copyright owner that effectively protect his or her copyright rights in a work, as opposed to those technological protection measures covered by subsection (a), which prevent unauthorized access to a copyrighted work. Unlike subsection (a), which prohibits the circumvention of access control technologies, subsection (b) does not, by itself, prohibit the circumvention of effective technological copyright protection measures.").
313 *Id.* at 12.

presence of cheats and bots, not to protect WoW's dynamic non-literal elements against copying."[314]

If a court finds that a defendant has violated Section (b)(1), the court might also find that the defendant has violated Section (a)(2). For example, in *Craigslist, Inc. v. Naturemarket, Inc.,* [315] online classified advertising website Craigslist alleged that defendant Naturemarket developed and distributed software that enabled Naturemarket customers to automatically post multiple ads on Craigslist and to harvest Craigslist user email addresses in order to send spam email messages. Both acts violate Craigslist's terms of service, and Craigslist attempts to prevent such automatic posting and harvesting by using a CAPTCHA program and telephone verification, which requires the user to enter a unique code, in an effort to block automated programs from accessing the site.[316] Craigslist alleged that Naturemarket copied portions of Craigslist's website in order to operate and develop its autoposter software. Naturemarket did not respond to Craigslist's complaint, and the district court granted default judgment to Craigslist, concluding that Craigslist's complaint stated viable claims under both Sections (a)(2) and (b)(1). Naturemarket violated Section (a)(2), the court concluded, applying the Ninth Circuit's broad interpretation of the statute, because it trafficked in a product that circumvented CAPTCHA and telephone verification, which "enabled unauthorized access to and copies of copyright-protected portions of Plaintiff's website."[317] The court concluded that because CAPTCHA protected plaintiff's copyright rights in the website, Craigslist stated a viable claim that Naturemarket violated Section (b)(1).[318]

In short, regardless of the circuit in which a Section 1201 dispute is adjudicated, a plaintiff who successfully states a Section (b)(1) claim might also will prevail under Section (a)(2). However, the reverse probably is less likely to be true. A successful Section (a)(2) claim, particularly in a jurisdiction that adopts the broad *MDY* reading of the statute, does not necessarily mean that the defendant also violated Section (b)(1), as Section (a)(2) does not require a link to copyright infringement.

5.3.3   Section 1201 Penalties

Violators of Section 1201 can face both civil actions and criminal prosecutions. Any person who is injured by a Section 1201 violation can bring a civil action against the violator in federal court. The plaintiff can seek injunctions

---

314 MDY Indus., LLC v. Blizzard Entm't, 629 F.3d 928, 954-55.
315 Craigslist, Inc. v. Naturemarket, Inc., 694 F. Supp. 2d 1039 (N.D. Cal. 2010).
316 *Id*. at 1048.
317 *Id*. at 1056.
318 *Id*.

preventing the circumvention or trafficking, impounding of a device used to violate Section 1201, damages, costs, attorney's fees, and the modification or destruction of a device used to violate the law.[319]

The plaintiff in a Section 1201 case can seek either actual damages or statutory damages. Actual damages are the actual costs that the Section 1201 violation caused for the plaintiff, along with any profits that the violator earned due to the illegal act, provided that they are not already taken account of in the other actual damages.[320] Statutory damages are a fixed amount per violation, set by the court as it "considers just." Violations of Section 1201 carry statutory damages between $200 and $2,500 per act of circumvention.[321] If the violator demonstrates that it "was not aware and had no reason to believe that its acts constituted a violation," the court is permitted to reduce or remit the damages award.[322]

Section 1201 violations also can trigger criminal prosecutions, but only if the violator acted "willfully and for purposes of commercial advantage or private financial gain."[323] The maximum sentence for a first offense is a $500,000 fine or five years in prison, and the maximum sentence for a subsequent offense is a $1 million fine or ten years in prison.[324] The statute of limitations for criminal prosecutions is five years. The government may not bring criminal prosecutions under Section 1201 against a "nonprofit library, archives, educational institution, or public broadcasting entity."[325]

5.3.4 Section 1201 Exemptions

Section 1201 has attracted a great deal of criticism from the cybersecurity community and consumer rights groups, who argue that the statute is not in the public interest because it prevents researchers from discovering vulnerabilities in software. As the Center for Democracy and Technology stated, the anti-circumvention provisions of Section (a)(1) mean that "a researcher who uncovers a software vulnerability by circumventing, for example, digital rights management (DRM) software, is breaking the law."[326] Critics also assert that Section 1201's prohibition on the distribution of tools that facilitate circumvention has had a chilling effect on online discussion about cybersecurity

---

319 17 U.S.C. § 1203(b).
320 17 U.S.C. § 1203(c)(2).
321 17 U.S.C. § 1203(c)(3).
322 17 U.S.C. § 1203(c)(5).
323 17 U.S.C. § 1204(a).
324 *Id.*
325 *Id.*
326 Erik Stallman, Center for Democracy and Technology, *Improve Cybersecurity by Allowing Vulnerability Research* (Feb. 13, 2015).

because publishers and Internet service providers (ISPs) fear that such discussions could lead to DMCA liability.[327]

Congress attempted to address these concerns by including a number of limited exceptions to the anti-circumvention provisions, though many critics say that these exceptions are not sufficient to address their concerns about the effects that Section 1201 has on cybersecurity, researchers, and consumers.

The most prominent—and flexible—exception allows the Librarian of Congress to temporarily exempt particular classes of works from Section (a)(l)'s anti-circumvention provisions, provided that the Librarian determines that the users of those works are "adversely affected by virtue of such prohibition in their ability to make noninfringing uses of that particular class of works[.]"[328] In making this determination, the Librarian is required to consider the availability of copyrighted works for use; the availability for use of works for nonprofit archival, preservation, and educational purposes; the impact that a Section 1201 prohibition would have on "criticism, comment, news reporting, teaching, scholarship, or research"; whether circumvention affects the market value of copyrighted works; and other factors that the Librarian considers appropriate.[329]

These Librarian-granted exceptions are somewhat limited. The Librarian can only grant them in a rulemaking proceeding that occurs once every three years. The exceptions are temporary, and expire after three years. Perhaps most important, the temporary exceptions *only* apply to the anti-circumvention provision of Section (a)(1); they do *not* apply to the anti-trafficking provisions of Sections (a)(2) and (b)(1).[330]

In October 2018, the Librarian of Congress issued its most recent triennial rulemaking for Section (a)(1) exemptions. As described in its overview of the 300-page rulemaking, the Librarian granted the following exemptions, as stated in Frequently Asked Questions drafted by the Copyright Office:

- Excerpts of motion pictures (including television programs and videos) for criticism and comment:
  - For educational uses,
    - By college and university or K-12 faculty and students

---

327 *See* Electronic Frontier Foundation, Unintended Consequences: Fifteen Years under the DMCA (Mar. 2013) ("Bowing to DMCA liability fears, online service providers and bulletin board operators have censored discussions of copy-protection systems, programmers have removed computer security programs from their websites, and students, scientists and security experts have stopped publishing details of their research").

328 17 U.S.C. § 1201(a)(1)(B).

329 17 U.S.C. § 1201(a)(1)(C).

330 *See* 17 U.S.C. § 1201(a)(1)(E) ("Neither the exception under subparagraph (B) from the applicability of the prohibition contained in subparagraph (A), nor any determination made in a rulemaking conducted under subparagraph (C), may be used as a defense in any action to enforce any provision of this title other than this paragraph.").

- By faculty of massive open online courses ("MOOCs")
- By educators and participants in digital and literacy programs offered by libraries, museums and other nonprofits
- For nonfiction multimedia e-books
- For uses in documentary films and other films where the use is in parody or for a biographical or historically significant nature
- For uses in noncommercial videos
- Motion pictures (including television programs and videos), for the provision of captioning and/or audio description by disability services offices or similar units at educational institutions for students with disabilities
- Literary works distributed electronically (i.e., e-books), for use with assistive technologies for persons who are blind, visually impaired or have print disabilities
- Literary works consisting of compilations of data generated by implanted medical devices and corresponding personal monitoring systems
- Computer programs that operate the following types of devices, to allow connection of a new or used device to an alternative wireless network ("unlocking"):
  - Cellphones
  - Tablets
  - Mobile hotspots
  - Wearable devices (e.g., smartwatches)
- Computer programs that operate the following types of devices, to allow the device to interoperate with or to remove software applications ("jailbreaking"):
  - Smartphones
  - Tablets and other all-purpose mobile computing devices
  - Smart TVs
  - Voice assistant devices
- Computer programs that control motorized land vehicles, including farm equipment, for purposes of diagnosis, repair, or modification of the vehicle, including to access diagnostic data
- Computer programs that control smartphones, home appliances, or home systems, for diagnosis, maintenance, or repair of the device or system
- Computer programs for purposes of good-faith security research
- Computer programs other than video games, for the preservation of computer programs and computer program-dependent materials by libraries, archives, and museums

- Video games for which outside server support has been discontinued, to allow individual play by gamers and preservation of games by libraries, archives, and museums (as well as necessary jailbreaking of console computer code for preservation uses only), and preservation of discontinued video games that never required server support
- Computer programs that operate 3D printers, to allow use of alternative feedstock[331]

The Librarian of Congress declined to provide the following exemptions:

- Audiovisual works, for broad-based space-shifting and format-shifting (declined due to lack of legal and factual support for exemption)
- Audiovisual works protected by HDCP/HDMI, for non-infringing uses (declined due to lack of legal and factual support for exemption)
- Access to avionics data (declined due to lack of factual support that access controls were protecting copyrighted works)[332]

Advocacy groups have criticized the complexity of the exceptions, and noted that a temporary Library of Congress rulemaking is perhaps not the best way to address the concerns of cybersecurity researchers and others.[333] Advocacy groups also asserted that the Librarian of Congress attempted to reach a middle ground among the users and rights holders, leading to unnecessarily complex exemptions that are difficult to implement in the real world.[334] Critics of Section 1201 have long expressed these concerns. In 1999, a year after Congress passed the DMCA, University of California-Berkeley law professor Pamela Samuelson wrote that "because none of the Librarian's findings last for more than a three-year period, copyright industry lobbyists will have multiple

---

331 U.S. Copyright Office, *Frequently Asked Questions About the Section 1201 Rulemaking*, available at https://www.copyright.gov/1201/2018/faqs.html.

332 *Id.*

333 Erik Stallman, Center for Democracy and Technology, *A Qualified Win for Cybersecurity Researchers in DMCA Triennial Rulemaking* (Oct. 27, 2015) ("The sheer complexity of some of the granted exemptions—and the need to re-request them every three years—suggests that DMCA rulemaking proceedings are simply not the best vehicle for industrial policymaking where copyright infringement is, at most, a tangential concern.").

334 KENDRA ALBERT, ELECTRONIC FRONTIER FOUNDATION, THE NEW DMCA SECTION 1201 EXEMPTION FOR VIDEO GAMES: A CLOSER LOOK (Nov. 13, 2015) ("The Register made a number of compromises on many of the exemptions, designed to find a middle ground between proponents and opponents. That eliminates much of the legal clarity that the exemptions are meant to provide").

opportunities to carve back or eliminate any user-friendly exceptions that the Librarian might have the temerity to recommend."[335]

In addition to the temporary exemptions that the Librarian of Congress grants every three years, the DMCA includes some permanent—but narrow— exceptions to Section (a)(1) for specified uses. As with the Librarian's temporary exceptions, these do not apply to the trafficking provisions of Sections (a)(2) or (b)(1) unless specified:

- *Nonprofit libraries, archives, and educational institutions.* Section 1201(d) exempts nonprofit libraries, archives, and educational institutions from Section (a)(1)'s anti-circumvention requirements to allow them to "make a good faith determination" whether to lawfully acquire a copy of a copyrighted work.[336] If a nonprofit library, archive, or educational institution circumvents access controls to make this determination, it may not retain the copy "longer than necessary" to determine whether to acquire the work, nor may it use the copy for purposes other than making this determination. This exception is not available if the organization already has an "identical copy" that "is not reasonably available in another form." The exemption is not available to libraries or archives that are closed to the public or only available to affiliated researchers.
- *Law enforcement and intelligence activities.* Under Section 1201(e), legal activities of federal, state, and local law enforcement, security, and intelligence agencies are not subject to *any* of the prohibitions in Section 1201 (Sections (a)(1), (a)(2), and (b)(1)). This includes the agencies' information security activities, which the statute defines as "activities carried out in order to identify and address the vulnerabilities of a government computer, computer system, or compute network."[337]
- *Reverse engineering for interoperability.* Section 1201(f) permits individuals who lawfully obtain the right to use a copy of a computer program to circumvent an access control technology without violating Section 1201, provided that the *only* purpose for which they circumvent the control is to identify and analyze the elements that are "necessary to achieve interoperability" with another program, and those elements have not been readily available to the user through other means.[338] Section 1201 defines "interoperability" as "the ability of computer programs to exchange information, and of such programs mutually to use the information which has been exchanged." In its report accompanying the DMCA, the Senate wrote that this exception was intended "to foster competition and innovation in the computer and software industry."[339]

---

335 Pamela Samuelson, *Intellectual Property and the Digital Economy: Why the Anti-Circumvention Regulations Need to Be Revised,* 14 BERKELEY TECH. L.J. 1, 41 n. 208 (1999).
336 17 U.S.C. § 1201(d).
337 17 U.S.C. § 1201(e).
338 17 U.S.C. § 1201(f).
339 S. REP. No. 105-190, at 13.

- *Encryption research.* Section 1201(g) provides a limited exception for "encryption research," which it defines as "activities necessary to identify and analyze flaws and vulnerabilities of encryption technologies applied to copyrighted works, if these activities are conducted to advance the state of knowledge in the field of encryption technology or to assist in the development of encryption products." The statute defines "encryption technology" as "the scrambling and descrambling of information using mathematical formulas or algorithms."

  The provision allows encryption researchers to circumvent an access control if (1) the researcher "lawfully obtained" the encrypted content, (2) the circumvention is "necessary to conduct" encryption research, (3) the researcher made a "good-faith effort to obtain authorization" to circumvent the control, and (4) the circumvention does not independently constitute copyright infringement or a violation of the CFAA. The exemption also allows researchers to provide the technological means of circumvention to a collaborating researcher.[340]

  To determine whether the researcher qualifies for this exemption, the statute lists three factors: (1) the manner in which the information derived from the research is circulated and whether the dissemination is "reasonably calculated to advance the state of knowledge or development of encryption technology;" (2) whether the researcher has an appropriate background, training, and experience in encryption technology; and (3) whether the researcher provides the results of the research to the copyright owner.[341]

  In its report accompanying the DMCA, senators wrote that the new law was intended to encourage—not discourage—development of encryption: "The goals of section 1201 would be poorly served if these provisions had the undesirable and unintended consequence of chilling legitimate research activities in the area of encryption. It is the view of the Committee, after having conducted extensive consultations, and having examined a number of hypothetical situations, that Section 1201 should not have such an unintended negative effect."[342]

  Some researchers have criticized this exemption for not providing the certainty necessary to conduct encryption research. In a petition to the Librarian of Congress, Johns Hopkins computer scientist Matthew D. Green wrote that the exemption includes "complex multifactor tests that cannot be evaluated *ex ante*, potential restrictions on the dissemination of research results, and requirements to seek authorization in advance of performing research."[343]

---

340 17 U.S.C § 1201(g).
341 *Id.*
342 S. Rep. No. 105-190, at 15.
343 Matthew D. Green, Petition for Exemption: Applied Cryptography, Security, and Reverse Engineering Research, Docket No. 2014-07.

- *Preventing minors from accessing the Internet.* Section 1201(h) instructs courts, when applying Sections (a)(1) and (a)(2) to a component or part, to consider the "necessity" of the component's or part's intended and actual incorporation in technology that does not violate the copyright law and has the "sole purpose" of preventing minors from accessing material on the Internet.[344] This is a relatively vague provision that does not give clear guidance as to the exact types of activities that are exempt from 1201 liability. The legislative history of the DMCA indicates that Congress intended to ensure that parents could install technology on their home computers to restrict their children's access to harmful material on the Internet.[345]

- *Protection of personally identifying information.* Section 1201(i) allows an individual to circumvent controls on copyrighted works in order to protect the individual's privacy, but only if the company that possesses the data failed to conspicuously disclose the collection and dissemination and provide the individual with the chance to opt out. An individual may circumvent access controls without violating Section(a)(1), provided that all of the following four conditions are met: (1) the access control or the content that it protects is capable of "collecting or disseminating personally identifying information reflecting the online activities of a natural person who seeks to gain access to the work protected;" (2) "in the normal course of its operation, the technological measure, or the work it protects, collects or disseminates personally identifying information about the person who seeks to gain access to the work protected, without providing conspicuous notice of such collection or dissemination to such person, and without providing such person with the capability to prevent or restrict such collection or dissemination;" (3) the circumvention has the "sole effect" of identifying and disabling the collection or dissemination of the personally identifying information; and (4) the circumvention is *only* conducted to prevent the personally identifiable information from being collected or disseminated.[346] The legislative history of the provision indicates that Congress intended this exception to apply only in cases when companies did not provide transparency and choice regarding personal information.[347]

---

344 17 U.S.C. § 1201(h).
345 H.R. Rep. No. 105-551, pt. 2, at 45 (expressing concern that the DMCA's anti-circumvention protections "might inadvertently make it unlawful for parents to protect their children from pornography and other harmful material available on the Internet, or have unintended legal consequences for manufacturers of products designed solely to enable parents to protect their children in this fashion").
346 17 U.S.C. § 1201(i).
347 H.R. Rep. No. 105-551, pt. 2, at 45 ("Only if there is no disclosure of privacy-related practices, or instances where consumers are left without the capability to disable the gathering of personal information, could a consumer circumvent a technological protection measure to protect his or her own privacy.").

- *Security testing.* Section 1201(j) creates an exemption to Section (a)(1) for certain forms of security testing, which the statute defines as accessing a computer "solely for the purpose of good faith testing, investigating, or correcting, a security flaw or vulnerability, with the authorization of the owner or operator" of the computer.[348] The statute provides the following two factors for consideration when determining whether the exemption applies: (1) whether the information obtained through testing was used "solely to promote the security of the owner or operator of the computer," or shared with the developer; and (2) whether the information was used in a way that facilitates copyright infringement or the violation of privacy or data security laws.

   Security researchers have argued that this exception is relatively toothless, and exposes them to great risk without providing sufficient certainty. For instance, Section 1201(j) explicitly states that the exemption does not apply if the testing violates another law, such as the CFAA. In light of the broad view of the CFAA in some courts, discussed in Section 5.1.2.2, there is a reasonable chance that this exception would not apply merely because a security test is viewed by a court as exceeding authorization.[349]

In sum, the seven permanent statutory exemptions to Section 1201 often do not provide cybersecurity researchers and consumers with the certainty that is necessary to feel safe in circumventing access controls, even if they have a good-faith reason to believe that the exception applies. Violating the DMCA could result in significant civil damages and, in some cases, criminal charges. The multifactor balancing tests are applied by a court only after the individual is accused of violating the DMCA. Therefore, it is impossible for the person to have certainty *before* circumventing an access control.

5.3.5   The First Amendment and DMCA Section 1201

In light of the uncertainty that Section 1201 has created for a number of researchers who work on encryption, cybersecurity, and in related fields, some critics assert that the statute violates the First Amendment's guarantee of freedom of speech. The gist of their argument is that software code is speech, and by prohibiting the distribution or discussion of certain types of code, Section 1201 censors speech and therefore violates the First Amendment.

---

348 17 U.S.C. § 1201(j).
349 Erik Stallman, Center for Democracy and Technology, *The Current DMCA Exemption Process Is a Computer Security Vulnerability* (Jan. 21, 2015) ("[A] researcher arguably violates the CFAA simply by exceeding the authorization given. Accordingly, a researcher who exceeds that authorization may be subject to liability under both the CFAA and the DMCA. Unsurprisingly, there is no reported case upholding a claim of good-faith security testing under this exception.").

In 2015 comments to the United States Copyright Office, a group of leading cybersecurity researchers expressed the primary First Amendment concerns with Section 1201:

> Academic and other research institutions can be risk-averse, advising faculty and students to steer clear of research with unclear liability; faculty advise students to work in areas less fraught with potential legal and public-relations challenges; and peer review may look unfavorably upon researchers whose work treads too closely to legal lines. Funders may be reluctant to support certain kinds of research. Academic publication venues are forced to wrestle with questions regarding the legality of research, despite its public value.[350]

In short, cybersecurity researchers say that fear of criminal prosecution and civil litigation under Section 1201 makes it incredibly difficult for them to conduct research on vulnerabilities in software and systems. The restrictions, they say, also make it difficult for them to communicate their findings via publications and conferences, having a chilling effect on speech. Researchers have raised these First Amendment objections to Section 1201 in a handful of court cases. To date, courts have not invalidated Section 1201 due to these concerns.

Among the highest profile of these cases emerged in 2001, when a group of academic researchers discovered a flaw in the copyright protection system that was used on audio CDs. The researchers had planned to present their findings at a large computer science conference, but they withdrew from the conference after receiving a threat from the RIAA, asserting that the publication of the research would violate the DMCA. The researchers then sued the recording industry, seeking a judgment from the court declaring that publication of the research would not violate Section 1201, and even if it did, applying the DMCA in that manner would violate the First Amendment. "In chilling publication and presentation of scientific research," they wrote in their complaint, "the DMCA wreaks havoc in the marketplace of ideas, not only the right to speak, but the right to receive information—the right to learn."[351] The court dismissed the case for lack of standing, and did not rule on the broader statutory and First Amendment arguments. The researchers did not appeal this ruling.

Later that year, however, the U.S. Court of Appeals for the Second Circuit did rule on the constitutionality of Section 1201 in another case. In *Universal City*

---

350 Comments of Ben Adida, et al. to the United States Copyright Office (May 21, 2015).
351 First Amended Complaint, Felten v. Recording Indus. Ass'n of Am., Case No. CV-01-2660 (GEB) (June 26, 2001).

Studios, Inc. v. *Corley,*[352] major movie studios sued Eric Corley, who published "DeCSS" code on his computer hacker website, 2600.com. He also linked to other sites that hosted DeCSS. DeCSS circumvented CSS, an encryption format that the major movie studios used to prevent copying of their DVDs. The movie studios sued Corley under Section (a)(2), seeking a permanent injunction to prevent him from both *posting* the DeCSS code and *linking* to other sites that host the code. After trial, the district court judge granted the permanent injunction. Corley appealed to the Second Circuit, primarily arguing that Section 1201, as applied to this case, violated the First Amendment.[353]

To understand how the court assessed this claim, it is necessary to know the general framework for First Amendment analysis. First, it is necessary to ask whether the law regulates speech. If the law regulates an activity other than speech, the First Amendment's free speech protections will not apply. Second, if a law does, in fact, regulate speech, then it is necessary to determine whether the law is *content-based* or *content-neutral.* If the law is content-based, then it will only survive a First Amendment challenge if the government demonstrates that it serves compelling governmental interests by the "least restrictive means available."[354] If the law is *content-neutral,* then a court will allow it if it furthers a "substantial government interest" that is "unrelated to the suppression of free expression," and the law is "narrowly tailored" so that it does not "burden substantially more speech than is necessary to further the government's legitimate interests."[355] The content-neutral analysis sets a much lower bar than the requirements for content-based restrictions. Accordingly, the constitutionality of a statute that restricts speech often hinges on whether a court classifies it as content-based or content-neutral.

Applying the First Amendment framework to the DeCSS case, the Second Circuit first determined that computer programs and code constitute "speech" that is protected by the First Amendment.[356] Acknowledging that computer code is different from more traditional forms of speech, such as literature, the court concluded that courts have long provided First Amendment protection to "dry information, devoid of advocacy, political relevance, or artistic expression."[357] The court likened programmers' communication via code to musicians' communication via musical notes.[358]

---

352 Universal City Studios v. Corley, 273 F.3d 429 (2d Cir. 2001).

353 *Id.* at 441–42.

354 *Id.* at 450.

355 *Id.* (internal quotation marks and citations omitted).

356 *Id.* at 446.

357 *Id.*

358 *Id.* at 448 ("Limiting First Amendment protection of programmers to descriptions of computer code (but not the code itself) would impede discourse among computer scholars, just as limiting protection for musicians to descriptions of musical scores (but not sequences of notes) would impede their exchange of ideas and expression.").

The next step in the analysis is to determine whether Section 1201's restrictions on publication of DeCSS and linking to other sites is content-based or content-neutral. The court reasoned that both restrictions are content-neutral. Corley argued that Section 1201's trafficking restrictions are content-based because they are specifically directed at communications regarding a particular topic: access control circumvention. The court disagreed, reasoning that Section 1201 and the district court's injunction target only the "non-speech" aspects of DeCSS: decrypting CSS.[359] Section 1201, as applied to DeCSS, is content-neutral, the Second Circuit reasoned, because it is not "concerned with whatever capacity DeCSS might have for conveying information to a human being."[360]

Applying the more lenient First Amendment test for content-neutral laws, the court concluded that Section 1201, as applied to this case, is constitutional. Prohibiting the posting of DeCSS code, the court ruled, serves a substantial government interest by "preventing unauthorized access to encrypted copyrighted material," and the government's actions are unrelated to suppressing free speech because it regulates DeCSS distribution "regardless of whether DeCSS code contains any information comprehensible by human beings that would qualify as speech."[361] The prohibition on posting DeCSS code does not burden substantially more speech than necessary, the court concluded. Although the court acknowledged that the unconditional prohibition on posting the code "is not absolutely necessary to preventing unauthorized access to copyrighted materials," Corley failed to demonstrate that the injunction burdens *substantially* more speech than is necessary. Had the court concluded that the injunction was content-based, it is unlikely that the injunction would have survived this challenge, since the government would have needed to demonstrate that the injunction is the *least* restrictive means to accomplish protect CSS-encrypted movies. The court suggested that the injunction's prohibition on *linking* to DeCSS code raises more difficult First Amendment issues, but ultimately it upheld the constitutionality of that prohibition as well.[362]

In more recent years, litigants have mounted similar First Amendment challenges to various aspects of Section 1201, but they have faced similar skepticism from courts.[363] Because the United States Supreme Court has not directly

---

359 *Id.* at 454.
360 *Id.*
361 *Id.* at 454.
362 *Id.* at 457–58.
363 *See, e.g.,* 321 Studios v. Metro Goldwyn Mayer Studios, 307 F. Supp. 2d 1085 (N.D. Cal. 2004) ("Congress determined that the DMCA was needed to protect copyrights and intellectual property rights; this Court finds that the challenged provisions further important and substantial government interests unrelated to the suppression of free expression, and that the incidental restrictions on First Amendment freedoms are no greater than essential to the furtherance of those interests.").

ruled on whether Section 1201 comports with the First Amendment, it is possible—though unlikely—that a court could invalidate the use of Section 1201 based on a First Amendment challenge.

5.4 Economic Espionage Act

The Economic Espionage Act prohibits the theft of U.S. companies' trade secrets, either to benefit a foreign government or to economically benefit anyone other than the owner. The statute was passed in 1996 to impose criminal penalties for both foreign and corporate espionage, and amended significantly in 2016 to allow companies to bring civil suits for trade secret theft. The evolution—and growing importance—of the Economic Espionage Act demonstrate the increasingly grave threat that trade secrets pose in the United States.

5.4.1 Origins of the Economic Espionage Act

At first glance, economic espionage and the theft of trade secrets may not appear to be of particular concern for cybersecurity professionals. However, the Economic Espionage Act is one of the first U.S. laws that was crafted with cybersecurity in mind. When Congress passed the Economic Espionage Act in 1996, companies were just beginning to consider how to integrate the Internet into their daily business operations. The companies also were taking greater advantage of computers and data centers for warehousing data that had long been contained only on paper and stored in folders and drawers.

As an increasing amount of data is stored on computers and in remote data centers, espionage and theft of trade secrets has become common, causing great economic risk for companies. Indeed, many executives view the theft of trade secrets as an even greater threat than the theft of personal information, because the theft of confidential business information such as trade secrets could undercut a company's entire economic model.

Companies have long protected their nontangible assets—information—with intellectual property laws. However, those laws provide only limited protection for much of the information that companies seek to keep confidential. Copyright law only protects creative expressions that are fixed in a medium. For example, although an email or report may be protected by copyright, the information contained in that report is not protected. Patent law offers protection only if the United States Patent and Trademark Office has approved a patent. The patent approval process is long and complex, and requires the applicant to demonstrate that the invention is nonobvious, useful, and new. A great deal of confidential business information, such as financial projections, sales statistics, and business plans, often is not covered under federal intellectual property laws.

The most likely source of protection for confidential corporate data is the many state laws that protect trade secrets. However, most of these laws do not provide sufficient penalties to deter corporate espionage. Moreover, the laws generally provide only for private civil litigation, so they rely on the victimized companies to investigate and litigate claims against the perpetrators.

Recognizing the need for a federal law to deter corporate espionage in the emerging information age, Congress drafted and enacted the Economic Espionage Act. In its report accompanying the bill, the House Judiciary Committee noted the growing number of espionage threats that companies were facing as their data was stored on computers and servers:

> Computer technology enables rapid and surreptitious duplica-tions of the information. Hundreds of pages of information can be loaded onto a small computer diskette, placed into a coat pocket, and taken from the legal owner. This material is a prime target for theft precisely because it costs so much to develop independently, because it is so valuable, and because there are virtually no penal-ties for its theft.[364]

The Judiciary Committee noted the particular dangers of espionage that arise from insider threats. "A great deal of the theft is committed by disgruntled indi-viduals or employees who hope to harm their former companies or line their own pockets," the committee wrote.[365] Indeed, many of the prosecutions and civil cases that have been brought under the Economic Espionage Act have involved insiders who have misused their access to corporate computer systems.

5.4.2 Criminal Prohibitions on Economic Espionage and Theft of Trade Secrets

The Economic Espionage Act contains two separate prohibitions: Section 1831 prohibits economic espionage to benefit a foreign government or entity, and Section 1832 prohibits the theft of trade secrets to benefit one company at the expense of another company.

The two portions of the law differ primarily regarding the purpose and intent behind the defendant's trade secret theft, as described in more detail in this section. Both sections, however, require the defendant to have committed one of the five following acts (edited modestly for clarity and brevity):

- Stealing, or without authorization appropriating, taking, carrying away, or concealing, or by fraud, artifice, or deception obtaining a trade secret.

---

364 H.R. REP. No. 104-788, at 5 (1996).
365 *Id.*

- Without authorization copying, duplicating, sketching, drawing, photographing, downloading, uploading, altering, destroying, photocopying, replicating, transmitting, delivering, sending, mailing, communicating, or conveying a trade secret.
- Receiving, buying, or possessing a trade secret, knowing the same to have been stolen or appropriated, obtained, or converted without authorization.
- Attempting to commit any of the aforesaid offenses.
- Conspiring with at least one other person to commit any of the first three offenses, and one or more of the conspirators do any act to effect the object of the conspiracy.[366]

Violations of Section 1831 carry prison time of up to 15 years and a fine of up to $5 million for an individual. Organizations that violate Section 1831 face a fine of up to $10 million or three times the value of the stolen trade secret, whichever is greater. Violations of Section 1832 carry prison time of up to ten years or a fine. Organizations that violate Section 1832 face a fine of up to $5 million, or three times the value of the stolen trade secret, whichever is greater.

Sections 1831 and 1832 apply to conduct that occurs outside of the United States, if either an act in furtherance of the violation was committed in the United States, or if the offender is a U.S. citizen or permanent resident alien, or an organization that is organized under U.S. laws.[367]

5.4.2.1 Definition of "Trade Secret"

Both Sections 1831 and 1832 only apply if the information at issue constitutes a "trade secret." The Economic Espionage Act broadly defines "trade secret" as:

> all forms and types of financial, business, scientific, technical, economic, or engineering information, including patterns, plans, compilations, program devices, formulas, designs, prototypes, methods, techniques, processes, procedures, programs, or codes, whether tangible or intangible, and whether or how stored, compiled, or memorialized physically, electronically, graphically, photographically, or in writing if—
>
> a) the owner thereof has taken reasonable measures to keep such information secret; and
> b) the information derives independent economic value, actual or potential, from not being generally known to, and not being readily ascertainable through proper means by, another person who can obtain economic value from the disclosure or use of the information.[368]

---

366 18 U.S.C. §§ 1831, 1832.
367 18 U.S.C. § 1837.
368 18 U.S.C. § 1839(3).

Congress modeled the Economic Espionage Act's definition of "trade secret" after the definition in the Uniform Trade Secrets Act, intending for the definition to broadly encompass many types of confidential information.[369]

In some cases, defendants argue that information is not a trade secret because the owner failed to take "reasonable measures" to keep the information secret. Although there is no precise checklist to determine whether companies have taken sufficiently reasonable measures, courts consider a wide range of factors, such as the number of people authorized to access the information, the security of the storage of the information, confidentiality agreements, and the company's information security and document destruction policies.[370]

Despite this broad definition of trade secrets, defendants often argue that the information is not a trade secret because the company failed to take reasonable measures to ensure secrecy. For example, in a 2008 criminal trial in Los Angeles, Tien Shiah was tried for violating Section 1832.[371] Shiah worked at a California company, and had accepted a job at another company. Before leaving his first employer, he allegedly amassed confidential electronic files on a laptop, and he also gathered hard copies. He believed this was a "toolkit" that documented his work.[372] Two years later, Shiah left his second employer, and created another "toolkit" with confidential documents.[373]

At trial, the judge concluded that, on balance, his second employer had taken reasonable steps to keep the information secret. The judge first noted that it is unnecessary to demonstrate that the company prevented even its own employees from seeing the data, as that would threaten internal productivity.[374] The proper inquiry is whether the company took reasonable steps to prevent *outsiders* from accessing the data. Among the steps that the company took to safeguard the data:

- Requiring confidentiality agreements.
- Using technical safeguards such as intrusion detection systems and firewalls.
- Requiring nondisclosure agreements for outside parties as a condition of accessing confidential information.
- Marking documents as confidential.

---

369 *See* H.R. Rep. No. 104-788 (1996), at 12 ("These general categories of information are included in the definition of trade secret for illustrative purposes and should not be read to limit the definition of trade secret. It is the Committee's intent that this definition be read broadly.").
370 *See* United States v. Chung, 659 F.3d 815, 825-26 (9th Cir. 2011).
371 United States v. Shiah, Case No. SA CR 06-92 DOC, 2008 U.S. Dist. LEXIS 11973 (C.D. Cal. Feb. 19, 2008).
372 *Id.* at *3.
373 *Id.* at *16.
374 *Id.* at *60–61.

- Physically securing its facilities with "a security guard, security cameras, and receptionists who monitored visitors."

However, the judge noted a few areas in which the employer could have improved its efforts to maintain secrecy of the data:

- Explain the confidentiality agreement to employees, and provide them with a copy for their records.
- Implement a "comprehensive system" to designate confidentiality of documents.
- Refer employees to the confidentiality agreement during their exit interviews.
- Ask employees at exit interview whether they copied any files.
- Inspect employee's computer upon termination to determine whether the employee has taken any confidential information.[375]

On balance, the court concluded, the employer's confidentiality practices were "generally effective," and the deficiencies "were not so extensive to qualify as unreasonable."[376] Despite the conclusion that the information constituted a trade secret, the judge found Shiah not guilty because the government failed to prove Shiah's intent to convert a trade secret for the benefit of anyone other than his former employer. The court's well-reasoned analysis in this case provides an example of the factors that courts will weigh when determining whether companies took reasonable steps to protect confidential information. Keep in mind that another court could just as easily have found that the employer did not take reasonable steps, depending on the weight that the court accorded to each protective measure.

Defendants also argue that information does not constitute a trade secret because the information does not derive independent economic value from not being known to another party.[377] To make this determination, courts typically consider "the degree to which the secret information confers a competitive advantage on its owner."[378] In general, courts have been willing to find that confidentiality of information creates independent value, and they typically do not require proof of an increase in value due to the confidentiality. In part, that is because the statute allows the economic value to be actual *or* potential.[379]

---

375 *Id*. at *61–66.
376 *Id*. at *68.
377 Until 2016, the statute required proof that "the information derives independent economic value, actual or potential, from not being generally known to, and not being readily ascertainable through proper means by, *the public*" (emphasis added). The Defend Trade Secrets Act of 2016 replaced "the public" with "another person who can obtain economic value from the disclosure or use of the information."
378 United States v. Chung, 659 F.3d 815, 826-27 (9th Cir. 2011).
379 *See* United States v. Jin, 733 F.3d 718 (7th Cir. 2013).

For instance, in the *Shiah* criminal prosecution, the court concluded that the information that Shiah allegedly copied had independent economic value due to its confidentiality. The pricing information, for instance, "would allow competitors to compete more effectively with respect to price by undermining [the employer's] pricing structure and also obtain more favorable terms from their suppliers."[380] Disclosure of information about the company's unreleased products would hurt the company's research and development efforts, the court reasoned.[381] Revealing the confidential customer information could harm the company's relationships with its customers, the court wrote.[382] The court recognized that some of the information in the files that Shiah allegedly copied was not confidential, such as information that already was publicly available, and Congress did not intend to accord trade secret status to such data.[383] Nonetheless, the information constituted a trade secret because at least *some* of it derived value from remaining confidential.[384]

5.4.2.2 "Knowing" Violations of the Economic Espionage Act

Both Sections 1831 and 1832 apply only to acts that are done "knowingly." Congress included this additional state-of-mind requirement to limit the application of the Economic Espionage Act to people who are aware that they are handling trade secrets. In the Senate Judiciary Committee's report accompanying the Economic Espionage Act, the legislators wrote that to knowingly commit an act in violation of the Economic Espionage Act requires "(1) an awareness of the nature of one's conduct, and (2) an awareness of or a firm belief in or knowledge to a substantial certainty of the existence of a relevant circumstance, such as whether the information is proprietary economic information as defined by this statute."[385]

5.4.2.3 Purpose and Intent Required under Section 1831: Economic Espionage

As mentioned earlier, Sections 1831 (Economic Espionage) and 1832 (Theft of Trade Secrets) apply to the same five acts involving the theft, copying, receipt, or purchase of trade secrets. The difference between the two sections is the purpose and intent behind these acts. Section 1831 involves a violation that is motivated by the desire to help a foreign government, whereas Section 1832

---

380 United States v. Shiah, Case No. SA CR 06-92 DOC, 2008 U.S. Dist. LEXIS 11973 (C.D. Cal. Feb. 19, 2008), at *58.

381 *Id.*

382 *Id.*

383 *Id.* at *59.

384 *Id.* ("Each of these files contained some information that derived value from not being generally known to the public, which is sufficient to satisfy the first prong of the trade secret test beyond a reasonable doubt.").

385 S. Rep. No. 104-359, at 16 (1996).

involves a violation that is motivated by the desire to help one company succeed and harm the victim. It is possible to see a defendant charged under *both* sections, if the act is intended to help both another country as well as a company in that country.

Section 1831 applies if the defendant knowingly committed the offense "intending or knowing that the offense will benefit any foreign government, foreign instrumentality, or foreign agent[.]"[386] In its 1996 report accompanying the Economic Espionage Act, the House Judiciary Committee stated that it intended for "benefit" to be interpreted "broadly":

> The defendant did not have to intend to confer an economic benefit to the foreign government, instrumentality, or agent, to himself, or to any third person. Rather, the government need only prove that the actor intended that his actions in copying or otherwise controlling the trade secret would benefit the foreign government, instrumentality, or agent in any way. Therefore, in this circumstance, benefit means not only an economic benefit but also reputational, strategic, or tactical benefit.[387]

Section 1831 explicitly states that it only applies if the foreign instrumentalities[388] and agents[389] are linked to a foreign government. Accordingly, an offense that is intended to benefit a foreign private company—and not the government—will not qualify as a Section 1831 violation (though it might fall under Section 1832).

For instance, Hanjuan Jin was indicted under both Sections 1831 and 1832 for allegedly stealing trade secrets from her former employer, Motorola, and moving to China with plans to work for a competing company. The judge conducted a bench trial (a trial that is decided by the judge, not a jury), and determined that although Jin violated Section 1832, there was insufficient evidence to convict her of economic espionage under Section 1831. The government argued that by providing the trade secrets to a Chinese company, Jin intended to benefit the People's Republic of China. The district court rejected this argument, concluding that "[t]here is certainly plenty of speculative proof that the PRC may have benefited from Jin's conduct, but such speculation does not

---

386 18 U.S.C. § 1831.

387 H.R. Rep. No. 104-788 (1996), at 11.

388 18 U.S.C. § 1839(1) ("the term 'foreign instrumentality' means any agency, bureau, ministry, component, institution, association, or any legal, commercial, or business organization, corporation, firm, or entity that is substantially owned, controlled, sponsored, commanded, managed, or dominated by a foreign government.").

389 18 U.S.C. § 1839(2) ("the term 'foreign agent' means any officer, employee, proxy, servant, delegate, or representative of a foreign government").

equate to proof beyond a reasonable doubt."[390] The *Jin* case demonstrates the difficulty of proving a Section 1831 violation. The government faces the heavy burden of demonstrating *beyond a reasonable doubt* that the defendant not only stole trade secrets but also did so with the intent or knowledge that the action would benefit a foreign government.

That is not to say that it is impossible to demonstrate that the defendant stole trade secrets with the intent of benefiting a foreign government. Consider a 2011 case from the U.S. Court of Appeals for the Ninth Circuit, *United States* v. *Chung*.[391] Dongfan Chung, a former Boeing engineer, was charged with violating Section 1831 because he allegedly provided Boeing trade secrets to China. Chung worked in Boeing facilities in the United States for more than three decades before retiring in 2002. During the 2005 search of the home of another criminal suspect, federal agents found a letter to Chung, from a Chinese government official, thanking Chung for providing information to China and requesting additional information about airplanes and space shuttles. This letter provided the agents with reason to investigate Chung. In 2006, with his consent, they searched his home and found more than 300,000 pages of documents from his employers.[392] They also learned that he gave a presentation in China about Boeing space shuttles. Chung was convicted at trial of violations of Section 1831, as well as other crimes.

Chung appealed the 1831 conviction. The Ninth Circuit held that there is "ample evidence" that Chung possessed the trade secrets with the intent of benefiting the Chinese government. "Defendant intended to benefit China by providing technical information responsive to requests from Chinese officials and by delivering presentations to Chinese engineers," the court wrote.[393] The *Chung* case shows courts' willingness to conclude that a Section 1831 defendant intended to benefit a foreign government based on compelling circumstantial evidence. Possessing the documents, and nothing more, probably would not have satisfied Section 1831's intent requirements. However, Chung's ongoing contacts with Chinese officials, coupled with his possession of trade secrets, was enough for the court to affirm his Section 1831 conviction.

5.4.2.4 Purpose and Intent Required under Section 1832: Theft of Trade Secrets

In recent years, prosecutors have brought a number of high-profile cases under Section 1832, likely owing to the fact that employees are increasingly transferring large amounts of data from their current employer to a future employer.

---

390 United States v. Jin, 833 F. Supp. 2d 977, 1020 (N.D. Ill. 2012), *aff'd on other grounds*, 733 F.3d 718 (7th Cir. 2013).
391 United States v. Chung, 659 F.3d 815 (9th Cir. 2011).
392 *Id.* at 819.
393 *Id.* at 828.

The abundance of portable digital media and unrestricted workplace Internet access makes such theft remarkably easy.

Section 1832 applies if the defendant knowingly commits one of the five offenses related to trade secrets "with intent to convert a trade secret, that is related to a product or service used in or intended for use in interstate or foreign commerce, to the economic benefit of anyone other than the owner thereof, and intending or knowing that the offense will injure any owner of that trade secret[.]"[394]

The requirement of "intent to convert a trade secret" means that the defendant must have intended to transfer the trade secret to an individual or entity other than the legally authorized owner. This is based on the tort of conversion,[395] which courts typically define as an "unauthorized assumption and exercise of the right of ownership over goods or personal chattels belonging to another, to the alteration of their condition or the exclusion of an owner's rights."[396] In the cyber realm, if an employee downloads thousands of pages of confidential sales documents, hoping to use them in a future job with a competitor, the employee intends to convert trade secrets.

Perhaps the most contentious—and complex—requirement is that the trade secret be related to a product or service used in or intended for use in interstate or foreign commerce. In fact, Congress has changed the precise wording of this requirement over the years as it has struggled to determine the scope of Section 1832.

When the Economic Espionage Act was initially introduced in the Senate, it did not require that the trade secret have any link to interstate or foreign commerce; instead, it imposed criminal penalties on any individual who steals "proprietary economic information having a value of not less than $100,000."[397] The House added an interstate or foreign commerce requirement, which applied to the conversion of any trade secret "that is related to or included in a product that is produced for or placed in interstate or foreign commerce."[398] That limitation was included in the bill that was enacted in 1996, and remained in effect until 2012.

That interstate commerce provision, however, raised some significant challenges for prosecutors and uncertainty for courts. What did it mean for a product to be produced for or placed in interstate commerce? And what if the trade secret related to a service, rather than a product? The

---

394 18 U.S.C. § 1832(a).
395 *See* Congressional Research Service, Stealing Trade Secrets and Economic Espionage: An Overview of the Economic Espionage Act (Aug. 19, 2016), at 3.
396 Variety Wholesalers v. Salem Logistics, 723 S.E.2d 744 (N.C. 2012).
397 S. 1556, 104th Cong. (1996); United States v. Aleynikov, 676 F.3d 71 (2d Cir. 2012).
398 S. 1556, 104th Cong. (1996).

limitations of this definition became apparent in a 2012 opinion from the U.S. Court of Appeals for the Second Circuit. In *United States v. Aleynikov,*[399] Sergey Aleynikov, a Goldman Sachs computer programmer, was charged with violating Section 1832. Prosecutors alleged that he stole source code for Goldman's high-frequency trading system, and had accepted a job with another company that was developing a separate high-frequency trading system.[400] Aleynikov was convicted, and he appealed, arguing that Goldman's high-frequency trading system was not a product that is produced for or placed in interstate commerce. Aleynikov argued that the high-frequency trading system was strictly for Goldman's internal use, and the company had no plans to sell or license the system. The Second Circuit agreed with Aleynikov and reversed his Section 1832 conviction. Even though the software helped Goldman *engage* in interstate and foreign commerce, the Second Circuit concluded that the statutory provision is far more limited, and only applies to products that are in the stream of commerce or are intended to be placed in the "stream of commerce."[401]

The *Aleynikov* decision quickly set off alarms throughout corporate America.[402] Corporations develop a great deal of proprietary technology that is intended strictly for internal use. The court's opinion suggested that employees would not be liable under the Economic Espionage Act for the theft of this valuable data. Within months of the Second Circuit's decision, members of Congress introduced the Theft of Trade Secrets Clarification Act of 2012. The bill's sponsors stated their intent to prevent future decisions such as *Aleynikov,* and the legislation passed without controversy.[403] The bill expanded the reach of Section 1832, applying to trade secrets that are "related to a product or service used in or intended for use in interstate or foreign commerce." This amendment significantly broadened the reach of

---

399 United States v. Aleynikov, 676 F.3d 71 (2d Cir. 2012).

400 *Id*. at 73–74.

401 *Id*. at 26–27 ("Because the HFT system was not designed to enter or pass in commerce, or make something that does, Aleynikov's theft of source code relating to that system was not an offense under the EEA.").

402 *See* TRADE SECRETS INSTITUTE, CASE REPORT: UNITED STATES V. ALEYNIKOV ("The February 2012 reversal of Aleynikov's conviction of trade secrets theft—especially the Second Circuit's ruling that Aleynikov was wrongly charged with espionage, since the code was not a product designed for interstate or foreign commerce—called into question the government's ability to prosecute theft of internal trading systems or other internal financial instruments under the Economic Espionage Act.").

403 *See* 158 CONG. REC. S6978 (statement of Sen. Leahy) (Nov. 27, 2012) ("The clarifying legislation that the Senate will pass today corrects the court's narrow reading to ensure that our federal criminal laws adequately address the theft of trade secrets related to a product or service used in interstate commerce. It is a straightforward fix, but an important one.").

Section 1832, allowing it to apply not only to products that are sold or licensed, but also to products *and* services that are *used in* interstate or foreign commerce. For instance, although Goldman's high-frequency trading system did not fall within the scope of the older version of Section 1832, it clearly is covered by the current version because the software is used in interstate and foreign commerce.

Section 1832 also is limited by the requirement that the act be "for the economic benefit" of anyone other than the owner. Courts have held that an employee does not violate Section 1832 merely by gaining skills and expertise at Employer A, quitting, and using those skills at Employer B. Individuals only violate Section 1832 if they use *confidential information* for the benefit of themselves or others, such as a new employer.[404]

5.4.3 Civil Actions for Trade Secret Misappropriation: The Defend Trade Secrets Act of 2016

Until 2016, the Economic Espionage Act was enforceable only by federal prosecutors. If a company wanted to obtain an injunction or recover damages for the theft of trade secrets, its only recourse was filing a lawsuit in state court under one of the 48 state trade secret misappropriation laws. Companies often were unable to effectively use state trade secret laws because the process was overly burdensome. Trade secret theft often affected a company's operations in all states, and bringing separate suits in each state would be impractical. Moreover, state courts often do not operate at the fast pace that is necessary to address trade secret theft involving a multinational company.

Recognizing the limitations of state trade secret laws, in 2014 members of Congress began to propose legislation to amend the Economic Espionage Act to allow companies to bring trade secret misappropriation lawsuits in federal court. They succeeded in 2016, when President Obama signed the Defend Trade Secrets Act of 2016. In his remarks at the bill signing, Obama touted the bill as necessary for global competition. "As many of you know, one of the biggest advantages that we've got in this global economy is that we innovate, we come up with new services, new goods, new products, new technologies,"

---

404 United States v. Martin, 228 F.3d 1, 11 (1st Cir. 2000) ("[I]t is clear that Congress did not intend to prohibit lawful competition such as the use of general skills or parallel development of a similar product, although it did mean to punish the disgruntled former employee who walks out of his former company with a computer diskette full of engineering schematics. In other words, 1832(a) was not designed to punish competition, even when such competition relies on the know-how of former employees of a direct competitor. It was, however, designed to prevent those employees (and their future employers) from taking advantage of confidential information gained, discovered, copied, or taken while employed elsewhere") (internal quotation marks and citations omitted).

Obama said. "Unfortunately, all too often, some of our competitors, instead of competing with us fairly, are trying to steal these trade secrets from American companies. And that means a loss of American jobs, a loss of American markets, a loss of American leadership."[405]

The primary component of the bill is a new civil remedy for trade secret misappropriation, allowing companies to directly sue under federal law if their trade secrets have been stolen. In the House Judiciary Committee report accompanying the bill, legislators expressed a desire to provide a "single, national standard for trade secret misappropriation with clear rules and predictability for everyone involved."[406] Congress recognized the close link between trade secret theft and cybersecurity, and noted that despite companies' efforts to improve their security measures, such theft has increasingly taken a toll on the U.S. economy.[407]

5.4.3.1 Definition of "Misappropriation"

The Defend Trade Secrets Act of 2016 (DTSA) allows companies to bring a federal civil suit if they have been the victims of misappropriation, a term that had not been previously used in the Economic Espionage Act. The bill provides two definitions for "misappropriation":

a) acquisition of a trade secret of another by a person who knows or has reason to know that the trade secret was acquired by improper means; or

b) disclosure or use of a trade secret of another without express or implied consent by a person who—

   i) used improper means to acquire knowledge of the trade secret;

   ii) at the time of disclosure or use, knew or had reason to know that the knowledge of the trade secret was—

      i) derived from or through a person who had used improper means to acquire the trade secret;

      ii) acquired under circumstances giving rise to a duty to maintain the secrecy of the trade secret or limit the use of the trade secret; or

      iii) derived from or through a person who owed a duty to the person seeking relief to maintain the secrecy of the trade secret or limit the use of the trade secret; or

---

405 WHITE HOUSE, *Remarks by the President at Signing of S. 1890, Defend Trade Secrets Act of 2016* (May 11, 2016).
406 H.R. REP. No. 114-529, at 6 (2016).
407 *Id.* at 4.

    iii) before a material change of the position of the person, knew or had reason to know that—
        i) the trade secret was a trade secret; and
        ii) knowledge of the trade secret had been acquired by accident or mistake.[408]

The term "improper means" is defined to include "theft, bribery, misrepresentation, breach or inducement of a breach of a duty to maintain secrecy, or espionage through electronic or other means[.]"[409] The term does not include lawful means of acquisition, including reverse engineering or independent derivation.[410]

The House Judiciary Committee report states that this definition is largely identical to that which is in the Uniform Trade Secrets Act, which is the basis for the 48 state trade secret laws. Congress used the state laws' definition "to make clear that this Act is not intended to alter the balance of current trade secret law or alter specific court decisions."[411]

For the first few years that the DTSA was on the books, courts appeared to maintain the state laws' broad definition of misappropriation. For instance, in 2018, the U.S. District Court for the Eastern District of Virginia denied a motion to dismiss a DTSA claim that satellite manufacturer Space Systems/Loral LLC brought against its competitor, Orbital ATK. Both companies did work for NASA. NASA allegedly notified Systems/Loral that an Orbital employee breached proprietary Systems/Loral data located on a NASA server, and Systems/Loral sued Orbital. The court concluded that Systems/Loral sufficiently stated a claim for misappropriation under the DTSA: "These facts taken as true satisfy the pleading requirement for misappropriation because it plausibly alleges 'acquisition of a trade secret of another by a person who knows or has reason to know that the trade secret was acquired by improper means.' The facts also support an inference of the 'disclosure ... of a trade secret ... without express or implied consent,' through 'improper means' and that Orbital at the very least 'knew or had reason to know that the trade secret was a trade secret,' and that it was 'acquired by accident or mistake.'"[412]

Because Congress intended for the DTSA's definition to mirror that of state laws, many courts have merged their analysis of state and federal trade secret claims when plaintiffs make claims under both laws. For instance, in a trade secret misappropriation claim brought under both the DTSA and Wisconsin's trade secret law, the court analyzed both claims simultaneously, noting that "the parties agree that substantively the [Wisconsin law] and DTSA are

---

408 18 U.S.C. § 1839(5).
409 18 U.S.C. § 1839(6).
410 *Id.*
411 *Id.* at 14.
412 Space Sys./Loral LLC v. Orbital ATK, 306 F. Supp. 3d 845, 854 (E.D. Va. 2018).

'essentially the same,' ... and that courts may look to the state [trade secrets law] when interpreting the DTSA."[413]

The Defend Trade Secrets Act provides three general types of relief that misappropriation victims may seek: (1) civil seizures, (2) injunctions and other equitable relief, and (3) damages.

5.4.3.2 Civil Seizures

In certain extraordinary circumstances, a company may go to federal court to seek an order for the seizure of property, if the seizure is necessary to prevent propagation or dissemination of the trade secret that has been misappropriated.[414] The company may apply for the seizure through an *ex parte* process, meaning that the other party need not be present to litigate the request. The House Judiciary Committee stated that it intends the civil seizure process to be used "in instances in which a defendant is seeking to flee the country or planning to disclose the trade secret to a third party immediately or is otherwise not amenable to the enforcement of the court's orders."[415]

For a court to grant a civil seizure motion, it must find the following to be clearly true:

- Other equitable relief would be inadequate.
- Denying the seizure would result in an "immediate and irreparable injury."
- The harm of denying the seizure outweighs the harm caused by the seizure.
- The applicant likely will succeed in demonstrating trade secret misappropriation.
- The person whose property is being seized actually has the trade secret.
- The application describes the location and subject of the proposed seizure with "reasonable particularity."
- The person against whom the seizure is being ordered, or other people, would make the property inaccessible to the court if notified.
- The applicant has not publicized the request for seizure.[416]

If a court issues a seizure order, it must set a hearing within seven days after the order has been issued. At the hearing, the applicant for the order has the burden of proving the facts that support the order. If the court determines that the applicant has not met that burden, the seizure order will be immediately modified or dissolved.[417]

---

413 Kuryakyn Holdings v. CIRO, 242 F. Supp. 3d 789 (W.D. Wis. 2017).
414 18 U.S.C. § 1836(b)(2)(A)(i).
415 H.R. Rep. No. 114-529, at 9–10 (2016).
416 18 U.S.C. § 1836(b)(2)(A)(ii).
417 18 U.S.C. § 1836(b)(2)(F).

Any party that has an interest in the matter seized may request an immediate hearing, which can be *ex parte,* to encrypt the seized material.[418]

5.4.3.3 Injunctions

A company that has been the victim of trade secret misappropriation may request an injunction to prevent actual or threatened misappropriation. Injunctions under this act may block threatened misappropriation, provided that they do not entirely prevent an individual from starting a new job. The injunction allows conditions to be placed on employment based on evidence of threatened misappropriation, but not only on information that the person knows. Such injunctions also may not conflict with state laws regarding restraints on trades or businesses.[419] The House Judiciary Committee stated that it added these limits on injunctive relief to "protect employee mobility," consistent with employment protection laws in many states.[420]

Injunctions also may require parties to take affirmative actions to protect a trade secret. In exceptional circumstances, injunctions may condition future use of a trade secret on the payment of a reasonable royalty, for a limited period of time.[421]

To obtain a preliminary injunction—often the first step in such litigation—plaintiffs must meet a high bar. For instance, in October 2017, the U.S. Court of Appeals reversed a preliminary injunction under the DTSA and the Colorado trade secrets statute in a case brought by a company against a former employee who, before leaving the company, allegedly asked his assistant for the contact information for 5,000 business contacts. The injunction prevented the former employee "from soliciting business from, or otherwise competing for the business of" any of the company's clients. The Tenth Circuit reversed the injunction, finding that the plaintiff failed to demonstrate "irreparable harm," which is a "significant risk that he or she will experience harm that cannot be compensated after the fact by money damages."[422]

5.4.3.4 Damages

The Defend Trade Secrets Act also enables plaintiffs to recover compensatory damages from the defendants. The DTSA allows plaintiffs to recover damages for actual loss caused by the misappropriation, as well as damages for unjust enrichment that are not included in the actual loss total.[423]

---

418 18 U.S.C. § 1836(b)(2)(H).
419 18 U.S.C. § 1836(b)(3)(A).
420 H.R. Rep. No. 114-529, at 12 (2016).
421 18 U.S.C. § 1836(b)(3)(A).
422 First Western Cap. Mgmt. v. Malamed, 874 F.3d 1136, 1141 (10th Cir. 2017).
423 18 U.S.C. § 1836(b)(3)(B)(i).

Alternatively, plaintiffs can seek to recover compensatory damages by requesting the imposition of a "reasonable royalty" for the defendant's unauthorized disclosure or use of the trade secret.[424] The House Judiciary Committee stated that it does not intend to encourage the use of reasonable royalties, and prefers alternative remedies.[425] If the court determines that the defendant "willfully and maliciously" misappropriated the trade secret, the plaintiff may recover exemplary damages of up to twice as much of the compensatory damages awarded.[426]

Although the DTSA is a relatively new statute, courts have indicated a willingness to allow federal claims to proceed in a similar manner as they do under the existing state trade secret laws. For instance, Teva Pharmaceuticals brought claims under, among other laws, the DTSA and Pennsylvania's trade secret laws against a former employee who allegedly provided confidential Teva documents to the chief executive of a competitor.[427] Teva also sued the competitor and its chief executive. Among the documents was a Complete Response Letter (CRL) from the Food and Drug Administration (FDA), containing confidential information regarding potential approval of a Teva drug. Two of the defendants argued that the FDA letter was not a trade secret. The court summarized both the DTSA and Pennsylvania trade secrets law as defining a "trade secret" as information that "(a) the owner has taken reasonable means to keep secret; (b) derives independent economic value, actual or potential, from being kept secret; (c) is not readily ascertainable by proper means; and (d) others who cannot readily access it would obtain economic value from its disclosure or use."[428] Applying this definition to the FDA letter, the court concluded that the information constitutes a trade secret: "These documents contain information that was not available outside Teva because it was classified as confidential and Teva took measures to restrict access to it. Its value was essential to Teva's maintaining an advantage over its competitors."[429]

5.4.3.5 Statute of Limitations

Plaintiffs must bring Economic Espionage Act civil actions within three years of the date the misappropriation was discovered or should have been discovered

---

424 18 U.S.C. § 1836(b)(3)(A).

425 H.R. Rep. No. 114-529, at 12 (2016) ("It is not the Committee's intent to encourage the use of reasonable royalties to resolve trade secret misappropriation. Rather, the Committee prefers other remedies that, first, halt the misappropriator's use and dissemination of the misappropriated trade secret and, second, make available appropriate damages.").

426 *Id.*

427 Teva Pharms. v. Sandhu, 291 F. Supp. 3d 659 (E.D. Pa. 2018).

428 *Id.* at 675.

429 *Id.*

through exercise of reasonable diligence.[430] This requirement is identical to the statute of limitations in the Uniform Trade Secrets Act.[431]

5.5 Budapest Convention on Cybercrime

An increasing number of cyberattacks on U.S. computers originate from outside the United States. In 2001, the Council of Europe recognized the need to address global cybercrime and drafted the Budapest Convention on Cybercrime. Nations that ratify the convention agree to incorporate a series of substantive requirements in their cybercrime statutes, and allow international cooperation in the investigation and prosecution of cross-border crime. As of early 2019, 61 nations had ratified the Budapest Convention. The United States ratified the Budapest Convention in 2006.[432]

The Budapest Convention requires member states to adopt measures that address the following offenses:

- Illegal access
- Illegal interception
- Data interference
- System interference
- Misuse of devices
- Computer-related forgery
- Computer-related fraud
- Offences related to child pornography
- Offences related to infringements of copyright and related rights
- Attempt and aiding or abetting
- Corporate liability[433]

The Budapest Convention also requires states to develop procedures to expedite the preservation of stored data, develop particular procedures for searching and seizing the data, empower its authorities to collect data in real time, and intercept content data. It also provides a framework for extradition of individuals for the covered computer crimes.[434]

---

430 18 U.S.C. § 1836(d).
431 H.R. REP. NO. 114-529, at 12 (2016).
432 *See* COUNCIL OF EUROPE, BUDAPEST CONVENTION AND RELATED STANDARDS, https://www.coe.int/en/web/cybercrime/the-budapest-convention.
433 *Id.*
434 *Id.*

One significant limitation of the Budapest Convention is that nations that are common sources of hacks against the United States, including Russia, North Korea, China, and Iran, are not parties to the convention. Therefore, they are not required to adopt the substantive and procedural requirements of the Budapest Convention. More importantly, they are not subject to the Budapest Convention's requirements to extradite computer criminals.

6

U.S. Government Cyber Structure and Public–Private Cybersecurity Partnerships

Much of this book focuses on the consequences that a company may face for inadequate cybersecurity, such as enforcement actions or lawsuits by the Federal Trade Commission or state attorneys general. However, the federal government's role in private sector cybersecurity is not merely that of a regulator. The government also operates a number of programs that are designed to help companies battle the ever-evolving field of cybersecurity threats. Cyberspace is unique in that it involves both public and private infrastructure, and therefore the federal government recognizes that it has a role in securing the Internet. Moreover, the federal government can act as a central repository of cybersecurity information.

This chapter first reviews the increasingly centralized civilian cybersecurity operations, many of which are located within the Department of Homeland Security (DHS). It next examines DHS's cybersecurity information-sharing program, created by the Cybersecurity Act of 2015. The chapter then reviews the voluntary Cybersecurity Framework developed by the National Institute of Standards and Technology. Finally, the chapter examines the U.S. military's ability to protect civilian networks and systems, and the limits placed on these activities by the Posse Comitatus Act.

6.1   U.S. Government's Civilian Cybersecurity Organization

The U.S. federal government does not have a single agency or department that is responsible for nationwide cybersecurity, as it does for health, education, housing, and other key policy issues. Due to the unique nature of cybersecurity, responsibilities are scattered throughout the federal government.

Many of the federal government's proactive cybersecurity programs are centered in the U.S. Department of Homeland Security, which has primary

Cybersecurity Law, Second Edition. Jeff Kosseff.
© 2020 John Wiley & Sons, Inc. Published 2020 by John Wiley & Sons, Inc.
Companion Website: www.wiley.com/go/kosseff/cybersecurity2e

responsibility for civilian (nonmilitary) cybersecurity. Over the years, statutes and presidential orders have increasingly consolidated civilian cybersecurity responsibilities within DHS.

Until 2018, DHS's cybersecurity operations were housed in the Office of Cybersecurity and Communications, part of DHS's National Protection and Programs Directorate (a broad organization that also includes programs to protect federal property and critical infrastructure from terrorism and natural disasters). Within the office was the National Cybersecurity and Communications Integration Center (NCCIC). And within NCCIC is the U.S. Computer Emergency Readiness Team (US-CERT), which provides round-the-clock monitoring for emerging cybersecurity threats, and issues alerts about significant cybersecurity issues that it has detected. Recognizing the need to elevate cybersecurity, in November 2018 Congress passed legislation that elevated all of the cybersecurity functions to the Cybersecurity and Infrastructure Security Agency, whose director now reports directly to the DHS secretary.[1]

In recent years, Congress and other officials have made clear that DHS plays a central role in coordinating civilian cybersecurity. In 2015, Congress passed the Cybersecurity Act of 2015, which, as described later in this chapter, provided limited legal immunity to encourage the private sector to share information about cybersecurity threats and defensive measures with the federal government. A lesser-publicized provision in that law significantly expanded the cybersecurity authorities of NCCIC. The provision, entitled the National Cybersecurity Protection Advancement Act of 2015, centralized the responsibility for cyber-threat information sharing within NCCIC (now part of the Cybersecurity and Infrastructure Security Agency). The statute also provides DHS with significant responsibility for nationwide cybersecurity planning.[2]

DHS, however, is far from the only federal agency or department that has taken some ownership of cybersecurity. The President also has advisers dedicated to cybersecurity, as does the President's National Security Council.

The U.S. State Department additionally has a cybersecurity coordinator who is dedicated to representing the nation on international cybersecurity issues. Among the issues that the State Department frequently discusses with other nations are export controls, international cybercrime standards, and cyber-threat sharing and incident response programs.

The U.S. Department of Commerce also is quite involved in helping U.S. businesses reduce the risk of data breaches and other incidents. The Commerce Department's National Institute of Standards and Technology has developed a

---

1 *See* Pub. L. No. 115-454.
2 *See* Pub. L. No. 114-113.

number of voluntary, nonbinding cybersecurity standards, including the Cybersecurity Framework discussed later in this chapter.[3]

The U.S. Justice Department's Computer Crimes and Intellectual Property Section leads the government's efforts in prosecuting cybercrimes. Among the many responsibilities of the section is partnering with the private sector and educating the sector about emerging cybercrime issues.[4]

Departments that focus on a particular industry often have attempted to help those industries ensure that they have adequate cybersecurity. For instance, the Food and Drug Administration has issued guidelines for the cybersecurity of medical devices, an issue that has long been seen as a serious national security concern.[5] The U.S. Energy Department long has listed cybersecurity of the electric grid among its top priorities, and has started a threat-sharing information exchange for utilities.[6] The Federal Communications Commission has offered cybersecurity resources to assist telecommunications providers in shoring up their network security.[7] The National Highway Traffic Safety Administration, part of the U.S. Department of Transportation, has been researching the cybersecurity risks associated with connected automobiles.[8]

In July 2016, President Obama issued Presidential Policy Directive 41 (PPD 41), which provides some guidance as to the responsibilities of the various federal agencies during a significant cybersecurity incident in either the public or private sector. The directive set forth the following roles and responsibilities:

- **Justice Department (and FBI)** is the lead agency for *threat response*, which includes law enforcement and national intelligence investigations, evidence gathering, threat mitigation, and information sharing.
- **Department of Homeland Security** is the lead agency for *asset response*, which includes helping companies and governments protect assets and mitigate harms.
- **Office of the Director of National Intelligence** is the lead agency for *intelligence support and related activities,* which includes "situational threat awareness and sharing of related intelligence, the integrated analysis of threat

---

3 *See* National Institute of Standards and Technology, Cybersecurity, https://www.nist.gov/topics/cybersecurity.
4 *See* Department of Justice, Computer Crime and Intellectual Property Section, https://www.justice.gov/criminal-ccips.
5 *See* Food & Drug Administration, Cybersecurity, https://www.fda.gov/medical-devices/digital-health/cybersecurity.
6 *See* Energy Department, Office of Cybersecurity, Energy Security, and Emergency Response, https://www.energy.gov/national-security-safety/cybersecurity.
7 *See* Federal Communications Commission, Cyber Security and Network Reliability, https://www.fcc.gov/general/cyber-security-and-network-reliability.
8 *See* National Highway Traffic Safety Administration, Vehicle Cybersecurity, https://www.nhtsa.gov/technology-innovation/vehicle-cybersecurity.

trends and events, the identification of knowledge gaps, and the ability to degrade or mitigate adversary threat capabilities."[9]

Although PPD 41 designates lead agencies for threat response, asset response, and intelligence support, it stresses the concept of "shared responsibility" during a cyber incident: "Individuals, the private sector, and government agencies have a shared vital interest and complementary roles and responsibilities in protecting the Nation from malicious cyber activity and managing cyber incidents and their consequences."[10] PPD 41 also recognizes a "unity of government effort" that urges coordination rather than compartmentalization of individual agency efforts: "Various government entities possess different roles, responsibilities, authorities, and capabilities that can all be brought to bear on cyber incidents. These efforts must be coordinated to achieve optimal results. Whichever Federal agency first becomes aware of a cyber incident will rapidly notify other relevant Federal agencies in order to facilitate a unified Federal response and ensure that the right combination of agencies responds to a particular incident."[11]

In September 2018, the Trump Administration released its National Cyber Strategy, which "recognizes that the United States is engaged in a continuous competition against strategic adversaries, rogue states, and terrorist and criminal networks."[12] The strategy's key pillars are:

- Defend the homeland by protecting networks, systems, functions, and data;
- Promote American prosperity by nurturing a secure, thriving digital economy and fostering strong domestic innovation;
- Preserve peace and security by strengthening the ability of the United States—in concert with allies and partners—to deter and, if necessary, punish those who use cyber tools for malicious purposes; and
- Expand American influence abroad to extend the key tenets of an open, interoperable, reliable, and secure Internet.[13]

6.2 Department of Homeland Security Information Sharing under the Cybersecurity Act of 2015

DHS has long operated the US-CERT, but the private sector has been hesitant to provide real-time threat information to the federal government because of

---

9 PRESIDENTIAL POLICY DIRECTIVE—UNITED STATES CYBER INCIDENT COORDINATION (July 26, 2016).

10 Id.

11 Id.

12 WHITE HOUSE, NATIONAL CYBER STRATEGY OF THE UNITED STATES OF AMERICA (2018), at 3.

13 Id. at 1.

concerns about liability under a wide range of laws, including antitrust and privacy. Recognizing this barrier, after years of heated debate, Congress in late 2015 passed, and President Obama signed, the Cybersecurity Act of 2015. The Cybersecurity Act has a number of components, including the affirmation of companies' ability to monitor and defend their networks, provisions that are discussed in Chapter 7 of this book. The new law also creates a greatly expanded platform by which private companies and the government can exchange information about cyber-threat indicators and defensive measures.

The information sharing—and limited immunity—apply only for the sharing or receipt of cyber-threat indicators or defensive measures. The statute broadly defines "cyber-threat indicator" as information that is necessary to describe or identify:

- malicious reconnaissance, including anomalous patterns of communications that appear to be transmitted for the purpose of gathering technical information related to a cybersecurity threat or security vulnerability;
- a method of defeating a security control or exploitation of a security vulnerability;
- a security vulnerability, including anomalous activity that appears to indicate the existence of a security vulnerability;
- a method of causing a user with legitimate access to an information system or information that is stored on, processed by, or transiting an information system to unwittingly enable the defeat of a security control or exploitation of a security vulnerability;
- malicious cyber command and control;
- the actual or potential harm caused by an incident including a description of the information exfiltrated as a result of a particular cybersecurity threat;
- any other attribute of a cybersecurity threat, if disclosure of such attribute is not otherwise prohibited by law; or
- any combination thereof.[14]

> ### Examples of Cyber-Threat Indicators
>
> In a June 2016 Guidance for nonfederal entities that seek to participate in the information-sharing program established under the Cybersecurity Act of 2015, the U.S. Department of Homeland Security provided these examples of cyber-threat indicators that the private sector could share with the government:
>
> - A company could report that its web server log files show that a particular IP address has sent web traffic that appears to be

---

14 6 U.S.C. § 1501(6).

testing whether the company's content management system has not been updated to patch a recent vulnerability.

- A security researcher could report on her discovery of a technique that permits unauthorized access to an industrial control system.
- A software publisher could report a vulnerability it has discovered in its software.
- A managed security service company could report a pattern of domain name lookups that it believes corresponds to malware infection.
- A manufacturer could report unexecuted malware found on its network.
- A researcher could report on the domain names or IP addresses associated with botnet command and control servers.
- An engineering company that suffers a computer intrusion could describe the types of engineering files that appear to have been exfiltrated, as a way of warning other companies with similar assets.
- A newspaper suffering a distributed denial-of-service attack to its website could report the IP addresses that are sending malicious traffic.

Source: DEPARTMENT OF HOMELAND SECURITY, DEPARTMENT OF JUSTICE, GUIDANCE TO ASSIST NON-FEDERAL ENTITIES TO SHARE CYBER THREAT INDICATORS AND DEFENSIVE MEASURES WITH FEDERAL ENTITIES UNDER THE CYBERSECURITY INFORMATION SHARING ACT OF 2015 (June 15, 2016).

The statute defines "defensive measure" as "an action, device, procedure, signature, technique, or other measure applied to an information system or information that is stored on, processed by, or transiting an information system that detects, prevents, or mitigates a known or suspected threat or security vulnerability."[15] The statute explicitly states that "defensive measure" does not include "a measure that destroys, renders unusable, provides unauthorized access to, or substantially harms an information system or information stored on, processed by, or transiting such information system" that is neither owned by the private entity that is operating the defensive measure or another entity that is "authorized to provide consent and has provided consent to that private entity for operation of the measure."[16]

To encourage sharing of information regarding cyber-threat indicators and defensive measures, the law provides limited immunity for companies that share information with other organizations or the federal government, via specific procedures promulgated by the Attorney General and Secretary of Homeland Security.[17] If a private entity complies with the requirements of the Cybersecurity

---

15 6 U.S.C. § 1501(7).
16 *Id.*
17 6 U.S.C. § 1505.

Act of 2015 and accompanying regulations, it will not be held liable for monitoring its systems for cyber threats. Moreover, private entities are not liable for properly sharing or receiving cyber-threat indicators under the Cybersecurity Act of 2015.

The immunity only applies for sharing information for a "cybersecurity purpose," which the statute defines as "the purpose of protecting an information system or information that is stored on, processed by, or transiting an information system from a cybersecurity threat or security vulnerability."[18] The statute defines "cybersecurity threat" as "an action, not protected by the First Amendment to the Constitution of the United States, on or through an information system that may result in an unauthorized effort to adversely impact the security, availability, confidentiality, or integrity of an information system or information that is stored on, processed by, or transiting an information system."[19] "Cybersecurity threat" does not include a violation of consumer terms of service or a licensing agreement.[20] This relatively narrow definition is intended to ensure that companies cannot gather and share private information with the government for reasons entirely unrelated to cybersecurity.

The limited immunity only applies if the private companies comply with DHS procedures—required under the Cybersecurity Act of 2015—to adequately secure the information from unauthorized access, and to review cyber-threat indicators *before sharing* and remove any information that is not directly related to the cybersecurity threat. For instance, imagine that a retailer has seen a specific type of attack resulting in the theft of its customers' payment card information. That retailer should not actually transmit to DHS the list of compromised customer names and payment card numbers, as it is difficult to imagine that such information would be directly related to the cybersecurity threat. Instead, the company should either describe the attack, or redact the personally identifiable information from the data that it sends to DHS.

The Cybersecurity Act of 2015 explicitly states that it does not create a duty for the private sector to share cyber threats, nor does it create a duty for the private sector to warn or act due to its receipt of cyber-threat information.[21] The Cybersecurity Act of 2015 requires DHS to create an information system that:

- accepts cyber-threat indicators and defensive measures from any nonfederal entity;
- ensures that federal entities receive the cyber-threat indicators in real time; and
- ensures that the sharing protects privacy rights and complies with other regulations.[22]

---

18 6 U.S.C. § 1501(4).
19 6 U.S.C. § 1501(5).
20 *Id.*
21 6 U.S.C. § 1505(c).
22 6 U.S.C. § 1504.

In 2016, DHS unveiled its Automated Indicator Sharing (AIS) system, operated by NCCIC and US-CERT as required by the new cybersecurity law. Private entities voluntarily receive and share indicators through AIS, typically anonymously unless they choose to have their name associated with the cyber-threat indicator. DHS states that it does not validate the cyber-threat indicators; instead, it shares indicators based on the volume and velocity of the tips that it receives, as quickly as possible.

DHS does not require companies to go through an extensive vetting process to use AIS. Instead, they must agree to its Terms of Use and connect to DHS's managed system.

As required by the Cybersecurity Act of 2015, DHS has built in a number of functions to protect privacy in the AIS. Among the protections are:

- using automated technology to delete unnecessary personally identifiable information;
- using human review of certain data to ensure privacy and proper functions;
- minimizing the data that DHS includes in cyber-threat indicator reports;
- only retaining the information that is necessary to combat cyber threats; and
- only collecting information that is used either for network defense or law enforcement.[23]

Even if companies do not participate in AIS, they may share cyber-threat indicators and defensive measures with DHS via its website or email.

Because the law was recently added to the books, as of publication of this book, we do not have any published court opinions that interpret the terms "cyber-threat indicator" or "cybersecurity threat." However, the broad language of the definitions suggests that if a service provider reasonably believes that email messages or other Internet traffic might help companies understand a cybersecurity threat, such as malware, then the service provider would be immune from lawsuits under the Cybersecurity Act—or any other federal or state laws, for that matter.

6.3 Critical Infrastructure Executive Order and the National Institute of Standards and Technology's Cybersecurity Framework

Over the past decade, policymakers have become increasingly concerned that companies have not developed adequate procedures and policies to guard

---

23 *See* Department of Homeland Security, Privacy Impact Assessment for Automated Indicator Sharing (Mar. 16, 2016); Department of Homeland Security, Privacy and Civil Liberties Final Guidelines: Cybersecurity Information Sharing Act of 2015 (June 15, 2018).

against cyber threats. This is particularly concerning because private companies operate a great deal of the power grids, communications networks, and other infrastructure that is central to the U.S. economy and national security.

In 2013, President Obama recognized this concern in an executive order regarding the cybersecurity of "critical infrastructure," which he broadly defined as "systems and assets, whether physical or virtual, so vital to the United States that the incapacity or destruction of such systems and assets would have a debilitating impact on security, national economic security, national public health or safety, or any combination of those matters."[24]

In the executive order, President Obama articulated a national policy "to enhance the security and resilience of the Nation's critical infrastructure and to maintain a cyber environment that encourages efficiency, innovation, and economic prosperity while promoting safety, security, business confidentiality, privacy, and civil liberties."[25] The executive order calls for achieving those goals through a "partnership" with the private sector. This overall approach is noteworthy because it does not call for new regulations or laws to force companies to adopt specific safeguards. The executive order appears to recognize that strong cybersecurity is in companies' best interests, and that the government can help companies achieve those goals.

The executive order directed the Attorney General, Secretary of Homeland Security, and Director of National Intelligence to establish a process for sharing information about cyber threats—a process that was later codified and expanded upon in the Cybersecurity Act of 2015's information-sharing program (described in section 6.2). The executive order also directed the Commerce Department's National Institute of Standards and Technology (NIST) to develop a voluntary cybersecurity framework for operators of critical infrastructure. The executive order directs NIST to incorporate industry feedback and align "policy, business and technological approaches to address cyber risks."

In February 2014, in response to the executive order, NIST released the Framework for Improving Critical Infrastructure Cybersecurity. The 39-page document draws on a number of existing security standards. The NIST Framework does not proscribe or prescribe specific technological solutions; rather, as its drafters state, it "provides organization and structure to today's multiple approaches to cybersecurity by assembling standards, guidelines, and practices that are working effectively in industry today." NIST emphasizes that its framework is not a "one-size-fits-all" cybersecurity solution, and that companies have a wide range of risks and are best suited to "determine activities that are important to critical service delivery and can prioritize investments to maximize the impact of each dollar spent."

---

24 EXECUTIVE ORDER—IMPROVING CRITICAL INFRASTRUCTURE CYBERSECURITY (Feb. 12, 2013).
25 *Id.*

The NIST Framework core consists of five key principles for cybersecurity risk management. The following list sets out the principles as stated by NIST, along with the implementation factors listed in the framework (edited slightly). The NIST Framework is presented in multiple charts; this book consolidates those principles into a single list for clarity and brevity:

- *Identify.* Understand the organization and the cybersecurity risks to its systems, assets, data, and capabilities. Among the components of this function:
  - Inventory software platforms and physical devices and systems.
  - Map organizational communications and data flows.
  - Catalogue external information systems.
  - Prioritize hardware, devices, data, time, personnel, and software based on their classification, criticality, and business value.
  - Establish cybersecurity roles and responsibilities for the workforce and third-party stakeholders, such as suppliers and customers.
  - Identify and communicate the organization's role in the supply chain, critical infrastructure, and industry sector.
  - Establish and communicate priorities for organizational mission, objectives, and activities.
  - Establish dependencies and critical functions for delivery of critical services.
  - Establish resilience requirements to support delivery of critical services at all operating states.
  - Establish and communicate organizational information security policy.
  - Coordinate and align cybersecurity roles and responsibilities with internal roles and external partners.
  - Understand and manage legal and regulatory requirements for cybersecurity, including privacy.
  - Address cybersecurity risks in governance and risk management processes.
  - Document and identify asset vulnerabilities.
  - Receive threat and vulnerability information from information-sharing forums.
  - Identify and document threats.
  - Identify potential business impacts.
  - Use threats, vulnerabilities, likelihoods, and impacts to determine risk.
  - Identify and prioritize risk responses.
  - Establish and run risk management processes.
  - Determine and clearly express organizational risk tolerance, in considering the organization's role in critical infrastructure and its sectoral risks.
  - Identify, establish, assess, manage, and agree to cyber supply-chain risk management processes and suppliers and third-party partners of information systems, and use contracts with these parties to implement appropriate security objectives.

- Routinely assess third parties' compliance with contractual obligations, and conduct response and recovery planning and testing with these providers.
- ***Protect.*** Implement safeguards to deliver services:
  - Manage, issue, verify, revoke, and audit identities and credentials for authorized devices, physical access to assets, and remote access.
  - Manage access permissions and authorizations, with the principles of least privilege and separation of duties.
  - Ensure that identities are proofed and bound to credentials and asserted in interactions.
  - Authenticate users, devices, and other assets commensurate with the risk of the transaction.
  - Protect network integrity, incorporating network segregation when possible.
  - Inform and train all users, and ensure that privileged users, senior executives, security personnel and third-party stakeholders understand roles and responsibilities.
  - Protect data at rest and in transit.
  - Formally manage assets throughout removal, transfers, and disposition.
  - Maintain adequate capacity to ensure data availability.
  - Implement protections against data leaks.
  - Use integrity-checking mechanisms to verify software, firmware, and information integrity.
  - Separate development and testing from the protection environment.
  - Use integrity-checking mechanisms to verify hardware integrity.
  - Create and maintain a baseline configuration of information technology and industrial control systems.
  - Implement a system development life cycle.
  - Implement configuration change control processes.
  - Periodically conduct, maintain, and test backups of information.
  - Meet policy and regulations regarding the physical operating environment.
  - Destroy data according to policy.
  - Continuously improve protection processes.
  - Share effectiveness of protection technologies with appropriate parties.
  - Implement, manage, and test response and recovery plans.
  - Include cybersecurity in human resources practices.
  - Develop and implement a vulnerability management plan.
  - Perform and log maintenance and repair of assets, and approve remote maintenance in a manner that prevents unauthorized access.
  - Develop and review audit logs.
  - Protect and restrict use of removable media.
  - Control access to systems according to the principle of least functionality.
  - Protect communications and control networks.

- Implement mechanisms such as failsafe, load balancing, and hot swap to achieve resilience requirements in normal and adverse situations.

- *Detect.* Continuously monitor the organization's systems and networks to more quickly become aware of cybersecurity incidents:

  - Establish and manage a baseline of network operations and expected data flows.
  - Analyze detected events to understand attack targets and methods.
  - Collect and correlate event data from multiple sources.
  - Determine the impact of events.
  - Establish incident alert thresholds.
  - Monitor network, physical environment, and personnel activity to detect cybersecurity events.
  - Detect malicious code and unauthorized mobile code.
  - Monitor external service provider activity.
  - Monitor for unauthorized personnel, connections, devices, and software.
  - Perform vulnerability scans.
  - Define roles and responsibilities to ensure accountability.
  - Ensure that detection activities comply with all applicable requirements.
  - Test detection processes.
  - Communicate event detection information to appropriate parties.
  - Continuously improve detection processes.

- *Respond.* Develop and implement a cybersecurity incident response program:

  - Execute a response plan during or after an event.
  - Ensure that personnel know their roles and order of operations when a response is needed.
  - Report events consistent with established criteria.
  - Share information consistent with response plans.
  - Coordinate with stakeholders consistent with response plans.
  - Voluntarily share information with external stakeholders.
  - Investigate notifications from detection systems.
  - Understand the impact of an incident.
  - Perform forensics.
  - Categorize incidents consistent with response plans.
  - Establish processes to receive, analyze, and respond to vulnerabilities disclosed to the organization from internal and external sources.
  - Contain and mitigate incidents.
  - Mitigate and document newly identified vulnerabilities as accepted risks.
  - Incorporate lessons learned into response plans and update response strategies.

- **Recover.** Develop and implement a plan to restore networks and systems after a cybersecurity incident:

  - Execute a recovery plan during or after an event.
  - Incorporate lessons learned into a response plan and update recovery strategy.
  - Manage public relations.
  - Repair reputation after an event.
  - Communicate recovery activities to internal stakeholders and executive and management team.

NIST Cybersecurity Framework Implementation Tiers

The NIST Cybersecurity Framework provides four "implementation tiers" that evaluate a company's "rigor and sophistication" in cybersecurity risk management. Tier 1 is the lowest level of rigor and sophistication, and Tier 4 is the highest. However, NIST recognizes that Tier 4 simply is not possible for all organizations. NIST suggests that companies determine the desirable tier, based on feasibility of implementation and risk tolerance. The following is NIST's description of each of the implementation tiers, as stated in the Framework:

Tier 1: Partial

- *Risk management process.* Organizational cybersecurity risk management practices are not formalized, and risk is managed in an ad hoc and sometimes reactive manner. Prioritization of cybersecurity activities may not be directly informed by organizational risk objectives, the threat environment, or business/mission requirements.
- *Integrated risk management program.* There is limited awareness of cybersecurity risk at the organizational level. The organization implements cybersecurity risk management on an irregular, case-by-case basis due to varied experience or information gained from outside sources. The organization may not have processes that enable cybersecurity information to be shared within the organization.
- *External participation.* The organization does not understand its role in the larger ecosystem with respect to either its dependencies or dependents. The organization does not collaborate with or receive information (e.g., threat intelligence, best practices, technologies) from other entities (e.g., buyers, suppliers, dependencies, dependents, ISAOs, researchers, governments), nor does it share information. The organization is generally unaware of the cyber supply chain risks of the products and services it provides and that it uses.

Tier 2: Risk Informed

- *Risk management process.* Risk management practices are approved by management but may not be established as organization-wide policy. Prioritization of cybersecurity activities and protection needs is directly informed by organizational risk objectives, the threat environment, or business/mission requirements.
- *Integrated risk management program.* There is an awareness of cybersecurity risk at the organizational level but an organization-wide approach to managing cybersecurity risk has not been established. Cybersecurity information is shared within the organization on an informal basis. Consideration of cybersecurity in organizational objectives and programs may occur at some but not all levels of the organization. Cyber risk assessment of organizational and external assets occurs, but is not typically repeatable or reoccurring.
- *External participation.* Generally, the organization understands its role in the larger ecosystem with respect to either its own dependencies or dependents, but has both. The organization collaborates with and receives some information from other entities and generates some of its own information, but may not share information with others. Additionally, the organization is aware of the cyber supply chain risks associated with the products and services it provides and uses, but does not act consistently or formally upon those risks.

Tier 3: Repeatable

- *Risk management process.* The organization's risk management practices are formally approved and expressed as policy. Organizational cybersecurity practices are regularly updated based on the application of risk management processes to changes in business/mission requirements and a changing threat and technology landscape.
- *Integrated risk management program.* There is an organization-wide approach to manage cybersecurity risk. Risk-informed policies, processes, and procedures are defined, implemented as intended, and reviewed. Consistent methods are in place to respond effectively to changes in risk. Personnel possess the knowledge and skills to perform their appointed roles and responsibilities. The organization consistently and accurately monitors cybersecurity risk of organizational assets. Senior cybersecurity and noncybersecurity executives communicate regularly regarding cybersecurity risk. Senior executives ensure consideration of cybersecurity through all lines of operation in the organization.
- *External participation.* The organization understands its role, dependencies, and dependents in the larger ecosystem and may contribute to the community's broader understanding of risks. It collaborates with and receives

information from other entities regularly that complements internally generated information, and shares information with other entities. The organization is aware of the cyber supply chain risks associated with the products and services it provides and that it uses. Additionally, it usually acts formally upon those risks, including mechanisms such as written agreements to communicate baseline requirements, governance structures (e.g., risk councils), and policy implementation and monitoring.

Tier 4: Adaptive

- *Risk management process.* The organization adapts its cybersecurity practices based on previous and current cybersecurity activities. Through a process of continuous improvement incorporating advanced cybersecurity technologies and practices, the organization actively adapts to a changing threat and technology landscape and responds in a timely and effective manner to evolving, sophisticated threats.
- *Integrated risk management program.* There is an organization-wide approach to managing cybersecurity risk that uses risk-informed policies, processes, and procedures to address potential cybersecurity events. The relationship between cybersecurity risk and organizational objectives is clearly understood and considered when making decisions. Senior executives monitor cybersecurity risk in the same context as financial risk and other organizational risks. The organizational budget is based on an understanding of the current and predicted risk environment and risk tolerance. Business units implement executive vision and analyze system-level risks in the context of the organizational risk tolerances. Cybersecurity risk management is part of the organizational culture and evolves from an awareness of previous activities and continuous awareness of activities on their systems and networks.
- *External participation.* The organization understands its role, dependencies, and dependents in the larger ecosystem and contributes to the community's broader understanding of risks. It receives, generates, and reviews prioritized information that informs continuous analysis of its risks as the threat and technology landscapes evolve. The organization shares that information internally and externally with other collaborators. The organization uses real-time or near real-time information to understand and consistently act upon cyber supply chain risks associated with the products and services it provides and that it uses. Additionally, it communicates proactively, using formal (e.g. agreements) and information mechanisms to develop and maintain strong supply chain relationships.

Source: National Institute of Standards and Technology, Framework for Improving Critical Infrastructure Cybersecurity, Version 1.1 (2018).

Keep in mind that the NIST Cybersecurity Framework is entirely voluntary, even for operators of the most critical infrastructure. NIST did not intend to create binding requirements, nor does it have the authority to do so.

However, companies are increasingly adopting the framework, in the manner they see fit, to strengthen their cybersecurity processes. The Cybersecurity Framework is increasingly becoming a de facto standard of care that companies expect their business partners to follow. Accordingly, it is in a company's best interests to demonstrate that it complies, to some extent, with the general principles articulated in the framework. Moreover, if a company experienced a breach or other cybersecurity incident, and subsequently faces a lawsuit or regulatory action, it might reduce the likelihood of liability if it could demonstrate the steps that it took to integrate the NIST Cybersecurity Framework into its operations.

Government agencies have recognized the value of the Cybersecurity Framework and have integrated it into their operations. For instance, in October 2015, the federal Office of Management and Budget, which is partly responsible for setting government-wide information technology policies, required federal agencies and departments to adopt the framework. Similarly, in 2014, the state of Virginia began requiring its agencies to adopt the framework. The Cybersecurity Framework is a good example of a public–private partnership that seeks to improve cybersecurity in the private sector without imposing regulations or the fear of costly litigation.

6.4 U.S. Military Involvement in Cybersecurity and the Posse Comitatus Act

This chapter has focused on *civilian* government agencies, such as DHS and NIST, that assist the private sector with cybersecurity. However, some of the most skilled government cybersecurity experts are in the military. Due to centuries-old restrictions, these experts face limits on their ability to help companies and individuals defend their systems and networks.

The National Security Agency (NSA), which is part of the U.S. Defense Department, specializes in signals intelligence—that is, intercepting foreign intelligence information. The NSA employs some of the world's leading code-breakers, who seek to intercept and decode foreign intelligence communications. NSA also operates an Information Assurance Directorate, which is charged with protecting the security of national security information.[26]

---

26 *See* NATIONAL SECURITY AGENCY, WHAT WE DO, https://www.nsa.gov/What-We-Do/.

Headquartered in the same location as NSA—and run by the same individual—is U.S. Cyber Command. As of publication of this book, policymakers had been discussing a proposal to separate NSA and Cyber Command. Cyber Command is charged with leading the Defense Department's defense of its information networks, and with conducting cyber operations on behalf of the U.S. military.[27]

In the Department of Defense's 2015 strategic report on cyber issues, it stated that the department "must work with its interagency partners, the private sector, and allied and partner nations to deter and if necessary defeat a cyberattack of significant consequence on the U.S. homeland and U.S. interests."[28] Likewise, the 2018 Cyber Command Vision states that Cyber Command "will prepare, operate, and collaborate with combatant commands, services, departments, allies, and industry to continuously thwart and contest hostile cyberspace actors wherever found."[29] Such a mission is sound, as the Defense Department has deep expertise in cyber, and protecting national security is clearly within the Department of Defense's missions. However, a long-standing legal rule known as posse comitatus in some cases may impose some limits on such actions.

The Posse Comitatus Act, passed in 1878, prohibits the use of the U.S. military to execute the laws. It states:

> Whoever, except in cases and under circumstances expressly authorized by the Constitution or Act of Congress, willfully uses any part of the Army or the Air Force as a posse comitatus or otherwise to execute the laws shall be fined under this title or imprisoned not more than two years, or both.[30]

Congress passed the law after the Civil War, in response to concerns of the former Confederacy that the federal government would use its military to create a police state.[31] Although the statute only mentions the Army and Air Force, regulations also apply the prohibition to the Navy and Marines. The Posse Comitatus Act does not apply to state National Guard forces or the U.S. Coast Guard.[32]

For the U.S. military to support domestic cyber defense, it must not be prohibited by the Posse Comitatus Act. Military cyber operations that enforce domestic laws must fall under another statute that provides an exception to the Posse Comitatus Act. Most notably, the Insurrection Act, which was passed in

---

27 *See* U.S. Cyber Command, Command Vision for U.S. Cyber Command (2018).

28 Department of Defense Cyber Strategy (Apr. 2015), at 14.

29 U.S. Cyber Command, Command Vision for U.S. Cyber Command (2018), at 7.

30 18 U.S.C. § 1385.

31 *See* Matt Matthews, The Posse Comitatus Act and the United States Army: A Historical Perspective (2006), at 23–34.

32 *See* Congressional Research Service, The Posse Comitatus Act and Related Matters: The Use of the Military to Execute Civilian Law (Nov. 6, 2018).

1807, before the Posse Comitatus Act, allows the president to use the armed forces to enforce laws or suppress rebellion if "unlawful obstructions, combinations, or assemblages, or rebellion against the authority of the United States, make it impracticable to enforce the laws of the United States in any State by the ordinary course of judicial proceedings."[33]

The Posse Comitatus Act only applies to *execution* of civilian laws. The military still may assist with non-law enforcement activities, such as protecting assets from a cyber attack, without raising Posse Comitatus Act concerns. A group of rules known as Defense Support of Civil Authorities allows the Defense Secretary to provide law enforcement with support, such as sharing relevant information collected during military training or operations.[34]

In its September 2015 update to its manual on defense support of civil operations, the Department of Defense addressed the types of cyber incidents that might allow the U.S. military to provide domestic government agencies with support. The Defense Department wrote that "[l]arge-scale cyber incidents may overwhelm government and private-sector resources by disrupting the internet and taxing critical infrastructure information systems," and that complications from these incidents "may threaten lives, property, the economy, and national security."[35] In such cases, the department wrote, its services "support the remediation, restoration, and protection of critical emergency telecommunication networks and infrastructure," and that "[c]yberspace technical assistance may be provided in response to a request from a lead federal agency."[36]

6.5 Vulnerabilities Equities Process

The U.S. government—particularly intelligence agencies such as the NSA—often has highly valuable, nonpublic information about cybersecurity vulnerabilities, or zero-day exploits. This sometimes leads to a clash in values: publicly disclosing the vulnerabilities to allow companies to patch them might benefit the companies and their consumers, but maintaining the secrecy of the vulnerabilities could allow the intelligence agency to continue to exploit the vulnerability to gather valuable intelligence.

To address these competing values, the U.S. government has maintained a "vulnerabilities equities process," in which it weighs the competing values and decides whether to withhold the public disclosure for a limited period of time. The government had disclosed the existence of the policy, and an Electronic

---

33 10 U.S.C. § 332.
34 10 U.S.C. § 371.
35 Joint Publication 3-28, Defense Support of Civil Authorities (Oct. 29, 2018).
36 Defense Department, Multi-Service Tactics, Techniques, and Procedures for Defense Support of Civil Authorities (Sept. 2015).

Frontier Foundation Freedom of Information Act request required the government to release a highly redacted version of its policy in 2015.[37]

In November 2017, the White House released a 14-page, unclassified version of its vulnerabilities equities policy.[38] The document provides the most public information to date about how the government addresses the sometimes-competing needs of intelligence gathering and cybersecurity. At the outset, the policy notes that the equities process is more than just a "binary" decision regarding whether to disclose vulnerabilities: "Other options that can be considered include disseminating mitigation information to certain entities without disclosing the particular vulnerability, limiting use of the vulnerability by the USG [U.S. government] in some way, informing U.S. and allied government entities of the vulnerability at a classified level, and using indirect means to inform the vendor of the vulnerability. All of these determinations must be informed by the understanding of risks of dissemination, the potential benefits of government use of the vulnerabilities, and the risks and benefits of all options in between."[39]

Decisions are made by an Equities Review Board, which is administered by the National Security Counsel and includes representatives of Office of Management and Budget, Office of the Director of National Intelligence, Central Intelligence Agency, and the Departments of Treasury, State, Justice, Homeland Security, Energy, Defense, and Commerce.[40]

The following material, drawn directly from the 2017 White House policy, sets forth the four equities that the board balances when weighing vulnerability disclosure decisions.

Part 1—Defensive Equity Considerations

1.A. Threat Considerations

- Where is the product used? How widely is it used?
- How broad is the range of products or versions affected?
- Are threat actors likely to exploit this vulnerability, if it were known to them?

1.B. Vulnerability Considerations

- What access must a threat actor possess to exploit this vulnerability?
- Is exploitation of this vulnerability alone sufficient to cause harm?
- How likely is it that threat actors will discover or acquire knowledge of this vulnerability?

---

37 *See* Electronic Frontier Foundation, *EFF v. NSA, ODNI—Vulnerabilities FOIA*, https://www.eff.org/cases/eff-v-nsa-odni-vulnerabilities-foia.
38 White House, Vulnerabilities Equities Policy and Process for the United States Government (Nov. 15, 2017).
39 *Id.* at 1.
40 *Id.* at 3–4.

1.C. Impact Considerations

- How much do users rely on the security of the product?
- How severe is the vulnerability? What are the potential consequences of exploitation of this vulnerability?
- What access or benefit does a threat actor gain by exploiting this vulnerability?
- What is the likelihood that adversaries will reverse engineer a patch, discover the vulnerability and use it against unpatched systems?
- Will enough USG information systems, U.S. businesses and/or consumers actually install the patch to offset the harm to security caused by educating attackers about the vulnerability?

1.D. Mitigation Considerations

- Can the product be configured to mitigate this vulnerability? Do other mechanisms exist to mitigate the risks from this vulnerability?
- Are impacts of this vulnerability mitigated by existing best-practice guidance, standard configurations, or security practices?
- If the vulnerability is disclosed, how likely is it that the vendor or another entity will develop and release a patch or update that effectively mitigates it?
- If a patch or update is released, how likely is it to be applied to vulnerable systems?
- How soon? What percentage of vulnerable systems will remain forever unpatched or unpatched for more than a year after the patch is released?
- Can exploitation of this vulnerability by threat actors be detected by USG or other members of the defensive community?

Part 2—Intelligence, Law Enforcement, and Operational Equity Considerations

2.A. Operational Value Considerations

- Can this vulnerability be exploited to support intelligence collection, cyber operations, or law enforcement evidence collection?
- What is the demonstrated value of this vulnerability for intelligence collection, cyber operations, and/or law enforcement evidence collection?
- What is its potential (future) value?
- What is the operational effectiveness of this vulnerability?

2.B. Operational Impact Considerations

- Does exploitation of this vulnerability provide specialized operational value against cyber threat actors or their operations? Against high-priority National Intelligence Priorities Framework (NIPF) or military targets? For protection of warfighters or civilians?

- Do alternative means exist to realize the operational benefits of exploiting this vulnerability?
- Would disclosing this vulnerability reveal any intelligence sources or methods?

Part 3—Commercial Equity Considerations

- If USG knowledge of this vulnerability were to be revealed, what risks could that pose for USG relationships with industry?

Part 4—International Partnership Equity Considerations

- If USG knowledge of this vulnerability were to be revealed, what risks could that pose for USG international relations?

Source: WHITE HOUSE, VULNERABILITY EQUITIES POLICY AND PROCESS FOR THE UNITED STATES GOVERNMENT (NOV. 2017).

7

Surveillance and Cyber

Any book about cybersecurity law would be incomplete without an examination of the constraints that both the government and private companies have on monitoring networks and sharing information. From the Fourth Amendment's prohibition on unreasonable searches and seizures to the Cybersecurity Act of 2015, both the government and companies face significant constraints on monitoring electronic traffic, even if their intention is to protect networks and users.

As discussed throughout this book, cybersecurity involves more than just preventing viruses and malware from infecting systems or flooding networks with denial-of-service attacks. Cybersecurity involves efforts by both the private and public sectors to secure the Internet and computer systems and to fight cybercrime. This chapter focuses on the tools that U.S. government entities have to conduct cyber operations, and the limits on the use of those tools.

This chapter first examines U.S. legal restrictions on government and private sector surveillance. We begin with a discussion of application of the Fourth Amendment to electronic content, and the general prohibition on warrantless searches and seizures by the government and government agents. We then examine the Electronic Communications Privacy Act and its three components: (1) the Stored Communications Act, which restricts government and private sector access to communications and data that are stored on servers and in the cloud; (2) the Wiretap Act, which restricts governments' and the private sector's ability to monitor data while it is in transit; and (3) the Title III/ pen register statute, which restricts the government's ability to obtain "non-content" information, such as the to/from lines of emails.

The section then examines the Communications Assistance for Law Enforcement Act, which requires telecommunications carriers and equipment makers to assist U.S. law enforcement with lawful surveillance. Finally, we examine the All Writs Act, and the government's attempts to use the

Cybersecurity Law, Second Edition. Jeff Kosseff.
© 2020 John Wiley & Sons, Inc. Published 2020 by John Wiley & Sons, Inc.
Companion Website: www.wiley.com/go/kosseff/cybersecurity2e

eighteenth-century law to compel smartphone manufacturers to help the government access encrypted information.

This chapter demonstrates that both constitutional and statutory restrictions on cyber surveillance and operations are still developing and that courts often are unsure what limits on government cyber operations are appropriate. The complexities are compounded because many of the restrictions are drawn from decades-old statutes that did not contemplate cloud computing, social media, and other technologies.

7.1 Fourth Amendment

The government's electronic surveillance is restricted by the Fourth Amendment. The Fourth Amendment is among the greatest constitutional limits on the government's ability to exercise power over individuals. If the government obtains evidence of a crime in a manner that violates the Fourth Amendment, none of the evidence gathered during that search or seizure can be admitted as evidence in the criminal trial of the individual whose rights were violated (though there are a few exceptions to this rule, as we'll discuss later). This section examines the Fourth Amendment's application to government surveillance and other actions in cyberspace.

The Fourth Amendment states:

> The right of the people to be secure in their persons, houses, papers, and effects, against unreasonable searches and seizures, shall not be violated, and no Warrants shall issue, but upon probable cause, supported by Oath or affirmation, and particularly describing the place to be searched, and the persons or things to be seized.

Since the nation's founding, the United States Supreme Court and lower courts have developed a wide range of factors and balancing tests that they apply to determine whether a government search or seizure has violated the Fourth Amendment. This book focuses primarily on the cases that involved government access to *information*. There is a long line of court cases assessing government access to physical objects (e.g., whether a police officer can search a car due to the smell of marijuana smoke). This chapter only reviews such cases to the extent that they are useful in understanding how the Fourth Amendment limits government cyber operations.

To best understand how courts analyze the Fourth Amendment, we have broken up the analysis into five questions. This is *not* the only way to conduct a Fourth Amendment analysis; indeed, scholars and courts approach these issues in a variety of ways and not necessarily in this order.[1] This book presents them in this order only to provide one way to approach Fourth Amendment analyses, which are inherently complex and depend on both the specific facts of the case and the court's approach to unsettled issues. Some of the questions have very easy answers, whereas others are far from settled:

1) Was the search or seizure conducted by a government entity (e.g., a police department) or government agent (e.g., a government contractor)?
2) Did the search or seizure involve an individual's reasonable expectation of privacy?
3) Did the government have a warrant?
4) If the government did not have a warrant, did an exception to the warrant requirement apply?
5) Was the search or seizure reasonable under the totality of the circumstances?

7.1.1 Was the Search or Seizure Conducted by a Government Entity or Government Agent?

The Fourth Amendment only restricts searches and seizures that are conducted by a *government entity* or by a *government agent* that is acting for the government. Like the other constitutional rights, the Fourth Amendment is subject to what is known as the state action doctrine: it only restricts the actions of the government, and not those of a private party. For instance, the government likely would violate the First Amendment by prohibiting Internet service providers from allowing their users to promote certain politicians on their websites. However, if the Internet service provider chose to prohibit its users from posting that content on their websites, the users would not be able to challenge that prohibition as a violation of the First Amendment. That is because the Internet service provider, acting independently, is not a state actor.[2] The same logic holds for the Fourth Amendment.

It is fairly simple to determine whether a government entity has conducted a search or seizure. In the United States, any federal, state, or local government agency or department is fully subject to the limits of the Fourth Amendment. For instance, if law enforcement officers obtain the email of a Los Angeles resident, they are subject to the Fourth Amendment regardless of whether they

---

1 For an example of a three-step framework for analyzing Fourth Amendment searches and seizures, *see* THOMAS K. CLANCY, ANALYTICAL STRUCTURE OF SEARCH AND SEIZURE CLAIMS, PRESENTATION TO WYOMING TRIAL COURTS (Apr. 2011).

2 *See* United States v. Jarrett, 338 F.3d 339, 344 (4th Cir. 2003) (holding that the Fourth Amendment does not apply to searches that are conducted "by private individuals acting in a private capacity.").

work for the Los Angeles Police Department, the California State Police, or the Federal Bureau of Investigation.

The more difficult question arises when a criminal defendant alleges that a *government agent* conducted a search. This is a particularly tricky task in cyber-related Fourth Amendment cases, because cyber infrastructure often is controlled by private companies that, at times, work with the government. In 1989, the United Supreme Court ruled that "[a]lthough the Fourth Amendment does not apply to a search or seizure, even an arbitrary one, effected by a private party on his own initiative, the Amendment protects against such intrusions if the private party acted as an instrument or agent of the Government."[3]

The Supreme Court has not defined precisely what it means to be an "instrument or agent" of the government. Lower courts have confronted the issue, and although their definitions vary somewhat, they generally have held that courts should consider the following factors when determining whether a private party acted as a government agent in conducting a search:

- Whether the government instigated the private party's search of the individual.
- The degree to which the government participated in the search.
- The degree of control that the government exercised over the search.
- Whether the private party was motivated by its own business interests or by the government.[4]

The "government agent" issue arises frequently in government prosecutions for online child pornography crimes. This is because the government often gathers evidence through a system established by federal law, which involves the participation of Internet service providers, the government, and a non-profit organization, the National Center for Missing and Exploited Children (NCMEC).

If online service providers (e.g., email services or Internet service providers) obtain actual knowledge that a customer appears to have violated federal child pornography laws, they are required by federal law to file a report with NCMEC.[5] NCMEC then reviews the report, as well as the apparent child pornography content, and if it determines that the content is in fact child pornography, it provides information to local, state, or federal law enforcement agencies. The federal law also provides legal immunity to the online service providers for their fulfillment of this duty, so that they cannot be sued for filing a NCMEC report if a customer appears to be exchanging child pornography on their services.[6]

---

3 Skinner v. Railway Labor Executives' Ass'n, 489 U.S. 602 (1989).
4 United States v. Silva, 554 F.3d 13, 16 (1st Cir. 2009).
5 18 U.S.C. § 2258A.
6 18 U.S.C. § 2258C.

Online service providers are not required to take any affirmative steps to look for child pornography. They are only required to file a report if they discover it on their services. Many service providers, however, voluntarily use automated scanning in an attempt to prevent the use of their services for illegal content. Often, the online services compare hash values of all user content with a NCMEC database of the hash values of known child pornography images.

When these automated searches lead to criminal prosecutions under federal child pornography laws, criminal defendants often challenge the admissibility of the evidence. They argue that the online service provider and NCMEC conducted a search of their private email or other online content, and that the warrantless search violated the Fourth Amendment. Courts typically have rejected such arguments, but they occasionally have been open to hearing defendants' Fourth Amendment claims in such cases.

For instance, in *United States* v. *Richardson*,[7] AOL used its image detection and filtering process (IDFP) to automatically scan hashes of customers' email content with NCMEC's database of hashes from known child pornography images. AOL detected a match for the email of its customer, Thomas McCoy Richardson, Jr., and filed a NCMEC report, as required by federal law. NCMEC provided the information to the North Carolina state police, who investigated and eventually discovered dozens of child pornography images and videos on Richardson's computer, leading Richardson to admit to police that he "sent and received" child pornography. Richardson was charged with federal child pornography crimes, and moved to suppress both the images and his statements, arguing that they were obtained due to a warrantless search of his AOL account. The gravamen of his argument was that AOL acted as a government agent when it scanned his account and reported the images to NCMEC, and violated the Fourth Amendment by conducting the search without a warrant. The U.S. Court of Appeals for the Fourth Circuit concluded that AOL was not a government agent and therefore was not subject to the Fourth Amendment warrant requirement. "There is nothing in the record to suggest that, in fact, law enforcement agents were involved in the search or investigation of Richardson's email transmissions until after AOL reported its discoveries to NCMEC," the court wrote. "Likewise, there is little evidence in this record to suggest that AOL intended to assist the Government in its case against Richardson."[8] Richardson argued that the mandatory reporting requirement in federal law effectively meant that AOL functioned as a government agent. The Fourth Circuit rejected this argument, reasoning that the law does not, in

---

7 United States v. Richardson, 607 F.3d 357 (4th Cir. 2010).
8 *Id*. at 364–65.

any way, obligate AOL to conduct the search in the first place. In fact, the statute explicitly states that providers are *not* obligated to conduct such searches. The child pornography statute, the court reasoned, "clears the way for ISPs to *report* violations of the child pornography laws, not investigate them."[9]

In similar Fourth Amendment challenges in child pornography cases, other courts have reached similar conclusions in cases in which the defendants have claimed that Internet service providers were government agents. Courts routinely hold that service providers have legitimate business interests—independent of the government—to automatically scan content and keep their services free of child pornography.[10]

A more difficult question arises when child pornography defendants argue not only that the online service providers acted as government agents, but also that NCMEC is a government agent. That is a tougher call, because NCMEC receives federal government funding and operates for the primary purpose of protecting children from exploitation. In *United States v. Keith*,[11] David Keith sought to suppress evidence collected in a search of his home and computer. The warrant for the search was supported, in part, by evidence of child pornography detected by AOL via its automated scanning of customer email accounts and included in a NCMEC report, which was used by state police in an investigation that eventually led to federal child pornography charges. Unlike other defendants, who only argued that their ISP acted as a government agent, Keith argued that both AOL *and* NCMEC were government agents and therefore subject to the Fourth Amendment. The federal court swiftly dismissed Keith's claim that AOL was a government agent, concluding that "AOL is motivated by its own wholly private interests in seeking to detect and deter the transmission of child pornography through its network facilities."[12] However, the court agreed with Keith's argument that NCMEC was a government agent. The court noted that the statute authorizing the NCMEC reporting program refers to the program as a "partnership" between NCMEC and the government, and that its examination of the files provided by AOL was "conducted for the sole purpose of assisting the prosecution of child pornography crimes."[13] Although AOL acted as a private party in scanning the content, the court reasoned, NCMEC

---

9 *Id*. at 367 (emphasis in original).
10 *See, e.g.*, United States v. Cameron, 699 F.3d 621, 638 (1st Cir. 2012) ("[T]here is no evidence that the government instigated the search, participated in the search, or coerced Yahoo! to conduct the search. Thus, if Yahoo! chose to implement a policy of searching for child pornography, it presumably did so for its own interests.").
11 United States v. Keith, 980 F. Supp. 2d 33 (D. Mass. 2013).
12 *Id*. at 40.
13 *Id*. at 41.

was a government agent when it expanded on the search. "Unlike AOL, which monitors its email traffic to serve its own business interest," the court wrote, "NCMEC's operation of the CyberTipline is intended to, and does, serve the public interest in crime prevention and prosecution, rather than a private interest."[14] However, the court did not suppress the evidence collected in the search of Keith's home because the warrant also relied on evidence of child pornography obtained by police after a Staples employee incidentally discovered potential child pornography file names while repairing Keith's laptop.[15]

The *Keith* opinion quickly set off alarms in the community of law enforcement, advocacy groups, and technology companies that seek to prevent the use of online services to distribute child pornography. A few years later, the Tenth Circuit released an even more defendant-friendly opinion, written in 2016 by then-Judge Neil Gorsuch, who would join the U.S. Supreme Court a year later. In *United States v. Ackerman*,[16] the Tenth Circuit reversed a district court's denial of a suppression order in a child pornography case that was commenced after NCMEC received a report from AOL based on the ISP's scanning. Due to NCMEC's congressional mandate and federal funding, Gorsuch concluded that NCMEC was not only a government agent, but it also qualified as a government entity. "Much as Amtrak was created by statute to assume functions previously carried out by private railroads, Congress passed statutes to fund and mandate various of NCMEC's functions soon after private parties incorporated it," Gorsuch wrote. "Today, NCMEC is statutorily required to perform over a dozen separate functions, a fact that evinces the sort of 'day-to-day' statutory control over its operations that the Court found tellingly present in the Amtrak cases. Law enforcement agents participate at varying levels in its daily operations, and government officials enjoy a sizeable presence on its board."[17]

7.1.2 Did the Search or Seizure Involve an Individual's Reasonable Expectation of Privacy?

If a government entity or government agency conducted a search or seizure, the Fourth Amendment applies only if the search or seizure involved the individual's protected privacy interests. In other words, did the individual have a reasonable expectation of privacy?

---

14 *Id.*
15 *Id.* at 46–47.
16 United States v. Ackerman, 831 F.3d 1292 (10th Cir. 2016).
17 *Id.* at 1297–98.

For electronic surveillance, the answer to this question traces back to a 1967 United States Supreme Court case, *Katz v. United States*.[18] FBI agents, acting without a search warrant, installed a listening device on a public payphone booth and heard the defendant discussing his illegal wagering operations. The defendant argued that his conviction was invalid because the FBI needed a warrant to conduct the surveillance. Until this decision, courts generally had focused on the physical characteristics of a search when determining whether the government invaded a constitutionally protected interest. In this case, the government argued that the defendant had no reasonable expectation of privacy because the defendant made the phone call from a public phone booth that was partly glass, so he could be seen by passersby while he was making the call. However, the Court found this argument unpersuasive, reasoning that "what he sought to exclude when he entered the booth was not the intruding eye—it was the uninvited ear."[19] The government also argued that the Fourth Amendment did not apply to the wiretap because the FBI did not physically penetrate the phone booth. The Court rejected this argument as well, concluding that "the Fourth Amendment protects people—and not simply 'areas'— against unreasonable searches and seizures," and that "the reach of that Amendment cannot turn upon the presence or absence of a physical intrusion into any given enclosure."[20] The Court reversed the defendant's conviction, concluding that the Fourth Amendment did, in fact, apply to electronic surveillance:

> The Government's activities in electronically listening to and recording the petitioner's words violated the privacy upon which he justifiably relied while using the telephone booth and thus constituted a "search and seizure" within the meaning of the Fourth Amendment. The fact that the electronic device employed to achieve that end did not happen to penetrate the wall of the booth can have no constitutional significance.[21]

The conclusion in the *Katz* case is among the most significant developments in Fourth Amendment history because it took the Fourth Amendment out of the exclusively physical realm and recognized that individuals could have a reasonable expectation of privacy in *information*. *Katz* set the groundwork for the modern Fourth Amendment disputes involving government surveillance of telephones, email, and other electronic communications.

---

18 Katz v. United States, 389 U.S. 347 (1967).
19 *Id*. at 352.
20 *Id*. at 353.
21 *Id*.

It is important to note that the Supreme Court in *Katz* did not conclude that individuals automatically have a reasonable expectation of privacy in *all* electronic communications. In an oft-cited concurrence in *Katz*, Justice Harlan articulated a two-prong test to determine whether a reasonable expectation of privacy exists for Fourth Amendment purposes:

1) whether the individual "exhibited an actual (subjective) expectation of privacy,"[22] and

2) whether that subjective expectation of privacy is "one that society is prepared to recognize as 'reasonable.'"[23]

In other words, under this two-pronged test, the Fourth Amendment only protects an individual if that individual *actually* expected privacy *and* that expectation was reasonable. In *Katz*, the Court concluded that the defendant expected that his phone conversation would be private, and that objectively, this expectation was reasonable.

For electronic surveillance, one of the biggest obstacles to finding a reasonable expectation of privacy is the third-party doctrine. Under this doctrine, individuals do not have a Fourth Amendment reasonable expectation of privacy in information once they have disclosed that information to an outside party. For instance, if Jack provides a secret document to Jill, and then Jill voluntarily provides that secret information to the police, Jack cannot claim that the police violated his Fourth Amendment rights by obtaining the information without a warrant. Of course, in the context of electronic surveillance, the third-party doctrine often is more difficult to parse.

The third-party doctrine, in the electronic surveillance realm, was most clearly articulated for communications data in a 1979 United States Supreme Court case, *Smith* v. *Maryland*.[24] In that case, the police asked a telephone company to install a pen register to document the numbers that were called by a robbery suspect. The phone company complied, even though the police did not have a warrant. Based on the information collected through the pen register, the police obtained a warrant to search the defendant's home, and he eventually was convicted of robbery. The United States Supreme Court distinguished this case from *Katz*, because pen registers only obtain lists of phone numbers, not the *contents* of the communications. This distinction is crucial, the Court reasoned, because people understand that they are voluntarily conveying the phone number that they are calling to the phone company. Therefore, under the first prong of Justice

---

22 *Id*. at 361 (Harlan, J., concurring).

23 *Id*.

24 Smith v. Maryland, 442 U.S. 735 (1979). The Supreme Court had recognized the third-party doctrine for bank records three years earlier, in United States v. Miller, 425 U.S. 435 (1976).

Harlan's *Katz* test, they should not have an actual expectation that the phone number is private:

> All telephone users realize that they must "convey" phone numbers to the telephone company, since it is through telephone company switching equipment that their calls are completed. All subscribers realize, moreover, that the phone company has facilities for making permanent records of the numbers they dial, for they see a list of their long-distance (toll) calls on their monthly bills.[25]

Moreover, the Court reasoned, even if individuals had a subjective expectation of privacy in phone numbers that they dialed, such an expectation would be objectively unreasonable:

> When he used his phone, petitioner voluntarily conveyed numerical information to the telephone company and "exposed" that information to its equipment in the ordinary course of business. In so doing, petitioner assumed the risk that the company would reveal to police the numbers he dialed. The switching equipment that processed those numbers is merely the modern counterpart of the operator who, in an earlier day, personally completed calls for the subscriber.[26]

Smith v. Maryland is perhaps the most significant limit on the Fourth Amendment rights created by *Katz*. It has been cited by advocates of the National Security Agency to justify its bulk metadata collection program (though the United States Supreme Court has not yet ruled on that issue). Under a broad reading of the doctrinal rule of *Smith v. Maryland,* NSA's program of collecting certain noncontent information of email and phone calls should similarly be exempt from Fourth Amendment scrutiny (and therefore not subject to a warrant requirement). But NSA critics argue that the Supreme Court, in 1979, did not anticipate the bulk collection of millions of sets of metadata when it decided *Smith v. Maryland*.[27]

---

25 *Smith,* 442 U.S. at 742.

26 *Id.* at 744.

27 *See* Hanni Fakhoury, Electronic Frontier Foundation, *Smith v. Maryland Turns 35, But Its Health Is Declining* (June 24, 2014) ("Ultimately, as more people have a subjective expectation of privacy in information exposed to others, these expectations also become ones that society is prepared to accept as reasonable. And if that's the case, then the Fourth Amendment should recognize that expectation of privacy as reasonable too. In other words, as more people do have an expectation of privacy in information they've turned over to third parties, it's the *Smith* decision, and not the expectation of privacy, that becomes unreasonable.").

A more difficult issue arises when individuals use an intermediary to communicate electronic information, such as email. Does the protective rule of *Katz* apply? Or does *Smith's* third-party doctrine prevent the application of the Fourth Amendment to government attempts to obtain stored email?

The United States Supreme Court has not addressed the issue directly. However, in 2010, the U.S. Court of Appeals for the Sixth Circuit addressed the issue in *United States v. Warshak*.[28] In that case, the government obtained thousands of emails from the ISP of a corporate executive, to help bring a fraud case against the executive. The government had not obtained a search warrant for the emails; instead, it used a subpoena that does not require a probable cause showing, and the defendant did not receive notice until more than a year after the email was disclosed. The Sixth Circuit held that although the Stored Communications Act (discussed later in this chapter) did not require a warrant for the emails at issue, the Fourth Amendment did. The court reasoned that the government must obtain a warrant to obtain paper mail delivered via the postal service, and "[g]iven the fundamental similarities between email and traditional forms of communication, it would defy common sense to afford emails lesser Fourth Amendment protection."[29] The court elaborated:

> If we accept that an email is analogous to a letter or a phone call, it is manifest that agents of the government cannot compel a commercial ISP to turn over the contents of an email without triggering the Fourth Amendment. An ISP is the intermediary that makes email communication possible. Emails must pass through an ISP's servers to reach their intended recipient. Thus, the ISP is the functional equivalent of a post office or a telephone company.[30]

Due to the *Warshak* decision, law enforcement in the Sixth Circuit— Kentucky, Michigan, Ohio, and Tennessee—is required under the Fourth Amendment to obtain warrants before compelling the disclosure of emails, regardless of the length of time an email has been stored. But *Warshak* is not binding in other parts of the United States. Since *Warshak*, federal prosecutors and law enforcement have generally sought warrants for emails, but they maintain that they are not constitutionally required to do so.[31]

There is a growing movement to reconsider the third-party doctrine because it makes little sense in the cyber age. Notably, in *United States v. Jones*,[32] the

---

28 631 F.3d 266 (6th Cir. 2010).

29 *Id*. at 285–86.

30 *Id*. at 286. The court, however, did not suppress the evidence, concluding that the government obtained it in good faith reliance on the Stored Communications Act.

31 Declan McCullagh, *DOJ: We Don't Need Warrants for E-Mail, Facebook Chats*, C-Net (May 8, 2013).

32 132 S. Ct. 945 (2012).

United States Supreme Court reversed the conviction of a criminal defendant because the evidence used against him was obtained via the warrantless installation of a GPS tracking device on his car. The majority opinion focused on the physical intrusion caused by the government's installation of the device on his property, an alternative to the traditional reasonable expectation of privacy analysis. Perhaps even more notable than the majority opinion was Justice Sotomayor's concurrence, in which she suggested that the Court should reconsider the third-party doctrine altogether:

> This approach is ill suited to the digital age, in which people reveal a great deal of information about themselves to third parties in the course of carrying out mundane tasks. People disclose the phone numbers that they dial or text to their cellular providers; the URLs that they visit and the e-mail addresses with which they correspond to their Internet service providers; and the books, groceries, and medications they purchase to online retailers ... [W]hatever the societal expectations, they can attain constitutionally protected status only if our Fourth Amendment jurisprudence ceases to treat secrecy as a prerequisite for privacy. I would not assume that all information voluntarily disclosed to some member of the public for a limited purpose is, for that reason alone, disentitled to Fourth Amendment protection.[33]

Justice Sotomayor's concurrence was noteworthy because, if it eventually is adopted by the majority, it would undercut decades of Fourth Amendment jurisprudence and expose a wide range of information to Fourth Amendment protection, even if it was disclosed to third parties. Microsoft, which has long been involved in battles over government surveillance, wrote in a 2014 blog post that Sotomayor's concurrence "looked forward and addressed directly the changing attitudes of a new generation that increasingly was comfortable sharing its personal information."[34]

Justice Sotomayor's concurrence received a great deal of attention, but because it was only the viewpoint of one Justice, it did not bind other courts. The question remained after her concurrence: In light of new technological developments since 1979, what remains of *Smith*? In 2018, the Supreme Court's ruling in *Carpenter v. United States*[35] suggested that although the Court is not yet willing to entirely repeal the third-party doctrine, it is increasingly reluctant to apply the doctrine to searches that reveal inherently private

---

33 *Id.* at 957 (Sotomayor, J., concurring).
34 *The Privacy Week That Was*, Microsoft Corporate Blogs (June 28, 2014), https://blogs. microsoft.com/on-the-issues/2014/06/28/the-privacy-week-that-was/.
35 Carpenter v. United States, 138 S. Ct. 2206 (2018).

information. The case involved cell site location information (CSLI), which is a record maintained by wireless carriers of the precise time that a customer's cell phone pinged a particular cell tower. The information can provide a virtual map of the general location of the customer. The FBI arrested four people for a series of store robberies, and obtained from an arrestee the names and cell phone numbers of people whom he identified as his accomplices. One of the suspected accomplices was Timothy Carpenter. The government obtained a court order for his CSLI under Section 2703(d) of the Stored Communications Act (described in Section 7.2.1), which does not require the probable cause showing demanded by a warrant. Instead, Section 2703(d) requires the government to present "specific and articulable facts showing that there are reasonable grounds to believe" that the government is requesting records that "are relevant and material to an ongoing criminal investigation."[36] This is a substantially less burdensome evidentiary requirement for law enforcement. The order required Carpenter's wireless carriers to provide the government with "cell/site sector [information] for [Carpenter's] telephone[] at call origination and at call termination for incoming and outgoing calls" during the entire four-month period during which the robberies took place.[37] In total, the order resulted in records that documented 12,898 cell tower pings over 127 days.[38] The data demonstrated that Carpenter was at the location of four of the robberies. He was indicted, tried, and convicted, sentenced to a prison term of more than 100 years.[39] He challenged the admissibility of the CSLI, which he stated was obtained in violation of his Fourth Amendment rights, but the United States Court of Appeals for the Sixth Circuit affirmed his conviction, ruling that he did not have a reasonable expectation of privacy in CSLI due to the third-party doctrine.[40]

The Supreme Court agreed to hear Carpenter's challenge to the Sixth Circuit opinion, and in a 5–4 opinion written by Chief Justice John Roberts, the Supreme Court overturned the Sixth Circuit and concluded that Carpenter's Fourth Amendment rights had been violated. Roberts acknowledged that the case "implicated" the third-party doctrine, but he reasoned that CSLI is quite different from the phone records at issue in *Smith*: "After all, when *Smith* was decided in 1979, few could have imagined a society in which a phone goes wherever its owner goes, conveying to the wireless carrier not just dialed digits, but a detailed and comprehensive record of the person's movements."[41]

---

36 *Id.* at 2212.
37 *Id.*
38 *Id.*
39 *Id.* at 2212–13.
40 *Id.* at 2213.
41 *Id.* at 2217.

Roberts pointed to "society's expectation" that law enforcement would not "secretly monitor" an individual for "a very long period."[42] The sweeping order that the FBI obtained for Carpenter's phone, he wrote, contradicted that expectation:

> Although such records are generated for commercial purposes, that distinction does not negate Carpenter's anticipation of privacy in his physical location. Mapping a cell phone's location over the course of 127 days provides an all-encompassing record of the holder's whereabouts. As with GPS information, the time-stamped data provides an intimate window into a person's life, revealing not only his particular movements, but through them his familial, political, professional, religious, and sexual associations. These location records hold for many Americans the privacies of life. And like GPS monitoring, cell phone tracking is remarkably easy, cheap, and efficient compared to traditional investigative tools. With just the click of a button, the Government can access each carrier's deep repository of historical location information at practically no expense.[43]

Roberts summarily rejected the government's contentions that the third-party doctrine blocks Carpenter's Fourth Amendment challenge: "The Government's position fails to contend with the seismic shifts in digital technology that made possible the tracking of not only Carpenter's location but also everyone else's, not for a short period but for years and years. Sprint Corporation and its competitors are not your typical witnesses. Unlike the nosy neighbor who keeps an eye on comings and goings, they are ever alert, and their memory is nearly infallible."[44]

Roberts stressed that he was not entirely abandoning the third-party doctrine, or questioning "conventional surveillance techniques and tools, such as security cameras." He made clear that his concern was with the *amount* and *scope* of information provided about Carpenter: "We decline to grant the state unrestricted access to a wireless carrier's database of physical location information. In light of the deeply revealing nature of CSLI, its depth, breadth, and comprehensive reach, and the inescapable and automatic nature of its collection, the fact that such information is gathered by a third party does not make it any less deserving of Fourth Amendment protection. The Government's acquisition of the cell-site records here was a search under that Amendment."[45]

---

42 *Id.*
43 *Id.* at 2217–18 (internal quotation marks and citations omitted).
44 *Id.* at 2219.
45 *Id.* at 2223.

Although the Supreme Court could have entirely abandoned the third-party doctrine in *Carpenter*, its ruling was narrower. The Court allowed the doctrine to survive, but imposed a limit on its application. As Orin Kerr wrote, Roberts based his reasoning on an "equilibrium-adjustment" theory by which it modifies the reach of its Fourth Amendment doctrine to address the realities of new technology. "If technology gives the government too much new power that can be abused based on old rules, the court expands legal protection to restore old levels of power and limit abuses," Kerr wrote. "On the flip side, if technology threatens to narrow government power too much that can unduly limit the government's ability to solve crimes under old rules, the court shrinks legal protection to restore old levels of power and ensure the government can still solve enough cases."[46]

Under the approach that Roberts adopted in *Carpenter*, courts will not be able to reflexively cite the third-party doctrine to uphold any warrantless search of information that was stored with a service provider or other third party. Instead, courts will need to conduct a searching, case-specific analysis of the scope and magnitude of each search. Although *Carpenter* provides lower courts with a general framework for approaching these tough and evolving questions, it leaves the precise application of this framework to the courts. Therefore, it is difficult to predict with much certainty how a court would react to a new technology used to obtain information.

7.1.3 Did the Government Have a Warrant?

If a government entity or government agent has conducted a search that invades a protected interest (i.e., where the individual had a reasonable expectation of privacy as in *Katz*, or where there was a physical invasion such as in *Jones*), the government typically must have a warrant supported by probable cause in order to comply with the Fourth Amendment. As Roberts wrote in *Carpenter*, "although the ultimate measure of the constitutionality of a governmental search is reasonableness, our cases establish that warrantless searches are typically unreasonable where a search is undertaken by law enforcement officials to discover evidence of criminal wrongdoing."[47]

In his dissent in *Carpenter*, Justice Alito wrote that unlike a physical search, the order for CSLI was "an order merely requiring a party to look through its own records and produce specified documents," and is therefore not subject to the probable cause requirement.[48] In his majority opinion in the case, Roberts

---

46 Orin Kerr, *Understanding the Supreme Court's Carpenter Decision*, Lawfare (June 22, 2018) [blog post].
47 Carpenter v. United States, 138 S. Ct. 2206, 2221 (2018) (internal quotation marks and citations omitted).
48 *Id.* at 2247 (Alito, J., dissenting).

dismissed Alito's argument as unsupported by precedent. "If the choice to proceed by subpoena provided a categorical limitation on Fourth Amendment protection, no type of record would ever be protected by the warrant requirement," Roberts wrote. "Under Justice Alito's view, private letters, digital contents of a cell phone—any personal information reduced to document form, in fact—may be collected by subpoena for no reason other than 'official curiosity.'"[49]

If a warrant is required, it must be issued by a "neutral and detached magistrate,"[50] who in some cases may be a judge, but also may be a magistrate whose primary job is to determine whether law enforcement has presented probable cause that the search will yield evidence that a crime has been or will be committed. Typically, the neutral magistrate bases the probable cause determination on an affidavit that law enforcement submits along with the search warrant request.

The United States Supreme Court has stated that the purpose of a warrant is to assure the citizen "that the intrusion is authorized by law, and that it is narrowly limited in its objectives and scope."[51] The "detached scrutiny" of a neutral magistrate "ensures an objective determination whether an intrusion is justified in any given case," the Court has stated.[52]

Generally, if a neutral magistrate issues a search warrant, it is very difficult for a defendant to later seek to suppress evidence gathered from the search on Fourth Amendment grounds. In *United States v. Leon*,[53] a criminal defendant in a drug case sought to suppress evidence that was collected under a search warrant that he claimed was not supported by probable cause. The United States Supreme Court declined to suppress the evidence, even though the warrant was not supported by probable cause. Because the police conducted the search in good faith pursuant to a warrant that they believed to be valid, the Court concluded that it should not suppress the evidence gathered by the search. "In the absence of an allegation that the magistrate abandoned his detached and neutral role, suppression is appropriate only if the officers were dishonest or reckless in preparing their affidavit or could not have harbored an objectively reasonable belief in the existence of probable cause," the Court wrote.[54] The "good-faith" exception makes it incredibly difficult to challenge a magistrate's probable cause determination, absent extreme recklessness or deceptive behavior by law enforcement.

One barrier to the use of warrants, however, is the "particularity" requirement. If a magistrate judge issues a warrant, the warrant must satisfy the

---

49 *Id.* at 2222 (majority opinion).
50 Coolidge v. New Hampshire, 403 U.S. 443, 449 (1971).
51 Skinner v. Ry. Labor Executives' Ass'n, 489 U.S. 602, 621–22 (1989).
52 *Id.* at 622.
53 United States v. Leon, 468 U.S. 897 (1984).
54 *Id.* at 926.

Fourth Amendment's explicit requirement for *particularity*, by describing the place to be searched as well as the persons or things to be seized.[55] This does not necessarily mean that the warrant must describe the precise evidence that law enforcement expects to collect.[56] In determining whether a warrant satisfied the particularity requirement, courts consider "(1) whether probable cause exists to seize all items of a particular type described in the warrant; (2) whether the warrant sets out objective standards by which executing officers can differentiate items subject to seizure from those which are not; and (3) whether the government was able to describe the items more particularly in light of the information available to it at the time the warrant was issued."[57]

Courts have recognized the difficulty of applying the particularity requirement to cyber searches, and they generally are deferential to law enforcement and magistrates. For instance, in *United States* v. *Adjani*,[58] the U.S. Court of Appeals for the Ninth Circuit refused to suppress evidence collected under a warrant that allowed the search and seizure of, among other things, "[a]ny computer equipment and storage device capable of being used to commit, further, or store evidence of the offense listed above."[59] The defendants argued that rather than allowing a "wholesale search" of their email, the warrant should have specified search terms. The court sympathized with this argument, but ultimately concluded that to "require such a pinpointed computer search, restricting the search to an email program or to specific search terms, would likely have failed to cast a sufficiently wide net to capture the evidence sought."[60] The court reasoned that computer files "are easy to disguise or rename," and therefore an overly limited search warrant would prevent law enforcement from collecting evidence.[61] Although search warrants for email and other electronic evidence must have some particularity, courts recognize that law enforcement needs some leeway to conduct legitimate searches of the vast amounts of electronic data.

---

55 *See* Groh v. Ramirez, 540 U.S. 551, 557 (2004) ("The fact that the *application* adequately described the 'things to be seized' does not save the *warrant* from its facial invalidity. The Fourth Amendment by its terms requires particularity in the warrant, not in the supporting documents."); Massachusetts v. Sheppard, 468 U.S. 981, 988, n.5 (1984) ("[A] warrant that fails to conform to the particularity requirement of the Fourth Amendment is unconstitutional").
56 *See* United States v. Spilotro, 800 F.2d 959, 963 (9th Cir. 1986) ("The specificity required in a warrant varies depending on the circumstances of the case and the type of items involved. Warrants which describe generic categories of items are not necessarily invalid if a more precise description of the items subject to seizure is not possible").
57 *Id.* at 963 (internal citations omitted).
58 United States v. Adjani, 452 F.3d 1140 (9th Cir. 2006).
59 *Id.* at 1144.
60 *Id.* at 1149–50.
61 *Id.* at 1150.

7.1.4   If the Government Did Not Have a Warrant, Did an Exception to the Warrant Requirement Apply?

If the government entity or a government agent conducts a *warrantless* search or seizure that invades a protected interest, the government must demonstrate that an exception to the warrant requirement applies. If the government does not convince the court that an exception applies, the evidence collected as a result of the search will be suppressed.

The courts have articulated a number of exceptions to the warrant requirement. Among the most commonly cited exceptions are:

- exigent circumstances;[62]
- searches incident to a lawful arrest, if the search is necessary to prevent the destruction of evidence or a detainee's escape, or harm to the police officer.[63]
- the individual provided consent for the search;[64]
- the evidence is in plain view (e.g., from the street, the police could see marijuana plants in the defendant's yard);[65]
- police have probable cause to search an automobile (a recognition that given the mobility of cars, it is difficult to obtain a warrant before searching them);[66] and
- programmatic searches and special needs unrelated to routine law enforcement purposes (e.g., drunk driving checkpoints, border searches, searches of students' lockers in schools, searches of parolees, and searches at large public gatherings to reduce the risk of terrorism).[67]

In 2014, the United States Supreme Court issued its opinion in *Riley v. California*.[68] The decision, involving the search incident to lawful arrest exception, has had a significant impact on cyber-related searches. When David Leon

---

62 *See* Kentucky v. King, 131 S. Ct. 1849, 1854 (2011) ("It is well established that 'exigent circumstances,' including the need to prevent the destruction of evidence, permit police officers to conduct an otherwise permissible search without first obtaining a warrant.").

63 *See* Arizona v. Gant, 556 U.S. 332 (2009) ("The exception derives from interests in officer safety and evidence preservation that are typically implicated in arrest situations.").

64 *See* Schneckloth v. Bustamonte, 412 U.S. 218, 222 (1973) ("[A] search authorized by consent is wholly valid").

65 *See* Kyllo v. United States, 533 U.S. 27, 42 (2001) ("[I]t is equally well settled that searches and seizures of property in plain view are presumptively reasonable.").

66 *See* Cardwell v. Lewis, 417 U.S. 583, 589 (1974) (plurality opinion) ("[T]he Court has recognized a distinction between the warrantless search and seizure of automobiles or other movable vehicles, on the one hand, and the search of a home or office, on the other. Generally, less stringent warrant requirements have been applied to vehicles.").

67 *See* Indianapolis v. Edmond, 531 U.S. 32, 37 (2000) ("[W]e have upheld certain regimes of suspicion-less searches where the program was designed to serve special needs, beyond the normal need for law enforcement.") (internal quotation marks and citation omitted).

68 Riley v. California, 134 S. Ct. 2473 (2014).

Riley was lawfully arrested for firearms possession, the police seized his smart-
phone, searched the text messages on the phone, and found messages that
indicated that Riley was associated with a street gang. Riley was convicted for
various gang-related offenses, and sought to overturn his conviction, arguing
that the police conducted a warrantless search of his phone. The Court agreed
with Riley and reversed his conviction, concluding that the search incident to
lawful arrest exception did not apply to the content stored on cell phones. The
exception applies when there is a concern that the arrestee will harm officers or
destroy evidence; the Court reasoned that neither concern is present in the
case of a cell phone.[69] The police could seize the cell phone, and obtain a warrant to search it. There was no danger that the data would be destroyed.
Particularly notable about the majority opinion, written by Chief Justice
Roberts, was the strong language that the Court used to caution law enforcement against warrantless searches of data:

> Our cases have recognized that the Fourth Amendment was the
> founding generation's response to the reviled "general warrants"
> and "writs of assistance" of the colonial era, which allowed British
> officers to rummage through homes in an unrestrained search for
> evidence of criminal activity. Opposition to such searches was in
> fact one of the driving forces behind the Revolution itself. In 1761,
> the patriot James Otis delivered a speech in Boston denouncing
> the use of writs of assistance. A young John Adams was there, and
> he would later write that "[e]very man of a crowded audience
> appeared to me to go away, as I did, ready to take arms against
> writs of assistance." According to Adams, Otis's speech was "the
> first scene of the first act of opposition to the arbitrary claims of
> Great Britain. Then and there the child Independence was born."
>
> Modern cell phones are not just another technological conveni-
> ence. With all they contain and all they may reveal, they hold for
> many Americans "the privacies of life." The fact that technology
> now allows an individual to carry such information in his hand
> does not make the information any less worthy of the protection
> for which the Founders fought. Our answer to the question of
> what police must do before searching a cell phone seized incident
> to an arrest is accordingly simple—get a warrant.[70]

The *Riley* opinion likely will have impacts that reach far beyond cases involving searches incident to lawful arrests. It is perhaps the Supreme Court's
strongest statement, since *Katz*, in opposition to the government's warrantless

---

69 *Id.* at 2485.
70 *Id.* at 2494–95 (internal citations omitted).

searches of criminal suspects' information. *Riley* is a clear indication that the Supreme Court believes that the Fourth Amendment applies just as much to electronic information as it does to physical objects. Although the case involved a relatively narrow issue related to the search of an arrestee, it likely will have a large impact on a wide range of future cyber-related Fourth Amendment cases.

7.1.5 Was the Search or Seizure Reasonable Under the Totality of the Circumstances?

The Fourth Amendment protects individuals against "unreasonable" searches and seizures. If the government obtains a warrant, that warrant is generally presumed to be reasonable.[71] If, however, the government conducts a search without a warrant, the government still must demonstrate that the search was "reasonable" and therefore did not violate the Fourth Amendment.[72]

To assess reasonableness of a search, courts conduct a "totality of the circumstances" analysis of the search, in which they evaluate "on the one hand, the degree to which it intrudes upon an individual's privacy and, on the other, the degree to which it is needed for the promotion of legitimate governmental interests."[73]

Courts have great leeway in determining the weight that they will accord to these often-competing values. A recent application, relevant to cyber searches, arose in the case of Jamshid Muhtorov, a legal permanent resident of the United States who was charged with providing material support to a designated terrorist organization. The government notified Muhtorov that it planned to use evidence that it had collected under Section 702 of the FISA Amendments Act of 2008, a program (colloquially known as "PRISM") that allows federal intelligence agencies to conduct electronic surveillance of targets who are believed to be located outside of the United States *and* are not United States citizens or legal residents. Although Muhtorov was located within the United States, the target of the surveillance apparently was not believed to be in the United States, and therefore the communications were collected under Section 702 (the content of the communications was classified and not included in the court opinion). Muhtorov asked the court to suppress the evidence collected under Section 702, arguing that it violated his Fourth Amendment rights.

---

71 "[S]earches pursuant to a warrant will rarely require any deep inquiry into reasonableness." Illinois v. Gates, 462 U.S. 213, 267 (1983) (White, J., concurring in judgment).

72 *See* Maryland v. King, 133 S. Ct. 1958, 1970 (2013) ("Even if a warrant is not required, a search is not beyond Fourth Amendment scrutiny; for it must be reasonable in its scope and manner of execution.").

73 Wyoming v. Houghton, 526 U.S. 295, 300 (1999).

A Colorado federal judge denied Muhtorov's motion to suppress. He found it unnecessary to rule whether this foreign intelligence gathering falls within the "special needs" exception to the warrant requirement (a conclusion reached by many other federal courts, but never addressed directly by the United States Supreme Court),[74] and instead validated the constitutionality by concluding that under the totality of the circumstances, the search was reasonable. The judge concluded both that Section 702, on its face, is constitutional, and that it was constitutionally applied to Muhtorov. Key to the judge's ruling was an extensive set of "minimization procedures" that the government uses to weed out information that is not related to foreign intelligence and to reduce the likelihood of searches being conducted of people who are either U.S. citizens or located in the United States. "I conclude on the record before me that a proper and supported application was filed, and that the targeting and minimization procedures forwarded were tailored to the government's legitimate foreign intelligence purposes and took into account the privacy interests of individuals whose communications would be incidentally acquired," the judge wrote.[75]

Ultimately, unless the Supreme Court has explicitly found a specific government practice to be reasonable or unreasonable, courts have a great deal of leeway under the totality-of-the-circumstances framework. Whether the government's needs outweigh the individual's privacy interests ultimately is a value judgment that likely will vary by court and judge. Accordingly, it often is difficult to predict, with certainty, whether a government search or seizure comports with the Fourth Amendment. This is particularly true with cyber searches, which often involve novel factual issues that have not yet been addressed by other courts.

7.2 Electronic Communications Privacy Act

In addition to satisfying the Fourth Amendment's requirements, the government must ensure that it isn't violating any statutes that restrict the government's ability to conduct electronic surveillance. The Electronic Communications Privacy Act (ECPA) is the most comprehensive U.S. law relating to cyber surveillance. ECPA limits the ability of government agencies, such as law enforcement, to obtain emails, monitor networks, and obtain Internet traffic logs. ECPA also imposes strict boundaries on the ability of service providers (e.g., phone companies and email service providers)

---

74 *Id.* ("I find the special need/foreign intelligence exception argument somewhat academic and limiting, because the standard ultimately is one of reasonableness, and it is on that standard that the constitutionality of § 702's warrantless surveillance authorization must be decided.").
75 United States v. Muhtorov, Criminal Case No. 12-cr-00033-JLK (D. Colo. Nov. 19, 2015).

to provide other private parties or the government with access to customer emails and other records.

ECPA is so central to cybersecurity because it severely limits the ability of both the government and the private sector to monitor networks for cybersecurity vulnerabilities and threats and to share the information. Moreover, it restricts the ability of law enforcement to monitor communications for kinetic threats (e.g., terrorist plots).

Congress passed much of ECPA in 1986. Although it has been amended since then, the heart of the law remains the same today as when it was passed more than three decades ago. This has led a number of critics to call for a full-scale overhaul of the statute.[76]

For now, however, ECPA remains the law of the land, and it shapes the cyber decisions of many companies and government agencies. This chapter provides an overview of the three sections of ECPA: the Stored Communications Act (SCA), the Wiretap Act, and the Pen Register Act. The Stored Communications Act regulates the ability of governments to compel release of—and service providers to disclose—stored communications such as email messages and cloud content. The Wiretap Act restricts the ability of the government to monitor communications while they are in transit. The Pen Register Act restricts the ability of government agencies and private parties to obtain noncontent information about telephone and email communications, such as phone numbers dialed and the to/from headers on email messages.

The three sections of ECPA provide very different safeguards and constraints regarding the ability of the government and private actors to access communications. As a 2006 article in the *Cardozo Law Review* observed:

> Whether an electronic communication is classified as "in transit" or "in storage" is crucial in determining how much privacy is afforded to that particular communication at any given moment. Under the Wiretap Act, private parties are never permitted to intercept communications, but there are certain circumstances under which law enforcement officers can follow specific procedures to receive temporary permission to engage in interception. The Wiretap Act affords significant procedural protections to electronic communications in transit to guard their privacy. However, those procedural protections are not afforded to the same communications when they are in electronic storage and covered by the SCA.[77]

---

76 *See, e.g.,* Elena Schneider, *Technology Companies Are Pressing Congress to Bolster Privacy Protections,* New York Times (May 26, 2014).
77 Samantha L. Martin, *Interpreting the Wiretap Act: Applying Ordinary Rules of Transit to the Internet Context,* 28 Cardozo L. Rev. 441, 443–44 (2006).

The entire text of ECPA is reprinted in Appendix E. This section is intended to provide an overview of the key concepts necessary to understanding how ECPA applies to cybersecurity.

7.2.1 Stored Communications Act

Data that is stored on a computer server or the cloud—such as email and files—may be covered by the Stored Communications Act. As the U.S. Court of Appeals for the Ninth Circuit observed, the SCA "reflects Congress's judgment that users have a legitimate interest in the confidentiality of communications in electronic storage at a communications facility."[78]

Indeed, when Congress passed the Stored Communications Act in 1986, it was addressing a very different technological landscape than exists today. For example, consider the Senate Judiciary Committee's explanation of the need for privacy protections for stored communications:

> With the advent of computerized recordkeeping systems, Americans have lost the ability to lock away a great deal of personal and business information. For example, physicians and hospitals maintain medical files in offsite data banks, businesses of all sizes transmit their records to remote computers to obtain sophisticated data processing services. These services as well as the providers of electronic mail create electronic copies of private correspondence for later reference. This information is processed for the benefit of the user but often it is maintained for approximately 3 months to ensure system integrity. For the person or business whose records are involved, the privacy or proprietary interest in that information should not change. Nevertheless, because it is subject to control by a third party computer operator, the information may be subject to no constitutional privacy protection.[79]

The SCA covers three general categories: (1) access to stored communications;[80] (2) voluntary disclosure of stored communications by service providers;[81] and (3) law enforcement agencies' attempts to compel service providers to disclose stored communications.[82]

---

78 Theofel v. Farey-Jones, 359 F.3d 1066 (9th Cir. 2004).
79 S. Rep. No. 99-541, at 3 (1986).
80 18 U.S.C. § 2701.
81 18 U.S.C. § 2702.
82 18 U.S.C. § 2703.

The first category can be seen as a supplement to the Computer Fraud and Abuse Act, which is described in Chapter 5. Indeed, criminal charges against computer hackers have been brought under both the SCA and CFAA. The second category involves the restrictions placed on a service provider's ability to disclose its users' information. In many ways, this is analogous to a privacy law. The third category limits the government's ability to require service providers to provide users' information. This section considers each of these SCA categories in turn.

Before examining each of these three categories, it is important to understand the scope of the SCA's applicability. The SCA applies to two types of services: electronic communication services (ECS) and remote computing services (RCS). The definitions of these services are important because the SCA imposes different requirements depending on whether a service is classified as an ECS or RCS. In many cases, a service provider may be both an ECS and an RCS.[83]

The SCA defines ECS as "any service which provides to users thereof the ability to send or receive wire or electronic communications,"[84] which are the "transfer of signs, signals, writing, images, sounds, data, or intelligence of any nature transmitted in whole or in part by a wire, radio, electromagnetic, photoelectronic or photooptical system that affects interstate or foreign commerce."[85] Many courts have held that unopened emails stored on servers or the cloud fall within the ECS rules.[86] Similarly, a secured website that is used to communicate has been held to be an ECS.[87] Moreover, courts have held that Internet access is an ECS,[88] as are cell phone service providers.[89] However,

---

83 *See In the Matter of the Application of the United States*, 665 F. Supp. 2d 1210, 1214 (D. Or. 2009) ("Today, most ISPs provide both ECS and RCS; thus, the distinction serves to define the service that is being provided at a particular time (or as to a particular piece of electronic communication at a particular time), rather than to define the service provider itself. The distinction is still essential, however, because different services have different protections.").

84 18 U.S.C. §§ 2510(15), 2711(1).

85 18 U.S.C. §§ 2510(12), 2711(1).

86 *See* United States Special Mkts. Ins. Consultants v. Lynch, Case No. 11 C 9181 (N.D. Ill. 2012) ("The cases cited by the parties and those located by this court's research have consistently held that Yahoo, AOL, and similar services are, indeed, the 'electronic communication services' contemplated by the SCA.").

87 *See* Konop v. Hawaiian Airlines, Inc., 302 F.3d 868, 879–80 (9th Cir. 2002) ("The parties agree that the relevant 'electronic communications service' is Konop's website, and that the website was in 'electronic storage.' ").

88 *In re* DoubleClick Inc. Privacy Litig., 154 F. Supp. 2d 497, 508 (S.D.N.Y. 2001) ("the 'service which provides to users thereof the ability to send or receive wire or electronic communications' is 'Internet access.' ").

89 *In re* Application of United States for an Order for Prosp. Cell, 460 F. Supp. 2d 448, 459 (S.D.N.Y. 2006) ("Cell phone service providers clearly fit within this definition.").

simply operating a website does not automatically cause a company to be treated as an ECS.[90]

The SCA defines RCS as "the provision to the public of computer storage or processing services by means of an electronic communications system."[91] The SCA defines "electronic communications system" as "any wire, radio, electromagnetic, photooptical or photoelectronic facilities for the transmission of wire or electronic communications, and any computer facilities or related electronic equipment for the electronic storage of such communications."[92] Further, the statute defines "electronic storage" as "(A) any temporary, intermediate storage of a wire or electronic communication incidental to the electronic transmission thereof; and (B) any storage of such communication by an electronic communication service for purposes of backup protection of such communication."[93] The definition of "electronic storage" is important when applying the SCA's limits on ECS providers, discussed below. Applying this web of definitions to modern technologies has proven challenging to litigators, prosecutors, and courts.

Keep in mind that Congress passed the SCA in 1986, long before the modern era of cloud computing. An article in *Duke Law & Technology Review* aptly observed that Congress passed ECPA (and SCA) "to promote technological innovation, encourage the commercial use of innovative communications systems, discourage unauthorized users from obtaining access to communications to which they are not a party, and establish clearer standards to protect both law enforcement officials from liability and the admissibility of legitimately obtained evidence."[94] Indeed, when passing the SCA, the Senate issued a report in which it provided the following explanation of its reasons for explicitly covering RCS:

> In the age of rapid computerization, a basic choice has faced the users of computer technology. That is, whether to process data inhouse on the user's own computer or on someone else's equipment. Over the years, remote computer service companies have developed to provide sophisticated and convenient computing services to subscribers and customers from remote facilities. Today businesses of all sizes—hospitals, banks and many others— use remote computing services for computer processing. This

---

90 *See In re* Jetblue Airways Corp. Privacy Litig., 379 F. Supp. 2d 299, 307 (E.D.N.Y. 2005) ("Mere operation of the website, however, does not transform JetBlue into a provider of internet access, just as the use of a telephone to accept telephone reservations does not transform the company into a provider of telephone service.").

91 18 U.S.C. § 2711(2).

92 18 U.S.C. § 2510(15).

93 18 U.S.C. § 2510(17).

94 Christopher J. Borchert, Fernando M. Pinguelo, & David Thaw, *Reasonable Expectations of Privacy Settings: Social Media and the Stored Communications Act*, 13 DUKE L. & TECH. REV. 36, 41 (2013) (internal quotation marks and citation omitted).

processing can be done with the customer or subscriber using the facilities of the remote computing service in essentially a time-sharing arrangement, or it can be accomplished by the service provider on the basis of information supplied by the subscriber or customer. Data is most often transmitted between these services and their customers by means of electronic communications.[95]

Although information technology habits have changed since 1986, the Senate's general explanation of the use of "remote facilities" continues to apply to the definition of RCS. Services such as cloud computing and data centers—in which data is stored remotely for long-term use—might fall under the definition of RCS.[96] In some cases, it may not be entirely clear whether a service is covered by the rules that govern an ECS or RCS.[97] For instance, email that is opened and then stored for many years—as is common practice—has been argued to be protected by both ECS and RCS rules.[98] The distinction between RCS and ECS is vital. As we will see, the designation may play an important role in determining the privacy protections that the SCA affords to a service's users.

One important point about the Stored Communications Act: although violations of the Fourth Amendment can provide grounds for a criminal defendant to move to suppress evidence collected via the illegal search, the SCA does not explicitly provide criminal defendants with a statutory right to suppress evidence collected in violation of the statute. As Orin Kerr wrote in 2004:

The current version of the SCA authorizes civil suits for violating the statute, but it does not contain a statutory suppression

---

95 Crispin v. Christian Audigier, Inc., 717 F. Supp. 2d 965, 979, *quoting* S. Rep. No. 99-541, at 10–11 (1986).

96 Quon v. Arch Wireless Operating Co., 529 F.3d 892, 902 (9th Cir. 2008) ("In light of the Report's elaboration upon what Congress intended by the term 'Remote Computer Services,' it is clear that, before the advent of advanced computer processing programs such as Microsoft Excel, businesses had to farm out sophisticated processing to a service that would process the information.").

97 *See* Orin Kerr, *A User's Guide to the Stored Communications Act—and a Legislator's Guide to Amending It,* 72 G.W. L. Rev. 1208, 1216 (2004). ("There are closer cases, however, and some of these closer cases are important ones. In particular, the proper treatment of opened e-mail is currently unclear. The traditional understanding has been that a copy of opened e-mail sitting on a server is protected by the RCS rules, not the ECS rules. The thinking is that when an e-mail customer leaves a copy of an already-accessed e-mail stored on a server, that copy is no longer 'incident to transmission' nor a backup copy of a file that is incident to transmission: rather, it is just in remote storage like any other file held by an RCS.").

98 *See id.*; Eric R. Hinz, *A Distinctionless Distinction, Why the RCS/ECS Distinction in the Stored Communications Act Does Not Work,* 88 Notre Dame L. Rev. 489, 496 (2012) ("An important point is that the designation of ECS or RCS refers to the specific service provided, not to the providers that facilitate the service. This is important because the services provided by one provider could be classified as an ECS at one point and an RCS at another.").

remedy. ... Congress could correct this problem by adding a statutory suppression remedy to the SCA. A suppression remedy would guarantee that criminal defendants challenge government and ISP practices under the SCA, giving courts cases and controversies in which to explain clearly how the statute works.[99]

7.2.1.1   Section 2701: Third-Party Hacking of Stored Communications

Section 2701 of the SCA makes it a criminal offense to access an ECS facility without authorization. The statute also allows victims of unauthorized access to bring civil claims. Think of this section as a restriction on the ability of outside parties to hack a stored communication. Although Section 2701 is part of the Stored Communications Act, at its core it is an anti-hacking law.[100]

The statute imposes criminal penalties on any individual who "(1) intentionally accesses without authorization a facility through which an electronic communication service is provided" or "(2) intentionally exceeds an authorization to access that facility," and, through either of those actions, "thereby obtains, alters, or prevents authorized access to a wire or electronic communication while it is in electronic storage in such system[.]"[101] Individuals who are convicted of this crime face fines and up to ten years in prison. The law allows service providers and individuals to file civil actions against violators.[102]

A limitation on this criminal provision is its application only to a *facility* through which an ECS is provided. Courts generally have held that hacking an individual's computer or smartphone does not constitute a violation of the SCA because that individual device is not a "facility"; instead, the unauthorized access must be of an email account, cloud service, or other ECS facility.[103] For instance, in 2012, a California federal judge dismissed a Section 2701 class action lawsuit against Apple alleging that its iOS devices violated plaintiffs' privacy rights by allowing third-party applications to collect information about users. The judge noted that although "the computer systems of an email provider, a bulletin board system, or an ISP are uncontroversial examples of facilities that provide electronic communications services to multiple users," individuals' computers, laptops, and mobile devices do not constitute "facilities."[104]

---

99 Kerr, *supra* note 97 at 1241 (describing why the lack of a statutory suppression remedy has "added to the confusion about the SCA.").

100 *Id.* at 1239 ("Section 2701 is a very close cousin of another criminal statute, 18 U.S.C. § 1030, sometimes known as the Computer Fraud and Abuse Act.").

101 18 U.S.C. § 2701(a).

102 18 U.S.C. § 2707.

103 *See, e.g.,* Cousineau v. Microsoft Corp., 6 F. Supp. 3d 1167, 1175 (W.D. Wash. 2014) ("In this situation, Plaintiff's phone did not provide location services to other users in a server-like fashion, but instead received the relevant services from Microsoft.").

104 *In re* iPhone Application Litig., 844 F. Supp. 2d 1040, 1057 (N.D. Cal. 2012).

Another significant limitation on this statute is the requirement that the access to the facility be "without authorization" or in excess of authorization. As with the CFAA, discussed in Chapter 5, it often is difficult for the government or civil plaintiffs to demonstrate that access was entirely without authorization or in excess of authorization. For instance, in a 2000 case in Michigan, a company accused its former manufacturer's representative of continuing to access the company's confidential sales information, which was stored on the network of one of its retailers, Kmart. The company alleged that the representative's continued access to the information, even after its termination, constituted a Section 2701 violation.[105] The district court disagreed and dismissed the lawsuit. Even though the manufacturer's representative continued to access the sales information after its termination—and it arguably had no need to do so—the court reasoned that Kmart continued to provide the representative with access to its network. "Where a party consents to another's access to its computer network, it cannot claim that such access was unauthorized," the court concluded.[106]

In contrast, the next year, a court allowed a Section 2701 class action lawsuit to proceed against Intuit, which the plaintiffs allege used website cookies to violate their privacy rights. The court reasoned that, unlike the Michigan case, "[p]laintiffs here allege that they did not authorize Defendant to access data contained in the cookies it implanted on Plaintiffs' computers."[107]

7.2.1.2 Section 2702: Restrictions on Service Providers' Ability to Disclose Stored Communications and Records to the Government and Private Parties

Section 2702 of the SCA restricts the ability of *both* ECS and RCS providers to voluntarily disclose both communications contents and consumer records. Disputes under this section commonly arise during discovery in civil cases; parties to litigation often subpoena service providers for emails, logs, and other records. Importantly, Section 2702 does not have an explicit exception that allows RCS and ECS providers to turn over information in civil discovery.[108]

The statute prohibits a public ECS provider from knowingly divulging to either the government *or* private parties "the contents of a communication while in electronic storage by that service."[109] As detailed in the next

---

105 Sherman & Co. v. Salton Maxim Housewares, 94 F. Supp. 2d 817 (E.D. Mich. 2000).
106 *Id*. at 821.
107 *In re* Intuit Privacy Litig., 138 F. Supp. 2d 1272, 1277 (C.D. Cal. 2001).
108 *See* Mintz v. Mark Bartelstein & Assocs., Inc., 885 F. Supp. 2d 987 (C.D. Cal. 2012) ("The SCA does not contain an exception for civil discovery subpoenas."); Flagg v. City of Detroit, 252 F.R.D. 346, 350 (E.D. Mich. 2008) ("[A]s noted by the courts and commentators alike, § 2702 lacks any language that explicitly authorizes a service provider to divulge the contents of a communication pursuant to a subpoena or court order.").
109 18 U.S.C. § 2702.

subsection, many courts have held that opened emails are no longer in "electronic storage," but the Ninth Circuit has disagreed.

Public RCS providers are prohibited from knowingly divulging contents of communications that are "carried or maintained" on the service on behalf of— and received via electronic transmission from—a subscriber or customer, for the purposes of storage or computer processing, unless the customer has provided authorization for other services.[110] The statute broadly defines "contents" to include "any information concerning the substance, purport, or meaning of that communication."[111]

In 2014, the Ninth Circuit provided a clear summary of the analysis to determine whether the restrictions apply to an RCS provider:

> Under the Stored Communications Act, a person or entity (1) providing remote computing service to the public (2) shall not knowingly divulge to any person or entity the contents of any communication (3) which is carried or maintained on that service ... on behalf of, and received by means of electronic transmission from (or created by means of computer processing of communications received by means of electronic transmission from), a subscriber or customer of such service (4) solely for the purpose of providing storage or computer processing services to such subscriber or customer, unless the provider is authorized to access the contents of any such communications to provide other services.[112]

Cloud services might qualify as RCS providers, but their coverage under Section 2702 is far from certain and might depend on the privacy protections that the service offers to its users.[113]

Keep in mind that Section 2702 only applies to ECS and RCS services that are provided *to the public*. This generally has been interpreted to include service

---

110 18 U.S.C. § 2702(a)(2)(B) (prohibiting the disclosure of communications contents that are on RCS "solely for the purpose of providing storage or computer processing services to such subscriber or customer, if the provider is not authorized to access the contents of any such communications for purposes of providing any services other than storage or computer processing.").

111 18 U.S.C. §§ 2510(8), 2711(1).

112 *In re* Zynga Privacy Litig., 750 F.3d 1098, 1104 (9th Cir. 2014) (internal quotation marks omitted).

113 *See* William Jeremy Robison, *Free at What Cost?: Cloud Computing Privacy Under the Stored Communications Act*, 98 Geo. L.J. 1195, 1222 (2010) ("Only when a cloud provider expressly limits its access to a customer's data for the purposes of providing computer storage or processing functions will the customer benefit from the Act's RCS provisions, including the protection from compelled disclosure by the government and civil litigants.").

providers that have customers; a purely internal email system (e.g., a private company's email and document storage server) likely would not be considered to be provided "to the public."[114] For instance, in a 1998 case, an Illinois federal judge rejected the argument that Section 2702 applies to an ECS provider "even if that provider maintains the system primarily for its own use and does not provide services to the general public."[115] The court concluded that "the statute covers any entity that provides electronic communication service (e.g., e-mail) to the community at large."[116]

Section 2702 contains a number of exceptions that allow service providers to disclose communications content under limited circumstances:

- *"to an addressee or intended recipient of such communication or an agent of such addressee or intended recipient"*[117] For example, Gmail can deliver the email to the address that is in the "to" line of the email.
- *If law enforcement obtains a warrant or other valid process that is authorized under another statute.*[118] For instance, Section 2703 of the SCA (discussed in Section 7.2.1.4), provides a few mechanisms for law enforcement to obtain valid process to compel service providers to disclose communications content. If the service providers receive this process, they will not be held liable for disclosure.
- *"with the lawful consent of the originator or an addressee or intended recipient of such communication, or the subscriber in the case of remote computing service."*[119]
- *"to a person employed or authorized or whose facilities are used to forward such communication to its destination."*[120] An example is an email provider that has to transmit a message through a third-party service provider in order for it to reach its intended destination.
- *As may be "necessarily incident to the rendition of the service or to the protection of the rights or to the protection of the rights or property of*

---

114 Simon M. Baker, *Unfriending the Stored Communications Act*, 22 DePaul J. Art Tech. & Intell. Prop. L. 75, 85 (2011) ("Although the SCA does not provide a definition of the word 'public,' an entity provides a service 'to the public' if it provides that service to 'the community at large' whether or not it charges a fee. This excludes systems that are proprietary or purely intra-company, or situations in which the services are only available to users with a special relationship to the entity providing the service.") (internal citations omitted).

115 Andersen Consulting LLP v. UOP, 991 F. Supp. 1041, 1042 (N.D. Ill. 1998); *see also* Kerr, *supra* note 97, at 1220 n.82 ("By implication, nonpublic providers can disclose without limitation under the SCA.").

116 Andersen Consulting LLP v. UOP, 991 F. Supp. 1041, 1042 (N.D. Ill. 1998).

117 18 U.S.C. § 2702(b)(1).

118 18 U.S.C. § 2702(b)(2).

119 18 U.S.C. § 2702(b)(3).

120 18 U.S.C. § 2702(b)(4).

the provider of the service.[121] This is one of the more controversial exceptions to Section 2702. For instance, in 2006, Apple contended that if an email provider did not comply with a civil subpoena issued by Apple for a customer's communications, the company could face court sanctions, and therefore providing the information protects the company's rights or property. The California Court of Appeal rejected this argument, concluding that the "effect of such an interpretation would be to permit disclosure whenever someone threatened the service provider with litigation."[122] However, few courts have directly addressed this exception, so it is not entirely clear exactly what types of disclosure *would* fall under this exception.

- *To the National Center for Missing and Exploited Children, in connection with a child pornography investigation.*[123] As discussed in Section 7.1 of this chapter (regarding the Fourth Amendment), 18 U.S.C. § 2258A requires all ECS and RCS providers to file a report with the National Center for Missing and Exploited Children if the providers obtain actual knowledge of an apparent violation of federal child pornography laws. Filing this report is explicitly exempt from the SCA.

- *To law enforcement, if the contents were inadvertently obtained by the service provider and appear to pertain to the commission of a crime.* No published court opinion has interpreted this provision, but based on court rulings regarding other exceptions to the SCA, for this exception to apply, a service provider likely would have to present substantial evidence that it obtained the contents "inadvertently."

- *"to a governmental entity, if the provider, in good faith, believes that an emergency involving danger of death or serious physical injury to any person requires disclosure without delay of communications relating to the emergency."*[124] For instance, one court suggested in nonbinding dicta to a case that if a service provider obtains credible evidence of potential child abuse, it is authorized to provide communications content to a government social services agency.[125]

Section 2702 allows RCS and ECS providers to divulge "a record or other information pertaining to a subscriber to or customer of such service" to nongovernmental entities, provided that the record does *not* include the *contents* of communications. Such records include subscriber names, addresses, and

---

121 18 U.S.C. § 2702(b)(5).
122 O'Grady v. Superior Ct., 44 Cal. Rptr. 3d 72 (Cal. Ct. App. 2006).
123 18 U.S.C. § 2702(b)(6).
124 18 U.S.C. § 2702(b)(7).
125 United States v. D'Andrea, 497 F. Supp. 2d 117 (D. Mass. 2007).

account use history.[126] However, RCS and ECS providers still are prohibited from disclosing customer records to government entities, unless (1) subject to a valid warrant, subpoena, or order under Section 2703; (2) with the customer's consent; (3) "as may be necessarily incident to the rendition of the service or to the protection of the rights or property of the provider of that service;" (4) to the government, if the provider believes in "good faith" that an emergency exists; or (5) to NCMEC in connection with a child pornography investigation.[127]

Individuals who believe that their SCA rights have been violated can file a civil action for actual and punitive damages.[128]

The Cybersecurity Act of 2015: Allowing Service Providers to Disclose and Monitor for Cybersecurity Threats. A 2015 law affirms the ability of RCS and ECS providers to disclose information about cybersecurity threats to the government and other organizations. In December 2015, Congress passed the Cybersecurity Act of 2015, which is intended to promote collaboration between the private sector and federal government on cybersecurity.

The Cybersecurity Act of 2015, described in Chapter 6, also may expand the ability of operators of computer networks and systems to monitor for cybersecurity threats without facing liability under the Stored Communications Act. The Cybersecurity Act allows private entities to monitor their own information systems—as well as information systems of other entities with consent—for "cybersecurity purposes."[129] It defines "cybersecurity purpose" as "the purpose of protecting an information system or information that is stored on, processed by, or transiting an information system from a cybersecurity threat or security vulnerability."[130]

The 2015 Act broadly defines "cybersecurity threat" as "an action, not protected by the First Amendment to the Constitution of the United States, on or through an information system that may result in an unauthorized effort to adversely impact the security, availability, confidentiality, or integrity of an information system or information that is stored on, processed by, or transiting an information system."[131] Cybersecurity threats do not include actions that merely violate a customer terms of service or licensing agreement. The Act defines "security vulnerability" as "any attribute of hardware, software, process, or procedure that could enable or facilitate the defeat of a security control."[132]

---

126 *See, e.g.,* United States v. Hambrick, 55 F. Supp. 2d 504 (W.D. Va. 1999) ("this court does not find that the ECPA has legislatively determined that an individual has a reasonable expectation of privacy in his name, address, social security number, credit card number, and proof of Internet connection.").

127 18 U.S.C. § 2702(c).

128 18 U.S.C. § 2707.

129 6 U.S.C. § 1503(a).

130 6 U.S.C. § 1501(4).

131 6 U.S.C. § 1501(5).

132 6 U.S.C. § 1501(17).

The statute also allows private companies to operate "defensive measures" for "cybersecurity purposes." However, the statute's definition of "defensive measures" is rather narrow, and explicitly excludes "hacking back" at a network that the company believes had attacked its network. The statute defines "defensive measure" as "an action, device, procedure, signature, technique, or other measure applied to an information system or information that is stored on, processed by, or transiting an information system that detects, prevents, or mitigates a known or suspected threat or security vulnerability."[133] The statute explicitly states that "defensive measure" does not include "a measure that destroys, renders unusable, provides unauthorized access to, or substantially harms an information system or information stored on, processed by, or transiting such information system" that is neither owned by the private entity that is operating the measure or another entity that is "authorized to provide consent and has provided consent to that private entity to operate the measure."[134]

Examples of Defensive Measures under the Cybersecurity Act of 2015

In June 2016, the U.S. Department of Homeland Security released guidance for the implementation of the Cybersecurity Act of 2015. It listed the following as illustrative examples of "defensive measures" under the statute:

- A computer program that identifies a pattern of malicious activity in web traffic flowing into an organization.
- A signature that could be loaded into a company's intrusion detection system in order to detect a spear phishing campaign with particular characteristics.
- A firewall rule that disallows a type of malicious traffic from entering a network.
- An algorithm that can search through a cache of network traffic to discover anomalous patterns that may indicate malicious activity.
- A technique for quickly matching, in an automated manner, the content of an organization's incoming Simple Mail Transfer Protocol (SMTP, a protocol commonly used for email) traffic against a set of content known to be associated with a specific cybersecurity threat without unacceptably degrading the speed of email delivery to end users.

Source: Department of Homeland Security and Department of Justice: Guidance to Assist Non-Federal Entities to Share Cyber Threat Indicators and Defensive Measures with Federal Entities under the Cybersecurity Information Sharing act of 2015.

---

133 6 U.S.C. § 1501(7).
134 *Id.*

7.2.1.3   Section 2703: Government's Ability to Require Service
Providers to Turn Over Stored Communications and Customer Records

Section 2703 of the SCA restricts the government's ability to compel ECS and RCS providers to disclose communications content and records. As we will see, this is not the only restriction on the government; in addition to the Section 2703 requirements, the government also must satisfy the requirements of the Fourth Amendment to the U.S. Constitution. In some cases, even if the SCA allows the government to compel disclosure, the Fourth Amendment may prevent it.

Section 2703's restrictions for the disclosure of communications content depend on whether the provider is an ECS or RCS provider, and the length of time the communications content has been stored. In short, electronic communications in electronic storage with ECS providers for 180 days or less receive more protection than other ECS communications (or any RCS communications).

Despite a general consensus that the 180-day distinction is arcane and wholly inapplicable to modern technology, the 1986 law remains the law of the land for now. Here is how it works: The government must obtain a court-issued warrant, supported by probable cause, to compel communications content from an ECS provider if that content has been "in electronic storage in an electronic communications system for one hundred and eighty days or less."[135] Some courts have concluded that once emails are opened, they are no longer in electronic storage—and therefore, not subject to the warrant requirement[136]—whereas others, particularly the Ninth Circuit in *Theofel v. Farey-Jones*, have reached an opposite conclusion and held that emails may be in "electronic storage" with ECS providers even if they were already opened.[137] In a 2009

---

135 18 U.S.C. § 2703; *see* United States v. Weaver, 636 F. Supp. 2d 769 (C.D. Ill. 2009) ("Thus, for emails less than 181 days old, the question of whether a warrant is necessary turns on whether the emails are 'in electronic storage' or are 'held or maintained ... solely for the purpose of providing storage or computer processing services to [the] subscriber or customer.'... If the emails the Government requested here are in electronic storage, Microsoft need not produce them without a warrant, but if they are held or maintained solely to provide the customer storage or computer processing services, Microsoft must comply with the Government's subpoena.").

136 United States v. Weaver, 636 F. Supp. 2d 769, 773 (C.D. Ill. 2009) ("Previously opened emails stored by Microsoft for Hotmail users are not in electronic storage, and the Government can obtain copies of such emails using a trial subpoena. Microsoft must comply with the Government's subpoena here.").

137 Theofel v. Farey-Jones, 359 F.3d 1066, 1075 (9th Cir. 2004) ("The ISP copy of the message functions as a 'backup' for the user. Notably, nothing in the Act requires that the backup protection be for the benefit of the ISP rather than the user. Storage under these circumstances thus literally falls within the statutory definition."). Orin Kerr has argued that the Ninth Circuit's interpretation is "quite implausible and hard to square with the statutory text." Kerr, *supra* note 97, at 1217. In contrast, Rebecca A. Fiss argues that the SCA should cover both unopened *and* opened emails. Pointing to the House and Senate reports regarding the SCA, Fiss argues that they "do not distinguish between read and unread communications, nor is any such distinction inherent in the rationale—messages that a user has read and left in his account for safekeeping are no less private and no less vulnerable to intrusion than unread messages." Rebecca A. Fiss, *Taking Back Electronic Storage*, 92 N.C. L. Rev. Addendum 76, 91–92 (2014).

guidebook on computer searches, the U.S. Justice Department noted that the broader interpretation has created practical difficulties in the Ninth Circuit, which is bound by *Theofel*: "There is no way for a service provider to determine whether a previously opened email on its servers is a backup for a copy of the email stored by a user on his computer, as the service provider simply cannot know whether the underlying email remains stored on the user's computer."[138] In jurisdictions that do not apply the Ninth Circuit's broad interpretation of "electronic storage," opened emails might receive the protections afforded to communications content stored with RCS providers.[139]

For SCA purposes, to obtain communications content that has been in electronic storage with an ECS provider for more than 180 days—or is stored with an RCS provider—the government is not required to obtain a warrant supported by probable cause. Instead, it also could obtain an administrative, grand jury, or trial subpoena, which requires a lower standard of proof than a warrant.[140] The rules differ depending on jurisdiction, but the government typically does not need to come anywhere close to demonstrating probable cause; however, the material sought must be relevant and related to the investigation or trial.[141] The government also may obtain this content by securing what is known as a "(d) order,"[142] which is because it is a mechanism created by subsection (d) of Section 2703 of the SCA. A federal or state court may issue a (d) order if the government "offers specific and articulable facts showing that there are reasonable grounds to believe that the contents of a wire or electronic communication, or the records or other information sought, are relevant and material to an ongoing criminal investigation."[143] Although this requires the government to provide some specific facts, this showing, as with a subpoena, is much lower than the probable cause required to obtain a warrant. A court can quash or modify a (d) order if the service provider files a motion which demonstrates that "the information or records requested are unusually voluminous in nature or compliance with such order otherwise would cause an undue burden on such provider."[144]

To obtain communications via a subpoena or (d) order, the government must provide prior notice to the subscriber or customer, unless it convinces a court to delay notice for up to 90 days because "there is reason to believe that notification of the existence of the court order [or subpoena] may have an adverse result[.]"[145]

---

138 Department of Justice, Searching and Seizing Computers and Obtaining Electronic Evidence in Criminal Investigations (2009) at 125.
139 *See* Kerr *supra* note 97, at 1216.
140 18 U.S.C. § 2703(b)(1)(B)(i).
141 *See, e.g.,* Fed. R. Crim. P. 17(c)(2) (allowing a court to quash or modify a criminal subpoena "if compliance would be unreasonable or oppressive").
142 18 U.S.C. § 2703(b)(1)(B)(ii).
143 18 U.S.C. § 2703(d).
144 *Id.*
145 18 U.S.C. § 2705(1)(A).

A number of critics say the 180-day distinction has become outdated and is often unworkable for modern communications. For this reason, members of both parties in Congress have long been attempting to amend the SCA to provide for the same level of protection regardless of the amount of time that a communication has been in storage. "In 2015, it is absurd that the government is free to rifle through Americans' emails that are older than six months," Sen. Ron Wyden, a sponsor of one such amendment, said in 2015. "Because of this arcane law, as technology advances, Americans' civil liberties are eroding."[146]

Moreover, as discussed in Section 7.1, some courts are beginning to hold that the Fourth Amendment requires a warrant for the government to obtain any communications, regardless of the length of time that they are stored. As of the publication of this book, momentum was building in Congress for an amendment to the Stored Communications Act that would eliminate the 180-day distinction and require the government to obtain a warrant for stored communications regardless of the length of time that they had been stored.

In recent years, as cloud computing has caused data to be stored around the globe, regardless of the location of the communications subjects, courts have grappled with the enforceability of SCA orders and warrants that seek data stored abroad.[147] The issue came to a head in Microsoft's challenge of a warrant issued in Manhattan federal court, seeking email from a Microsoft account that was stored in a Microsoft data center in Ireland.[148] Microsoft asked the district court to quash the warrant, arguing that the Stored Communications Act did not authorize warrants for data stored outside of the United States. The district judge denied Microsoft's motion, but the United States Court of Appeals for the Second Circuit reversed in a 2016 opinion. "When, in 1986, Congress passed the Stored Communications Act as part of the broader Electronic Communications Privacy Act, its aim was to protect user privacy in the context of new technology that required a user's interaction with a service provider," Judge Susan L. Carney wrote for the three-judge panel. "Neither explicitly nor implicitly does the statute envision the application of its warrant provisions overseas. Three decades ago, international boundaries were not so

---

146 Grant Gross, *U.S. Lawmakers Introduce Two Bills to Protect Email Privacy*, PC World (Feb. 12, 2015).

147 *See* Andrew J. Pecoraro, *Drawing Lines in the Cloud: Implications of Extraterritorial Limits to the Stored Communications Act*, 51 Creighton L. Rev. 75 (2017) (concluding that "the location of data is a problematic factor to rely upon" and arguing "that the SCA should be interpreted to reach data stored overseas held by electronic service providers that are subject to U.S. jurisdiction, but that such a warrant should be quashed upon a prima facie showing that the target of the investigation is not a U.S. national or the target is not acting in the United States, or that retrieving the data would violate the laws of the country in which the data is being stored.").

148 Microsoft v. United States, 829 F.3d 197 (2d Cir. 2016).

routinely crossed as they are today, when service providers rely on worldwide networks of hardware to satisfy users' 21st-century demands for access and speed and their related, evolving expectations of privacy."[149]

The federal government petitioned the Supreme Court to review the Second Circuit opinion, and the Supreme Court granted certiorari and held oral arguments in February 2018. The next month—before the Supreme Court issued an opinion—Congress effectively mooted the case by passing the Clarifying Lawful Overseas Use of Data (CLOUD) Act, which explicitly creates circumstances in which a U.S. warrant could reach extraterritorially to data stored abroad. In its findings, Congress wrote that "conflicting legal obligations" arise when the SCA "requires disclosure of electronic data that foreign law prohibits communications-service providers from disclosing."[150]

The CLOUD Act addresses the ambiguity that caused the Microsoft dispute by requiring ECS and RCS providers to "comply with the obligations of this chapter to preserve, backup, or disclose the contents of a wire or electronic communication and any record or other information pertaining to a customer or subscriber within such provider's possession, custody, or control, regardless of whether such communication, record, or other information is located within or outside of the United States."[151] However, the law contains provisions that are designed to provide some privacy protections. The CLOUD Act allows the U.S. Attorney General to enter bilateral executive agreements with other countries to allow each country's legal process to access data stored in the other country, subject to a number of substantive and procedural privacy safeguards.[152] Most notably, a service provider can request that a judge quash an SCA order if the provider "reasonably believes" that "the customer or subscriber is not a United States person and does not reside in the United States" and "that the required disclosure would create a material risk that the provider" would violate a foreign government's laws, provided that the United States has an executive agreement with that government.[153] The court may quash the SCA order only if: (1) the disclosure of data "would cause the provider to violate the laws" of the foreign government; (2) "based on the totality of the circumstances, the interests of justice dictate that the legal process should be modified or quashed;" and (3) "the customer or subscriber is not a United States person and does not reside in the United States."[154] If the United States does not have an executive agreement with a nation whose laws

---

149 *Id*. at 201.
150 H.R. Rep. No. 1625, Division 5, Sec. 102(5).
151 18 U.S.C. § 2713.
152 18 U.S.C. § 2523.
153 18 U.S.C. § 2703(h)(2)(A).
154 18 U.S.C. § 2703(h)(2)(B).

allegedly would be violated by the order, the service provider still could bring a common-law challenge to an SCA order.[155]

Executive agreements under the CLOUD Act are reciprocal; they create a process for foreign governments to issue orders to obtain data that is stored by U.S. providers. However, the statute imposes substantial limits on the agreements. To enter into an executive agreement with another country, the Attorney General, with the Secretary of State concurring, must file a written certification to Congress stating, among other things, that "the domestic law of the foreign government, including the implementation of that law, affords robust substantive and procedural protections for privacy and civil liberties in light of the data collection and activities of the foreign government that will be subject to the agreement" and that the other government "has adopted appropriate procedures to minimize the acquisition, retention, and dissemination of information concerning United States persons subject to the agreement."[156] The agreement must restrict the foreign government's orders issued under the agreement so that, among other things, they (1) do not "intentionally target a United States person or a person located in the United States;" (2) do "not target a non-United States person located outside the United States if the purpose is to obtain information concerning a United States person or a person located in the United States;" (3) are "for the purpose of obtaining information relating to the prevention, detection, investigation, or prosecution of serious crime, including terrorism;" and (4) "identify a specific person, account, address, or personal device, or any other specific identifier as the object of the order."[157] The order must comply with the foreign government's domestic law, "be based on requirements for a reasonable justification based on articulable and credible facts, particularity, legality, and severity regarding the conduct under investigation," and be subject to review.[158] (The full list of requirements is in Section 2523 of ECPA, reprinted in full in Appendix E of this book.)

7.2.2 Wiretap Act

As its name suggests, the Stored Communications Act restricts the disclosure and procurement of communications that are stored on a medium

---

155 H.R. Rep. No. 1625, Division 5, § 103(c) ("Nothing in this section, or an amendment made by this section, shall be construed to modify or otherwise affect the common law standards governing the availability or application of comity analysis to other types of compulsory process or to instances of compulsory process issued under section 2703 of title 18, United States Code, as amended by this section, and not covered under subsection (h)(2) of such section 2703.").
156 18 U.S.C. § 2523(b)(2).
157 18 U.S.C. § 2523(b)(4)(D).
158 *Id.*

(e.g., a server). In contrast, the Wiretap Act[159] restricts the ability of the government and private parties to intercept communications as they are in transit.

The Wiretap Act, passed as Title III of the Omnibus Crime Control and Safe Streets Act of 1968, contains a broad, general prohibition on the intentional interception, procurement, and use of electronic, wire, or oral communications.[160] The statute also prohibits the intentional interception or disclosure of the contents of unlawfully intercepted communications.[161] As the U.S. Court of Appeals for the First Circuit accurately summarized, a typical claim of a Wiretap Act violation consists of a demonstration that the defendant "(1) intentionally (2) intercepted, endeavored to intercept or procured another person to intercept or endeavor to intercept (3) the contents of (4) an electronic communication (5) using a device."[162]

The Wiretap Act uses the same definition of "contents" as the SCA: "any information concerning the substance, purport, or meaning of that communication."[163] Courts generally have interpreted this definition broadly to include personally identifiable information such as names and birthdates.[164] However, data automatically generated about the call, such as the call time and duration, is not considered "content" that is covered by the Wiretap Act.[165] Violations of the Wiretap Act carry criminal fines and prison time of up to five years.[166] The statute also allows the victims of Wiretap Act violations to file civil lawsuits for damages and equitable relief.[167]

The Wiretap Act's broad prohibitions contain a number of exceptions. Among the most commonly cited exceptions are these.

First, the Wiretap Act does not prohibit an employee of a communications provider from intercepting, disclosing, or using communications for any activity "which is a necessary incident to the rendition of his service or to the protection of the rights or property of the provider of that service."[168] As one court noted, this exception "has been repeatedly interpreted by Courts to authorize telephone companies to intercept and monitor calls placed over their facilities

---

159 18 U.S.C. §§ 2510–22.
160 18 U.S.C. § 2511.
161 *Id.*
162 *In re* Pharmatrak, 329 F.3d 9, 18 (1st Cir. 2003).
163 18 U.S.C. § 2510(8).
164 *See In re* Pharmatrak, 329 F.3d 9, 18 (1st Cir. 2003).
165 *See In re* iPhone Application Litig., 844 F. Supp. 2d 1040, 1061 (N.D. Cal. 2012) ("'[c]ontent' is limited to information the user intended to communicate, such as the words spoken in a phone call.").
166 18 U.S.C. § 2511(4)(a).
167 18 U.S.C. § 2520.
168 18 U.S.C § 2511(2)(a)(i).

in order to combat fraud and theft of service."[169] Similarly, this exception enables employers to monitor employee email accounts without facing Wiretap Act charges.[170] The law also provides law enforcement with a limited ability to intercept a "computer trespasser's communications" with the service provider's authorization.

Second, communications providers may "provide information, facilities, or technical assistance to persons authorized by law to intercept wire, oral, or electronic communications or to conduct electronic surveillance" pursuant to a court order under Section 704 of the Foreign Intelligence Surveillance Act or if a top Justice Department official certifies the existence of an emergency situation.[171]

Third, a Federal Communications Commission employee, conducting normal enforcement responsibilities, may "intercept a wire or electronic communication, or oral communication transmitted by radio, or to disclose or use the information thereby obtained."[172]

Fourth, a "person acting under color of law" (such as a law enforcement officer) who is party to a communication is not subject to the Wiretap Act's prohibitions.[173] Relatedly, the Wiretap Act does not restrict such interception if at least one party to the communication has provided consent.[174] In other words, if one of the parties to a phone conversation or email exchange is an undercover officer, or a private party acting on behalf of law enforcement, then the Wiretap Act would not restrict the government's interception of that phone call.

Fifth, a private individual may intercept a communication if that individual is a party to the communication, or if one of the parties provided consent.[175] However, this exception does not apply if the interception is conducted to commit a criminal or tortious act that violates a state or federal law.[176]

The most significant exception to the Wiretap Act, for government purposes, allows law enforcement to seek a court order for the interception of wire, oral, or electronic communications.[177] Under this exception, law enforcement must fulfill a number of requirements before obtaining an order that allows them to intercept communications.

---

169 United States v. Villanueva, 32 F. Supp. 2d 635, 639 (S.D.N.Y. 1998).

170 *In re* Info. Mgmt. Servs., Inc. Derivative Litig., 81 A.3d 278, 294 (Del. Ct. Chancery 2013) ("Employers monitor email (or reserve the right to do so) in large part to protect their property and to guard against potential liability.").

171 18 U.S.C. § 2511(2)(a)(ii).

172 18 U.S.C. § 2511(2)(b).

173 18 U.S.C. § 2511(2)(c).

174 *Id.*

175 18 U.S.C. § 2511(2)(d).

176 For a complete list of state recording laws, *see* REPORTER'S COMMITTEE FOR FREEDOM OF THE PRESS, REPORTER'S REPORTING GUIDE, https://www.rcfp.org/rcfp/orders/docs/RECORDING.pdf.

177 18 U.S.C. § 2518.

Applications for wiretap orders must contain the identity of the officer seeking the information, with a "full and complete statement of the facts," including:

> (i) details as to the particular offense that has been, is being, or is about to be committed, (ii) [when possible] a particular description of the nature and location of the facilities from which or the place where the communication is to be intercepted, (iii) a particular description of the type of communications sought to be intercepted, (iv) the identity of the person, if known, committing the offense and whose communications are to be intercepted.[178]

Wiretap orders may only be based on probable cause of one of a list of a series of serious crimes, which appears in 18 U.S.C. § 2516 (reprinted in Appendix E of this book). The application also must describe whether other investigative procedures have been attempted, the period of time for which interception has been attempted, and a statement concerning previous applications for wiretaps.[179]

After reviewing the application, the judge may grant the order only after finding that there is probable cause to believe that the target of the wiretap is committing, has committed, or soon will commit a particular serious criminal offense *and* that there is probable cause to believe that communications concerning the offense will be obtained via the wiretap.[180] The court also must find that "normal investigative procedures have been tried and have failed or reasonably appear to be unlikely to succeed if tried or to be too dangerous."[181] The court also generally must find that there is probable cause to believe that the Internet connection or other communications facility that is being wiretapped is being used by the target of the investigation.[182]

In short, before a court will grant a wiretap order, it must determine that probable cause exists for three different elements: (1) that the target has committed, is committing, or soon will commit a crime; (2) that the wiretap will lead to information about this crime; and (3) that the target will use the communications facilities specified in the wiretap application. This is a relatively high standard to meet. As one court held, probable cause for a wiretap application requires a "reasonable and common sense" evaluation of all of the facts:

> Under this standard, the question that must be decided in issuing a warrant is whether there is probable cause to believe that

---

178 *Id.*
179 *Id.*
180 18 U.S.C. § 2518(3).
181 *Id.*
182 *Id.*

evidence of a crime will be uncovered. Obviously, certainty is not required at this stage, and the exact quantum of support required has frequently been described as "a fair probability," but more than a "mere suspicion," that such evidence will be discovered. Facts can amount to a fair probability without being proof beyond a reasonable doubt or even a prima facie showing.[183]

In other words, although a court need not be certain that the wiretap will uncover evidence of a crime, law enforcement must make a substantial showing of probable cause in order to obtain a wiretap order.

A wiretap order may be authorized for no longer than 30 days.[184] If law enforcement needs an extension, then it must seek an extension of up to 30 more days. As one federal appeals court stated, the Wiretap Act intends law enforcement "to adopt minimization techniques to reduce to a practical minimum the interception of conversations unrelated to the criminal activity under investigation."[185]

The Wiretap Act applies to many media; it limits the ability of private parties and law enforcement to intercept electronic communications while in transit. Accordingly, the Wiretap Act applies not only to phone calls, but also to email messages, instant messages, text messages, and other communications that are intercepted while in transit.[186]

7.2.3 Pen Register Act

As described in Section 7.1, the United States Supreme Court has held that the Fourth Amendment does not restrict the government's use of pen registers to obtain noncontent information, such as logs of telephone numbers and other metadata (though post-*Carpenter*, that may be changing). In 1986, Congress passed Chapter 206 of the ECPA, known as the Pen Register Act, which imposes some restrictions on the collection of some noncontent data, though not nearly as extensive as the limits imposed by the Fourth Amendment.

The Pen Register Act restricts the real-time collection of noncontent communications data by the government and private parties. The statute applies to "pen registers," which it defines as devices or processes that record "dialing, routing, addressing, or signaling information" of a wire or electronic communication.[187]

---

183 United States v. Alfano, 838 F.2d 158, 161–62 (6th Cir. 1988).
184 18 U.S.C. § 2518(5).
185 United States v. Carey, No. 14-50222 (9th Cir. Sept. 7, 2016) (internal quotation marks and citation omitted).
186 *See* Luis v. Zang, No. 14-3601 (6th Cir. Aug. 16, 2016).
187 18 U.S.C. § 3127.

It also applies to "trap and trace devices," which record the metadata of incoming communications.[188]

The Pen Register Act does not apply to the contents of communications; those are regulated under the Wiretap Act. In 2001, as part of the PATRIOT Act, Congress amended the Pen Register Act to clarify that it applies to the metadata of electronic communications, such as email. However, the subject line of emails is typically considered to be content, and therefore is not covered by the Pen Register Act.

The Pen Register Act imposes a general prohibition[189] on the use of pen register and trap and trace devices, with a few key exceptions, including:

- if the pen register or trap and trace device is related to the "operation, maintenance, and testing" of a communications service;[190]
- if the pen register or trap and trace device is related to the protection of the communications providers or their users to keep the service free of abuse or unlawful service use;[191]
- if the user has consented;[192] or
- if the government has obtained a court order under Section 3123 of the Pen Register Act.[193]

Section 3123 does *not* require the government to demonstrate probable cause that a crime has occurred or will occur. Instead, law enforcement must satisfy the more lenient requirement of certifying that "information likely to be obtained by such installation and use is relevant to an ongoing criminal investigation."[194]

A Section 3123 order must specify the identity of the person to whom a telephone line or facility is leased, the identity of the person who is the subject of the investigation, the attributes of the communications to which the order applies, and a statement of the offense to which the information likely to be obtained by the device relates.[195] The orders may not exceed 60 days, but may be extended by new court order for up to 60 days.[196] Communications providers are prohibited from disclosing the existence of a pen register or trap and trace order unless directed by the issuing court.[197]

---

188 *Id.*
189 18 U.S.C. § 3121.
190 18 U.S.C. § 3121(b)(1).
191 18 U.S.C. § 3121(b)(2).
192 18 U.S.C. § 3121(b)(2).
193 18 U.S.C. § 3121(a).
194 18 U.S.C. § 3123(a)(1).
195 18 U.S.C. § 3123(b)(1).
196 18 U.S.C. § 3123(c).
197 18 U.S.C. § 3123(d).

7.2.4   National Security Letters

Among the most controversial aspects of the 2001 USA PATRIOT Act, passed after the September 11, 2001, terrorist attacks, was an expansion of the government's ability to issue national security letters.[198] National security letters are administrative subpoenas that allow the government to secretly obtain certain information relevant to national security investigations. The law has since been amended modestly to address some concerns of privacy advocates.

The National Security Letter provision of the Stored Communications Act[199] allows the Federal Bureau of Investigation (FBI) to provide a wire or electronic communication service provider with a name, phone number, or account number and request the associated name, address, length of service, and local and long-distance toll billing records of that person or account. Rather than obtain court approval, an FBI official need only certify in writing that "the name, address, length of service, and toll billing records sought are relevant to an authorized investigation to protect against international terrorism or clandestine intelligence activities."[200] If the request does not include local and long-distance toll billing records, the FBI need only certify that the *information* it is attempting to obtain is relevant to an investigation. The national security letter may not be issued solely due to an individual's First Amendment protected activities (e.g., organizing a lawful protest).[201]

The National Security Letter statute prohibits communications service providers from revealing the existence of a national security letter to any person, provided that the FBI certifies that the absence of a disclosure prohibition would result in a danger to U.S. national security, interference with a criminal, counterterrorism, or counterintelligence investigation or diplomatic relations, or "danger to the life or physical safety of any person."[202] If a communications provider receives such a nondisclosure order, it is permitted to disclose the existence of the national security letter to people to whom disclosure is "necessary" for compliance, an attorney to receive legal advice, or others approved by the FBI.[203] Individuals to whom the providers have disclosed the existence of a national security letter also are bound by the gag order.[204]

---

198 Pub. L. No. 107-56 (Oct. 26, 2001).
199 18 U.S.C. § 2709. The PATRIOT Act also amended the Gramm-Leach-Bliley Act to allow national security letters for financial records, 12 U.S.C. § 3414(a)(5)(A), and the Fair Credit Reporting Act to allow national security letters for consumer reports, 15 U.S.C. § 1681u.
200 18 U.S.C. § 2709(b)(1).
201 18 U.S.C. § 2709(b)(2).
202 18 U.S.C. § 2709(c)(1).
203 18 U.S.C. § 2709(c)(2).
204 *Id.*

In 2006 and 2015, Congress amended the National Security Letter statute to allow for a limited form of judicial review.[205] If a service provider receives a nondisclosure order associated with a national security letter, it may notify the government that it wishes to have a court review the order, or file a petition for review in federal court. Within 30 days of receiving notification, the government must ask a federal court for an order prohibiting disclosure.[206] The application must include a certification from a senior Justice Department or FBI official explaining why an absence of a prohibition on disclosure may result in threats to national security, investigations, diplomatic relations, or physical safety.[207] The federal court will approve the nondisclosure order only if it agrees with the government's allegations in its application.[208]

7.3 Communications Assistance for Law Enforcement Act (CALEA)

This chapter has examined the limits on the government's ability to obtain information about individuals' communications. If the government is permitted to obtain the information, it still must have cooperation from communications providers, such as phone companies and Internet service providers.

That's where the Communications Assistance for Law Enforcement Act (CALEA)[209] comes in. The statute, passed in 1994, requires telecommunications carriers to assist law enforcement in conducting electronic surveillance under lawful warrants and court orders.

The Federal Communications Commission (FCC), which enforces CALEA, has broadly applied CALEA's requirements not only to traditional phone companies like AT&T and Verizon but also to Voice Over Internet Protocol and broadband service providers.[210]

CALEA requires telecommunications providers that "provide a customer or subscriber with the ability to originate, terminate, or direct communications" to ensure that their systems and networks are capable of expeditiously assisting the government in conducting lawfully authorized electronic surveillance.[211]

CALEA also requires telecommunications providers to secure their law enforcement assistant technology to "ensure that any interception of

---

205 18 U.S.C. § 3511; Pub. L. No. 109-177.

206 18 U.S.C. § 3511(b)(1)(B).

207 *Id.*

208 *Id.*

209 47 U.S.C. §§ 1001–10.

210 *In re* Communications Assistance for Law Enforcement Act and Broadband Access and Servs., ET Docket No. 04-295 (May 12, 2006).

211 47 U.S.C. § 1002.

communications or access to call-identifying information effected within its switching premises can be activated only in accordance with a court order or other lawful authorization and with the affirmative intervention of an individual officer or employee of the carrier acting in accordance with regulations prescribed by the Commission."[212]

The FCC has stated that telecommunications providers are free to develop their own solutions to ensure that their systems comply with CALEA's requirements.[213]

CALEA's requirements are primarily focused on telecommunications providers. The requirements do not apply to information services or telecommunications equipment.[214] Nor does CALEA require telecommunications carriers to help the government decrypt communications, unless the carrier provided the encryption and possesses the key or other information necessary to decrypt.[215]

7.4 Encryption and the All Writs Act

One of the most prominent cyber-related surveillance disputes in recent years has involved government access to encrypted communications. This is not a new debate; indeed, in the 1990s, the government failed in its attempt to require technology companies to include a "backdoor" to allow law enforcement access to encrypted communications. The debate re-emerged in 2016, as encryption was the default setting on a number of smartphones and mobile apps. The FBI and state and local law enforcement increasingly became concerned that even if they had a lawful warrant, supported by probable cause, to search a mobile device, they would be unable to do so because the data was encrypted.

No statute explicitly requires phone manufacturers to assist the government with carrying out a search warrant, as there is not an equivalent of CALEA for device makers. Rather, the government seeks such assistance under the All Writs Act, a statute which states that "all courts established by Act of Congress may issue all writs necessary or appropriate in aid of their respective jurisdictions and agreeable to the usages and principles of law."[216] The United States

---

212 47 U.S.C. § 1004.
213 *See* Federal Communications Commission, Communications Assistance for Law Enforcement Act ("A telecommunications carrier may comply with CALEA in different ways. First, the carrier may develop its own compliance solution for its unique network. Second, the carrier may purchase a compliance solution from vendors, including the manufacturers of the equipment it is using to provide the service. Third, the carrier may purchase a compliance solution from a trusted third party (TPP).").
214 47 U.S.C. § 1002(b)(2).
215 47 U.S.C. § 1002(b)(3).
216 28 U.S.C. § 1651(a).

Supreme Court has stated that this statute is "a residual source of authority to issue writs that are not otherwise covered by statute."[217] In other words, the government sought to use the All Writs Act as a catchall statute to order Apple to help it carry out a search warrant.

No binding appellate court ruling had explicitly required a company such as Apple to help the government defeat encryption. The government relied largely on a 1977 United States Supreme Court case, *United States v. New York Telephone Co.*,[218] in which the Court held that the All Writs Act requires a phone company to assist the FBI with carrying out a pen register order. The Court concluded that the Act extends "to persons who, though not parties to the original action or engaged in wrongdoing, are in a position to frustrate the implementation of a court order or the proper administration of justice, ... and encompasses even those who have not taken any affirmative action to hinder justice."[219] Courts also have held that the All Writs Act requires, among other things, credit card companies to provide records to law enforcement[220] and landlords to provide law enforcement with security camera footage.[221]

A federal judge in Brooklyn ruled in 2016 that the All Writs Act does not require Apple to assist law enforcement in accessing an encrypted iPhone. In that case, the federal Drug Enforcement Agency received a warrant to search the residence of a drug-trafficking suspect, who said that he had forgotten the code to the phone. Among the items that the agents obtained in the search was an iPhone 5S.[222] The government then obtained a warrant to search the iPhone. The government requested Apple's technical assistance to unlock the phone, and Apple said that it would provide the assistance only if it was ordered to do

---

217 Pennsylvania Bureau of Correction v. United States Marshals Serv., 474 U.S. 34, 43 (1985).

218 United States v. New York Tel. Co., 434 U.S. 159 (1977).

219 *Id.* at 174.

220 United States v. Hall, 583 F. Supp. 717, 722 (E.D. Va. 1984) ("Credit card corporations routinely, indeed monthly, compile a list of all the purchases and the amounts of those purchases, the so-called cash advances, and the amount of those advances, and present them to their customers for payment. All that is involved in complying with this court order is duplicating these records for the government by punching a few buttons.").

221 *In re* Application of United States for an Order Directing X to Provide Access to Videotapes, No. 03-89 (D. Md. Aug. 22, 2003) (unpublished) ("[A]n order pursuant to the All Writs Act is both necessary and appropriate in the instant case. First, an arrest warrant has been issued for defendant Y by a judge of this court. Second, the investigating agent has stated that defendant Y has disappeared; that efforts to locate defendant Y have been unsuccessful; that it is likely defendant Y maintains contact with his/her spouse and may visit the apartment complex where the spouse resides; and that it is likely the requested access to security videotapes will provide information concerning defendant Y's current whereabouts, thereby preventing frustration of this court's previously issued arrest warrant.").

222 *In re* Order Requiring Apple, Inc. to Assist in the Execution of a Search Warrant Issued by This Court, No. 15-MC-1902 (JO) (E.D.N.Y. Feb. 29, 2016).

so by a court. The government requested a court order under the All Writs Act, and Apple opposed the request, arguing that the statute does not require Apple to write code to help circumvent the device's security features.

The U.S. District Court for the Eastern District of New York rejected the government's application for an order compelling Apple's assistance. Central to the court's ruling was the fact that Congress passed CALEA, which requires telecommunications carriers to assist law enforcement in carrying out search warrants but explicitly excludes "information service providers" such as Apple. If Congress had intended to require companies such as Apple to assist law enforcement, the court reasoned, Congress would have explicitly included the companies within the scope of CALEA or a similar statute. The court reasoned that if it were to adopt the government's broad reading of the All Writs Act, it would transform the statute "from a limited gap-filling statute that ensures the smooth functioning of the judiciary itself into a mechanism for upending the separation of powers by delegating to the judiciary a legislative power bounded only by Congress's superior ability to prohibit or preempt."[223]

The court noted that the All Writs Act was enacted by the First Congress in 1789, during a time when the Founders divided distinct and discrete powers among the three branches of government. The court stated that it was difficult to imagine the Founders passing the All Writs Act with the intention of providing the executive branch with such broad powers. "The government's interpretation of the breadth of authority the AWA confers on courts of limited jurisdiction thus raises serious doubts about how such a statute could withstand constitutional scrutiny under the separation of powers doctrine," the court wrote. "It would attribute to the First Congress an anomalous diminishment of its own authority (to deny a request to increase the executive's investigative powers it deemed inadvisable simply by declining to enact it) as well as an equally implausible intention to confer essentially unlimited legislative powers on the judiciary."[224]

The Eastern District of New York opinion, while emphatic, is not binding on any court. Accordingly, there is a chance that another court—including an appellate court, which issues binding opinions—could view the All Writs Act in a more expansive light. Moreover, many law enforcement advocates are pushing Congress to pass a CALEA-like law that would explicitly require companies such as Apple to assist law enforcement with unlocking devices. In short, it is likely that technology companies' compelled assistance to law enforcement will continue to be a hotly debated issue in the judicial, legislative, and executive branches.

---

223 *Id.* at 26.
224 *Id.* at 29.

7.5 Encrypted Devices and the Fifth Amendment

In the Brooklyn iPhone case described in Section 7.4, the government stated that it needed Apple's assistance in unlocking the phone because the phone's owner claimed to have forgotten the code. What if an individual simply refuses to unlock or decrypt the phone or computer? Can the government compel the person to provide access to the contents of the phone?

This issue has increasingly arisen in the past decade, as iPhones and other encrypted devices and computers have become more prevalent. Even if the government obtains a warrant, supported by probable cause, to search the phone, it may be unable to do so without the person's assistance.

When confronted with a compelled decryption order, criminal suspects are increasingly raising their Fifth Amendment rights against self-incrimination. The Fifth Amendment states that an individual shall not "be compelled in any criminal case to be a witness against himself."[225] The Supreme Court has stated that this means that if the state "proposes to convict and punish an individual," it must "produce the evidence against him by the independent labor of its officers, not by the simple, cruel expedient of forcing it from his own lips."[226] In short, the government may not force a criminal suspect to testify against herself in a criminal case.

The Supreme Court has articulated clear limits on this self-incrimination privilege. It only applies to government actions that require a criminal suspect to "disclose the contents of his own mind."[227] In a 2000 opinion, the Supreme Court outlined some types of acts that are *not* covered by the self-incrimination privilege:

> As Justice Holmes observed, there is a significant difference between the use of compulsion to extort communications from a defendant and compelling a person to engage in conduct that may be incriminating. Thus, even though the act may provide incriminating evidence, a criminal suspect may be compelled to put on a shirt, to provide a blood sample or handwriting exemplar, or to make a recording of his voice. The act of exhibiting such physical characteristics is not the same as a sworn communication by a witness that relates either express or implied assertions of fact or belief. ... Similarly, the fact that incriminating evidence may be the byproduct of obedience to a regulatory requirement, such as filing an income tax return, maintaining required records, or

---

225 U.S. Const. amend. V.
226 Estelle v. Smith, 451 U.S. 454, 462 (1981).
227 Curcio v. United States, 354 U.S. 118, 128 (1957).

> reporting an accident, does not clothe such required conduct with the testimonial privilege.[228]

In other words, the Fifth Amendment does not allow a person to decline to provide *any evidence* or perform *any act* that might produce self-incriminatory evidence. Instead, the question is whether the government is compelling the individual to self-incriminate by *testifying*, or providing the contents of his mind.

So how does this framework apply to government orders to compel individuals to assist in accessing their devices and computers? The caselaw is not entirely settled. In one of the earliest compelled decryption cases to reach a federal appellate court, the U.S. Court of Appeals for the Eleventh Circuit invalidated a grand jury subpoena requiring a suspect, with the pseudonym John Doe, in a child pornography case to produce the "unencrypted contents" of password-encrypted hard drives because law enforcement was unable to decrypt the drives.[229] The Eleventh Circuit concluded that requiring the individual to decrypt the hard drives would be testimonial because "the decryption and production of the hard drives would require the use of the contents of Doe's mind and could not be fairly characterized as a physical act that would be nontestimonial in nature," the unanimous panel reasoned. "We conclude that the decryption and production would be tantamount to testimony by Doe of his knowledge of the existence and location of potentially incriminating files; of his possession, control, and access to the encrypted portions of the drives; and of his capability to decrypt the files."[230] The government argued that the order merely required Doe to produce unencrypted files and not to testify, but the court rejected this reasoning. "Requiring Doe to use a decryption password is most certainly more akin to requiring the production of a combination because both demand the use of the contents of the mind, and the production is accompanied by the implied factual statements noted above that could prove to be incriminatory," the court wrote.[231]

The government also asked the Eleventh Circuit to uphold the decryption order under an exception to the self-incrimination rule known as the foregone conclusion doctrine. Under that doctrine, testimony is permissible if it "adds little or nothing to the sum total of the Government's information[.]"[232] The Eleventh Circuit concluded that the foregone conclusion doctrine did not apply in this case because "[n]othing in the record before us reveals that the Government knows whether any files exist and are located on the hard drives;

---

228 United States v. Hubbell, 530 U.S. 27, 34–35 (2000).
229 *In re* Grand Jury Subpoena Duces Tecum, 670 F.3d 1335 (11th Cir. 2012).
230 *Id*. at 1346.
231 *Id*.
232 Fisher v. United States, 425 U.S. 391, 411 (1976).

what's more, nothing in the record illustrates that the Government knows with reasonable particularity that Doe is even capable of accessing the encrypted portions of the drives."[233]

In some recent cases, however, courts have held that the foregone conclusion doctrine allows compelled decryption orders. For instance, in 2017, the U.S. Court of Appeals for the Third Circuit considered a decryption order in an investigation into another John Doe's potential access of online child pornography. The government managed to decrypt his computer, which indicated that names of potential child pornography files were located on encrypted external hard drives.[234] Although Doe provided police with the password to his iPhone, he did not provide access to an encrypted application on the phone that forensic analysts believed also contained child pornography. Doe's sister told police that she had seen child pornography on the external hard drives.[235]

A magistrate judge approved an order for Doe to produce, in an unencrypted form, his phone, computer, and the hard drives, and denied his motion to quash the order, which was based on the Fifth Amendment.[236] Doe then stated that he had forgotten the passwords to the hard drives, and the court held Doe in civil contempt, placing him in custody until he decrypted the drives.[237] Doe then appealed, arguing that the order violated his Fifth Amendment rights.

On appeal, the Third Circuit ruled that Doe failed to properly preserve his right to appeal the denial to quash the initial decryption order on Fifth Amendment grounds. Assuming that it could consider the Fifth Amendment objections at this stage, the Third Circuit ruled, the magistrate judge did not commit plain error in concluding that the foregone conclusion doctrine would bar Doe's challenge:

> The affidavit supporting the search warrant states that an investigation led to the identification of Doe as a user of an internet file sharing network that was used to access child pornography. When executing a search of Doe's residence, forensic analysts found the encrypted devices, and Doe does not dispute their existence or his ownership of them. Once the analysts accessed Doe's Mac Pro Computer, they found one image depicting a pubescent girl in a sexually suggestive position and logs that suggested the user had visited groups with titles common in child exploitation. Doe's sister then reported that she had witnessed Doe unlock his Mac Pro while connected to the hard drives to show her hundreds of

---

233 *In re* Grand Jury Subpoena Duces Tecum, 670 F.3d at 1356.
234 United States v. Apple MacPro Computer, 851 F.3d 238, 242 (3d Cir. 2017).
235 *Id.* at 243.
236 *Id.*
237 *Id.* at 243–44.

pictures and videos of child pornography. Forensic analysts also found an additional 2,015 videos and photographs in an encrypted application on Doe's phone, which Doe had opened for the police by entering a password.[238]

The magistrate judge's order differed from the decryption order that the Eleventh Circuit considered, the Third Circuit reasoned, because for the magistrate judge's order, "the Government has provided evidence to show both that files exist on the encrypted portions of the devices and that Doe can access them."[239] The Third Circuit emphasized that its review was limited to plain error, and it was "not concluding that the Government's knowledge of the content of the devices is necessarily the correct focus of the 'foregone conclusion' inquiry in the context of a compelled decryption order." Rather, the Court stated, "a very sound argument can be made that the foregone conclusion doctrine properly focuses on whether the Government already knows the testimony that is implicit in the act of production," which in this case would be that Doe knows the password for the devices.

The Third and Eleventh Circuit cases dealt with production of passwords or codes to decrypt devices or computers. Increasingly, biometrics such as fingerprints and facial recognition can be used to unlock encrypted phones and devices. Although the case law is far from settled, courts are less likely to determine that compelled use of biometrics to decrypt devices violates self-incrimination strictures. In 2017, the Minnesota Court of Appeals affirmed a district court order requiring a burglary suspect to use his fingerprint to unlock his phone.[240] The defendant relied on the Eleventh Circuit's opinion to assert that the order violated his Fifth Amendment rights. The Minnesota court rejected that argument, concluding that an order requiring the defendant to unlock the phone with his fingerprint did not require him "to disclose any knowledge he might have or speak his guilt."[241] Requiring him to produce his fingerprint "is no more testimonial than furnishing a blood sample, providing handwriting or voice exemplars, standing in a lineup, or wearing particular clothing," the court wrote.[242]

---

238 *Id.* at 249.
239 *Id.*
240 State v. Diamond, 890 N.W.2d 143 (Minn. Ct. App. 2017).
241 *Id.* at 150.
242 *Id.* at 151.

8

Cybersecurity and Federal Government Contractors

Federal government contracting is a multibillion-dollar industry in the United States. Companies provide a wide range of services to the federal government, ranging from information technology to janitorial services to management consulting. To the extent that any of these businesses exchange data with the federal government, they must comply with a wide range of cybersecurity laws and regulations.

In recent years, Congress and federal agencies have intensified their scrutiny of contractors' cybersecurity practices, in the aftermath of contractor Edward Snowden's leak of massive volumes of classified National Security Agency documents and the breach of millions of Americans' security clearance applications with the Office of Personnel Management. This chapter provides a broad overview of the laws and regulations that are most likely to affect the cybersecurity of government contractors.

In short, cybersecurity requirements for government contractors depend on the types of information they handle. All contractors that handle federal government information systems must comply with the recently overhauled Federal Information Security Management Act and adopt controls that are structured around the National Institute of Standards and Technology's *Special Publication 800-53*, which sets baseline requirements for cybersecurity of government information. Contractors that handle classified information must comply with much more stringent requirements set by the Defense Security Service in the *National Industrial Security Program Operating Manual* (*NISPOM*). Recently, government regulators have created new requirements for contractors who handle information that, though not classified, is considered sensitive enough to warrant special protections. This new category, known as controlled unclassified information (CUI), likely will result in many federal contractors being required to significantly strengthen their cybersecurity practices.

Cybersecurity Law, Second Edition. Jeff Kosseff.
© 2020 John Wiley & Sons, Inc. Published 2020 by John Wiley & Sons, Inc.
Companion Website: www.wiley.com/go/kosseff/cybersecurity2e

8.1   Federal Information Security Management Act

In 2002, Congress passed the Federal Information Security Management Act (FISMA),[1] which established a framework for agencies to manage their information security. In 2014, in light of the tremendously more complex web of cybersecurity threats, Congress overhauled FISMA by passing the Federal Information Security Modernization Act of 2014.[2] FISMA's requirements affect the information security of not only government agencies, but also their contractors and subcontractors.

In its report accompanying the 2014 FISMA legislation, the Senate Homeland Security and Government Affairs Committee wrote that a revision to FISMA was urgent in light of the rapidly changing landscape of cybersecurity threats:

> Over the past two decades, the growth of the Internet and the country's increasing use of interconnected networks to conduct its business has led to significant economic growth and innovation. However, this ever-increasing reliance upon the Internet has also unintentionally enabled new threats to develop.[3]

One challenge under the original 2002 version of FISMA is that it did not explicitly delegate cybersecurity functions to DHS, which did not reflect the reality in 2014 that DHS "performs a variety of functions, including providing cybersecurity services for federal civilian agencies across the government, under a patchwork of other authorities," the legislators wrote in 2014.[4] Under the 2014 amendment, FISMA delegates a great deal of responsibility for cybersecurity to individual federal departments and agencies, but it also centralizes many cybersecurity functions within the Office of Management and Budget and Department of Homeland Security. The Office of Management and Budget is charged with developing government-wide information security policies, standards, and guidelines, requiring agencies to adopt adequate information security protections, and coordinating with the National Institute of Standards and Technology on standards and guidelines (discussed later in this chapter).[5] The Department of Homeland Security is responsible for developing government-wide requirements on reporting security incidents, for annual agency cybersecurity reports, for risk mitigation requirements, for monitoring agency information security, and for providing operational and technical assistance to agencies.[6]

---

1 44 U.S.C. § 3552 *et seq.*
2 Pub. L. No. 113-283.
3 S. Rep. No. 113-256 (2014), at 2.
4 *Id.* at 3.
5 44 U.S.C. § 3553.
6 *Id.*

The updated FISMA also requires federal agency heads to take a number of steps to increase their agencies' cybersecurity. Among the responsibilities of each agency head are the following:

- Implementing information security protections that are commensurate "with the risk and magnitude of the harm resulting from unauthorized access, use, disclosure, disruption, modification, or destruction of" information collected, used, or maintained by the agency or a contractor.
- Ensuring that senior agency officials conduct information security risk assessments, implement necessary protections, and periodically test and evaluate information security controls.
- Delegating information security compliance authority to agency chief information officers.
- Overseeing agency information security training.
- Annually reporting on the effectiveness of agency information security controls.
- Holding all personnel accountable for complying with an agency-wide information security program.[7]

FISMA requires each agency to develop a comprehensive information security program that contains the following elements:

- Periodic risk assessments.
- Policies and procedures that are based on the risk assessments.
- Subordinate plans for information security.
- Security training for agency employees and contractors.
- Annual testing and evaluation of information security policies and procedures.
- Remedial action to correct security flaws.
- Security incident detection, reporting, and response procedures.
- Continuity of operations plans for information systems.[8]

Notably, the updated FISMA requires agencies to "expeditiously" notify the House and Senate Judiciary Committees of data breaches.[9] The notices must be provided within 30 days of discovery of the breach, and must include:

- a general description of the breach,
- an estimate of the number of individuals whose information was disclosed,
- an assessment of the risk of harm to those individuals,
- a description of any circumstances that require a delay in notifying affected individuals, and
- an estimate of when the agency will notify individuals.[10]

---

7 44 U.S.C. § 3554.
8 *Id.*
9 44 U.S.C. § 3553.
10 *Id.*

In the Senate committee report accompanying the 2014 bill, legislators wrote of the importance of imposing a stringent notification requirement on agencies. "When it comes to responding to a data breach and notifying the public, it is very important for the federal government to be transparent and lead by example," the committee wrote.[11]

8.2   NIST Information Security Controls for Government Agencies and Contractors

FISMA delegates responsibility for specific information security standards to the National Institute of Standards and Technology (NIST), an agency within the U.S. Department of Commerce. NIST has produced a number of detailed standards for various aspects of information security at government agencies and their contractors. Perhaps the two most influential NIST documents are *Federal Information Processing Standards 200 (FIPS 200)* and *NIST Special Publication 800-53 (SP 800-53)*, which set baseline categories for information security controls. These documents constitute the baseline information security standard for the federal government and its contractors and subcontractors that operate federal information systems. More sensitive information, such as classified information and defense information, is covered by even more stringent requirements, discussed later in this chapter.

Under *FIPS 200*, agencies and contractors must implement minimum information security requirements. To implement these minimum information security requirements, agencies and contractors must select from security controls that are listed in *SP 800-53*. *SP 800-53* runs to nearly 500 pages and details dozens of security controls. Organizations select from the menu of controls based on whether their information systems are classified as low-impact, moderate-impact, or high-impact (with higher-impact systems receiving the more stringent controls). The following list covers the 17 minimum information security requirements from *FIPS 200*, along with some of the corresponding categories of security controls as stated in *SP 800-53*. The list is modestly edited for clarity and brevity, and may not reflect the latest changes to the requirements; accordingly, businesses should consult the most current versions of *FIPS 200* and *SP 800-53*:

- *Access control.* Agencies and contractors must ensure that only authorized users, processes, and devices are permitted to access information systems. Security control categories include:
  o Access control policy and procedures
  o Account management
  o Access enforcement

---

11 S. Rep. No. 113-256 (2014), at 7.

- o Information flow enforcement
- o Separation of duties
- o Least privilege
- o Unsuccessful log-on attempts
- o System use notification
- o Previous log-on notification
- o Concurrent session control
- o Session lock
- o Session termination
- o Supervision and review of access control
- o Permitted actions without identification or authentication
- o Security attributes
- o Remote access
- o Wireless access
- o Mobile access
- o External information system use
- o Information sharing
- o Publicly accessible content
- o Data mining protection
- *Awareness and training.* Agencies and contractors must ensure that managers and personnel are adequately trained regarding information security. Security control categories include:
  - o Security awareness and training policy and procedures
  - o Role-based security training
  - o Security training records
  - o Contacts with security groups and associations
- *Audit and accountability.* System audit records must enable monitoring, analysis, investigation, and reporting of unauthorized activity on an information system. Actions must be traceable to individual users. Security control categories include:
  - o Audit and accountability policy and procedures
  - o Audit events
  - o Content of audit records
  - o Audit storage capacity
  - o Response to audit processing failures
  - o Audit review, analysis, and reporting
  - o Time stamps
  - o Protection of audit information
  - o Nonrepudiation
  - o Session audit
  - o Cross-organizational audit
- *Certification, accreditation, and security assessments.* Periodic assessments of security controls will determine whether the current systems are

effective and suggest corrections for deficiencies. Security control categories include:

o Security assessments
o System interconnections
o Security certification
o Continuous monitoring
o Penetration testing

- *Configuration management.* Federal agencies and contractors must establish and maintain baseline inventories and configurations of hardware, software, firmware, and other information systems. Security control categories include:

o Baseline configuration
o Configuration change control
o Security impact analysis
o Least functionality
o Information system component inventory
o Software usage restrictions
o User-installed software

- *Contingency planning.* Agencies and contractors are required to develop plans for operating information systems during emergencies, such as natural disasters, to ensure continuity of operations. Security control categories include:

o Contingency plan
o Contingency training
o Contingency plan testing
o Alternate storage site
o Information system backup

- *Identification and authentication.* Authorized users (and their devices and processes) must be accurately identified in order to prevent unauthorized access. Security control categories include:

o Identification and authentication of organizational users
o Device identification and authentication
o Identifier management
o Service identification and authentication

- *Incident response.* Agencies and contractors must develop comprehensive plans to detect, contain, and respond to information security incidents and to report incidents to the appropriate officials and authorities. Security control categories include:

o Incident response training
o Incident response testing
o Incident handling
o Incident monitoring
o Incident reporting
o Incident response plan

- *Maintenance.* Agencies and contractors must regularly maintain their information systems and security controls. Security control categories include:
  - Maintenance tools
  - Maintenance personnel
  - Timely maintenance
- *Media protection.* Agencies and contractors must limit access to information system media to authorized users and permanently wipe information systems media before disposal. Security control categories include:
  - Media access
  - Media storage
  - Media sanitization
  - Media use
  - Media downgrading
- *Physical and environmental protection.* Physical access to information systems must be restricted to authorized individuals. Organizations also must protect their information systems from environmental hazards and ensure that they have adequate environmental controls in the physical facilities that contain information systems. Security control categories include:
  - Physical access authorization
  - Monitoring physical access
  - Visitor access records
  - Emergency power
  - Fire protection
  - Temperature and humidity controls
  - Water damage protection
- *Planning.* Information security plans must describe the security controls that the agency or contractor has implemented, as well as the rules of behavior for those who access the information systems. Security control categories include:
  - System security plan
  - Rules of behavior
  - Privacy impact assessment
  - Central management
- *Personnel security.* Agencies and contractors must take steps to ensure that employees and service providers who have access to information systems are trustworthy and meet specified security criteria. The organizations also should ensure that when an employee or service provider is transferred or terminated, the information systems are protected, and that personnel are formally sanctioned for failing to comply with information security policies and procedures. Security control categories include:
  - Personnel screening
  - Access agreements
  - Third-party personnel security

- **Risk assessment.** Agencies and contractors must periodically conduct assessments of their information security, considering their operations, assets, and individuals. Security control categories include:
  - o Security categorization
  - o Vulnerability scanning
  - o Technical surveillance countermeasures survey
- **System and services acquisition.** Agencies and contractors must ensure that they have sufficient resources for information security, use a system development life cycle process for information security, restrict use and installation of software, and ensure that their third-party providers maintain adequate information security. Security control categories include:
  - o Allocation of resources
  - o Acquisition process
  - o Software usage restrictions
  - o User-installed software
  - o Developer configuration management
  - o Tamper resistance and detection
- **System and communications protection.** Organizations must monitor and protect their information systems at external boundaries and key internal boundaries, and employ architectural designs, software development techniques, and systems engineering principles that promote information security. Security control categories include:
  - o Security function isolation
  - o Denial-of-service protection
  - o Boundary protection
  - o Transmission confidentiality
  - o Cryptographic key establishment and management
  - o Session authenticity
  - o Covert channel analysis
- **System and information integrity.** Agencies and contractors are required to identify, report, and correct flaws in the information system; protect information systems from malicious code; and monitor security alerts and advisories and respond appropriately. Security control categories include:
  - o Flaw remediation
  - o Malicious code protection
  - o Information system monitoring
  - o Software, firmware, and information integrity
  - o Predictable failure prevention

8.3 Classified Information Cybersecurity

In addition to the general cybersecurity requirements of *FIPS 200* and *SP 800-53*, contractors face heightened requirements if they are dealing with sensitive government information. The most restrictive requirements apply to contractors that process classified information.

Cybersecurity requirements for contractors that process classified government information are set by the Defense Security Service (DSS). DSS publishes the *National Industrial Security Program Operating Manual* (*NISPOM*), which sets the rules for industry's access to classified information.

Chapter 8 of *NISPOM* establishes the information security requirements for contractor information systems that are used to capture, create, store, process, or distribute classified information. Among the key requirements of Chapter 8 of *NISPOM* are the following, largely as stated in *NISPOM* but edited substantially for clarity and brevity:[12]

- *Information security program.* The contractor must maintain a risk-based set of management, operational, and technical controls, including policies and procedures to reduce security risks, information security training for all users, testing and evaluation of all security policies and procedures, incident detection and response plans, continuity of operations plans, and a self-inspection plan.

- *System security plan.* The contractor must have a system security plan that documents its information security protections and controls, and includes supporting documentation (e.g., a risk assessment, plan of action, and configuration checklist).

- *Information Systems (IS) security manager.* The contractor must designate a qualified IS security manager who is responsible for implementing the IS program, monitoring compliance, verifying self-inspections, certifying in writing that the system security plan has been implemented and controls are in place, briefing users on their information security responsibilities and ensuring necessary training.

- *Information system users.* All users are required to comply with the security program, be accountable for their actions on an information system, not share authentication mechanisms, protect authentication mechanisms at the highest classification level and most restrictive category of information to which that mechanism permits access, and be subject to monitoring of activity on a classified network.

- *Assessment and authorization.* Contractors must work with the government agency to assess security controls in order to receive an authorization to handle classified information. A contractor will be re-evaluated for authorization to handle classified information at least once every three years. All security-related changes must be approved in advance by the government agency.

---

12 For the complete and current version of Chapter 8, please consult the full text of *NISPOM*, which is available via the Defense Security Service website, www.dss.mil.

- **Systems and services controls.** Contractors must allocate "sufficient resources" to information security. As part of their routine assessment and self-inspection, contractors must assess and monitor security controls.
- **Risk assessment.** Contractors must conduct a comprehensive risk assessment, categorizing the potential impact level for confidentiality based on the information's classification, and monitoring changes to the information system that may affect security.
- **Personnel security.** Employees who access classified systems must meet the security requirements (e.g., a clearance). Once an employee no longer requires access to the system, the authentication credentials must be disabled. The contractor must review audit logs to determine whether any employees fail to comply with security policies.
- **Physical and environmental protection.** Contractors must limit physical access to information systems, protect the physical plant, and protect against environmental hazards.
- **Configuration management.** Contractors must implement baseline configurations and information system inventories.
- **Maintenance.** Contractors must perform necessary maintenance, such as patch management, and provide controls on the tools and personnel used for the maintenance.
- **Integrity.** Contractors must protect systems from malicious code.
- **Media protection.** Contractors must mark all media with level of authorization until a classification review is conducted, and limit access to the classified information.
- **Incident response.** Contractors must implement incident detection processes and immediately report any incidents to government agencies.
- **Authentication and access.** Contractors must identify users, authenticate them, and limit access to authorized users, according to the types of transactions and functions to which each user is permitted access.
- **Audit and accountability.** Contractors must create audit records to enable monitoring of activity on their systems.
- **System and communications protection.** Contractors must monitor, control, and protect organizational communications.

In 2011, as cyber threats to classified information increased in frequency and magnitude, President Obama issued Executive Order 13587, entitled "Structural Reforms to Improve the Security of Classified Networks and the Responsible Sharing and Safeguarding of Classified Information." The executive order seeks to "ensure coordinated interagency development and reliable implementation of policies and minimum standards regarding information security, personnel security, and systems security; address both internal and external security threats and vulnerabilities; and provide policies and minimum standards for sharing classified information both within and outside the Federal Government."

The executive order requires all agencies that operate or access classified computer networks to designate a senior official for classified information sharing and safeguarding, implement an insider threat detection and prevention program, and perform self-assessments of compliance. In response to the executive order, DSS amended *NISPOM* in May 2016 to require contractors that handle classified information to create an insider threat program. Contractors must create an insider threat program plan that describes:

- the contractor's capability to gather relevant insider threat information;
- the contractor's procedures to report that an individual potentially poses an insider threat; to deter employees from becoming insider threats; and to mitigate insider threat risks; and
- corporate-wide plans to address requirements for cleared facilities.

Contractors must conduct annual self-inspections and certifications of their insider threat programs, and they must report behaviors that indicate insider threats. They also must implement a system or process that identifies negligence or carelessness in handling classified information. Contractors are further required to provide insider threat awareness training to all cleared employees at least once a year.

8.4 Covered Defense Information and Controlled Unclassified Information

Even if information is not classified, it may be subject to more stringent cybersecurity requirements if it is sufficiently sensitive. In 2010, President Obama issued Executive Order 13556, which called for adequate safeguards of "controlled unclassified information" (CUI), which it defined as "unclassified information throughout the executive branch that requires safeguarding or dissemination controls[.]" The National Archives and Records Administration (NARA) is responsible for implementing the safeguards throughout the executive branch, and has issued rules for safeguarding civilian government agencies' CUI.[13]

Additionally, in 2015, the Defense Department overhauled its contractor cybersecurity rules for its sensitive, yet unclassified, information.[14] The rules apply to agencies and contractors that handle "covered defense information,"

---

13 32 C.F.R. pt. 2002.
14 Department of Defense, Defense Acquisition Regulations Supplement: Network Penetration Reporting and Contracting for Cloud Services, 80 Fed. Reg. 51739 (Aug. 26, 2015).

which is the Defense Department's version of CUI. The Defense Department's regulations define "covered defense information" as:

> unclassified controlled technical information or other informa-
> tion, as described in the Controlled Unclassified Information
> (CUI) Registry at http://www.archives.gov/cui/registry/category-
> list.html, that requires safeguarding or dissemination controls
> pursuant to and consistent with law, regulations, and Government-
> wide policies, and is—
>
> (1) Marked or otherwise identified in the contract, task order,
> or delivery order and provided to the contractor by or on behalf of
> DoD in support of the performance of the contract; or
>
> (2) Collected, developed, received, transmitted, used, or stored
> by or on behalf of the contractor in support of the performance of
> the contract.[15]

In practice, "covered defense information" is so broad that it can include virtually all aspects of a defense contractor's business, even its contract with the Defense Department. Even if a defense contractor does not handle any classified information, it likely is covered by these new cybersecurity rules. For that reason, the new regulations were met with significant consternation among the defense contracting community.

The two primary requirements of the Defense Department regulations are an expedited security incident reporting requirement and compliance with a more stringent NIST security framework for sensitive but unclassified information. Under the new regulations, contractors and subcontractors that handle covered defense information are required to "rapidly report" cyber incidents to the Defense Department within 72 hours of discovery.[16] This is among the shortest breach reporting requirements in the United States, and it puts significant pressure on defense contractors to quickly gather the necessary information after discovering an incident.

The regulations broadly define "cyber incident" as "actions taken through the use of computer networks that result in a compromise or an actual or potentially adverse effect on an information system and/or the information residing therein."[17] Accordingly, the reporting requirement applies not only to data breaches, but also to any attacks or incidents that could harm covered defense information on the contractor's network or systems.

The NARA and Defense Department regulations also require contractors and subcontractors handling covered defense information to comply with

---

15 48 C.F.R. § 252.204-7012.
16 *Id.*
17 *Id.*

NIST's *Special Publication 800-171* (*SP 800-171*), *Protecting Controlled Unclassified Information in Nonfederal Information Systems and Organizations*. As seen in the following list, *SP 800-171*'s requirements adopt the "moderate" control level of *SP 800-53*.

In August 2015, the Office of Management and Budget issued proposed guidance in which it instructs agencies to require contractors that handle CUI to comply with *SP 800-171* on nonfederal information systems. In short, *SP 800-171* will eventually become the de facto cybersecurity standard for many federal contractors.

Here are some of the key security requirements of the new standard for contractors that handle covered defense information on nonfederal systems, as stated in *SP 800-171* (modestly edited for clarity and brevity):

- *Access control.*
  - o Limit system access to authorized users, processes acting on behalf of authorized users, and devices (including other systems).
  - o Limit system access to types of transactions and functions that authorized users are permitted to execute.
  - o Control the flow of controlled unclassified information ("CUI") in accordance with approved authorizations.
  - o Separate the duties of individuals to reduce the risk of malevolent activity without collusion.
  - o Employ the principle of least privilege, including for specific security functions and privileged accounts.
  - o Use nonprivileged accounts or roles when accessing nonsecurity functions.
  - o Prevent nonprivileged users from executing privileged functions and audit the execution of such functions.
  - o Limit unsuccessful log-on attempts.
  - o Provide privacy and security notices consistent with applicable CUI rules.
  - o Use session lock with pattern-hiding displays to prevent access and viewing of data after a period of inactivity.
  - o Terminate (automatically) a user session after a defined condition.
  - o Monitor and control remote access sessions.
  - o Employ cryptographic mechanisms to protect confidentiality of remote access sessions.
  - o Route remote access via managed access control points.
  - o Authorize remote execution of privileged commands and remote access to security-relevant information.
  - o Authorize wireless access prior to allowing such connections.
  - o Protect wireless access using authentication and encryption.
  - o Control connection of mobile devices.
  - o Encrypt CUI on mobile devices and mobile computing platforms.

- o Verify and control/limit connections to and use of external information systems.
- o Limit use of portable storage devices on external systems.
- o Control CUI posted or processed on publicly accessible systems.
- *Awareness and training.*
  - o Ensure that managers, systems administrators, and users of organizational information systems are made aware of the security risks associated with their activities and of the applicable policies, standards, and procedures related to the security of those systems.
  - o Ensure that personnel are trained to carry out their assigned information security-related duties and responsibilities.
  - o Provide security awareness training on recognizing and reporting potential indicators of insider threat.
- *Audit and accountability.*
  - o Create and retain system audit logs and records to the extent needed to enable the monitoring, analysis, investigation, and reporting of unlawful or unauthorized system activity.
  - o Ensure that the actions of individual system users can be uniquely traced to those users so that they can be held accountable for their actions.
  - o Review and update audited events.
  - o Alert in the event of an audit logging process failure.
  - o Correlate audit record review, analysis, and reporting processes for investigation and response to indications of unlawful, unauthorized, suspicious, or unusual activity.
  - o Provide audit reduction and report generation to support on-demand analysis and reporting.
  - o Provide a system capability that compares and synchronizes internal system clocks with an authoritative source to generate time stamps for audit records.
  - o Protect audit information and audit tools from unauthorized access, modification, and deletion.
  - o Limit management of audit logging functionality to a subset of privileged users.
- *Configuration management.*
  - o Establish and maintain baseline configurations and inventories of organizational information systems (e.g., hardware, software, firmware, and documentation) throughout the respective system development life cycles.
  - o Establish and enforce security configuration settings for information technology projects employed in organizational information systems.
  - o Track, review, approve/disapprove, and log changes to information systems.
  - o Analyze the security impact of changes prior to implementation.

o Define, document, approve, and enforce physical and logical access restrictions associated with changes to organizational systems.
o Employ the principle of least functionality by configuring organizational systems to provide only essential capabilities.
o Restrict, disable, and prevent the use of nonessential programs, functions, ports, protocols, and services.
o Apply denial-by-exception (blacklisting) policy to prevent the use of unauthorized software or deny-all, permit-by-exception (whitelisting) policy to allow the execution of authorized software.
o Control and monitor user-installed software.

- *Identification and authentication.*
  o Identify system users, processes acting on behalf of users, and devices.
  o Authenticate (or verify) the identities of those users, processes, or devices, as a prerequisite to allowing access to organizational information systems.
  o Use multifactor authentication for local and network access to privileged accounts.
  o Prevent reuse of identifiers for a defined period.
  o Disable identifiers after a defined period of inactivity.
  o Enforce a minimum password complexity and change of characters when new passwords are created.
  o Prohibit password reuse for a specified number of generations.
  o Allow temporary password use for system log-ons with an immediate change to a permanent password.
  o Store and transmit only encrypted representation of passwords.
  o Obscure feedback of authentication information.

- *Incident response.*
  o Establish an operational incident-handling capability for organizational systems that includes adequate preparation, detection, analysis, containment, recovery, and user response activities.
  o Track, document, and report incidents to appropriate officials and/or authorities both internal and external to the organization.
  o Test the organizational incident response capability.

- *Maintenance.*
  o Perform maintenance on organizational systems.
  o Provide controls on the tools, techniques, mechanisms, and personnel used to conduct system maintenance.
  o Ensure that equipment removed for off-site maintenance is sanitized of any CUI.
  o Check media containing diagnostic and test programs for malicious code before the media are used in the information system.
  o Require multifactor authentication to establish nonlocal maintenance sessions via external network connections and terminate such connections when nonlocal maintenance is complete.

o Supervise the maintenance activities of maintenance personnel without required access authorization.

- *Media protection.*
  o Protect (i.e., physically control and securely store) system media containing CUI, both paper and digital.
  o Limit access to CUI on system media to authorized users.
  o Sanitize or destroy system media containing CUI before disposal or release for reuse.
  o Mark media with necessary CUI markings and distribution limitations.
  o Control access to media containing CUI and maintain accountability for media during transport out of controlled areas.
  o Implement cryptographic mechanisms to protect the confidentiality of CUI stored on digital media during transport unless otherwise protected by alternative physical safeguards.
  o Control the of removable media on system components.
  o Prohibit the use of portable storage devices when such devices have no identifiable owner.
  o Protect the confidentiality of backup CUI at storage locations.
- *Personnel security.*
  o Screen individuals prior to authorizing access to organizational systems containing CUI.
  o Ensure that organizational systems containing CUI are protected during and after personnel actions such as terminations and transfers.
- *Physical protection.*
  o Limit physical access to organizational systems, equipment, and the respective operating environments to authorized individuals.
  o Protect and monitor the physical facility and support infrastructure for organizational systems.
  o Escort visitors and monitor visitor activity.
  o Maintain audit logs of physical access.
  o Control and manage physical access devices.
  o Enforce safeguarding measures for CUI at alternate work sites (e.g., telework sites).
- *Risk assessment.*
  o Periodically assess the risk to organizational operations (including mission, functions, image, or reputation), organizational assets, and individuals, resulting from the operation of organizational systems and the associated processing, storage, or transmission of CUI.
  o Scan for vulnerabilities in organizational systems and applications periodically and when new vulnerabilities affecting those systems are identified.
  o Remediate vulnerabilities in accordance with risk assessments.

- *Security assessment.*
  - Periodically assess the security controls in organizational systems to determine if the controls are effective in their application.
  - Develop and implement plans of action designed to correct deficiencies and reduce or eliminate vulnerabilities in organizational systems.
  - Monitor security controls on an ongoing basis to ensure the continued effectiveness of the controls.
- *System and communications protection.*
  - Monitor, control, and protect organizational communications (i.e., information transmitted or received by organizational systems) at the external boundaries and key internal boundaries of organizational systems.
  - Employ architectural designs, software development techniques, and systems engineering principles that promote effective information security within organizational systems.
  - Separate user functionality from system management functionality.
  - Prevent unauthorized and unintended information transfer via shared system resources.
  - Implement subnetworks for publicly accessible system components that are physically or logically separated from internal networks.
  - Deny network communications traffic by default and allow network communications traffic by exception (i.e., deny-all, permit-by-exception).
  - Prevent remote devices from simultaneously establishing nonremote connections with organizational systems and communicating via some other connection to resources in external networks (i.e., split networking).
  - Implement cryptographic mechanisms to prevent unauthorized disclosure of CUI during transmission unless otherwise protected by alternative physical safeguards.
  - Terminate network connections associated with communications sessions at the end of the sessions or after a defined period of inactivity.
  - Establish and manage cryptographic keys for cryptography when used to protect the confidentiality of CUI.
  - Prohibit remote activation of collaborative computing devices, and provide an indication of devices in use to users present at the device.
  - Control and monitor the use of mobile code.
  - Control and monitor the use of Voice over Internet Protocol (VoIP) technologies.
  - Protect the authenticity of communications sessions.
  - Protect the confidentiality of CUI at rest.
- *System and information integrity.*
  - Identify, report, and correct information and information system flaws in a timely manner.

o Provide protection from malicious code at designated locations within organizational systems.
o Monitor system security alerts and advisories and take appropriate actions in response.
o Update malicious code protection mechanisms when new releases are available.
o Perform periodic scans of organizational systems and real-time scans of files from external sources as files are downloaded, opened, or executed.
o Monitor the organizational systems, including inbound and outbound communications traffic, to detect attacks and indicators of potential attacks.
o Identify unauthorized use of organizational systems.

9

Privacy Laws

Thus far we have focused primarily on laws that affect the security of data, systems, and networks, and the ability of the government and the private sector to conduct surveillance on this infrastructure to prevent cybercrime and other harms. However, an examination of cybersecurity law would be incomplete without an overview of privacy law.

Privacy law limits companies' collection, use, sharing, and retention of personal information. Although data security laws provide the safeguards that companies must have in place to prevent hackers from accessing customer data, privacy law restricts companies' ability to use customer data. For instance, privacy law may prevent a company from selling customer web-browsing activities to third-party marketers, building customer profiles based on the videos they view online, or using facial recognition.

Some might argue that privacy law is outside the scope of cybersecurity law, and they may be correct. At least under some conceptions of cybersecurity law, it is irrelevant how companies choose to legitimately use customer data. However, cybersecurity is an emerging field and there is no single, settled definition of the term. Nevertheless, privacy does often intersect with cybersecurity; consequently, all cybersecurity professionals should have a basic understanding of privacy legal principles.

Any examination of cybersecurity law would be incomplete without an overview of the legal restrictions on the use and disclosure of personal information. As with data security, the Federal Trade Commission regulates privacy under Section 5 of the FTC Act, which prohibits unfair and deceptive trade practices. However, the United States, unlike other jurisdictions, such as the European Union and Canada, does not have a general privacy law that applies to all companies. Instead, privacy regulation in the United States, like data security regulation, is a web of federal and state laws, some of which focus on specific industries or types of data. This chapter provides an overview of the regulation of privacy under Section 5 of the

Cybersecurity Law, Second Edition. Jeff Kosseff.
© 2020 John Wiley & Sons, Inc. Published 2020 by John Wiley & Sons, Inc.
Companion Website: www.wiley.com/go/kosseff/cybersecurity2e

FTC Act, as well as the most prominent federal and state privacy laws that restrict the private sector's cyber-related use and disclosure of personal information.[1]

9.1 Section 5 of the FTC Act and Privacy

As described more thoroughly in Chapter 1, Section 5 of the Federal Trade Commission Act declares illegal "unfair or deceptive acts or practices in or affecting commerce."[2] The statute states that "unfair" practices are those that cause or are likely to cause "substantial injury to consumers which is not reasonably avoidable by consumers themselves and not outweighed by countervailing benefits to consumers or to competition."[3]

As with data security, the FTC has not promulgated privacy regulations under Section 5. Rather, it takes a case-by-case approach to determine whether a company's privacy practices are unfair or deceptive. In general, the FTC expects companies to disclose material aspects of the manner in which they disclose personal data (i.e., if they share information with third parties) and to be honest in their statements about data processing (i.e., not lie in their privacy policies). Transparency, full disclosure, and honesty are among the most important principles in complying with the FTC's privacy expectations. Unlike data protection regulators in other countries, the FTC does not impose a specific set of data privacy requirements on all companies.

Honesty is perhaps the FTC's most important expectation for companies' privacy practices. The FTC provides companies with tremendous flexibility in determining how to collect, use, and share customers' personal information, but it expects that companies will accurately disclose these practices to consumers. If a company does not disclose a material practice—or, even worse, misrepresents it—the FTC may bring an enforcement action.

For example, in August 2012, the FTC announced a $22.5 million civil penalty against Google for violating a previous privacy-related consent order. The FTC alleged that Google surreptitiously placed advertising tracking cookies in consumers' Safari web browsers, allowing targeted advertising via Google's DoubleClick advertising network. This contradicted Google's representation to Safari users that Safari's default setting effectively blocks such cookies, and therefore they did not need to take any actions to opt out of targeted advertisements. Typically, the FTC settles privacy and data security cases by

---

1 This chapter is limited to privacy laws that impact *private sector* cybersecurity. This chapter does not cover privacy laws that apply primarily to government entities or schools (e.g., the Family Educational Rights and Privacy Act) or to practices that typically do not involve cyber (e.g., the Telephone Consumer Protection Act).
2 15 U.S.C. § 45(a)(1).
3 15 U.S.C. § 45(n).

entering into consent orders that require a company to take specific remedial actions, and it does not fine the offending company initially. However, the FTC imposed the $22.5 million penalty because Google already was operating under a 2011 consent order, arising from alleged misrepresentation of its privacy practices on a social network, Google Buzz. In a statement accompanying the $22.5 million fine, the FTC stated that the penalty "signals to Google and other companies that the Commission will vigorously enforce its orders."

Similarly, in 2011, the FTC announced a settlement and consent decree with Facebook arising from allegations about the social network's privacy practices. Among other things, the FTC alleged that Facebook made users' friends lists public without providing advance warning. Additionally, the FTC alleged that Facebook's "Friends Only" setting still allowed user content to be shared with third-party applications used by the users' friends. "Facebook is obligated to keep the promises about privacy that it makes to its hundreds of millions of users," Jon Leibowitz, then-Chairman of the FTC, said in a news release. "Facebook's innovation does not have to come at the expense of consumer privacy. The FTC action will ensure it will not."[4]

Companies that tout their privacy protections in their marketing to consumers must ensure that their products and services live up to those promises. For instance, in May 2014, the FTC reached a settlement with Snapchat, a mobile messaging application that marketed the fact that messages sent via the service would "disappear forever" after a specified amount of time.[5] The FTC brought the complaint because users could circumvent this requirement, and store the messages beyond the expiration date.

The FTC in recent years has increasingly focused on particularly sensitive data collected by new technologies, such as geolocation. For instance, in December 2013, it announced a settlement with Goldenshores Technologies, the creator of an Android flashlight app. The FTC alleged that the company provided third parties, including ad networks, with users' precise location and unique device identifiers, but it did not disclose this sharing in its privacy policy. Moreover, the FTC states that when customers first opened the app, they had an option to "accept" or "refuse" the end user licensing agreement (EULA), but that this presented a "false choice" because the information already had been sent to third parties after the app was downloaded. "In truth and in fact, consumers cannot prevent the [app] from ever collecting or using their device's data," the FTC wrote in its complaint against the company. "Regardless of whether consumers accept or refuse the terms of the EULA, the [app] transmits, or causes the transmission of, device data as soon as the consumer launches the application and before they have chosen to accept or refuse the terms[.]"[6]

---

4 Federal Trade Commission, *Facebook Settles FTC Charges that It Deceived Consumers by Failing to Keep Privacy Promises* (Nov. 29, 2011) [press release].
5 *In re* Snapchat, Docket No. C-4501 (2014).
6 *In re* Goldenshores Techs. LLC, Docket No. C-4446.

The White House Consumer Privacy Bill of Rights

In February 2012, shortly before the FTC released its privacy report, President Obama's White House released a Consumer Privacy Bill of Rights. The document, which is entirely nonbinding, demonstrates the Obama White House's core beliefs in flexible but clear privacy requirements for the private sector. Many of these values also are seen in the FTC privacy report. The White House proposed incorporating this policy into binding law, but Congress never enacted the legislation. Although the White House Consumer Privacy Bill of Rights is not binding, it is a good reflection of state and federal regulators' expectations of companies that handle customers' personal information. Below is the full text of the Consumer Privacy Bill of Rights:

The Consumer Privacy Bill of Rights applies to *personal data,* which means any data, including aggregations of data, which is linkable to a specific individual. Personal data may include data that is linked to a specific computer or other device. The Administration supports Federal legislation that adopts the principles of the Consumer Privacy Bill of Rights. Even without legislation, the Administration will convene multistakeholder processes that use these rights as a template for codes of conduct that are enforceable by the Federal Trade Commission. These elements—the Consumer Privacy Bill of Rights, codes of conduct and strong enforcement—will increase interoperability between the U.S. consumer data privacy framework and those of our international partners.

1) **Individual Control: Consumers have a right to exercise control over what personal data companies collect from them and how they use it.** Companies should provide consumers appropriate control over the personal data that consumers share with others and over how companies collect, use, or disclose personal data. Companies should enable these choices by providing consumers with easily used and accessible mechanisms that reflect the scale, scope, and sensitivity of the personal data that they collect, use, or disclose, as well as the sensitivity of the uses they make of personal data. Companies should offer consumers clear and simple choices, presented at times and in ways that enable consumers to make meaningful decisions about personal data collection, use, and disclosure. Companies should offer consumers means to withdraw or limit consent that are as accessible and easily used as the methods for granting consent in the first place.

2) **Transparency: Consumers have a right to easily understandable and accessible information about privacy and security practices.** At times and in places that are most useful to enabling consumers to gain a meaningful understanding of privacy risks and the ability to exercise Individual Control, companies should provide clear descriptions of what personal data they collect, why they need the data, how they will use it, when they will delete the data or de-identify it from consumers, and whether and for what purposes they may share personal data with third parties.

3) **Respect for Context: Consumers have a right to expect that companies will collect, use, and disclose personal data in ways that are consistent with the context in which consumers provide the data.** Companies should limit their use and disclosure of personal data to those purposes that are consistent with both the relationship that they have with consumers and the context in which consumers originally disclosed the data, unless required by law to do otherwise. If companies will use and disclose personal data for other purposes, they should provide heightened Transparency and Individual Control by disclosing these other purposes in a manner that is prominent and easily actionable by consumers at the time of data collection. If, subsequent to collection, companies decide to use or disclose personal data for purposes that are inconsistent with the context in which the data was disclosed, they must provide heightened measures of Transparency and Individual Choice. Finally, the age and familiarity with technology of consumers who engage with a company are important elements of context. Companies should fulfill the obligations under this principle in ways that are appropriate for the age and sophistication of consumers. In particular, the principles in the Consumer Privacy Bill of Rights may require greater protections for personal data obtained from children and teenagers than for adults.

4) **Security: Consumers have a right to secure and responsible handling of personal data.** Companies should assess the privacy and security risks associated with their personal data practices and maintain reasonable safeguards to control risks such as loss; unauthorized access, use, destruction, or modification; and improper disclosure.

5) **Access and Accuracy: Consumers have a right to access and correct personal data in usable formats, in a manner that is appropriate to the sensitivity of the data and the risk of adverse consequences to consumers if the data is inaccurate.** Companies should use reasonable measures to ensure they maintain accurate personal data. Companies also should provide consumers with reasonable access to personal data that they collect or maintain about them, as well as the appropriate means and opportunity to correct inaccurate data or request its deletion or use limitation. Companies that handle personal data should construe this principle in a manner consistent with freedom of expression and freedom of the press. In determining what measures they may use to maintain accuracy and to provide access, correction, deletion, or suppression capabilities to consumers, companies may also consider the scale, scope, and sensitivity of the personal data that they collect or maintain and the likelihood that its use may expose consumers to financial, physical, or other material harm.

6) **Focused Collection: Consumers have a right to reasonable limits on the personal data that companies collect and retain.** Companies should collect only as much personal data as they need to accomplish purposes

specified under the Respect for Context principle. Companies should securely dispose of or de-identify personal data once they no longer need it, unless they are under a legal obligation to do otherwise.

7) **Accountability: Consumers have a right to have personal data handled by companies with appropriate measures in place to assure they adhere to the Consumer Privacy Bill of Rights.** Companies should be accountable to enforcement authorities and consumers for adhering to these principles. Companies also should hold employees responsible for adhering to these principles. To achieve this end, companies should train their employees as appropriate to handle personal data consistently with these principles and regularly evaluate their performance in this regard. Where appropriate, companies should conduct full audits. Companies that disclose personal data to third parties should at minimum ensure that the recipients are under enforceable contractual obligations to adhere to these principles, unless they are required by law to do otherwise.

Source: White House, Consumer Data Privacy in a Networked World: A Framework for Protecting Privacy and Promoting Innovation in the Global Digital Economy (Feb. 2012), app. A.

9.2 Health Insurance Portability and Accountability Act

Although the FTC has not enacted specific privacy regulations for all companies, some sectors are legally required to abide by detailed privacy regulations. Among the most restrictive is healthcare, owing in part to the sensitive nature of health records.

Chapter 3 described the data security and breach notification requirements of the Health Insurance Portability and Accountability Act (HIPAA), enforced by the U.S. Department of Health and Human Services.[7] Also under HIPAA, the department has adopted a Privacy Rule, which limits the ability of health plans, healthcare providers, healthcare clearinghouses, and their business associates to use and disclose "protected health information," which is information that relates to an individual's "physical or mental health or condition," healthcare services, or healthcare payments.[8] The Privacy Rule only applies if the information identifies the individual; it does not apply to the use or disclosure of de-identified information.

---

7 Pub. L. No. 104-191, 110 Stat. 1936 (1996).
8 45 C.F.R. § 160.103.

The Privacy Rule allows covered entities to use and disclose protected health information:

- To the individual.
- For treatment.
- For payment.
- For healthcare.
- Incidental to a permitted use or disclosure.
- If the person has consented.
- For use in a facility directory or to notify family or friends of care, provided that the individual has the opportunity to agree or object (if the individual is incapacitated, the use or disclosure may be deemed to be in the individual's best interests).
- If the use or disclosure is in the public interest, which the law defines as one of the following categories as provided by the regulations: (1) required by law; (2) for public health activities; (3) regarding victims of abuse, neglect, or domestic violence; (4) for health oversight activities, such as criminal investigations of a health provider; (5) for judicial and administrative proceedings; (6) for law enforcement purposes; (7) information about decedents; (8) for cadaveric organ, eye, or tissue donation purposes; (9) for research purposes; (10) to avert a serious threat to health or safety; (11) for specialized government functions, such as military and national security activities; and (12) for workers' compensation.[9]

If the use or disclosure is not explicitly covered by one of these categories, the covered entity or business associate is required to obtain the individual's *written* authorization, which specifically allows the use and disclosure. For instance, in order for a healthcare provider to be permitted to use an individual's protected health information for marketing purposes, the written authorization must explicitly give permission to use the data for marketing.[10]

When covered entities and business associates use or disclose protected health information, they typically must make "reasonable efforts" to use or disclose the "minimum necessary" information only for the intended purpose. In other words, if a health insurer needs the healthcare provider's records of a patient's most recent physical in order to process its payment, the healthcare provider should not provide the insurer with records from the patient's ten most recent visits. The "minimum necessary" limit does not apply in a few select cases—notably if needed for treatment, disclosed to the individual who is the subject of the information, or if disclosed under an authorization by the individual.[11]

---

9 45 C.F.R. §§ 164.502–164.514.
10 45 C.F.R. § 164.508.
11 45 C.F.R. § 164.502(b).

Covered entities also must fulfill a number of administrative requirements under the Privacy Rule. They must designate a privacy official responsible for implementation of their privacy policies and procedures. Covered entities also must train all of their employees regarding protected health information.[12] HIPAA further imposes a number of data security requirements, which are discussed in Chapter 3.

The HIPAA Privacy Rule also requires covered entities to provide consumers with "adequate notice of the uses and disclosures of protected health information that may be made by the covered entity, and of the individual's rights and the covered entity's legal duties with respect to protected health information."[13]

In addition to restricting the use and disclosure of protected health information, HIPAA provides individuals with a relatively broad right of access to their information.[14] Individuals do not, however, have a right to access psychotherapy notes or information that is compiled in reasonable anticipation of, or for use in, a civil, criminal, or administrative action or proceeding.[15]

9.3 Gramm-Leach-Bliley Act and California Financial Information Privacy Act

As with health information, nonpublic financial data also receives special protection under U.S. law. The Gramm-Leach-Bliley Act (GLBA), the data security requirements of which were discussed in Chapter 3, also imposes privacy requirements on financial institutions. GLBA's privacy requirements, known as the Privacy Rule, generally are less burdensome than the HIPAA requirements that healthcare providers face, owing in part to the greater sensitivity of healthcare data.

GLBA imposes two general requirements: notice and choice. Under the notice requirement, a financial institution generally must provide customers with privacy notices at the time that the relationship with the customer is formed and at least once a year after that.[16] The notices must provide "clear and conspicuous disclosure" of the institution's privacy practices, including its policies for disclosure of "nonpublic personal information" to nonaffiliated parties, and other disclosures.[17] Financial regulators have developed model privacy notices that

---

12 45 C.F.R. § 164.530.
13 45 C.F.R. § 520.
14 45 C.F.R. § 164.524.
15 *Id.*
16 15 U.S.C. § 6803.
17 *Id.*

could satisfy this requirement.[18] In 2018, the Consumer Financial Protection Bureau adopted a new regulation that allows certain institutions to be exempt from the annual notice requirement, provided that they do not share nonpublic personal information with unaffiliated third parties.[19]

GLBA's Privacy Rule also requires financial institutions to allow users to choose whether to permit certain types of information sharing. If the financial institution is sharing information with a nonaffiliated third party that is performing services for the financial institution (e.g., marketing the institution's services), the institution does not need to provide the user with choice before sharing the data. However, if the financial institution intends to disclose nonpublic personal information to nonaffiliated third parties for other purposes (e.g., to market another company's services), the institution first must clearly and conspicuously notify the individual of the planned sharing and provide the individual with an opportunity to opt out *before* the institution shares the information.[20]

A California law imposes more restrictive choice requirements on financial institutions. The California Financial Information Privacy Act, also known as SB-1,[21] requires companies to receive *opt-in* consent from consumers before sharing their data with most unaffiliated third parties (unless the sharing is necessary to provide the financial services to the customers). This opt-in requirement is significantly more restrictive than GLBA's opt-out requirement because opt-in requires the customer to provide explicit consent before the sharing occurs. In contrast, under the opt-out system, if a customer does nothing after receiving notice, the information sharing is permitted. The California Financial Information Privacy Act also restricts financial institutions' ability to share information with *affiliated* entities. To do so under the California law, customers must obtain opt-out consent. This also is more restrictive than the GLBA Privacy Rule, which does not restrict financial institutions' sharing of data among affiliated companies.

9.4 CAN-SPAM Act

In the early 2000s, as email was becoming an important component of business and personal lives, policy makers focused on the increasing volume of

---

18 The FTC's model privacy notice is available at https://www.ftc.gov/system/files/ documents/rules/privacy-consumer-financial-information-financial-privacy-rule/ privacymodelform_optout.pdf. The model form developed by banking regulators and the SEC is available at https://www.sec.gov/rules/final/2009/34-61003_modelprivacyform.pdf.
19 12 C.F.R. § 1016.
20 15 U.S.C. § 6802.
21 CAL. FIN. CODE §§ 4050–60.

junk "spam" email messages that were flooding inboxes around the nation. States began to develop their own patchwork of anti-spam laws, and in 2003, Congress passed a single national restriction on spam, the Controlling the Assault of Non-Solicited Pornography and Marketing Act of 2003 (CAN SPAM Act).[22]

In a report accompanying the legislation, the Senate Commerce Committee wrote that the "inconvenience and intrusiveness to consumers of large volumes of spam are exacerbated by the fact that, in many instances, the senders of spam purposefully disguise the source or content of the e-mail by falsifying or including misleading information in the email's 'from', 'reply-to', or 'subject' lines."[23] Moreover, the legislators noted "that nearly all spam being sent today is considered untraceable back to its original source without extensive and costly investigation."[24]

The law is enforced by the Federal Trade Commission and Federal Communications Commission.[25] The statute has been criticized by some consumer groups because it preempts more stringent state laws and prevents consumers from bringing private lawsuits against spammers.

Among the key requirements of the CAN SPAM Act are the following:

- *Prohibition of false or misleading transmission information.* The CAN SPAM Act prohibits the senders of commercial email messages from using false header information, including email addresses or IP addresses. The statute states that header information is misleading "if it fails to identify accurately a protected computer used to initiate the message because the person initiating the message knowingly uses another protected computer to relay or retransmit the message for purposes of disguising its origin."[26]
- *Prohibition of deceptive subject headings.* Senders of commercial email messages may not use a subject line that "would be likely to mislead a recipient, acting reasonably under the circumstances, about a material fact regarding the contents or subject matter of the message[.]"[27]
- *Return address or opt-out.* Senders of commercial email must include a return email address or other mechanism (e.g., a link) that allows recipients to request not to receive commercial emails in the future. Once a sender receives such a request, it must stop sending commercial emails to that address within ten business days.[28]

---

22 15 U.S.C. § 7701 *et seq.*
23 S. Rep. No. 108-102 (2003).
24 *Id.* at 4.
25 15 U.S.C. § 7704.
26 15 U.S.C. § 7704(a)(1).
27 15 U.S.C. § 7704(a)(2).
28 15 U.S.C. § 7704(a)(3)–(4).

- *Identification of email as advertisement.* Commercial email must contain a "clear and conspicuous identification" that the email is an advertisement or solicitation, a notice of the opportunity to decline to receive further email, and a valid *physical* mailing address of the sender.[29]

Companies that violate the CAN SPAM Act can face FTC penalties of up to $42,530 *per email.*

9.5   Video Privacy Protection Act

The Video Privacy Protection Act (VPPA),[30] passed in 1988 in an effort to protect the privacy of videocassette rental information, has had a surprisingly large impact on the data processing abilities of websites and apps that deliver online video content.

Congress passed the VPPA in response to a newspaper's publication of the video rental records of Judge Robert Bork, who had been nominated to the United States Supreme Court. The VPPA prevents "video tape service providers" from knowingly disclosing an individual's personally identifiable video requests or viewing habits, unless the individual has provided informed, written consent. This consent may be provided online. The requirement is rather broad, though it contains a few exceptions, including disclosures that are incidental to the ordinary course of business for the service provider (debt collection activities, order fulfillment, request processing, and the transfer of ownership) or to law enforcement under a warrant, subpoena, or court order. Companies may use opt-out consent to share only customers' names and addresses, providing that their video viewing information is not disclosed.[31]

Why should websites and apps be concerned about a law that restricts the ability of "video tape service providers" to share information? The statute rather broadly defines "video tape service providers" as "any person, engaged in the business, in or affecting interstate or foreign commerce, of rental, sale, or delivery of prerecorded video cassette tapes or similar audio visual materials[.]"[32] This definition is broad enough to encompass not only video rental stores, but also websites and apps that provide video (whether it be streaming movies, television shows, or news clips). For instance, in 2012, a federal court ruled that Hulu's online movie streaming is covered by the VPPA because Hulu provides "similar audio visual materials."[33]

---

29 15 U.S.C. § 7704(a)(5).
30 18 U.S.C. § 2710.
31 *Id.*
32 *Id.*
33 *In re* Hulu Privacy Litig., No. C 11-03764 LB, 2012 WL 3282960 (N.D. Cal. Aug. 10, 2012).

VPPA disputes often arise when websites or apps provide individually identifiable video viewing information to third-party analytics companies. Unless
companies can convince a court that they are not covered by the VPPA or an
exception applies, they must obtain a very specific form of consent from the
consumer in order to share the data. The VPPA requires that the request for
consent be "distinct and separate" from any other legal or financial notice.[34] For
instance, to obtain a consumer's consent online, the provider must use a separate online pop-up ad seeking consent to disclose video viewing information,
and the customer must take an affirmative act, such as clicking "I agree." The
notice may not be buried in a larger privacy policy or terms of service. Once a
website or app obtains consent, it may share video viewing information for two
years, or until the consumer revokes consent.

Companies have good reason to care about compliance with the VPPA. The
statute allows damages of at least $2,500 *per violation*. This large amount
makes the VPPA a particularly attractive tool for class action plaintiffs' lawyers.
Imagine that a newspaper's website shared the video viewing information of
100,000 registered users with its online analytics provider and did not obtain
proper consent. A VPPA class action lawsuit could recover $250 million. For
this reason, it is important that companies take extra precautions to ensure
that they obtain adequate consent before sharing video viewing information.

A number of states have enacted statutes that are similar to the VPPA. One
notable state law is the Michigan Video Rental Privacy Act, which is broader than
the VPPA. The Michigan law restricts information sharing by companies that are
"engaged in the business of selling at retail, renting, or lending books or other
written materials, sound recordings, or video recordings."[35] In 2014, a federal
court ruled that this includes not only online video providers but also magazines
that share information about their subscribers.[36] Accordingly, at least for
Michigan subscribers, companies must be careful about sharing subscriber
information not only for videos but also for virtually all forms of online content.

9.6 Children's Online Privacy Protection Act

The Children's Online Privacy Protection Act (COPPA)[37] restricts the online
collection of personal information from minors who are under 13 years old.
The Federal Trade Commission has promulgated regulations[38] under COPPA
and enforces the law.

---

34 18 U.S.C. § 2710.
35 Mich. Comp. Laws § 445.1712.
36 Kinder v. Meredith Corp., Case No. 14-cv-11284 (E.D. Mich. Aug. 26, 2014).
37 15 U.S.C. §§ 6501–6505.
38 16 C.F.R. § 312.

COPPA applies to two types of website and online services: (1) those that are directed to children under 13, and (2) those that have actual knowledge that they are collecting or maintaining information from children under 13. To determine whether a website or online service is directed to children under 13, the FTC's regulations state that the commission considers:

- subject matter;
- visual content;
- use of animated characters or child-oriented activities and incentives, music or other audio content;
- age of models;
- presence of celebrities who appeal to children
- language or other characteristics of the service; and
- whether advertising promoting or appearing on the website or online service is directed to children.[39]

Websites and online services that are covered under COPPA must provide clear notice on their sites about the information that they collect from children, how they use the information, and their disclosure practices for this information. The websites and services must obtain "verifiable parental consent" before collecting, using, or disclosing any personal information from children under 13. The FTC broadly defines "personal information" as including:

- first and last name;
- physical mailing address;
- online contact information;
- screen or user name that functions as online contact information;
- telephone number;
- social security number;
- persistent identifier "that can be used to recognize a user over time and across different websites or online services";
- photograph, video, or audio file, where such file contains a child's image or voice;
- geolocation information that can identify the street and city or town; or
- information regarding the child or the child's parents, collected along with an identifier described above.[40]

To obtain verifiable parental consent, the regulations state, websites and online services must use methods that are "reasonably calculated, in light of available technology, to ensure that the person providing consent is the child's

---

39 16 C.F.R. § 312.2.
40 *Id.*

parent."[41] Included among the examples of such methods listed in the regulations are:

- requiring a parent to sign a consent form and return it by postal mail, fax, or electronic scan;
- requiring parent to use a payment card that notifies the account holder of a transaction;
- having parent call a toll-free number;
- having parent connect to company via video-conference; and
- verifying government-issued identification by comparing it against databases.[42]

If a website or online service is collecting personal information only for internal operations, and will not disclose it to any outside party, it also can obtain parental consent using the "email plus" method, in which the parent provides consent via a return email message, provided that the website or online service also takes an additional confirming step, either (1) requesting in the initial message that the parent include a phone number or mailing address to which the operator can send a confirming phone call or letter, or (2) after a "reasonable" delay, sending another email confirming consent.[43]

Even if a website or online service has obtained verifiable parental consent, it must provide parents with an ongoing opportunity to access the personal information collected from their children, delete the information, and prevent further use or collection of the information.[44] The websites and online services also are required to maintain the confidentiality, security, and integrity of information, though the regulations do not specify particular data security safeguards that the companies must enact.[45]

If the FTC determines that a website or online service has violated COPPA, it can bring an enforcement action in court, seeking damages of up to $42,530 per violation. For instance, in 2011, the FTC secured a $3 million settlement for alleged COPPA violations. Playdom, which develops online multi-player games, operated a website called Pony Stars, a virtual online world directed to children. The FTC alleged that from 2006 to 2010, hundreds of thousands of children registered for Pony Stars, even though Playdom did not properly obtain verifiable parental consent, nor did it properly post a COPPA-compliant privacy policy.[46]

---

41 16 C.F.R. § 312.5(b).
42 *Id.*
43 FEDERAL TRADE COMMISSION, COMPLYING WITH COPPA: FREQUENTLY ASKED QUESTIONS (Mar. 20, 2015).
44 *Id.*
45 *Id.*
46 Federal Trade Commission, *Operators of Online 'Virtual Worlds' to Pay $3 Million to Settle FTC Charges That They Illegally Collected and Disclosed Children's Personal Information* (May 12, 2011) [press release].

9.7   California Online Privacy Laws

Some of the most stringent online privacy laws were adopted not by Congress but by the California state legislature. Although the laws only apply to California residents, they have become de facto requirements for most companies that conduct business in the United States. In addition to the California Financial Information Privacy Act, described earlier, California has imposed requirements on companies via the California Online Privacy Protection Act (CalOPPA), the California Shine the Light law, and the California "Eraser Button" law.

9.7.1   California Online Privacy Protection Act (CalOPPA)

Until 2004, many U.S. websites did not contain privacy policies. The general rule had been that companies do not need to post a privacy policy, but if they did, the policy must accurately reflect the company's data processing practices. This rule changed in 2004, when CalOPPA went into effect. The statute requires all operators of commercial websites or online services that collect personally identifiable information about California customers to "conspicuously" post a privacy policy.[47] The privacy policy must, at minimum, contain the following elements:

- The categories of personally identifiable information collected about individual consumers.
- The categories of third parties with whom the website or service may share the personally identifiable information.
- A description of any process that the website or service maintains for consumers to "review and request changes" to their personally identifiable information.
- A description of the process by which the website or service notifies customers of "material changes" to their privacy policies.
- The effective date of the privacy policy.
- A description of the website or service's response to web browser "Do Not Track" signals or similar mechanisms.
- A disclosure of whether other parties may collect personally identifiable information about a consumer's online activities "over time and across different websites" when the consumer uses the website or service.[48]

CalOPPA defines personally identifiable information as individually identifiable information including:

- first and last name
- home or other physical address

---

47 Cal. Bus. & Prof. Code § 22575.
48 *Id.*

- email address
- phone number
- social security number
- any other identifier that permits physical or online contacting of an individual
- information collected by the website or service that is maintained in a personally identifiable form in combination with one of the identifiers above.[49]

Since it went into effect, CalOPPA has effectively set a nationwide requirement that all companies post a privacy policy describing how they handle customers' personal information. The California Attorney General aggressively enforces the policy, and in recent years has taken the position that CalOPPA also requires mobile apps to post privacy policies.

9.7.2 California Shine the Light Law

In 2005, the California Shine the Light law[50] went into effect, instituting additional privacy requirements for websites. The statute applies to businesses that have established business relationships with customers and have disclosed their personal information in the past calendar year to third parties for direct marketing.

The following are the categories of personal information under the California Shine the Light law:

- name and address
- email address
- age
- date of birth
- children's names
- email or other addresses of children
- number of children
- age or gender of children
- height
- weight
- race
- religion
- occupation
- phone number
- education
- political party affiliation

---

49 *Id.*
50 CAL. CIV. CODE § 1798.83.

- medical condition
- drugs, therapies, or medical products or equipment used
- kind of product the customer purchased, leased, or rented
- real property purchased, leased, or rented
- kind of service provided
- social security number
- bank account number
- credit card number
- debit card number
- bank or investment account, debit card, or credit card balance
- payment history
- information regarding an individual's creditworthiness, assets, income, or liabilities

Upon request from a customer, a business that is covered by this statute must provide the following information to the customer, for free:

- A list of the "categories of personal information" that the business has disclosed to third parties for direct marketing purposes.
- The "names and addresses of all third parties that received personal information from the business for the third parties' direct marketing purposes;"
- Examples of the types of services and products that were marketed for the third parties, if the "nature of the third parties' business" cannot be "reasonably determined" by their names.

Businesses that are required to comply with the California Shine the Light law must designate mailing and email addresses (or, at their discretion, a toll-free phone or fax number), to which customers may direct requests for information. Businesses must take one of the following steps to ensure compliance with the law:

- "Notify all agents and managers who directly supervise employees who regularly have contact with customers of the designated addresses or numbers or the means to obtain those addresses or numbers and instruct those employees that customers who inquire about the business's privacy practices or the business's compliance with this section shall be informed of the designated addresses or numbers or the means to obtain the addresses or numbers";
- From the website home page, include a link to a page entitled "Your Privacy Rights" or title a new section "Your Privacy Rights" within the larger privacy policy. The section must describe the customer's rights under the California Shine the Light law and provide the necessary contact details to obtain the information; or

- "Make the designated addresses or numbers, or means to obtain the designated addresses or numbers, readily available upon request of a customer at every place of business in California where the business or its agents regularly have contact with customers."[51]

Businesses also may comply with this requirement by stating in their privacy policy that either (1) they do not disclose their customers' personal information for the third parties' direct marketing purposes unless the customer opts in or (2) the business will not disclose personal information to third parties for the third parties' direct marketing purposes if the customer opts out (provided that the customer is notified of this right and provided with a "cost-free" method to exercise that right).

Companies that receive requests under the Shine the Light law must respond within 30 days. If the request is received in a manner other than by use of the designated addresses or phone numbers, the business generally must respond within 150 days.

Businesses with fewer than 20 full-time or part-time employees are exempt from the California Shine the Light law, and businesses are not required to respond to a single customer more than once per calendar year.

9.7.3 California Minor "Eraser Law"

California's latest endeavor in the online privacy law area went into effect in 2015. Known as the "eraser law,"[52] the statute imposes a number of restrictions on websites, online services, and apps that are directed to minors. Unlike the federal COPPA, which only applies to minors under the age of 13, the California law applies if the website, service, or app is targeted at minors under 18.

A website, service, or app is considered to be "directed to minors" and therefore covered by the statute if it "is created for the purpose of reaching an audience that is predominately comprised of minors, and is not intended for a more general audience comprised of adults."[53] The statute is known as the "eraser law" because it provides minors with a limited ability to request the removal of certain information.

The statute requires covered websites, services, and apps to allow minors who are registered users to request and obtain removal of content and information that the minor posted on the service. The sites must notify minor registered users of the instructions to remove the data.[54]

---

51 *Id.*
52 Cal. Bus. & Prof. Code §§ 22580–81.
53 *Id.*
54 *Id.*

Covered websites, services, and apps are not required to remove content or information under any of the following circumstances:

- Another state or federal law requires the service to "maintain the content or information."
- The content was stored or posted by a third party other than the minor.
- The content is anonymized so that the minor is not individually identifiable.
- The minor failed to request removal of the content, as instructed by the site.
- The minor has been compensated for the content.[55]

This statute received a great deal of media attention because it allows users to request the removal of certain content. However, the right is limited. First, it only applies if the minor was a registered user, and it only covers content that the *minor* provided. If, for example, the minor's friend posted personal information about the minor on a social media site, the minor would not have a right to request removal.

Less discussed in the media coverage, but perhaps more significant, are the restrictions that the statute places on online marketing. It prohibits covered websites, services, and apps from marketing certain categories of products and services:

- alcoholic beverages
- firearms or handguns
- ammunition or reloaded ammunition
- handgun safety certificates
- aerosol container of paint that is capable of defacing property
- etching cream that is capable of defacing property
- tobacco, cigarette, or cigarette papers, or blunt wraps, or any other preparation of tobacco; any other instrument or paraphernalia that is designed for the smoking or ingestion of tobacco; products prepared from tobacco, or any controlled substance
- BB devices
- dangerous fireworks
- tanning in an ultraviolet tanning device
- dietary supplement products containing ephedrine group alkaloids
- tickets or shares in a lottery game
- *Salvia divinorum* or Salvinorin A, or any substance or material containing *Salvia divinorum* or Salvinorin A
- body branding
- permanent tattoo
- drug paraphernalia

---

55 *Id.*

- electronic cigarette
- obscene matter
- a less lethal weapon

9.8 California Consumer Privacy Act

One of the biggest developments in the privacy world in 2018 was California's quick passage of the California Consumer Privacy Act. The law, which is scheduled to go into effect in 2020, incorporates some data protection elements of Europe's General Data Protection Regulation (GDPR), which is described in Chapter 10 of this book. Although the statute is not as onerous as the GDPR, it contains a number of requirements that companies may need to address, particularly if they had determined that they were not subject to the GDPR's requirements.[56]

The statute applies to companies that do business in California, collect personal information from California consumers, and fall into at least one of the following three categories:

- Gross annual revenues above $25 million;
- "Alone or in combination, annually buys, receives for the business' commercial purposes, sells, or shares for commercial purposes, alone or in combination, the personal information of 50,000" California residents, households, or devices; or
- "Derives 50 percent or more of its annual revenues" from selling California residents' personal information.[57]

The statute defines "personal information" quite broadly, to include any information:

> that identifies, relates to, describes, is capable of being associated with, or could reasonably be linked, directly or indirectly, with a particular consumer or household. Personal information includes, but is not limited to, the following:
>
> (A) Identifiers such as a real name, alias, postal address, unique personal identifier, online identifier Internet Protocol address, email address, account name, social security number, driver's license number, passport number, or other similar identifiers.

---

56 This book went to production in the spring of 2019, as the California legislature was considering additional amendments to the CCPA. This section describes the CCPA as of March 2019. It may have changed substantively since then, so it is important to consult the current version of the law as amended.

57 CAL. CIV. CODE § 1798.140(c).

(B) Any categories of personal information described in subdivision (e) of Section 1798.80.

(C) Characteristics of protected classifications under California or federal law.

(D) Commercial information, including records of personal property, products or services purchased, obtained, or considered, or other purchasing or consuming histories or tendencies.

(E) Biometric information.

(F) Internet or other electronic network activity information, including, but not limited to, browsing history, search history, and information regarding a consumer's interaction with an Internet Web site, application, or advertisement.

(G) Geolocation data.

(H) Audio, electronic, visual, thermal, olfactory, or similar information.

(I) Professional or employment-related information.

(J) Education information, defined as information that is not publicly available personally identifiable information as defined in the Family Educational Rights and Privacy Act (20 U.S.C. section 1232g, 34 C.F.R. Part 99).[58]

If CCPA applies, a business faces many requirements, including:

- The business must display a privacy policy that describes customers' rights under the statute, personal information that the business collected over the past year, referring to the categories of personal information listed above, and other disclosures.[59]
- Upon request from a consumer, the business must disclose the "categories and specific pieces of personal information the business has collected."[60]
- Subject to a number of exceptions (such as free speech, completing transactions, and security), fulfill requests that the business "delete any personal information about the consumer which the business has collected from the consumer."[61]
- If the business sells personal information to third parties, the business must allow the consumer to opt out, subject to some exceptions.[62]
- The business cannot discriminate against consumers for exercising their rights under CCPA.[63]

---

58 Cal. Civ. Code § 1798.140(o).
59 Cal. Civ. Code § 1798.130(a)(5).
60 Cal. Civ. Code § 1798.100.
61 Cal. Civ. Code § 1798.105.
62 Cal. Civ. Code § 1798.120.
63 Cal. Civ. Code § 1798.125(a).

- If a service provider receives personal information from the business, the contract must prohibit the service provider "from retaining, using, or disclosing the personal information for any purpose other than for the specific purpose of performing the services specified in the contract for the business, or as otherwise permitted by this title, including retaining, using, or disclosing the personal information for a commercial purpose other than providing the services specified in the contract with the business."[64]

The statute is mostly enforced by the California Attorney General's office, which has the ability to issue fines of up to $2,500 per violation, or $7,500 per intentional violation. The California Attorney General also can develop compliance guidelines. The statute does provide a private right of action for consumers whose unencrypted and unredacted personal information is "subject to an unauthorized access and exfiltration, theft, or disclosure as a result of the business' violation of the duty to implement and maintain reasonable security procedures and practices appropriate to the nature of the information to protect the personal information."[65] Damages for these breach claims are the greater of: (1) $100 to $750 per consumer per incident; or (2) actual damages.

As this book was being published in 2019, the California legislature was considering a number of substantive and procedural amendments to the CCPA. Accordingly, it is important to consult the most current version of the statute when structuring compliance programs.

9.9 Illinois Biometric Information Privacy Act

The Illinois Biometric Information Privacy Act[66] is being increasingly used by plaintiffs' lawyers to limit online services' use of facial recognition and other new technologies. The statute prohibits companies from obtaining or disclosing "biometric identifiers or biometric information" unless the companies first obtain the individuals' opt-in consent.

The statute broadly defines "biometric identifier" to include "a retina or iris scan, fingerprint, voiceprint, or scan of hand or face geometry." The statute excludes a number of types of information from the definition of "biometric identifier," including photographs, writing samples, and physical descriptions of individuals. The statute defines "biometric information" as "any information, regardless of how it is captured, converted, stored, or shared, based on an individual's biometric identifier used to identify an individual."[67] The statute

---

64 CAL. CIV. CODE § 1798.140(v).
65 CAL. CIV. CODE § 1798.150.
66 740 ILL. COMP. STAT. 14.
67 *Id.*

prohibits the collection, receipt, or exchange of covered biometric identifiers unless the company first does the following:

1) informs the subject or the subject's legally authorized representative in writing that a biometric identifier or biometric information is being collected or stored;
2) informs the subject or the subject's legally authorized representative in writing of the specific purpose and length of term for which a biometric identifier or biometric information is being collected, stored, and used; and
3) receives a written release executed by the subject of the biometric identifier or biometric information or the subject's legally authorized representative.[68]

Private parties can bring lawsuits under the statute for up to $5,000 *per violation*. As with other statutes, this can lead to significant, bet-the-company damages if a plaintiff brings a class action lawsuit on behalf of thousands of customers.

The statute received significant attention in May 2016 when a federal judge refused to dismiss a class action lawsuit brought under the statute against Facebook. The plaintiffs claimed that Facebook violated the Illinois law with its "Tag Suggestions" program, in which Facebook scans photos uploaded by users and uses facial recognition to suggest that the users tag the photo subjects by name. Facebook moved to dismiss the lawsuit, claiming that the statute did not apply because it explicitly states that it does not cover photographs. The court disagreed and denied the motion to dismiss, reasoning that Facebook's facial recognition technology constitutes a "scan of face geometry," which is covered by the statute. The court reasoned that the exclusion for photographs is "better understood to mean paper prints of photographs, not digitized images stored as a computer file and uploaded to the Internet."[69]

The *Facebook* decision is significant because it broadly applies the Illinois law to facial recognition technologies. Companies must ensure that they obtain adequate consent before using facial recognition or other new technologies, or they could find themselves on the hook for significant penalties under the Illinois law.

Companies must pay particular attention to the Illinois state law because Illinois courts have indicated a willingness to allow claims even if the plaintiffs have not alleged actual harm. Chapter 2 discussed the requirement, in federal courts, for plaintiffs to allege an "injury in fact" to establish standing. In contrast, plaintiffs can bring claims under the Illinois biometric privacy law in Illinois state courts, which do not impose the same standing requirements.

---

68 *Id.*
69 *In re* Facebook Biometric Info. Privacy Litig., Case No. 15-cv-03747-JD (N.D. Cal. May 5, 2016).

In a 2019 case, the Illinois Supreme Court allowed a lawsuit under the biometric privacy law to proceed against Six Flags Entertainment Corporation, even though the company claimed that the plaintiff "had suffered no actual or threatened injury and therefore lacked standing to sue[.]"[70] The court concluded that pleading "actual harm" is unnecessary, and that the violation of the biometric privacy law "in itself, is sufficient to support the individual's or customer's statutory cause of action."[71]

70 Rosenbach v. Six Flags Entm't Corp., 2019 IL 123186 (Ill. 2019).
71 *Id.*

10

International Cybersecurity Law

The preceding chapters focused primarily on the cybersecurity obligations that U.S. companies face within the United States. However, many U.S. companies must worry not only about U.S. laws and regulations but also about the laws and regulations of other nations. In this chapter, we review the primary cybersecurity and privacy laws of the five largest U.S. trading partners: the European Union, Canada, China, Mexico, and Japan.

As this chapter demonstrates, other jurisdictions have more clearly articulated a comprehensive data security and privacy legal framework than the United States has. The U.S. cybersecurity and privacy laws often vary by sector (and, in some cases, by state), whereas other large countries have adopted across-the-board laws that severely restrict the collection, storage, use, and disclosure of personal information.

At the outset, many of the other jurisdictions' laws, unlike many of those in the United States, focus on the terms "data controller" and "data processor." This is a key distinction that, under many of these laws, affects the legal responsibilities of companies. The definitions vary by jurisdiction, but the easiest way to view this distinction generally is that data *controllers* help determine precisely how data is used, distributed, shared, collected, or otherwise processed, whereas data *processors* merely follow instructions from the data controllers. For instance, an employer that collects tax information from its employees is a data controller. The third-party payroll company that issues the employer's paychecks likely is a data processor. In many countries, the data controller is responsible for the practices of the data processor.

This chapter is intended to be a high-level overview of the cybersecurity legal frameworks in these countries, to provide U.S. businesses with a general understanding of their obligations. In some cases, the chapter is based on English translations of laws and regulations that are published primarily in foreign languages. Moreover, there may be additional local and regional laws

Cybersecurity Law, Second Edition. Jeff Kosseff.
© 2020 John Wiley & Sons, Inc. Published 2020 by John Wiley & Sons, Inc.
Companion Website: www.wiley.com/go/kosseff/cybersecurity2e

that alter a particular company's responsibilities. Accordingly, companies should consult with local counsel about non-U.S. legal requirements.

10.1 European Union

In 2016, the European Union replaced its 1995 data protection law, Directive 95/46/EC of the European Parliament, with the General Data Protection Regulation (GDPR). The GDPR establishes the data protection rules to which member states must adhere, though there is some flexibility for the states to pass "derogations" from particular portions of the GDPR. The GDPR went into effect in May 2018.

Europe views privacy as a fundamental human right, and therefore its requirements for privacy and data security generally are more stringent than those in the United States. This section first outlines the key components of the GDPR, and then examines the methods by which U.S. companies can obtain legal approval to process the data of EU residents.

Although the GDPR does not apply to all U.S. companies, it contains some provisions that allow it to apply extraterritorially, even if the company does not have any operations or employees in the European Union. If a company is not "established" in the European Union, the GDPR's requirements still apply if the processing is related to either (1) "the offering of goods or services, irrespective of whether a payment of the data subject is required, to such data subjects in the Union," or (2) "the monitoring of their behaviour as far as their behaviour takes place within the Union."[1]

In a recital provided along with the GDPR territoriality rule, European officials clarified that a company is not "offering" goods or services to Europeans and therefore subject to the GDPR merely because its website is accessible in Europe. Instead, they look to "factors such as the use of a language or a currency generally used in one or more Member States with the possibility of ordering goods and services in that other language, or the mentioning of customers or users who are in the Union[.]"[2]

This relatively limited instruction has left many companies based outside of Europe confused as to what exactly triggers the requirement to comply with the GDPR. In November 2018 guidelines, the European Data Protection Board released guidance on the GDPR's territorial scope.[3] The board stressed that even if a company is not located in the European Union, it may be subject to the GDPR merely by targeting data subjects in the European Union: that is, by

---

1 General Data Protection Regulation (GDPR), art. 3.
2 GDPR, Recital 23.
3 European Data Protection Board, Guidelines 3/2018 on the territorial scope of the GDPR (Article 3)—Version for public consultation (adopted November 16, 2018).

offering goods or services to them. Relying on caselaw, the board identified the following factors as potentially relevant to a determination as to whether a company is "offering goods or services" to European data subjects:

> The EU or at least one Member State is designated by name with reference to the good or service offered;
>
> The data controller or processor pays a search engine operator for an internet referencing service in order to facilitate access to its site by consumers in the Union; or the controller or processor has launched marketing and advertisement campaigns directed at an EU country audience;
>
> The international nature of the activity at issue, such as certain tourist activities;
>
> The mention of dedicated addresses or phone numbers to be reached from an EU country;
>
> The use of a top-level domain name other than that of the third country in which the controller or processor is established, for example ".de", or the use of neutral top-level domain names such as ".eu";
>
> The description of travel instructions from one or more other EU Member States to the place where the service is provided;
>
> The mention of an international clientele composed of customers domiciled in various EU Member States, in particular by presentation of accounts written by such customers;
>
> The use of a language or a currency other than that generally used in the trader's country, especially a language or currency of one or more EU Member states;
>
> The data controller offers the delivery of goods in EU Member States.[4]

The board also stressed that the GDPR could apply based on a non-EU company monitoring the behavior of data subjects in Europe. "The EDPB does not consider that any online collection or analysis of personal data of individuals in the EU would automatically count as 'monitoring,'" the board wrote. "It will be necessary to consider the controller's purpose for processing the data and, in particular, any subsequent behavioural analysis or profiling techniques involving that data."[5]

The GDPR applies to the processing (i.e., collecting, using, storing, or disclosing) of "personal data" of EU residents, regardless of whether that processing

---

4 *Id.* at 15–16.
5 *Id.* at 18.

occurs in the European Union or another jurisdiction. The GDPR broadly defines "personal data" as "any information that is relating to an identified or identifiable natural person ('data subject'); an identifiable natural person is one who can be identified, directly or indirectly, in particular by reference to an identifier such as a name, an identification number, location data, an online identifier or to one or more factors specific to the physical, physiological, genetic, mental, economic, cultural or social identity of that natural person[.]"[6] In other words, information may be personal data even if it does not contain the individual's name, provided that the individual could be identified by that data. For instance, information about the income of an individual who lives at a particular address likely would be considered personal data, even if the individual's name was not used, because that information could be traced to the individual who lives at that address.

The GDPR applies to two general types of companies: controllers (the entity that "determines the purposes and means of the processing of personal data") and processors (the entity that "processes personal data on behalf of the controller"). Controllers are responsible for ensuring that their processors provide "sufficient guarantees to implement appropriate technical and organizational measures in such a manner that processing will meet the requirements" of the GDPR.[7]

What does it mean to comply with the GDPR? The GDPR imposes the following general principles for the processing of personal data:

- *Lawfulness, fairness, and transparency.* Companies must employ lawful, fair, and transparent processing of personal data.
- *Purpose limitation.* Companies must collect personal information for "specified, explicit, and legitimate purposes." Companies must explicitly state the purposes for which they are collecting personal data, and they may not expand upon those uses.
- *Data minimization.* Companies must collect only what is necessary for the stated purposes.
- *Accuracy.* Companies must take "every reasonable step" to ensure that the personal data they handle is accurate and up-to-date.
- *Storage limitation.* Companies must allow identification of data subjects only for as long as necessary to achieve the stated purposes.
- *Integrity and confidentiality.* Companies must protect data from unauthorized access, loss, or destruction via "appropriate technical or organizational measures."[8]

---

6 GDPR art. 4(1).
7 GDPR art. 28.
8 GDPR art. 5(1).

Companies must devote significant time to analyzing the "lawfulness"—or "legal basis"—of their processing of European data. Processing of personal data is lawful only if one of the following conditions is satisfied:

- The individual has provided consent for processing of the personal data. If the data subject provides consent via a written declaration[,] that consent must be "clearly distinguishable" from other issues, intelligible, and easily accessible. Individuals must be able to revoke their consent at any time. Parents must provide consent for children.
- The individual is subject to a contract for which processing is necessary.
- Processing is necessary for the controller of the data to comply with a legal obligation.
- Processing is necessary to protect "the vital interests of the data subject or of another natural person."
- Processing is necessary to perform a task in the "public interest" or under the data controller's official authority.
- Processing is necessary for the "legitimate interests pursued by the controller or by a third party, except where such interests are overridden by the interests or fundamental rights and freedoms of the data subject which require protection of personal data, in particular where the data subject is a child."[9]

The GDPR imposes additional restrictions on the processing of "special categories" of particularly sensitive data, which it defines as data that reveals "racial or ethnic origin, political opinions, religious or philosophical beliefs, or trade union membership, and the processing of genetic data, biometric data for the purpose of uniquely identifying a natural person, data concerning health or data concerning a natural person's sex life or sexual orientation[.]"[10] Typically, the data may be processed only if the individual has provided explicit consent for the processing of that sensitive data, or if another narrow exception applies.[11]

The processing of personal data must further be "transparent." If the personal data is collected from the data subject, the company must clearly and intelligibly provide the data subject with the following information:

- The contact information for the data controller and, if applicable, its data protection officer.
- The purposes for the processing and legal basis, and, if applicable, the legitimate interests that the controller or a third party is pursuing.
- The recipients or categories of recipients of the personal data.

---

9 GDPR arts. 6–8.
10 GDPR art. 9.
11 *Id.*

- Whether the data controller plans to transfer the personal data to another jurisdiction.
- The length of time the personal data will be stored.
- The right to request access to and erasure of personal data.
- The right to withdraw consent under certain circumstances.
- The right to complain to a supervisory authority.
- Whether the provision of the personal data is required by statute or contract and the consequences of the data subject's failure to provide the personal data.
- Existence of automated decisionmaking, such as profiling.[12]

The GDPR provides data subjects with a "right of access" to their data. At a data subject's request, a controller must provide the data subject with copies of the subject's personal data, as well as the following:

> the purposes of the processing;
> the categories of personal data concerned;
> the recipients or categories of recipient to whom the personal data have been or will be disclosed, in particular recipients in third countries or international organisations;
> where possible, the envisaged period for which the personal data will be stored, or, if not possible, the criteria used to determine that period;
> the existence of the right to request from the controller rectification or erasure of personal data or restriction of processing of personal data concerning the data subject or to object to such processing;
> the right to lodge a complaint with a supervisory authority;
> where the personal data are not collected from the data subject, any available information as to their source;
> the existence of automated decision-making, including profiling.[13]

The GDPR allows data subjects not only to review this data, but also to obtain "the rectification of inaccurate personal data concerning him or her."[14]

Among the most discussed provisions of the GDPR is Article 17, which provides a "right to be forgotten." Under this provision, data subjects have a qualified right to request that data controllers erase personal data if they can demonstrate that one of the following circumstances exists:

- The personal data is no longer necessary to serve the purposes for which it was collected or processed.

---

12 GDPR art. 13.
13 GDPR art. 15.
14 GDPR art. 16.

- The data subject has withdrawn the consent that allowed the personal data to be collected and there are no other grounds for processing.
- The data subject objects and the controller fails to demonstrate "compelling legitimate grounds for the processing which override the interests, rights and freedoms of the data subject or for the establishment, exercise or defence of legal claims."
- The personal data was processed unlawfully.
- The EU or member state requires erasure under a different law.
- The personal data was collected from a child under 16 for information services.[15]

The GDPR states that controllers are not required to delete data if processing is necessary "for exercising the right of freedom of expression and information."[16] This reflects the EU belief that the right-to-be-forgotten request must balance, on the one hand, the right of individual privacy and, on the other hand, the right to free speech.

The GDPR does not explicitly state the specific data security measures that companies must implement for personal data. Rather, it instructs controllers and processors to "implement appropriate technical and organizational measures to ensure a level of security appropriate to the risk." Among the considerations that the GDPR suggests companies apply when making these determinations are:

- pseudonymization;
- encryption;
- data security safeguards;
- resilience, including the ability to recover quickly after incidents; and
- regular testing of technical and organizational security measures.[17]

The United Kingdom Information Commissioner's Office released GDPR guidance which suggests that companies consider the following security factors:

- system security—the security of your network and information systems, including those which process personal data;
- data security—the security of the data you hold within your systems, e.g. ensuring appropriate access controls are in place and that data is held securely;
- online security—e.g. the security of your website and any other online service or application that you use; and

---

15 GDPR art. 17.
16 *Id.*
17 GDPR art. 32.

- device security—including policies on Bring-your-own-Device (BYOD) if you offer it.[18]

Significant among the additions in the GDPR is a data breach notification requirement (long a feature of U.S. law, as discussed in Chapter 1). If a company experiences a breach of personal data, the controller must without undue delay, and, if feasible, within 72 hours, notify government regulators.[19] If the controller fails to notify the government within 72 hours, it must provide a reason for the delay.

The notification to regulators must contain the following information:

- Nature of the data breach.
- Categories and number of data subjects.
- Categories and number of personal data records involved.
- Name and contact details of the controller's data protection officer and other contact points.
- Likely consequences of the breach.
- Measures taken to mitigate the adverse effects of the breach.[20]

Controllers also are required to notify individuals of data breaches if they determine that the breach "is likely to result in a high risk to the rights and freedoms of the individuals."[21] The GDPR does not require the notices to be sent within a specified time period, but rather states that individuals should be notified "without undue delay." The individual notices must contain all of the information that must be sent to regulators, except for the description of the nature of the breach and categories and number of data subjects and personal data records.[22]

Notification to individuals is not required under one of the following circumstances:

- The controller had implemented encryption or other safeguards that render the personal data unintelligible.
- The controller took subsequent measures that "ensure that the high risk to the rights and freedoms of data subjects" likely will not materialize.
- The individual notices would "involve disproportionate effort." In this case, the controller must provide the notice via a public communication.[23]

For U.S. companies, a significant concern raised by the GDPR (as by the earlier 1995 Directive) is the restriction of transfers of Europeans' personal data to

---

18 United Kingdom Information Security Office, Guide to the General Data Protection Regulation: Security.
19 GDPR art. 33.
20 *Id.*
21 GDPR art. 34.
22 *Id.*
23 *Id.*

third countries. Europeans' personal information may only be transferred to a company outside of the United States if one of the following circumstances exists:

- The nation to which the data is being transferred has been deemed by the European Commission to have "adequate" protection for personal data. The Commission makes this determination based on its evaluation of the nation's rule of law, respect for human rights, data protection regulation, and international commitments regarding personal data. The United States is not among the countries deemed by the European Union to have "adequate" data protection.
- The foreign company has adopted binding corporate rules that impose significant restrictions (similar to those in the GDPR) on personal data processing.
- The foreign company agrees to handle the Europeans' data pursuant to standard contractual clauses that have been adopted by the European Commission.
- The foreign company agrees to "binding and enforceable commitments" regarding safeguards and data subjects' rights via an approved code of conduct or certification mechanism.[24]

Many U.S. companies had used a certification program known as "Safe Harbor" to process data of European residents. The Safe Harbor framework, which was negotiated by U.S. and EU officials, required U.S. companies to self-certify that they complied with specified data protection principles. However, in October 2015, the Court of Justice of the European Union struck down the Safe Harbor program,[25] concluding that U.S. government foreign intelligence surveillance programs revealed by Edward Snowden rendered the Safe Harbor's protections inadequate.

Because so many U.S. companies relied on the Safe Harbor framework to conduct business with Europe, government officials throughout the United States and European Union quickly began negotiating a new certification framework to replace Safe Harbor. The result is a new arrangement known as the Privacy Shield, which the European Commission approved in July 2016.

The Privacy Shield requires participating U.S. companies to adhere to the following privacy principles:

- *Notice.* Companies must inform data subjects about the type of data collected, purposes, right of access, choice, and other elements regarding the processing.[26]

---

24 GDPR arts. 44–50.
25 Case C-362/14, Schrems v. Data Protection Comm'r, E.C.R. [2015].
26 COMMISSION IMPLEMENTING DECISION OF 12.7.2016 PURSUANT TO DIRECTIVE 95/46/EC OF THE EUROPEAN PARLIAMENT AND OF THE COUNCIL ON THE ADEQUACY OF THE PROTECTION PROVIDED BY THE EU–U.S. PRIVACY SHIELD.

- ***Data integrity and purpose limitation.*** Companies must limit their processing of personal data to the stated purpose.
- ***Choice.*** Individuals must have an opportunity to opt out of processing that is materially different from the original purpose. Individuals must be provided opt-in choices for sensitive information.
- ***Security.*** Companies must implement "reasonable and appropriate" security measures and contractually require service providers to do the same.
- ***Access.*** Data subjects have the right to access their personal information, though this access may be limited "in exceptional circumstances." Individuals may correct, amend, or delete inaccurate information.
- ***Recourse, enforcement, and liability.*** Companies must ensure compliance with the Privacy Shield and annually certify their compliance. Companies also must implement redress procedures to handle complaints about their personal data processing. This compliance is subject to investigation and enforcement by U.S. regulators.
- ***Accountability for onward transfer.*** Before transferring Europeans' data to another country, the U.S. company must ensure that adequate protections are in place to guarantee the same level of protection as the Privacy Shield.[27]

To address the concerns about U.S. government surveillance that led to the invalidation of the Safe Harbor agreement, the United States agreed to limits on and oversight of its surveillance programs, and to a redress mechanism for EU residents.

The GDPR also requires covered companies to enter into extensive contracts with third-party processors that handle Europeans' personal information. In the year before the GDPR went into effect in May 2018, companies devoted significant time—and incurred significant legal expenses—to amend their existing vendor contracts to comply with the GDPR's requirements for data protection agreements. The GDPR requires that the contract impose the following obligations on processors:

a) processes the personal data only on documented instructions from the controller, including with regard to transfers of personal data to a third country or an international organisation, unless required to do so by Union or Member State law to which the processor is subject; in such a case, the processor shall inform the controller of that legal requirement before processing, unless that law prohibits such information on important grounds of public interest;

b) ensures that persons authorised to process the personal data have committed themselves to confidentiality or are under an appropriate statutory obligation of confidentiality;

---

27 *Id*. at 2.1.

c) takes all measures required pursuant to Article 32;

d) respects the conditions referred to in paragraphs 2 and 4 for engaging another processor;

e) taking into account the nature of the processing, assists the controller by appropriate technical and organisational measures, insofar as this is possible, for the fulfilment of the controller's obligation to respond to requests for exercising the data subject's rights laid down in Chapter III;

f) assists the controller in ensuring compliance with the obligations pursuant to Articles 32 to 36 taking into account the nature of processing and the information available to the processor;

g) at the choice of the controller, deletes or returns all the personal data to the controller after the end of the provision of services relating to processing, and deletes existing copies unless Union or Member State law requires storage of the personal data;

h) makes available to the controller all information necessary to demonstrate compliance with the obligations laid down in this Article and allow for and contribute to audits, including inspections, conducted by the controller or another auditor mandated by the controller.[28]

In addition to the GDPR, in 2016 the European Union separately passed the EU Network and Information Security Directive (NIS Directive),[29] which sets security requirements for operators of "essential services." The NIS Directive provides the following criteria for determining whether an organization operates essential services:

a) an entity provides a service which is essential for the maintenance of critical societal and/or economic activities;

b) the provision of that service depends on network and information systems; and

c) an incident would have significant disruptive effects on the provision of that service.[30]

The NIS Directive lists the following sectors among operators of "essential services": energy, transport, banking, financial market infrastructures, health,

---

28 GDPR art. 28.
29 Directive (EU) 2016/1148 of the European Parliament and of the Council of 6 July 2016 concerning measures for a high common level of security of network and information systems across the Union ("NIS Directive").
30 Id. at art. 5(2).

drinking water supply and distribution, and digital infrastructure.[31] The Directive also imposes security requirements on certain "digital service providers" such as cloud providers and search engines.

The NIS Directive creates structures for companies and government entities to work together to protect services. It requires member states to designate at least one Computer Security Incident Response Team (CSIRT)[32] to effectively act as national monitors and coordinators after cybersecurity incidents.[33] The directive also requires that EU states "ensure that operators of essential services take appropriate and proportionate technical and organisational measures to manage the risks posed to the security of network and information systems which they use in their operations."[34] States also must ensure that covered companies issue notifications of cybersecurity incidents.[35]

When the European Commission adopted the NIS Directive in 2016, officials marked it as a significant milestone in EU cybersecurity. "The Directive on Security of Network and Information Systems is the first comprehensive piece of EU legislation on cybersecurity and a fundamental building block for our work in this area," European Commission Vice-President Andrus Ansip said at the time. "It requires companies in critical sectors—such as energy, transport, banking and health—to adopt risk management practices and report major incidents that can affect the Digital Single Market to their national authorities which will, in turn, be able to carry out better capacity-building with greater cross-border cooperation inside the EU."[36]

10.2 Canada

Canada's primary privacy and data security law is the Personal Information Protection and Electronic Documents Act (PIPEDA). Unlike the U.S. patchwork of industry-specific privacy and data security laws, PIPEDA sets a national standard for the use, disclosure, and protection of identifiable information about a Canadian resident.

PIPEDA's requirements are divided into ten principles, as set forth in Schedule 1 of the law (the following is a truncated and edited summary; make sure to consult with the full and most recent version of PIPEDA):

- *Accountability.* Companies must designate privacy and data security compliance with specified employees (e.g., chief privacy officers and chief

---

31 *Id.* at Annex II.
32 *Id.* at art. 9.
33 *Id.* at Annex I.
34 *Id.* at art. 14.
35 *Id.*
36 European Commission, Statement by Vice-President Ansip and Commissioner Oettinger welcoming the adoption of the first EU-wide rules on cybersecurity (July 6, 2016).

information security officers), and provide the identity of these employees upon request. Companies must contractually require that their service providers protect Canadians' personal information. Companies also are required to develop procedures to protect personal information and respond to complaints and inquiries about their privacy procedures, train staff regarding these procedures, and clearly explain how the company handles privacy issues.[37]

- ***Identifying purposes.*** Companies must identify the purposes for which they collect personal information at or before the time of collection. PIPEDA allows companies to communicate the purpose orally or in writing. To use information for a new purpose that was not identified at collection, companies must obtain the individual's consent for the new purpose.[38]

- ***Consent.*** With some exceptions, companies must obtain knowing consent of individuals before collecting, using, or disclosing their personal information. Companies generally should obtain consent when they collect the data. The law allows companies to obtain consent via a number of methods, including an application form, a checkoff box, orally, or at the time that the individuals use the company's product or service. Individuals "may withdraw consent at any time, subject to legal or contractual restrictions and reasonable notice." PIPEDA allows limited exceptions to the consent requirement, including legal, medical, and security reasons.[39]

- ***Limiting collection.*** Companies may only collect personal information that is "necessary for the purposes identified by the organization." This applies both to the volume and types of information that companies collect. For instance, if a company collects personal information in order to provide telecommunications services, it likely cannot justify collecting customers' health information. Companies also must collect information by "fair and lawful means." They cannot deceive customers to obtain the information, and they must comply with all other legal requirements.[40]

- ***Limiting use, disclosure, and retention.*** Companies may only disclose and use personal information for the stated purposes. For example, if a retailer obtains a customer's address in order to process a purchase, it may not sell

---

37 PIPEDA § 4.1.
38 PIPEDA § 4.2.
39 PIPEDA § 4.3 ("For example, legal, medical, or security reasons may make it impossible or impractical to seek consent. When information is being collected for the detection and prevention of fraud or for law enforcement, seeking the consent of the individual might defeat the purpose of collecting the information. Seeking consent may be impossible or inappropriate when the individual is a minor, seriously ill, or mentally incapacitated. In addition, organizations that do not have a direct relationship with the individual may not always be able to seek consent. For example, seeking consent may be impractical for a charity or a direct-marketing firm that wishes to acquire a mailing list from another organization. In such cases, the organization providing the list would be expected to obtain consent before disclosing personal information.").
40 PIPEDA § 4.4.

that information to a third-party marketing firm unless that purpose was explicitly stated (and consent was obtained). Companies also must dispose of personal information once it is "no longer required to fulfil the identified purposes."[41]

- *Accuracy.* Companies must ensure that the personal information they maintain is "as accurate, complete, and up-to-date as is necessary for the purposes for which it is to be used." This principle is intended to reduce the likelihood that a decision about an individual (e.g., an employment offer or credit approval) is made based on inaccurate information.[42]

- *Safeguards.* Whereas many of the principles focus more on privacy concerns with personal information, this principle is more directly targeted at data security. The principle generally requires companies to protect personal information with security safeguards that are "appropriate to the sensitivity of the information." Companies should implement three types of safeguards: (1) physical measures (e.g., limiting access to offices where personal information is stored); (2) organizational measures (e.g., requiring background checks for employees who have access to particularly sensitive personal information); and (3) technological measures (e.g., encryption). The statute requires companies to ensure that employees understand that they must protect the confidentiality of all personal information.[43]

The Privacy Commissioner of Canada, which oversees implementation of PIPEDA, stated that the following are examples of "reasonable" safeguards:

- o Risk management
- o Security policies
- o Human resources security
- o Physical security
- o Technical security
- o Incident management
- o Business continuity planning.[44]

The Privacy Commissioner suggests that companies consider the following factors when assessing the reasonableness of security safeguards:

- o Sensitivity of the personal information
- o Foreseeable risks
- o Likelihood of damage occurring
- o Medium and format of the record containing the personal information

---

41 PIPEDA § 4.5.
42 PIPEDA § 4.6.
43 PIPEDA § 4.7.
44 Office of the Privacy Commissioner of Canada, Securing Personal Information: A Self-Assessment Tool for Organizations.

- o Potential harm that could be caused by an incident
- o Cost of preventative measures.[45]

- *Openness.* Companies must openly tell individuals how they handle personal information. The statute encourages companies to use a "generally understandable" form that includes: the contact information for the employee who is responsible for personal information policies and practices and receives complaints; how to access personal information; a description of the categories of personal information that the company maintains, and how it uses that information; "a copy of any brochures or other information that explain the organization's policies, standards, or codes"; and the personal information that is provided to affiliates, subsidiaries, and other corporate relatives. The notice about its privacy practices may be given online, provided over the phone, communicated via a brochure, or other methods.[46]

- *Individual access.* If a Canadian resident requests the personal information that a company has maintained, used, or disclosed about that resident, the company must provide that information to the individual, and allow the individual to challenge the accuracy and completeness of the information. The statute allows for some exception to this requirement, such as instances in which it would be "prohibitively costly" to provide the personal information to the individual, when there are legal restrictions on the disclosure, or if the information contains personal information about other individuals. The individual has the opportunity to challenge the completeness and accuracy of the data, and if the company fails to satisfactorily resolve the individual's concerns, the company must document "the substance of the unresolved challenge" and transmit those concerns to any third parties that have access to the individual's personal information.[47]

- *Challenging compliance.* Canada provides individuals with the right to challenge companies' compliance with PIPEDA. This is a marked difference from many U.S. federal privacy laws, such as Section 5 of the FTC Act and HIPAA, which are enforceable only by government agencies. In Canada, companies must implement a complaint process and make those procedures easily available to individuals. Companies are required to investigate all complaints and take appropriate measures to rectify any valid concerns.[48]

In 2015, Canada amended PIPEDA to require data breach notifications. If a company determines that a data breach "creates a real risk of significant harm to an individual," it must file a report with the Privacy Commissioner and notify

---

45 *Id.*
46 PIPEDA § 4.8.
47 PIPEDA § 4.9.
48 PIPEDA § 4.10.

the individual.[49] PIPEDA defines "significant harm" as including "bodily harm, humiliation, damage to reputation or relationships, loss of employment, business or professional opportunities, financial loss, identity theft, negative effects on the credit record and damage to or loss of property."[50] In determining whether a real risk of significant harm has arisen from a data breach, PIPEDA instructs companies to consider the sensitivity of the breached personal information, the probability that the information has been or will be misused, and any other prescribed factors.[51]

The breach notice must "contain sufficient information to allow the individual to understand the significance to them of the breach and to take steps, if any are possible, to reduce the risk of harm that could result from it or to mitigate that harm."[52] Notice must be provided "as soon as feasible" after the company determines that a breach has occurred.

Three provinces—Alberta, Quebec, and British Columbia—are not covered by PIPEDA because they have passed separate privacy and data security laws. These laws are substantially similar to PIPEDA and rely on the same basic concepts such as purpose limitation, consent, and openness.[53]

10.3 China

Although China has enacted some privacy and data security laws, it is unclear how aggressively the government or courts will enforce those laws, as China does not have government regulators that are as dedicated to data protection and privacy as those in the European Union and Canada. Indeed, China has long faced criticism for the restrictions it places on individuals' use of the Internet.[54] Nonetheless, there are a number of privacy and data security laws that apply to companies doing business in China, and the government has proposed further restrictions.

---

49 PIPEDA § 10.1.

50 *Id.*

51 *Id.*

52 *Id.*

53 *See* Office of the Privacy Commissioner of Canada, Legal Information Related to PIPEDA, Substantially Similar Provincial Legislation ("Several provincial statutes have also been deemed substantially similar to PIPEDA. Under paragraph 26(2)(b) of PIPEDA, the Governor in Council can exempt an organization, a class of organizations, an activity or a class of activities from the application of PIPEDA with respect to the collection, use or disclosure of personal information that occurs within a province that has passed legislation deemed to be substantially similar to the PIPEDA.").

54 Human Rights Watch, World Report 2015: China ("The Chinese government targeted the Internet and the press with further restrictions in 2014. All media are already subject to pervasive control and censorship. The government maintains a nationwide Internet firewall to exclude politically unacceptable information.").

In perhaps the most significant development, in 2016, the Standing Committee of the 12th National People's Congress passed the Cybersecurity Law of the People's Republic of China. The law, which went into effect on June 1, 2017, focuses on a number of issues, including personal information, critical infrastructure, and cybersecurity products. The law has 79 articles with a number of detailed requirements. A few of the key provisions are highlighted here.

It is difficult to predict with certainty how the new law will affect U.S. companies. According to an unofficial English language translation from the New America Foundation, the cybersecurity law imposes the following obligations on network operators:

1) Formulate internal security management systems and operating rules, determine persons who are responsible for cybersecurity, and implement cybersecurity protection responsibility;
2) Adopt technical measures to prevent computer viruses, cyber attacks, network intrusions, and other actions endangering cybersecurity;
3) Adopt technical measures for monitoring and recording network operational statuses and cybersecurity incidents, and follow provisions to store network logs for at least six months;
4) Adopt measures such as data classification, backup of important data, and encryption;
5) Other obligations provided by law or administrative regulations.[55]

The law requires network operators to take a number of reactive and proactive cybersecurity measures. "Providers of network products and services must not install malicious programs; when discovering that their products and services have security flaws or vulnerabilities, they shall immediately adopt remedial measures, and follow provisions to promptly inform users and report to the competent departments," the law instructs. "Providers of network products and services shall provide security maintenance for their products and services, and they must not terminate the provision of security maintenance during the time limits or period agreed on with clients."[56] The law requires "specialized cybersecurity products" and "critical network equipment" to "follow national standards and mandatory requirements, and be security certified by a qualified establishment or meet the requirements of a security inspection, before being sold or provided."[57] The law requires network operators to "provide technical support and assistance to public security organs and national security organs that are safeguarding national security and investigating criminal activities in accordance with the law."[58]

---

55 Rogier Creemers, Paul Triolo, & Graham Webster, New America Foundation, Translation: Cybersecurity Law of the People's Republic of China (Effective June 1, 2017), Art. 21.
56 *Id.* at Art. 22.
57 *Id.* at Art. 23.
58 *Id.* at Art. 28.

The cybersecurity law also establishes a number of mechanisms for protecting personal information. Network providers that collect and use personal information must "abide by the principles of legality, propriety, and necessity; they shall publish rules for collection and use, explicitly stating the purposes, means, and scope for collecting or using information, and obtain the consent of the persons whose data is gathered."[59] The law does not specify precisely how to comply with those principles. The law restricts the actions that companies may take to obtain personal information: companies may not "steal or use other illegal methods to acquire personal information, and must not unlawfully sell or unlawfully provide others with personal information."[60]

Among the most publicized provisions of China's cybersecurity law is its data localization provision, which in many cases requires that a category of organizations known as "critical information infrastructure operators" that "gather or produce personal information or important data during operations within the mainland territory of the People's Republic of China, shall store it within mainland China."[61] The law states that critical information infrastructure operators are organizations whose destruction, loss of functionality, or data leakage "might seriously endanger national security, national welfare, the people's livelihood, or the public interest."[62]

The cybersecurity law was not China's first official statement involving security. In 2013, China expanded on its expectations for Internet and telecommunications companies' handling of personal information when China's Ministry of Industry and Information Technology released the Information Security Technology Guidelines for Personal Information Protection on Public and Commercial Service Information Systems.[63] According to an unofficial English translation, these advisory guidelines define "personal information" as "[c]omputer data that is handled in computer systems that are related to a specific natural person, and that can be used independently or in combination with other information to distinguish that specific natural person."[64] The voluntary guidelines present eight principles:

- *Clear purpose.* Companies must have a "specific, clear, and reasonable purpose" to handle personal information, and they may not alter that purpose unless the data subject is first made aware of the change.

---

59 *Id.* at Art. 41.
60 *Id.* at Art. 44.
61 *Id.* at Art. 37. If it is "truly necessary" to transfer data abroad, the operators must abide by state-ordered procedures.
62 *Id.* at Art. 31.
63 Information Security Technology Guidelines for Personal Information Protection on Public and Commercial Service Information Systems (as translated on the China Copyright and Media blog, chinacopyrightandmedia.wordpress.com) (Aug. 9, 2013).
64 *Id.*

- *Least sufficient use.* Companies may only use "the smallest amount of information related to the purpose" that is necessary to accomplish the purpose, and must delete personal information "in the shortest time."
- *Open notification.* Companies must properly notify data subjects of their handling of personal information in "clear, easily understandable, and appropriate ways."
- *Individual consent.* Companies must obtain consent from data subjects *before* handling their personal information.
- *Quality guarantee.* Companies must guarantee that they will keep personal information "secret, intact, and usable."
- *Security guarantee.* Companies must implement sufficient administrative and technical safeguards "that are suited to the possibility and gravity of harm to personal information, protecting personal information security, preventing retrieval or disclosure of information without the authorization of the personal information, and the loss, leakage, destruction, and alteration of personal information."
- *Honest implementation.* Companies must abide by the promises that they made regarding the handling of personal information.
- *Clear responsibilities.* Companies must clarify the responsibilities for handling personal information and record handling processes so that they can be easily traced.[65]

Additionally, in 2012, a significant statement about privacy from the Chinese government came from the Standing Committee of the National People's Congress. The Standing Committee issued the Decision on Strengthening Network Information Protection ("Decision"), which imposed new privacy obligations on certain companies.[66] It is unclear precisely how broadly the decision is intended to apply. According to an unofficial English translation, the Decision applies to "internet service providers and other enterprises and institutions that collect or use citizens' personal electronic information in the course of their business."[67] The Decision requires these companies to "abide by the principles of legality, legitimacy, and necessity," and to "clearly indicate the objective, methods, and scope of collection and use of information, and obtain agreement from the person whose data is collected[.]"[68] The Decision also requires covered companies to "strictly preserve the secrecy of citizens' individual electronic information they collect in their business activities," and states that companies may not "divulge, distort, or damage" the data or "sell or illegally provide" the data to other persons. Covered companies are required to

---

65 *Id.*
66 National People's Congress Standing Committee Decision concerning Strengthening Network Information Protection (as translated on the China Copyright and Media blog, chinacopyrightandmedia.wordpress.com) (Dec. 29, 2012).
67 *Id.*
68 *Id.*

"adopt technological measures and other necessary measures to ensure information security and prevent ... citizens' individual electronic information collected during business activities [from being] divulged, damaged, or lost."[69]

In a 2015 report, European privacy experts criticized the "easily evident" shortcomings of the 2012 China decision, as compared with the EU data protection regime: "[I]t is lacking in scope (Internet only), in enforcement mechanism (none whatsoever), in basic data subject rights (none whatsoever), as well as, in its principle-setting (their list does not include all of the principles in the EU data protection approach)."[70] The EU report did, however, concede that if the China Decision is seen as a "first attempt" at data protection, "then the Decision does present certain merits, mostly in the form of basic data protection elements that may be found in its text."[71]

In 2013, China amended its Consumer Protection Law to reiterate the privacy principles of the Standing Committee's 2012 Decision restrictions on companies that collect and use the personal information of Chinese residents. According to an unofficial translation, the amendment states, in relevant part:

> Proprietors collecting and using consumers' personal information shall abide by principles of legality, propriety and necessity, explicitly stating the purposes, means and scope for collecting or using information, and obtaining the consumers' consent. Proprietors collecting or using consumers' personal information shall disclose their rules for their collection or use of this information, and must not collect or use information in violation of laws, regulations or agreements between the parties.
>
> Proprietors and their employees must keep consumers' personal information they collect strictly confidential and must not disclose, sell, or illegally provide it to others. Proprietors shall employ technical measures and other necessary measures to ensure information security, and to prevent consumers' personal information from being disclosed or lost. In situations where information has been or might be disclosed or lost, proprietors shall immediately adopt remedial measures.
>
> Proprietors must not send commercial information to consumers without their consent or upon their request of consumers, or where they have clearly refused it.[72]

---

69 *Id.*

70 EUROPEAN PARLIAMENT, DIRECTORATE-GENERAL FOR INTERNAL POLICIES, POLICY DEPARTMENT, CITIZENS' RIGHTS AND CONSTITUTIONAL AFFAIRS, THE DATA PROTECTION REGIME IN CHINA (2015).

71 *Id.*

72 Consumer Protection Law art. 29 (as translated by China Law Translate, http://chinalawtranslate.com/consumer-protection-law-including-2013-amendments/?lang=en).

Moreover, the amended law states that businesses "who harm consumers' human dignity, infringe upon consumers' personal freedom or upon consumers' lawful right to protect personal information, shall cease infringement, restore consumers' reputation, eliminate the impact, make formal apologies, and compensate consumers for losses."[73]

These amendments to the Consumer Protection Law impose fairly stringent general restrictions on companies that handle personal information, similar to the principles in the European Union's GDPR.[74] However, some commentators have questioned how aggressively this law can be enforced, as China does not have data protection authorities similar to those in the European Union.[75]

10.4 Mexico

In 2010, Mexico enacted the Federal Law on the Protection of Personal Data Possessed by Private Persons. Many of the restrictions and rights specified in this law are similar to those in the EU data protection regime, though they are not identical. A key difference is that unlike the European Union, Mexico does not restrict the export of personal information to countries with "adequate" privacy protections. Additionally, Mexico's law places a greater responsibility on data controllers, even when the data is in the hands of a third party.

Mexico's privacy law broadly applies to all privacy companies' processing and handling of Mexican residents' "personal data," which the statute defines as "[a]ny information concerning an identified or identifiable individual."[76] Mexico's law requires data controllers to adhere to the following principles:

- Controllers may not violate any **legal restrictions** on the collection and processing of personal data.[77]
- The law requires a "reasonable expectation of privacy" in all instances in which personal data is processed, recognizing "the trust any one person

---

73 *Id*. at art. 29.

74 *See* Tiffany Li & Zhou Zhou, *Who Cares About Chinese Privacy Law? Well, You Should*, THE PRIVACY ADVISOR (Sept 21, 2015) ("So while Chinese privacy law is still fairly undeveloped, China has made significant strides in recent years to create new laws governing data privacy and confidentiality of personal information. Some of the major principles inherent in the highest level Chinese privacy laws are similar to international privacy norms[.]").

75 EUROPEAN PARLIAMENT, THE DATA PROTECTION REGIME IN CHINA, *supra* note 70 ("[I]f judged from a data protection point of view the amended Chinese consumer law could not possibly amount to a data protection regime, because it is missing both in scope (purpose of the legislation) as well as in principles, rights and enforcement mechanism.").

76 Official English translation of the Federal Law on Protection of Personal Data Held by Private Parties (via Mexico's National Institute of Transparency, Access to Information and Protection of Personal Data).

77 *Id*. at art. 7.

places in another for personal data provided to be treated pursuant to any agreement of the parties in the terms established by this Law."[78] The law prohibits companies from obtaining data **deceptively or fraudulently**.[79]

- In general, controllers must obtain **consent** from data subjects before their personal data is collected or processed. Consent may be inferred if the individual receives a privacy notice disclosing the processing and does not object. Otherwise, Mexico's law requires express consent, and it allows consent to be provided verbally, in writing, electronically, via other technology, or "by unmistakable indications." Consent for financial or asset data processing must be provided expressly. Individuals may revoke consent at any time.[80]

  o *Consent for sensitive personal data.* The statute imposes more stringent consent requirements for the processing of "sensitive personal data," which is defined as personal data "touching on the most private areas of the data owner's life, or whose misuse might lead to discrimination or involve a serious risk for said data owner." Among the categories of personal data that the statute categorizes as sensitive are those that reveal "racial or ethnic origin, present and future health status, genetic information, religious, philosophical and moral beliefs, union membership, political views, [and] sexual preference." For such sensitive personal data, controllers must obtain express written consent from the data owner via a signature, electronic signature, "or any authentication mechanism established for such purpose."[81]

  Exceptions to consent. The statute does not require consent in the following circumstances: (1) any law allows processing without consent, (2) the personal data is publicly available, (3) the data is subject to a "prior dissociation procedure," (4) the processing fulfills a "legal relationship" between the data owner and controller, (5) "an emergency situation that could potentially harm an individual in his person or property," (6) the processing is necessary for health treatment, or (7) a "competent authority" issues a resolution.

- The controller is responsible for ensuring that the personal data is **correct, up-to-date, and relevant**. Once the data is "no longer necessary for the fulfillment of the objectives set forth in the privacy notice and applicable law," the controller must delete the data.[82]

- Personal data may only be processed for the **purposes** articulated in the privacy notice.[83]

---

78 *Id.*
79 *Id.*
80 *Id.* at art. 8.
81 *Id.* at art. 9.
82 *Id.* at art. 11.
83 *Id.* at art. 12.

- Personal data may only be processed "as **necessary, appropriate and relevant** with relation to the purposes set out in the privacy notice." The statute explicitly requires controllers to "make reasonable efforts to limit the processing period" of sensitive personal data to the minimum required.[84]
- Data controllers are responsible for ensuring compliance with Mexico's privacy laws, even if the data is processed by a third party at the controller's request. The statue requires the controller to take "all necessary and sufficient action" to ensure that all **third parties** respect the privacy notice that has been provided to the individual.[85]
- Controllers must provide a **privacy notice** that informs individuals "what information is collected on them and why."[86] Notices must contain (1) identity and domicile of the controller; (2) purposes for the processing; (3) options for data subjects to limit use or disclosure of the data; (4) procedures for individuals to exercise rights of access, rectification, cancellation, or objection; (5) if applicable, where the data will be transferred; and (6) how individuals will be notified of changes to the privacy notice.[87]

The law also provides data owners the following rights regarding their personal information:

- Access to their personal information;[88]
- Rectification of inaccurate or incomplete personal information;[89]
- The ability to "cancel" their personal data,[90] subject to a number of exceptions;[91] and
- The right to "object" to their personal data being processed.[92]

In addition to these general privacy-related principles, Mexico's privacy law requires all processors of personal data to implement physical, technical, and administrative data security safeguards.[93] Although Mexico's privacy statute does not specify the necessary safeguards, the Ministry of the Economy has elaborated on the security requirements in regulations that implemented the statute.[94]

---

84 *Id.* at art. 13.
85 *Id.* at art. 14.
86 *Id.* at art. 15.
87 *Id.* at art. 16.
88 *Id.* at art. 23.
89 *Id.* at art. 24.
90 *Id.* at art. 25.
91 *Id.* at art. 26.
92 *Id.* at art. 27.
93 *Id.* at art. 19.
94 Official English Translation of Regulations to the Federal Law on the Protection of Personal Data Held by Private Parties (Dec. 21, 2011).

According to the regulations, data controllers must consider the following factors when determining security measures for personal data:

- "Inherent risk" for the type of data
- Sensitivity of the data
- Technological development
- Potential consequences for the individuals if the security is violated[95]

Controllers also should attempt to account for the number of data subjects whose personal information is stored, previous vulnerabilities that the controllers have encountered, the risk based on the value that the personal data might have to an unauthorized third party, and other factors that impact risk or result from other laws or regulations.[96]

The regulations state that controllers must take the following actions, at minimum, to secure personal data:

- Inventory all processing systems and personal data.
- Determine duties of personal data processors.
- Conduct a risk analysis for personal data.
- Establish security measures.
- Conduct a gap analysis to determine the necessary security measures that are missing.
- Develop a plan to fill the gaps identified in the gap analysis.
- Review and audit data security.
- Provide data security training for all personnel.
- Maintain records of personal data storage media.[97]

Controllers are required to document all of these security measures, and to update them.[98]

If a breach occurs, the controller must undertake an "exhaustive review of the magnitude of the breach[.]"[99] If the review concludes that the breach significantly prejudices the data subjects' property or rights, the controller is required to issue a breach notification to the data subject "without delay[.]"[100] The notice must include, at a minimum, (1) a description of the breach, (2) an inventory of the types of personal data that potentially were compromised, (3) recommendations for the data subject to protect his or her interests, (4) "corrective actions implemented immediately," and (5) instructions to obtain more

---

95 *Id.* at art. 60.
96 *Id.*
97 *Id.* at art. 61.
98 *Id.* at arts. 61–62.
99 *Id.* at art. 61.
100 *Id.*

information about the breach.[101] The controller also is required to conduct a thorough analysis of the cause of the breach and implement "corrective, preventative, and improvement steps" to avoid another breach in the future.[102]

10.5 Japan

In Japan, privacy and data security law largely is governed by a 2003 statute, the Act on the Protection of Personal Information (APPI).[103] The statute is similar to the comprehensive EU approach to data regulation, and certainly is more stringent than the U.S. sectoral approach. Indeed, Japan's privacy and data security protections are among the most comprehensive in Asia.

However, Japan's privacy law also lacks some of the features of Europe's. For instance, Japan does not impose additional restrictions on "sensitive" personal information. Moreover, unlike the European data protection regime, the APPI does not distinguish between controllers and processors. Japan's law also does not require other countries' data protection laws to be "adequate" before allowing a foreign data transfer.

Among the notable features of APPI is its relatively broad definition of the "personal information" that is protected by the statute. APPI defines "personal information" as "information about a living individual which can identify the specific individual by name, date of birth or other description contained in such information (including such information as will allow easy reference to other information and will enable the identification of the specific individual)."[104] In other words, Japan considers not only personal information to be data that could help identify an individual, but it also includes data that could lead to *other* data that could help identify an individual. The restrictions apply to all "business operators" that handle personal information.[105]

In 2015, Japan's legislature amended APPI, with the goal of implementing the new provisions by the end of 2017. Because some of the details of the implementation of the amended law have yet to be finalized and the English-language translation of the amendments is not yet available, this section summarizes the 2003 law, followed by an overview of reported changes.

Japan's privacy and data security laws, like those of Europe, suggest that personal information protection is a human right. APPI sets out a general "basic principle" that companies should cautiously handle Japanese residents'

---

101 *Id.* at art. 65.
102 *Id.* at art. 66.
103 Unofficial English Translation of the Act on the Protection of Personal Information (Act No. 57 of 2003), http://www.cas.go.jp/jp/seisaku/hourei/data/APPI.pdf.
104 *Id.* at art. 2.
105 *Id.*

personal information "under the philosophy of respecting the personalities of individuals[.]"[106]

The following are among the key duties that 2003 APPI imposes on business operators that handle Japanese residents' personal information:

- **_Purpose of utilization._** Business operators must specify the "purpose of utilization" when they handle personal information, and they may not unreasonably change the scope of that purpose. Business operators must obtain _prior consent_ to handle personal information beyond the initial scope stated in the purpose of utilization.[107]

- **_Proper acquisition._** Business operators may not use "deception or other wrongful means" to acquire personal information.[108]

- **_Notice._** At the time that a business operator obtains personal information, it must "promptly notify" the individual of the purpose of utilization (either directly or via a public announcement). The notice requirement does not apply if the notice could harm individuals or property or the rights or legitimate interests of the business operator. The notice requirement also does not apply when it is necessary to comply with law enforcement or if the purpose "is clear in consideration of the circumstances of the acquisition."[109]

- **_Accuracy._** Business operators must "endeavor to maintain" accurate and up-to-date personal information that is "necessary" to achieve the purpose of utilization.[110]

- **_Security controls._** The statute requires business operators to "take necessary and proper measures for the prevention of leakage, loss, or damage, and for other security control of the personal data."[111] The statute does not specify the particular safeguards that businesses must implement to satisfy this requirement.

- **_Employee supervision._** Business operators must "exercise necessary and appropriate supervision" to ensure that employees properly handle personal information.[112]

- **_Transfers to third parties._** Business operators generally may not provide personal information to third parties without prior consent from the data subjects. This prohibition does not apply in a few exceptional cases: (1) if the transfer is based on laws or regulations, (2) if the transfer is necessary to protect individuals or property and consent is difficult to obtain, (3) if public

---

106 _Id._ at art. 3.
107 _Id._ at arts. 15–16.
108 _Id._ at art. 17.
109 _Id._ at art. 18.
110 _Id._ at art. 19.
111 _Id._ at art. 20.
112 _Id._ at art. 21.

health or child welfare is involved and consent is difficult to obtain, and (4) if it is necessary to cooperate with government.[113]

- **Public privacy notice.** Business operators must post a publicly accessible document that contains the following information: (1) the name of the business operator who is handling the personal information, (2) the purpose of utilization for retained personal data, (3) procedures for handling requests regarding personal information from data subjects, and (4) any other information required by Cabinet Order.[114]

- **Correction of data.** Business operators generally must correct, add, or delete personal data at the request of the data subject.[115]

- **Discontinuance.** APPI provides data subjects with the right to request a business to "discontinue using or to erase such retained personal data as may lead to the identification of the person on the ground that the retained personal data" violates certain provisions of the Act.[116]

In September 2015, the Japanese National Diet passed a bill that contained the first significant amendments to APPI since its passage more than a decade earlier. The changes went into effect in 2017. Here are some of the significant changes:[117]

- Allowing companies to share certain data with third parties unless the data subject "opts out" (a more lenient standard than the 2003 law's opt-in requirement).[118]

- Under certain circumstances, disclosure of anonymized or pseudonymous data will not require individual consent.[119]

- Additional protection for "sensitive information," similar to the European Union.[120]

- The creation of a Privacy Protection Commission, which will enforce Japan's privacy law. The commission, which was formed in August 2016, will determine many of the details of the implementation of the amended law.[121]

In an analysis of the amendments to APPI, law firm Alston & Bird noted some similarities to the GDPR: "For example, most of the provisions under the

---

113 *Id.* at art. 23.
114 *Id.* at art. 24.
115 *Id.* at art. 26.
116 *Id.* at art. 27.
117 Brian Caster, DLA Piper, *New Amendments to Japanese Privacy Law* (Sept. 26, 2015); Eric Kosinski, White and Case, *Transfer of Personal Data Under Japan's Amended Personal Information Protection Act* (Oct. 3, 2015).
118 Caster, *supra* note 117; Kosinski, *supra* note 117.
119 Caster, *supra* note 117; Kosinski, *supra* note 117.
120 Caster, *supra* note 117; Kosinski, *supra* note 117.
121 Caster, *supra* note 117; Kosinski, *supra* note 117.

Amended APPI will have extra-territorial applications if entities outside Japan collect personal information through the supply of goods or services to individuals in Japan even when entities do not have offices in Japan. The Amended APPI will also introduce a new cross-border data transfer framework. Under the new cross-border data transfer framework, individuals' prior consent is required for cross-border transfer of personal data unless one of the exemptions applies."[122]

---

122 Maki DePalo, *May 30 Is Fast Approaching—Are You Ready for Compliance with the Amended Act on Protection of Personal Information in Japan?*, ALSTON & BIRD PRIVACY BLOG (Apr. 11, 2017).

11

Cyber and the Law of War

Increasingly, cyberattacks against the United States are attributed to other nations. In particular, Russia, North Korea, Iran, and China have engaged in persistent hostile cyber campaigns against U.S. government and private sector systems. China obtained U.S. workers' security applications from the Office of Personnel Management. North Korea launched an aggressive campaign against Sony Entertainment. Russia hacked the computers of U.S. political campaigns during the 2016 election.[1]

International legal norms provide the framework for responding to such actions. This chapter provides a high-level overview of the criteria that nations use to determine whether they have the right to engage in self-defense. Our international legal system has developed a set of rules that govern both the criteria that justify going to war (known as *jus ad bellum*) and the rules of conduct that apply once war has begun (*jus in bello*). *Jus ad bellum* is governed by a number of international agreements, most notably the United Nations Charter. Other agreements, most notably the Geneva Conventions, govern *jus in bello*. This chapter focuses on *jus ad bellum*.

The rules for *jus ad bellum* are based on decades of agreements, international legal precedent, and informal understandings among countries. Accordingly, the rules apply most easily to purely kinetic attacks, such as the use of ground troops or bombs. These legal norms, however, do not explicitly apply to cyberattacks. The United Nations Charter was signed in 1945, and the Geneva Conventions were signed four years later. Cyberwarfare, let alone the modern Internet, was not a factor as these rules first developed.

In 2009, recognizing the need to understand how these rules apply to modern cyberwarfare, Michael Schmitt, a professor at the U.S. Naval War College, convened a group of international legal experts, via the NATO Cooperative Cyber

---

1 Much of this chapter appeared in a book chapter, written by this book's author, in HOUBING SONG ET AL. (eds.), SECURITY AND PRIVACY IN CYBER-PHYSICAL SYSTEMS: FOUNDATIONS, PRINCIPLES AND APPLICATIONS (Wiley, 2017).

Cybersecurity Law, Second Edition. Jeff Kosseff.
© 2020 John Wiley & Sons, Inc. Published 2020 by John Wiley & Sons, Inc.
Companion Website: www.wiley.com/go/kosseff/cybersecurity2e

Defence Centre of Excellence, "in an effort to examine how extant legal norms apply to this new form of cyber warfare."[2] In 2013, the group produced the *Tallinn Manual*, which reviews applicable international law and sets forth 95 blackletter rules that describe how they might apply to cyberwarfare. In 2017, the group released *Tallinn Manual 2.0*, which expanded to 154 rules and addressed developments in cyber threats and warfare. It is important to note that the *Tallinn Manual* is not a definitive list of binding legal rules. In fact, there were a number of important issues on which the group of legal experts were unable to reach a consensus, demonstrating the difficulty of applying traditional law-of-war principles to the cyber domain. However, the *Tallinn Manual* is the clearest and most useful international guidance to date regarding the many questions regarding cyber and the law of armed conflict. As a 2017 article aptly described, the *Tallinn Manual* is "a tremendously useful starting point for assessing the challenging intersection of many areas of the law."[3]

This chapter focuses on *jus ad bellum*. Specifically, it asks: When is an action in cyberspace a use of force that violates international legal principles? And what types of responses are warranted by a state whose systems were attacked?

This framework draws on the analytical framework from the *Tallinn Manual*, International Court of Justice rulings, and other binding and non binding statements of international law. The following questions guide the *jus ad bellum* analysis:

- Was the cyberattack a "use of force" that violates international law?
- If the attack was a use of force, was that force attributable to a state?
- Did the use of force constitute an "armed attack" that entitles the target to self-defense?
- If the use of force was an armed attack, what types of self-defense are justified?
- If the nation experiences hostile cyber actions that fall short of use of force or armed attacks, what options are available?

11.1   Was the Cyberattack a "Use of Force" that Violates International Law?

This chapter focuses on cyberattacks that constitute a "use of force." Although other acts—such as the theft of government employees' background check application information—may raise serious national security concerns, they

---

2 Michael N. Schmitt, ed., Tallinn Manual 2.0 on the International Law Applicable to Cyber Operations (2017) (hereinafter "Tallinn Manual"), at 1.
3 Robert E. Barnsby & Shane R. Reeves, *Give Them an Inch, They'll Take a Terabyte: How States May Interpret* Tallinn Manual 2.0's *International Human Rights Chapter*, 95 Tex. L. Rev. 1515, 1529 (2017).

generally do not rise to the level of a use of force. As Herbert S. Lin wrote in 2010, "[b]ased largely on historical precedents, nations appear to agree that a variety of unfriendly actions, including unfavorable trade decisions, space-based surveillance, boycotts, severance of diplomatic relations, denial of communications, espionage, economic competition or sanctions, and economic and political coercion do not rise to the threshold of a use of force, regardless of the scale of their effects."[4]

Rule 68 of the *Tallinn Manual* states that a cyber operation "that constitutes a threat or use of force against the territorial integrity or political independence of any State, or that is in any other manner inconsistent with the purposes of the United Nations, is unlawful."[5] The concept of "use of force" originates from Article 2(4) of the United Nations Charter, which states that UN members "shall refrain in their international relations from the threat or use of force against the territorial integrity or political independence of any State, or in any other manner inconsistent with the Purposes of the United Nations."[6] Article 51 of the United Nations Charter creates a limited exception to this general rule, stating that the charter shall not "impair the inherent right of individual or collective self-defense if an armed attack occurs against a Member of the United Nations."[7] (We discuss what constitutes an "armed attack" later in this section.)

Some legal experts long believed that a "use of force" could only be a traditional, kinetic attack, such as a bombing. As one report on the subject noted, the traditional law of armed conflict "emphasizes death or physical injury to people and destruction of physical property as criteria for the definitions of 'use of force' and 'armed attack.'"[8] As cyber has emerged as an integral part of our economy and everyday lives, however, it has become largely accepted that some cyberattacks can constitute unlawful use of force that implicate warfare law. As Matthew Waxman wrote, "[o]ffensive cyber attack capabilities such as taking down government or private computer systems share some similarities with kinetic military force, economic coercion and subversion, yet also have unique characteristics and are evolving rapidly." Waxman argues that the potential for such attacks "raises difficult line-drawing questions and requires re-examination of previous US legal strategy toward Charter interpretation."[9]

So, what is a "use of force?" The United Nations Charter does not provide a comprehensive definition of the term. The authors of the *Tallinn Manual*

---

4 Herbert S. Lin, *Offensive Cyber Operations and the Use of Force*, 4 J. OF NAT'L SECURITY L. & POL'Y 63, 72 (2010).

5 TALLINN MANUAL at 329.

6 U.N. Charter art. 2(4).

7 *Id.*, art. 51.

8 W. OWENS ET AL., eds., TECHNOLOGY, POLICY, LAW, AND ETHICS REGARDING U.S. ACQUISITION AND USE OF CYBERATTACK CAPABILITIES (National Research Council, 2009), 253.

9 Matthew Waxman, *Cyber Attacks as "Force" Under UN Charter Article 2(4)*, 87 INT'L L. STUD. 43 (2011).

reviewed the history of the charter's drafting in 1945 and observed that the drafters refused to include economic coercion as a use of force. The *Tallinn Manual* also notes that the United Nations General Assembly stated that the "use of force" does not necessarily include *all* "forms of pressure, including those of a political or economic character, which have the effect of threatening the territorial integrity or political independence of any State."[10]

The most authoritative guidance as to what constitutes a use of force comes from a 1986 ruling in *Nicaragua v. United States* by the International Court of Justice, which adjudicates disputes under the United Nations Charter.[11] In that case, Nicaragua claimed that the United States engaged in an unlawful use of force by supporting the Contras, a group that was rebelling against the Nicaraguan government. The Court agreed with Nicaragua, concluding that "the arming and training of the *contras* can certainly be said to involve the threat or use of force against Nicaragua[.]" However, the Court also concluded that "the mere supply of funds to the *contras,* while undoubtedly an act of intervention in the internal affairs of Nicaragua ... does not in itself amount to a use of force." In other words, the Court found that intentionally providing weapons to be used against a state is a use of force; merely providing funds does not necessarily constitute use of force. Applying this precedent, the authors of the *Tallinn Manual* concluded that "a State that provides an organized armed group with malware and the training necessary to carry out cyber operations against another State has engaged in a use of force against the latter so long as that supply and training enable the group to conduct cyber operations that amount to a use of force."[12]

To determine whether a cyber act constitutes a use of force, the authors of the *Tallinn Manual* developed a multifactor balancing test. The factors to consider are:

- **Severity:** The *Tallinn Manual* authors conclude that severity is the most important factor in determining whether an act in cyberspace constitutes a use of force.[13]
- **Immediacy:** A cyberattack is more likely to constitute an unlawful use of force if its effects are immediate.[14]
- **Directness:** If a cyberattack is highly attenuated from its eventual effects, it is less likely to be an unlawful use of force. Therefore, a direct attack that damages a system is far more likely to be a use of force than the propagation of a botnet that eventually reaches the same system and causes a slowdown.

---

10 TALLINN MANUAL at 331.
11 Nicaragua v. United States, 1986 I.C.J. 14 (June 27).
12 TALLINN MANUAL at 332.
13 TALLINN MANUAL at 334.
14 *Id.*

- **Invasiveness**: The *Tallinn Manual* defines invasiveness as the extent to which cyberattacks "intrude into the target State or its cyber systems contrary to the interests of that State."[15] A cyberattack on a device that is operated by the government or a military contractor is more likely to constitute a use of force than a cyberattack on a physical system that is operated by a company that is entirely unrelated to the government's interests.
- **Measurability of effects**: A cyberattack is more likely to be seen as a use of force if its effects are readily visible and quantifiable.[16] For instance, a cyberattack on a manufacturing plant likely could be easily quantified in terms of the number of machines damaged and the harm caused, making it more likely to be seen as a use of force.
- **Military character**: A cyberattack that is connected to the military is more likely to be seen as a use of force as one that is not.[17] For instance, a cyberattack deployed by military cyber operators is more likely to be seen as a use of force than one carried out by a private actor.
- **State involvement**: Similarly, the *Tallinn Manual* states that if a government's nonmilitary actors—such as intelligence agencies—are involved in a cyberattack, the attack is more likely to be viewed as a use of force.[18]

It is important to note that each of these factors, standing alone, often does not provide a dispositive answer as to whether a cyberattack constitutes an unlawful use of force (though in some cases, severity will be dispositive).[19] A government would consider all of these factors and the totality of the circumstances surrounding a cyberattack to determine whether it has experienced a use of force.

11.2 If the Attack Was a Use of Force, Was that Force Attributable to a State?

States are only responsible for cyberattacks that are "attributable" to them.[20] An act is attributable to a state if it is carried out by an "organ" of the state, such as the military, an intelligence agency, or another government agency. The

---

15 *Id.*
16 *Id.* at 335.
17 *Id.* at 336.
18 *Id.*
19 *Id.* at 337.
20 *See* Ido Kilovaty, *Evaluation in the Light of the* Tallinn Manual *on the International Law Applicable to Cyber Warfare*, Cyber Warfare and the Jus Ad Bellum Challenges, at 105 (2014) ("A state engaging in self-defense measures must first identify the state responsible for the armed attack. The assumption of state responsibility for international law is that a state can be held liable if the illegal acts or omission[s] were conducted on behalf of the state by a state organ, or if the state instructed, gave directions or controlled the non-state entity.").

nonbinding Draft Articles on Responsibility of States for Internationally Wrongful Acts, which sets the general analytical framework for attribution, indicates that the conduct "of any State organ shall be considered an act of that State under international law, whether the organ exercises legislative, executive, judicial or any other functions, whatever position it holds in the organization of the State, and whatever its character as an organ of the central Government or of a territorial unit of the State."[21]

The primary exception to that rule is if a state later condones actions taken by a private entity. The Draft Articles on Responsibility notes that conduct "which is not attributable to a State under the preceding articles shall nevertheless be considered an act of that State under international law if and to the extent that the State acknowledges and adopts the conduct in question as its own."[22] Thus, if an independent hacktivist launches a cyberattack that exploits a power grid in another country, the attack initially is not attributable to a state. However, if a state subsequently exploits that vulnerability by using it to launch its own attacks, then the initial attack can be attributable to the state as well.

To be sure, attribution is not an easy task, even for nations with sophisticated cyber forensics operations. As the U.S. Office of the Director of National Intelligence wrote in its 2018 *Guide to Cyber Attribution*: "There is no simple technical process or automated solution to determine responsibility for cyber operations. This painstaking work in many cases requires several weeks or months of analyzing intelligence and forensics."[23]

11.3 Did the Use of Force Constitute an "Armed Attack" that Entitles the Target to Self-Defense?

Our analysis to this point has focused on whether a cyberattack is a use of force that violates international law. However, our inquiry does not end there. The logical follow-up question is whether that use of force entitles the target nation to respond with kinetic or cyber force.[24]

Under *jus ad bellum*, the answer to that question hinges on whether the initial action constitutes an "armed attack." Article 51 of the United Nations Charter states that nothing in the Charter "shall impair the inherent right of

---

21 United Nations Draft Articles on Responsibility of States for Internationally Wrongful Acts.

22 *Id.*

23 Office of the Director of National Intelligence, A Guide to Cyber Attribution (Sept. 14, 2018), at 2.

24 *See* Andrew C. Foltz, *Stuxnet, Schmitt Analysis, and the Cyber "Use-of-Force" Debate*, 67 JFQ (2012) ("Importantly, it is not the use of force, but rather an 'armed attack' that triggers a state's right to use force in self-defense.").

individual or collective self-defence if an armed attack occurs against a Member of the United Nations, until the Security Council has taken the measures necessary to maintain international peace and security."[25] The United States government has long contended that the distinction between use of force and armed attack is immaterial, and that any use of force triggers the right to self-defense. However, other nations believe that self-defense is permissible only in the event of an armed attack.

The Charter does not define "armed attack," but the International Court of Justice, in the *Nicaragua* opinion, wrote that an armed attack is "the most grave" form of "use of force." This means that an attack that qualifies as a "use of force" may not rise to the level of an "armed attack" that allows self-defense. The *Nicaragua* opinion does not provide an exhaustive definition of "armed attack," but noted that it is "not merely action by regular armed forces across an international border": it can also include "the sending by or on behalf of a State of armed bands, groups, irregulars or mercenaries, which carry out acts of armed force against another State of such gravity as to amount to … an armed attack."[26]

In the cyber context, it is clear that the bar is quite high for an action to constitute an armed attack.[27] The *Tallinn Manual*'s authors agree that certain acts, such as intelligence gathering and temporary interruption of noncritical services, are not armed attacks.[28] The *Manual*'s authors "took the view that the law is unclear as to the precise point at which the effects of a cyber operation qualify that operation as an armed attack."[29] They also agreed that it is "unsettled" as to whether acts that do not cause "injury, death, damage, or destruction, but which otherwise have extensive negative effects" are armed attacks.[30]

Since the September 11 attacks, officials in the United States and Europe have increasingly taken the position that self-defense includes not only retaliation for past attacks, but also the prevention of future imminent attacks. In 2002, the U.S. National Security Council wrote:

> The United States has long maintained the option of preemptive actions to counter a sufficient threat to our national security. The greater the threat, the greater is the risk of inaction—and the more

---

25 U.N. Charter art. 51.

26 Nicaragua v. United States, *supra* n. 11; TALLINN MANUAL at 344.

27 *See* W. Boothby et al., *When Is a Cyberattack a Use of Force or an Armed Attack?* 45 IEEE COMPUTER 8, 82–84 (2012) ("Not all cyberattacks are uses of force or armed attacks. In fact, no cyberattack to date has been proven to be an armed attack. However, it's technically feasible to carry out armed attacks in cyberspace, and some states have publicly acknowledged that cyberoperations are an indispensable part of modern warfare.").

28 TALLINN MANUAL at 341.

29 *Id.* at 342.

30 *Id.*

compelling the case for taking anticipatory action to defend ourselves, even if uncertainty remains as to the time and place of the
enemy's attack. To forestall or prevent such hostile acts by our
adversaries, the United States will, if necessary, act preemptively.[31]

Moreover, nations are increasingly viewing self-defense as an action that can
be done abroad, in addition to domestically. For instance, in 2003, the European
Council took a broad approach to self-defense:

Our traditional concept of self-defence—up to and including the
Cold War—was based on the threat of invasion. With the new
threats, the first line of defence will often be abroad.[32]

An attack on a cyber-physical system is more likely than other types of
cyberattacks to meet the armed-attack threshold.[33] Although not dispositive, a
use of force is more likely to be viewed as an armed attack if it causes physical
damage to property or individuals. If the number of cyber-physical attacks
increases in the coming years, this likely will lead to an increase in states' exercise of self-defensive measures.

It is important to note that the United States does not subscribe to the international law view that self-defense is permitted only in the context of an armed
attack. As Ryan Goodman wrote in 2018, "the United States has long maintained that a State can use force in self defense in response to any amount of
force by another state."[34]

11.4 If the Use of Force Was an Armed Attack, What Types of Self-Defense Are Justified?

Even when self-defense is permitted under *jus ad bellum*, the defender faces
significant limits as to the scope and method of response. The customary rules
of "necessity" and "proportionality" impose these restrictions.

---

31 U.S. National Security Council, The National Security Strategy of the United
States of America 6 (2002).
32 Council of the European Union, A Secure Europe in a Better World: European
Security Strategy (2003), at 7.
33 *See* Reese Nguyen, *Navigating Jus Ad Bellum in the Age of Cyber Warfare*, 101 Calif. L. Rev.
1079, 1084 (2013) (proposing that "cyber attacks constitute 'armed attack' when they are aimed at
causing irreversible disruption or physical damage to a cyber-physical system (CPS), which is a
physical system monitored or controlled by computers.").
34 Ryan Goodman, *Cyber Operations and the U.S. Definition of "Armed Attack,"* JustSecurity
(Mar. 8, 2018).

Under the rule of necessity, a nation "may be justified in taking certain measures which it considers to be 'necessary' for the protection of its essential security interests."[35] Although the necessity concept sounds rigid, in practice, it often is not a significant barrier to acts conducted in self-defense in response to attacks by other states. When a state is attacked by another state, scholars recently noted, "there seems to be an almost irrefutable presumption here that such a use of force in self-defense would pass the test of necessity."[36] However, if the state is responding to a nonstate actor, or if there is not an ongoing use of force, "necessity becomes a critical gateway for considering whether a forcible response is permitted at all."[37]

In the cyber realm, whether necessity exists turns on "the existence, or lack, of alternative courses of action that do not rise to the level of a use of force. Should passive (as distinct from active) cyber defences like firewalls be adequate to reliably and completely thwart a cyber armed attack, other measures, whether cyber or kinetic, at the level of use of force are impermissible."[38]

The rule of proportionality is separate from necessity. For self-defense to be proportional, the state must "limit self-defense actions to the amount of force required to defeat an ongoing attack or to deter a future attack."[39] Proportionality "serves to identify the situations in which the unilateral use of force is permissible; and it serves to determine the intensity and the magnitude of military action."[40]

To be sure, "proportionality" may have different meanings to different government officials and scholars. David Kretzmer noted that proportionality "is invariably an elusive concept" that "becomes even more so when used in a context which is as highly loaded as the right of a state to use force in self defense."[41] He posited that "the main source of disagreement and confusion flows from the lack of consensus over the legitimate ends of force employed by a state that is exercising its inherent right to self defense."[42]

Legal scholars have articulated various general guidelines for proportionality under *jus ad bellum*, though these frameworks do not contain bright-line rules. Proportionality has been described as requiring "an assessment as to whether

---

35 Oil Platforms (Islamic Republic of Iran v. United States of Am.), Judgment, I.C.J. Rep. 2003, p. 161 (Nov. 6, 2003).
36 D. Akande & T. Lieflander, *Clarifying Necessity, Imminence, and Proportionality in the Law of Self-Defense*, Am. J. Int'l L. 563 (2013).
37 *Id.*
38 Tallinn Manual at 349.
39 David E. Graham, *Cyber Threats and the Law of War*, 4 J. Nat'l Sec. L. & Pol'y 87, 89 (2010).
40 Enzo Cannizzaro, Contextualizing Proportionality: Jus Ad Bellum and Jus In Bello in the Lebanese War (International Review of the Red Cross 2006).
41 David Kretzmer, *The Inherent Right to Self-Defence and Proportionality in* Jus Ad Bellum, 24 European J. Int'l L. 235 (2013).
42 *Id.*

the overall evil a war would cause was balanced by the good that would be achieved."[43] In other words, even if a nation has been the victim of an armed attack, it must consider whether defensive actions would result, on balance, in social good. Of course, such a broad balancing test could be easily manipulated to reach a desired result. Proportionality does not mean that the defensive action must take the same magnitude or form as the initial armed attack. The authors of the *Tallinn Manual* believe that it is possible for a cyber-based act of self-defense to be appropriate in response to a kinetic use of force, or vice versa.[44]

The rules of necessity and proportionality require a state to closely examine the extent of an armed attack before determining a response. For instance, if State A launches a cyberattack that leads to a one-hour shutdown of a manufacturing plant in State B, it is unlikely that *jus ad bellum* would allow State B to respond with significant kinetic force, such as ground troops. However, if the cyberattack led to serious property damage and injuries to individuals, then it is far more likely that a significant kinetic or cyber response would be seen as necessary and proportionate.

It also is likely that, under *jus ad bellum*, a state would be justified in engaging in limited preventative measures if it has reason to believe that an attack on its systems is imminent. The state would be able to justify reasonable self-defensive actions as necessary to prevent imminent and immediate threats.

11.5 If the Nation Experiences Hostile Cyber Actions that Fall Short of Use of Force or Armed Attacks, What Options Are Available?

As evidenced by the constant barrage of threats that governments and businesses face, bad acts in cyberspace abound, often at the direction of state actors. But these cyber threats typically do not rise to the level of armed attack or even use of force. In those cases, nations are not entitled under international law to exercise self-defense (as discussed in Section 11.4). There are cases in which an aggressor does not use force, but does use cyber as a means to violate the state's sovereignty or intervene in its inherently domestic affairs, such as by interfering with its election systems. In those cases, the target state is entitled to use lower-intensity countermeasures, which are intended to cause the adversary to cease the unlawful acts.[45]

To be sure, countermeasures typically are more limited than many forms of self-defense that are used in response to armed attacks. The *Tallinn Manual* says that an injured state may only take countermeasures "to induce a

---

43 J. Gardam, *Proportionality and Force in International Law*, Am. J. Int'l L. 391 (1993).
44 Tallinn Manual at 349.
45 Articles on Responsibility at 75.

responsible State to comply with the legal obligations it owes an injured State,"[46] and countermeasures "must be proportionate to the injury to which they respond."[47] According to the *Draft Articles on Responsibility*, countermeasures "are not intended as a form of punishment for wrongful conduct, but as an instrument for achieving compliance with the obligations of the responsible State."[48]

Michael Schmitt, in a 2013 book, noted that "[f]ew, if any, cyber activities have crossed the armed attack threshold," although "malicious cyber operations below that level are commonplace."[49] Countermeasures, he wrote, "can prove an effective response option for States facing harmful cyber operations," though he cautioned that "due to various limitations on their use, they are no panacea."[50]

In a 2017 article, Eric Jensen and Sean Watts summarized the importance of countermeasures to cyber:

> Given the decentralized, self-governing nature of international law, countermeasures are an important form of international law self-help. The modern conception of countermeasures grew out of the traditional concept of reprisals and now replaces the traditional concept of nonforceful reprisals that occur outside of armed conflict.[51]

To understand when countermeasures could be used in cyberspace, consider a scenario in which State A continuously transmits malware to federal government computers of State B. The malware slows down government functions, but is not anywhere near the level of the use of force or armed attack. Still, it interferes with inherently governmental functions and infringes the sovereignty and governmental functions of State B. Under this scenario, State B likely would be entitled to deploy a targeted distributed denial-of-service (DDOS) attack on the State A computers that are the source of this malware. Had State A not transmitted the malware, State B's DDOS attack likely would have constituted an illegal infringement of State A's sovereignty. Yet because State A intervened in State B's domestic affairs, State B is permitted to exercise low-intensity countermeasures to cause State A to stop its illegal cyber operations.

---

46 TALLINN MANUAL at 116.
47 *Id*. at 127.
48 Articles on Responsibility at 130.
49 Michael N. Schmitt, *Cyber Activities and the Law of Countermeasures*, in PEACETIME REGIME FOR STATE ACTIVITIES IN CYBERSPACE (2013), at 659.
50 *Id*. at 660.
51 Eric Jensen & Sean Watts, *A Cyber Duty of Due Diligence: Gentle Civilizer or Crude Destabilizer?*, 95 TEX. L. REV. 1555, 1563 (2017).

Additionally, targets of cyber operations may take actions that are legal, yet nonetheless adversarial. For instance, a nation that is the target of a cyberattack may enact sanctions against the aggressor. The target also may launch a public campaign to attempt to convince the aggressor's leaders to cease their conduct. Such legal acts are known as retorsion.[52]

A nation also may gather information about the cyber capabilities of an adversary. There is no *per se* prohibition of the use of espionage under international law. The U.S. Department of Defense, for instance, states that "unauthorized intrusions into computer networks solely to acquire information" will be treated as "traditional intelligence and counter-intelligence activities under international law."[53]

Indeed, the concepts of countermeasures, retorsion, and espionage appear to have taken on even greater importance to U.S. military cyber operations in recent years, in recognition of the fact that the United States faces persistent cyber aggression which, though below the level of a use of force, poses substantial threats to national security, individual liberties, and the economy. In a September 2018 summary of its cyber strategy, the U.S. Defense Department stated that it will "defend forward to disrupt or halt malicious cyber activity at its source, including activity that falls below the level of armed conflict."[54] Such actions to "defend forward" necessarily rely on countermeasures and other responses that fall below the use-of-force threshold.

---

52 Troy Anderson, *Fitting a Virtual Peg into a Round Hole: Why Existing International Law Fails to Govern Cyber Reprisals*, 34 ARIZ. J. INT'L & COMP. L. 135 (2016) ("Examples of retorsion include: cessation of trade (that has not been contracted in an international agreement), suspension of diplomatic relations, and expulsion of diplomats, travelers, and other nationals of the country retaliated against; a quintessential example is found in the Obama administration's expulsion of Russian diplomats in response to the Russian cyber-attack of hacking.").
53 OFFICE OF GENERAL COUNSEL, DEPARTMENT OF DEFENSE, DEPARTMENT OF DEFENSE LAW OF WAR MANUAL (June 2015, updated December 2016), at 1016.
54 U.S. Department of Defense, *Summary, Department of Defense Cyber Strategy* (2018), at 1.

Appendix A

Text of Section 5 of the FTC Act

Section 5 of the Federal Trade Commission Act, described in Chapter 1, is the primary law under which the federal government regulates data security. Although the statute does not explicitly mention data security or cybersecurity, the FTC has long interpreted its prohibition on unfair and deceptive trade practices as authority for the Commission to penalize companies for particularly egregious data security practices.

[15 U.S.C.] §45. Unfair methods of competition unlawful; prevention by Commission

(a) **Declaration of unlawfulness; power to prohibit unfair practices; inapplicability to foreign trade**

(1) Unfair methods of competition in or affecting commerce, and unfair or deceptive acts or practices in or affecting commerce, are hereby declared unlawful.

(2) The Commission is hereby empowered and directed to prevent persons, partnerships, or corporations, except banks, savings and loan institutions described in section 57a(f)(3) of this title, Federal credit unions described in section 57a(f)(4) of this title, common carriers subject to the Acts to regulate commerce, air carriers and foreign air carriers subject to part A of subtitle VII of title 49, and persons, partnerships, or corporations insofar as they are subject to the Packers and Stockyards Act, 1921, as amended [7 U.S.C. 181 *et seq.*], except as provided in section 406(b) of said Act [7 U.S.C. 227(b)], from using unfair methods of competition in or affecting commerce and unfair or deceptive acts or practices in or affecting commerce.

(3) This subsection shall not apply to unfair methods of competition involvingcommercewithforeignnations(otherthanimportcommerce)unless—

Cybersecurity Law, Second Edition. Jeff Kosseff.
© 2020 John Wiley & Sons, Inc. Published 2020 by John Wiley & Sons, Inc.
Companion Website: www.wiley.com/go/kosseff/cybersecurity2e

(A)   such methods of competition have a direct, substantial, and reasonably foreseeable effect—

(i) on commerce which is not commerce with foreign nations, or on import commerce with foreign nations; or

(ii) on export commerce with foreign nations, of a person engaged in such commerce in the United States; and

(B)   such effect gives rise to a claim under the provisions of this subsection, other than this paragraph.

If this subsection applies to such methods of competition only because of the operation of subparagraph (A)(ii), this subsection shall apply to such conduct only for injury to export business in the United States.

(4)   (A) For purposes of subsection (a), the term "unfair or deceptive acts or practices" includes such acts or practices involving foreign commerce that—

(i)   cause or are likely to cause reasonably foreseeable injury within the United States; or

(ii) involve material conduct occurring within the United States.

(B)   All remedies available to the Commission with respect to unfair and deceptive acts or practices shall be available for acts and practices described in this paragraph, including restitution to domestic or foreign victims.

(b) Proceeding by Commission; modifying and setting aside orders

Whenever the Commission shall have reason to believe that any such person, partnership, or corporation has been or is using any unfair method of competition or unfair or deceptive act or practice in or affecting commerce, and if it shall appear to the Commission that a proceeding by it in respect thereof would be to the interest of the public, it shall issue and serve upon such person, partnership, or corporation a complaint stating its charges in that respect and containing a notice of a hearing upon a day and at a place therein fixed at least thirty days after the service of said complaint. The person, partnership, or corporation so complained of shall have the right to appear at the place and time so fixed and show cause why an order should not be entered by the Commission requiring such person, partnership, or corporation to cease and desist from the violation of the law so charged in said complaint. Any person, partnership, or corporation may make application, and upon good cause shown may be allowed by the Commission to intervene and appear in said proceeding by counsel or in person. The testimony in any such proceeding shall be reduced to writing and filed in the office of the Commission. If upon such hearing the Commission shall be of the opinion that the method of competition or the act or practice in question is prohibited by this subchapter, it shall make a report in writing in which it shall state its findings as to the facts and shall issue and cause to be served on such person, partnership, or corporation an order requiring such person, partnership, or corporation to cease and desist from using such method of competition or such act or practice. Until the expiration of the time allowed for filing a petition for review, if no such petition has been duly filed within such time, or, if a petition for review has been filed within such time then until the record in the proceeding has been filed in a court of appeals of the United States, as hereinafter provided, the Commission may at any time, upon such notice and in such manner as it shall deem proper, modify or set aside, in whole or in part, any report or any order made or issued by it under this section. After the expiration of the time allowed for filing a petition for review, if no such petition has been duly filed within such time, the Commission may at any time, after notice and opportunity for hearing, reopen and alter, modify, or set aside, in whole or in part any report or order made or issued by it under this section, whenever in the opinion of the Commission conditions of fact or of law have so changed as to require such action or if the public interest shall so require, except that (1) the said person, partnership, or corporation may, within sixty days after service upon him or it of said report or order entered after such a reopening, obtain a review thereof in the appropriate court of appeals of the United States, in the manner provided in subsection (c) of this section; and (2) in the case of an order, the Commission shall reopen any such order to consider whether such order (including any affirmative relief provision contained in such order) should be altered, modified, or set aside, in whole or in part, if the person, partnership, or corporation involved files a request with the Commission which makes a satisfactory showing that changed conditions of law or fact require such order to be altered, modified, or set aside, in whole or in part. The Commission shall determine whether to alter, modify, or set aside any order of the Commission in response to a request made by a person, partnership, or corporation under paragraph[1] (2) not later than 120 days after the date of the filing of such request.

(c)   Review of order; rehearing

Any person, partnership, or corporation required by an order of the Commission to cease and desist from using any method of competition or act or practice may obtain a review of such order in the court of appeals of the United States, within any circuit where the method of competition or the act or practice in question was used or where such person, partnership, or corporation resides or carries on business, by filing in the court, within sixty days from the date of the service of such order, a written petition praying

---

1 *So in original. Probably should be "clause".*

that the order of the Commission be set aside. A copy of such petition shall be forthwith transmitted by the clerk of the court to the Commission, and thereupon the Commission shall file in the court the record in the proceeding, as provided in section 2112 of title 28. Upon such filing of the petition the court shall have jurisdiction of the proceeding and of the question determined therein concurrently with the Commission until the filing of the record and shall have power to make and enter a decree affirming, modifying, or setting aside the order of the Commission, and enforcing the same to the extent that such order is affirmed and to issue such writs as are ancillary to its jurisdiction or are necessary in its judgement to prevent injury to the public or to competitors pendente lite. The findings of the Commission as to the facts, if supported by evidence, shall be conclusive. To the extent that the order of the Commission is affirmed, the court shall thereupon issue its own order commanding obedience to the terms of such order of the Commission. If either party shall apply to the court for leave to adduce additional evidence, and shall show to the satisfaction of the court that such additional evidence is material and that there were reasonable grounds for the failure to adduce such evidence in the proceeding before the Commission, the court may order such additional evidence to be taken before the Commission and to be adduced upon the hearing in such manner and upon such terms and conditions as to the court may seem proper. The Commission may modify its findings as to the facts, or make new findings, by reason of the additional evidence so taken, and it shall file such modified or new findings, which, if supported by evidence, shall be conclusive, and its recommendation, if any, for the modification or setting aside of its original order, with the return of such additional evidence. The judgment and decree of the court shall be final, except that the same shall be subject to review by the Supreme Court upon certiorari, as provided in section 1254 of title 28.

(d) Jurisdiction of court

Upon the filing of the record with it the jurisdiction of the court of appeals of the United States to affirm, enforce, modify, or set aside orders of the Commission shall be exclusive.

(e) Exemption from liability

No order of the Commission or judgement of court to enforce the same shall in anywise relieve or absolve any person, partnership, or corporation from any liability under the Antitrust Acts.

(f) Service of complaints, orders and other processes; return

Complaints, orders, and other processes of the Commission under this section may be served by anyone duly authorized by the Commission, either (a) by delivering a copy thereof to the person to be served, or to a member of the partnership to be served, or the president, secretary, or other executive officer or a director of the corporation to be served; or (b) by leaving a copy thereof at the residence or the principal office or place of business of such person, partnership, or corporation; or (c) by mailing a copy thereof by registered mail or by certified mail addressed to such person, partnership, or corporation at his or its residence or principal office or place of business. The verified return by the person so serving said complaint, order, or other process setting forth the manner of said service shall be proof of the same, and the return post office receipt for said complaint, order, or other process mailed by registered mail or by certified mail as aforesaid shall be proof of the service of the same.

(g) Finality of order

An order of the Commission to cease and desist shall become final—

(1) Upon the expiration of the time allowed for filing a petition for review, if no such petition has been duly filed within such time; but the Commission may thereafter modify or set aside its order to the extent provided in the last sentence of subsection (b).

(2) Except as to any order provision subject to paragraph (4), upon the sixtieth day after such order is served, if a petition for review has been duly filed; except that any such order may be stayed, in whole or in part and subject to such conditions as may be appropriate, by—

(A) the Commission;

(B) an appropriate court of appeals of the United States, if (i) a petition for review of such order is pending in such court, and (ii) an application for such a stay was previously submitted to the Commission and the Commission, within the 30-day period eginning on the date the application was received by the Commission, either denied the application or did not grant or deny the application; or

(C) the Supreme Court, if an applicable petition for certiorari is pending.

(3) For purposes of subsection (m)(l)(B) of this section and of section 57b(a)(2) of this title, if a petition for review of the order of the Commission has been filed—

(A) upon the expiration of the time allowed for filing a petition for certiorari, if the order of the Commission has been affirmed or the petition for review has been dismissed by the court of appeals and no petition for certiorari has been duly filed;

(B) upon the denial of a petition for certiorari, if the order of the Commission has been affirmed or the petition for review has been dismissed by the court of appeals; or

(C) upon the expiration of 30 days from the date of issuance of a mandate of the Supreme Court directing that the order of the Commission be affirmed or the petition for review be dismissed.

(4)   In the case of an order provision requiring a person, partnership, or corporation to divest itself of stock, other share capital, or assets, if a petition for review of such order of the Commission has been filed—

(A) upon the expiration of the time allowed for filing a petition for certiorari, if the order of the Commission has been affirmed or the petition for review has been dismissed by the court of appeals and no petition for certiorari has been duly filed;

(B) upon the denial of a petition for certiorari, if the order of the Commission has been affirmed or the petition for review has been dismissed by the court of appeals; or

(C) upon the expiration of 30 days from the date of issuance of a mandate of the Supreme Court directing that the order of the Commission be affirmed or the petition for review be dismissed.

(h)   Modification or setting aside of order by Supreme Court

If the Supreme Court directs that the order of the Commission be modified or set aside, the order of the Commission rendered in accordance with the mandate of the Supreme Court shall become final upon the expiration of thirty days from the time it was rendered, unless within such thirty days either party has instituted proceedings to have such order corrected to accord with the mandate, in which event the order of the Commission shall become final when so corrected.

(i)   Modification or setting aside of order by Court of Appeals

If the order of the Commission is modified or set aside by the court of appeals, and if (1) the time allowed for filing a petition for certiorari has expired and no such petition has been duly filed, or (2) the petition for certiorari has been denied, or (3) the decision of the court has been affirmed by the Supreme Court, then the order of the Commission rendered in accordance with the mandate of the court of appeals shall become final on the expiration of thirty days from the time such order of the Commission was rendered, unless within such thirty days either party has instituted proceedings to have such order corrected so that it will accord with the mandate, in which event the order of the Commission shall become final when so corrected.

(j)   Rehearing upon order or remand

If the Supreme Court orders a rehearing; or if the case is remanded by the court of appeals to the Commission for a rehearing, and if (1) the time allowed for filing a petition for certiorari has expired, and no such petition has been duly filed, or (2) the petition for certiorari has been denied, or (3) the decision of the court has been affirmed by the Supreme Court, then the order of the Commission rendered upon such rehearing shall become final in the same manner as though no prior order of the Commission had been rendered.

(k) "Mandate" defined

As used in this section the term "mandate", in case a mandate has been recalled prior to the expiration of thirty days from the date of issuance thereof, means the final mandate.

(l) Penalty for violation of order; injunctions and other appropriate equitable relief

Any person, partnership, or corporation who violates an order of the Commission after it has become final, and while such order is in effect, shall forfeit and pay to the United States a civil penalty of not more than $10,000 for each violation, which shall accrue to the United States and may be recovered in a civil action brought by the Attorney General of the United States. Each separate violation of such an order shall be a separate offense, except that in a case of a violation through continuing failure to obey or neglect to obey a final order of the Commission, each day of continuance of such failure or neglect shall be deemed a separate offense. In such actions, the United States district courts are empowered to grant mandatory injunctions and such other and further equitable relief as they deem appropriate in the enforcement of such final orders of the Commission.

(m) Civil actions for recovery of penalties for knowing violations of rules and cease and desist orders respecting unfair or deceptive acts or practices; jurisdiction; maximum amount of penalties; continuing violations; de novo determinations; compromise or settlement procedure

(1) (A) The Commission may commence a civil action to recover a civil penalty in a district court of the United States against any person, partnership, or corporation which violates any rule under this subchapter respecting unfair or deceptive acts or practices (other than an interpretive rule or a rule violation of which the Commission has provided is not an unfair or deceptive act or practice in violation of subsection (a)(1) of this section) with actual knowledge or knowledge fairly implied on the basis of objective circumstances that such act is unfair or deceptive and is prohibited by such rule. In such action, such person, partnership, or corporation shall be liable for a civil penalty of not more than $10,000 for each violation.

(B) If the Commission determines in a proceeding under subsection (b) of this section that any act or practice is unfair or deceptive, and issues a final cease and desist order, other than a consent order, with respect to such act or practice, then the Commission may commence a civil action to obtain a civil penalty in a district court of the

United States against any person, partnership, or corporation which engages in such act or practice—

(1) after such cease and desist order becomes final (whether or not such person, partnership, or corporation was subject to such cease and desist order), and

(2) with actual knowledge that such act or practice is unfair or deceptive and is unlawful under subsection (a)(1) of this section.

In such action, such person, partnership, or corporation shall be liable for a civil penalty of not more than $10,000 for each violation.

(C) In the case of a violation through continuing failure to comply with a rule or with subsection (a)(1) of this section, each day of continuance of such failure shall be treated as a separate violation, for purposes of subparagraphs (A) and (B). In determining the amount of such a civil penalty, the court shall take into account the degree of culpability, any history of prior such conduct, ability to pay, effect on ability to continue to do business, and such other matters as justice may require.

(2) If the cease and desist order establishing that the act or practice is unfair or deceptive was not issued against the defendant in a civil penalty action under paragraph (1)(B) the issues of fact in such action against such defendant shall be tried de novo. Upon request of any party to such an action against such defendant, the court shall also review the determination of law made by the Commission in the proceeding under subsection (b) of this section that the act or practice which was the subject of such proceeding constituted an unfair or deceptive act or practice in violation of subsection (a) of this section.

(3) The Commission may compromise or settle any action for a civil penalty if such compromise or settlement is accompanied by a public statement of its reasons and is approved by the court.

(n) Standard of proof; public policy considerations

The Commission shall have no authority under this section or section 57a of this title to declare unlawful an act or practice on the grounds that such act or practice is unfair unless the act or practice causes or is likely to cause substantial injury to consumers which is not reasonably avoidable by consumers themselves and not outweighed by countervailing benefits to consumers or to competition. In determining whether an act or practice is unfair, the Commission may consider established public policies as evidence to be considered with all other evidence. Such public policy considerations may not serve as a primary basis for such determination.

Appendix B

Summary of State Data Breach Notification Laws

Section 1.2 of this book describes the common requirements of the data breach notification laws in 50 states and the District of Columbia. These summaries focus on the obligations of private companies; government agencies also often face separate notice obligations if they experience data breaches. For ease of reference, particularly for companies that are dealing with a data breach, this appendix summarizes key provisions of each of these laws as they relate to private companies' obligations, including the types of personal information that trigger the breach notice requirement, significant exceptions to that requirement, and notice and format of breach notices.

Note that most state notification laws allow electronic notice; in all of these instances, consent to receive notices electronically often must be consistent with the federal E-SIGN Act. The breach notice laws typically apply to the unauthorized acquisition of covered personal information.

For ease of reference, this appendix includes many of the most important parts of the state laws, rather than mere reprints of the full statutes. However, the state laws do have additional requirements that are specific to the state. Moreover, the breach notification laws could have been amended since the publication of this book; indeed, typically at least a few states each year amend their breach notice laws. Accordingly, legal counsel always should review the current version of the applicable breach notice laws to confirm requirements.

Alabama

Alabama, SB318 (2018)

Categories of covered personal information: An individual's first name or first initial and last name, in combination with at least one of the following elements: (1) Social Security number, (2) driver's license, military ID, or

Cybersecurity Law, Second Edition. Jeff Kosseff.
© 2020 John Wiley & Sons, Inc. Published 2020 by John Wiley & Sons, Inc.
Companion Website: www.wiley.com/go/kosseff/cybersecurity2e

state ID card number, (3) credit card or debit card number and personal code if applicable, and passwords or PINS or other access codes for financial accounts, (4) medical records, health insurance policy number or subscriber ID number, or (5) user name/email address in combination with password or security question and answer that could access the account.

Exceptions to notice requirement: (1) If all of the personal information was encrypted, provided that the encryption key was not also disclosed; (2) if after a good-faith investigation, the company determines that the incident is not "reasonably likely to cause substantial harm to the individuals to whom the information relates;" and (3) if the company is "subject to or regulated by federal laws, rules, regulations, procedures, or guidance on data breach notification established or enforced by the federal government."

Timing of notice to individuals: Disclosure must be made within 45 calendar days and "as expeditiously as possible and without unreasonable delay, taking into account the time necessary to allow the covered entity to conduct an investigation." Federal or state law enforcement may request a delay if notice "would interfere with a criminal investigation or national security."

Requirements for notice to individual (form and content): Three options: (1) written document sent to most recent known mailing address; (2) email; or (3) substitute notice if the cost of providing notice would exceed $500,000, the number of "affected individuals" exceeds 100,000, or the company does not have sufficient information to provide notice. Substitute notice consists of email if the address is known, conspicuously posting disclosure on the company's website for 30 days, and notice to print and broadcast media "including major media in urban and rural areas where the affected individuals reside."

The notice to individuals must include the date of the breach, a description of the affected information, a description of the actions the company is taking in response to the breach, a description of how the individual can protect against identity theft, and contact information for the company.

Notice to state regulators or consumer reporting agencies/credit bureaus: If more than 1,000 Alabama residents receive breach notices, the State Attorney General must be notified within 45 calendar days if the company determines that there is a risk of harm and therefore individual notice is necessary. Notice to the Attorney General must include a synopsis of the breach, the approximate number of Alabama residents affected, and services that the company provided to affected

Alabama residents. Notice to credit bureaus "without unreasonable delay" is required if more than 1,000 Alabama residents are notified.

Alaska

Alaska Stat. § 45.48.010 *et seq.*

Categories of covered personal information: An individual's first name or first initial and last name, in combination with at least one of the following elements: (1) Social Security number, (2) driver's license or state ID card number, or (3) credit card or debit card number and personal code if applicable, and passwords or PINS or other access codes for financial accounts.

Exceptions to notice requirement: (1) If all of the personal information was encrypted, "and the encryption key has been accessed or acquired;" or (2) if after an appropriate investigation and a written notification to the Alaska Attorney General, the company determines that "there is not a reasonable likelihood that harm to consumers whose personal information has been acquired has resulted or will result from the breach," but the company must retain this documentation for five years.

Timing of notice to individuals: Disclosure must be made "in the most expeditious time possible and without unreasonable delay" unless a delay is necessary for law enforcement or to determine the scope of the breach and restore system integrity.

Requirements for notice to individual (form and content): Three options: (1) written document sent to most recent known mailing address; (2) email if that is the company's primary method of communication with the individual; or (3) substitute notice if the cost of providing notice would exceed $150,000, the affected class in the state exceeds 300,000, or the company does not have sufficient information to provide notice. Substitute notice consists of email if the address is known, conspicuously posting disclosure on the company's website, and notice to major statewide media.

Notice to state regulators or consumer reporting agencies/credit bureaus: The State Attorney General must be notified if the company determines that there is not a risk of harm and therefore individual notice is unnecessary. Notice to credit bureaus is required if more than 1,000 Alaska residents are notified, but this requirement does not apply if the company is subject to the Gramm-Leach-Bliley Act.

Arizona

Ariz. Rev. Stat. § 44-7501

Categories of covered personal information: An individual's first name or first initial and last name in combination with at least one of the following: (1) Social Security number; (2) driver's license or state ID number; (3) financial account or credit card or debit card number in combination with required security code, access code, or passcode (if necessary for access); (4) "a private key that is unique to an individual and that is used to authenticate or sign an electronic record;" (5) health insurance ID number; (6) medical record; (7) passport number; (8) taxpayer ID number; or (9) biometric data. Separately, the law covers a user name or email address, when combined with a password or security question and answer that allows access to the account.

Exceptions to notice requirement: The notice requirement does not apply to (1) information that is encrypted or redacted; (2) if after "reasonable investigation" the company determines that the breach did not result in and is not "reasonably likely" to result in "substantial economic loss to affected individuals"; (3) if the company is subject to GLBA or HIPAA; (4) if the company complies with the notification requirements of its "primary or functional federal regulator," or (5) if the company follows its own notification procedures as part of an information security policy that is consistent with the Arizona law, including the 45-day notice requirement.

Timing of notice to individuals: Companies must provide notice within 45 days of determination of the breach.

Requirements for notice to individual (form and content): (1) Written notice; (2) electronic notice if the company has the covered individuals' email addresses; (3) telephonic notice, provided it is not prerecorded; or (4) substitute notice if the cost of other notice would exceed $50,000, the "affected class of subject individuals to be notified" is greater than 100,000 individuals, or the company does not have sufficient contact information. Substitute notice consists of (1) email notice when available and (2) conspicuous posting of the notice on the company's website for at least 45 days. The company also must write a letter to the Attorney General explaining the facts that justify the substitute notice.

Notice to state regulators or consumer reporting agencies/credit bureaus: If the company is required to notify at least 1,000 Arizona residents, it also must notify the Arizona Attorney General and the three credit bureaus within 45 days.

Arkansas

Ark. Code § 4-110-103 *et seq.*

Categories of covered personal information: First name or first initial and last name in combination with one or more of the following: (1) Social Security number; (2) driver's license or state ID number; (3) financial account number, credit card number or debit card number in combination with any code or password necessary to access financial account; or (4) medical information.

Exceptions to notice requirement: (1) If personal information is encrypted or redacted; (2) if after a reasonable investigation the company determines there is not a "reasonable likelihood of harm" to customers; (3) if the business "is regulated by a state or federal law that provides greater protection to personal information and at least as thorough disclosure requirements for breaches of the security of personal information than that provided" under the Arkansas breach notice law; or (4) if the business "maintains its own notification procedures as part of an information security policy" and is otherwise consistent with the law's timing requirements, provided that the company follows its internal policies.

Timing of notice to individuals: Individual notice must be made "in the most expedient time and manner possible and without unreasonable delay," consistent with the needs of law enforcement and to determine the scope of the breach and restore system integrity.

Requirements for notice to individual (form and content): (1) Written notice; (2) email notice; or (3) substitute notice if the cost of notifying would exceed $250,000, the "affected class of persons to be notified" is greater than 500,000, or the company does not have sufficient contact information. Substitute notice consists of email notice when an address is available, conspicuous posting of the notice on the company's website, and notification by statewide media.

Notice to state regulators or consumer reporting agencies/credit bureaus: Not required.

California

Cal. Civ. Code § 1798.82

Categories of covered personal information: (1) An individual's first name or first initial and last name in combination with at least one of the following: (a) Social Security number; (b) driver's license or state ID card number; (c) financial account number, credit or debit card number, in combination with any required code or password; (d) medical information; (e) health insurance information; or (f) information collected through an automated license plate recognition system; or

(2)   a user name or email address, in combination with a password or Social Security question and answer that would permit access to an online account.

Exceptions to notice requirement: (1) If the data is encrypted and the key was not acquired by an unauthorized individual; or (2) if a company complies with its internal information security policy notification procedures, consistent with the timing requirements of the statute. If a HIPAA-covered entity complies with HIPAA's breach notice requirements, it is not required to follow the California breach notice law's requirements for specific content to be included in the notification.

Timing of notice to individuals: In the "most expedient time possible and without unreasonable delay," consistent with needs of law enforcement or to determine the scope of the breach and restore system integrity.

Requirements for notice to individual (form and content): (1) Written notice; (2) email notice; or (3) substitute notice, if the company demonstrates that the cost of notice would exceed $250,000, the "affected class of subject persons to be notified exceeds 500,000," or the company does not have sufficient contact information. Substitute notice consists of email notice when available, conspicuous posting of the notice on the company's website for at least thirty days; and (3) notification to major statewide media.

If the breach only involved the credentials for an online account, the company should send password-reset credentials. It should not email the notice to the breached email account.

The notice must be "written in plain language" and be titled "Notice of Data Breach."

The notice must contain: (1) name and contact information of company; (2) list of categories of personal information compromised; (3) if possible, the date or estimated date or ranges of the breach; (4) date of notice; (5) whether notice was delayed due to law enforcement investigation, if possible; (6) general description of the data breach, if possible; (7) toll-free phone numbers and addresses of major credit reporting agencies, and an offer for 12 months of free identity theft prevention and mitigation services, if Social Security or ID card number was exposed.

Companies also may choose to provide "[i]nformation about what the person or business has done to protect individuals whose information has been breached" and "[a]dvice on steps that the person whose information has been breached may take to protect himself or herself," though these elements are not mandatory.

This notice should be presented under the following headings: "What Happened," "What Information Was Involved," "What We Are Doing," "What You Can Do," and "For More Information."

Notice to state regulators or consumer reporting agencies/credit bureaus: If a company notifies more than 500 California residents due to a single data breach, the company must submit a single sample copy of the notice to the California Attorney General. Note that these sample copies are made publicly available on the California Attorney General's website.

Colorado

Colo. Rev. Stat. § 6-1-716

Categories of covered personal information: First name or first initial and last name in combination with at least one of the following: (1) Social Security number; (2) driver's license or ID card number; (3) account number or credit or debit card number, along with code or password necessary to access financial account; (4) student, military, or passport identification number; (5) medical records; (6) health insurance number; or (7) biometric data. Separately, the law covers a user name or email address, when combined with a password or security question and answer that allows access to the account.

Exceptions to notice requirement: (1) If the personal information is encrypted, redacted, or "secured by any other method rendering the name or the element unreadable or unusable;" (2) if after an investigation the company concludes that misuse of the information "has not occurred and is not reasonably likely to occur;" (3) if a company "is regulated by state or federal law" and "maintains procedures for a breach of the security of the system pursuant to the laws, rules, regulations, guidances, or guidelines established by its primary or functional state or federal regulator;" or (4) if the company follows its internal notification procedures "as part of an information security policy for the treatment of personal information" and is consistent with the statute's timing requirements.

Timing of notice to individuals: Disclosure must be provided within 30 days and "in the most expedient time possible and without unreasonable delay," subject to the needs of law enforcement and to determine the scope of the breach and restore system integrity.

Requirements for notice to individual (form and content): (1) Written notice to mailing address listed in company's records; (2) telephonic notice; (3) electronic notice, if that is the company's primary method of communicating with the individual; or (4) substitute notice if the company demonstrates that the cost of notice exceeds $250,000, at least 250,000 Colorado residents would have to be notified, or the company does not have sufficient contact information. Substitute notice consists of email notice when available, conspicuous posting of the notice on the company's website, and notification to major statewide media.

Notice must include: (1) the date of the breach; (2) a description of the personal information at issue in the breach; (3) the company's contact information; (4) toll-free phone numbers, addresses, and websites for the three credit bureaus and the FTC; and (5) "a statement that the resident can obtain information from the Federal Trade Commission and the credit reporting agencies about fraud alerts and security freezes."

Notice to state regulators or consumer reporting agencies/credit bureaus: Notice to the state Attorney General is required if 500 or more Coloradans are notified. Notice to credit reporting agencies is required, provided that more than 1,000 Colorado residents are notified, and the company is not covered by the Gramm-Leach-Bliley Act. The notice to credit reporting agencies must state the date that the notice will be provided and the number of Colorado residents who will receive the notices.

Connecticut

Conn. Gen. Stat. § 36A-701b

Categories of covered personal information: An individual's first name or first initial and last name in combination with at least one of the following: (1) Social Security number; (2) driver's license or state ID card number; or (3) account number, credit or debit card number, in combination with any required code or password to access the financial account.

Exceptions to notice requirement: (1) Information that has been "secured by encryption or by any other method or technology that renders the personal information unreadable or unusable;" (2) if, after investigation and consultation with relevant law enforcement agencies, the company determines that breach will not "likely result in harm" to individuals whose information was exposed; (3) if a company maintains a breach procedure under the rules of the Gramm-Leach-Bliley Act, provided that the company notifies the individuals and the Connecticut Attorney General; or (4) if the company maintains its "own security breach procedures as part of an information security policy for the treatment of personal information and otherwise complies with the timing requirements of this section," provided that it complies with the statute's timing requirements and notifies the Connecticut Attorney General.

Timing of notice to individuals: Individuals must be notified without unreasonable delay, and within 90 days of discovery of the incident, subject to the needs of law enforcement, to identify individuals, and restore system integrity.

Requirements for notice to individual (form and content): (1) Written notice; (2) telephone notice; (3) electronic notice; or (4) substitute notice, if the costs of notification would exceed $250,000, "the affected class of subject persons to be notified" is greater than 500,000 people, or the company does not have sufficient contact information. Substitute notice consists of email when the address is available, conspicuous posting of the notice on the company's website, and notification to major statewide media, including newspapers, radio, and television.

For breaches involving social security numbers, companies must provide "appropriate identity theft protection services, and, if applicable, identity theft mitigation services" for at least 12 months.

Notice to state regulators or consumer reporting agencies/credit bureaus: If any Connecticut residents are notified, the Connecticut Attorney General also must receive notification at the same time or earlier.

Delaware

Del. Code tit. 6, § 12B-101 *et seq*.

Categories of covered personal information: An individual's first name or first initial and last name along with at least one of the following: (1) Social Security number; (2) driver's license or state ID card number; (3) account or credit or debit card number, along with any required code or password; (4) user name or email address, when combined with a password or security question and answer that allows access to the account; (5) passport number; (6) medical records; (7) health insurance number; (8) biometric data; and (9) taxpayer identification number.

Exceptions to notice requirement: (1) If the personal information was encrypted, "unless such unauthorized acquisition includes, or is reasonably believed to include, the encryption key and the person that owns or licenses the encrypted information has a reasonable belief that the encryption key could render that personal information readable or useable;" (2) if, after an appropriate investigation, the company "reasonably determines that the breach of security is unlikely to result in harm to the individuals whose personal information has been breached;" (3) a company regulated by state or federal law, including but not limited to HIPAA and GLBA, and "maintains procedures for a breach of security pursuant to the laws, rules, regulations, guidance, or guidelines established by its primary or functional state or federal regulator;" or (4) a company that follows the notification requirements of its information security policy, provided that the "procedures are otherwise consistent with the timing requirements" of the Delaware breach notice law.

Timing of notice to individuals: Notice must be provided within 60 days and "without unreasonable delay," except as needed legitimately for law enforcement, to determine scope of the breach, and to restore system integrity.

Requirements for notice to individual (form and content): (1) Written notice; (2) telephonic notice; (3) electronic notice; or (4) substitute notice, if the total cost of notification will exceed $75,000, more than 100,000 Delaware residents must be notified, or the company does not have sufficient contact information. Substitute notice consists of email notice if the company has email addresses, conspicuous posting of the notice on the company's website, and notice to major statewide media.

If Social Security numbers were breached, the company must offer credit monitoring services for at least a year.

Notice to state regulators or consumer reporting agencies/credit bureaus: If more than 500 Delaware residents are notified, the company must notify the Delaware Attorney General.

District of Columbia

D.C. Code Mun. Regs. § 28-3851 *et seq.*

Categories of covered personal information: (1) Individual's first name or first initial and last name, or phone number, or address, and at least one of the following: (a) Social Security number; (b) driver's license or

D.C. ID card number; or (c) credit card or debit card number; or (2) any other number or code or combination of numbers or codes that allows access to or use of a financial or credit account.

Exceptions to notice requirement: (1) If the data is "rendered secure, so as to be unusable by an unauthorized third party" (i.e., encryption); (2) a company that notifies pursuant to the Gramm-Leach-Bliley Act; or (3) a company that "maintains its own notification procedures as part of an information security policy for the treatment of personal information and is otherwise consistent with the timing requirements" of the D.C. breach notice law, provided that the company notifies individuals "in accordance with its policies, reasonably calculated to give actual notice to persons to whom notice is otherwise required to be given[.]"

Timing of notice to individuals: Notice is required in the "most expedient time possible and without unreasonable delay," consistent with legitimate needs of law enforcement and with the need to determine the scope of the breach and restore system integrity.

Requirements for notice to individual (form and content): (1) Written notice; (2) electronic notice; or (3) substitute notice, if the company's total cost of notification would exceed $50,000, the number of D.C. residents requiring notification exceeds 100,000, or the company does not have sufficient contact information. Substitute notice consists of email notice when an address is available, conspicuous posting of the notice on the company's website, and notice to major local and, if applicable, national media.

Notice to state regulators or consumer reporting agencies/credit bureaus: No notice to D.C. regulators required. Notice to credit reporting agencies required if more than 1,000 D.C. residents are notified. The credit reporting agency notices must describe the "timing, distribution and content" of the individual notices.

Florida

Fla. Stat. § 501.171

Categories of covered personal information: An individual's first name or first initial and last name in combination with any one or more of the following: (1) Social Security number; (2) driver's license or ID card number, passport number, military ID number, or similar number on a government document used to verify identity; (3) financial account or credit or debit card number, in combination with required code or password; (4) information regarding medical history, mental or physical condition, or medical treatment or diagnosis by healthcare professional; or (5) health insurance policy number or subscriber ID number and any unique identifier used by health insurer to verify identity.

Separately, Florida's notification law covers a user name or email address, in combination with a password or security question and answer that would permit access to an online account. The notification requirement applies even if the individual's name is not disclosed.

Exceptions to notice requirement: (1) If the information was "encrypted, secured, or modified by any other method or technology that removes elements that personally identify an individual or that otherwise renders the information unusable;" (2) if after investigation and consulting with law enforcement, the company "reasonably determines that the disclosure has not and will not likely result in identity theft or any other financial harm" to individuals, provided that the company documents this determination, provides the written documentation to the Florida Department of Legal Affairs within 30 days, and retains the determination for five years; or (3) if the entity follows the breach notice provisions for its primary or functional federal regulator and provides a copy of this notice to the Florida Department of Legal Affairs.

Timing of notice to individuals: Notice must be made "as expeditiously as practicable and without unreasonable delay," but no longer than 30 days after determination of a breach or reason to believe the breach has occurred, unless there is a written request from a law enforcement agency.

Requirements for notice to individual (form and content): (1) Written notice; (2) email notice; or (3) substitute notice if cost of notifying exceeds $250,000, "the affected individuals exceed 500,000 persons," or the company does not have contact information. Substitute notice consists of a conspicuous notice on the company's website and notice in print and broadcast media, including major media in urban and rural areas where the affected individuals reside.

Notices to individuals must include the date, estimated date, or date range of the breach, a description of the personal information at issue in the breach, and contact information for the company.

Third-party agents that suffer a data breach must notify the company whose customers' information is breached within ten days of "the determination of the breach of security or reason to believe the breach occurred." When the company receives a notice from a third-party agent, the company should provide the required individual notices.

Notice to state regulators or consumer reporting agencies/credit bureaus: If more than 500 Florida residents' personal information is compromised, companies must inform the Florida Department of Legal Affairs within 30 days after a breach is discovered. The written notice must include a synopsis of the events surrounding the breach; the number of Floridians affected; services offered for free to individuals related to the breach; a copy of the individual notice; and the name, address, phone number, and email address of the company for more information about the breach.

Companies must provide written notice to credit reporting agencies if more than 1,000 Florida residents' personal information is compromised.

Georgia

Ga. Code § 10-1-910 *et seq.*

Categories of covered personal information: Georgia's breach notice law only applies to breaches of the systems of "information brokers" or companies that maintain data on behalf of information brokers. The statute defines "information broker" as "any person or entity who, for monetary fees or dues, engages in whole or in part in the business of collecting, assembling, evaluating, compiling, reporting, transmitting, transferring, or communicating information concerning individuals for the primary purpose of furnishing personal information to nonaffiliated third parties, but does not include any governmental agency whose records are maintained primarily for traffic safety, law enforcement, or licensing purposes."

The statute defines "personal information" as an individual's first name or first initial and last name in combination with at least one of the following: (1) Social Security number; (2) driver's license or state ID card number; (3) financial account number or credit card or debit card number, along with any required access codes or passwords; (4) account passwords or personal ID numbers or other access codes; or (5) any of the previous four items when not in connection with individual's name if the information would be sufficient to conduct identity theft.

Exceptions to notice requirement: (1) If the information is encrypted or redacted; or (2) an information broker provides notice pursuant to its internal information security policy, provided that the internal policy's notice requirements is "otherwise consistent" with the Georgia breach notice statute's timing requirements.

Timing of notice to individuals: Notice must be provided in the "most expedient time possible and without unreasonable delay," consistent with the needs of law enforcement and any "measures necessary to determine the scope of the breach and restore the reasonable integrity, security, and confidentiality of the data system."

Requirements for notice to individual (form and content): (1) Written notice; (2) electronic notice; or (3) substitute notice, if the cost of providing notice would exceed $50,000, more than 100,000 Georgia residents would be notified, or the information broker does not have sufficient contact information. Substitute notice consists of email notice if addresses are available, conspicuous posting on the information broker's webpage, and notification to major statewide media.

Notice to state regulators or consumer reporting agencies/credit bureaus: If more than 10,000 Georgia residents are notified, the information broker must also notify the credit reporting agencies.

Hawaii

Haw. Rev. Stat. § 487N-1 *et seq*.

Categories of covered personal information: A person's first name or first initial and last name in combination with at least one of the following: (1) Social Security number; (2) driver's license number or state ID card number; or (3) financial account number, credit or debit card number, access code, or password.

Exceptions to notice requirement: (1) If the information was encrypted, and the "confidential process key" was not accessed; (2) if the information was redacted; (3) if the company determines that there has not been an "illegal use of the personal information," and that an illegal use is not "reasonably likely to occur" and "create a risk of harm" to individuals; (4) a "financial institution that is subject to the federal Interagency Guidance on Response Programs for Unauthorized Access to Customer Information and Customer Notice;" or (5) a "health plan or healthcare provider that is subject to and in compliance with the standards for privacy or individually identifiable health information and the security standards for the protection of electronic health information of the Health Insurance Portability and Accountability Act of 1996."

Timing of notice to individuals: Notice should be made "without unreasonable delay," consistent with the needs of law enforcement and with measures necessary to determine contact information and scope of the breach, and "with any measures necessary to determine sufficient contact information, determine the scope of the breach, and restore the reasonable integrity, security, and confidentiality of the data system."

Requirements for notice to individual (form and content): (1) Written notice to last available address on record; (2) electronic notice; (3) telephone notice as long as contact is made directly with affected person; or (4) substitute notice if the cost of notice would exceed $100,000, the "affected class of subject persons to be notified" is greater than 200,000, or the business does not have sufficient contact information. Substitute notice consists of email if addresses are available, conspicuous posting of the notice on the company's website, and notification to major statewide media.

Notice must describe the incident in general terms, along with the type of personal information that was breached, the steps the company took to prevent further access, a telephone number for more information, and advice to "remain vigilant by reviewing financial account records and monitoring free credit reports."

Notice to state regulators or consumer reporting agencies/credit bureaus: If the company notifies more than 1,000 Hawaii residents, it also must notify the Hawaii Office of Consumer Protection and the major credit reporting agencies. The notices should disclose the timing, distribution, and content of the notice.

Idaho

Idaho Code § 28-51-104 *et seq.*

Categories of covered personal information: An individual's first name or first initial and last name in combination with at least one of the following: (1) Social Security number; (2) driver's license or state ID card number; or (3) financial account number, or credit or debit card number, along with any required code or password.

Exceptions to notice requirement: (1) If the information is encrypted; (2) if an investigation determines that misuse of information has not occurred and is not "reasonably likely to occur;" (3) a company regulated by state or federal law that maintains procedures for data breach notification, provided that the company complies with those procedures; or (4) if the company "maintains its own notice procedures as part of an information security policy for the treatment of personal information" and those "procedures are otherwise consistent with the timing requirements" of the Idaho breach notice law.

Timing of notice to individuals: Notice must be provided to individuals in the "most expedient time possible and without unreasonable delay," consistent with needs of law enforcement and "any measures necessary to determine the scope of the breach, to identify the individuals affected, and to restore the reasonable integrity of the computerized data system."

Requirements for notice to individual (form and content): (1) Written notice; (2) telephonic notice; (3) electronic notice; and (4) substitute notice, if the cost of notice would exceed $25,000, more than 50,000 Idaho residents would have to be notified, or the company does not have sufficient contact information. Substitute notice consists of email notice to available addresses, conspicuous posting on the company's website, and notice to major statewide media.

Notice to state regulators or consumer reporting agencies/credit bureaus: Not required.

Illinois

815 Ill. Comp. Stat. § 530/1 *et seq.*

Categories of covered personal information: An individual's first name or first initial and last name in combination with at least one of the following: (1) Social Security number; (2) driver's license or state ID card number; (3) financial account number or credit or debit card number, along with any required code or password, (4) medical information; (5) health insurance information; or (6) unique biometric data. Separately, the law covers "[u]ser name or email address, in combination with a password or security question and answer that would permit access to an online account, when either the user name or email address or password or security question and answer are not encrypted or redacted or are encrypted or redacted but the keys to unencrypt or unredact or otherwise read the data elements have been obtained through the breach of security."

Exceptions to notice requirement: (1) If data is encrypted or redacted, provided that "the keys to unencrypt or unredact or otherwise read the name or data elements have been acquired without authorization through the breach of security;" or (2) if the company notifies individuals under "its own notification procedures as part of an information security policy for the treatment of personal information," provided that the internal policy "is otherwise consistent with the timing requirements" of the Illinois breach notice law.

Timing of notice to individuals: Notice must be provided in the "most expedient time possible and without unreasonable delay," consistent with "any measures necessary to determine the scope of the breach and restore the reasonable integrity, security, and confidentiality of the data system."

Requirements for notice to individual (form and content): (1) Written notice; (2) electronic notice; or (3) substitute notice, if the cost of providing notice would exceed $250,000, the "affected class of subject persons to be notified" is greater than 500,000, or the company does not have sufficient contact information. Substitute notice must be provided via email if an address is available, conspicuous posting on the company's website, and notification to statewide media.

The notice must include toll-free phone numbers for the credit reporting agencies; toll-free phone number, address, and web address for the FTC; and a statement that these sources can provide information about fraud alerts and credit freezes. The notice must not include the number of Illinois residents whose data was compromised.

Notice to state regulators or consumer reporting agencies/credit bureaus: Not required.

Indiana

Ind. Code § 24-4.9-2-2 *et seq.*

Categories of covered personal information: First name or first initial and last name, along with at least one of the following: (1) driver's license or state ID card number; (2) credit card number; or (3) financial account number or debit card number in combination with a security code, password, or access code. Separately, an unencrypted and unredacted social security number is considered to be personal information, even if it is not disclosed with an individual's name.

Exceptions to notice requirement: (1) encrypted information, unless that information "was or may have been acquired by an unauthorized person with access to the encryption key;" (2) if the company does not know or should not have known that the breach "resulted in or could result in identity deception, ... identity theft, or fraud;" (3) a company that "maintains its own disclosure procedures as part of an information privacy, security policy, or compliance plan" under the USA PATRIOT Act, Executive Order 13224, Driver's Privacy Protection Act, Fair Credit Reporting Act, GLBA, or HIPAA, provided that the policy or plan requires that "Indiana residents be notified of a breach of the security of the data without unreasonable delay and the data base owner complies with the data base owner's information privacy, security policy, or compliance plan;" or (4) a financial institution that complies with the Interagency Guidance's disclosure rules.

Timing of notice to individuals: Notice is required without unreasonable delay. A delay is reasonable if "necessary to restore the integrity of the computer system," "necessary to discovery the scope of the breach," or "in response to a request from the attorney general or a law enforcement agency to delay disclosure because disclosure will ... impede a criminal or civil investigation or jeopardize national security."

Requirements for notice to individual (form and content): (1) Written notice; (2) telephonic notice; (3) fax notice; (4) email; or (5) substitute notice, if the total cost of notice exceeds $250,000 or more than 500,000 "subject persons" would be notified. Substitute notice must be provided via a conspicuous posting on the company's website and notice to major news reporting media in the geographic area where Indiana residents affected by the data breach reside.

Notice to state regulators or consumer reporting agencies/credit bureaus: If any individuals are notified, the company must notify the Indiana Attorney General. If more than 1,000 Indiana residents are notified, the company also must notify the major credit reporting agencies.

Iowa

Iowa Code § 715c.1 *et seq.*

Categories of covered personal information: An individual's first name or first initial in combination with at least one of the following: (1) Social Security number; (2) driver's license or government identification number; (3) financial account number, credit card number, or debit card number, along with any required code or password; (4) "unique electronic identifier or routing code," combined with any required security code, access code, or password that would enable access to a financial account; or (5) unique biometric data (i.e., retinal image or fingerprint).

Exceptions to notice requirement: (1) If data is encrypted and key is not accessed, or if the data is redacted (the statute defines "encryption" as "use of an algorithmic process pursuant to accepted industry standards to transform data into a form in which the data is rendered unreadable or unusable without the use of a confidential process or key"); (2) after investigation or consulting with law enforcement, the company determines there is "no reasonable likelihood of financial harm" to the affected individuals, provided that the company documents this determination in writing and retains the documentation for five years; (3) the company complies with disclosure "rules, regulations, procedures, guidance, or guidelines" of its "primary or functional federal regulator," provided that the requirements provide protection at least equal to that under the Iowa law; or (4) the company is covered by GLBA and complies with its notice requirements.

Timing of notice to individuals: In the "most expeditious manner possible and without unreasonable delay," consistent with the "legitimate needs of law enforcement" and "any measures necessary to sufficiently determine contact information for the affected consumers, determine the scope of the breach, and restore the reasonable integrity, security, and confidentiality of the data."

Requirements for notice to individual (form and content): (1) Written notice; (2) electronic notice; or (3) substitute notice, if the cost of providing notice would exceed $250,000, the "affected class of consumers to be notified" is greater than 350,000 people, or the company does not have sufficient contact information. Substitute notice consists of email to available addresses, conspicuous posting of the notice on the company's website, and notification to major statewide media.

Notices must contain a description of the breach, the approximate date of the breach, the type of personal information breached, contact information for consumer reporting agencies, and advice to the consumer to report suspected identity theft to local law enforcement or the Iowa Attorney General.

Notice to state regulators or consumer reporting agencies/credit bureaus: If 500 or more Iowa residents are notified, the company must notify the director of the consumer protection division of the Iowa Attorney General's office within five business days of notifying the Iowa residents. The law does not require notification of credit bureaus.

Kansas

Kansas Stat. § 50-7a01 *et seq.*

Categories of covered personal information: An individual's first name or first initial and last name along with at least one of the following: (1) Social Security number; (2) driver's license or state ID card number; or (3) financial account or credit or debit card number, along with any required code or password.

Exceptions to notice requirement: (1) If the information is encrypted, which the statute defines as "transformation of data through the use of algorithmic process into a form in which there is a low probability of assigning meaning without the use of a confidential process or key, or securing the information by another method that renders the data elements unreadable or unusable;" (2) if an investigation concludes that "the misuse of information" has not occurred and is not "reasonably likely to occur;" (3) a company regulated by state or federal law that "maintains procedures for a breach of the security of the system pursuant to the laws, rules, regulations, guidances or guidelines established by its primary or functional state or federal regulator;" or (4) if the company maintains and follows "its own notification procedures as part of an information security policy for the treatment of personal information," consistent with the timing requirements of the Kansas breach notice law.

Timing of notice to individuals: In the "most expedient time possible and without unreasonable delay, consistent with the legitimate needs of law enforcement and consistent with any measures necessary to determine the scope of the breach and to restore the reasonable integrity of the computerized system."

Requirements for notice to individual (form and content): (1) Written notice; (2) electronic notice; or (3) substitute notice, if the cost of providing notice would exceed $100,000, the "affected class of consumers to be notified" exceeds 5,000, or the company does not have sufficient contact information. Substitute notice consists of email to available addresses, conspicuous posting of the notice on the company's website, and notification to major statewide media.

Notice to state regulators or consumer reporting agencies/credit bureaus: A company must notify credit reporting agencies of the timing, content, and distribution of notices if the company notified more than 1,000 Kansas residents.

Kentucky

Ky. Rev. Stat. § 365.732

Categories of covered personal information: An individual's first name or first initial and last name along with at least one of the following: (1) Social Security number; (2) driver's license or state ID card number; or (3) financial account or credit or debit card number, along with any required code or password.

Exceptions to notice requirement: (1) If the information is encrypted or redacted; (2) if the company does not "reasonably believe" that the breach "has caused or will cause, identity theft or fraud" against any Kentucky resident; (3) a company subject to GLBA or HIPAA; or (4) if the company follows and maintains "its own notification procedures as part of an information security policy for the treatment of personally identifiable information, and is otherwise consistent with the timing requirements" of the Kentucky breach notice law.

Timing of notice to individuals: In the "most expedient time possible and without unreasonable delay," consistent with legitimate law enforcement needs and "any measures necessary to determine the scope of the breach and restore the reasonable integrity of the data system."

Requirements for notice to individual (form and content): (1) Written notice; (2) electronic notice; or (3) substitute notice, if the cost of providing notice would exceed $250,000, the "affected class of subject persons to be notified" is greater than 500,000 people, or the company does not have sufficient contact information. Substitute notice consists of email to available addresses, conspicuous posting of the notice on the company's website, and notification to major statewide media.

Notice to state regulators or consumer reporting agencies/credit bureaus: A company must notify credit reporting agencies of the timing, content, and distribution of notices if the company notified more than 1,000 Kentucky residents.

Louisiana

La. Stat. § 51:3071 *et seq.*

Categories of covered personal information: An individual's first name or first initial and last name along with at least one of the following: (1) Social

Security number; (2) driver's license or state ID card number; (3) account or credit or debit card number, along with any required code or password, (4) passport number, or (5) biometric data.

Exceptions to notice requirement: (1) If the information is encrypted or redacted; (2) if "after a reasonable investigation, the person or business determines there is no reasonable likelihood of harm" to Louisianans, provided that the business retains a written copy of the determination for five years from the breach's discovery; (3) a financial institution subject to and in compliance with Interagency Guidance; or (4) if the company follows the security breach notification procedures of its information security policy, consistent with this statute's timing requirements.

Timing of notice to individuals: Within 60 days of discovery of the breach, and "in the most expedient time possible and without unreasonable delay," consistent with legitimate law enforcement needs and measures that are necessary to determine the scope of the breach, prevent further disclosure, and restore system integrity. If the notification is delayed, the company must provide a written explanation to the state Attorney General within 60 days.

Requirements for notice to individual (form and content): (1) Written notice; (2) electronic notice; or (3) substitute notice, if the cost of providing notice would exceed $100,000, the "affected class of persons to be notified" is greater than 100,000 people, or the company does not have sufficient contact information. Substitute notice consists of email to available addresses, conspicuous posting of the notice on the company's website, and notification to major statewide media.

Notice to state regulators or consumer reporting agencies/credit bureaus: A company must notify the Consumer Protection Section of the Office of the Louisiana Attorney General within ten days of notifying Louisiana residents. The notice should include the names of all Louisiana citizens who were notified of the breach.

Maine

Me. Rev. Stat. tit. 10, § 1346 *et seq.*

Categories of covered personal information: An individual's first name or first initial and last name along with at least one of the following: (1) Social Security number; (2) driver's license or state ID card number; (3) financial account or credit or debit card number, along with any required code or password; or (4) account passwords or PIN numbers or other access codes. Alternatively, any of those four data elements, without the individual's name, if the information "would be sufficient to permit a person to fraudulently assume or attempt to assume the identity of the person whose information was compromised."

Exceptions to notice requirement: (1) If the information is encrypted or redacted (the statute defines "encryption" as "disguising of data using generally accepted practices"); (2) if after conducting "in good faith a reasonable and prompt investigation" the company determines that it is not "reasonably possible" that the information could be misused (though this exception does not apply to information brokers); (3) if the company "complies with the security breach notification requirements of rules, regulations, procedures or guidelines established pursuant to federal law" or Maine law, provided they are at least as protective as the requirements of the Maine breach notice law.

Timing of notice to individuals: Disclosure must occur "as expediently as possible and without unreasonable delay, consistent with the legitimate needs of law enforcement pursuant" or "with measures necessary to determine the scope of the security breach and restore the reasonable integrity, security and confidentiality of the data in the system."

Requirements for notice to individual (form and content): (1) Written notice; (2) electronic notice; or (3) substitute notice, if the cost of providing notice would exceed $5000, the "affected class of individuals to be notified exceeds 1,000," or the company does not have sufficient contact information. Substitute notice consists of email to available addresses, conspicuous posting of the notice on the company's website, and notification to major statewide media.

Notice to state regulators or consumer reporting agencies/credit bureaus: A company that notifies Maine residents must notify the Maine Department of Professional and Financial Regulation or, if not regulated by that department, the Maine Attorney General. If the company notifies more than 1,000 Maine residents, the company must notify credit reporting agencies of the breach date, estimated number of people affected, and date of individual notification.

Maryland

Md. Code, Com. Law § 14-3501 *et seq.*

Categories of covered personal information: An individual's first name or first initial and last name along with at least one of the following: (1)

Social Security or passport number; (2) driver's license or state ID card number; (3) financial account or credit or debit card number, along with any required code or password; (4) an individual taxpayer identification number; (5) health information; (6) health insurance information; and (7) biometric data. Separately, the law covers a "user name or e-mail address in combination with a password or security question and answer that permits access to an individual's e-mail account."

Exceptions to notice requirement: (1) If the information is encrypted or redacted (the statute defines "encrypted" as "the protection of data in electronic or optical form using an encryption technology that renders the data indecipherable without an associated cryptographic key necessary to enable decryption of the data"); (2) if an investigation determines there is not a reasonable likelihood of misuse of the information, provided that the company retains written documentation of this determination for three years; (3) if the company is subject to rules of a primary or functional federal or state regulator; or (4) a financial institution subject to and complies with GLBA.

Timing of notice to individuals: Notification should be provided within 45 days of the conclusion of an investigation, and "as soon as reasonably practicable." Delay is permitted if "a law enforcement agency determines that the notification will impede a criminal investigation or jeopardize homeland or national security" or to "determine the scope of the breach of the security of a system, identify the individuals affected, or restore the integrity of the system."

Requirements for notice to individual (form and content): (1) Written notice; (2) electronic notice; (3) telephone notice; or (4) substitute notice, if the cost of providing notice would exceed $100,000, the "affected class of individuals to be notified exceeds 175,000," or the company does not have sufficient contact information. Substitute notice consists of email to available addresses, conspicuous posting of the notice on the company's website, and notification to major statewide media.

Notices must contain descriptions of the types of data breached; the company's contact information; the toll-free phone numbers and addresses for the credit reporting agencies; the toll-free telephone number, addresses, and websites for the FTC and Maryland Attorney General; and a statement that individuals can obtain information about identity theft from these sources.

Notice to state regulators or consumer reporting agencies/credit bureaus: A company must notify the Maryland Attorney General *before* notifying Maryland residents. If more than 1,000 Maryland residents are notified, credit bureaus also should be notified, and the notice should state the timing, content, and distribution of the individual notices.

Massachusetts

Mass. Gen. Laws ch. 93H, § 3

Categories of covered personal information: An individual's first name or first initial and last name along with at least one of the following: (1) Social Security number; (2) driver's license or state ID card number; or (3) financial account or credit or debit card number, along with any required code or password.

Exceptions to notice requirement: (1) If the information is encrypted with at least a 128-bit process and the key was not accessed; or (2) if the company maintains and follows "procedures for responding to a breach of security pursuant to federal laws, rules, regulations, guidance, or guidelines," provided that the company notifies Massachusetts residents and Massachusetts officials.

The statute does not have the standard risk-of-harm exception. Instead, it requires notification if a company "(1) knows or has reason to know of a breach of security or (2) when the person or agency knows or has reason to know that the personal information of such resident was acquired or used by an unauthorized person or used for an unauthorized purpose."

Timing of notice to individuals: Notification must be provided "as soon as practicable and without unreasonable delay." Delay is permitted "if a law enforcement agency determines that provision of such notice may impede a criminal investigation and has notified the attorney general, in writing, thereof and informs the person or agency of such determination." The company must "cooperate with law enforcement in its investigation of any breach of security or unauthorized acquisition or use, which shall include the sharing of information relevant to the incident, provided however, that such disclosure shall not require the disclosure of confidential business information or trade secrets."

Requirements for notice to individual (form and content): (1) Written notice; (2) electronic notice; or (3) substitute notice, if the cost of providing notice would exceed $250,000, more than 500,000 Massachusetts residents would have to be notified, or the company does not have sufficient contact information. Substitute notice consists of email to available addresses, conspicuous posting of the notice on the company's website, and notification to major statewide media.

The notice must include the consumer's right to obtain a police report, and instructions to request a security freeze, including fees paid to consumer reporting agencies. The notice must *not* describe the nature of the breach or the number of Massachusetts residents affected.

Notice to state regulators or consumer reporting agencies/credit bureaus: A company must notify the Massachusetts Attorney General and Director of Consumer Affairs and Business Regulation. The notice should describe the breach, the number of affected Massachusetts residents, and steps taken to remediate harm.

Michigan

Mich. Comp. Laws §§ 445.63, 445.72

Categories of covered personal information: An individual's first name or first initial and last name along with at least one of the following: (1) Social Security number; (2) driver's license or state ID card number; or (3) financial account or credit or debit card number, along with any required code or password.

Exceptions to notice requirement: (1) If the personal information was encrypted and the key was not disclosed (the statute defines "encrypted" as "transformation of data through the use of an algorithmic process into a form in which there is a low probability of assigning meaning without use of a confidential process or key, or securing information by another method that renders the data elements unreadable or unusable"); (2) if the company determines that the breach "has not or is not likely to cause substantial loss or injury to, or result in identity theft of" a Michigan resident; (3) "financial institution that is subject to, and has notification procedures in place that are subject to examination by the financial institution's appropriate regulator for compliance with" the Interagency Guidance under GLBA; or (4) a company subject to and in compliance with HIPAA.

Timing of notice to individuals: Notice must be provided "without unreasonable delay," except as needed legitimately for law enforcement or to "take any measures necessary to determine the scope of the security breach and restore the reasonable integrity of the database."

Requirements for notice to individual (form and content): (1) Written notice; (2) telephonic notice, subject to consent and format restrictions specified in the statute; (3) electronic notice, subject to consent and format restrictions specified in the statute; or (4) substitute notice, if the total cost of notification will exceed $250,000, more than 500,000 Michigan residents must be notified, or the company does not have sufficient contact information. Substitute notice consists of email notice if the company has email addresses; conspicuous posting of the notice on the company's website, and notice to major statewide media that includes a telephone number to obtain assistance and information.

Notices must be written in a "clear and conspicuous manner;" describe the breach in general terms; describe the type of personal information that is the subject of the unauthorized access or use, if applicable; describe remediation steps to prevent further breaches; include phone number for additional information; and remind recipients of the need to remain vigilant for identity theft and fraud.

Notice to state regulators or consumer reporting agencies/credit bureaus: Notice to major credit reporting agencies is required if more than 1,000 Michigan residents receive breach notices (though this does not apply to GLBA-covered companies). The notice must state the date of the notices that were sent to individuals.

Minnesota

Minn. Stat. § 325E.61 *et seq.*

Categories of covered personal information: An individual's first name or first initial and last name along with at least one of the following: (1) Social Security number; (2) driver's license or state ID card number; or (3) financial account or credit or debit card number, along with any required code or password.

Exceptions to notice requirement: (1) if the personal information was "secured by encryption or another method of technology that makes electronic data unreadable or unusable," provided that the key was not accessed; (2) a company that qualifies as a "financial institution" under GLBA; or (3) a company that follows "its own notification procedures as part of an information security policy for the treatment of personal information," provided that the timing of notification is consistent with the Minnesota breach notice law.

Timing of notice to individuals: Notice must be provided "in the most expedient time possible and without unreasonable delay," except as needed legitimately for law enforcement or "any measures necessary to determine the scope of the breach, identify the individuals affected, and restore the reasonable integrity of the data system."

Requirements for notice to individual (form and content): (1) Written notice; (2) electronic notice; or (3) substitute notice, if the total cost of notification will exceed $250,000, the "affected class of subject persons to be notified exceeds 500,000," or the company does not have sufficient contact information. Substitute notice consists of email notice if the company has email addresses, conspicuous posting of the notice on the company's website, and notice to major statewide media.

Notice to state regulators or consumer reporting agencies/credit bureaus: If a company determines that more than 500 Minnesota residents must be notified, the company must notify the major consumer reporting agencies, within 48 hours of the determination, of the timing, distribution, and content of the notices.

Mississippi

Miss. Code § 75-24-29

Categories of covered personal information: An individual's first name or first initial and last name along with at least one of the following: (1) Social Security number; (2) driver's license or state ID card number; or (3) financial account or credit or debit card number, along with any required code or password.

Exceptions to notice requirement: (1) If the personal information was "secured by encryption or by any other method or technology that renders the personal information unreadable or unusable;" (2) if after "appropriate investigation," the company "reasonably determines that the breach will not likely result in harm to the affected individuals;" (3) a company that maintains and follows a breach notice procedure under the rules of GLBA; or (4) a company that follows "an information security policy for the treatment of personal information" and the timing is consistent with this statute.

Timing of notice to individuals: Notice must be provided "without unreasonable delay," except as needed legitimately for law enforcement to "determine the nature and scope of the incident, to identify the affected individuals, or to restore the reasonable integrity of the data system."

Requirements for notice to individual (form and content): (1) Written notice; (2) telephone notice; (3) electronic notice; or (4) substitute notice, if the total cost of notification will exceed $5,000, the "affected class of subject persons to be notified" is greater than 5,000 people, or the company does not have sufficient contact information. Substitute notice consists of email notice if the company has email addresses; conspicuous posting of the notice on the company's website; and notice to major state-wide media, including newspapers, radio, and television.

Notice to state regulators or consumer reporting agencies/credit bureaus: Not required.

Missouri

Mo. Rev. Stat. § 407.1500

Categories of covered personal information: An individual's first name or first initial and last name along with at least one of the following: (1) Social Security number; (2) driver's license or state ID card number; (3) financial account or credit or debit card number, along with any required code or password; (4) "unique electronic identifier or routing code," along with any required code or password to access a financial account; (5) medical information; or (6) health insurance information.

Exceptions to notice requirement: (1) If the personal information was encrypted or redacted ("encryption" is defined as "the use of an algorithmic process to transform data into a form in which the data is rendered unreadable or unusable without the use of a confidential process or key"); (2) if after an "appropriate investigation" or consultation with law enforcement, the company "determines that a risk of identity theft or other fraud to any consumer is not reasonably likely to occur as a result of the breach," provided that the company documents this finding in writing and maintains it for five years; (3) a company "maintains procedures for a breach of the security of the system pursuant to the laws, rules, regulations, guidances, or guidelines established by its primary or functional state or federal regulator;" (4) a financial institution subject to the Interagency Guidance, GLBA, or the National Credit Union Administration regulations; or (5) a company that follows "its own notice procedures as part of an information security policy for the treatment of personal information," and the timing is consistent with the Missouri breach notice law.

Timing of notice to individuals: Notice must be provided "without unreasonable delay," except as needed legitimately for law enforcement or consistent with "any measures necessary to determine sufficient contact information and to determine the scope of the breach and restore the reasonable integrity, security, and confidentiality of the data system."

Requirements for notice to individual (form and content): (1) Written notice; (2) electronic notice; (3) telephone notice, if affected customers are directly contacted; or (4) substitute notice, if the total cost of notification will exceed $100,000, the "class of affected consumers to be notified" is greater than 150,000, or the company does not have sufficient contact information. Substitute notice consists of email notice if the company has email addresses, conspicuous posting of the notice on the company's website, and notice to major statewide media.

The notice should contain a description of the incident "in general terms;" the type of personal information obtained; a phone number for further information and assistance, if one exists; contact information for consumer reporting agencies; and advice that the consumer should "remain vigilant by reviewing account statements and monitoring free credit reports."

Notice to state regulators or consumer reporting agencies/credit bureaus: If a company determines that more than 1,000 Missouri residents must be notified, the company must notify the Missouri Attorney General's office and the major consumer reporting agencies of the timing, distribution, and content of the notices.

Montana

Mont. Code § 30-14-1701 *et seq.*

Categories of covered personal information: An individual's first name or first initial and last name along with at least one of the following: (1) Social Security number; (2) driver's license or state ID card number; (3) financial account or credit or debit card number, along with any required code or password; (4) medical record information; (5) taxpayer identification number; or (6) IRS-issued identity protection personal identification number.

Exceptions to notice requirement: (1) If the information is encrypted; (2) if the breach did not cause and is not "reasonably believed to cause" loss or injury to a Montana resident; or (3) if the company follows "its own notification procedures as part of an information security policy for the treatment of personal information" and "does not unreasonably delay notice."

Timing of notice to individuals: Notice must be provided "without unreasonable delay," consistent with legitimate law enforcement needs or "any measures necessary to determine the scope of the breach and restore the reasonable integrity of the data system."

Requirements for notice to individual (form and content): (1) Written notice; (2) electronic notice; (3) telephone notice; or (4) substitute notice, if the cost of providing notice would exceed $250,000, the "affected class of subject persons to be notified exceeds 500,000," or the company does not have sufficient contact information. Substitute notice consists of email to available addresses, conspicuous posting of the notice on the company's website, and notification to major statewide media.

Notice to state regulators or consumer reporting agencies/credit bureaus: When a company notifies Montana residents of a breach, it must simultaneously submit an electronic copy of the notice and a statement with the "date and method of distribution" of the individual notices to the Montana Attorney General's consumer protection office. The copy must not contain any personally identifiable information about the individual notice recipients. The statute does not require reports to the consumer reporting bureaus, but if the individual notices state that individuals may obtain copies of their files from the bureaus, the company must coordinate with the bureaus on the timing, content, and distribution of the individual notices. The coordination cannot unreasonably delay individual notices.

Nebraska

Neb. Rev. Stat. § 87-801 *et seq.*

Categories of covered personal information: (a) An individual's first name or first initial and last name along with at least one of the following: (1) Social Security number; (2) driver's license or state ID card number; (3) financial account or credit or debit card number, along with any required code or password; (4) unique electronic identification number or routing code, in combination with any required security code, access code, or password; or (5) "unique biometric data," such as a fingerprint, voice print, or retinal or iris image, or other unique physical representation; or

(b) a user name or email address, along with the password or security question that allows access to an online user account.

Exceptions to notice requirement: (1) If the information is encrypted, provided that the key was not accessed, or if the information was redacted (the statute defines "encrypted" as "converted by use of an algorithmic process to transform data into a form in which the data is rendered unreadable or unusable without use of a confidential process or key"); (2) if an investigation determines that use of information about a Nebraska resident for an unauthorized purpose has not occurred and is not "reasonably likely" to occur; (3) a company "regulated by state or federal law and that maintains procedures for a breach of the security of the system pursuant to the laws, rules, regulations, guidances, or guidelines established by its primary or functional state or federal regulator;" or (4) if the company follows "its own notice procedures which are part of an information security policy for the treatment of personal information," consistent with this statute's timing requirements.

Timing of notice to individuals: Notice must be made "as soon as possible and without unreasonable delay," consistent with "the legitimate needs of law enforcement and consistent with any measures necessary to determine the scope of the breach and to restore the reasonable integrity of the computerized data system."

Requirements for notice to individual (form and content): (1) Written notice; (2) electronic notice; (3) telephone notice; or (4) substitute notice, if the cost of providing notice would exceed $75,000, more than 100,000 Nebraska residents would have to be notified, or the company does not have sufficient contact information. Substitute notice consists of email to available addresses, conspicuous posting of the notice on the company's website, and notification to major statewide media.

If the company has ten or fewer employees and the cost of notice would exceed $10,000, substitute notice consists of (1) email to known addresses; (2) notification by a paid advertisement in a local newspaper in the geographic area in which the company is located, provided that the ad covers at least a quarter of a page in the newspaper and is published at least once a week for three consecutive weeks; (3) conspicuous posting on the company's website; and (4) notification to major media outlets in the geographic area in which the company is located.

Notice to state regulators or consumer reporting agencies/credit bureaus: If a company notifies Nebraska residents of a data breach, it must also notify the Nebraska Attorney General concurrently or before it notifies the individuals.

Nevada

Nev. Rev. Stat. § 603A.010 *et seq.*

Categories of covered personal information: First name or first initial and last name in combination with one or more of the following: (1) Social Security number (not including last four digits of number); (2) driver's license or state ID number; (3) financial account number, credit card number, or debit card number, in combination with any code or password necessary to access financial account; (4) medical identification number or health insurance identification number; or (5) a "user name, unique identifier or electronic mail address in combination with a password, access code or security question and answer that would permit access to an online account."

Exceptions to notice requirement: (1) If personal information is encrypted; (2) if the company is subject to and complies with GLBA's breach notice requirements; or (3) if the business follows "its own notification policies and procedures as part of an information security policy for the treatment of personal information" and is otherwise consistent with the law's timing requirements.

Timing of notice to individuals: Individual notice must be made in the "most expedient time possible and without unreasonable delay," consistent with the needs of law enforcement or "any measures necessary to determine the scope of the breach and restore the reasonable integrity of the system data."

Requirements for notice to individual (form and content): (1) Written notice; (2) electronic notice; or (3) substitute notice if the cost of notifying would exceed $250,000, the "affected class of subject persons to be notified" is greater than 500,000, or the company does not have sufficient contact information. Substitute notice consists of email notice when an address is available, conspicuous posting of the notice on the company's website, and notification to major statewide media.

Notice to state regulators or consumer reporting agencies/credit bureaus: If more than 1,000 Nevada residents are notified for one incident, the company must notify the major consumer reporting agencies of the time the notification was distributed and the content of the notification.

New Hampshire

N.H. Rev. Stat. § 359-C20

Categories of covered personal information: First name or first initial and last name in combination with one or more of the following: (1) Social Security number; (2) driver's license or state ID number; or (3) financial account number, credit card number, or debit card number, in combination with any code or password necessary to access financial account.

Exceptions to notice requirement: (1) If personal information is encrypted (the statute defines "encrypted" as "transformation of data through the use of an algorithmic process into a form for which there is a low probability of assigning meaning without use of a confidential process or key, or securing the information by another method that renders the data elements completely unreadable or unusable"); (2) if the company determines that misuse of the information has not occurred and is not "reasonably likely" to occur; or (3) a company subject to N.H. Rev. Stat. Ann. § 358-A:3 (e.g., a financial institution) and maintains procedures consistent with rules issued by a state or federal regulator.

Timing of notice to individuals: Individual notice must be made "as quickly as possible" after the company determines there is a risk of harm. Delay is permissible "if a law enforcement agency, or national or homeland security agency determines that the notification will impede a criminal investigation or jeopardize national or homeland security."

Requirements for notice to individual (form and content): (1) Written notice; (2) telephone notice; (3) electronic notice, if it was primary means of communication with individual; (4) substitute notice if the cost of notifying would exceed $5,000, the "affected class of subject individuals to be notified exceeds 1,000," or the company does not have sufficient contact information. Substitute notice consists of email notice when an address is available, conspicuous posting of the notice on the company's website, and notification to major statewide media; or (5) notice under the company's internal notification procedures maintained as part of an information security program.

The notice must include a description of the incident "in general terms," the approximate date of the breach, the type of personal information obtained due to the breach, and the telephone contact information for the company.

Notice to state regulators or consumer reporting agencies/credit bureaus: If the company notifies any individuals in New Hampshire, it also must notify the New Hampshire Attorney General's office of the anticipated date of the individual notice and the approximate number of New Hampshire residents who will be notified. The statute does not require companies to provide names of affected residents. Companies subject to N.H. Rev. Stat. Ann. § 358-A:3 (e.g., financial institutions) should notify their primary regulator rather than the New Hampshire Attorney General's office.

If more than 1,000 New Hampshire residents are notified for one incident, the company must notify the major consumer reporting agencies of the time the notification was distributed and the content of the notification. (Companies subject to GLBA need not notify credit bureaus.)

New Jersey

N.J. Stat. § 56:8-163

Categories of covered personal information: An individual's first name or first initial and last name along with at least one of the following: (1) Social Security number; (2) driver's license or state ID card number; or (3) financial account or credit or debit card number, along with any required code or password. "Dissociated" data that, if linked, would be personal information is considered to be personal information "if the means to link the dissociated data were accessed in connection with access to the dissociated data."

Exceptions to notice requirement: (1) If the information has "been secured by encryption or by any other method or technology that renders the personal information unreadable or unusable;" (2) if the business "establishes that misuse of the information is not reasonably possible" and retains a written documentation of that determination for five years; or (3) if the company follows "its own notification procedures as part of an information security policy for the treatment of personal information," provided that the procedures are "otherwise consistent with the requirements" of the New Jersey law.

Timing of notice to individuals: Notification must be provided "in the most expedient time possible and without unreasonable delay," consistent with legitimate law enforcement needs and "measures necessary to determine the scope of the breach and restore the reasonable integrity of the data system."

Requirements for notice to individual (form and content): (1) Written notice; (2) electronic notice; or (3) substitute notice, if the cost of providing notice would exceed $250,000, the "affected class of subject persons to be notified exceeds 500,000," or the company does not have sufficient contact information. Substitute notice consists of email to available addresses, conspicuous posting of the notice on the company's website, and notification to major statewide media.

Notice to state regulators or consumer reporting agencies/credit bureaus: A company must notify the New Jersey Division of State Police *before* notifying individuals. Note that it is rare for a state breach notice law to require notice to a state official before notifying consumers, so it is always important to keep the New Jersey law in mind if dealing with a breach of New Jersey residents' personal information.

If a company notifies more than 1,000 New Jersey residents, it should, without unreasonable delay, notify all consumer reporting agencies of the timing, distribution, and content of the notices.

New Mexico

H.B. 15 (2017)

Categories of covered personal information: First name or first initial and last name in combination with one or more of the following: (1) Social Security number; (2) driver's license or government ID number; (3) financial account number, credit card number, or debit card number in combination with any code or password necessary to access financial account; or (4) biometric data.

Exceptions to notice requirement: (1) If personal information is encrypted or redacted, provided that the key was not acquired; (2) if "after an appropriate investigation," the company "determines that the security breach does not give rise to a significant risk of identity theft or fraud;" (3) if the business follows "its own notice procedures as part of an information security policy for the treatment of personal identifying information" and its procedures are consistent with the New Mexico statute's timing requirements and is otherwise consistent with the timing requirements of that law.

Timing of notice to individuals: Within 45 calendar days of discovering the breach, and in "the most expedient time possible," unless a delay is necessary to "determine the scope of the security breach and restore the integrity, security and confidentiality of the data system" or is requested by law enforcement.

Requirements for notice to individual (form and content): (1) Written notice; (2) email notice; or (3) substitute notice if the cost of notifying would exceed $100,000, more than 50,000 residents of New Mexico would have to be notified, or the company does not have sufficient contact information. Substitute notice consists of email notice when an address is available, conspicuous posting of the notice on the company's website, and notification to statewide media and the state Attorney General.

Notice must include:

- The company's contact information;
- Categories of personal information suspected to have been breached;
- Date of the breach;
- A "general description" of the breach;
- Toll-free phone numbers for the credit bureaus;
- "advice that directs the recipient to review personal account statements and credit reports, as applicable, to detect errors resulting from the security breach" and
- Advice about the individual's rights under the federal Fair Credit Reporting Act.

Notice to state regulators or consumer reporting agencies/credit bureaus: If a single data breach results in notice to more than 1,000 New Mexico residents, the company must notify the state Attorney General and major credit bureaus within 45 days, unless a delay is permitted. The notification must include the number of notified New Mexico residents and a copy of the notice to individuals.

New York

N.Y. Gen. Bus. Law § 899-aa

Categories of covered personal information: Any "information concerning a natural person which, because of name, number, personal mark, or other identifier, can be used to identify such natural person" along with at least one of the following: (1) Social Security number; (2)

driver's license or state ID card number; or (3) financial account or credit or debit card number, along with any required code or password.

Exceptions to notice requirement: (1) If the personal information was encrypted and the key was not accessed; (2) if the company determines that the unauthorized acquisition did not compromise "the security, confidentiality, or integrity of personal information," after considering the following factors: (a) indications that the information is in the "physical possession and control of an unauthorized person;" (b) indications that "the information has been downloaded or copied;" and (c) indications that the information was "used by an unauthorized person, such as fraudulent accounts opened or instances of identity theft reported."

Timing of notice to individuals: Notice must be provided in the "most expedient time possible and without unreasonable delay," except as needed legitimately for law enforcement and "any measures necessary to determine the scope of the breach and restore the reasonable integrity of the system."

Requirements for notice to individual (form and content): (1) Written notice; (2) telephone notice; (3) electronic notice; or (4) substitute notice, if the total cost of notification will exceed $250,000, the "affected class of subject persons to be notified" is greater than 500,000, or the company does not have sufficient contact information. Substitute notice consists of email notice if the company has email addresses, conspicuous posting of the notice on the company's website, and notice to major statewide media.

The notice must include contact information for the company, and a description of the categories of information believed to have been acquired.

Notice to state regulators or consumer reporting agencies/credit bureaus: Any time that New York residents are notified of a data breach, the company should notify the New York Attorney General, the New York Department of State, and the New York Division of State Police of the timing, content, and distribution of the notices and the approximate number of New York residents affected. The notice must not delay notification of individuals.

If more than 5,000 New York residents are notified at one time, the company must notify the consumer reporting agencies of the timing, content, and distribution of the notices and approximate number of New York residents affected.

North Carolina

N.C. Gen. Stat § 75-65

Categories of covered personal information: An individual's first name or first initial and last name along with at least one of the following: (1) Social Security number; (2) driver's license or state ID card number; or (3) checking account number; (4) savings account number; (5) credit card number; (6) debit card number; (7) personal identification code; (8) electronic identification numbers, electronic mail names or addresses, Internet account numbers, or Internet identification names; (9) digital signatures; (10) any other numbers or information that can be used to access a person's financial resources; (11) biometric data; (12) fingerprints; (13) passwords; or (14) parent's legal surname prior to marriage.

Exceptions to notice requirement: (1) If the personal information was encrypted and the key has not been accessed ("encryption" is defined as the "use of an algorithmic process to transform data into a form in which the data is rendered unreadable or unusable without use of a confidential process or key"); (2) if "illegal use of the personal information" has not occurred, is not "reasonably likely to occur," and does not create "a material risk of harm to a consumer;" or (3) a financial institution that complies with the GLBA Interagency Guidance.

Timing of notice to individuals: Notice must be provided "without unreasonable delay," except as needed legitimately for law enforcement and "consistent with any measures necessary to determine sufficient contact information, determine the scope of the breach and restore the reasonable integrity, security, and confidentiality of the data system."

Requirements for notice to individual (form and content): (1) Written notice; (2) telephone notice; (3) electronic notice; or (4) substitute notice, if the total cost of notification will exceed $250,000, the "affected class of subject persons to be notified exceeds 500,000," or the company does not have sufficient contact information. Substitute notice consists of email notice if the company has email addresses; conspicuous posting of the notice on the company's website, and notice to major statewide media.

The notice must contain a description of the incident "in general terms;" a description of the categories of personal information that were subject to unauthorized access; a description of the steps the business took to prevent further unauthorized access; a phone number for further information and assistance; advice to "remain vigilant by reviewing account statements and monitoring free credit reports;" toll-free numbers and addresses for the major consumer reporting agencies; and toll-free numbers, addresses, and website addresses for the FTC and North Carolina Attorney General's office, along with a statement that the individual "can obtain information from these sources about preventing identity theft."

Notice to state regulators or consumer reporting agencies/credit bureaus: If any North Carolina residents are notified, the company must notify the North Carolina Attorney General's Consumer Protection Division, without unreasonable delay, of the nature of the breach, the number of consumers affected, steps taken to investigate the breach, steps taken to prevent a similar breach in the future, and information regarding the timing, distribution, and content of the notice.

If a company notifies more than 1,000 North Carolina residents at once, the company must notify the consumer reporting agencies of the timing, distribution, and content of the individual notices.

North Dakota

N.D. Cent. Code § 51-30-01 *et seq.*

Categories of covered personal information: An individual's first name or first initial and last name along with at least one of the following: (1) Social Security number; (2) driver's license or state ID card number; (3) financial account or credit or debit card number, along with any required code or password; (4) date of birth; (5) mother's maiden name; (6) medical information; (7) health insurance information; (8) employee identification number along with any required code or password; or (9) digitized or other electronic signature.

Exceptions to notice requirement: (1) If the information is encrypted or otherwise rendered "otherwise unreadable or unusable;" (2) a financial institution that complies with notice requirements of the Interagency Guidance; or (3) if the company follows "its own notification procedures as part of an information security policy for the treatment of personal information," consistent with the timing requirements of the North Dakota breach notice law.

Timing of notice to individuals: In the "most expedient time possible and without unreasonable delay," consistent with legitimate law enforcement needs and "any measures necessary to determine the scope of the breach and to restore the integrity of the data system."

Requirements for notice to individual (form and content): (1) Written notice; (2) electronic notice; or (3) substitute notice, if the cost of providing notice would exceed $250,000, the "affected class of subject persons to be notified" is greater than 500,000 people, or the company does not have sufficient contact information. Substitute notice consists of email to available addresses, conspicuous posting of the notice on the company's website, and notification to major statewide media.

Notice to state regulators or consumer reporting agencies/credit bureaus: If a company notifies more than 250 individuals of a data breach, it must disclose the breach to the North Dakota Attorney General by mail or email.

Ohio

Ohio Rev. Code § 1349.19 *et seq.*

Categories of covered personal information: First name or first initial and last name in combination with at least one of the following: (1) Social Security number; (2) driver's license or ID card number; or (3) account number or credit or debit card number, along with code or password necessary to access financial account. Personal information does not include information that already had lawfully been made publicly available by or to the news media.

Exceptions to notice requirement: (1) Encrypted or redacted personal information (the statute defines "encryption" as "the use of an algorithmic process to transform data into a form in which there is a low probability of assigning meaning without use of a confidential process or key"); (2) if the company does not "reasonably" believe that the breach will cause a "material risk of identity theft or other fraud" to Ohio residents; (3) if the company is a financial institution, trust company, or credit union or affiliate of such, and is required by federal law to issue breach notices to affected customers; or (4) if the company is a covered entity that is regulated under HIPAA.

Timing of notice to individuals: Disclosure must be provided in the "most expedient time possible," but no later than 45 days after discovery or notification of the breach, subject to legitimate needs of law enforcement and "consistent with any measures necessary to determine the scope of the breach, including which residents' personal information was accessed and acquired, and to restore the reasonable integrity of the data system."

Requirements for notice to individual (form and content): (1) Written notice; (2) telephonic notice; (3) electronic notice, if that is the company's primary method of communicating with the individual; or (4) substitute notice if the company demonstrates that the cost of notice exceeds $250,000, at least 500,000 Ohio residents would have to be notified, or the company does not have sufficient contact information. Substitute notice consists of email notice when available; conspicuous posting of the notice on the company's website; and notification to major media outlets, when the cumulative total readership, viewing audience, or listening audience combined is equal to at least 75 percent of Ohio's population.

Separately, Ohio allows another form of substitute notice if the company has ten or fewer employees and the cost of notice would exceed $10,000. In this case, the substitute notice must include (1) notice by a paid advertisement in a local newspaper that is distributed in the area in which the company is located, with the advertisement covering at least one-quarter of a page and published at least weekly for three consecutive weeks; (2) conspicuous posting of the notice on the company's website; and (3) notice to major media outlets in the company's geographic area.

Notice to state regulators or consumer reporting agencies/credit bureaus: Notice to state regulators not required. Notice to credit reporting agencies is required if more than 1,000 Ohio residents are notified. The notice to credit reporting agencies must describe the timing, distribution, and content of the individual breach notices.

Oklahoma

Okla. Stat. tit. 24, §§ 162–164

Categories of covered personal information: First name or first initial and last name in combination with at least one of the following: (1) Social Security number; (2) driver's license or ID card number; or (3) financial account number or credit or debit card number, along with code or password necessary to access financial accounts.

Exceptions to notice requirement: (1) Redacted or encrypted personal information, provided that the key was not accessed; (2) if the breach did not cause and is not reasonably believed to cause "identity theft or other fraud;" (3) a financial institution that complies with the federal Interagency Guidance on breach notification; (4) a company that "complies with the notification requirements or procedures pursuant to the rules, regulation, procedures, or guidelines established by the primary or functional federal regulator;" or (5) if the company follows "its own notification procedures as part of an information privacy or security policy for the treatment of personal information" and is consistent with the timing requirements of the Oklahoma breach notice law.

Timing of notice to individuals: Disclosure must be provided "without unreasonable delay," though delay is permitted "if a law enforcement agency determines and advises the individual or entity that the notice will impede a criminal or civil investigation or homeland or national security."

Requirements for notice to individual (form and content): (1) Written notice to postal address listed in company's records; (2) telephonic notice; (3) electronic notice; (4) substitute notice if the company demonstrates that the cost of notice exceeds $50,000, at least 100,000 Oklahoma residents would have to be notified, or the company does not have sufficient contact information. Substitute notice consists of at least two of the following methods: email notice when available, conspicuous posting of the notice on the company's website, and notification to major statewide media.

Notice to state regulators or consumer reporting agencies/credit bureaus: Not required.

Oregon

Or. Rev. Stat. § 646A.600 *et seq.*

Categories of covered personal information: First name or first initial and last name in combination with at least one of the following: (1) Social Security number; (2) driver's license or ID card number; (3) passport number or other identification number issued by the United States; (4) financial account number or credit or debit card number, along with code or password necessary to access financial account, or "any other information or combination of information that a person reasonably knows or should know would permit access to the consumer's financial account;" (5) data from "automatic measurements of a consumer's physical characteristics" (e.g., fingerprint or retinal scans) that are used to authenticate a consumer's identity for a transaction; (6) health insurance policy number or health insurance subscriber identification number in combination with unique identifiers used by health insurers; or (7) information about medical history, medical or physical condition, medical diagnosis, or treatment. These seven categories of information—without an individual's name—still could be considered personal information if they would enable identity theft.

Exceptions to notice requirement: (1) Encrypted or redacted personal information; (2) if, after an appropriate investigation or consultation with law enforcement, the company "reasonably determines" that the consumers are "unlikely to suffer harm" (this determination must be documented in writing and retained for at least five years); (3) if a company follows notification rules that its "primary or functional federal regulator adopts, promulgates or issues in rules, regulations, procedures, guidelines or guidance, if the rules, regulations, procedures, guidelines or guidance provide greater protection to personal information and disclosure requirements at least as thorough as the protections and disclosure requirements provided" under the Oregon breach notice law; (4) the company is a financial institution that complies with GLBA; or (5) if the company follows its internal notification procedures and those procedures are consistent with the statute's timing requirements.

Timing of notice to individuals: Disclosure must be provided within 45 days of discovery or notification of the breach, and in the most "expeditious manner possible" and "without unreasonable delay," consistent with legitimate needs of law enforcement and "consistent with any measures that are necessary to determine sufficient contact information for the affected consumer, determine the scope of the breach of security and restore the reasonable integrity, security and confidentiality of the personal information."

Requirements for notice to individual (form and content): (1) Written notice; (2) telephonic notice, if the company directly contacts the consumer by that means; (3) electronic notice, if that is the company's customary method of communicating with the individual; or (4) substitute notice if the company demonstrates that the cost of notice exceeds $250,000, the "affected class of consumers exceeds 350,000," or the company does not have sufficient contact information. Substitute notice consists of email notice when available, conspicuous posting of the notice on the company's website, and notification to major statewide television and media.

Notice must contain a description of the data breach "in general terms;" the approximate date of the breach; the type of personal information that was subject to the breach; contact information for the company that was subject to the breach; contact information for credit bureaus; and advice to report suspected identity theft to law enforcement, including the Attorney General and the Federal Trade Commission.

If the company provides free credit monitoring or identity theft prevention and mitigation services, the company cannot condition the services on the individual providing a credit card or debit card number, or on the purchase of any other service. If the services are offered for a fee, the company "must separately, distinctly, clearly, and conspicuously disclose in the offer for the additional credit monitoring services or identity theft prevention and mitigation services" that the company will charge a fee.

Notice to state regulators or consumer reporting agencies/credit bureaus: If the number of affected Oregon residents exceeds 250, the company, either in writing or electronically, must provide the Oregon Attorney General with the same notice provided to consumers. Notice to credit reporting agencies without unreasonable delay is required, provided that more than 1,000 Oregon residents are affected. The notice to credit bureaus should include the notice provided to individuals, and any police report number assigned to the data breach.

Pennsylvania

73 Pa. Cons. Stat. § 2301 *et seq.*

Categories of covered personal information: First name or first initial and last name in combination with at least one of the following: (1) Social Security number; (2) driver's license or ID card number; or (3) financial account number or credit or debit card number, along with code or password necessary to access financial account.

Exceptions to notice requirement: (1) Redacted or encrypted information, if the key was not accessed; (2) if the company does not "reasonably" believe that the breach has caused or will cause "loss or injury" to a Pennsylvania resident; (3) if a company "complies with the notification requirements or procedures pursuant to the rules, regulations, procedures or guidelines established by the entity's primary or functional Federal regulator;" (4) if the company is a financial institution that complies with the Interagency Guidance procedures; or (5) if the company follows "its own notification procedures as part of an information privacy or security policy for the treatment of personal information," provided that the policy is "consistent with the notice requirements" of the Pennsylvania breach notice law.

Timing of notice to individuals: Disclosure must be provided "without unreasonable delay," except to determine the scope of the breach and restore the reasonable integrity of the data system, or at the written request of law enforcement.

Requirements for notice to individual (form and content): (1) Written notice to the last known postal address; (2) telephonic notice, if the individual can reasonably be expected to receive it and the notice clearly and conspicuously describes the incident generally and verifies personal information but does not require the customer to provide personal information, and the customer is provided with a phone number or website for further information or assistance; (3) electronic notice, if a prior business relationship exists and the company has a valid email address for the individual; or (4) substitute notice if the company demonstrates that the cost of notice exceeds $100,000, the "affected class of subject persons to be notified exceeds 175,000," or the company does not have sufficient contact information. Substitute notice consists of email notice when available, conspicuous posting of the notice on the company's website, and notification to major statewide media.

Notice to state regulators or consumer reporting agencies/credit bureaus: Notice to state regulators is not required. Notice to credit reporting agencies is required, provided that more than 1,000 Pennsylvania residents are notified. The notice to credit reporting agencies must state the timing, distribution, and number of individual notices.

Rhode Island

R.I. Gen. Laws § 11-49.3-3 *et seq.*

Categories of covered personal information: First name or first initial and last name in combination with at least one of the following: (1) Social Security number; (2) driver's license or ID card number; (3) financial account number or credit or debit card number, along with code or password necessary to access financial account; (4) medical or health insurance information; or (5) email address with any security code, access code, or password that would allow access to a personal, medical, insurance, or financial account.

Exceptions to notice requirement: (1) Encrypted personal information (the statute defines "encrypted" as "transformation of data through the use of a one hundred twenty-eight (128) bit or higher algorithmic process into a form in which there is a low probability of assigning meaning without use of a confidential process or key. Data shall not be considered to be encrypted if it is acquired in combination with any key, security code, or password that would permit access to the encrypted data"); (2) if the company determines that the breach does not pose "a significant risk of identity theft" to Rhode Island residents; (3) if the company follows "a security breach procedure pursuant to the rules, regulations, procedures, or guidelines established by the primary or functional regulator;" (4) the company is a financial institution that complies with the GLBA Interagency Guidelines; (5) the company is a health-related company that complies with HIPAA's breach notification procedures; or (6) if the company follows "its own security breach procedures as part of an information security policy for the treatment of personal information" and is consistent with the timing requirements of the Rhode Island breach notice law.

Timing of notice to individuals: Disclosure must be provided in the "most expedient time possible," but no later than 45 days after confirmation of the breach and the ability to ascertain the information required to fulfill the notice requirements, "consistent with the legitimate needs of law enforcement."

Requirements for notice to individual (form and content): (1) Written notice; (2) electronic notice; or (3) substitute notice if the company demonstrates that the cost of notice exceeds $25,000, the "affected class of subject persons to be notified exceeds" 50,000 people, or the company does not have sufficient contact information. Substitute notice consists of email notice when available, conspicuous posting of the notice on the company's website, and notification to major statewide media.

The individual notices should contain (1) a "general and brief description" of the breach, including how it occurred and the number of affected individuals; (2) the type of information that was breached; (3) date (or estimated date) of the breach; (4) date of discovery of the breach; (5) description of remediation services, including toll-free phone numbers and websites for credit reporting agencies, remediation service providers, and the Rhode Island Attorney General; and (6) a "clear and concise" description of the consumer's ability to file or obtain a police report regarding the data breach, how the individual can request a security freeze on financial accounts, and the fees that consumers may be required to pay to credit bureaus for these remedies.

Notice to state regulators or consumer reporting agencies/credit bureaus: Notice to the Attorney General and the major credit bureaus is required if more than 500 Rhode Island residents are notified. The notices should describe the timing, content, and distribution of the individual notices and the approximate number of affected individuals. These notices are not grounds to delay individual notifications.

South Carolina

S.C. Code § 39-1-90

Categories of covered personal information: First name or first initial and last name in combination with at least one of the following: (1) Social Security number; (2) driver's license or ID card number; (3) financial account number or credit or debit card number, along with code or password necessary to access financial account; or (4) "other numbers or information which may be used to access a person's financial accounts or numbers or information issued by a governmental or regulatory entity that uniquely will identify an individual."

Exceptions to notice requirement: (1) if the information has been "rendered unusable through encryption, redaction, or other methods;" (2) if the company concludes that "illegal use of the information" has not occurred, is "not reasonably likely to occur," and does not create a "material risk of harm" to a South Carolina resident; (3) if a company is a financial institution or bank subject to GLBA; (4) if the company is a financial institution subject to and complying with the GLBA Interagency Guidance; or (5) if the company follows "its own notification procedures as part of an information security policy for the treatment of personal identifying information" and issues a notification that is consistent with the timing requirements of the South Carolina breach notice law.

Timing of notice to individuals: Disclosure must be provided in the "most expedient time possible and without unreasonable delay," subject to law enforcement's legitimate needs, or consistent with "measures necessary to determine the scope of the breach and restore the reasonable integrity of the data system."

Requirements for notice to individual (form and content): (1) Written notice; (2) telephonic notice; (3) electronic notice, if that is the company's primary method of communicating with the individual; or (4) substitute notice if the company demonstrates that the cost of notice exceeds $250,000, the "affected class of subject persons to be notified" is greater than 500,000 people, or the company does not have sufficient contact information. Substitute notice consists of email notice when available, conspicuous posting of the notice on the company's website, and notification to major statewide media.

Notice to state regulators or consumer reporting agencies/credit bureaus: If more than 1,000 South Carolina residents are notified, the company must notify without unreasonable delay the Consumer

Protection Division of the South Carolina Department of Consumer Affairs and the major credit bureaus of the timing, distribution, and content of the notices to individuals.

South Dakota

S.B. 62, 2018 (to be codified)

Categories of covered personal information: First name or first initial and last name in combination with at least one of the following: (1) Social Security number; (2) driver's license or ID card number; (3) financial account number or credit or debit card number, along with code or password necessary to access financial accounts; (4) health information; or (5) "an identification number assigned to a person by the person's employer in combination with any required security code, access code, password, or biometric data generated from measurements of human body characteristics for authentication purposes."

Exceptions to notice requirement: (1) Encrypted or redacted personal information; (2) if the company, after investigating and notifying the state Attorney General, "reasonably determines that the breach will not likely result in harm to the affected person," provided that the company retains the written documentation of this determination for at least three years; (3) if a company is regulated by a federal law or regulation, such as HIPAA or GLBA, regarding data breach notification; (4) if the company concludes that illegal use of the information has not occurred, is "not reasonably likely to occur," and does not create a "material risk of harm" to a South Carolina resident; or (5) if the company follows its own internal notification policy.

Timing of notice to individuals: Disclosure must be provided within 60 days of discovery or notification of the breach, unless law enforcement's legitimate needs require a delay.

Requirements for notice to individual (form and content): (1) Written notice; (2) electronic notice, if that is the company's primary method of communicating with the individual; or (3) substitute notice if the company demonstrates that the cost of notice exceeds $250,000, the "affected class of persons to be notified" is greater than 500,000 people, or the company does not have sufficient contact information. Substitute notice consists of email notice when available, conspicuous posting of the notice on the company's website, and notification to major statewide media.

Notice to state regulators or consumer reporting agencies/credit bureaus: The company must notify the credit bureaus of any breach without unreasonable delay. If more than 250 residents are notified, the company must notify the state Attorney General.

Tennessee

Tenn. Code § 47-18-2107(a)

Categories of covered personal information: First name or first initial and last name in combination with at least one of the following: (1) Social Security number; (2) driver's license or ID card number; or (3) account number or credit or debit card number, along with code or password necessary to access financial account.

Exceptions to notice requirement: (1) if the data is encrypted, provided that the key was not accessed; (2) if the company determines that the breach did not "materially" compromise the security, confidentiality, or integrity of personal information; (3) if the company is subject to GLBA; (4) if the company is subject to HIPAA; or (5) if the company complies with "its own notification procedures as part of an information security policy for the treatment of personal information" and is consistent with the timing requirements of the Tennessee breach notification law.

Timing of notice to individuals: Disclosure must be provided immediately, but no later than 45 days from the discovery or notification of the breach, unless the legitimate needs of law enforcement require a delay.

Requirements for notice to individual (form and content): (1) Written notice; (2) electronic notice; or (3) substitute notice if the company demonstrates that the cost of notice exceeds $250,000, the "affected class of subject persons to be notified" is greater than 500,000 people, or the company does not have sufficient contact information. Substitute notice consists of email notice when available, conspicuous posting of the notice on the company's website, and notification to major statewide media.

Notice to state regulators or consumer reporting agencies/credit bureaus: Notice to state regulators is not required. Notice to credit reporting agencies is required, provided that more than 1,000 Tennessee residents are notified. The notice to credit reporting agencies must describe the timing, distribution, and content of the individual notices.

Texas

Tex. Bus. & Com. Code § 521.001 *et seq.*

Categories of covered personal information: The Texas statute applies to "sensitive personal information," which includes two general categories. The first category includes first name or first initial and last name in combination with at least one of the following: (1) Social Security number; (2) driver's license or ID card number; or (3) financial account number or credit or debit card number, along with code or password necessary to access financial account. The second category includes sensitive information that identifies an individual and relates to (1) the physical or mental health or condition of the individual; (2) the provision of health care to the individual; or (3) payment for the provision of health care to the individual.

Some commentators have suggested that the Texas statute could be read to suggest that it requires companies to provide notice even if the affected individuals do not live in Texas, though no court has ruled on this issue.

Exceptions to notice requirement: (1) Encrypted data, provided that the accessor does not have the decryption key; or (2) if the company follows its "own notification procedures as part of an information security policy for the treatment of sensitive personal information" and is consistent with the timing requirements of the Texas breach notification statute.

Timing of notice to individuals: Disclosure must be made "as quickly as possible," except if a delay is requested by law enforcement or "as necessary to determine the scope of the breach and restore the reasonable integrity of the data system."

Requirements for notice to individual (form and content): (1) Written notice to last known address; (2) electronic notice; or (3) substitute notice if the company demonstrates that the cost of notice exceeds $250,000, the "number of affected persons exceeds 500,000," or the company does not have sufficient contact information. Substitute notice consists of email notice when available, conspicuous posting of the notice on the company's website, and notification published in or broadcast on major statewide media.

Notice to state regulators or consumer reporting agencies/credit bureaus: Notice to state regulators is not required. Notice to credit reporting agencies is required, provided that more than 10,000 people are notified under this law. The notice to credit reporting agencies must state the timing, distribution, and content of the individual notices.

Utah

Utah Code § 13-44-101 *et seq.*

Categories of covered personal information: First name or first initial and last name in combination with at least one of the following: (1) Social Security number; (2) driver's license or ID card number; or (3) financial account number or credit or debit card number, along with code or password necessary to access financial account.

Exceptions to notice requirement: (1) If the personal information is encrypted or protected by another method that renders the data unreadable or unusable; (2) if a "reasonable and prompt investigation" conducted in good faith determines that "misuses of personal information for identity theft or fraud purposes" has neither occurred nor is "reasonably likely to occur;" (3) if a company is "regulated by state or federal law and maintains procedures for a breach of system security under applicable law established by the primary state or federal regulator," provided that it follows that system's notification rules; or (4) if the company follows its "own notification procedures as part of an information security policy for the treatment of personal information" that is consistent with the timing requirements of the Utah breach notice law.

Timing of notice to individuals: Disclosure must be provided in "the most expedient time possible and without unreasonable delay," subject to the needs of law enforcement and to determine the scope of the breach and restore system integrity.

Requirements for notice to individual (form and content): (1) Written notice via first-class mail to the individual's most recent address; (2) telephonic notice, including via automatic dialing technology that is not legally prohibited; (3) electronic notice, if that is the company's primary method of communicating with the individual; or (4) for Utah residents for whom the other notification methods are "not feasible," publishing a notice in a general circulation newspaper. Unlike most other states, Utah does not allow the standard form of substitute notice.

Notice to state regulators or consumer reporting agencies/credit bureaus: Notice is not required.

Vermont

Vt. Stat. Ann. tit. 9, § 2430 *et seq.*

Categories of covered personal information: First name or first initial and last name in combination with at least one of the following: (1) Social Security number; (2) driver's license or ID card number; (3) financial account number or credit or debit card number, along with code or password necessary to access financial account; or (4) account passwords, PINS, or other codes that could access a financial account.

Exceptions to notice requirement: (1) Information that is encrypted, redacted, or "protected by another method that renders [it] unreadable or unusable by unauthorized persons;" (2) the company determines that misuse of personal information is "not reasonably possible" and notifies the Vermont Attorney General or Vermont Department of Financial Regulation of this determination; or (3) if a company is a financial institution that is subject to the GLBA Interagency Guidance.

Timing of notice to individuals: Disclosure must be provided "in the most expedient time possible and without unreasonable delay," but not later than 45 days after the discovery or notification, subject to law enforcement's "legitimate needs" or consistent "with any measures necessary to determine the scope of the security breach and restore the reasonable integrity, security, and confidentiality of the data system."

Requirements for notice to individual (form and content): (1) Written notice to the individual's residence; (2) telephonic notice, provided that telephonic contact is made directly with each affected individual and not via a prerecorded message; (3) electronic notice, if the company has a valid email address; or (4) substitute notice if the company demonstrates that the cost of notice exceeds $5,000, the "class of affected consumers to be provided written or telephonic notice exceeds 5,000," or the company does not have sufficient contact information. Substitute notice consists of conspicuous posting of the notice on the company's website and notification to major statewide and regional media.

Individual notices must contain (1) a description of the breach; (2) the type of personal information that was breached; (3) the steps that the company took to protect against further unauthorized access; (4) a toll-free number for more information; (5) advice to "remain vigilant" by reviewing account statements and free credit reports; and (6) date of the breach.

Notice to state regulators or consumer reporting agencies/credit bureaus: Vermont requires two forms of notice to state regulators.

First, the Vermont Attorney General or Department of Financial Regulation must be notified of the dates of the breach and discovery, along with a preliminary description, within 14 business days, consistent with the needs of law enforcement. Companies must notify state regulators no later than when they notify consumers. In other words, if a company notifies consumers seven days after discovering a breach, it must notify Vermont regulators at the same time that it notifies consumers, even though the 14-day period has not elapsed. If, before the breach occurs, the company swears in writing to the Attorney General that it maintains written security policies and procedures and responds to breaches in a manner consistent with Vermont law, the company need only notify state regulators of the date of the breach and discovery of the breach before it notifies individuals.

Second, when companies notify Vermont residents of data breaches, they also must provide Vermont regulators with a copy of the individual notice and the number of Vermont residents who were notified.

If more than 1,000 consumers are notified, the company shall notify credit bureaus, without unreasonable delay, of the timing, distribution, and content of the notice.

Data brokers: Separate from its standard data breach notice law, as of 2019, Vermont began requiring data brokers to annually report data breaches to the Vermont Secretary of State. Data brokers must report breaches of individuals' names, addresses, birth dates, places of birth, mother's maiden names, biometric data, immediate family members' names or addresses, social security numbers or other government-issued identification numbers, or "other information that, alone or in combination with the other information sold or licensed, would allow a reasonable person to identify the consumer with reasonable certainty."

Virginia

Va. Code § 18.2-186.6

Categories of covered personal information: First name or first initial and last name in combination with at least one of the following: (1) Social Security number; (2) driver's license or ID card number; or (3) financial account number or credit or debit card number, along with code or password necessary to access financial account.

Exceptions to notice requirement: (1) Encrypted or redacted personal information; (2) if the company does not reasonably believe that the breach "has caused or will cause identity theft or other fraud" to a Virginia resident; (3) if the company follows its internal notification procedures and is consistent with the timing requirements of the statute; or (4) if the company is subject to and complies with the notification requirements of GLBA or the requirements of its primary or functional state or federal regulator.

Timing of notice to individuals: Disclosure must be provided "without unreasonable delay," subject to the needs of law enforcement and to determine the scope of the breach and restore system integrity.

Requirements for notice to individual (form and content): (1) Written notice to the last known postal address listed in the company's records; (2) telephonic notice; (3) electronic notice; or (4) substitute notice if the company demonstrates that the cost of notice exceeds $50,000, at least 100,000 Virginia residents would have to be notified, or the company does not have sufficient contact information. Substitute notice consists of email notice when available, conspicuous posting of the notice on the company's website, and notification to major state-wide media.

Notice must describe: (1) the incident "in general terms;" (2) the categories of personal information subject to the breach; (3) the general steps taken to protect the information from further unauthorized access; (4) a phone number for more information, if one exists; and (5) advice to "remain vigilant by reviewing account statements and monitoring free credit reports."

Notice to state regulators or consumer reporting agencies/credit bureaus: Notice of the timing, distribution, and content of the individual notices must be sent to the Virginia Attorney General and consumer reporting agencies "without unreasonable delay" if more than 1,000 Virginia residents are notified at one time.

Income tax data breach: If a company experiences a breach of "computerized data relating to income tax withheld," it must notify the Virginia Attorney General "without unreasonable delay." Covered data includes a taxpayer identification number combined with the income tax withheld, provided that the company "reasonably believes" that the breach "has caused or will cause, identity theft or other fraud." For employers, the requirement only applies to the company's own employees, and not to customers or others. If notice is required, the company must provide the Virginia Attorney General with its name and federal employer identification number.

Washington State

Wash. Rev. Code § 19.255.010

Categories of covered personal information: First name or first initial and last name in combination with at least one of the following: (1) Social Security number; (2) driver's license or ID card number; or (3) financial account number or credit or debit card number, along with code or password necessary to access financial account.

Exceptions to notice requirement: (1) the information is encrypted; (2) if the company determines that the breach is "not reasonably likely to subject consumers to a risk of harm;" (3) if the company follows "its own notification procedures as part of an information security policy for the treatment of personal information" and is consistent with the timing requirements of the Washington state breach notice law; or (4) if the company is subject to and complies with the notification requirements of HIPAA or the GLBA financial institution Interagency Guidelines.

Timing of notice to individuals: Disclosure must be provided in the "most expedient time possible and without unreasonable delay," and no later than 45 days after discovery of the breach, unless requested by law enforcement or "due to any measures necessary to determine the scope of the breach and restore the reasonable integrity of the data system."

Requirements for notice to individual (form and content): (1) Written notice; (2) electronic notice; or (3) substitute notice if the company demonstrates that the cost of notice exceeds $250,000, the "affected class of subject persons to be notified" is greater than 500,000 people, or the company does not have sufficient contact information. Substitute notice consists of email notice when available, conspicuous posting of the notice on the company's website, and notification to major statewide media.

Notices must be written in "plain language" and include (1) name and contact information of the company, (2) a list of the categories of personal information at issue, and (3) toll-free telephone numbers of the major credit reporting agencies if personal information was exposed.

Notice to state regulators or consumer reporting agencies/credit bureaus: If a company is required to notify more than 500 Washington state residents of a breach, it must electronically submit a sample copy of that notification, without personally identifiable information, to the Washington

State Attorney General, along with the number of Washington State residents affected (or an estimate if the exact number is unknown). Credit bureau notification is not required.

West Virginia

W. Va. Code § 46A-2A-101 *et seq.*

Categories of covered personal information: First name or first initial and last name in combination with at least one of the following: (1) Social Security number; (2) driver's license or ID card number; or (3) financial account number or credit or debit card number, along with code or password necessary to access financial account.

Exceptions to notice requirement: (1) Encrypted or redacted personal information ("encrypted" is defined as "transformation of data through the use of an algorithmic process into a form in which there is a low probability of assigning meaning without use of a confidential process or key or securing the information by another method that renders the data elements unreadable or unusable"); (2) if the company does not "reasonably believe that the breach has caused or will cause identity theft or other fraud" to a West Virginia resident; (3) if the company "complies with the notification requirements or procedures pursuant to the rules, regulation, procedures or guidelines established by the entity's primary or functional regulator;" (4) if a company is subject to and follows the financial institution federal Interagency Guidance for notifications; or (5) if the company follows "its own notification procedures as part of an information privacy or security policy for the treatment of personal information" and is consistent with the timing requirements of the West Virginia breach notice law.

Timing of notice to individuals: Disclosure must be provided "without unreasonable delay," subject to "any measures necessary to determine the scope of the breach and to restore the reasonable integrity of the system." Additionally, the company may delay notice if "a law-enforcement agency determines and advises the individual or entity that the notice will impede a criminal or civil investigation or homeland or national security."

Requirements for notice to individual (form and content): (1) Written notice to postal address of the individual; (2) telephonic notice; (3) electronic notice; or (4) substitute notice if the company demonstrates that the cost of notice exceeds $50,000, at least 100,000 West Virginia residents would have to be notified, or the company does not have sufficient contact information. Substitute notice consists of email notice when available, conspicuous posting of the notice on the company's website, and notification to major statewide media.

Notice to state regulators or consumer reporting agencies/credit bureaus: Notice to state regulators is not required. If more than 1,000 West Virginia residents are notified, the company also must notify the credit reporting agencies of the timing, distribution, and content of the notices. This requirement does not apply to financial institutions that are subject to GLBA.

Wisconsin

Wis. Stat. § 134.98

Categories of covered personal information: First name or first initial and last name in combination with at least one of the following: (1) Social Security number; (2) driver's license or ID card number; (3) financial account number or credit or debit card number, along with code or password necessary to access financial account; (4) DNA profile; or (5) unique biometric data, including fingerprint, voice print, retinal or iris image, or other unique physical representation.

Exceptions to notice requirement: (1) Encrypted or redacted personal information; (2) if the breach "does not create a material risk of identity theft or fraud to the subject of the personal information;" or (3) if a company is subject to and follows the financial institution federal Interagency Guidance for notifications or HIPAA's notification procedures.

Timing of notice to individuals: Disclosure must be provided "within a reasonable time," not to exceed 45 days after the company learns of the breach. Reasonableness determinations should consider the number of notices required and methods of communication available. Notice may be delayed at the request of law enforcement.

Requirements for notice to individual (form and content): The notice must be provided by mail or the method the company has previously used to communicate with the individual. If, with reasonable diligence, the company cannot determine the individual's mailing address and has not previously communicated with the individual, the company must use a "method reasonably calculated to provide actual notice to the subject of the personal information."

The individual notice should indicate that the company knows of a breach of personal information pertaining to the individual.

Notice to state regulators or consumer reporting agencies/credit bureaus: Notice to state regulators is not required. If more than 1,000 Wisconsin residents are notified, the company also must notify the credit reporting agencies of the timing, distribution, and content of the notices.

Wyoming

Wyo. Stat. § 40-12-501 *et seq.*

Categories of covered personal information: First name or first initial and last name in combination with at least one of the following: (1) Social Security number; (2) driver's license number; (3) financial account number, credit card number, or debit card number in combination with any security code or password that would allow access to a financial account; (4) tribal identification card; (5) federal or state government-issued ID card; (6) shared secrets or security tokens that are known to be used for data-based authentication; (7) username or email address in combination with a password; (8) birth or marriage certificate; (9) medical information; (10) health insurance information; (10) unique biometric data; or (11) individual taxpayer ID number.

Exceptions to notice requirement: (1) Encrypted or redacted personal information; (2) if an investigation determines that misuse of the personal information has not occurred and is not "reasonably likely to occur;" (3) if a company is subject to and follows the financial institution federal Interagency Guidance for notifications; or (4) if the company follows its internal notification procedures and is consistent with the timing requirements of the state statute.

Timing of notice to individuals: Disclosure must be provided in the "most expedient time possible and without unreasonable delay" consistent with legitimate needs of law enforcement and measures necessary to determine the scope of the breach and restore reasonable integrity of the data system.

Requirements for notice to individual (form and content): (1) Written notice; (2) electronic notice; or (3) substitute notice if the company demonstrates that "the affected class of subject persons to be notified exceeds ten thousand (10,000) for Wyoming-based persons or businesses and five hundred thousand (500,000) for all other businesses operating but not based in Wyoming"; or if the company does not have sufficient contact information. Substitute notice consists of conspicuous posting of the notice on the company's website, and notification to major statewide media.

Individual notices must contain, at minimum, (1) a toll-free phone number to contact the company and learn the contact information for major credit bureaus; (2) the types of personal information that were reasonably believed to have been breached; (3) a general description of the breach; (4) the approximate date of the breach, if determinable; (5) the steps taken by the company to prevent further harm; (6) advice to remain vigilant by reviewing account statements and monitoring credit reports; and (7) whether notification was delayed due to a law enforcement investigation, if that is possible to determine at the time of the notice.

Notice to state regulators or consumer reporting agencies/credit bureaus: Notice to state regulators and credit bureaus is not required.

Appendix C

Text of Section 1201 of the Digital Millennium Copyright Act

Section 1201 of the Digital Millennium Copyright Act, examined in Chapter 5, restricts the circumvention of controls that protect copyrighted materials. In practice, this can create significant obstacles for cybersecurity researchers who seek to test software for vulnerabilities. Here is the full text of Section 1201.

17 U.S.C. §1201. Circumvention of copyright protection systems

(a)   Violations Regarding Circumvention of Technological Measures.

(1)   (A) No person shall circumvent a technological measure that effectively controls access to a work protected under this title. The prohibition contained in the preceding sentence shall take effect at the end of the 2-year period beginning on the date of the enactment of this chapter.

(B)   The prohibition contained in subparagraph (A) shall not apply to persons who are users of a copyrighted work which is in a particular class of works, if such persons are, or are likely to be in the succeeding 3-year period, adversely affected by virtue of such prohibition in their ability to make noninfringing uses of that particular class of works under this title, as determined under subparagraph (C).

(C)   During the 2-year period described in subparagraph (A), and during each succeeding 3-year period, the Librarian of Congress, upon the recommendation of the Register of Copyrights, who shall consult with the Assistant Secretary for Communications and Information of the Department of Commerce and report and comment on his or her views in making such recommendation, shall make the determination in a rulemaking proceeding for purposes of subparagraph (B) of whether persons who are users of a copyrighted work are, or are likely

Cybersecurity Law, Second Edition. Jeff Kosseff.
© 2020 John Wiley & Sons, Inc. Published 2020 by John Wiley & Sons, Inc.
Companion Website: www.wiley.com/go/kosseff/cybersecurity2e

to be in the succeeding 3-year period, adversely affected by the prohibition under subparagraph (A) in their ability to make noninfringing uses under this title of a particular class of copyrighted works. In conducting such rulemaking, the Librarian shall examine—

(i) the availability for use of copyrighted works;

(ii) the availability for use of works for nonprofit archival, preservation, and educational purposes;

(iii) the impact that the prohibition on the circumvention of technological measures applied to copyrighted works has on criticism, comment, news reporting, teaching, scholarship, or research;

(iv) the effect of circumvention of technological measures on the market for or value of copyrighted works; and

(v) such other factors as the Librarian considers appropriate.

(D) The Librarian shall publish any class of copyrighted works for which the Librarian has determined, pursuant to the rulemaking conducted under subparagraph (C), that noninfringing uses by persons who are users of a copyrighted work are, or are likely to be, adversely affected, and the prohibition contained in subparagraph (A) shall not apply to such users with respect to such class of works for the ensuing 3-year period.

(E) Neither the exception under subparagraph (B) from the applicability of the prohibition contained in subparagraph (A), nor any determination made in a rulemaking conducted under subparagraph (C), may be used as a defense in any action to enforce any provision of this title other than this paragraph.

(2) No person shall manufacture, import, offer to the public, provide, or otherwise traffic in any technology, product, service, device, component, or part thereof, that—

(A) is primarily designed or produced for the purpose of circumventing a technological measure that effectively controls access to a work protected under this title;

(B) has only limited commercially significant purpose or use other than to circumvent a technological measure that effectively controls access to a work protected under this title; or

(C) is marketed by that person or another acting in concert with that person with that person's knowledge for use in circumventing a technological measure that effectively controls access to a work protected under this title.

(3) As used in this subsection—

(A) to "circumvent a technological measure" means to descramble a scrambled work, to decrypt an encrypted work, or otherwise to avoid, bypass, remove, deactivate, or impair a technological measure, without the authority of the copyright owner; and

(B) a technological measure "effectively controls access to a work" if the measure, in the ordinary course of its operation, requires the application of information, or a process or a treatment, with the authority of the copyright owner, to gain access to the work.

(b) Additional Violations.—(1) No person shall manufacture, import, offer to the public, provide, or otherwise traffic in any technology, product, service, device, component, or part thereof, that—

(A) is primarily designed or produced for the purpose of circumventing protection afforded by a technological measure that effectively protects a right of a copyright owner under this title in a work or a portion thereof;

(B) has only limited commercially significant purpose or use other than to circumvent protection afforded by a technological measure that effectively protects a right of a copyright owner under this title in a work or a portion thereof; or

(C) is marketed by that person or another acting in concert with that person with that person's knowledge for use in circumventing protection afforded by a technological measure that effectively protects a right of a copyright owner under this title in a work or a portion thereof.

(2) As used in this subsection—

(A) to "circumvent protection afforded by a technological measure" means avoiding, bypassing, removing, deactivating, or otherwise impairing a technological measure; and

(B) a technological measure "effectively protects a right of a copyright owner under this title" if the measure, in the ordinary course of its operation, prevents, restricts, or otherwise limits the exercise of a right of a copyright owner under this title.

(c) Other Rights, Etc., Not Affected.—(1) Nothing in this section shall affect rights, remedies, limitations, or defenses to copyright infringement, including fair use, under this title.

(2) Nothing in this section shall enlarge or diminish vicarious or contributory liability for copyright infringement in connection with any technology, product, service, device, component, or part thereof.

(3) Nothing in this section shall require that the design of, or design and selection of parts and components for, a consumer electronics, telecommunications, or computing product provide for a response to any particular technological measure, so long as such part or component, or the product in which such part or component is integrated, does not otherwise fall within the prohibitions of subsection (a)(2) or (b)(1).

(4)   Nothing in this section shall enlarge or diminish any rights of free speech or the press for activities using consumer electronics, telecommunications, or computing products.

(d) Exemption for Nonprofit Libraries, Archives, and Educational Institutions.—(1) A nonprofit library, archives, or educational institution which gains access to a commercially exploited copyrighted work solely in order to make a good faith determination of whether to acquire a copy of that work for the sole purpose of engaging in conduct permitted under this title shall not be in violation of subsection (a)(1)(A). A copy of a work to which access has been gained under this paragraph—

(A) may not be retained longer than necessary to make such good faith determination; and

(B) may not be used for any other purpose.

(2) The exemption made available under paragraph (1) shall only apply with respect to a work when an identical copy of that work is not reasonably available in another form.

(3) A nonprofit library, archives, or educational institution that willfully for the purpose of commercial advantage or financial gain violates paragraph (1)—

(A) shall, for the first offense, be subject to the civil remedies under section 1203; and

(B) shall, for repeated or subsequent offenses, in addition to the civil remedies under section 1203, forfeit the exemption provided under paragraph (1).

(4) This subsection may not be used as a defense to a claim under subsection (a)(2) or (b), nor may this subsection permit a nonprofit library, archives, or educational institution to manufacture, import, offer to the public, provide, or otherwise traffic in any technology, product, service, component, or part thereof, which circumvents a technological measure.

(5) In order for a library or archives to qualify for the exemption under this subsection, the collections of that library or archives shall be—

(A) open to the public; or

(B) available not only to researchers affiliated with the library or archives or with the institution of which it is a part, but also to other persons doing research in a specialized field.

(e)   Law Enforcement, Intelligence, and Other Government Activities.— This section does not prohibit any lawfully authorized investigative, protective, information security, or intelligence activity of an officer, agent, or employee of the United States, a State, or a political subdivision of a State, or a person acting pursuant to a contract with the United States, a State, or a political subdivision of a State. For purposes of this subsection, the term "information security" means activities carried out in order to identify and address the vulnerabilities of a government computer, computer system, or computer network.

(f)   Reverse Engineering.—Notwithstanding the provisions of subsection (a)(1)(A), a person who has lawfully obtained the right to use a copy of a computer program may circumvent a technological measure that effectively controls access to a particular portion of that program for the sole purpose of identifying and analyzing those elements of the program that are necessary to achieve interoperability of an independently created computer program with other programs, and that have not previously been readily available to the person engaging in the circumvention, to the extent any such acts of identification and analysis do not constitute infringement under this title.

(2)   Notwithstanding the provisions of subsections (a)(2) and (b), a person may develop and employ technological means to circumvent a technological measure, or to circumvent protection afforded by a technological measure, in order to enable the identification and analysis under paragraph (1), or for the purpose of enabling interoperability of an independently created computer program with other programs, if such means are necessary to achieve such interoperability, to the extent that doing so does not constitute infringement under this title.

(3)   The information acquired through the acts permitted under paragraph (1), and the means permitted under paragraph (2), may be made available to others if the person referred to in paragraph (1) or (2), as the case may be, provides such information or means solely for the purpose of enabling interoperability of an independently created computer program with other programs, and to the extent that doing so does not constitute infringement under this title or violate applicable law other than this section.

(4)   For purposes of this subsection, the term "interoperability" means the ability of computer programs to exchange information, and of such programs mutually to use the information which has been exchanged.

(g)   Encryption Research.—

(1)   Definitions.—For purposes of this subsection—

(A)   the term "encryption research" means activities necessary to identify and analyze flaws and vulnerabilities of encryption technologies applied to copyrighted works, if these activities are conducted to advance the state of knowledge in the field of encryption technology or to assist in the development of encryption products; and

(B)   the term "encryption technology" means the scrambling and descrambling of information using mathematical formulas or algorithms.

(2)   Permissible acts of encryption research.—Notwithstanding the provisions of subsection (a)(1)(A), it is not a violation of that subsection for a person to circumvent a technological measure as applied to a copy, phonorecord, performance, or display of a published work in the course of an act of good faith encryption research if—

(A)   the person lawfully obtained the encrypted copy, phonorecord, performance, or display of the published work;

(B)   such act is necessary to conduct such encryption research;

(C)   the person made a good faith effort to obtain authorization before the circumvention; and

(D)   such act does not constitute infringement under this title or a violation of applicable law other than this section, including section 1030 of title 18 and those provisions of title 18 amended by the Computer Fraud and Abuse Act of 1986.

(3)   Factors in determining exemption.—In determining whether a person qualifies for the exemption under paragraph (2), the factors to be considered shall include—

(A)   whether the information derived from the encryption research was disseminated, and if so, whether it was disseminated in a manner reasonably calculated to advance the state of knowledge or development of encryption technology, versus whether it was disseminated in a manner that facilitates infringement under this title or a violation of applicable law other than this section, including a violation of privacy or breach of security;

(B)   whether the person is engaged in a legitimate course of study, is employed, or is appropriately trained or experienced, in the field of encryption technology; and

(C)   whether the person provides the copyright owner of the work to which the technological measure is applied with notice of the findings and documentation of the research, and the time when such notice is provided.

(4)   Use of technological means for research activities.— Notwithstanding the provisions of subsection (a)(2), it is not a violation of that subsection for a person to—

(A)   develop and employ technological means to circumvent a technological measure for the sole purpose of that person performing the acts of good faith encryption research described in paragraph (2); and

(B) provide the technological means to another person with whom he or she is working collaboratively for the purpose of conducting the acts of good faith encryption research described in paragraph (2) or for the purpose of having that other person verify his or her acts of good faith encryption research described in paragraph (2).

(5) Report to Congress.—Not later than 1 year after the date of the enactment of this chapter, the Register of Copyrights and the Assistant Secretary for Communications and Information of the Department of Commerce shall jointly report to the Congress on the effect this subsection has had on—

(A) encryption research and the development of encryption technology;

(B) the adequacy and effectiveness of technological measures designed to protect copyrighted works; and

(C) protection of copyright owners against the unauthorized access to their encrypted copyrighted works.
The report shall include legislative recommendations, if any.

(h) Exceptions Regarding Minors.—In applying subsection (a) to a component or part, the court may consider the necessity for its intended and actual incorporation in a technology, product, service, or device, which—

(1) does not itself violate the provisions of this title; and

(2) has the sole purpose to prevent the access of minors to material on the Internet.

(i) Protection of Personally Identifying Information.—

(1) Circumvention permitted.—Notwithstanding the provisions of subsection (a)(1)(A), it is not a violation of that subsection for a person to circumvent a technological measure that effectively controls access to a work protected under this title, if—

(A) the technological measure, or the work it protects, contains the capability of collecting or disseminating personally identifying information reflecting the online activities of a natural person who seeks to gain access to the work protected;

(B) in the normal course of its operation, the technological measure, or the work it protects, collects or disseminates personally identifying information about the person who seeks to gain access to the work protected, without providing conspicuous notice of such collection or dissemination to such person, and without providing such person with the capability to prevent or restrict such collection or dissemination;

(C)   the act of circumvention has the sole effect of identifying and disabling the capability described in subparagraph (A), and has no other effect on the ability of any person to gain access to any work; and

(D)   the act of circumvention is carried out solely for the purpose of preventing the collection or dissemination of personally identifying information about a natural person who seeks to gain access to the work protected, and is not in violation of any other law.

(2)   Inapplicability to certain technological measures.—This subsection does not apply to a technological measure, or a work it protects, that does not collect or disseminate personally identifying information and that is disclosed to a user as not having or using such capability.

(j)   Security Testing.—

(1)   Definition.—For purposes of this subsection, the term "security testing" means accessing a computer, computer system, or computer network, solely for the purpose of good faith testing, investigating, or correcting, a security flaw or vulnerability, with the authorization of the owner or operator of such computer, computer system, or computer network.

(2)   Permissible acts of security testing.—Notwithstanding the provisions of subsection (a)(1)(A), it is not a violation of that subsection for a person to engage in an act of security testing, if such act does not constitute infringement under this title or a violation of applicable law other than this section, including section 1030 of title 18 and those provisions of title 18 amended by the Computer Fraud and Abuse Act of 1986.

(3)   Factors in determining exemption.—In determining whether a person qualifies for the exemption under paragraph (2), the factors to be considered shall include—

(A)   whether the information derived from the security testing was used solely to promote the security of the owner or operator of such computer, computer system or computer network, or shared directly with the developer of such computer, computer system, or computer network; and

(B)   whether the information derived from the security testing was used or maintained in a manner that does not facilitate infringement under this title or a violation of applicable law other than this section, including a violation of privacy or breach of security.

(4)   Use of technological means for security testing.—Notwithstanding the provisions of subsection (a)(2), it is not a violation of that subsection for a person to develop, produce, distribute or employ technological means for the sole purpose of performing the acts of security testing described in

subsection (2),[1] provided such technological means does not otherwise violate section (a)(2).[2]

(k) Certain Analog Devices and Certain Technological Measures.—

(1) Certain analog devices.—

(A) Effective 18 months after the date of the enactment of this chapter, no person shall manufacture, import, offer to the public, provide or otherwise traffic in any—

(i) VHS format analog video cassette recorder unless such recorder conforms to the automatic gain control copy control technology;

(ii) 8mm format analog video cassette camcorder unless such camcorder conforms to the automatic gain control technology;

(iii) Beta format analog video cassette recorder, unless such recorder conforms to the automatic gain control copy control technology, except that this requirement shall not apply until there are 1,000 Beta format analog video cassette recorders sold in the United States in any one calendar year after the date of the enactment of this chapter;

(iv) 8mm format analog video cassette recorder that is not an analog video cassette camcorder, unless such recorder conforms to the automatic gain control copy control technology, except that this requirement shall not apply until there are 20,000 such recorders sold in the United States in any one calendar year after the date of the enactment of this chapter; or

(v) analog video cassette recorder that records using an NTSC format video input and that is not otherwise covered under clauses (i) through (iv), unless such device conforms to the automatic gain control copy control technology.

(B) Effective on the date of the enactment of this chapter, no person shall manufacture, import, offer to the public, provide or otherwise traffic in—

(i) any VHS format analog video cassette recorder or any 8mm format analog video cassette recorder if the design of the model of such recorder has been modified after such date of enactment so that a model of recorder that previously conformed to the automatic gain control copy control technology no longer conforms to such technology; or

---

1 *So in original. Probably should be subsection "(a)(2),".*
2 *So in original. Probably should be "subsection".*

(ii) any VHS format analog video cassette recorder, or any 8mm format analog video cassette recorder that is not an 8mm analog video cassette camcorder, if the design of the model of such recorder has been modified after such date of enactment so that a model of recorder that previously conformed to the four-line colorstripe copy control technology no longer conforms to such technology.

Manufacturers that have not previously manufactured or sold a VHS format analog video cassette recorder, or an 8mm format analog cassette recorder, shall be required to conform to the four-line colorstripe copy control technology in the initial model of any such recorder manufactured after the date of the enactment of this chapter, and thereafter to continue conforming to the four-line colorstripe copy control technology. For purposes of this subparagraph, an analog video cassette recorder "conforms to" the four-line colorstripe copy control technology if it records a signal that, when played back by the playback function of that recorder in the normal viewing mode, exhibits, on a reference display device, a display containing distracting visible lines through portions of the viewable picture.

(2) Certain encoding restrictions.—No person shall apply the automatic gain control copy control technology or colorstripe copy control technology to prevent or limit consumer copying except such copying—

(A) of a single transmission, or specified group of transmissions, of live events or of audiovisual works for which a member of the public has exercised choice in selecting the transmissions, including the content of the transmissions or the time of receipt of such transmissions, or both, and as to which such member is charged a separate fee for each such transmission or specified group of transmissions;

(B) from a copy of a transmission of a live event or an audiovisual work if such transmission is provided by a channel or service where payment is made by a member of the public for such channel or service in the form of a subscription fee that entitles the member of the public to receive all of the programming contained in such channel or service;

(C) from a physical medium containing one or more prerecorded audiovisual works; or

(D) from a copy of a transmission described in subparagraph (A) or from a copy made from a physical medium described in subparagraph (C).

In the event that a transmission meets both the conditions set forth in subparagraph (A) and those set forth in subparagraph (B), the transmission shall be treated as a transmission described in subparagraph (A).

(3) Inapplicability.—This subsection shall not—

(A) require any analog video cassette camcorder to conform to the automatic gain control copy control technology with respect to any video signal received through a camera lens;

(B) apply to the manufacture, importation, offer for sale, provision of, or other trafficking in, any professional analog video cassette recorder; or

(C) apply to the offer for sale or provision of, or other trafficking in, any previously owned analog video cassette recorder, if such recorder was legally manufactured and sold when new and not subsequently modified in violation of paragraph (1)(B).

(4) Definitions.—For purposes of this subsection:

(A) An "analog video cassette recorder" means a device that records, or a device that includes a function that records, on electromagnetic tape in an analog format the electronic impulses produced by the video and audio portions of a television program, motion picture, or other form of audiovisual work.

(B) An "analog video cassette camcorder" means an analog video cassette recorder that contains a recording function that operates through a camera lens and through a video input that may be connected with a television or other video playback device.

(C) An analog video cassette recorder "conforms" to the automatic gain control copy control technology if it—

(i) detects one or more of the elements of such technology and does not record the motion picture or transmission protected by such technology; or

(ii) records a signal that, when played back, exhibits a meaningfully distorted or degraded display.

(D) The term "professional analog video cassette recorder" means an analog video cassette recorder that is designed, manufactured, marketed, and intended for use by a person who regularly employs such a device for a lawful business or industrial use, including making, performing, displaying, distributing, or transmitting copies of motion pictures on a commercial scale.

(E) The terms "VHS format" "8mm format", "Beta format", "automatic gain control copy control technology", "colorstripe copy control technology", "four-line version of the colorstripe copy control technology", and "NTSC" have the meanings that are commonly understood in the consumer electronics and motion picture industries as of the date of the enactment of this chapter.

(5) Violations.—Any violation of paragraph (1) of this subsection shall be treated as a violation of subsection (b)(1) of this section. Any violation of paragraph (2) of this subsection shall be deemed an "act of circumvention" for the purposes of section 1203(c)(3)(A) of this chapter.

Appendix D

Text of the Computer Fraud and Abuse Act

The Computer Fraud and Abuse Act, 18 U.S.C. § 1030, described in Chapter 5, is the primary law by which the federal government prosecutes computer hacking. The CFAA also allows hacking victims to bring civil suits against hackers in certain circumstances. Many states have their own computer hacking laws, some of which are modeled after the CFAA but are not identical.

§ 1030. Fraud and related activity in connection with computers

(a) Whoever—

(1) having knowingly accessed a computer without authorization or exceeding authorized access, and by means of such conduct having obtained information that has been determined by the United States Government pursuant to an Executive order or statute to require protection against unauthorized disclosure for reasons of national defense or foreign relations, or any restricted data, as defined in paragraph y. of section 11 of the Atomic Energy Act of 1954, with reason to believe that such information so obtained could be used to the injury of the United States, or to the advantage of any foreign nation willfully communicates, delivers, transmits, or causes to be communicated, delivered, or transmitted, or attempts to communicate, deliver, transmit or cause to be communicated, delivered, or transmitted the same to any person not entitled to receive it, or willfully retains the same and fails to deliver it to the officer or employee of the United States entitled to receive it;

(2) intentionally accesses a computer without authorization or exceeds authorized access, and thereby obtains—

(A) information contained in a financial record of a financial institution, or of a card issuer as defined in section 1602(n) of title 15, or contained in a file of a consumer reporting agency on a consumer,

Cybersecurity Law, Second Edition. Jeff Kosseff.
© 2020 John Wiley & Sons, Inc. Published 2020 by John Wiley & Sons, Inc.
Companion Website: www.wiley.com/go/kosseff/cybersecurity2e

as such terms are defined in the Fair Credit Reporting Act (15 U.S.C. 1681 *et seq.*);

(B) information from any department or agency of the United States; or

(C) information from any protected computer;

(3) intentionally, without authorization to access any nonpublic computer of a department or agency of the United States, accesses such a computer of that department or agency that is exclusively for the use of the Government of the United States or, in the case of a computer not exclusively for such use, is used by or for the Government of the United States and such conduct affects that use by or for the Government of the United States;

(4) knowingly and with intent to defraud, accesses a protected computer without authorization, or exceeds authorized access, and by means of such conduct furthers the intended fraud and obtains anything of value, unless the object of the fraud and the thing obtained consists only of the use of the computer and the value of such use is not more than $5,000 in any 1-year period;

(5) (A) knowingly causes the transmission of a program, information, code, or command, and as a result of such conduct, intentionally causes damage without authorization, to a protected computer;

(B) intentionally accesses a protected computer without authorization, and as a result of such conduct, recklessly causes damage; or

(C) intentionally accesses a protected computer without authorization, and as a result of such conduct, causes damage and loss.

(6) knowingly and with intent to defraud traffics (as defined in section 1029) in any password or similar information through which a computer may be accessed without authorization, if—

(A) such trafficking affects interstate or foreign commerce; or

(B) such computer is used by or for the Government of the United States;

(7) with intent to extort from any person any money or other thing of value, transmits in interstate or foreign commerce any communication containing any—

(A) threat to cause damage to a protected computer;

(B) threat to obtain information from a protected computer without authorization or in excess of authorization or to impair the confidentiality of information obtained from a protected computer without authorization or by exceeding authorized access; or

(C) demand or request for money or other thing of value in relation to damage to a protected computer, where such damage was caused to facilitate the extortion;

shall be punished as provided in subsection (c) of this section.

(b)   Whoever conspires to commit or attempts to commit an offense under subsection (a) of this section shall be punished as provided in subsection (c) of this section.

(c)   The punishment for an offense under subsection (a) or (b) of this section is—

(1)   (A)   a fine under this title or imprisonment for not more than ten years, or both, in the case of an offense under subsection (a)(1) of this section which does not occur after a conviction for another offense under this section, or an attempt to commit an offense punishable under this subparagraph; and

(B)   a fine under this title or imprisonment for not more than twenty years, or both, in the case of an offense under subsection (a)(1) of this section which occurs after a conviction for another offense under this section, or an attempt to commit an offense punishable under this subparagraph;

(2)   (A)   except as provided in subparagraph (B), a fine under this title or imprisonment for not more than one year, or both, in the case of an offense under subsection (a)(2), (a)(3), or (a)(6) of this section which does not occur after a conviction for another offense under this section, or an attempt to commit an offense punishable under this subparagraph;

(B)   a fine under this title or imprisonment for not more than 5 years, or both, in the case of an offense under subsection (a)(2), or an attempt to commit an offense punishable under this subparagraph, if—

(i)   the offense was committed for purposes of commercial advantage or private financial gain;

(ii)   the offense was committed in furtherance of any criminal or tortious act in violation of the Constitution or laws of the United States or of any State; or

(iii) the value of the information obtained exceeds $5,000; and

(C)   a fine under this title or imprisonment for not more than ten years, or both, in the case of an offense under subsection (a)(2), (a)(3) or (a)(6) of this section which occurs after a conviction for another offense under this section, or an attempt to commit an offense punishable under this subparagraph;

(3)   (A)   a fine under this title or imprisonment for not more than five years, or both, in the case of an offense under subsection (a)(4) or (a)(7) of this section which does not occur after a conviction for another offense under this section, or an attempt to commit an offense punishable under this subparagraph; and

(B)   a fine under this title or imprisonment for not more than ten years, or both, in the case of an offense under subsection (a)(4), [4] or (a)(7) of this section which occurs after a conviction for another offense under this section, or an attempt to commit an offense punishable under this subparagraph;

(4)   (A) except as provided in subparagraphs (E) and (F), a fine under this title, imprisonment for not more than 5 years, or both, in the case of—

(i)   an offense under subsection (a)(5)(B), which does not occur after a conviction for another offense under this section, if the offense caused (or, in the case of an attempted offense, would, if completed, have caused)—

(I)   loss to 1 or more persons during any 1-year period (and, for purposes of an investigation, prosecution, or other proceeding brought by the United States only, loss resulting from a related course of conduct affecting 1 or more other protected computers) aggregating at least $5,000 in value;

(II)   the modification or impairment, or potential modification or impairment, of the medical examination, diagnosis, treatment, or care of 1 or more individuals;

(III)   physical injury to any person;

(IV)   a threat to public health or safety;

(V)   damage affecting a computer used by or for an entity of the United States Government in furtherance of the administration of justice, national defense, or national security; or

(VI)   damage affecting 10 or more protected computers during any 1-year period; or

(ii)   an attempt to commit an offense punishable under this subparagraph;

(B)   except as provided in subparagraphs (E) and (F), a fine under this title, imprisonment for not more than 10 years, or both, in the case of—

(i)   an offense under subsection (a)(5)(A), which does not occur after a conviction for another offense under this section, if the offense caused (or, in the case of an attempted offense, would, if completed, have caused) a harm provided in subclauses (I) through (VI) of subparagraph (A)(i); or

(ii)   an attempt to commit an offense punishable under this subparagraph;

(C)   except as provided in subparagraphs (E) and (F), a fine under this title, imprisonment for not more than 20 years, or both, in the case of—

(i)   an offense or an attempt to commit an offense under sub-paragraphs (A) or (B) of subsection (a)(5) that occurs after a conviction for another offense under this section; or

(ii)   an attempt to commit an offense punishable under this subparagraph;

(D)   a fine under this title, imprisonment for not more than 10 years, or both, in the case of—

(i)   an offense or an attempt to commit an offense under subsection (a)(5)(C) that occurs after a conviction for another offense under this section; or

(ii)   an attempt to commit an offense punishable under this subparagraph;

(E)   if the offender attempts to cause or knowingly or recklessly causes serious bodily injury from conduct in violation of subsection (a)(5) (A), a fine under this title, imprisonment for not more than 20 years, or both;

(F)   if the offender attempts to cause or knowingly or recklessly causes death from conduct in violation of subsection (a)(5)(A), a fine under this title, imprisonment for any term of years or for life, or both; or

(G)   a fine under this title, imprisonment for not more than 1 year, or both, for—

(i)   any other offense under subsection (a)(5); or

(ii)   an attempt to commit an offense punishable under this subparagraph.

(d)   (1) The United States Secret Service shall, in addition to any other agency having such authority, have the authority to investigate offenses under this section.

(2)   The Federal Bureau of Investigation shall have primary authority to investigate offenses under subsection (a)(1) for any cases involving espionage, foreign counterintelligence, information protected against unauthorized disclosure for reasons of national defense or foreign relations, or Restricted Data (as that term is defined in section 11y of the Atomic Energy Act of 1954 (42 U.S.C. 2014(y)), except for offenses affecting the duties of the United States Secret Service pursuant to section 3056(a) of this title.

(3)   Such authority shall be exercised in accordance with an agreement which shall be entered into by the Secretary of the Treasury and the Attorney General.

(e)   As used in this section—

(1)   the term "computer" means an electronic, magnetic, optical, electrochemical, or other high speed data processing device performing logical, arithmetic, or storage functions, and includes any data storage facility or communications facility directly related to or operating in conjunction with

such device, but such term does not include an automated typewriter or typesetter, a portable hand held calculator, or other similar device;

(2) the term "protected computer" means a computer—

(A) exclusively for the use of a financial institution or the United States Government, or, in the case of a computer not exclusively for such use, used by or for a financial institution or the United States Government and the conduct constituting the offense affects that use by or for the financial institution or the Government; or

(B) which is used in or affecting interstate or foreign commerce or communication, including a computer located outside the United States that is used in a manner that affects interstate or foreign commerce or communication of the United States;

(3) the term "State" includes the District of Columbia, the Commonwealth of Puerto Rico, and any other commonwealth, possession or territory of the United States;

(4) the term "financial institution" means—

(A) an institution, with deposits insured by the Federal Deposit Insurance Corporation;

(B) the Federal Reserve or a member of the Federal Reserve including any Federal Reserve Bank;

(C) a credit union with accounts insured by the National Credit Union Administration;

(D) a member of the Federal home loan bank system and any home loan bank;

(E) any institution of the Farm Credit System under the Farm Credit Act of 1971;

(F) a broker-dealer registered with the Securities and Exchange Commission pursuant to section 15 of the Securities Exchange Act of 1934;

(G) the Securities Investor Protection Corporation;

(H) a branch or agency of a foreign bank (as such terms are defined in paragraphs (1) and (3) of section 1(b) of the International Banking Act of 1978); and

(I) an organization operating under section 25 or section 25(a) 1 of the Federal Reserve Act;

(5) the term "financial record" means information derived from any record held by a financial institution pertaining to a customer's relationship with the financial institution;

(6) the term "exceeds authorized access" means to access a computer with authorization and to use such access to obtain or alter information in the computer that the accesser is not entitled so to obtain or alter;

(7) the term "department of the United States" means the legislative or judicial branch of the Government or one of the executive departments enumerated in section 101 of title 5;

(8) the term "damage" means any impairment to the integrity or availability of data, a program, a system, or information;

(9) the term "government entity" includes the Government of the United States, any State or political subdivision of the United States, any foreign country, and any state, province, municipality, or other political subdivision of a foreign country;

(10) the term "conviction" shall include a conviction under the law of any State for a crime punishable by imprisonment for more than 1 year, an element of which is unauthorized access, or exceeding authorized access, to a computer;

(11) the term "loss" means any reasonable cost to any victim, including the cost of responding to an offense, conducting a damage assessment, and restoring the data, program, system, or information to its condition prior to the offense, and any revenue lost, cost incurred, or other consequential damages incurred because of interruption of service; and

(12) the term "person" means any individual, firm, corporation, educational institution, financial institution, governmental entity, or legal or other entity.

(f) This section does not prohibit any lawfully authorized investigative, protective, or intelligence activity of a law enforcement agency of the United States, a State, or a political subdivision of a State, or of an intelligence agency of the United States.

(g) Any person who suffers damage or loss by reason of a violation of this section may maintain a civil action against the violator to obtain compensatory damages and injunctive relief or other equitable relief. A civil action for a violation of this section may be brought only if the conduct involves 1 of the factors set forth in subclauses (I), (II), (III), (IV), or (V) of subsection (c)(4)(A)(i). Damages for a violation involving only conduct described in subsection (c)(4)(A)(i)(I) are limited to economic damages. No action may be brought under this subsection unless such action is begun within 2 years of the date of the act complained of or the date of the discovery of the damage. No action may be brought under this subsection for the negligent design or manufacture of computer hardware, computer software, or firmware.

(h) The Attorney General and the Secretary of the Treasury shall report to the Congress annually, during the first 3 years following the date of the enactment of this subsection, concerning investigations and prosecutions under subsection (a)(5).

(i) (1) The court, in imposing sentence on any person convicted of a violation of this section, or convicted of conspiracy to violate this section, shall order, in addition to any other sentence imposed and irrespective of any provision of State law, that such person forfeit to the United States—

   (A) such person's interest in any personal property that was used or intended to be used to commit or to facilitate the commission of such violation; and

   (B) any property, real or personal, constituting or derived from, any proceeds that such person obtained, directly or indirectly, as a result of such violation.

(2) The criminal forfeiture of property under this subsection, any seizure and disposition thereof, and any judicial proceeding in relation thereto, shall be governed by the provisions of section 413 of the Comprehensive Drug Abuse Prevention and Control Act of 1970 (21 U.S.C. 853), except subsection (d) of that section.

(j) For purposes of subsection (i), the following shall be subject to forfeiture to the United States and no property right shall exist in them:

(1) Any personal property used or intended to be used to commit or to facilitate the commission of any violation of this section, or a conspiracy to violate this section.

(2) Any property, real or personal, which constitutes or is derived from proceeds traceable to any violation of this section, or a conspiracy to violate this section.

Appendix E

Text of the Electronic Communications Privacy Act

The Electronic Communications Privacy Act (ECPA), discussed in Chapter 7, is actually a combination of three different provisions. Title I, known as the Wiretap Act, restricts interception of communications while in transit. Title II, known as the Stored Communications Act, restricts the disclosure of communications contents that are stored on a server or in the cloud. Title III, known as the Pen Register Statute, limits the government's ability to obtain noncontent communications data (e.g., a list of phone numbers dialed or the to/from lines of email messages).

Title I (Wiretap Act), 18 U.S.C §§ 2510–2523

§2510. Definitions

As used in this chapter—

(1) "wire communication" means any aural transfer made in whole or in part through the use of facilities for the transmission of communications by the aid of wire, cable, or other like connection between the point of origin and the point of reception (including the use of such connection in a switching station) furnished or operated by any person engaged in providing or operating such facilities for the transmission of interstate or foreign communications or communications affecting interstate or foreign commerce;

(2) "oral communication" means any oral communication uttered by a person exhibiting an expectation that such communication is not subject to interception under circumstances justifying such expectation, but such term does not include any electronic communication;

(3) "State" means any State of the United States, the District of Columbia, the Commonwealth of Puerto Rico, and any territory or possession of the United States;

Cybersecurity Law, Second Edition. Jeff Kosseff.
© 2020 John Wiley & Sons, Inc. Published 2020 by John Wiley & Sons, Inc.
Companion Website: www.wiley.com/go/kosseff/cybersecurity2e

(4) "intercept" means the aural or other acquisition of the contents of any wire, electronic, or oral communication through the use of any electronic, mechanical, or other device.[1]

(5) "electronic, mechanical, or other device" means any device or apparatus which can be used to intercept a wire, oral, or electronic communication other than—

(a) any telephone or telegraph instrument, equipment or facility, or any component thereof, (i) furnished to the subscriber or user by a provider of wire or electronic communication service in the ordinary course of its business and being used by the subscriber or user in the ordinary course of its business or furnished by such subscriber or user for connection to the facilities of such service and used in the ordinary course of its business; or (ii) being used by a provider of wire or electronic communication service in the ordinary course of its business, or by an investigative or law enforcement officer in the ordinary course of his duties;

(b) a hearing aid or similar device being used to correct subnormal hearing to not better than normal;

(6) "person" means any employee, or agent of the United States or any State or political subdivision thereof, and any individual, partnership, association, joint stock company, trust, or corporation;

(7) "Investigative or law enforcement officer" means any officer of the United States or of a State or political subdivision thereof, who is empowered by law to conduct investigations of or to make arrests for offenses enumerated in this chapter, and any attorney authorized by law to prosecute or participate in the prosecution of such offenses;

(8) "contents" when used with respect to any wire, oral, or electronic communication, includes any information concerning the substance, purport, or meaning of that communication;

(9) "Judge of competent jurisdiction" means—

(a) a judge of a United States district court or a United States court of appeals; and

(b) a judge of any court of general criminal jurisdiction of a State who is authorized by a statute of that State to enter orders authorizing interceptions of wire, oral, or electronic communications;

(10) "communication common carrier" has the meaning given that term in section 3 of the Communications Act of 1934;

---

1 So in original. The period probably should be a semicolon.

(11) "aggrieved person" means a person who was a party to any intercepted wire, oral, or electronic communication or a person against whom the interception was directed;

(12) "electronic communication" means any transfer of signs, signals, writing, images, sounds, data, or intelligence of any nature transmitted in whole or in part by a wire, radio, electromagnetic, photoelectronic or photooptical system that affects interstate or foreign commerce, but does not include—

(A) any wire or oral communication;

(B) any communication made through a tone-only paging device;

(C) any communication from a tracking device (as defined in section 3117 of this title); or

(D) electronic funds transfer information stored by a financial institution in a communications system used for the electronic storage and transfer of funds;

(13) "user" means any person or entity who—

(A) uses an electronic communication service; and

(B) is duly authorized by the provider of such service to engage in such use;

(14) "electronic communications system" means any wire, radio, electromagnetic, photooptical or photoelectronic facilities for the transmission of wire or electronic communications, and any computer facilities or related electronic equipment for the electronic storage of such communications;

(15) "electronic communication service" means any service which provides to users thereof the ability to send or receive wire or electronic communications;

(16) "readily accessible to the general public" means, with respect to a radio communication, that such communication is not—

(A) scrambled or encrypted;

(B) transmitted using modulation techniques whose essential parameters have been withheld from the public with the intention of preserving the privacy of such communication;

(C) carried on a subcarrier or other signal subsidiary to a radio transmission;

(D) transmitted over a communication system provided by a common carrier, unless the communication is a tone only paging system communication; or

(E) transmitted on frequencies allocated under part 25, subpart D, E, or F of part 74, or part 94 of the Rules of the Federal Communications Commission, unless, in the case of a communication transmitted on a frequency allocated under part 74 that is not exclusively allocated to broadcast auxiliary services, the communication is a two-way voice communication by radio;

(17) "electronic storage" means—

(A) any temporary, intermediate storage of a wire or electronic communication incidental to the electronic transmission thereof; and

(B) any storage of such communication by an electronic communication service for purposes of backup protection of such communication;

(18) "aural transfer" means a transfer containing the human voice at any point between and including the point of origin and the point of reception;

(19) "foreign intelligence information", for purposes of section 2517(6) of this title, means—

(A) information, whether or not concerning a United States person, that relates to the ability of the United States to protect against—

(i)   actual or potential attack or other grave hostile acts of a foreign power or an agent of a foreign power;

(ii) sabotage or international terrorism by a foreign power or an agent of a foreign power; or

(iii) clandestine intelligence activities by an intelligence service or network of a foreign power or by an agent of a foreign power; or

(B) information, whether or not concerning a United States person, with respect to a foreign power or foreign territory that relates to—

(i)   the national defense or the security of the United States; or

(ii) the conduct of the foreign affairs of the United States;

(20) "protected computer" has the meaning set forth in section 1030; and

(21) "computer trespasser"—

(A) means a person who accesses a protected computer without authorization and thus has no reasonable expectation of privacy in any communication transmitted to, through, or from the protected computer; and

(B) does not include a person known by the owner or operator of the protected computer to have an existing contractual relationship with the owner or operator of the protected computer for access to all or part of the protected computer.

§2511. Interception and disclosure of wire, oral, or electronic communications prohibited

(1) Except as otherwise specifically provided in this chapter any person who—

(a) intentionally intercepts, endeavors to intercept, or procures any other person to intercept or endeavor to intercept, any wire, oral, or electronic communication;

(b) intentionally uses, endeavors to use, or procures any other person to use or endeavor to use any electronic, mechanical, or other device to intercept any oral communication when—

(i) such device is affixed to, or otherwise transmits a signal through, a wire, cable, or other like connection used in wire communication; or

(ii) such device transmits communications by radio, or interferes with the transmission of such communication; or

(iii) such person knows, or has reason to know, that such device or any component thereof has been sent through the mail or transported in interstate or foreign commerce; or

(iv) such use or endeavor to use (A) takes place on the premises of any business or other commercial establishment the operations of which affect interstate or foreign commerce; or (B) obtains or is for the purpose of obtaining information relating to the operations of any business or other commercial establishment the operations of which affect interstate or foreign commerce; or

(v) such person acts in the District of Columbia, the Commonwealth of Puerto Rico, or any territory or possession of the United States;

(c) intentionally discloses, or endeavors to disclose, to any other person the contents of any wire, oral, or electronic communication, knowing or having reason to know that the information was obtained through the interception of a wire, oral, or electronic communication in violation of this subsection;

(d) intentionally uses, or endeavors to use, the contents of any wire, oral, or electronic communication, knowing or having reason to know that the information was obtained through the interception of a wire, oral, or electronic communication in violation of this subsection; or

(e) (i) intentionally discloses, or endeavors to disclose, to any other person the contents of any wire, oral, or electronic communication, intercepted by means authorized by sections 2511(2)(a)(ii), 2511(2)(b)-(c), 2511(2)(e), 2516, and 2518 of this chapter, (ii) knowing or having reason to know that the information was obtained through the interception of such a communication in connection with a criminal investigation, (iii) having obtained or received the information in connection with a criminal investigation, and (iv) with intent to improperly obstruct, impede, or interfere with a duly authorized criminal investigation, shall be punished as provided in subsection (4) or shall be subject to suit as provided in subsection (5).

(2) (a) (i) It shall not be unlawful under this chapter for an operator of a switchboard, or an officer, employee, or agent of a provider of wire or electronic communication service, whose facilities are used in the transmission of a wire or

electronic communication, to intercept, disclose, or use that communication in the normal course of his employment while engaged in any activity which is a necessary incident to the rendition of his service or to the protection of the rights or property of the provider of that service, except that a provider of wire communication service to the public shall not utilize service observing or random monitoring except for mechanical or service quality control checks.

(ii) Notwithstanding any other law, providers of wire or electronic communication service, their officers, employees, and agents, landlords, custodians, or other persons, are authorized to provide information, facilities, or technical assistance to persons authorized by law to intercept wire, oral, or electronic communications or to conduct electronic surveillance, as defined in section 101 of the Foreign Intelligence Surveillance Act of 1978, if such provider, its officers, employees, or agents, landlord, custodian, or other specified person, has been provided with—

(A) a court order directing such assistance or a court order pursuant to section 704 of the Foreign Intelligence Surveillance Act of 1978 signed by the authorizing judge, or

(B) certification in writing by a person specified in section 2518(7) of this title or the Attorney General of the United States that no warrant or court order is required by law, that all statutory requirements have been met, and that the specified assistance is required,

setting forth the period of time during which the provision of the information, facilities, or technical assistance is authorized and specifying the information, facilities, or technical assistance required. No provider of wire or electronic communication service, officer, employee, or agent thereof, or landlord, custodian, or other specified person shall disclose the existence of any interception or surveillance or the device used to accomplish the interception or surveillance with respect to which the person has been furnished a court order or certification under this chapter, except as may otherwise be required by legal process and then only after prior notification to the Attorney General or to the principal prosecuting attorney of a State or any political subdivision of a State, as may be appropriate. Any such disclosure, shall render such person liable for the civil damages provided for in section 2520. No cause of action shall lie in any court against any provider of wire or electronic communication service, its officers, employees, or agents, landlord, custodian, or other specified person for providing information, facilities, or assistance in accordance with the terms of a court order, statutory authorization, or certification under this chapter.

(iii) If a certification under subparagraph (ii)(B) for assistance to obtain foreign intelligence information is based on statutory authority, the certification shall identify the specific statutory provision and shall certify that the statutory requirements have been met.

(b)   It shall not be unlawful under this chapter for an officer, employee, or agent of the Federal Communications Commission, in the normal course of his employment and in discharge of the monitoring responsibilities exercised by the Commission in the enforcement of chapter 5 of title 47 of the United States Code, to intercept a wire or electronic communication, or oral communication transmitted by radio, or to disclose or use the information thereby obtained.

(c)   It shall not be unlawful under this chapter for a person acting under color of law to intercept a wire, oral, or electronic communication, where such person is a party to the communication or one of the parties to the communication has given prior consent to such interception.

(d)   It shall not be unlawful under this chapter for a person not acting under color of law to intercept a wire, oral, or electronic communication where such person is a party to the communication or where one of the parties to the communication has given prior consent to such interception unless such communication is intercepted for the purpose of committing any criminal or tortious act in violation of the Constitution or laws of the United States or of any State.

(e)   Notwithstanding any other provision of this title or section 705 or 706 of the Communications Act of 1934, it shall not be unlawful for an officer, employee, or agent of the United States in the normal course of his official duty to conduct electronic surveillance, as defined in section 101 of the Foreign Intelligence Surveillance Act of 1978, as authorized by that Act.

(f)   Nothing contained in this chapter or chapter 121 or 206 of this title, or section 705 of the Communications Act of 1934, shall be deemed to affect the acquisition by the United States Government of foreign intelligence information from international or foreign communications, or foreign intelligence activities conducted in accordance with otherwise applicable Federal law involving a foreign electronic communications system, utilizing a means other than electronic surveillance as defined in section 101 of the Foreign Intelligence Surveillance Act of 1978, and procedures in this chapter or chapter 121 and the Foreign Intelligence Surveillance Act of 1978 shall be the exclusive means by which electronic surveillance, as defined in section 101 of such Act, and the interception of domestic wire, oral, and electronic communications may be conducted.

(g)   It shall not be unlawful under this chapter or chapter 121 of this title for any person—

(i)   to intercept or access an electronic communication made through an electronic communication system that is configured so that such electronic communication is readily accessible to the general public;

(ii) to intercept any radio communication which is transmitted—

(I) by any station for the use of the general public, or that relates to ships, aircraft, vehicles, or persons in distress;

(II) by any governmental, law enforcement, civil defense, private land mobile, or public safety communications system, including police and fire, readily accessible to the general public;

(III) by a station operating on an authorized frequency within the bands allocated to the amateur, citizens band, or general mobile radio services; or

(IV) by any marine or aeronautical communications system;

(iii) to engage in any conduct which—

(I) is prohibited by section 633 of the Communications Act of 1934; or

(II) is excepted from the application of section 705(a) of the Communications Act of 1934 by section 705(b) of that Act;

(iv) to intercept any wire or electronic communication the transmission of which is causing harmful interference to any lawfully operating station or consumer electronic equipment, to the extent necessary to identify the source of such interference; or

(v) for other users of the same frequency to intercept any radio communication made through a system that utilizes frequencies monitored by individuals engaged in the provision or the use of such system, if such communication is not scrambled or encrypted.

(h) It shall not be unlawful under this chapter—

(i) to use a pen register or a trap and trace device (as those terms are defined for the purposes of chapter 206 (relating to pen registers and trap and trace devices) of this title); or

(ii) for a provider of electronic communication service to record the fact that a wire or electronic communication was initiated or completed in order to protect such provider, another provider furnishing service toward the completion of the wire or electronic communication, or a user of that service, from fraudulent, unlawful or abusive use of such service.

(i) It shall not be unlawful under this chapter for a person acting under color of law to intercept the wire or electronic communications of a computer trespasser transmitted to, through, or from the protected computer, if—

> (I)   the owner or operator of the protected computer authorizes the interception of the computer trespasser's communications on the protected computer;
> (II)   the person acting under color of law is lawfully engaged in an investigation;
> (III) the person acting under color of law has reasonable grounds to believe that the contents of the computer trespasser's communications will be relevant to the investigation; and
> (IV) such interception does not acquire communications other than those transmitted to or from the computer trespasser.

(j)   It shall not be unlawful under this chapter for a provider of electronic communication service to the public or remote computing service to intercept or disclose the contents of a wire or electronic communication in response to an order from a foreign government that is subject to an executive agreement that the Attorney General has determined and certified to Congress satisfies section 2523.

(3)   (a) Except as provided in paragraph (b) of this subsection, a person or entity providing an electronic communication service to the public shall not intentionally divulge the contents of any communication (other than one to such person or entity, or an agent thereof) while in transmission on that service to any person or entity other than an addressee or intended recipient of such communication or an agent of such addressee or intended recipient.

> (b) A person or entity providing electronic communication service to the public may divulge the contents of any such communication—

> (i)   as otherwise authorized in section 2511 (2) (a) or 2517 of this title;
> (ii)   with the lawful consent of the originator or any addressee or intended recipient of such communication;
> (iii) to a person employed or authorized, or whose facilities are used, to forward such communication to its destination; or
> (iv) which were inadvertently obtained by the service provider and which appear to pertain to the commission of a crime, if such divulgence is made to a law enforcement agency.

(4)   (a) Except as provided in paragraph (b) of this subsection or in subsection (5), whoever violates subsection (1) of this section shall be fined under this title or imprisoned not more than five years, or both.

(b) Conduct otherwise an offense under this subsection that consists of or relates to the interception of a satellite transmission that is not encrypted or scrambled and that is transmitted—

> (i) to a broadcasting station for purposes of retransmission to the general public; or
>
> (ii) as an audio subcarrier intended for redistribution to facilities open to the public, but not including data transmissions or telephone calls,

is not an offense under this subsection unless the conduct is for the purposes of direct or indirect commercial advantage or private financial gain.

(5) (a) (i) If the communication is—

(A) a private satellite video communication that is not scrambled or encrypted and the conduct in violation of this chapter is the private viewing of that communication and is not for a tortious or illegal purpose or for purposes of direct or indirect commercial advantage or private commercial gain; or

(B) a radio communication that is transmitted on frequencies allocated under subpart D of part 74 of the rules of the Federal Communications Commission that is not scrambled or encrypted and the conduct in violation of this chapter is not for a tortious or illegal purpose or for purposes of direct or indirect commercial advantage or private commercial gain,

then the person who engages in such conduct shall be subject to suit by the Federal Government in a court of competent jurisdiction.

(ii) In an action under this subsection—

(A) if the violation of this chapter is a first offense for the person under paragraph (a) of subsection (4) and such person has not been found liable in a civil action under section 2520 of this title, the Federal Government shall be entitled to appropriate injunctive relief; and

(B) if the violation of this chapter is a second or subsequent offense under paragraph (a) of subsection (4) or such person has been found liable in any prior civil action under section 2520, the person shall be subject to a mandatory $500 civil fine.

(b) The court may use any means within its authority to enforce an injunction issued under paragraph (ii)(A), and shall impose a civil fine of not less than $500 for each violation of such an injunction.

§2512. Manufacture, distribution, possession, and advertising of wire, oral, or electronic communication intercepting devices prohibited

(1) Except as otherwise specifically provided in this chapter, any person who intentionally—

(a)   sends through the mail, or sends or carries in interstate or foreign commerce, any electronic, mechanical, or other device, knowing or having reason to know that the design of such device renders it primarily useful for the purpose of the surreptitious interception of wire, oral, or electronic communications;

(b)   manufactures, assembles, possesses, or sells any electronic, mechanical, or other device, knowing or having reason to know that the design of such device renders it primarily useful for the purpose of the surreptitious interception of wire, oral, or electronic communications, and that such device or any component thereof has been or will be sent through the mail or transported in interstate or foreign commerce; or

(c)   places in any newspaper, magazine, handbill, or other publication or disseminates by electronic means any advertisement of—

> (i)   any electronic, mechanical, or other device knowing or having reason to know that the design of such device renders it primarily useful for the purpose of the surreptitious interception of wire, oral, or electronic communications; or
>
> (ii)   any other electronic, mechanical, or other device, where such advertisement promotes the use of such device for the purpose of the surreptitious interception of wire, oral, or electronic communications,

knowing the content of the advertisement and knowing or having reason to know that such advertisement will be sent through the mail or transported in interstate or foreign commerce,

shall be fined under this title or imprisoned not more than five years, or both.

(2)   It shall not be unlawful under this section for—

(a)   a provider of wire or electronic communication service or an officer, agent, or employee of, or a person under contract with, such a provider, in the normal course of the business of providing that wire or electronic communication service, or

(b)   an officer, agent, or employee of, or a person under contract with, the United States, a State, or a political subdivision thereof, in the normal course of the activities of the United States, a State, or a political subdivision thereof,

to send through the mail, send or carry in interstate or foreign commerce, or manufacture, assemble, possess, or sell any electronic, mechanical, or other device knowing or having reason to know that the design of such device renders it primarily useful for the purpose of the surreptitious interception of wire, oral, or electronic communications.

(3)   It shall not be unlawful under this section to advertise for sale a device described in subsection (1) of this section if the advertisement is mailed, sent, or carried in interstate or foreign commerce solely to a domestic provider of wire or electronic communication service or to an agency of the United States, a State, or a political subdivision thereof which is duly authorized to use such device.

§2513. Confiscation of wire, oral, or electronic communication intercepting devices

Any electronic, mechanical, or other device used, sent, carried, manufactured, assembled, possessed, sold, or advertised in violation of section 2511 or section 2512 of this chapter may be seized and forfeited to the United States. All provisions of law relating to (1) the seizure, summary and judicial forfeiture, and condemnation of vessels, vehicles, merchandise, and baggage for violations of the customs laws contained in title 19 of the United States Code, (2) the disposition of such vessels, vehicles, merchandise, and baggage or the proceeds from the sale thereof, (3) the remission or mitigation of such forfeiture, (4) the compromise of claims, and (5) the award of compensation to informers in respect of such forfeitures, shall apply to seizures and forfeitures incurred, or alleged to have been incurred, under the provisions of this section, insofar as applicable and not inconsistent with the provisions of this section; except that such duties as are imposed upon the collector of customs or any other person with respect to the seizure and forfeiture of vessels, vehicles, merchandise, and baggage under the provisions of the customs laws contained in title 19 of the United States Code shall be performed with respect to seizure and forfeiture of electronic, mechanical, or other intercepting devices under this section by such officers, agents, or other persons as may be authorized or designated for that purpose by the Attorney General.

§2514. Repealed

§2515. Prohibition of use as evidence of intercepted wire or oral communications

Whenever any wire or oral communication has been intercepted, no part of the contents of such communication and no evidence derived therefrom may be received in evidence in any trial, hearing, or other proceeding in or before any court, grand jury, department, officer, agency, regulatory body, legislative committee, or other authority of the United States, a State, or a political subdivision thereof if the disclosure of that information would be in violation of this chapter.

§2516. Authorization for interception of wire, oral, or electronic communications

(1)   The Attorney General, Deputy Attorney General, Associate Attorney General,[1] or any Assistant Attorney General, any acting Assistant Attorney General, or any Deputy Assistant Attorney General or acting Deputy Assistant Attorney General in the Criminal Division or National Security Division specially designated by the Attorney General, may authorize an application to a Federal judge of competent jurisdiction for, and such judge may grant in conformity with section 2518 of this chapter an order authorizing or approving the interception of wire or oral communications by the Federal Bureau of Investigation, or a Federal agency having responsibility for the investigation of the offense as to which the application is made, when such interception may provide or has provided evidence of—

(a)   any offense punishable by death or by imprisonment for more than one year under sections 2122 and 2274 through 2277 of title 42 of the United States Code (relating to the enforcement of the Atomic Energy Act of 1954), section 2284 of title 42 of the United States Code (relating to sabotage of nuclear facilities or fuel), or under the following chapters of this title: chapter 10 (relating to biological weapons), chapter 37 (relating to espionage), chapter 55 (relating to kidnapping), chapter 90 (relating to protection of trade secrets), chapter 105 (relating to sabotage), chapter 115 (relating to treason), chapter 102 (relating to riots), chapter 65 (relating to malicious mischief), chapter 111 (relating to destruction of vessels), or chapter 81 (relating to piracy);

(b)   a violation of section 186 or section 501(c) of title 29, United States Code (dealing with restrictions on payments and loans to labor organizations), or any offense which involves murder, kidnapping, robbery, or extortion, and which is punishable under this title;

(c)   any offense which is punishable under the following sections of this title: section 37 (relating to violence at international airports), section 43 (relating to animal enterprise terrorism), section 81 (arson within special maritime and territorial jurisdiction), section 201 (bribery of public officials and witnesses), section 215 (relating to bribery of bank officials), section 224 (bribery in sporting contests), subsection (d), (e), (f), (g), (h), or (i) of section 844 (unlawful use of explosives), section 1032 (relating to concealment of assets), section 1084 (transmission of wagering information), section 751 (relating to escape), section 832 (relating to nuclear and weapons of mass destruction threats), section 842 (relating to explosive materials), section 930 (relating to possession of weapons in Federal

---

1 *See 1984 Amendment note below* [not reproduced in this appendix].

facilities), section 1014 (relating to loans and credit applications generally; renewals and discounts), section 1114 (relating to officers and employees of the United States), section 1116 (relating to protection of foreign officials), sections 1503, 1512, and 1513 (influencing or injuring an officer, juror, or witness generally), section 1510 (obstruction of criminal investigations), section 1511 (obstruction of State or local law enforcement), section 1581 (peonage), section 1584 (involuntary servitude), section 1589 (forced labor), section 1590 (trafficking with respect to peonage, slavery, involuntary servitude, or forced labor), section 1591 (sex trafficking of children by force, fraud, or coercion), section 1592 (unlawful conduct with respect to documents in furtherance of trafficking, peonage, slavery, involuntary servitude, or forced labor), section 1751 (Presidential and Presidential staff assassination, kidnapping, and assault), section 1951 (interference with commerce by threats or violence), section 1952 (interstate and foreign travel or transportation in aid of racketeering enterprises), section 1958 (relating to use of interstate commerce facilities in the commission of murder for hire), section 1959 (relating to violent crimes in aid of racketeering activity), section 1954 (offer, acceptance, or solicitation to influence operations of employee benefit plan), section 1955 (prohibition of business enterprises of gambling), section 1956 (laundering of monetary instruments), section 1957 (relating to engaging in monetary transactions in property derived from specified unlawful activity), section 659 (theft from interstate shipment), section 664 (embezzlement from pension and welfare funds), section 1343 (fraud by wire, radio, or television), section 1344 (relating to bank fraud), section 1992 (relating to terrorist attacks against mass transportation), sections 2251 and 2252 (sexual exploitation of children), section 2251A (selling or buying of children), section 2252A (relating to material constituting or containing child pornography), section 1466A (relating to child obscenity), section 2260 (production of sexually explicit depictions of a minor for importation into the United States), sections 2421, 2422, 2423, and 2425 (relating to transportation for illegal sexual activity and related crimes), sections 2312, 2313, 2314, and 2315 (interstate transportation of stolen property), section 2321 (relating to trafficking in certain motor vehicles or motor vehicle parts), section 2340A (relating to torture), section 1203 (relating to hostage taking), section 1029 (relating to fraud and related activity in connection with access devices), section 3146 (relating to penalty for failure to appear), section 3521(b)(3) (relating to witness relocation and assistance), section 32 (relating to destruction of aircraft or aircraft facilities), section 38 (relating to aircraft parts fraud), section 1963 (violations with respect to racketeer influenced and corrupt organizations), section 115 (relating to threatening or retaliating against a Federal official), section 1341 (relating to mail fraud), a felony violation of section 1030 (relating to computer fraud and abuse), section 351 (violations with respect to congressional, Cabinet, or Supreme Court assassinations, kidnapping, and assault), section 831 (relating to prohibited transactions involving nuclear materials), section 33 (relating to destruction of motor vehicles or motor vehicle facilities), section 175 (relating to biological weapons), section 175c (relating to variola virus), section 956 (conspiracy to harm persons or property overseas), a felony violation of section 1028 (relating to production of false identification documentation), section 1425 (relating to the procurement of citizenship or nationalization unlawfully), section 1426 (relating to the reproduction of naturalization or citizenship papers), section 1427 (relating to the sale of naturalization or citizenship papers), section 1541 (relating to passport issuance without authority), section 1542 (relating to false statements in passport applications), section 1543 (relating to forgery or false use of passports), section 1544 (relating to misuse of passports), or section 1546 (relating to fraud and misuse of visas, permits, and other documents);

(d)   any offense involving counterfeiting punishable under section 471, 472, or 473 of this title;

(e)   any offense involving fraud connected with a case under title 11 or the manufacture, importation, receiving, concealment, buying, selling, or otherwise dealing in narcotic drugs, marihuana, or other dangerous drugs, punishable under any law of the United States;

(f)   any offense including extortionate credit transactions under sections 892, 893, or 894 of this title;

(g)   a violation of section 5322 of title 31, United States Code (dealing with the reporting of currency transactions), or section 5324 of title 31, United States Code (relating to structuring transactions to evade reporting requirement prohibited);

(h)   any felony violation of sections 2511 and 2512 (relating to interception and disclosure of certain communications and to certain intercepting devices) of this title;

(i)   any felony violation of chapter 71 (relating to obscenity) of this title;

(j)   any violation of section 60123(b) (relating to destruction of a natural gas pipeline), section 46502 (relating to aircraft piracy), the second sentence of section 46504 (relating to assault on a flight crew with dangerous weapon), or section 46505(b)(3) or (c) (relating to explosive or incendiary devices, or endangerment of human life, by means of weapons on aircraft) of title 49;

(k)   any criminal violation of section 2778 of title 22 (relating to the Arms Export Control Act);

(l)   the location of any fugitive from justice from an offense described in this section;

(m) a violation of section 274, 277, or 278 of the Immigration and Nationality Act (8 U.S.C. 1324, 1327, or 1328) (relating to the smuggling of aliens);

(n) any felony violation of sections 922 and 924 of title 18, United States Code (relating to firearms);

(o) any violation of section 5861 of the Internal Revenue Code of 1986 (relating to firearms);

(p) a felony violation of section 1028 (relating to production of false identification documents), section 1542 (relating to false statements in passport applications), section 1546 (relating to fraud and misuse of visas, permits, and other documents), section 1028A (relating to aggravated identity theft) of this title or a violation of section 274, 277, or 278 of the Immigration and Nationality Act (relating to the smuggling of aliens); or

(q) any criminal violation of section 229 (relating to chemical weapons) or section 2332, 2332a, 2332b, 2332d, 2332f, 2332g, 2332h 3 2339, 2339A, 2339B, 2339C, or 2339D of this title (relating to terrorism);

(r) any criminal violation of section 1 (relating to illegal restraints of trade or commerce), 2 (relating to illegal monopolizing of trade or commerce), or 3 (relating to illegal restraints of trade or commerce in territories or the District of Columbia) of the Sherman Act (15 U.S.C. 1, 2, 3);

(s) any violation of section 670 (relating to theft of medical products); or

(t) any conspiracy to commit any offense described in any subparagraph of this paragraph.

(2) The principal prosecuting attorney of any State, or the principal prosecuting attorney of any political subdivision thereof, if such attorney is authorized by a statute of that State to make application to a State court judge of competent jurisdiction for an order authorizing or approving the interception of wire, oral, or electronic communications, may apply to such judge for, and such judge may grant in conformity with section 2518 of this chapter and with the applicable State statute an order authorizing, or approving the interception of wire, oral, or electronic communications by investigative or law enforcement officers having responsibility for the investigation of the offense as to which the application is made, when such interception may provide or has provided evidence of the commission of the offense of murder, kidnapping human trafficking, child sexual exploitation, child pornography production, gambling, robbery, bribery, extortion, or dealing in narcotic drugs, marihuana or other dangerous drugs, or other crime dangerous to life, limb, or property, and punishable by imprisonment for more than one year, designated in any applicable State statute authorizing such interception, or any conspiracy to commit any of the foregoing offenses.

(3) Any attorney for the Government (as such term is defined for the purposes of the Federal Rules of Criminal Procedure) may authorize an application to a Federal judge of competent jurisdiction for, and such judge may grant, in conformity with section 2518 of this title, an order authorizing or approving the interception of electronic communications by an investigative or law enforcement officer having responsibility for the investigation of the offense as to which the application is made, when such interception may provide or has provided evidence of any Federal felony.

§2517. Authorization for disclosure and use of intercepted wire, oral, or electronic communications

(1) Any investigative or law enforcement officer who, by any means authorized by this chapter, has obtained knowledge of the contents of any wire, oral, or electronic communication, or evidence derived therefrom, may disclose such contents to another investigative or law enforcement officer to the extent that such disclosure is appropriate to the proper performance of the official duties of the officer making or receiving the disclosure.

(2) Any investigative or law enforcement officer who, by any means authorized by this chapter, has obtained knowledge of the contents of any wire, oral, or electronic communication or evidence derived therefrom may use such contents to the extent such use is appropriate to the proper performance of his official duties.

(3) Any person who has received, by any means authorized by this chapter, any information concerning a wire, oral, or electronic communication, or evidence derived therefrom intercepted in accordance with the provisions of this chapter may disclose the contents of that communication or such derivative evidence while giving testimony under oath or affirmation in any proceeding held under the authority of the United States or of any State or political subdivision thereof.

(4) No otherwise privileged wire, oral, or electronic communication intercepted in accordance with, or in violation of, the provisions of this chapter shall lose its privileged character.

(5) When an investigative or law enforcement officer, while engaged in intercepting wire, oral, or electronic communications in the manner authorized herein, intercepts wire, oral, or electronic communications relating to offenses other than those specified in the order of authorization or approval, the contents thereof, and evidence derived therefrom, may be disclosed or used as provided in subsections (1) and (2) of this section. Such contents and any evidence derived therefrom may be used under subsection (3) of this section when authorized or approved by a judge of competent jurisdiction where such judge finds on subsequent application that the contents were otherwise

intercepted in accordance with the provisions of this chapter. Such application shall be made as soon as practicable.

(6) Any investigative or law enforcement officer, or attorney for the Government, who by any means authorized by this chapter, has obtained knowledge of the contents of any wire, oral, or electronic communication, or evidence derived therefrom, may disclose such contents to any other Federal law enforcement, intelligence, protective, immigration, national defense, or national security official to the extent that such contents include foreign intelligence or counterintelligence (as defined in section 3 of the National Security Act of 1947 (50 U.S.C. 401a)),[1] or foreign intelligence information (as defined in subsection (19) of section 2510 of this title), to assist the official who is to receive that information in the performance of his official duties. Any Federal official who receives information pursuant to this provision may use that information only as necessary in the conduct of that person's official duties subject to any limitations on the unauthorized disclosure of such information.

(7) Any investigative or law enforcement officer, or other Federal official in carrying out official duties as such Federal official, who by any means authorized by this chapter, has obtained knowledge of the contents of any wire, oral, or electronic communication, or evidence derived therefrom, may disclose such contents or derivative evidence to a foreign investigative or law enforcement officer to the extent that such disclosure is appropriate to the proper performance of the official duties of the officer making or receiving the disclosure, and foreign investigative or law enforcement officers may use or disclose such contents or derivative evidence to the extent such use or disclosure is appropriate to the proper performance of their official duties.

(8) Any investigative or law enforcement officer, or other Federal official in carrying out official duties as such Federal official, who by any means authorized by this chapter, has obtained knowledge of the contents of any wire, oral, or electronic communication, or evidence derived therefrom, may disclose such contents or derivative evidence to any appropriate Federal, State, local, or foreign government official to the extent that such contents or derivative evidence reveals a threat of actual or potential attack or other grave hostile acts of a foreign power or an agent of a foreign power, domestic or international sabotage, domestic or international terrorism, or clandestine intelligence gathering activities by an intelligence service or network of a foreign power or by an agent of a foreign power, within the United States or elsewhere, for the purpose of preventing or responding to such a threat. Any official who receives information pursuant to this provision may use that information only as necessary in the conduct of that person's official duties subject to any limitations on the unauthorized disclosure of such

---

1 *See References in Text note below* [not reproduced in this Appendix].

information, and any State, local, or foreign official who receives information pursuant to this provision may use that information only consistent with such guidelines as the Attorney General and Director of Central Intelligence shall jointly issue.

§2518. Procedure for interception of wire, oral, or electronic communications

(1)   Each application for an order authorizing or approving the interception of a wire, oral, or electronic communication under this chapter shall be made in writing upon oath or affirmation to a judge of competent jurisdiction and shall state the applicant's authority to make such application. Each application shall include the following information:

(a)   the identity of the investigative or law enforcement officer making the application, and the officer authorizing the application;

(b)   a full and complete statement of the facts and circumstances relied upon by the applicant, to justify his belief that an order should be issued, including (i) details as to the particular offense that has been, is being, or is about to be committed, (ii) except as provided in subsection (11), a particular description of the nature and location of the facilities from which or the place where the communication is to be intercepted, (iii) a particular description of the type of communications sought to be intercepted, (iv) the identity of the person, if known, committing the offense and whose communications are to be intercepted;

(c)   a full and complete statement as to whether or not other investigative procedures have been tried and failed or why they reasonably appear to be unlikely to succeed if tried or to be too dangerous;

(d)   a statement of the period of time for which the interception is required to be maintained. If the nature of the investigation is such that the authorization for interception should not automatically terminate when the described type of communication has been first obtained, a particular description of facts establishing probable cause to believe that additional communications of the same type will occur thereafter;

(e)   a full and complete statement of the facts concerning all previous applications known to the individual authorizing and making the application, made to any judge for authorization to intercept, or for approval of interceptions of, wire, oral, or electronic communications involving any of the same persons, facilities or places specified in the application, and the action taken by the judge on each such application; and

(f)   where the application is for the extension of an order, a statement setting forth the results thus far obtained from the interception, or a reasonable explanation of the failure to obtain such results.

(2)   The judge may require the applicant to furnish additional testimony or documentary evidence in support of the application.

(3)   Upon such application the judge may enter an ex parte order, as requested or as modified, authorizing or approving interception of wire, oral, or electronic communications within the territorial jurisdiction of the court in which the judge is sitting (and outside that jurisdiction but within the United States in the case of a mobile interception device authorized by a Federal court within such jurisdiction), if the judge determines on the basis of the facts submitted by the applicant that—

(a)   there is probable cause for belief that an individual is committing, has committed, or is about to commit a particular offense enumerated in section 2516 of this chapter;

(b)   there is probable cause for belief that particular communications concerning that offense will be obtained through such interception;

(c)   normal investigative procedures have been tried and have failed or reasonably appear to be unlikely to succeed if tried or to be too dangerous;

(d)   except as provided in subsection (11), there is probable cause for belief that the facilities from which, or the place where, the wire, oral, or electronic communications are to be intercepted are being used, or are about to be used, in connection with the commission of such offense, or are leased to, listed in the name of, or commonly used by such person.

(4)   Each order authorizing or approving the interception of any wire, oral, or electronic communication under this chapter shall specify—

(a)   the identity of the person, if known, whose communications are to be intercepted;

(b)   the nature and location of the communications facilities as to which, or the place where, authority to intercept is granted;

(c)   a particular description of the type of communication sought to be intercepted, and a statement of the particular offense to which it relates;

(d)   the identity of the agency authorized to intercept the communications, and of the person authorizing the application; and

(e)   the period of time during which such interception is authorized, including a statement as to whether or not the interception shall automatically terminate when the described communication has been first obtained.

An order authorizing the interception of a wire, oral, or electronic communication under this chapter shall, upon request of the applicant, direct that a provider of wire or electronic communication service, landlord, custodian or other person shall furnish the applicant forthwith all information, facilities, and technical assistance necessary to accomplish the interception unobtrusively and with a minimum of interference with the services that such service provider, landlord, custodian, or person is according the person whose communications are to be intercepted. Any provider of wire or electronic communication service, landlord, custodian or other person furnishing such facilities or technical assistance shall be compensated therefor by the applicant for reasonable expenses incurred in providing such facilities or assistance. Pursuant to section 2522 of this chapter, an order may also be issued to enforce the assistance capability and capacity requirements under the Communications Assistance for Law Enforcement Act.

(5)   No order entered under this section may authorize or approve the interception of any wire, oral, or electronic communication for any period longer than is necessary to achieve the objective of the authorization, nor in any event longer than thirty days. Such thirty-day period begins on the earlier of the day on which the investigative or law enforcement officer first begins to conduct an interception under the order or ten days after the order is entered. Extensions of an order may be granted, but only upon application for an extension made in accordance with subsection (1) of this section and the court making the findings required by subsection (3) of this section. The period of extension shall be no longer than the authorizing judge deems necessary to achieve the purposes for which it was granted and in no event for longer than thirty days. Every order and extension thereof shall contain a provision that the authorization to intercept shall be executed as soon as practicable, shall be conducted in such a way as to minimize the interception of communications not otherwise subject to interception under this chapter, and must terminate upon attainment of the authorized objective, or in any event in thirty days. In the event the intercepted communication is in a code or foreign language, and an expert in that foreign language or code is not reasonably available during the interception period, minimization may be accomplished as soon as practicable after such interception. An interception under this chapter may be conducted in whole or in part by Government personnel, or by an individual operating under a contract with the Government, acting under the supervision of an investigative or law enforcement officer authorized to conduct the interception.

(6)   Whenever an order authorizing interception is entered pursuant to this chapter, the order may require reports to be made to the judge who issued the order showing what progress has been made toward achievement of the authorized objective and the need for continued interception. Such reports shall be made at such intervals as the judge may require.

(7)   Notwithstanding any other provision of this chapter, any investigative or law enforcement officer, specially designated by the Attorney General, the Deputy Attorney General, the Associate Attorney General, or by the principal

prosecuting attorney of any State or subdivision thereof acting pursuant to a statute of that State, who reasonably determines that—

  (a) an emergency situation exists that involves—
    (i) immediate danger of death or serious physical injury to any person,
    (ii) conspiratorial activities threatening the national security interest, or
    (iii) conspiratorial activities characteristic of organized crime,

that requires a wire, oral, or electronic communication to be intercepted before an order authorizing such interception can, with due diligence, be obtained, and

  (b) there are grounds upon which an order could be entered under this chapter to authorize such interception,

may intercept such wire, oral, or electronic communication if an application for an order approving the interception is made in accordance with this section within forty-eight hours after the interception has occurred, or begins to occur. In the absence of an order, such interception shall immediately terminate when the communication sought is obtained or when the application for the order is denied, whichever is earlier. In the event such application for approval is denied, or in any other case where the interception is terminated without an order having been issued, the contents of any wire, oral, or electronic communication intercepted shall be treated as having been obtained in violation of this chapter, and an inventory shall be served as provided for in subsection (d) of this section on the person named in the application.

(8) (a) The contents of any wire, oral, or electronic communication intercepted by any means authorized by this chapter shall, if possible, be recorded on tape or wire or other comparable device. The recording of the contents of any wire, oral, or electronic communication under this subsection shall be done in such a way as will protect the recording from editing or other alterations. Immediately upon the expiration of the period of the order, or extensions thereof, such recordings shall be made available to the judge issuing such order and sealed under his directions. Custody of the recordings shall be wherever the judge orders. They shall not be destroyed except upon an order of the issuing or denying judge and in any event shall be kept for ten years. Duplicate recordings may be made for use or disclosure pursuant to the provisions of subsections (1) and (2) of section 2517 of this chapter for investigations. The presence of the seal provided for by this subsection, or a satisfactory explanation for the absence thereof, shall be a prerequisite for the use or disclosure of the contents of any wire, oral, or electronic communication or evidence derived therefrom under subsection (3) of section 2517.

(b)   Applications made and orders granted under this chapter shall be sealed by the judge. Custody of the applications and orders shall be wherever the judge directs. Such applications and orders shall be disclosed only upon a showing of good cause before a judge of competent jurisdiction and shall not be destroyed except on order of the issuing or denying judge, and in any event shall be kept for ten years.

(c)   Any violation of the provisions of this subsection may be punished as contempt of the issuing or denying judge.

(d)   Within a reasonable time but not later than ninety days after the filing of an application for an order of approval under section 2518(7)(b) which is denied or the termination of the period of an order or extensions thereof, the issuing or denying judge shall cause to be served, on the persons named in the order or the application, and such other parties to intercepted communications as the judge may determine in his discretion that is in the interest of justice, an inventory which shall include notice of—

(1)   the fact of the entry of the order or the application;

(2)   the date of the entry and the period of authorized, approved or disapproved interception, or the denial of the application; and

(3)   the fact that during the period wire, oral, or electronic communications were or were not intercepted.

The judge, upon the filing of a motion, may in his discretion make available to such person or his counsel for inspection such portions of the intercepted communications, applications and orders as the judge determines to be in the interest of justice. On an ex parte showing of good cause to a judge of competent jurisdiction the serving of the inventory required by this subsection may be postponed.

(9)   The contents of any wire, oral, or electronic communication intercepted pursuant to this chapter or evidence derived therefrom shall not be received in evidence or otherwise disclosed in any trial, hearing, or other proceeding in a Federal or State court unless each party, not less than ten days before the trial, hearing, or proceeding, has been furnished with a copy of the court order, and accompanying application, under which the interception was authorized or approved. This ten-day period may be waived by the judge if he finds that it was not possible to furnish the party with the above information ten days before the trial, hearing, or proceeding and that the party will not be prejudiced by the delay in receiving such information.

(10) (a) Any aggrieved person in any trial, hearing, or proceeding in or before any court, department, officer, agency, regulatory body, or other authority of the United States, a State, or a political subdivision thereof, may move to

suppress the contents of any wire or oral communication intercepted pursuant to this chapter, or evidence derived therefrom, on the grounds that—

(i) the communication was unlawfully intercepted;

(ii) the order of authorization or approval under which it was intercepted is insufficient on its face; or

(iii) the interception was not made in conformity with the order of authorization or approval.

Such motion shall be made before the trial, hearing, or proceeding unless there was no opportunity to make such motion or the person was not aware of the grounds of the motion. If the motion is granted, the contents of the intercepted wire or oral communication, or evidence derived therefrom, shall be treated as having been obtained in violation of this chapter. The judge, upon the filing of such motion by the aggrieved person, may in his discretion make available to the aggrieved person or his counsel for inspection such portions of the intercepted communication or evidence derived therefrom as the judge determines to be in the interests of justice.

(b) In addition to any other right to appeal, the United States shall have the right to appeal from an order granting a motion to suppress made under paragraph (a) of this subsection, or the denial of an application for an order of approval, if the United States attorney shall certify to the judge or other official granting such motion or denying such application that the appeal is not taken for purposes of delay. Such appeal shall be taken within thirty days after the date the order was entered and shall be diligently prosecuted.

(c) The remedies and sanctions described in this chapter with respect to the interception of electronic communications are the only judicial remedies and sanctions for nonconstitutional violations of this chapter involving such communications.

(11) The requirements of subsections (l)(b)(ii) and (3)(d) of this section relating to the specification of the facilities from which, or the place where, the communication is to be intercepted do not apply if—

(a) in the case of an application with respect to the interception of an oral communication—

(i) the application is by a Federal investigative or law enforcement officer and is approved by the Attorney General, the Deputy Attorney General, the Associate Attorney General, an Assistant Attorney General, or an acting Assistant Attorney General;

(ii) the application contains a full and complete statement as to why such specification is not practical and identifies the person committing the offense and whose communications are to be intercepted; and

(iii) the judge finds that such specification is not practical; and

(b) in the case of an application with respect to a wire or electronic communication—

(i) the application is by a Federal investigative or law enforcement officer and is approved by the Attorney General, the Deputy Attorney General, the Associate Attorney General, an Assistant Attorney General, or an acting Assistant Attorney General;

(ii) the application identifies the person believed to be committing the offense and whose communications are to be intercepted and the applicant makes a showing that there is probable cause to believe that the person's actions could have the effect of thwarting interception from a specified facility;

(iii) the judge finds that such showing has been adequately made; and

(iv) the order authorizing or approving the interception is limited to interception only for such time as it is reasonable to presume that the person identified in the application is or was reasonably proximate to the instrument through which such communication will be or was transmitted.

(12) An interception of a communication under an order with respect to which the requirements of subsections (1)(b)(ii) and (3)(d) of this section do not apply by reason of subsection (11)(a) shall not begin until the place where the communication is to be intercepted is ascertained by the person implementing the interception order. A provider of wire or electronic communications service that has received an order as provided for in subsection (11)(b) may move the court to modify or quash the order on the ground that its assistance with respect to the interception cannot be performed in a timely or reasonable fashion. The court, upon notice to the government, shall decide such a motion expeditiously.

§2519. Reports concerning intercepted wire, oral, or electronic communications

(1) In January of each year, any judge who has issued an order (or an extension thereof) under section 2518 that expired during the preceding year, or who has denied approval of an interception during that year, shall report to the Administrative Office of the United States Courts—

(a) the fact that an order or extension was applied for;

(b) the kind of order or extension applied for (including whether or not the order was an order with respect to which the requirements of sections 2518(l)(b)(ii) and 2518(3)(d) of this title did not apply by reason of section 2518(11) of this title);

(c) the fact that the order or extension was granted as applied for, was modified, or was denied;

(d) the period of interceptions authorized by the order, and the number and duration of any extensions of the order;

(e) the offense specified in the order or application, or extension of an order;

(f) the identity of the applying investigative or law enforcement officer and agency making the application and the person authorizing the application; and

(g) the nature of the facilities from which or the place where communications were to be intercepted.

(2) In March of each year the Attorney General, an Assistant Attorney General specially designated by the Attorney General, or the principal prosecuting attorney of a State, or the principal prosecuting attorney for any political subdivision of a State, shall report to the Administrative Office of the United States Courts—

(a) the information required by paragraphs (a) through (g) of subsection (1) of this section with respect to each application for an order or extension made during the preceding calendar year;

(b) a general description of the interceptions made under such order or extension, including (i) the approximate nature and frequency of incriminating communications intercepted, (ii) the approximate nature and frequency of other communications intercepted, (iii) the approximate number of persons whose communications were intercepted, (iv) the number of orders in which encryption was encountered and whether such encryption prevented law enforcement from obtaining the plain text of communications intercepted pursuant to such order, and (v) the approximate nature, amount, and cost of the manpower and other resources used in the interceptions;

(c) the number of arrests resulting from interceptions made under such order or extension, and the offenses for which arrests were made;

(d) the number of trials resulting from such interceptions;

(e) the number of motions to suppress made with respect to such interceptions, and the number granted or denied;

(f) the number of convictions resulting from such interceptions and the offenses for which the convictions were obtained and a general assessment of the importance of the interceptions; and

(g) the information required by paragraphs (b) through (f) of this subsection with respect to orders or extensions obtained in a preceding calendar year.

(3) In June of each year the Director of the Administrative Office of the United States Courts shall transmit to the Congress a full and complete report

concerning the number of applications for orders authorizing or approving the interception of wire, oral, or electronic communications pursuant to this chapter and the number of orders and extensions granted or denied pursuant to this chapter during the preceding calendar year. Such report shall include a summary and analysis of the data required to be filed with the Administrative Office by subsections (1) and (2) of this section. The Director of the Administrative Office of the United States Courts is authorized to issue binding regulations dealing with the content and form of the reports required to be filed by subsections (1) and (2) of this section.

§2520. Recovery of civil damages authorized

(a)   In General.—Except as provided in section 2511(2)(a)(ii), any person whose wire, oral, or electronic communication is intercepted, disclosed, or intentionally used in violation of this chapter may in a civil action recover from the person or entity, other than the United States, which engaged in that violation such relief as may be appropriate.

(b)   Relief.—In an action under this section, appropriate relief includes—

(1)   such preliminary and other equitable or declaratory relief as may be appropriate;

(2)   damages under subsection (c) and punitive damages in appropriate cases; and

(3)   a reasonable attorney's fee and other litigation costs reasonably incurred.

(c)   Computation of Damages.—

(1)   In an action under this section, if the conduct in violation of this chapter is the private viewing of a private satellite video communication that is not scrambled or encrypted or if the communication is a radio communication that is transmitted on frequencies allocated under subpart D of part 74 of the rules of the Federal Communications Commission that is not scrambled or encrypted and the conduct is not for a tortious or illegal purpose or for purposes of direct or indirect commercial advantage or private commercial gain, then the court shall assess damages as follows:

(A)   If the person who engaged in that conduct has not previously been enjoined under section 2511(5) and has not been found liable in a prior civil action under this section, the court shall assess the greater of the sum of actual damages suffered by the plaintiff, or statutory damages of not less than $50 and not more than $500.

(B)   If, on one prior occasion, the person who engaged in that conduct has been enjoined under section 2511(5) or has been found liable in a civil action under this section, the court shall assess the greater of the sum of actual damages suffered by the plaintiff, or statutory damages of not less than $100 and not more than $1000.

(2) In any other action under this section, the court may assess as damages whichever is the greater of—

  (A) the sum of the actual damages suffered by the plaintiff and any profits made by the violator as a result of the violation; or
  (B) statutory damages of whichever is the greater of $100 a day for each day of violation or $10,000.

(d) Defense.—A good faith reliance on—

  (1) a court warrant or order, a grand jury subpoena, a legislative authorization, or a statutory authorization;
  (2) a request of an investigative or law enforcement officer under section 2518(7) of this title; or
  (3) a good faith determination that section 2511(3), 2511(2)(i), or 2511(2)(j) of this title permitted the conduct complained of;

is a complete defense against any civil or criminal action brought under this chapter or any other law.

(e) Limitation.—A civil action under this section may not be commenced later than two years after the date upon which the claimant first has a reasonable opportunity to discover the violation.

(f) Administrative Discipline.—If a court or appropriate department or agency determines that the United States or any of its departments or agencies has violated any provision of this chapter, and the court or appropriate department or agency finds that the circumstances surrounding the violation raise serious questions about whether or not an officer or employee of the United States acted willfully or intentionally with respect to the violation, the department or agency shall, upon receipt of a true and correct copy of the decision and findings of the court or appropriate department or agency promptly initiate a proceeding to determine whether disciplinary action against the officer or employee is warranted. If the head of the department or agency involved determines that disciplinary action is not warranted, he or she shall notify the Inspector General with jurisdiction over the department or agency concerned and shall provide the Inspector General with the reasons for such determination.

(g) Improper Disclosure Is Violation.—Any willful disclosure or use by an investigative or law enforcement officer or governmental entity of information beyond the extent permitted by section 2517 is a violation of this chapter for purposes of section 2520(a).

§2521. Injunction against illegal interception

Whenever it shall appear that any person is engaged or is about to engage in any act which constitutes or will constitute a felony violation of this chapter, the Attorney General may initiate a civil action in a district court of the United States to enjoin such violation. The court shall proceed as soon as practicable to the hearing and determination of such an action, and may, at any time before final determination, enter such a restraining order or prohibition, or take such other action, as is warranted to prevent a continuing and substantial injury to the United States or to any person or class of persons for whose protection the action is brought. A proceeding under this section is governed by the Federal Rules of Civil Procedure, except that, if an indictment has been returned against the respondent, discovery is governed by the Federal Rules of Criminal Procedure.

§2522. Enforcement of the Communications Assistance for Law Enforcement Act

(a) Enforcement by Court Issuing Surveillance Order.—If a court authorizing an interception under this chapter, a State statute, or the Foreign Intelligence Surveillance Act of 1978 (50 U.S.C. 1801 *et seq.)* or authorizing use of a pen register or a trap and trace device under chapter 206 or a State statute finds that a telecommunications carrier has failed to comply with the requirements of the Communications Assistance for Law Enforcement Act, the court may, in accordance with section 108 of such Act, direct that the carrier comply forthwith and may direct that a provider of support services to the carrier or the manufacturer of the carrier's transmission or switching equipment furnish forthwith modifications necessary for the carrier to comply.

(b) Enforcement Upon Application by Attorney General.—The Attorney General may, in a civil action in the appropriate United States district court, obtain an order, in accordance with section 108 of the Communications Assistance for Law Enforcement Act, directing that a telecommunications carrier, a manufacturer of telecommunications transmission or switching equipment, or a provider of telecommunications support services comply with such Act.

(c) Civil Penalty.—

(1) In general.—A court issuing an order under this section against a telecommunications carrier, a manufacturer of telecommunications transmission or switching equipment, or a provider of telecommunications support services may impose a civil penalty of up to $10,000 per day for each day in violation after the issuance of the order or after such future date as the court may specify.

(2) Considerations.—In determining whether to impose a civil penalty and in determining its amount, the court shall take into account—

(A) the nature, circumstances, and extent of the violation;

(B) the violator's ability to pay, the violator's good faith efforts to comply in a timely manner, any effect on the violator's ability to continue to do business, the degree of culpability, and the length of any delay in undertaking efforts to comply; and

(C) such other matters as justice may require.

(d) Definitions.—As used in this section, the terms defined in section 102 of the Communications Assistance for Law Enforcement Act have the meanings provided, respectively, in such section.

§2523. Executive agreements on access to data by foreign governments

(a) Definitions.—In this section—

(1) the term "lawfully admitted for permanent residence" has the meaning given the term in section 101(a) of the Immigration and Nationality Act (8 U.S.C. 1101(a)); and

(2) the term "United States person" means a citizen or national of the United States, an alien lawfully admitted for permanent residence, an unincorporated association a substantial number of members of which are citizens of the United States or aliens lawfully admitted for permanent residence, or a corporation that is incorporated in the United States.

(b) Executive Agreement Requirements.—For purposes of this chapter, chapter 121, and chapter 206, an executive agreement governing access by a foreign government to data subject to this chapter, chapter 121, or chapter 206 shall be considered to satisfy the requirements of this section if the Attorney General, with the concurrence of the Secretary of State, determines, and submits a written certification of such determination to Congress, including a written certification and explanation of each consideration in paragraphs (1), (2), (3), and (4), that—

(1) the domestic law of the foreign government, including the implementation of that law, affords robust substantive and procedural protections for privacy and civil liberties in light of the data collection and activities of the foreign government that will be subject to the agreement, if—

(A) such a determination under this section takes into account, as appropriate, credible information and expert input; and

(B) the factors to be met in making such a determination include whether the foreign government—

(i) has adequate substantive and procedural laws on cyber-crime and electronic evidence, as demonstrated by being a party to the Convention on Cybercrime, done at Budapest November 23, 2001, and entered into force January 7, 2004, or through domestic laws that are consistent with definitions and the requirements set forth in chapters I and II of that Convention;

(ii) demonstrates respect for the rule of law and principles of nondiscrimination;

(iii) adheres to applicable international human rights obligations and commitments or demonstrates respect for international universal human rights, including—

(I) protection from arbitrary and unlawful interference with privacy;

(II) fair trial rights;

(III) freedom of expression, association, and peaceful assembly;

(IV) prohibitions on arbitrary arrest and detention; and

(V) prohibitions against torture and cruel, inhuman, or degrading treatment or punishment;

(iv) has clear legal mandates and procedures governing those entities of the foreign government that are authorized to seek data under the executive agreement, including procedures through which those authorities collect, retain, use, and share data, and effective oversight of these activities;

(v) has sufficient mechanisms to provide accountability and appropriate transparency regarding the collection and use of electronic data by the foreign government; and

(vi) demonstrates a commitment to promote and protect the global free flow of information and the open, distributed, and interconnected nature of the Internet;

(2) the foreign government has adopted appropriate procedures to minimize the acquisition, retention, and dissemination of information concerning United States persons subject to the agreement;

(3) the terms of the agreement shall not create any obligation that providers be capable of decrypting data or limitation that prevents providers from decrypting data; and

(4) the agreement requires that, with respect to any order that is subject to the agreement—

(A) the foreign government may not intentionally target a United States person or a person located in the United States, and shall adopt targeting procedures designed to meet this requirement;

(B)   the foreign government may not target a non-United States person located outside the United States if the purpose is to obtain information concerning a United States person or a person located in the United States;

(C)   the foreign government may not issue an order at the request of or to obtain information to provide to the United States Government or a third-party government, nor shall the foreign government be required to share any information produced with the United States Government or a third-party government;

(D)   an order issued by the foreign government—

(i)   shall be for the purpose of obtaining information relating to the prevention, detection, investigation, or prosecution of serious crime, including terrorism;

(ii)   shall identify a specific person, account, address, or personal device, or any other specific identifier as the object of the order;

(iii)   shall be in compliance with the domestic law of that country, and any obligation for a provider of an electronic communications service or a remote computing service to produce data shall derive solely from that law;

(iv)   shall be based on requirements for a reasonable justification based on articulable and credible facts, particularity, legality, and severity regarding the conduct under investigation;

(v)   shall be subject to review or oversight by a court, judge, magistrate, or other independent authority prior to, or in proceedings regarding, enforcement of the order; and

(vi)   in the case of an order for the interception of wire or electronic communications, and any extensions thereof, shall require that the interception order—

(I)   be for a fixed, limited duration; and

(II)   may not last longer than is reasonably necessary to accomplish the approved purposes of the order; and

(III)   be issued only if the same information could not reasonably be obtained by another less intrusive method;

(E)   an order issued by the foreign government may not be used to infringe freedom of speech;

(F)   the foreign government shall promptly review material collected pursuant to the agreement and store any unreviewed communications on a secure system accessible only to those persons trained in applicable procedures;

(G)   the foreign government shall, using procedures that, to the maximum extent possible, meet the definition of minimization procedures in section 101 of the Foreign Intelligence Surveillance Act of 1978 (50 U.S.C. 1801), segregate, seal, or delete, and not disseminate material found not to be information that is, or is necessary to understand or assess the importance of information that is, relevant to the prevention, detection, investigation, or prosecution of serious crime, including terrorism, or necessary to protect against a threat of death or serious bodily harm to any person;

(H) the foreign government may not disseminate the content of a communication of a United States person to United States authorities unless the communication may be disseminated pursuant to subparagraph (G) and relates to significant harm, or the threat thereof, to the United States or United States persons, including crimes involving national security such as terrorism, significant violent crime, child exploitation, transnational organized crime, or significant financial fraud;

(I)   the foreign government shall afford reciprocal rights of data access, to include, where applicable, removing restrictions on communications service providers, including providers subject to United States jurisdiction, and thereby allow them to respond to valid legal process sought by a governmental entity (as defined in section 2711) if foreign law would otherwise prohibit communications-service providers from disclosing the data;

(J)   the foreign government shall agree to periodic review of compliance by the foreign government with the terms of the agreement to be conducted by the United States Government; and

(K) the United States Government shall reserve the right to render the agreement inapplicable as to any order for which the United States Government concludes the agreement may not properly be invoked.

(c)   Limitation on Judicial Review.—A determination or certification made by the Attorney General under subsection (b) shall not be subject to judicial or administrative review.

(d)   Effective Date of Certification.—

(1) Notice.—Not later than 7 days after the date on which the Attorney General certifies an executive agreement under subsection (b), the Attorney General shall provide notice of the determination under subsection (b) and a copy of the executive agreement to Congress, including—

(A) the Committee on the Judiciary and the Committee on Foreign Relations of the Senate; and

(B) the Committee on the Judiciary and the Committee on Foreign Affairs of the House of Representatives.

(2) Entry into force.—An executive agreement that is determined and certified by the Attorney General to satisfy the requirements of this section shall enter into force not earlier than the date that is 180 days after the date on which notice is provided under paragraph (1), unless Congress enacts a joint resolution of disapproval in accordance with paragraph (4).

(3) Requests for information.—Upon request by the Chairman or Ranking Member of a congressional committee described in paragraph (1), the head of an agency shall promptly furnish a summary of factors considered in determining that the foreign government satisfies the requirements of this section.

(4) Congressional review.—

(A) Joint resolution defined.—In this paragraph, the term "joint resolution" means only a joint resolution—

(i) introduced during the 180-day period described in paragraph (2);

(ii) which does not have a preamble;

(iii) the title of which is as follows: "Joint resolution disapproving the executive agreement signed by the United States and ____.", the blank space being appropriately filled in; and

(iv) the matter after the resolving clause of which is as follows: "That Congress disapproves the executive agreement governing access by ___ to certain electronic data as submitted by the Attorney General on ___.", the blank spaces being appropriately filled in.

(B) Joint resolution enacted.—Notwithstanding any other provision of this section, if not later than 180 days after the date on which notice is provided to Congress under paragraph (1), there is enacted into law a joint resolution disapproving of an executive agreement under this section, the executive agreement shall not enter into force.

(C) Introduction.—During the 180-day period described in subparagraph (B), a joint resolution of disapproval may be introduced—

(i) in the House of Representatives, by the majority leader or the minority leader; and

(ii) in the Senate, by the majority leader (or the majority leader's designee) or the minority leader (or the minority leader's designee).

(5) Floor consideration in house of representatives.—If a committee of the House of Representatives to which a joint resolution of disapproval has been referred has not reported the joint resolution within 120 days after

the date of referral, that committee shall be discharged from further consideration of the joint resolution.

    (6) Consideration in the senate.—

        (A) Committee referral.—A joint resolution of disapproval introduced in the Senate shall be referred jointly—

            (i) to the Committee on the Judiciary; and
            (ii) to the Committee on Foreign Relations.

        (B) Reporting and discharge.—If a committee to which a joint resolution of disapproval was referred has not reported the joint resolution within 120 days after the date of referral of the joint resolution, that committee shall be discharged from further consideration of the joint resolution and the joint resolution shall be placed on the appropriate calendar.

        (C) Proceeding to consideration.—It is in order at any time after both the Committee on the Judiciary and the Committee on Foreign Relations report a joint resolution of disapproval to the Senate or have been discharged from consideration of such a joint resolution (even though a previous motion to the same effect has been disagreed to) to move to proceed to the consideration of the joint resolution, and all points of order against the joint resolution (and against consideration of the joint resolution) are waived. The motion is not debatable or subject to a motion to postpone. A motion to reconsider the vote by which the motion is agreed to or disagreed to shall not be in order.

        (D) Consideration in the senate.—In the Senate, consideration of the joint resolution, and on all debatable motions and appeals in connection therewith, shall be limited to not more than 10 hours, which shall be divided equally between those favoring and those opposing the joint resolution. A motion further to limit debate is in order and not debatable. An amendment to, or a motion to postpone, or a motion to proceed to the consideration of other business, or a motion to recommit the joint resolution is not in order.

        (E) Consideration of veto messages.—Debate in the Senate of any veto message with respect to a joint resolution of disapproval, including all debatable motions and appeals in connection with the joint resolution, shall be limited to 10 hours, to be equally divided between, and controlled by, the majority leader and the minority leader or their designees.

    (7) Rules relating to senate and house of representatives.—

        (A) Treatment of senate joint resolution in house.—In the House of Representatives, the following procedures shall apply to a joint resolution of disapproval received from the Senate (unless the House has already passed a joint resolution relating to the same proposed action):

(i) The joint resolution shall be referred to the appropriate committees.

(ii) If a committee to which a joint resolution has been referred has not reported the joint resolution within 7 days after the date of referral, that committee shall be discharged from further consideration of the joint resolution.

(iii) Beginning on the third legislative day after each committee to which a joint resolution has been referred reports the joint resolution to the House or has been discharged from further consideration thereof, it shall be in order to move to proceed to consider the joint resolution in the House. All points of order against the motion are waived. Such a motion shall not be in order after the House has disposed of a motion to proceed on the joint resolution. The previous question shall be considered as ordered on the motion to its adoption without intervening motion. The motion shall not be debatable. A motion to reconsider the vote by which the motion is disposed of shall not be in order.

(iv) The joint resolution shall be considered as read. All points of order against the joint resolution and against its consideration are waived. The previous question shall be considered as ordered on the joint resolution to final passage without intervening motion except 2 hours of debate equally divided and controlled by the sponsor of the joint resolution (or a designee) and an opponent. A motion to reconsider the vote on passage of the joint resolution shall not be in order.

(B) Treatment of house joint resolution in senate.—

(i) If, before the passage by the Senate of a joint resolution of disapproval, the Senate receives an identical joint resolution from the House of Representatives, the following procedures shall apply:

(I) That joint resolution shall not be referred to a committee.

(II) With respect to that joint resolution—

(aa) the procedure in the Senate shall be the same as if no joint resolution had been received from the House of Representatives; but

(bb) the vote on passage shall be on the joint resolution from the House of Representatives.

(ii) If, following passage of a joint resolution of disapproval in the Senate, the Senate receives an identical joint resolution from the House of Representatives, that joint resolution shall be placed on the appropriate Senate calendar.

(iii) If a joint resolution of disapproval is received from the House, and no companion joint resolution has been introduced in the Senate, the Senate procedures under this subsection shall apply to the House joint resolution.

(C) Application to revenue measures.—The provisions of this paragraph shall not apply in the House of Representatives to a joint resolution of disapproval that is a revenue measure.

(8) Rules of house of representatives and senate.—This subsection is enacted by Congress—

(A) as an exercise of the rulemaking power of the Senate and the House of Representatives, respectively, and as such is deemed a part of the rules of each House, respectively, and supersedes other rules only to the extent that it is inconsistent with such rules; and

(B) with full recognition of the constitutional right of either House to change the rules (so far as relating to the procedure of that House) at any time, in the same manner, and to the same extent as in the case of any other rule of that House.

(e) Renewal of Determination.—

(1) In general.—The Attorney General, with the concurrence of the Secretary of State, shall review and may renew a determination under subsection (b) every 5 years.

(2) Report.—Upon renewing a determination under subsection (b), the Attorney General shall file a report with the Committee on the Judiciary and the Committee on Foreign Relations of the Senate and the Committee on the Judiciary and the Committee on Foreign Affairs of the House of Representatives describing—

(A) the reasons for the renewal;

(B) any substantive changes to the agreement or to the relevant laws or procedures of the foreign government since the original determination or, in the case of a second or subsequent renewal, since the last renewal; and

(C) how the agreement has been implemented and what problems or controversies, if any, have arisen as a result of the agreement or its implementation.

(3) Nonrenewal.—If a determination is not renewed under paragraph (1), the agreement shall no longer be considered to satisfy the requirements of this section.

(f) Revisions to Agreement.—A revision to an agreement under this section shall be treated as a new agreement for purposes of this section and shall be subject to the certification requirement under subsection (b), and to the proceduresundersubsection(d),exceptthatforpurposesofarevisiontoanagreement—

(1) the applicable time period under paragraphs (2), (4)(A)(i), (4)(B), and (4)(C) of subsection (d) shall be 90 days after the date notice is provided under subsection (d)(1); and

(2) the applicable time period under paragraphs (5) and (6)(B) of subsection (d) shall be 60 days after the date notice is provided under subsection (d)(1).

(g) Publication.—Any determination or certification under subsection (b) regarding an executive agreement under this section, including any termination or renewal of such an agreement, shall be published in the Federal Register as soon as is reasonably practicable.

(h) Minimization Procedures.—A United States authority that receives the content of a communication described in subsection (b)(4)(H) from a foreign government in accordance with an executive agreement under this section shall use procedures that, to the maximum extent possible, meet the definition of minimization procedures in section 101 of the Foreign Intelligence Surveillance Act of 1978 (50 U.S.C. 1801) to appropriately protect nonpublicly available information concerning United States persons.

Title II (Stored Communications Act), 18 U.S.C. §§ 2701–2713

Stored Wire and Electronic Communications and Transactional Records Access Act

§2701. Unlawful access to stored communications

(a) Offense.—Except as provided in subsection (c) of this section whoever—

(1) intentionally accesses without authorization a facility through which an electronic communication service is provided; or

(2) intentionally exceeds an authorization to access that facility;

and thereby obtains, alters, or prevents authorized access to a wire or electronic communication while it is in electronic storage in such system shall be punished as provided in subsection (b) of this section.

(b) Punishment.—The punishment for an offense under subsection (a) of this section is—

(1) if the offense is committed for purposes of commercial advantage, malicious destruction or damage, or private commercial gain, or in further-ance of any criminal or tortious act in violation of the Constitution or laws of the United States or any State—

(A) a fine under this title or imprisonment for not more than 5 years, or both, in the case of a first offense under this subparagraph; and

(B) a fine under this title or imprisonment for not more than 10 years, or both, for any subsequent offense under this subparagraph; and

(2) in any other case—

(A) a fine under this title or imprisonment for not more than 1 year or both, in the case of a first offense under this paragraph; and

(B) a fine under this title or imprisonment for not more than 5 years, or both, in the case of an offense under this subparagraph that occurs after a conviction of another offense under this section.

(c) Exceptions.—Subsection (a) of this section does not apply with respect to conduct authorized—

(1) by the person or entity providing a wire or electronic communica-tions service;

(2) by a user of that service with respect to a communication of or intended for that user; or

(3) in section 2703, 2704 or 2518 of this title.

§2702. Voluntary disclosure of customer communications or records

(a) Prohibitions.—Except as provided in subsection (b) or (c)—

(1) a person or entity providing an electronic communication service to the public shall not knowingly divulge to any person or entity the con-tents of a communication while in electronic storage by that service; and

(2) a person or entity providing remote computing service to the pub-lic shall not knowingly divulge to any person or entity the contents of any communication which is carried or maintained on that service—

(A) on behalf of, and received by means of electronic transmis-sion from (or created by means of computer processing of communica-tions received by means of electronic transmission from), a subscriber or customer of such service;

(B)   solely for the purpose of providing storage or computer processing services to such subscriber or customer, if the provider is not authorized to access the contents of any such communications for purposes of providing any services other than storage or computer processing; and

(3)   a provider of remote computing service or electronic communication service to the public shall not knowingly divulge a record or other information pertaining to a subscriber to or customer of such service (not including the contents of communications covered by paragraph (1) or (2)) to any governmental entity.

(b)   Exceptions for disclosure of communications.—A provider described in subsection (a) may divulge the contents of a communication—

(1)   to an addressee or intended recipient of such communication or an agent of such addressee or intended recipient;

(2)   as otherwise authorized in section 2517, 2511(2)(a), or 2703 of this title;

(3)   with the lawful consent of the originator or an addressee or intended recipient of such communication, or the subscriber in the case of remote computing service;

(4)   to a person employed or authorized or whose facilities are used to forward such communication to its destination;

(5)   as may be necessarily incident to the rendition of the service or to the protection of the rights or property of the provider of that service;

(6)   to the National Center for Missing and Exploited Children, in connection with a report submitted thereto under section 2258A;

(7)   to a law enforcement agency—

(A)   if the contents—

(i)   were inadvertently obtained by the service provider; and
(ii)   appear to pertain to the commission of a crime;

[(B)   repealed]

(8)   to a governmental entity, if the provider, in good faith, believes that an emergency involving danger of death or serious physical injury to any person requires disclosure without delay of communications relating to the emergency; or

(9)   to a foreign government pursuant to an order from a foreign government that is subject to an executive agreement that the Attorney General has determined and certified to Congress satisfies section 2523.

(c)   Exceptions for Disclosure of Customer Records.—A provider described in subsection (a) may divulge a record or other information pertaining to a subscriber to or customer of such service (not including the contents of communications covered by subsection (a)(1) or (a)(2))—

(1) as otherwise authorized in section 2703;

(2) with the lawful consent of the customer or subscriber;

(3) as may be necessarily incident to the rendition of the service or to the protection of the rights or property of the provider of that service;

(4) to a governmental entity, if the provider, in good faith, believes that an emergency involving danger of death or serious physical injury to any person requires disclosure without delay of information relating to the emergency;

(5) to the National Center for Missing and Exploited Children, in connection with a report submitted thereto under section 2258A;

(6) to any person other than a governmental entity; or

(7) to a foreign government pursuant to an order from a foreign government that is subject to an executive agreement that the Attorney General has determined and certified to Congress satisfies section 2523.

(d) Reporting of Emergency Disclosures.—On an annual basis, the Attorney General shall submit to the Committee on the Judiciary of the House of Representatives and the Committee on the Judiciary of the Senate a report containing—

(1) the number of accounts from which the Department of Justice has received voluntary disclosures under subsection (b)(8);

(2) a summary of the basis for disclosure in those instances where—

(A) voluntary disclosures under subsection (b)(8) were made to the Department of Justice; and

(B) the investigation pertaining to those disclosures was closed without the filing of criminal charges; and

(3) the number of accounts from which the Department of Justice has received voluntary disclosures under subsection (c)(4).

§ 2703. Required disclosure of customer communications or records

(a) Contents of Wire or Electronic Communications in Electronic Storage.—A governmental entity may require the disclosure by a provider of electronic communication service of the contents of a wire or electronic communication, that is in electronic storage in an electronic communications system for one hundred and eighty days or less, only pursuant to a warrant issued using the procedures described in the Federal Rules of Criminal Procedure (or, in the case of a State court, issued using State warrant procedures) by a court of competent jurisdiction. A governmental entity may require the disclosure by a provider of electronic communications services of the contents of a wire or electronic communication that has been in electronic storage in an electronic communications system for more than one hundred and eighty days by the means available under subsection (b) of this section.

(b)   Contents of Wire or Electronic Communications in a Remote Computing Service.— (1)   A governmental entity may require a provider of remote computing service to disclose the contents of any wire or electronic communication to which this paragraph is made applicable by paragraph (2) of this subsection—

(A)   without required notice to the subscriber or customer, if the governmental entity obtains a warrant issued using the procedures described in the Federal Rules of Criminal Procedure (or, in the case of a State court, issued using State warrant procedures) by a court of competent jurisdiction; or

(B)   with prior notice from the governmental entity to the subscriber or customer if the governmental entity—

(i)   uses an administrative subpoena authorized by a Federal or State statute or a Federal or State grand jury or trial subpoena; or

(ii)   obtains a court order for such disclosure under subsection (d) of this section;

except that delayed notice may be given pursuant to section 2705 of this title.

(2)   Paragraph (1) is applicable with respect to any wire or electronic communication that is held or maintained on that service—

(A)   on behalf of, and received by means of electronic transmission from (or created by means of computer processing of communications received by means of electronic transmission from), a subscriber or customer of such remote computing service; and

(B)   solely for the purpose of providing storage or computer processing services to such subscriber or customer, if the provider is not authorized to access the contents of any such communications for purposes of providing any services other than storage or computer processing.

(c)   Records Concerning Electronic Communication Service or Remote Computing Service.—

(1)   A governmental entity may require a provider of electronic communication service or remote computing service to disclose a record or other information pertaining to a subscriber to or customer of such service

(not including the contents of communications) only when the governmental entity—

    (A) obtains a warrant issued using the procedures described in the Federal Rules of Criminal Procedure (or, in the case of a State court, issued using State warrant procedures) by a court of competent jurisdiction;

    (B) obtains a court order for such disclosure under subsection (d) of this section;

    (C) has the consent of the subscriber or customer to such disclosure;

    (D) submits a formal written request relevant to a law enforcement investigation concerning telemarketing fraud for the name, address, and place of business of a subscriber or customer of such provider, which subscriber or customer is engaged in telemarketing (as such term is defined in section 2325 of this title); or

    (E) seeks information under paragraph (2).

    (2) A provider of electronic communication service or remote computing service shall disclose to a governmental entity the—

    (A) name;

    (B) address;

    (C) local and long distance telephone connection records, or records of session times and durations;

    (D) length of service (including start date) and types of service utilized;

    (E) telephone or instrument number or other subscriber number or identity, including any temporarily assigned network address; and

    (F) means and source of payment for such service (including any credit card or bank account number),

of a subscriber to or customer of such service when the governmental entity uses an administrative subpoena authorized by a Federal or State statute or a Federal or State grand jury or trial subpoena or any means available under paragraph (1).

    (3) A governmental entity receiving records or information under this subsection is not required to provide notice to a subscriber or customer.

    (d) Requirements for Court Order.—A court order for disclosure under subsection (b) or (c) may be issued by any court that is a court of competent jurisdiction and shall issue only if the governmental entity offers specific and articulable facts showing that there are reasonable grounds to believe that the contents of a wire or electronic communication, or the records or other information sought, are relevant and material to an ongoing criminal investigation. In the case of a State governmental authority, such a court order shall not issue if prohibited by the law of such State. A court issuing an order pursuant to this section, on a motion made promptly by the service provider, may quash or modify such order, if the information or records requested are unusually voluminous in nature or compliance with such order otherwise would cause an undue burden on such provider.

(e) No Cause of Action Against a Provider Disclosing Information Under This Chapter.—No cause of action shall lie in any court against any provider of wire or electronic communication service, its officers, employees, agents, or other specified persons for providing information, facilities, or assistance in accordance with the terms of a court order, warrant, subpoena, statutory authorization, or certification under this chapter.

(f) Requirement To Preserve Evidence.—

(1) In general.—A provider of wire or electronic communication services or a remote computing service, upon the request of a governmental entity, shall take all necessary steps to preserve records and other evidence in its possession pending the issuance of a court order or other process.

(2) Period of retention.—Records referred to in paragraph (1) shall be retained for a period of 90 days, which shall be extended for an additional 90-day period upon a renewed request by the governmental entity.

(g) Presence of Officer Not Required.—Notwithstanding section 3105 of this title, the presence of an officer shall not be required for service or execution of a search warrant issued in accordance with this chapter requiring disclosure by a provider of electronic communications service or remote computing service of the contents of communications or records or other information pertaining to a subscriber to or customer of such service.

(i) Comity Analysis and Disclosure of Information Regarding Legal Process Seeking Contents of Wire or Electronic Communication.—

(1) Definitions.—In this subsection—

(A) the term 'qualifying foreign government' means a foreign government—

(i) with which the United States has an executive agreement that has entered into force under section 2523; and

(ii) the laws of which provide to electronic communication service providers and remote computing service providers substantive and procedural opportunities similar to those provided under paragraphs (2) and (5); and

(B) the term 'United States person' has the meaning given the term in section 2523.

(2)   Motions to quash or modify.—

(A)   A provider of electronic communication service to the public or remote computing service, that is being required to disclose pursuant to legal process issued under this section the contents of a wire or electronic communication of a subscriber or customer, may file a motion to modify or quash the legal process where the provider reasonably believes—

(i)   that the customer or subscriber is not a United States person and does not reside in the United States; and
(ii)   that the required disclosure would create a material risk that the provider would violate the laws of a qualifying foreign government.

Such a motion shall be filed not later than 14 days after the date on which the provider was served with the legal process, absent agreement with the government or permission from the court to extend the deadline based on an application made within the 14 days. The right to move to quash is without prejudice to any other grounds to move to quash or defenses thereto, but it shall be the sole basis for moving to quash on the grounds of a conflict of law related to a qualifying foreign government.

(B)   Upon receipt of a motion filed pursuant to subparagraph (A), the court shall afford the governmental entity that applied for or issued the legal process under this section the opportunity to respond. The court may modify or quash the legal process, as appropriate, only if the court finds that—

(i)   the required disclosure would cause the provider to violate the laws of a qualifying foreign government;
(ii)   based on the totality of the circumstances, the interests of justice dictate that the legal process should be modified or quashed; and
(iii)   the customer or subscriber is not a United States person and does not reside in the United States.

(3)   Comity analysis.—For purposes of making a determination under paragraph (2)(B)(ii), the court shall take into account, as appropriate—

(A)   the interests of the United States, including the investigative interests of the governmental entity seeking to require the disclosure;
(B)   the interests of the qualifying foreign government in preventing any prohibited disclosure;
(C)   the likelihood, extent, and nature of penalties to the provider or any employees of the provider as a result of inconsistent legal requirements imposed on the provider;

(D) the location and nationality of the subscriber or customer whose communications are being sought, if known, and the nature and extent of the subscriber or customer's connection to the United States, or if the legal process has been sought on behalf of a foreign authority pursuant to section 3512, the nature and extent of the subscriber or customer's connection to the foreign authority's country;

(E) the nature and extent of the provider's ties to and presence in the United States;

(F) the importance to the investigation of the information required to be disclosed;

(G) the likelihood of timely and effective access to the information required to be disclosed through means that would cause less serious negative consequences; and

(H) if the legal process has been sought on behalf of a foreign authority pursuant to section 3512, the investigative interests of the foreign authority making the request for assistance.

(4) Disclosure obligations during pendency of challenge.—A service provider shall preserve, but not be obligated to produce, information sought during the pendency of a motion brought under this subsection, unless the court finds that immediate production is necessary to prevent an adverse result identified in section 2705(a)(2).

(5) Disclosure to qualifying foreign government.—

(A) It shall not constitute a violation of a protective order issued under section 2705 for a provider of electronic communication service to the public or remote computing service to disclose to the entity within a qualifying foreign government, designated in an executive agreement under section 2523, the fact of the existence of legal process issued under this section seeking the contents of a wire or electronic communication of a customer or subscriber who is a national or resident of the qualifying foreign government.

(B) Nothing in this paragraph shall be construed to modify or otherwise affect any other authority to make a motion to modify or quash a protective order issued under section 2705.

§2704. Backup preservation

(a) Backup Preservation.—

(1) A governmental entity acting under section 2703(b)(2) may include in its subpoena or court order a requirement that the service provider to whom the request is directed create a backup copy of the contents of the electronic communications sought in order to preserve those

communications. Without notifying the subscriber or customer of such subpoena or court order, such service provider shall create such backup copy as soon as practicable consistent with its regular business practices and shall confirm to the governmental entity that such backup copy has been made. Such backup copy shall be created within two business days after receipt by the service provider of the subpoena or court order.

(2)   Notice to the subscriber or customer shall be made by the governmental entity within three days after receipt of such confirmation, unless such notice is delayed pursuant to section 2705(a).

(3)   The service provider shall not destroy such backup copy until the later of—

(A)   the delivery of the information; or

(B)   the resolution of any proceedings (including appeals of any proceeding) concerning the government's subpoena or court order.

(4)   The service provider shall release such backup copy to the requesting governmental entity no sooner than fourteen days after the governmental entity's notice to the subscriber or customer if such service provider—

(A)   has not received notice from the subscriber or customer that the subscriber or customer has challenged the governmental entity's request; and

(B)   has not initiated proceedings to challenge the request of the governmental entity.

(5)   A governmental entity may seek to require the creation of a backup copy under subsection (a)(1) of this section if in its sole discretion such entity determines that there is reason to believe that notification under section 2703 of this title of the existence of the subpoena or court order may result in destruction of or tampering with evidence. This determination is not subject to challenge by the subscriber or customer or service provider.

(b)   Customer Challenges.—

(1)   Within fourteen days after notice by the governmental entity to the subscriber or customer under subsection (a)(2) of this section, such subscriber or customer may file a motion to quash such subpoena or vacate such court order, with copies served upon the governmental entity and with written notice of such challenge to the service provider. A motion to vacate a court order shall be filed in the court which issued such order. A motion to quash a subpoena shall be filed in the appropriate United States district court or State court. Such motion or application shall contain an affidavit or sworn statement—

(A)   stating that the applicant is a customer or subscriber to the service from which the contents of electronic communications maintained for him have been sought; and

(B)   stating the applicant's reasons for believing that the records sought are not relevant to a legitimate law enforcement inquiry or that there has not been substantial compliance with the provisions of this chapter in some other respect.

(2)   Service shall be made under this section upon a governmental entity by delivering or mailing by registered or certified mail a copy of the papers to the person, office, or department specified in the notice which the customer has received pursuant to this chapter. For the purposes of this section, the term "delivery" has the meaning given that term in the Federal Rules of Civil Procedure.

(3)   If the court finds that the customer has complied with paragraphs (1) and (2) of this subsection, the court shall order the governmental entity to file a sworn response, which may be filed in camera if the governmental entity includes in its response the reasons which make in camera review appropriate. If the court is unable to determine the motion or application on the basis of the parties' initial allegations and response, the court may conduct such additional proceedings as it deems appropriate. All such proceedings shall be completed and the motion or application decided as soon as practicable after the filing of the governmental entity's response.

(4)   If the court finds that the applicant is not the subscriber or customer for whom the communications sought by the governmental entity are maintained, or that there is a reason to believe that the law enforcement inquiry is legitimate and that the communications sought are relevant to that inquiry, it shall deny the motion or application and order such process enforced. If the court finds that the applicant is the subscriber or customer for whom the communications sought by the governmental entity are maintained, and that there is not a reason to believe that the communications sought are relevant to a legitimate law enforcement inquiry, or that there has not been substantial compliance with the provisions of this chapter, it shall order the process quashed.

(5)   A court order denying a motion or application under this section shall not be deemed a final order and no interlocutory appeal may be taken therefrom by the customer.

§2705. Delayed notice

(a)   Delay of Notification.—

(1)   A governmental entity acting under section 2703(b) of this title may—

(A)   where a court order is sought, include in the application a request, which the court shall grant, for an order delaying the notification required under section 2703(b) of this title for a period not to exceed ninety days, if the court determines that there is reason to believe that notification of the existence of the court order may have an adverse result described in paragraph (2) of this subsection; or

(B)   where an administrative subpoena authorized by a Federal or State statute or a Federal or State grand jury subpoena is obtained, delay the notification required under section 2703(b) of this title for a period not to exceed ninety days upon the execution of a written certification of a supervisory official that there is reason to believe that notification of the existence of the subpoena may have an adverse result described in paragraph (2) of this subsection.

(2)   An adverse result for the purposes of paragraph (1) of this subsection is—

(A)   endangering the life or physical safety of an individual;

(B)   flight from prosecution;

(C)   destruction of or tampering with evidence;

(D)   intimidation of potential witnesses; or

(E)   otherwise seriously jeopardizing an investigation or unduly delaying a trial.

(3)   The governmental entity shall maintain a true copy of certification under paragraph (1)(B).

(4)   Extensions of the delay of notification provided in section 2703 of up to ninety days each may be granted by the court upon application, or by certification by a governmental entity, but only in accordance with subsection (b) of this section.

(5)   Upon expiration of the period of delay of notification under paragraph (1) or (4) of this subsection, the governmental entity shall serve upon, or deliver by registered or first-class mail to, the customer or subscriber a copy of the process or request together with notice that—

(A)   states with reasonable specificity the nature of the law enforcement inquiry; and

(B)   informs such customer or subscriber—

(i)   that information maintained for such customer or subscriber by the service provider named in such process or request was supplied to or requested by that governmental authority and the date on which the supplying or request took place;

(ii)   that notification of such customer or subscriber was delayed;

(iii) what governmental entity or court made the certification or determination pursuant to which that delay was made; and

(iv)   which provision of this chapter allowed such delay.

(6) As used in this subsection, the term "supervisory official" means the investigative agent in charge or assistant investigative agent in charge or an equivalent of an investigating agency's headquarters or regional office, or the chief prosecuting attorney or the first assistant prosecuting attorney or an equivalent of a prosecuting attorney's headquarters or regional office.

(b) Preclusion of Notice to Subject of Governmental Access.—A governmental entity acting under section 2703, when it is not required to notify the subscriber or customer under section 2703(b)(1), or to the extent that it may delay such notice pursuant to subsection (a) of this section, may apply to a court for an order commanding a provider of electronic communications service or remote computing service to whom a warrant, subpoena, or court order is directed, for such period as the court deems appropriate, not to notify any other person of the existence of the warrant, subpoena, or court order. The court shall enter such an order if it determines that there is reason to believe that notification of the existence of the warrant, subpoena, or court order will result in—

(1) endangering the life or physical safety of an individual;
(2) flight from prosecution;
(3) destruction of or tampering with evidence;
(4) intimidation of potential witnesses; or
(5) otherwise seriously jeopardizing an investigation or unduly delaying a trial.

§2706. Cost reimbursement

(a) Payment.—Except as otherwise provided in subsection (c), a governmental entity obtaining the contents of communications, records, or other information under section 2702, 2703, or 2704 of this title shall pay to the person or entity assembling or providing such information a fee for reimbursement for such costs as are reasonably necessary and which have been directly incurred in searching for, assembling, reproducing, or otherwise providing such information. Such reimbursable costs shall include any costs due to necessary disruption of normal operations of any electronic communication service or remote computing service in which such information may be stored.

(b) Amount.—The amount of the fee provided by subsection (a) shall be as mutually agreed by the governmental entity and the person or entity providing the information, or, in the absence of agreement, shall be as determined by the court which issued the order for production of such information (or the court before which a criminal prosecution relating to such information would be brought, if no court order was issued for production of the information).

(c) Exception.—The requirement of subsection (a) of this section does not apply with respect to records or other information maintained by a communications common carrier that relate to telephone toll records and telephone listings obtained under section 2703 of this title. The court may, however, order a payment as described in subsection (a) if the court determines the information required is unusually voluminous in nature or otherwise caused an undue burden on the provider.

§2707. Civil action

(a)   Cause of Action.—Except as provided in section 2703(e), any provider of electronic communication service, subscriber, or other person aggrieved by any violation of this chapter in which the conduct constituting the violation is engaged in with a knowing or intentional state of mind may, in a civil action, recover from the person or entity, other than the United States, which engaged in that violation such relief as may be appropriate.

(b)   Relief.—In a civil action under this section, appropriate relief includes—

(1)   such preliminary and other equitable or declaratory relief as may be appropriate;

(2)   damages under subsection (c); and

(3)   a reasonable attorney's fee and other litigation costs reasonably incurred.

(c)   Damages.—The court may assess as damages in a civil action under this section the sum of the actual damages suffered by the plaintiff and any profits made by the violator as a result of the violation, but in no case shall a person entitled to recover receive less than the sum of $1,000. If the violation is willful or intentional, the court may assess punitive damages. In the case of a successful action to enforce liability under this section, the court may assess the costs of the action, together with reasonable attorney fees determined by the court.

(d)   Administrative Discipline.—If a court or appropriate department or agency determines that the United States or any of its departments or agencies has violated any provision of this chapter, and the court or appropriate department or agency finds that the circumstances surrounding the violation raise serious questions about whether or not an officer or employee of the United States acted willfully or intentionally with respect to the violation, the department or agency shall, upon receipt of a true and correct copy of the decision and findings of the court or appropriate department or agency promptly initiate a proceeding to determine whether disciplinary action against the officer or employee is warranted. If the head of the department or agency involved determines that disciplinary action is not warranted, he or she shall notify the Inspector General with jurisdiction over the department or agency concerned and shall provide the Inspector General with the reasons for such determination.

(e) Defense.—A good faith reliance on—

(1) a court warrant or order, a grand jury subpoena, a legislative authorization, or a statutory authorization (including a request of a governmental entity under section 2703(f) of this title);

(2) a request of an investigative or law enforcement officer under section 2518(7) of this title; or

(3) a good faith determination that section 2511(3) of this title permitted the conduct complained of;

is a complete defense to any civil or criminal action brought under this chapter or any other law.

(f) Limitation.—A civil action under this section may not be commenced later than two years after the date upon which the claimant first discovered or had a reasonable opportunity to discover the violation.

(g) Improper Disclosure.—Any willful disclosure of a "record", as that term is defined in section 552a(a) of title 5, United States Code, obtained by an investigative or law enforcement officer, or a governmental entity, pursuant to section 2703 of this title, or from a device installed pursuant to section 3123 or 3125 of this title, that is not a disclosure made in the proper performance of the official functions of the officer or governmental entity making the disclosure, is a violation of this chapter. This provision shall not apply to information previously lawfully disclosed (prior to the commencement of any civil or administrative proceeding under this chapter) to the public by a Federal, State, or local governmental entity or by the plaintiff in a civil action under this chapter.

§2708. Exclusivity of remedies

The remedies and sanctions described in this chapter are the only judicial remedies and sanctions for nonconstitutional violations of this chapter.

§2709. Counterintelligence access to telephone toll and transactional records

(a) Duty to Provide.—A wire or electronic communication service provider shall comply with a request for subscriber information and toll billing records information, or electronic communication transactional records in its custody or possession made by the Director of the Federal Bureau of Investigation under subsection (b) of this section.

(b) Required Certification.—The Director of the Federal Bureau of Investigation, or his designee in a position not lower than Deputy Assistant

Director at Bureau headquarters or a Special Agent in Charge in a Bureau field office designated by the Director, may, using a term that specifically identifies a person, entity, telephone number, or account as the basis for a request—

(1) request the name, address, length of service, and local and long distance toll billing records of a person or entity if the Director (or his designee) certifies in writing to the wire or electronic communication service provider to which the request is made that the name, address, length of service, and toll billing records sought are relevant to an authorized investigation to protect against international terrorism or clandestine intelligence activities, provided that such an investigation of a United States person is not conducted solely on the basis of activities protected by the first amendment to the Constitution of the United States; and

(2) request the name, address, and length of service of a person or entity if the Director (or his designee) certifies in writing to the wire or electronic communication service provider to which the request is made that the information sought is relevant to an authorized investigation to protect against international terrorism or clandestine intelligence activities, provided that such an investigation of a United States person is not conducted solely upon the basis of activities protected by the first amendment to the Constitution of the United States.

(c) Prohibition of Certain Disclosure.—

(1) Prohibition.—

(A) In general.—If a certification is issued under subparagraph (B) and notice of the right to judicial review under subsection (d) is provided, no wire or electronic communication service provider that receives a request under subsection (b), or officer, employee, or agent thereof, shall disclose to any person that the Federal Bureau of Investigation has sought or obtained access to information or records under this section.

(B) Certification.—The requirements of subparagraph (A) shall apply if the Director of the Federal Bureau of Investigation, or a designee of the Director whose rank shall be no lower than Deputy Assistant Director at Bureau headquarters or a Special Agent in Charge of a Bureau field office, certifies that the absence of a prohibition of disclosure under this subsection may result in—

(i) a danger to the national security of the United States;

(ii) interference with a criminal, counterterrorism, or counterintelligence investigation;

(iii) interference with diplomatic relations; or

(iv) danger to the life or physical safety of any person.

(2) Exception.—

(A) In general.—A wire or electronic communication service provider that receives a request under subsection (b), or officer, employee, or agent thereof, may disclose information otherwise subject to any applicable nondisclosure requirement to—

(i) those persons to whom disclosure is necessary in order to comply with the request;

(ii) an attorney in order to obtain legal advice or assistance regarding the request; or

(iii) other persons as permitted by the Director of the Federal Bureau of Investigation or the designee of the Director.

(B) Application.—A person to whom disclosure is made under subparagraph (A) shall be subject to the nondisclosure requirements applicable to a person to whom a request is issued under subsection (b) in the same manner as the person to whom the request is issued.

(C) Notice.—Any recipient that discloses to a person described in subparagraph (A) information otherwise subject to a nondisclosure requirement shall notify the person of the applicable nondisclosure requirement.

(D) Identification of disclosure recipients.—At the request of the Director of the Federal Bureau of Investigation or the designee of the Director, any person making or intending to make a disclosure under clause (i) or (iii) of subparagraph (A) shall identify to the Director or such designee the person to whom such disclosure will be made or to whom such disclosure was made prior to the request.

(d) Judicial Review.—

(1) In general.—A request under subsection (b) or a nondisclosure requirement imposed in connection with such request under subsection (c) shall be subject to judicial review under section 3511.

(2) Notice.—A request under subsection (b) shall include notice of the availability of judicial review described in paragraph (1).

(e) Dissemination by Bureau.—The Federal Bureau of Investigation may disseminate information and records obtained under this section only as provided in guidelines approved by the Attorney General for foreign intelligence collection and foreign counterintelligence investigations conducted by the Federal Bureau of Investigation, and, with respect to dissemination to an agency of the United States, only if such information is clearly relevant to the authorized responsibilities of such agency.

(f) Requirement That Certain Congressional Bodies Be Informed.—On a semiannual basis the Director of the Federal Bureau of Investigation shall fully inform the Permanent Select Committee on Intelligence of the House of Representatives and the Select Committee on Intelligence of the Senate, and the Committee on the Judiciary of the House of Representatives and the Committee on the Judiciary of the Senate, concerning all requests made under subsection (b) of this section.

(g)   Libraries.—A library (as that term is defined in section 213(1) of the Library Services and Technology Act (20 U.S.C. 9122(1)), the services of which include access to the Internet, books, journals, magazines, newspapers, or other similar forms of communication in print or digitally by patrons for their use, review, examination, or circulation, is not a wire or electronic communication service provider for purposes of this section, unless the library is providing the services defined in section 2510(15) ("electronic communication service") of this title.

[§2710 not reproduced (part of the Video Privacy Protection Act (VPPA); see Chapter 9]

§2711. Definitions for chapter

As used in this chapter—

(1)   the terms defined in section 2510 of this title have, respectively, the definitions given such terms in that section;

(2)   the term "remote computing service" means the provision to the public of computer storage or processing services by means of an electronic communications system;

(3)   the term "court of competent jurisdiction" includes—

(A) any district court of the United States (including a magistrate judge of such a court) or any United States court of appeals that—

(i)   has jurisdiction over the offense being investigated;

(ii)   is in or for a district in which the provider of a wire or electronic communication service is located or in which the wire or electronic communications, records, or other information are stored; or

(iii)   is acting on a request for foreign assistance pursuant to section 3512 of this title; or

(B) a court of general criminal jurisdiction of a State authorized by the law of that State to issue search warrants;

(C) a court-martial or other proceeding under chapter 47 of title 10 (the Uniform Code of Military Justice) to which a military judge has been detailed; and

(4)   the term "governmental entity" means a department or agency of the United States or any State or political subdivision thereof.

§2712. Civil actions against the United States

(a) In General.—Any person who is aggrieved by any willful violation of this chapter or of chapter 119 of this title or of sections 106(a), 305(a), or 405(a) of the Foreign Intelligence Surveillance Act of 1978 (50 U.S.C. 1801 *et seq.)* may commence an action in United States District Court against the United States to recover money damages. In any such action, if a person who is aggrieved successfully establishes such a violation of this chapter or of chapter 119 of this title or of the above specific provisions of title 50, the Court may assess as damages—

(1) actual damages, but not less than $10,000, whichever amount is greater; and

(2) litigation costs, reasonably incurred.

(b) Procedures.—

(1) Any action against the United States under this section may be commenced only after a claim is presented to the appropriate department or agency under the procedures of the Federal Tort Claims Act, as set forth in title 28, United States Code.

(2) Any action against the United States under this section shall be forever barred unless it is presented in writing to the appropriate Federal agency within 2 years after such claim accrues or unless action is begun within 6 months after the date of mailing, by certified or registered mail, of notice of final denial of the claim by the agency to which it was presented. The claim shall accrue on the date upon which the claimant first has a reasonable opportunity to discover the violation.

(3) Any action under this section shall be tried to the court without a jury.

(4) Notwithstanding any other provision of law, the procedures set forth in section 106(f), 305(g), or 405(f) of the Foreign Intelligence Surveillance Act of 1978 (50 U.S.C. 1801 *et seq.*) shall be the exclusive means by which materials governed by those sections may be reviewed.

(5) An amount equal to any award against the United States under this section shall be reimbursed by the department or agency concerned to the fund described in section 1304 of title 31, United States Code, out of any appropriation, fund, or other account (excluding any part of such appropriation, fund, or account that is available for the enforcement of any Federal law) that is available for the operating expenses of the department or agency concerned.

(c) Administrative Discipline.—If a court or appropriate department or agency determines that the United States or any of its departments or agencies has violated any provision of this chapter, and the court or appropriate department or agency finds that the circumstances surrounding the violation raise serious questions about whether or not an officer or employee of the United States acted willfully or intentionally with respect to the violation, the department or agency shall, upon receipt of a true and correct copy of the decision and findings of the court or appropriate department or agency promptly initiate a proceeding to determine whether disciplinary action against the officer or employee is warranted. If the head of the department or agency involved determines that disciplinary action is not warranted, he or she shall notify the Inspector General with jurisdiction over the department or agency concerned and shall provide the Inspector General with the reasons for such determination.

(d) Exclusive Remedy.—Any action against the United States under this subsection shall be the exclusive remedy against the United States for any claims within the purview of this section.

(e) Stay of Proceedings.—

(1) Upon the motion of the United States, the court shall stay any action commenced under this section if the court determines that civil discovery will adversely affect the ability of the Government to conduct a related investigation or the prosecution of a related criminal case. Such a stay shall toll the limitations periods of paragraph (2) of subsection (b).

(2) In this subsection, the terms "related criminal case" and "related investigation" mean an actual prosecution or investigation in progress at the time at which the request for the stay or any subsequent motion to lift the stay is made. In determining whether an investigation or a criminal case is related to an action commenced under this section, the court shall consider the degree of similarity between the parties, witnesses, facts, and circumstances involved in the 2 proceedings, without requiring that any one or more factors be identical.

(3) In requesting a stay under paragraph (1), the Government may, in appropriate cases, submit evidence ex parte in order to avoid disclosing any matter that may adversely affect a related investigation or a related criminal case. If the Government makes such an ex parte submission, the plaintiff shall be given an opportunity to make a submission to the court, not ex parte, and the court may, in its discretion, request further information from either party.

§2713. Required preservation and disclosure of communications and records

A provider of electronic communication service or remote computing service shall comply with the obligations of this chapter to preserve, backup, or disclose the contents of a wire or electronic communication and any record or other information pertaining to a customer or subscriber within such provider's possession, custody, or control, regardless of whether such communication, record, or other information is located within or outside of the United States.

Title III (Pen Registers and Trap and Trace Devices), 18 U.S.C. §§ 3121–3127

§3121. General prohibition on pen register and trap and trace device use; exception

(a) In General.—Except as provided in this section, no person may install or use a pen register or a trap and trace device without first obtaining a court order under section 3123 of this title or under the Foreign Intelligence Surveillance Act of 1978 (50 U.S.C. 1801 *et seq.*), or an order from a foreign government that is subject to an executive agreement that the Attorney General has determined and certified to Congress satisfies section 2523.

(b) Exception.—The prohibition of subsection (a) does not apply with respect to the use of a pen register or a trap and trace device by a provider of electronic or wire communication service—

(1) relating to the operation, maintenance, and testing of a wire or electronic communication service or to the protection of the rights or property of such provider, or to the protection of users of that service from abuse of service or unlawful use of service; or

(2) to record the fact that a wire or electronic communication was initiated or completed in order to protect such provider, another provider furnishing service toward the completion of the wire communication, or a user of that service, from fraudulent, unlawful or abusive use of service; or (3) where the consent of the user of that service has been obtained.

(c) Limitation.—A government agency authorized to install and use a pen register or trap and trace device under this chapter or under State law shall use technology reasonably available to it that restricts the recording or decoding of electronic or other impulses to the dialing, routing, addressing, and signaling information utilized in the processing and transmitting of wire or electronic communications so as not to include the contents of any wire or electronic communications.

(d) Penalty.—Whoever knowingly violates subsection (a) shall be fined under this title or imprisoned not more than one year, or both.

§3122. Application for an order for a pen register or a trap and trace device

(a) Application.—

(1) An attorney for the Government may make application for an order or an extension of an order under section 3123 of this title authorizing or approving the installation and use of a pen register or a trap and trace device under this chapter, in writing under oath or equivalent affirmation, to a court of competent jurisdiction.

(2) Unless prohibited by State law, a State investigative or law enforcement officer may make application for an order or an extension of an order under section 3123 of this title authorizing or approving the installation and use of a pen register or a trap and trace device under this chapter, in writing under oath or equivalent affirmation, to a court of competent jurisdiction of such State.

(b) Contents of Application.—An application under subsection (a) of this section shall include—

(1) the identity of the attorney for the Government or the State law enforcement or investigative officer making the application and the identity of the law enforcement agency conducting the investigation; and

(2) a certification by the applicant that the information likely to be obtained is relevant to an ongoing criminal investigation being conducted by that agency.

§3123. Issuance of an order for a pen register or a trap and trace device

(a) In General.—

(1) Attorney for the government.—Upon an application made under section 3122(a)(1), the court shall enter an ex parte order authorizing the installation and use of a pen register or trap and trace device anywhere within the United States, if the court finds that the attorney for the Government has certified to the court that the information likely to be obtained by such installation and use is relevant to an ongoing criminal investigation. The order, upon service of that order, shall apply to any person or entity providing wire or electronic communication service in the United States whose assistance may facilitate the execution of the order. Whenever such an order is served on any person or entity not specifically named in the order, upon request of such person or entity, the attorney for the Government or law enforcement or investigative officer that is serving

the order shall provide written or electronic certification that the order applies to the person or entity being served.

(2) State investigative or law enforcement officer.—Upon an application made under section 3122(a)(2), the court shall enter an ex parte order authorizing the installation and use of a pen register or trap and trace device within the jurisdiction of the court, if the court finds that the State law enforcement or investigative officer has certified to the court that the information likely to be obtained by such installation and use is relevant to an ongoing criminal investigation.

(3) (A) Where the law enforcement agency implementing an ex parte order under this subsection seeks to do so by installing and using its own pen register or trap and trace device on a packet-switched data network of a provider of electronic communication service to the public, the agency shall ensure that a record will be maintained which will identify—

(i) any officer or officers who installed the device and any officer or officers who accessed the device to obtain information from the network;

(ii) the date and time the device was installed, the date and time the device was uninstalled, and the date, time, and duration of each time the device is accessed to obtain information;

(iii) the configuration of the device at the time of its installation and any subsequent modification thereof; and

(iv) any information which has been collected by the device.

To the extent that the pen register or trap and trace device can be set automatically to record this information electronically, the record shall be maintained electronically throughout the installation and use of such device.

(B) The record maintained under subparagraph (A) shall be provided ex parte and under seal to the court which entered the ex parte order authorizing the installation and use of the device within 30 days after termination of the order (including any extensions thereof).

(b) Contents of Order.—An order issued under this section—

(1) shall specify—

(A) the identity, if known, of the person to whom is leased or in whose name is listed the telephone line or other facility to which the pen register or trap and trace device is to be attached or applied;

(B) the identity, if known, of the person who is the subject of the criminal investigation;

(C) the attributes of the communications to which the order applies, including the number or other identifier and, if known, the location of the telephone line or other facility to which the pen register or trap and trace device is to be attached or applied, and, in the case of an order authorizing installation and use of a trap and trace device under subsection (a)(2), the geographic limits of the order; and

(D) a statement of the offense to which the information likely to be obtained by the pen register or trap and trace device relates; and

(2) shall direct, upon the request of the applicant, the furnishing of information, facilities, and technical assistance necessary to accomplish the installation of the pen register or trap and trace device under section 3124 of this title.

(c) Time Period and Extensions.—

(1) An order issued under this section shall authorize the installation and use of a pen register or a trap and trace device for a period not to exceed sixty days.

(2) Extensions of such an order may be granted, but only upon an application for an order under section 3122 of this title and upon the judicial finding required by subsection (a) of this section. The period of extension shall be for a period not to exceed sixty days.

(d) Nondisclosure of Existence of Pen Register or a Trap and Trace Device.—An order authorizing or approving the installation and use of a pen register or a trap and trace device shall direct that—

(1) the order be sealed until otherwise ordered by the court; and

(2) the person owning or leasing the line or other facility to which the pen register or a trap and trace device is attached or applied, or who is obligated by the order to provide assistance to the applicant, not disclose the existence of the pen register or trap and trace device or the existence of the investigation to the listed subscriber, or to any other person, unless or until otherwise ordered by the court.

§3124. Assistance in installation and use of a pen register or a trap and trace device

(a) Pen Registers.—Upon the request of an attorney for the Government or an officer of a law enforcement agency authorized to install and use a pen register under this chapter, a provider of wire or electronic communication service, landlord, custodian, or other person shall furnish such investigative or law enforcement officer forthwith all information, facilities, and technical assistance necessary to accomplish the installation of the pen register unobtrusively and with a minimum of interference with the services that the person so ordered by the court accords the party with respect to whom the installation and use is to take place, if such assistance is directed by a court order as provided in section 3123(b)(2) of this title.

(b)   Trap and Trace Device.—Upon the request of an attorney for the Government or an officer of a law enforcement agency authorized to receive the results of a trap and trace device under this chapter, a provider of a wire or electronic communication service, landlord, custodian, or other person shall install such device forthwith on the appropriate line or other facility and shall furnish such investigative or law enforcement officer all additional information, facilities and technical assistance including installation and operation of the device unobtrusively and with a minimum of interference with the services that the person so ordered by the court accords the party with respect to whom the installation and use is to take place, if such installation and assistance is directed by a court order as provided in section 3123(b)(2) of this title. Unless otherwise ordered by the court, the results of the trap and trace device shall be furnished, pursuant to section 3123(b) or section 3125 of this title, to the officer of a law enforcement agency, designated in the court order, at reasonable intervals during regular business hours for the duration of the order.

(c)   Compensation.—A provider of a wire or electronic communication service, landlord, custodian, or other person who furnishes facilities or technical assistance pursuant to this section shall be reasonably compensated for such reasonable expenses incurred in providing such facilities and assistance.

(d)   No Cause of Action Against a Provider Disclosing Information Under This Chapter.—No cause of action shall lie in any court against any provider of a wire or electronic communication service, its officers, employees, agents, or other specified persons for providing information, facilities, or assistance in accordance with a court order under this chapter, request pursuant to section 3125 of this title, or an order from a foreign government that is subject to an executive agreement that the Attorney General has determined and certified to Congress satisfies section 2523.

(e)   Defense.—A good faith reliance on a court order under this chapter, a request pursuant to section 3125 of this title, a legislative authorization, a statutory authorization, or a good faith determination that the conduct complained of was permitted by an order from a foreign government that is subject to executive agreement that the Attorney General has determined and certified to Congress satisfies section 2523, is a complete defense against any civil or criminal action brought under this chapter or any other law.

(f)   Communications Assistance Enforcement Orders.—Pursuant to section 2522, an order may be issued to enforce the assistance capability and capacity requirements under the Communications Assistance for Law Enforcement Act.

§3125. Emergency pen register and trap and trace device installation

(a) Notwithstanding any other provision of this chapter, any investigative or law enforcement officer, specially designated by the Attorney General, the Deputy Attorney General, the Associate Attorney General, any Assistant Attorney General, any acting Assistant Attorney General, or any Deputy Assistant Attorney General, or by the principal prosecuting attorney of any State or subdivision thereof acting pursuant to a statute of that State, who reasonably determines that—

    (1) an emergency situation exists that involves—

        (A) immediate danger of death or serious bodily injury to any person;

        (B) conspiratorial activities characteristic of organized crime;

        (C) an immediate threat to a national security interest; or

        (D) an ongoing attack on a protected computer (as defined in section 1030) that constitutes a crime punishable by a term of imprisonment greater than one year;

that requires the installation and use of a pen register or a trap and trace device before an order authorizing such installation and use can, with due diligence, be obtained, and

    (2) there are grounds upon which an order could be entered under this chapter to authorize such installation and use;

may have installed and use a pen register or trap and trace device if, within forty-eight hours after the installation has occurred, or begins to occur, an order approving the installation or use is issued in accordance with section 3123 of this title.

(b) In the absence of an authorizing order, such use shall immediately terminate when the information sought is obtained, when the application for the order is denied or when forty-eight hours have lapsed since the installation of the pen register or trap and trace device, whichever is earlier.

(c) The knowing installation or use by any investigative or law enforcement officer of a pen register or trap and trace device pursuant to subsection (a) without application for the authorizing order within forty-eight hours of the installation shall constitute a violation of this chapter.

(d) A provider of a wire or electronic service, landlord, custodian, or other person who furnished facilities or technical assistance pursuant to this section shall be reasonably compensated for such reasonable expenses incurred in providing such facilities and assistance.

§3126. Reports concerning pen registers and trap and trace devices

The Attorney General shall annually report to Congress on the number of pen register orders and orders for trap and trace devices applied for by law enforcement agencies of the Department of Justice, which report shall include information concerning—

(1) the period of interceptions authorized by the order, and the number and duration of any extensions of the order;

(2) the offense specified in the order or application, or extension of an order;

(3) the number of investigations involved;

(4) the number and nature of the facilities affected; and

(5) the identity, including district, of the applying investigative or law enforcement agency making the application and the person authorizing the order.

§3127. Definitions for chapter

As used in this chapter—

(1) the terms "wire communication", "electronic communication", "electronic communication service", and "contents" have the meanings set forth for such terms in section 2510 of this title;

(2) the term "court of competent jurisdiction" means—

(A) any district court of the United States (including a magistrate judge of such a court) or any United States court of appeals that—

(i) has jurisdiction over the offense being investigated;

(ii) is in or for a district in which the provider of a wire or electronic communication service is located;

(iii) is in or for a district in which a landlord, custodian, or other person subject to subsections (a) or (b) of section 3124 of this title is located; or

(iv) is acting on a request for foreign assistance pursuant to section 3512 of this title; or

(B) a court of general criminal jurisdiction of a State authorized by the law of that State to enter orders authorizing the use of a pen register or a trap and trace device;

(3) the term "pen register" means a device or process which records or decodes dialing, routing, addressing, or signaling information transmitted by an instrument or facility from which a wire or electronic communication is transmitted, provided, however, that such information shall not include the

contents of any communication, but such term does not include any device or process used by a provider or customer of a wire or electronic communication service for billing, or recording as an incident to billing, for communications services provided by such provider or any device or process used by a provider or customer of a wire communication service for cost accounting or other like purposes in the ordinary course of its business;

(4)   the term "trap and trace device" means a device or process which captures the incoming electronic or other impulses which identify the originating number or other dialing, routing, addressing, and signaling information reasonably likely to identify the source of a wire or electronic communication, provided, however, that such information shall not include the contents of any communication;

(5)   the term "attorney for the Government" has the meaning given such term for the purposes of the Federal Rules of Criminal Procedure; and

(6)   the term "State" means a State, the District of Columbia, Puerto Rico, and any other possession or territory of the United States.

Appendix F

Key Cybersecurity Court Opinions

Although cybersecurity law relies heavily on statutes, regulations, and agency guidance, the legal rules increasingly are being shaped by court opinions. Because this book is intended not only as a desk reference, but also as a textbook for undergraduate, graduate, and law school classes, this appendix includes excerpted court opinions from some of the most important cybersecurity-related cases to date. This appendix, which is new to the second edition of this book, is intended for use in law school courses and other classes that rely, at least in part, on the case learning method. I recommend first reading the overview in the main chapters, and then reading the accompanying cases to see the issues explored by the judges in greater depth.

The cases also are useful for reference for those working in the cybersecurity field. However, these excerpts do not contain the full opinions, and are heavily truncated. Many case and record citations have been deleted without ellipses or brackets to note the deletion; lengthier redactions (of multiple paragraphs) are indicated with either ellipses or a bracketed summary. Most footnotes were deleted, unless I deemed them necessary to provide context to the reader. Accordingly, if you plan to rely on these cases or cite them in a document, always check the full opinion rather than the excerpts in this book.

The following list is a summary of the opinion excerpts in this appendix.

Cases to accompany Chapter 1:

- *Federal Trade Commission v. Wyndham* (scope of FTC's data security authority under the unfairness prong of Section 5 of the FTC Act)
- *LabMD v. Federal Trade Commission* (specificity required for FTC data security orders)

Cases to accompany Chapter 2:

- *Krottner v. Starbucks Corp.* (broad view of Article III standing in private data security litigation)

Cybersecurity Law, Second Edition. Jeff Kosseff.
© 2020 John Wiley & Sons, Inc. Published 2020 by John Wiley & Sons, Inc.
Companion Website: www.wiley.com/go/kosseff/cybersecurity2e

- *Reilly v. Ceridian* (narrow view of Article III standing in private data security litigation)
- *In re Target Corporation Customer Data Security Breach Litigation* (court ruling on the merits of state law claims for data breach notification laws and negligence in a data breach class action)

Case to accompany Chapter 4:

- *In re The Home Depot Shareholder Derivative Litigation* (shareholder derivative claim against officers and directors of a company that experienced a data breach)

Cases to accompany Chapter 5:

- *United States v. Rodriguez* (broad view of "exceeds authorized access" under the Computer Fraud and Abuse Act)
- *United States v. Nosal ("Nosal I")* (narrow view of "exceeds authorized access" under the Computer Fraud and Abuse Act)
- *United States v. Nosal ("Nosal II")* (interpretation of "without authorization" under the Computer Fraud and Abuse Act)
- *International Airport Centers v. Citrin* (interpreting the scope of the CFAA's provisions regarding damage to computers)

Cases to accompany Chapter 7:

- *Katz v. United States* (development of the "reasonable expectation of privacy" test under the Fourth Amendment)
- *Smith v. Maryland* (development of the third party doctrine exception to *Katz*)
- *Carpenter v. United States* (the Supreme Court's 2018 application of the Fourth Amendment to cell-site location information)
- *United States v. Keith* (whether a private party that searches a person's online content is a government agent subject to the Fourth Amendment requirements)
- *United States v. Warshak* (the applicability of the Fourth Amendment to email)

Federal Trade Commission v. Wyndham, 799 F.3d 236 (3d Cir. 2015)
This opinion, discussed in Chapter 1, marks the first time that a federal appellate court ruled on the authority of the Federal Trade Commission to bring data security actions under Section 5 of the FTC Act. The Third Circuit's opinion validates the FTC's longstanding position that Section 5 provides it with the authority to regulate data security.

August 24, 2015

Opinion Judge Thomas L. Ambro, Circuit Judge:
The Federal Trade Commission Act prohibits "unfair or deceptive acts or practices in or affecting commerce." 15 U.S.C. § 45(a). In 2005 the Federal Trade

Commission began bringing administrative actions under this provision against companies with allegedly deficient cybersecurity that failed to protect consumer data against hackers. The vast majority of these cases have ended in settlement. On three occasions in 2008 and 2009 hackers successfully accessed Wyndham Worldwide Corporation's computer systems. In total, they stole personal and financial information for hundreds of thousands of consumers leading to over $10.6 million dollars in fraudulent charges. The FTC filed suit in federal District Court, alleging that Wyndham's conduct was an unfair practice and that its privacy policy was deceptive. The District Court denied Wyndham's motion to dismiss, and we granted interlocutory appeal on two issues: whether the FTC has authority to regulate cybersecurity under the unfairness prong of § 45(a); and, if so, whether Wyndham had fair notice its specific cybersecurity practices could fall short of that provision.[1] We affirm the District Court.

I. Background

A. Wyndham's Cybersecurity

Wyndham Worldwide is a hospitality company that franchises and manages hotels and sells timeshares through three subsidiaries. Wyndham licensed its brand name to approximately 90 independently owned hotels. Each Wyndham-branded hotel has a property management system that processes consumer information that includes names, home addresses, email addresses, telephone numbers, payment card account numbers, expiration dates, and security codes. Wyndham "manage[s]" these systems and requires the hotels to "purchase and configure" them to its own specifications. It also operates a computer network in Phoenix, Arizona, that connects its data center with the property management systems of each of the Wyndham-branded hotels.

The FTC alleges that, at least since April 2008, Wyndham engaged in unfair cybersecurity practices that, "taken together, unreasonably and unnecessarily exposed consumers' personal data to unauthorized access and theft." This claim is fleshed out as follows.

1. The company allowed Wyndham-branded hotels to store payment card information in clear readable text.
2. Wyndham allowed the use of easily guessed passwords to access the property management systems. For example, to gain "remote access to at least one hotel's system," which was developed by Micros Systems, Inc., the user ID and password were both "micros."

---

1 On appeal, Wyndham also argues that the FTC fails the pleading requirements of an unfairness claim. As Wyndham did not request and we did not grant interlocutory appeal on this issue, we decline to address it.

3. Wyndham failed to use "readily available security measures"—such as fire-walls—to "limit access between [the] hotels' property management systems, . . . corporate network, and the Internet."

4. Wyndham allowed hotel property management systems to connect to its network without taking appropriate cybersecurity precautions. It did not ensure that the hotels implemented "adequate information security policies and procedures." Also, it knowingly allowed at least one hotel to connect to the Wyndham network with an out-of-date operating system that had not received a security update in over three years. It allowed hotel servers to connect to Wyndham's network even though "default user IDs and passwords were enabled . . . , which were easily available to hackers through simple Internet searches." And, because it failed to maintain an "adequate[] inventory [of] computers connected to [Wyndham's] network [to] manage the devices," it was unable to identify the source of at least one of the cybersecurity attacks.

5. Wyndham failed to "adequately restrict" the access of third-party vendors to its network and the servers of Wyndham-branded hotels. For example, it did not "restrict[] connections to specified IP addresses or grant[] temporary, limited access, as necessary."

6. It failed to employ "reasonable measures to detect and prevent unauthorized access" to its computer network or to "conduct security investigations."

7. It did not follow "proper incident response procedures." The hackers used similar methods in each attack, and yet Wyndham failed to monitor its network for malware used in the previous intrusions. . . .

B. The Three Cybersecurity Attacks

As noted, on three occasions in 2008 and 2009 hackers accessed Wyndham's network and the property management systems of Wyndham-branded hotels. In April 2008, hackers first broke into the local network of a hotel in Phoenix, Arizona, which was connected to Wyndham's network and the Internet. They then used the brute-force method—repeatedly guessing users' login IDs and passwords—to access an administrator account on Wyndham's network. This enabled them to obtain consumer data on computers throughout the network. In total, the hackers obtained unencrypted information for over 500,000 accounts, which they sent to a domain in Russia.

In March 2009, hackers attacked again, this time by accessing Wyndham's network through an administrative account. The FTC claims that Wyndham was unaware of the attack for two months until consumers filed complaints about fraudulent charges. Wyndham then discovered "memory-scraping malware" used in the previous attack on more than thirty hotels' computer systems. The FTC asserts that, due to Wyndham's "failure to monitor [the network] for the malware used in the previous attack, hackers had unauthorized access to [its] network for approximately two months." In this second attack, the hackers obtained unencrypted payment card information for approximately 50,000 consumers from the property management systems of 39 hotels.

Hackers in late 2009 breached Wyndham's cybersecurity a third time by accessing an administrator account on one of its networks. Because Wyndham "had still not adequately limited access between . . . the Wyndham-branded hotels' property management systems, [Wyndham's network], and the Internet," the hackers had access to the property management servers of multiple hotels. Wyndham only learned of the intrusion in January 2010 when a credit card company received complaints from cardholders. In this third attack, hackers obtained payment card information for approximately 69,000 customers from the property management systems of 28 hotels.

The FTC alleges that, in total, the hackers obtained payment card information from over 619,000 consumers, which (as noted) resulted in at least $10.6 million in fraud loss. It further states that consumers suffered financial injury through "unreimbursed fraudulent charges, increased costs, and lost access to funds or credit," and that they "expended time and money resolving fraudulent charges and mitigating subsequent harm."

C. Procedural History

The FTC filed suit in the U.S. District Court for the District of Arizona in June 2012 claiming that Wyndham engaged in "unfair" and "deceptive" practices in violation of § 45(a). At Wyndham's request, the Court transferred the case to the U.S. District Court for the District of New Jersey. Wyndham then filed a Rule 12(b)(6) motion to dismiss both the unfair practice and deceptive practice claims. The District Court denied the motion but certified its decision on the unfairness claim for interlocutory appeal. We granted Wyndham's application for appeal. . . .

III. FTC's Regulatory Authority Under § 45(a)

A. Legal Background

The Federal Trade Commission Act of 1914 prohibited "unfair methods of competition in commerce." Congress "explicitly considered, and rejected, the notion that it reduce the ambiguity of the phrase 'unfair methods of competition' . . . by enumerating the particular practices to which it was intended to apply." . . .

After several early cases limited "unfair methods of competition" to practices harming competitors and not consumers, Congress inserted an additional prohibition in § 45(a) against "unfair or deceptive acts or practices in or affecting commerce."

For the next few decades, the FTC interpreted the unfair-practices prong primarily through agency adjudication. But in 1964 it issued a "Statement of Basis and Purpose" for unfair or deceptive advertising and labeling of cigarettes, which explained that the following three factors governed unfairness determinations:

> (1) whether the practice, without necessarily having been previously considered unlawful, offends public policy as it has been established by statutes, the common law, or otherwise—whether, in other words, it is within at least the penumbra of some common-law, statutory or other established concept of unfairness; (2) whether it is immoral, unethical, oppressive, or unscrupulous; [and] (3) whether it causes substantial injury to consumers (or competitors or other businessmen).

Almost a decade later, the Supreme Court implicitly approved these factors, apparently acknowledging their applicability to contexts other than cigarette advertising and labeling. The Court also held that, under the policy statement, the FTC could deem a practice unfair based on the third prong—substantial consumer injury—without finding that at least one of the other two prongs was also satisfied.

During the 1970s, the FTC embarked on a controversial campaign to regulate children's advertising through the unfair-practices prong of § 45(a). At the request of Congress, the FTC issued a second policy statement in 1980 that clarified the three factors. It explained that public policy considerations are relevant in determining whether a particular practice causes substantial consumer injury. Next, it "abandoned" the "theory of immoral or unscrupulous conduct . . . altogether" as an "independent" basis for an unfairness claim. . . . And finally, the Commission explained that "[u]njustified consumer injury is the primary focus of the FTC Act" and that such an injury "[b]y itself . . . can be sufficient to warrant a finding of unfairness." This "does not mean that every consumer injury is legally 'unfair.'"

> [t]o justify a finding of unfairness the injury must satisfy three tests. [1] It must be substantial; [2] it must not be outweighed by any countervailing benefits to consumers or competition that the practice produces; and [3] it must be an injury that consumers themselves could not reasonably have avoided.

In 1994, Congress codified the 1980 Policy Statement at 15 U.S.C. § 45(n):

> The Commission shall have no authority under this section . . . to declare unlawful an act or practice on the grounds that such act or practice is unfair unless the act or practice causes or is likely to cause substantial injury to consumers which is not reasonably avoidable by consumers themselves and not outweighed by countervailing benefits to consumers or to competition. In determining

whether an act or practice is unfair, the Commission may consider established public policies as evidence to be considered with all other evidence. Such public policy considerations may not serve as a primary basis for such determination.

Like the 1980 Policy Statement, § 45(n) requires substantial injury that is not reasonably avoidable by consumers and that is not outweighed by the benefits to consumers or competition. It also acknowledges the potential significance of public policy and does not expressly require that an unfair practice be immoral, unethical, unscrupulous, or oppressive.

B. Plain Meaning of Unfairness

Wyndham argues (for the first time on appeal) that the three requirements of 15 U.S.C. § 45(n) are necessary but insufficient conditions of an unfair practice and that the plain meaning of the word "unfair" imposes independent require-ments that are not met here. Arguably, § 45(n) may not identify all of the requirements for an unfairness claim. (While the provision forbids the FTC from declaring an act unfair "unless" the act satisfies the three specified requirements, it does not answer whether these are the only requirements for a finding of unfairness.) Even if so, some of Wyndham's proposed requirements are unpersuasive, and the rest are satisfied by the allegations in the FTC's complaint.

First, citing *FTC v. R.F. Keppel & Brother, Inc.*, Wyndham argues that conduct is only unfair when it injures consumers "through unscrupulous or unethical behavior." But *Keppel* nowhere says that unfair conduct must be unscrupulous or unethical. Moreover, in *Sperry* the Supreme Court rejected the view that the FTC's 1964 policy statement required unfair conduct to be "unscrupulous" or "unethical." Wyndham points to no subsequent FTC policy statements, adjudi-cations, judicial opinions, or statutes that would suggest any change since *Sperry*.

Next, citing one dictionary, Wyndham argues that a practice is only "unfair" if it is "not equitable" or is "marked by injustice, partiality, or deception." Whether these are requirements of an unfairness claim makes little difference here. A company does not act equitably when it publishes a privacy policy to attract customers who are concerned about data privacy, fails to make good on that promise by investing inadequate resources in cybersecurity, exposes its unsuspecting customers to substantial financial injury, and retains the profits of their business.

We recognize this analysis of unfairness encompasses some facts relevant to the FTC's deceptive practices claim. But facts relevant to unfairness and decep-tion claims frequently overlap. … We cannot completely disentangle the two theories here. The FTC argued in the District Court that consumers could not reasonably avoid injury by booking with another hotel chain because Wyndham had published a misleading privacy policy that overstated its cybersecurity. ... Wyndham did not challenge this argument in the District Court nor does it do so now. If Wyndham's conduct satisfies the reasonably avoidable requirement at least partially because of its privacy policy—an inference we find plausible at this stage of the litigation—then the policy is directly relevant to whether Wyndham's conduct was unfair.

Continuing on, Wyndham asserts that a business "does not treat its customers in an 'unfair' manner when the business itself is victimized by criminals." It offers no reasoning or authority for this principle, and we can think of none ourselves. Although unfairness claims usually involve actual and completed harms, they may also be brought on the basis of likely rather than actual injury. And the FTC Act expressly contemplates the possibility that conduct can be unfair before actual injury occurs. ... More importantly, that a company's conduct was not the most proximate cause of an injury generally does not immunize liability from foreseeable harms. ... For good reason, Wyndham does not argue that the cybersecurity intrusions were unforeseeable. That would be particularly implausible as to the second and third attacks.

Finally, Wyndham posits a *reductio ad absurdum*, arguing that if the FTC's unfairness authority extends to Wyndham's conduct, then the FTC also has the authority to "regulate the locks on hotel room doors, . . . to require every store in the land to post an armed guard at the door," and to sue supermarkets that are "sloppy about sweeping up banana peels." The argument is alarmist to say the least. And it invites the tart retort that, were Wyndham a supermarket, leaving so many banana peels all over the place that 619,000 customers fall hardly suggests it should be immune from liability under § 45(a).

We are therefore not persuaded by Wyndham's arguments that the alleged conduct falls outside the plain meaning of "unfair."

C. Subsequent Congressional Action

Wyndham next argues that, even if cybersecurity were covered by § 45(a) as initially enacted, three legislative acts since the subsection was amended in 1938 have reshaped the provision's meaning to exclude cybersecurity. A recent amendment to the Fair Credit Reporting Act directed the FTC and other agencies to develop regulations for the proper disposal of consumer data. The Gramm-Leach-Bliley Act required the FTC to establish standards for financial institutions to protect consumers' personal information. And the Children's Online Privacy Protection Act ordered the FTC to promulgate regulations requiring children's websites, among other things, to provide notice of "what information is collected from children . . . , how the operator uses such information, and the operator's disclosure practices for such information." Wyndham contends these "tailored grants of substantive authority to the FTC in the cybersecurity field would be inexplicable if the Commission already had general substantive authority over this field." Citing *FDA v. Brown & Williamson*

Tobacco Corp., 529 U.S. 120, 143 (2000), Wyndham concludes that Congress excluded cybersecurity from the FTC's unfairness authority by enacting these measures.

We are not persuaded. The inference to congressional intent based on post-enactment legislative activity in *Brown & Williamson* was far stronger. There, the Food and Drug Administration had repeatedly disclaimed regulatory authority over tobacco products for decades. During that period, Congress enacted six statutes regulating tobacco. The FDA later shifted its position, claiming authority over tobacco products. The Supreme Court held that Congress excluded tobacco-related products from the FDA's authority in enacting the statutes. As tobacco products would necessarily be banned if subject to the FDA's regulatory authority, any interpretation to the contrary would contradict congressional intent to regulate rather than ban tobacco products outright. Wyndham does not argue that recent privacy laws contradict reading corporate cybersecurity into § 45(a). Instead, it merely asserts that Congress had no reason to enact them if the FTC could already regulate cybersecurity through that provision.

We disagree that Congress lacked reason to pass the recent legislation if the FTC already had regulatory authority over some cybersecurity issues. The Fair Credit Reporting Act requires (rather than authorizes) the FTC to issue regulations ..., and expands the scope of the FTC's authority. The Gramm-Leach-Bliley Act similarly requires the FTC to promulgate regulations. And the Children's Online Privacy Protection Act required the FTC to issue regulations and empowered it to do so under the procedures of the Administrative Procedure Act, rather than the more burdensome Magnuson-Moss procedures under which the FTC must usually issue regulations. Thus none of the recent privacy legislation was "inexplicable" if the FTC already had some authority to regulate corporate cybersecurity through § 45(a).

Next, Wyndham claims that the FTC's interpretation of § 45(a) is "inconsistent with its repeated efforts to obtain from Congress the very authority it purports to wield here." Yet again we disagree. In two of the statements cited by Wyndham, the FTC clearly said that some cybersecurity practices are "unfair" under the statute. . . .

In the two other cited statements, given in 1998 and 2000, the FTC only acknowledged that it cannot require companies to adopt "fair information practice policies." These policies would protect consumers from far more than the kind of "substantial injury" typically covered by § 45(a). In addition to imposing some cybersecurity requirements, they would require companies to give notice about what data they collect from consumers, to permit those consumers to decide how the data is used, and to permit them to review and correct inaccuracies. As the FTC explained in the District Court, the primary concern driving the adoption of these policies in the late 1990s was that "companies . . . were capable of collecting enormous amounts of information about consumers, and people were suddenly realizing this." The FTC thus could not require companies to adopt broad fair information practice policies because they were "just collecting th[e] information, and consumers [were not] injured." Our conclusion is this: that the FTC later brought unfairness actions against companies whose inadequate cybersecurity resulted in consumer harm is not inconsistent with the agency's earlier position.

Having rejected Wyndham's arguments that its conduct cannot be unfair, we assume for the remainder of this opinion that it was.

IV. Fair Notice

A conviction or punishment violates the Due Process Clause of our Constitution if the statute or regulation under which it is obtained fails to provide a person of ordinary intelligence fair notice of what is prohibited, or is so standardless that it authorizes or encourages seriously discriminatory enforcement. Wyndham claims that, notwithstanding whether its conduct was unfair under § 45(a), the FTC failed to give fair notice of the specific cybersecurity standards the company was required to follow.

A. Legal Standard

The level of required notice for a person to be subject to liability varies by circumstance. In *Bouie v. City of Columbia*, the Supreme Court held that a "judicial construction of a criminal statute" violates due process if it is "unexpected and indefensible by reference to the law which had been expressed prior to the conduct in issue." The precise meaning of "unexpected and indefensible" is not entirely clear, but we and our sister circuits frequently use language implying that a conviction violates due process if the defendant could not reasonably foresee that a court might adopt the new interpretation of the statute.

The fair notice doctrine extends to civil cases, particularly where a penalty is imposed. "Lesser degrees of specificity" are allowed in civil cases because the consequences are smaller than in the criminal context. The standards are especially lax for civil statutes that regulate economic activities. For those statutes, a party lacks fair notice when the relevant standard is "so vague as to be no rule or standard at all." *CMR D.N. Corp. v. City of Phila[delphia]*, 703 F.3d 612, 631-32 (3d Cir. 2013).

A different set of considerations is implicated when agencies are involved in statutory or regulatory interpretation. Broadly speaking, agencies interpret in at least three contexts. One is where an agency administers a statute without any special authority to create new rights or obligations. When disputes arise under this kind of agency interpretation, the courts give respect to the agency's view to the extent it is persuasive, but they retain the primary responsibility for construing the statute. As such, the standard of notice afforded to litigants about the meaning of the statute is not dissimilar to the standard of notice for civil statutes generally because the court, not the agency, is the ultimate arbiter of the statute's meaning.

The second context is where an agency exercises its authority to fill gaps in a statutory scheme. There the agency is primarily responsible for interpreting the statute because the courts must defer to any reasonable construction it adopts. Courts appear to apply a more stringent standard of notice to civil regulations than civil statutes: parties are entitled to have "ascertainable certainty" of what conduct is legally required by the regulation.

The third context is where an agency interprets the meaning of its own regulation. Here also courts typically must defer to the agency's reasonable interpretation. We and several of our sister circuits have stated that private parties are entitled to know with "ascertainable certainty" an agency's interpretation of its regulation. . . .

A higher standard of fair notice applies in the second and third contexts than in the typical civil statutory interpretation case because agencies engage in interpretation differently than courts. In resolving ambiguity in statutes or regulations, courts generally adopt the best or most reasonable interpretation. But, as the agency is often free to adopt any reasonable construction, it may impose higher legal obligations than required by the best interpretation. . . .

Wyndham argues it was entitled to "ascertainable certainty" of the FTC's interpretation of what specific cybersecurity practices are required by § 45(a). Yet it has contended repeatedly—no less than seven separate occasions in this case—that there is no FTC rule or adjudication about cybersecurity that merits deference here. The necessary implication, one that Wyndham itself has explicitly drawn on two occasions noted below, is that federal courts are to interpret § 45(a) in the first instance to decide whether Wyndham's conduct was unfair.

Wyndham's argument has focused on the FTC's motion to dismiss order in *LabMD*, an administrative case in which the agency is pursuing an unfairness claim based on allegedly inadequate cybersecurity. Wyndham first argued in the District Court that the *LabMD* Order does not merit *Chevron* deference because "self-serving, litigation-driven decisions . . . are entitled to no deference at all" and because the opinion adopted an impermissible construction of the statute.

Second, Wyndham switched gears in its opening brief on appeal to us, arguing that *LabMD* does not merit *Chevron* deference because courts owe no deference to an agency's interpretation of the "boundaries of Congress' statutory delegation of authority to the agency."

Third, in its reply brief it argued again that *LabMD* does not merit *Chevron* deference because it adopted an impermissible construction of the statute.

Fourth, Wyndham switched gears once more in a Rule 28(j) letter, arguing that *LabMD* does not merit *Chevron* deference because the decision was nonfinal.

Fifth, at oral argument we asked Wyndham whether the FTC has decided that cybersecurity practices are unfair. Counsel answered: "No. I don't think consent decrees count, I don't think the 2007 brochure counts, and I don't think *Chevron* deference applies. So are . . . they asking this federal court in the first instance . . . [?] I think the answer to that question is yes . . . ."

Sixth, due to our continuing confusion about the parties' positions on a number of issues in the case, we asked for supplemental briefing on certain questions, including whether the FTC had declared that cybersecurity practices can be unfair. In response, Wyndham asserted that "the FTC has not declared unreasonable cybersecurity practices 'unfair.'" Wyndham explained further: "It follows from [our] answer to [that] question that the FTC is asking the federal courts to determine in the first instance that unreasonable cybersecurity practices qualify as 'unfair' trade practices under the FTC Act."

Seventh, and most recently, Wyndham submitted a Rule 28(j) letter arguing that *LabMD* does not merit *Chevron* deference because it decided a question of "deep economic and political significance."

Wyndham's position is unmistakable: the FTC has not yet declared that cybersecurity practices can be unfair; there is no relevant FTC rule, adjudication or document that merits deference; and the FTC is asking the federal courts to interpret § 45(a) in the first instance to decide whether it prohibits the alleged conduct here. The implication of this position is similarly clear: if the federal courts are to decide whether Wyndham's conduct was unfair in the first instance under the statute without deferring to any FTC interpretation, then this case involves ordinary judicial interpretation of a civil statute, and the ascertainable certainty standard does not apply. The relevant question is not whether Wyndham had fair notice of the FTC's interpretation of the statute, but whether Wyndham had fair notice of what the statute itself requires.

Indeed, at oral argument we asked Wyndham whether the cases cited in its brief that apply the "ascertainable certainty" standard—all of which involve a court reviewing an agency adjudication or at least a court being asked to defer to an agency interpretation—apply where the court is to decide the meaning of the statute in the first instance. Wyndham's counsel responded, "I think it would, your Honor. I think if you go to *Ford Motor* [*Co. v. FTC,*] I think that's what was happening there." But *Ford Motor* is readily distinguishable. Unlike Wyndham, the petitioners there did not bring a fair notice claim under the Due Process Clause. Instead, they argued that, per *NLRB v. Bell Aerospace Co.*, 416 U.S. 267 (1974), the FTC abused its discretion by proceeding through agency adjudication rather than rulemaking. More importantly, the Ninth Circuit was reviewing an agency adjudication; it was not interpreting the meaning of the FTC Act in the first instance.

In addition, our understanding of Wyndham's position is consistent with the District Court's opinion, which concluded that the FTC has stated a claim under § 45(a) based on the Court's interpretation of the statute and without any reference to *LabMD* or any other agency adjudication or regulation.

We thus conclude that Wyndham was not entitled to know with ascertainable certainty the FTC's interpretation of what cybersecurity practices are required by § 45(a). Instead, the relevant question in this appeal is whether Wyndham had fair notice that its conduct could fall within the meaning of the statute. If later proceedings in this case develop such that the proper resolution is to defer to an agency interpretation that gives rise to Wyndham's liability, we leave to that time a fuller exploration of the level of notice required. For now, however, it is enough to say that we accept Wyndham's forceful contention that we are interpreting the FTC Act (as the District Court did). As a necessary consequence, Wyndham is only entitled to notice of the meaning of the statute and not to the agency's interpretation of the statute.

B. Did Wyndham Have Fair Notice of the Meaning of § 45(a)?

Having decided that Wyndham is entitled to notice of the meaning of the statute, we next consider whether the case should be dismissed based on fair notice principles. We do not read Wyndham's briefs as arguing the company lacked fair notice that cybersecurity practices can, as a general matter, form the basis of an unfair practice under § 45(a). Wyndham argues instead it lacked notice of what specific cybersecurity practices are necessary to avoid liability. We have little trouble rejecting this claim.

To begin with, Wyndham's briefing focuses on the FTC's failure to give notice of its interpretation of the statute and does not meaningfully argue that the statute itself fails fair notice principles. We think it imprudent to hold a 100-year-old statute unconstitutional as applied to the facts of this case when we have not expressly been asked to do so.

Moreover, Wyndham is entitled to a relatively low level of statutory notice for several reasons. Subsection 45(a) does not implicate any constitutional rights here. It is a civil rather than criminal statute. And statutes regulating economic activity receive a "less strict" test because their subject matter is often more narrow, and because businesses, which face economic demands to plan behavior carefully, can be expected to consult relevant legislation in advance of action.

In this context, the relevant legal rule is not "so vague as to be no rule or standard at all." Subsection 45(n) asks whether "the act or practice causes or is likely to cause substantial injury to consumers which is not reasonably avoidable by consumers themselves and not outweighed by countervailing benefits to consumers or to competition." While far from precise, this standard informs parties that the relevant inquiry here is a cost-benefit analysis. . . . We acknowledge there will be borderline cases where it is unclear if a particular company's conduct falls below the requisite legal threshold. But under a due process analysis a company is not entitled to such precision as would eliminate all close calls. Fair notice is satisfied here as long as the company can reasonably foresee that a court could construe its conduct as falling within the meaning of the statute.

What appears to us is that Wyndham's fair notice claim must be reviewed as an as-applied challenge. Yet Wyndham does not argue that its cybersecurity practices survive a reasonable interpretation of the cost-benefit analysis required by § 45(n). One sentence in Wyndham's reply brief says that its "view of what data-security practices are unreasonable . . . is not necessarily the same as the FTC's." Too little and too late.

Wyndham's as-applied challenge falls well short given the allegations in the FTC's complaint. As the FTC points out in its brief, the complaint does not allege that Wyndham used weak firewalls, IP address restrictions, encryption software, and passwords. Rather, it alleges that Wyndham failed to use any firewall at critical network points, did not restrict specific IP addresses at all, did not use any encryption for certain customer files, and did not require some users to change their default or factory-setting passwords at all. Wyndham did not respond to this argument in its reply brief.

Wyndham's as-applied challenge is even weaker given it was hacked not one or two, but three, times. At least after the second attack, it should have been painfully clear to Wyndham that a court could find its conduct failed the cost-benefit analysis. That said, we leave for another day whether Wyndham's alleged cybersecurity practices do in fact fail, an issue the parties did not brief. We merely note that certainly after the second time Wyndham was hacked, it was on notice of the possibility that a court could find that its practices fail the cost-benefit analysis.

Several other considerations reinforce our conclusion that Wyndham's fair notice challenge fails. In 2007 the FTC issued a guidebook, *Protecting Personal Information: A Guide for Business*, which describes a "checklist[]" of practices that form a "sound data security plan." The guidebook does not state that any particular practice is required by § 45(a) but it does counsel against many of the specific practices alleged here. For instance, it recommends that companies "consider encrypting sensitive information that is stored on [a] computer net-work . . . [, c]heck . . . software vendors' websites regularly for alerts about new vulnerabilities, and implement policies for installing vendor-approved patches." It recommends using "a firewall to protect [a] computer from hacker attacks while it is connected to the Internet," deciding "whether [to] install a `border' firewall where [a] network connects to the Internet," and setting access controls that "determine who gets through the firewall and what they will be allowed to see . . . to allow only trusted employees with a legitimate business need to access the network." It recommends "requiring that employees use `strong' passwords" and cautions that "[h]ackers will first try words like . . . the software's default password[] and other easy-to-guess choices." And it recommends implementing a "breach response plan," which includes "[i]nvestigat[ing] security incidents immediately and tak[ing] steps to close off existing vulnerabilities or threats to personal information."

As the agency responsible for administering the statute, the FTC's expert views about the characteristics of a "sound data security plan" could certainly have helped Wyndham determine in advance that its conduct might not survive the cost-benefit analysis.

Before the attacks, the FTC also filed complaints and entered into consent decrees in administrative cases raising unfairness claims based on inadequate corporate cybersecurity. The agency published these materials on its website and provided notice of proposed consent orders in the Federal Register. Wyndham responds that the complaints cannot satisfy fair notice principles because they are not "adjudications on the merits." But even where the "ascertainable certainty" standard applies to fair notice claims, courts regularly consider materials that are neither regulations nor "adjudications on the merits." . . . That the FTC commissioners—who must vote on whether to issue a complaint—believe that alleged cybersecurity practices fail the cost-benefit analysis of § 45(n) certainly helps companies with similar practices apprehend the possibility that their cybersecurity could fail as well.

Wyndham next contends that the individual allegations in the complaints are too vague to be relevant to the fair notice analysis. It does not, however, identify any specific examples. . . . [T]he individual allegations were specific and similar to those here in at least one of the four or five cybersecurity-related unfair-practice complaints that issued prior to the first attack.

Wyndham also argues that, even if the individual allegations are not vague, the complaints "fail to spell out what specific cybersecurity practices . . . actually triggered the alleged violation, . . . provid[ing] only a . . . description of certain alleged problems that, 'taken together,'" fail the cost-benefit analysis. We part with it on two fronts. First, even if the complaints do not specify which allegations, in the Commission's view, form the necessary and sufficient conditions of the alleged violation, they can still help companies apprehend the possibility of liability under the statute. Second, . . . Wyndham cannot argue that the complaints fail to give notice of the necessary and sufficient conditions of an alleged § 45(a) violation when all of the allegations in at least one of the relevant four or five complaints have close corollaries here.

V. Conclusion

The three requirements in § 45(n) may be necessary rather than sufficient conditions of an unfair practice, but we are not persuaded that any other requirements proposed by Wyndham pose a serious challenge to the FTC's claim here. Furthermore, Wyndham repeatedly argued there is no FTC interpretation of § 45(a) or (n) to which the federal courts must defer in this case, and, as a result, the courts must interpret the meaning of the statute as it applies to Wyndham's conduct in the first instance. Thus, Wyndham cannot argue it was entitled to know with ascertainable certainty the cybersecurity standards by which the FTC expected it to conform. Instead, the company can only claim that it lacked fair notice of the meaning of the statute itself—a theory it did not meaningfully raise and that we strongly suspect would be unpersuasive under the facts of this case.

We thus affirm the District Court's decision.

LabMD v. Federal Trade Commission, 894 F.3d 1221 (11th Cir. 2018)

LabMD's challenge to an FTC data security cease-and-desist order, discussed in Chapter 1, hinged on LabMD's claim that the order lacked sufficient specificity. Just as the Third Circuit's opinion in Wyndham *was a significant victory for the FTC's data security enforcement efforts, the Eleventh Circuit's opinion in LabMD represented a potential limitation on future efforts.*

June 6, 2018

Opinion by Gerald B. Tjoflat, Circuit Judge:

This is an enforcement action brought by the Federal Trade Commission ("FTC" or "Commission") against LabMD, Inc., alleging that LabMD's data-security program was inadequate and thus constituted an "unfair act or practice" under Section 5(a) of the Federal Trade Commission Act (the "FTC Act" or "Act"). Following a trial before an administrative law judge ("ALJ"), the Commission issued a cease and desist order directing LabMD to create and implement a variety of protective measures. LabMD petitions this Court to vacate the order, arguing that the order is unenforceable because it does not direct LabMD to cease committing an unfair act or practice within the meaning of Section 5(a). We agree and accordingly vacate the order.

I.

A.

LabMD is a now-defunct medical laboratory that previously conducted diagnostic testing for cancer. It used medical specimen samples, along with relevant patient information, to provide physicians with diagnoses. Given the nature of its work, LabMD was subject to data-security regulations issued under the Health Insurance Portability and Accountability Act of 1996, known colloquially as HIPAA. LabMD employed a data-security program in an effort to comply with those regulations.

Sometime in 2005, contrary to LabMD policy, a peer-to-peer file-sharing application called LimeWire was installed on a computer used by LabMD's billing manager. LimeWire is an application commonly used for sharing and downloading music and videos over the Internet. It connects to the "Gnutella" network, which during the relevant period had two to five million people logged in at any given time. Those using LimeWire and connected to the Gnutella network can browse directories and download files that other users on the network designate for sharing. The billing manager designated the contents of the "My Documents" folder on her computer for sharing, exposing the contents to the other users. Between July 2007 and May 2008, this folder contained a 1,718-page file (the "1718 File") with the personal information of 9,300 consumers, including names, dates of birth, social security numbers, laboratory test codes, and, for some, health insurance company names, addresses, and policy numbers.

In February 2008, Tiversa Holding Corporation, an entity specializing in data security, used LimeWire to download the 1718 File. Tiversa began contacting LabMD months later, offering to sell its remediation services to LabMD. LabMD refused Tiversa's services and removed LimeWire from the billing manager's computer. Tiversa's solicitations stopped in July 2008, after LabMD instructed Tiversa to direct any further communications to LabMD's lawyer. In 2009, Tiversa arranged for the delivery of the 1718 File to the FTC.

B.

In August 2013, the Commission, following an extensive investigation, issued an administrative complaint against LabMD and assigned an ALJ to the case. The complaint alleged that LabMD had committed an "unfair act or practice" prohibited by Section 5(a) by "engag[ing] in a number of practices that, taken together, failed to provide reasonable and appropriate security for personal information on its computer networks." Rather than allege specific acts or practices that LabMD engaged in, however, the FTC's complaint set forth a number of data-security measures that LabMD failed to perform. LabMD answered the complaint, denying it had engaged in the conduct alleged and asserting several affirmative defenses, among them that the Commission lacked authority under Section 5 of the Act to regulate its handling of the personal information in its computer networks.

After answering the FTC's complaint, LabMD filed a motion to dismiss it for failure to state a case cognizable under Section 5. The motion essentially replicated the assertions in LabMD's answer. Under the FTC's Rules of Practice, the Commission, rather than the ALJ, ruled on the motion to dismiss. The Commission denied the motion, concluding that it had authority under Section 5(a) to prosecute the charge of unfairness asserted in its complaint.

Following discovery, LabMD filed a motion for summary judgment, presenting arguments similar to those made in support of its motion to dismiss. As before, the motion was submitted to the Commission to decide. It denied the motion on the ground that there were genuine factual disputes relating to LabMD's liability "for engaging in unfair acts or practices in violation of

Section 5(a)," necessitating an evidentiary hearing. An evidentiary hearing was held before the ALJ in July 2015.

After considering the parties' submissions, the ALJ dismissed the FTC's complaint, concluding that the FTC failed to prove that LabMD had committed unfair acts or practices in neglecting to provide adequate security for the personal information lodged in its computer networks. Namely, the FTC failed to prove that LabMD's "alleged failure to employ reasonable data security . . . caused or is likely to cause substantial injury to consumers," as required by Section 5(n) of the Act, 15 U.S.C. § 45(n). Because there was no substantial injury or likelihood thereof, there could be no unfair act or practice.

The FTC appealed the ALJ's decision, which under 16 C.F.R. § 3.52 brought the decision before the full Commission for review. In July 2016, reviewing the ALJ's findings of fact and conclusions of law de novo, the FTC reversed the ALJ's decision.

The FTC first found that LabMD "failed to implement reasonable security measures to protect the sensitive consumer information on its computer network." Therefore, LabMD's "data security practices were unfair under Section 5." In particular, LabMD failed to adequately secure its computer network, employ suitable risk-assessment tools, provide data-security training to its employees, and adequately restrict and monitor the computer practices of those using its network. Because of these deficiencies, the Commission continued, LimeWire was able to be installed on the LabMD billing manager's computer, and Tiversa was ultimately able to download the 1718 File. The Commission then held that, contrary to the ALJ's decision, the evidence showed that Section 5(n)'s "substantial injury" prong was met in two ways: the unauthorized disclosure of the 1718 File itself caused intangible privacy harm, and the mere exposure of the 1718 File on LimeWire was likely to cause substantial injury. The FTC went on to conclude that Section 5(n)'s other requirements were also met.

Next, the Commission addressed and rejected LabMD's arguments that Section 5(a)'s "unfairness" standard—which, according to the Commission, is a reasonableness standard—is void for vagueness and that the Commission failed to provide fair notice of what data-security practices were adequate under Section 5(a). The FTC then entered an order vacating the ALJ's decision and enjoining LabMD to install a data-security program that comported with the FTC's standard of reasonableness. See generally Appendix. The order is to terminate on either July 28, 2036, or twenty years "from the most recent date that the [FTC] files a complaint . . . in federal court alleging any violation of the order, whichever comes later."

C.

LabMD petitioned this Court to review the FTC's decision. LabMD then moved to stay enforcement of the FTC's cease and desist order pending review, arguing that compliance with the order was unfeasible given LabMD's defunct status and de minimis assets. After an FTC response urging against the stay, we granted LabMD's motion.

II.

Now, LabMD argues that the Commission's cease and desist order is unenforceable because the order does not direct it to cease committing an unfair "act or practice" within the meaning of Section 5(a). . . .

A.

[The Eleventh Circuit provided much of the same statutory history of Section 5 of the FTC Act as the Third Circuit did in the *Wyndham* case excerpted earlier in this appendix.]

B.

Here, the FTC's complaint alleges that LimeWire was installed on the computer used by LabMD's billing manager. This installation was contrary to company policy. The complaint then alleges that LimeWire's installation caused the 1718 File, which consisted of consumers' personal information, to be exposed. The 1718 File's exposure caused consumers injury by infringing upon their right of privacy. Thus, the complaint alleges that LimeWire was installed in defiance of LabMD policy and caused the alleged consumer injury. Had the complaint stopped there, a narrowly drawn and easily enforceable order might have followed, commanding LabMD to eliminate the possibility that employees could install unauthorized programs on their computers.

But the complaint continues past this single allegation of wrongdoing, adding that LimeWire's installation was not the only conduct that caused the 1718 File to be exposed. It also alleges broadly that LabMD "engaged in a number of practices that, taken together, failed to provide reasonable and appropriate security for personal information on its computer networks." The complaint then provides a litany of security measures that LabMD failed to employ, each setting out in general terms a deficiency in LabMD's data-security protocol. Because LabMD failed to employ these measures, the Commission's theory goes, LimeWire was able to be installed on the billing manager's computer. LabMD's policy forbidding employees from installing programs like LimeWire was insufficient.

The FTC's complaint, therefore, uses LimeWire's installation, and the 1718 File's exposure, as an entry point to broadly allege that LabMD's data-security operations are deficient as a whole. Aside from the installation of LimeWire on a company computer, the complaint alleges no specific unfair acts or practices engaged in by LabMD. Rather, it was LabMD's multiple, unspecified failures to act in creating and operating its data-security program that amounted to an unfair act or practice. Given the breadth of these failures, the Commission attached to its complaint a proposed order which would regulate all aspects of LabMD's data-security program—sweeping prophylactic measures to collectively reduce the possibility of employees installing unauthorized programs on their computers and thus exposing consumer information. The proposed cease and desist order, which is identical in all relevant respects to the order the FTC ultimately issued, identifies no specific unfair acts or practices from which LabMD must abstain and instead requires LabMD to implement and maintain a data-security program "reasonably designed" to the Commission's satisfaction. . . .

The decision on which the FTC based its final cease and desist order exhibits more of the same. The FTC found that LabMD "failed to implement reasonable security measures to protect the sensitive consumer information on its computer network" and that the failure caused substantial consumer injury. In effect, the decision held that LabMD's failure to act in various ways to protect consumer data rendered its entire data-security operation an unfair act or practice. The broad cease and desist order now at issue, according to the Commission, was therefore justified.

* * *

The first question LabMD's petition for review presents is whether LabMD's failure to implement and maintain a reasonably designed data-security program constituted an unfair act or practice within the ambit of Section 5(a). The FTC declared that it did because such failure caused substantial injury to consumers' right of privacy, and it issued a cease and desist order to avoid further injury.

The Commission must find the standards of unfairness it enforces in "clear and well-established" policies that are expressed in the Constitution, statutes, or the common law. The Commission's decision in this case does not explicitly cite the source of the standard of unfairness it used in holding that LabMD's failure to implement and maintain a reasonably designed data-security program constituted an unfair act or practice. It is apparent to us, though, that the source is the common law of negligence. According to the Restatement (Second) of Torts § 281 (Am. Law Inst. 1965), Statement of the Elements of a Cause of Action for Negligence,

> [an] actor is liable for an invasion of an interest of another, if:
> a) the interest invaded is protected against unintentional invasion, and
> b) the conduct of the actor is negligent with respect to the other, or a class of persons within which [the other] is included, and
> c) the actor's conduct is a legal cause of the invasion, and
> d) the other has not so conducted himself as to disable himself from bringing an action for such invasion.

The gist of the Commission's complaint and its decision is this: The consumers' right of privacy is protected against unintentional invasion. LabMD unintentionally invaded their right, and its deficient data-security program was a legal cause. Section 5(a) empowers the Commission to "prevent persons, partnerships, or corporations . . . . from using unfair . . . acts or practices." The law of negligence, the Commission's action implies, is a source that provides standards for determining whether an act or practice is unfair, so a person, partnership, or corporation that negligently infringes a consumer interest protected against unintentional invasion may be held accountable under Section 5(a). We will assume arguendo that the Commission is correct and that LabMD's negligent failure to design and maintain a reasonable data-security program invaded consumers' right of privacy and thus constituted an unfair act or practice.

The second question LabMD's petition for review presents is whether the Commission's cease and desist order, founded upon LabMD's general negligent failure to act, is enforceable. We answer this question in the negative. We illustrate why by first laying out the FTC Act's enforcement and remedial schemes and then by demonstrating the problems that enforcing the order would pose.

III.

The FTC carries out its Section 5(a) mission to prevent unfair acts or practices in two ways: formal rulemaking and case-by-case litigation.

The Commission is authorized under 15 U.S.C. § 57a to prescribe rules "which define with specificity" unfair acts or practices within the meaning of Section 5(a). Once a rule takes effect, it becomes in essence an addendum to Section 5(a)'s phrase "unfair . . . acts or practices"; the rule puts the public on notice that a particular act or practice is unfair. The FTC enforces its rules in the federal district courts. Under 15 U.S.C. § 45(m)(1)(A), the Commission may bring an action to recover a civil penalty against any person, partnership or corporation that knowingly violates a rule. This case does not involve the enforcement of an FTC-promulgated rule.

What is involved here is the FTC's establishment of an unfair act or practice through litigation. Because Congress thought impossible the task of legislating a comprehensive list of unfair acts or practices, it authorized the Commission to establish unfair acts or practices through case-by-case litigation. In the litigation context, once an act or practice is adjudged to be unfair, the act or practice becomes in effect—like an FTC-promulgated rule—an addendum to Section 5(a).

The FTC Act provides two forums for such litigation. The Commission may choose to prosecute its claim that an act or practice is unfair before an ALJ, with appellate review before the full Commission and then in a federal court of appeals. . . . Or, under Section 13(b) of the Act, it may prosecute its claim before a federal district judge, with appellate review also in a federal court of appeals.

Assume a factual scenario in which the Commission believes a certain act or practice is unfair. It should not matter which of the two forums the Commission chooses to prosecute its claim. The result should be the same. As we explain below, the ALJ and the district judge use materially identical procedural rules in processing the case to judgment and both apply the same substantive law to the facts. Further, putting any venue differences aside, the same court of appeals reviews their decisions.

A.

We consider the Commission's first option, litigation before an ALJ. The Commission issues an administrative complaint against a party it has reason to believe is engaging in an unfair act or practice and seeks a cease and desist order. The Commission prosecutes the complaint before an ALJ whom it designates, in accordance with its Rules of Practice. Under these Rules, the complaint must provide, among other things, "[a] clear and concise factual statement sufficient to inform each respondent with reasonable definiteness of the type of acts or practices alleged to be in violation of the law." If the respondent files a motion to dismiss the complaint, the motion is referred to the Commission for a ruling. If the motion is denied, the respondent files an answer. From that point on, the proceedings before the ALJ resemble the proceedings in an action for injunctive relief in federal district court. If the ALJ finds that the respondent has been engaging in the unfair act or practice alleged and will likely continue doing so, the ALJ enters a cease and desist order enjoining the respondent from engaging in the unfair conduct. If not, the ALJ dismisses the Commission's complaint. Either way, the ALJ's decision is appealable to the FTC, and the FTC's decision is in turn reviewable in a federal court of appeals.

Suppose the Commission chooses the second option, litigation before a federal district judge under Section 13(b). If the Commission has reason to believe a party is engaging in an unfair act or practice, it seeks an injunction by filing in district court a complaint that sets forth "well-pleaded facts . . . permit[ting] the court to infer more than the mere possibility of misconduct." Although the case is tried pursuant to the Federal Rules of Civil Procedure, not the FTC Rules of Practice, it is handled essentially as it would be before the ALJ. If the district judge finds that the defendant has been engaging in the unfair act or practice alleged and will likely continue doing so, the judge enjoins the defendant from engaging in such conduct. Whatever the court's decision, it is reviewable in the court of appeals.

Assume the result is the same in both litigation forums. The ALJ enters a cease and desist order; the district court issues an injunction. Appellate review would reach the same result regardless of the trial forum (assuming that venue is laid in the same court of appeals). Assume further that both coercive orders are affirmed by the court of appeals. The cease and desist order and the injunction address the same behavior and contain the same command: discontinue engaging in a specific unfair act or practice.

With the cease and desist order or the injunction in hand, the Commission may proceed in two ways against a party who violates its terms. The Commission may seek the imposition of either a civil penalty or civil-contempt sanction. We explain below the procedures the Commission invokes in pursuing these respective remedies.

B.

1.

Under Section 5(l), the Commission may bring a civil-penalty action in district court should the respondent violate a final cease and desist order. The Commission's complaint would allege that the defendant is subject to an existing cease and desist order and has violated its terms. For each separate violation of the order—or, in the case of a continuing violation, for each day in violation—the district court may impose a penalty of up to $41,484. Section 5(l) also empowers the district court to grant an injunction if the Commission proves that the violation is likely to continue and an injunction is necessary to enforce the order.

If the Commission has obtained an injunction in district court requiring the defendant to discontinue an unfair act or practice, it may invoke the district court's civil-contempt power should the defendant disobey. Rather than filing a complaint, as in a Section 5(l) action, the Commission simply moves the district court for an order requiring the defendant to show cause why it should not be held in contempt for engaging in conduct the injunction specifically enjoined. If the court is satisfied that the conduct is forbidden, it issues a show cause order. Then, if at the show cause hearing the Commission establishes by clear and convincing proof that the defendant engaged in the forbidden conduct and that the defendant "had the ability to comply" with the injunctive provision at issue, the court may adjudicate the defendant in civil contempt and impose appropriate sanctions.

2.

The concept of specificity is crucial to both modes of enforcement. We start with civil penalties for violations of cease and desist orders. Nothing in the FTC Act addresses what content must go into a cease and desist order. The FTC Rule of Practice governing Commission complaints, however, states that a complaint must contain "[a] clear and concise factual statement sufficient to inform each respondent with reasonable definiteness of the type of acts or practices alleged to be in violation of the law." It follows that the remedy the complaint seeks must comport with this requirement of reasonable definiteness. Moreover, given the severity of the civil penalties a district court may impose for the violation of a cease and desist order, the order's prohibitions must be stated with clarity and precision. The United States Supreme Court emphasized this point in *FTC v. Colgate-Palmolive Co.*, stating,

> [T]his Court has . . . warned that an order's prohibitions should be clear and precise in order that they may be understood by those against whom they are directed, and that [t]he severity of possible penalties prescribed . . . for violations of orders which have become final underlines the necessity for fashioning orders which are, at the outset, sufficiently clear and precise to avoid raising serious questions as to their meaning and application.

The imposition of penalties upon a party for violating an imprecise cease and desist order—up to $41,484 per violation or day in violation—may constitute a denial of due process.

Specificity is equally important in the fashioning and enforcement of an injunction consequent to an action brought in district court under Section 13(b). Federal Rule of Civil Procedure 65(d)(1) requires that an injunctive order state the reasons for its coercive provisions, state the provisions "specifically," and describe the acts restrained or required "in reasonable detail." The Supreme Court has stated that Rule 65(d)(1)'s "specificity provisions . . . are no mere technical requirements. The Rule was designed to prevent uncertainty and confusion on the part of those faced with injunctive orders, and to avoid the possible founding of a contempt citation on a decree too vague to be understood." *Schmidt v. Lessard*, 414 U.S. 473, 476 (1974). Indeed, "[t]he most fundamental postulates of our legal order forbid the imposition of a penalty for disobeying a command that defies comprehension." *Int'l Longshoremen's Ass'n, Local 1291 v. Phila. Marine Trade Ass'n*, 389 U.S. 64, 76 (1967). Being held in contempt and sanctioned pursuant to an insufficiently specific injunction is therefore a denial of due process.

In sum, the prohibitions contained in cease and desist orders and injunctions must be specific. Otherwise, they may be unenforceable. Both coercive orders are also governed by the same standard of specificity, as the stakes involved for a violation are the same—severe penalties or sanctions.

C.

In the case at hand, the cease and desist order contains no prohibitions. It does not instruct LabMD to stop committing a specific act or practice. Rather, it commands LabMD to overhaul and replace its data-security program to meet an indeterminable standard of reasonableness. This command is unenforceable. Its unenforceability is made clear if we imagine what would take place if the

Commission sought the order's enforcement. As we have explained, the standards a district court would apply are essentially the same whether it is entertaining the Commission's action for the imposition of a penalty or the Commission's motion for an order requiring the enjoined defendant to show cause why it should not be adjudicated in contempt. For ease of discussion, we posit a scenario in which the Commission obtained the coercive order it entered in this case from a district court, and now seeks to enforce the order. The Commission moves the district court for an order requiring LabMD to show cause why it should not be held in contempt for violating the following injunctive provision:

> [T]he respondent shall . . . establish and implement, and thereafter maintain, a comprehensive information security program that is reasonably designed to protect the security, confidentiality, and integrity of personal information collected from or about consumers. . . .. Such program. . . shall contain administrative, technical, and physical safeguards appropriate to respondent's size and complexity, the nature and scope of respondent's activities, and the sensitivity of the personal information collected from or about consumers . . . .

The Commission's motion alleges that LabMD's program failed to implement "x" and is therefore not "reasonably designed." The court concludes that the Commission's alleged failure is within the provision's language and orders LabMD to show cause why it should not be held in contempt.

At the show cause hearing, LabMD calls an expert who testifies that the data-security program LabMD implemented complies with the injunctive provision at issue. The expert testifies that "x" is not a necessary component of a reasonably designed data-security program. The Commission, in response, calls an expert who disagrees. At this point, the district court undertakes to determine which of the two equally qualified experts correctly read the injunctive provision. Nothing in the provision, however, indicates which expert is correct. The provision contains no mention of "x" and is devoid of any meaningful standard informing the court of what constitutes a "reasonably designed" data-security program. The court therefore has no choice but to conclude that the Commission has not proven—and indeed cannot prove—LabMD's alleged violation by clear and convincing evidence.

If the court held otherwise and ordered LabMD to implement "x," the court would have effectively modified the injunction at a show cause hearing. This would open the door to future modifications, all improperly made at show cause hearings. Pretend that LabMD implemented "x" pursuant to the court's order, but the FTC, which is continually monitoring LabMD's compliance with the court's injunction, finds that "x" failed to bring the system up to the FTC's conception of reasonableness. So, the FTC again moves the district court for an order to show cause. This time, its motion alleges that LabMD failed to implement "y," another item the Commission thinks necessary to any reasonable data-security program. Does the court side with the Commission, modify the injunction, and order the implementation of "y"? Suppose "y" fails. Does another show cause hearing result in a third modification requiring the implementation of "z"?

The practical effect of repeatedly modifying the injunction at show cause hearings is that the district court is put in the position of managing LabMD's business in accordance with the Commission's wishes. It would be as if the Commission was LabMD's chief executive officer and the court was its operating officer. It is self-evident that this micromanaging is beyond the scope of court oversight contemplated by injunction law.

This all serves to show that an injunction identical to the FTC cease and desist order at issue would be unenforceable under a district court's contempt power. Because the standards governing the coercive enforcement of injunctions and cease and desist orders are the same, it follows that the Commission's cease and desist order is itself unenforceable.

IV.

In sum, assuming arguendo that LabMD's negligent failure to implement and maintain a reasonable data-security program constituted an unfair act or practice under Section 5(a), the Commission's cease and desist order is nonetheless unenforceable. It does not enjoin a specific act or practice. Instead, it mandates a complete overhaul of LabMD's data-security program and says precious little about how this is to be accomplished. Moreover, it effectually charges the district court with managing the overhaul. This is a scheme Congress could not have envisioned. We therefore grant LabMD's petition for review and vacate the Commission's order.

Krottner v. Starbucks Corp., 628 F.3d 1139 (9th Cir. 2010)

For a private party to bring a lawsuit in federal court arising from a data breach, that plaintiff must demonstrate that he or she has "standing" to sue under Article III of the U.S. Constitution. As discussed in Chapter 2, courts are split as to what level of injury a plaintiff must have to sue a company over a breach of the plaintiff's personal information. The Krottner *opinion represents the Ninth Circuit's relatively broad approach to standing in data breach cases.*

December 14, 2010

Opinion by Milan D. Smith, Circuit Judge:

Plaintiffs-Appellants Laura Krottner, Ishaya Shamasa, and Joseph Lalli appeal the district court's dismissal of their negligence and breach of contract claims against Starbucks Corporation. Plaintiffs-Appellants are current or former Starbucks employees whose names, addresses, and social security numbers were stored on a laptop that was stolen from Starbucks. Their complaints allege that, in failing to protect Plaintiffs-Appellants' personal data, Starbucks acted negligently and breached an implied contract under Washington law.

Affirming the district court, we hold that Plaintiffs-Appellants, whose personal information has been stolen but not misused, have suffered an injury sufficient to confer standing under Article III, Section 2 of the U.S. Constitution. We affirm the dismissal of their state-law claims in a memorandum disposition filed contemporaneously with this opinion.

FACTUAL AND PROCEDURAL BACKGROUND

On October 29, 2008, someone stole a laptop from Starbucks. The laptop contained the unencrypted names, addresses, and social security numbers of approximately 97,000 Starbucks employees.

On November 19, 2008, Starbucks sent a letter to Plaintiffs-Appellants and other affected employees alerting them to the theft and stating that Starbucks had "no indication that the private information has been misused." Nonetheless, the letter continued,

> As a precaution, we ask that you monitor your financial accounts carefully for suspicious activity and take appropriate steps to protect yourself against potential identity theft. To assist you in protecting this effort [sic], Starbucks has partnered with Equifax to offer, at no cost to you, credit watch services for the next year.

Krottner and Shamasa allege that after receiving the letter, they enrolled in the free credit watch services that Starbucks offered. Krottner alleges that she "has been extra vigilant about watching her banking and 401(k) accounts," spending a "substantial amount of time doing so," and will pay out-of-pocket for credit monitoring services once the free service expires. Lalli alleges that he "has spent and continues to spend substantial amounts of time checking his 401(k) and bank accounts," has placed fraud alerts on his credit cards, and "has generalized anxiety and stress regarding the situation." Shamasa alleges that his bank notified him in December 2008 that someone had attempted to open a new account using his social security number. The bank closed the account, and Shamasa does not allege that he suffered any financial loss.

Plaintiffs-Appellants filed two nearly identical putative class action complaints against Starbucks, alleging negligence and breach of implied contract. On August 14, 2009, the district court granted Starbucks's motion to dismiss, holding that Plaintiffs-Appellants have standing under Article III but had failed to allege a cognizable injury under Washington law.

DISCUSSION

We have an independent obligation to examine standing to determine whether it comports with the case or controversy requirement of Article III, Section 2 of the Constitution. . . . The case or controversy requirement, which constitutes "the irreducible constitutional minimum of standing," *Lujan v. Defenders of Wildlife*, 504 U.S. 555, 560 (1992), requires that a plaintiff show

> (1) it has suffered an 'injury in fact' that is (a) concrete and particularized and (b) actual or imminent, not conjectural or hypothetical; (2) the injury is fairly traceable to the challenged action of the defendant; and (3) it is likely, as opposed to merely speculative, that the injury will be redressed by a favorable decision.

Friends of the Earth, Inc. v. Laidlaw Envtl. Servs. (TOC), Inc., 528 U.S. 167, 180-81 (2000). The party asserting federal jurisdiction bears the burden of establishing these requirements at every stage of the litigation, as it does for "any other essential element of the case." *Cent. Delta Water Agency v. United States*, 306 F.3d 938, 947 (9th Cir. 2002). On appeal from a motion to dismiss, a plaintiff need only show that the facts alleged, if proven, would confer standing.

It was undisputed before the district court that Plaintiffs-Appellants had sufficiently alleged causation and redressability, the second and third standing requirements. We thus turn to the first standing requirement: whether Plaintiffs-Appellants adequately alleged an injury-in-fact. Lalli's allegation that he "has generalized anxiety and stress" as a result of the laptop theft is the only present injury that Plaintiffs-Appellants allege. This is sufficient to confer standing, but only as to Lalli. . . .

Plaintiffs-Appellants' remaining allegations concern their increased risk of future identity theft. Krottner and Shamasa enrolled in credit watch services, but Starbucks provided those services at no cost to affected employees. Krottner and Lalli allege that they have been vigilant in monitoring their accounts—that is, in guarding against future identity theft—but they do not allege that any theft has actually occurred. Shamasa alleges that someone attempted to open a bank account in his name, but that the bank closed the account before he suffered any loss.

Although we have not previously determined whether an increased risk of identity theft constitutes an injury-in-fact, we have addressed future harm in other contexts, holding that "the possibility of future injury may be sufficient to confer standing on plaintiffs; threatened injury constitutes 'injury in fact.'" *Cent. Delta Water Agency*, 306 F.3d at 947. More specifically,

> [a] plaintiff may allege a future injury in order to comply with [the injury-in-fact] requirement, but only if he or she "is immediately

in danger of sustaining some direct injury as the result of the challenged . . . conduct and the injury or threat of injury is both real
and immediate, not conjectural or hypothetical."

Scott v. Pasadena Unified Sch. Dist., 306 F.3d 646, 656 (9th Cir. 2002). Thus,
in the context of environmental claims, a plaintiff may challenge governmental
action that creates "a credible threat of harm" before the potential harm, or
even a statutory violation, has occurred. Similarly, a plaintiff seeking to compel
funding of a medical monitoring program after exposure to toxic substances
satisfies the injury-in-fact requirement if he is unable to receive medical
screening . . . .

In *Pisciotta v. Old National Bancorp*, the Seventh Circuit extended that
reasoning to the identity-theft context, holding that plaintiffs whose data
had been stolen but not yet misused had suffered an injury-in-fact sufficient to confer Article III standing. In *Pisciotta*, the plaintiffs' only alleged
injury was the increased risk that their personal data would be misused in
the future; none alleged any completed financial or other loss. The court
surveyed case law addressing toxic substance, medical monitoring, and
environmental claims in the Second, Fourth, Sixth, and Ninth Circuits. It
concluded:

> As many of our sister circuits have noted, the injury-in-fact
> requirement can be satisfied by a threat of future harm or by an
> act which harms the plaintiff only by increasing the risk of future
> harm that the plaintiff would have otherwise faced, absent the
> defendant's actions. We concur in this view. Once the plaintiffs'
> allegations establish at least this level of injury, the fact that the
> plaintiffs anticipate that some greater potential harm might fol-
> low the defendant's act does not affect the standing inquiry.

Because the plaintiffs had alleged an act that increased their risk of future
harm, they had alleged an injury-in-fact sufficient to confer standing.

The Sixth Circuit, while not explicitly analyzing the issue, appears to disagree. In *Lambert v. Hartman*, the plaintiff alleged both that she had suffered
financial loss as a result of identity theft and that the theft had exposed her
to the risk of additional, future identity theft. The *Lambert* court held that
the plaintiff's actual financial injuries resulting from the theft of her personal data were sufficient to confer standing. It also noted, without analysis,
that the risk of future identity theft was "somewhat 'hypothetical' and
'conjectural.'"

On these facts, we reach a different conclusion. If a plaintiff faces "a credible
threat of harm," and that harm is "both real and immediate, not conjectural or
hypothetical," the plaintiff has met the injury-in-fact requirement for standing

under Article III. Here, Plaintiffs-Appellants have alleged a credible threat of real and immediate harm stemming from the theft of a laptop containing their unencrypted personal data. Were Plaintiffs-Appellants' allegations more conjectural or hypothetical—for example, if no laptop had been stolen, and Plaintiffs had sued based on the risk that it would be stolen at some point in the future—we would find the threat far less credible. On these facts, however, Plaintiffs-Appellants have sufficiently alleged an injury-in-fact for purposes of Article III standing.

Reilly v. Ceridian, 664 F.3d 38 (3d Cir. 2011)

The Ninth Circuit's opinion in Krottner *represents a relatively expansive view of Article III standing in data breach cases. This opinion, also discussed in Chapter 2, represents the narrower approach that many courts have taken, requiring a stronger showing of injury before allowing a data breach lawsuit to proceed.*

December 12, 2011

Opinion by Rugerro J. Aldisert, Senior Circuit Judge:

Kathy Reilly and Patricia Pluemacher, individually and on behalf of all others similarly situated, appeal from an order of the United States District Court for the District of New Jersey, which granted Ceridian Corporation's motion to dismiss for lack of standing, and alternatively, failure to state a claim. Appellants contend that (1) they have standing to bring their claims in federal court, and (2) they stated a claim that adequately alleged cognizable damage, injury, and ascertainable loss. We hold that Appellants lack standing and do not reach the merits of the substantive issue. We will therefore affirm.

I.

A.

Ceridian is a payroll processing firm with its principal place of business in Bloomington, Minnesota. To process its commercial business customers' payrolls, Ceridian collects information about its customers' employees. This information may include employees' names, addresses, social security numbers, dates of birth, and bank account information.

Reilly and Pluemacher were employees of the Brach Eichler law firm, a Ceridian customer, until September 2003. Ceridian entered into contracts with Appellants' employer and the employers of the proposed class members to provide payroll processing services.

On or about December 22, 2009, Ceridian suffered a security breach. An unknown hacker infiltrated Ceridian's Powerpay system and potentially gained access to personal and financial information belonging to Appellants and approximately 27,000 employees at 1,900 companies. It is not known whether the hacker read, copied, or understood the data.

Working with law enforcement and professional investigators, Ceridian determined what information the hacker may have accessed. On about January 29, 2010, Ceridian sent letters to the potential identity theft victims, informing them of the breach: "[S]ome of your personal information . . . may have been illegally accessed by an unauthorized hacker. . . . [T]he information accessed included your first name, last name, social security number and, in several cases, birth date and/or the bank account that is used for direct deposit." Ceridian arranged to provide the potentially affected individuals with one year of free credit monitoring and identity theft protection. Individuals had until April 30, 2010, to enroll in the free program, and Ceridian included instructions on how to do so within its letter.

B.

On October 7, 2010, Appellants filed a complaint against Ceridian, on behalf of themselves and all others similarly situated, in the United States District Court for the District of New Jersey. Appellants alleged that they: (1) have an increased risk of identity theft, (2) incurred costs to monitor their credit activity, and (3) suffered from emotional distress.

On December 15, 2010, Ceridian filed a motion to dismiss pursuant to Rules 12(b)(1) and 12(b)(6), Federal Rules of Civil Procedure, for lack of standing and failure to state a claim. On February 22, 2011, the District Court granted Ceridian's motion, holding that Appellants lacked Article III standing. The Court further held that, assuming Appellants had standing, they nonetheless failed to adequately allege the damage, injury, and ascertainable loss elements of their claims. Appellants timely filed their Notice of Appeal on March 18, 2011. . . .

III.

Appellants' allegations of hypothetical, future injury do not establish standing under Article III. For the following reasons we will therefore affirm the District Court's dismissal.

A.

[Similar summary of general Article III standing doctrine as provided in *Krottner*]

B.

We conclude that Appellants' allegations of hypothetical, future injury are insufficient to establish standing. Appellants' contentions rely on speculation that the hacker: (1) read, copied, and understood their personal information;

(2) intends to commit future criminal acts by misusing the information; and (3) is able to use such information to the detriment of Appellants by making unauthorized transactions in Appellants' names. Unless and until these conjectures come true, Appellants have not suffered any injury; there has been no misuse of the information, and thus, no harm.

The Supreme Court has consistently dismissed cases for lack of standing when the alleged future harm is neither imminent nor certainly impending. For example, the *Lujan* Court addressed whether plaintiffs had standing when seeking to enjoin the funding of activities that threatened certain species' habitats. The Court held that plaintiffs' claim that they would visit the project sites "some day" did not meet the requirement that their injury be "imminent." Appellants' allegations here are even more speculative than those at issue in *Lujan*. There, the acts necessary to make the injury "imminent" were within plaintiffs' own control, because all plaintiffs needed to do was travel to the site to see the alleged destruction of wildlife take place. Yet, notwithstanding their stated intent to travel to the site at some point in the future—which the Court had no reason to doubt—their harm was not imminent enough to confer standing. Here, Appellants' alleged increased risk of future injury is even more attenuated, because it is dependent on entirely speculative, future actions of an unknown third-party.

The requirement that an injury be "certainly impending" is best illustrated by *City of Los Angeles v. Lyons*, 461 U.S. 95, 103 (1983). There, the Court held that a plaintiff lacked standing to enjoin the Los Angeles Police Department from using a controversial chokehold technique on arrestees. Although the plaintiff had already once been subjected to this maneuver, the future harm he sought to enjoin depended on the police again arresting and choking him. Unlike the plaintiff in *Lyons*, Appellants in this case have yet to suffer any harm, and their alleged increased risk of future injury is nothing more than speculation. As such, the alleged injury is not "certainly impending."

Our Court, too, has refused to confer standing when plaintiffs fail to allege an imminent injury-in-fact. For example, although the plaintiffs in [*Storino v. Borough of Point Pleasant Beach*, 322 F. 3d 293 (3d Cir. 2003)] contended that a municipal ordinance would eventually result in a commercially undesirable zoning change, we held that the allegation of future economic damage was too conjectural and insufficient to meet the "injury in fact" requirement. As we stated in that case, "one cannot describe how the [plaintiffs] will be injured without beginning the explanation with the word 'if.' The prospective damages, described by the [plaintiffs] as certain, are, in reality, conjectural." Similarly, we cannot now describe how Appellants will be injured in this case without beginning our explanation with the word "if": if the hacker read, copied, and understood the hacked information, and if the hacker attempts to use the information, and if he does so successfully, only then will Appellants have suffered an injury.

C.

In this increasingly digitized world, a number of courts have had occasion to decide whether the "risk of future harm" posed by data security breaches confers standing on persons whose information may have been accessed. Most courts have held that such plaintiffs lack standing because the harm is too speculative. . . . We agree with the holdings in those cases. Here, no evidence suggests that the data has been—or will ever be—misused. The present test is actuality, not hypothetical speculations concerning the possibility of future injury. Appellants' allegations of an increased risk of identity theft resulting from a security breach are therefore insufficient to secure standing. . . .

Principally relying on *Pisciotta v. Old National Bancorp*, 499 F.3d 629 (7th Cir. 2007), Appellants contend that an increased risk of identity theft is itself a harm sufficient to confer standing. In *Pisciotta*, plaintiffs brought a class action against a bank after its website had been hacked, alleging that the bank failed to adequately secure the personal information it solicited (such as names, addresses, birthdates, and social security numbers) when consumers applied for banking services on its website. The named plaintiffs did not allege "any completed direct financial loss to their accounts" nor that they "already had been the victim of identity theft as a result of the breach." The court, nonetheless, held that plaintiffs had standing, concluding, without explanation, that the "injury-in-fact requirement can be satisfied by a threat of future harm or by an act which harms the plaintiff only by increasing the risk of future harm that the plaintiff would have otherwise faced, absent the defendant's actions."

Appellants rely as well on *Krottner v. Starbucks Corp.*, 628 F.3d 1139 (9th Cir. 2010), in which the Court of Appeals for the Ninth Circuit conferred standing under circumstances much different from those present here. There, plaintiffs' "names, addresses, and social security numbers were stored on a laptop that was stolen from Starbucks." The court concluded that plaintiffs met the standing requirement through their allegations of "a credible threat of real and immediate harm stemming from the theft of a laptop containing their unencrypted personal data." Appellants here contend that we should follow *Pisciotta* and *Krottner* and hold that the "credible threat of real and immediate harm" stemming from the security breach of Ceridian's Powerpay system satisfies the standing requirement.

But these cases have little persuasive value here; in *Pisciotta* and *Krottner*, the threatened harms were significantly more "imminent" and "certainly impending" than the alleged harm here. In *Pisciotta*, there was evidence that "the [hacker's] intrusion was sophisticated, intentional and malicious." In *Krottner*, someone attempted to open a bank account with a plaintiff's information following the physical theft of the laptop.[2] Here, there is no evidence that the

---

2 The bank closed the account before any financial loss occurred.

intrusion was intentional or malicious. Appellants have alleged no misuse, and therefore, no injury. Indeed, no identifiable taking occurred; all that is known is that a firewall was penetrated. Appellants' string of hypothetical injuries do not meet the requirement of an "actual or imminent" injury.

D.

Neither *Pisciotta* nor *Krottner*, moreover, discussed the constitutional standing requirements and how they apply to generalized data theft situations. Indeed, the *Pisciotta* court did not mention—let alone discuss—the requirement that a threatened injury must be "imminent" and "certainly impending" to confer standing. Instead of making a determination as to whether the alleged injury was "certainly impending," both courts simply analogized data-security-breach situations to defective-medical-device, toxic-substance-exposure, or environmental-injury cases.

Still, Appellants urge us to adopt those courts' skimpy rationale for three reasons. First, Appellants here expended monies on credit monitoring and insurance to protect their safety, just as plaintiffs in defective-medical-device and toxic-substance-exposure cases expend monies on medical monitoring. Second, members of this putative class may very well have suffered emotional distress from the incident, which also represents a bodily injury, just as plaintiffs in the medical-device and toxic-tort cases have suffered physical injuries. . . . Third, injury to one's identity is extraordinarily unique and money may not even compensate one for the injuries sustained, just as environmental injury is unique and monetary compensation may not adequately return plaintiffs to their original position. . . . Based on these analogies, Appellants contend they have established standing here. These analogies do not persuade us, because defective-medical-device and toxic-substance-exposure cases confer standing based on two important factors not present in data breach cases.

First, in those cases, an injury has undoubtedly occurred. In medical-device cases, a defective device has been implanted into the human body with a quantifiable risk of failure. Similarly, exposure to a toxic substance causes injury; cells are damaged and a disease mechanism has been introduced. . . . Hence, the damage has been done; we just cannot yet quantify how it will manifest itself.

In data breach cases where no misuse is alleged, however, there has been no injury—indeed, no change in the status quo. Here, Appellants' credit card statements are exactly the same today as they would have been had Ceridian's database never been hacked. Moreover, there is no quantifiable risk of damage in the future. Any damages that may occur here are entirely speculative and dependent on the skill and intent of the hacker.

Second, standing in medical-device and toxic-tort cases hinges on human health concerns. Courts resist strictly applying the "actual injury" test when the future harm involves human suffering or premature death. . . . The deceased, after all, have little use for compensation. This case implicates none of these concerns. The hacker did not change or injure Appellants' bodies; any harm that may occur—if all of Appellants' stated fears are actually realized—may be redressed in due time through money damages after the harm occurs with no fear that litigants will be dead or disabled from the onset of the injury.

An analogy to environmental injury cases fails as well. As the Court of Appeals for the Ninth Circuit explained in *Central Delta Water Agency*, standing is unique in the environmental context because monetary compensation may not adequately return plaintiffs to their original position. In a data breach case, however, there is no reason to believe that monetary compensation will not return plaintiffs to their original position completely—if the hacked information is actually read, copied, understood, and misused to a plaintiff's detriment. To the contrary, unlike priceless "mountains majesty," the thing feared lost here is simple cash, which is easily and precisely compensable with a monetary award. We therefore decline to analogize this case to those cases in the medical device, toxic tort or environmental injury contexts.

E.

Finally, we conclude that Appellants' alleged time and money expenditures to monitor their financial information do not establish standing, because costs incurred to watch for a speculative chain of future events based on hypothetical future criminal acts are no more "actual" injuries than the alleged "increased risk of injury" which forms the basis for Appellants' claims. . . . That a plaintiff has willingly incurred costs to protect against an alleged increased risk of identity theft is not enough to demonstrate a "concrete and particularized" or "actual or imminent" injury. . . .

Although Appellants have incurred expenses to monitor their accounts and "to protect their personal and financial information from imminent misuse and/or identity theft," they have not done so as a result of any actual injury (e.g. because their private information was misused or their identities stolen). Rather, they prophylactically spent money to ease fears of future third-party criminality. Such misuse is only speculative—not imminent. The claim that they incurred expenses in anticipation of future harm, therefore, is not sufficient to confer standing.

IV.

The District Court correctly held that Appellants failed to plead specific facts demonstrating they have standing to bring this suit under Article III, because Appellants' allegations of an increased risk of identity theft as a result of the security breach are hypothetical, future injuries, and are therefore insufficient to establish standing. For the reasons set forth, we will AFFIRM the District Court's order granting Ceridian's motion to dismiss.

In re **Target Corporation Customer Data Security Breach Litigation**, 66 F. Supp. 3d 1154 (D. Minn. 2014)

Chapter 2 discusses how judges have ruled on the merits of claims in class-action lawsuits filed against companies that have experienced data breaches of personal information. Among the most comprehensive of those opinions was Minnesota Federal Judge Paul A. Magnuson's split ruling in the lawsuit filed against Target on behalf of a class of customers. The ruling systematically walked through the laundry list of claims, and determined whether the complaint sufficiently stated a claim or should be dismissed. The opinion was more than 11,000 words, and covered standing, state consumer protection laws, state data breach notice laws, negligence, breach of implied contract, breach of contract, bailment, and unjust enrichment. To illustrate Magnuson's approach, this excerpt contains his analysis of the data breach notification and negligence claims.

December 18, 2014

Opinion by Paul A. Magnuson, District Judge

BACKGROUND

This case arises out of one of the largest breaches of payment-card security in United States retail history: over a period of more than three weeks during the 2013 holiday shopping season, computer hackers stole credit- and debit-card information and other personal information for approximately 110 million customers of Target's retail stores. Plaintiffs are a putative class of consumers who used their credit or debit cards at Target stores during the period of the security breach, and whose personal financial information was compromised as a result of the breach. Indeed, many of the 114 named Plaintiffs allege that they actually incurred unauthorized charges; lost access to their accounts; and/or were forced to pay sums such as late fees, card-replacement fees, and credit monitoring costs because the hackers misused their personal financial information.

The Judicial Panel on Multidistrict Litigation consolidated all federal litigation into this case, which is divided into two tracks: one for cases brought by financial institutions and one for cases brought by consumers. In this Motion, Target asks the Court to dismiss the First Amended Consolidated Class Action Complaint filed in the consumer cases.

Plaintiffs' Complaint raises seven claims. Count One contends that Target violated the consumer protection laws of 49 states (all states save Alaska) and the District of Columbia. Count Two alleges a similar violation with respect to the data breach statutes of 38 states. Count III asserts that Target was negligent in failing to safeguard its customers' data. Count IV raises a claim for breach of an implied contract as to Plaintiffs who were not Target REDcard cardholders, and Count V claims a breach of contract as to Plaintiffs who were Target REDcard cardholders. Count VI claims a bailment, and Count VII claims unjust enrichment. Target seeks dismissal of all claims, contending that the 121-page, 356-paragraph Complaint lacks sufficient detail to support Plaintiffs' allegations. . . .

Data Breach Notice Statutes

In Count II, Plaintiffs contend that Target violated the data-breach notice statutes of 38 jurisdictions.

1. *Damages*

Plaintiffs allege that Target violated the data-breach notice statutes of these jurisdictions by failing "to provide timely and accurate notice of the Target data breach." Target contends that all of Plaintiffs' data-breach-statute claims fail because Plaintiffs cannot show any damages flowing from the alleged violation of the statutes. In the main, Plaintiffs' delayed-notice damages are "would not have shopped at Target" damages. Target maintains that because Plaintiffs have not alleged when they shopped at Target, they cannot establish any damages from allegedly delayed notice. In other words, because no Plaintiff alleges that he or she shopped at Target on a specific date after Target knew or should have known about the breach but before Target notified consumers about the breach, no Plaintiff can establish "would not have shopped" damages.

This argument is premature. Plaintiffs have pled a "short and plain statement" of their claims, Fed.R.Civ.P. 8(a)(2); discovery will be required to flesh out which Plaintiffs are entitled to claim "would not have shopped" damages. In addition, Plaintiffs allege that Target should have found out about the breach immediately, so that notice potentially could have gone out mere days after the breach. If that is true, then nearly every putative class member may be able to claim "would not have shopped" damages. Target's Motion on this point is denied.

2. *Private Right of Action*

According to Target, 29 of the 38 data-breach notice statutes on which Plaintiffs base their claims provide no private right of action. Plaintiffs concede this point as to the claims under Florida, Oklahoma, and Utah law, and have withdrawn those claims. Plaintiffs contend, however, that they are entitled to maintain their claims under the remaining 26 states' laws either through eight of the states' consumer-protection statutes or by determining that there should be a private right of action despite the statute not explicitly providing one.

Target responds that, of the eight data-breach notice statutes that reference consumer-protection laws, only six of those are potentially enforceable through the state's consumer-protection law, because North Dakota and

Oregon give enforcement authority for the data-breach notice statute to government officials. . . .

But again, the statutes are not as cut-and-dried as Target contends. North Dakota's statute states that the "attorney general may enforce this chapter." But the section also states that "[a] violation of this chapter is deemed a violation of [the consumer-protection statute]," and that the "remedies . . . of this chapter are not exclusive and are in addition to all other causes of action, remedies, and penalties under [the consumer-protection statute]. . . ." Target does not dispute that North Dakota's consumer-protection statute contains a private right of action. Thus, absent a case construing North Dakota law to preclude private enforcement of the data-breach notice statute, Plaintiffs have plausibly claimed that there is a private right of action under that statute.

Similarly, the Oregon statute provides that the director may enforce the data-breach notice statute, but the same section states that "the director may order compensation to consumers only upon a finding that enforcement of the rights of the consumers by private civil action would be so burdensome or expensive as to be impractical." This section implies that private civil actions are available, and without any contrary authority, Plaintiffs have plausibly alleged that they are entitled to private enforcement of Oregon's data-breach notice statute.

As to the six states that explicitly allow enforcement of the data-breach notice statute through the consumer-protection statute, Target contends that Plaintiffs have not sufficiently pled that the data-breach violation is a violation of the state's consumer-protection law. But Plaintiffs have pled both a violation of each state's consumer-protection law and a violation of the state's data-breach notice statute. Such pleading puts Target on notice of the claims against them. Plaintiffs' data-breach claims under these states—Alaska, Illinois, Maryland, Montana, New Jersey, North Carolina, North Dakota, and Oregon—survive Target's Motion.

Finally, there are 14 states that either provide for attorney general enforcement in what Plaintiffs contend is "permissive, non-exclusive language" and four states that are silent as to the enforcement of the data-breach notice statute. Aside from Minnesota's data-breach notice statute, the parties do not discuss any of the remaining 17 states' statutes specifically in their briefs, instead relying on the summary of each state's law provided in their respective appendices. The appendices are intended to assist the Court, but instead serve to obfuscate the issues and make determining each parties' arguments and each state's law difficult. The Court understands that the parties operate under Court-imposed word-count limitations, but in the future they would be better served by requesting an extension of those limits, rather than attempting to reference legal principles buried in lengthy appendices.

There are two types of enforcement provisions typically found in state data-breach notice statutes: Attorney General or government enforcement only, or states in which the enforcement provision is either ambiguous or explicitly non-exclusive. And as noted, four states' laws are silent as to enforcement. To simplify the following discussion, the Court categorizes each of the remaining states as either Attorney General/government enforcement only, ambiguous/non-exclusive enforcement, or no enforcement provision.

3. Attorney General enforcement only

The Arkansas data-breach notice statute provides that a "violation of this chapter is punishable by action of the Attorney General under the provisions of § 4-88-101 et seq." This is clear—only the Arkansas attorney general may enforce the Arkansas data-breach notice statute. Merely because the statute references the broader Arkansas consumer-protection statute does not mean that all of the remedies from the consumer-protection statute are available under the data-breach notice statute. There is no private right of action for violations of the Arkansas data-breach notice statute and Plaintiffs' Arkansas claim is dismissed.

Connecticut's data-breach notice statute provides that violations of the statute "shall be enforced by the Attorney General." As with Arkansas, this language clearly limits enforcement power to the state's attorney general and Plaintiffs' Connecticut claim is dismissed.

Idaho's law provides that "the primary regulator may bring a civil action to enforce compliance" with the state's data-breach notice statute. There is no provision for any other enforcement action, and Plaintiffs' Idaho claim is dismissed.

Massachusetts's data-breach notice statute provides similarly that the "attorney general may bring an action . . . to remedy violations of this chapter." Plaintiffs' Massachusetts claim is dismissed.

Minnesota's data-breach notice statute provides that the "attorney general shall enforce this section . . . under section 8.31." Plaintiffs argue that the reference to § 8.31 gives individuals private-enforcement rights, because § 8.31 gives the attorney general non-exclusive authority to prosecute violations of certain statutes, and because subdivision 3a of § 8.31 allows private individuals to sue under the statutes referenced in § 8.31. Plaintiffs' interpretation stretches the language of the statute beyond the breaking point, however. Minnesota's data-breach notice statute provides that the "attorney general shall" enforce the statute; that language is unambiguous. Plaintiffs' Minnesota claim is dismissed.

Similarly, Nebraska law provides that "the Attorney General may issue subpoenas and seek and recover direct economic damages for each affected Nebraska resident injured by a violation of the" data-breach notice statute. There is no provision for any other enforcement of the statute. Plaintiffs' Nebraska claim is dismissed.

Nevada's enforcement provision limits enforcement to a temporary or permanent injunction, and provides that "the Attorney General or district attorney may bring an action" to obtain that injunction. Nevada law also provides that a data collector may bring a civil action against a person who steals personal information from the data collector's records, but that situation is not present here. Plaintiffs' Nevada claim is dismissed.

Texas's data-breach notice statute provides only for attorney general enforcement, stating repeatedly that "[t]he attorney general may bring an action to recover the civil penalt[-y,-ies] imposed under this subsection," and that "the attorney general may bring an action . . . to restrain the violation by a temporary restraining order or by a permanent or temporary injunction." Plaintiffs' Texas claim is dismissed.

4. Ambiguous language or non-exclusive remedies

Colorado's data-breach notice statute provides that the "attorney general may bring an action . . . to address violations of this section," but also provides that the "provisions of this section are not exclusive." This permissive language is, as Plaintiffs' argue, at least ambiguous as to whether there is a private right of action under Colorado law. Given the procedural posture of this Motion, which requires the Court to view the law in the light most favorable to Plaintiffs, and absent any authority construing this ambiguity to exclude private rights of action, Plaintiffs' Colorado claim will not be dismissed.

Delaware's statute provides that "the Attorney General may bring an action . . . to address the violations of this chapter." The statute further provides that its provisions "are not exclusive." As in Colorado, it is at least ambiguous whether there is a private right of action. Plaintiffs' Delaware claim will not be dismissed.

In Iowa, a violation of the data-breach notice statute

> is an unlawful practice [under the consumer-protection statute] and, in addition to the remedies provided to the attorney general [in the consumer-protection statute], the attorney general may seek and obtain an order that a party held to violate this section pay damages to the attorney general on behalf of a person injured by this violation.

The statute further provides, however, that the "rights and remedies available under this section are cumulative to each other and to any other rights and remedies available under the law." This is at least ambiguous as to whether private enforcement is permissible, and Plaintiffs' Iowa claim will not be dismissed.

Kansas's data-breach enforcement provision is substantially similar to Delaware's. It provides that "the attorney general is empowered to bring an action . . . to address violations of this section" and also states that the enforcement provisions are "not exclusive." Plaintiffs' claim under Kansas law will not be dismissed.

Michigan law provides for a civil fine for a violation of the data-breach notice statute, and that the "attorney general or a prosecuting attorney may bring an action to recover" that fine. The statute also provides that the quoted subsection 13 does "not affect the availability of any civil remedy for a violation of state or federal law." This implies that consumers may bring a civil action to enforce Michigan's data-breach notice statute through Michigan's consumer-protection statute or other laws. Plaintiff's Michigan claim will not be dismissed.

Wyoming provides that the "attorney general may bring an action in law or equity to address any violation of the data-breach notice statute, and that the "provisions of this section are not exclusive." Plaintiffs' Wyoming claim will not be dismissed.

5. No enforcement provision

Georgia's data-breach-notice statute is silent as to enforcement. Neither party cites any case regarding how a court should interpret silence as to enforcement under Georgia law, and absent any such authority, Plaintiffs have plausibly alleged that private enforcement is possible and their Georgia claim survives.

Kentucky's statute is likewise silent. But Kentucky law elsewhere provides that a "person injured by the violation of any statute may recover from the offender such damages as he sustained by reason of the violation." This section gives a private right of action for a violation of Kentucky's data-breach notice statute. Plaintiffs' Kentucky claim will not be dismissed.

Rhode Island's statute provides that "[e]ach violation of this chapter is a civil violation for which a penalty of not more than a hundred dollars ($100) per occurrence and not more than twenty-five thousand dollars ($25,000) may be adjudged against a defendant." ... "When a statute does not plainly provide for a private cause of action [for damages], such a right cannot be inferred.'" *Stebbins v. Wells*, 818 A.2d 711, 716 (R.I. 2003). Plaintiffs have offered no contrary authority on Rhode Island's statutory interpretation principles. Plaintiffs' Rhode Island claim is dismissed.

Wisconsin's statute, like Georgia's, is silent on enforcement. Plaintiffs' Wisconsin claim will not be dismissed.

6. Conclusion

Plaintiffs have withdrawn their claims under Florida, Oklahoma, and Utah law. In addition, the data-breach notice statutes of Arkansas, Connecticut, Idaho, Massachusetts, Minnesota, Nebraska, Nevada, and Texas allow for enforcement only by the state's attorney general or other government official, and the Rhode Island statute's silence on enforcement is to be construed as prohibiting private rights of action. Plaintiffs' claims under these states' laws are therefore dismissed. Plaintiffs have plausibly alleged data-breach notice claims from 26 states.

Negligence

Target argues that Plaintiffs' negligence claim must be dismissed because Plaintiffs have failed to allege any damages that were caused by the breaches of duty they allege. Alternatively, Target contends that many states bar negligence claims for economic losses, and Target seeks the dismissal of the negligence claims brought under those states' laws.

A claim of negligence requires a plaintiff to allege four elements: duty, breach, causation, and injury.[3] Plaintiffs allege two different duties to support their negligence claims. First, Plaintiffs claim that Target had the duty "to exercise reasonable care in obtaining, retaining, securing, safeguarding, deleting and protecting [Plaintiffs'] personal and financial information in its possession from being compromised, lost, stolen, accessed and misused by unauthorized persons." Plaintiffs also allege that "Target owed a duty to timely and accurately disclose . . . that [Plaintiffs'] personal and financial information had been or was reasonably believed to have been compromised." For purposes of this Motion, Target does not dispute that Plaintiffs have plausibly alleged the existence of a duty. Target contends, however, that Plaintiffs have failed to allege any damages caused by the alleged breaches of duty, and that in any event some of Plaintiffs' negligence claims are barred by the economic loss rule.

1. Damages

Most of Target's contentions about damages are the same as those discussed previously with respect to standing. Those arguments, as discussed, are premature.

Target raises one new argument: that Plaintiffs have not alleged any damages whatsoever flowing from the alleged delay in notifying them of the breach. The Complaint contends that timely disclosure of the breach would have allowed Plaintiffs to "take appropriate measures to avoid unauthorized charges . . . , cancel or change usernames and passwords on compromised accounts, monitor their account information and credit reports for fraudulent activity, contact their banks . . . , obtain credit monitoring services and take other steps to mitigate or ameliorate the damages caused by Target's misconduct." Although Target would like a more detailed explanation of what damages were caused by the delayed breach notification, the allegations in the Complaint are not fatally insufficient. Rather, those allegations are a "short and plain statement," Fed.R.Civ.P. 8(a)(2), that plausibly alleges that Plaintiffs suffered damage as a result of the delay. Plaintiffs' negligence claim will not be dismissed on this basis.

---

3 These elements are substantially identical in every jurisdiction in which Plaintiffs raise a negligence claim.

2. Economic Loss Rule

The economic loss rule "bars a plaintiff from recovering for purely economic losses under a tort theory of negligence." *In re Michaels Stores Pin Pad Litig.*, 830 F.Supp.2d 518, 528 (N.D. Ill. 2011). It reflects the belief "that tort law affords the proper remedy for loss arising from personal injury or damages to one's property, whereas contract law and the Uniform Commercial Code provide the appropriate remedy for economic loss stemming from diminished commercial expectations without related injury to person or property."

Target's opening brief contends that the economic loss rule bars Plaintiffs' negligence claims in 20 states. Target's reply brief seems to narrow that to 12 states, stating that in eight of those original 20 states "the economic loss rule does not bar plaintiffs' negligence claims absent some contractual duty." Thus, Target appears to concede that only 12 states would apply the economic loss rule to bar Plaintiffs' claims here. However, Target's reply brief appendix lists only 11 states that it argues would apply the economic loss rule to facts similar to this case, and although the parties did not clarify the issue at the hearing, the Court will assume that only these 11 states are at issue.

Courts in five of these states—California, Georgia, Illinois, Massachusetts, and Pennsylvania—have faced data-breach claims such as those here; all of these courts dismissed the negligence claims based on the economic loss rule. Plaintiffs contend that these decisions are wrong and do not correctly apply the laws of the states in two ways. First, Plaintiffs assert that each state recognizes an independent-duty exception to the economic loss rule, so the rule does not apply where the duty alleged is an independent duty that does not arise from commercial expectations. Target appears to concede that the duty on which Plaintiffs rely is an independent duty that, in some jurisdictions, takes Plaintiffs' negligence claims out of the economic loss rule. Plaintiffs also contend that some states recognize a "special relationship" exception to the economic loss rule, and again, Target does not take issue with this premise but contends that this case does not fit this exception in some of the jurisdictions. According to Target, the 11 states in Target's reply appendix—including the five from which there are data-breach cases on point—either do not recognize the independent-duty exception, are states in which the exception is narrowly drawn to exclude the duty alleged here, or are states in which the special-relationship exception does not include the situation at issue. The Court will discuss these 11 states in alphabetical order.

a. Alaska

Plaintiffs contend that Alaska recognizes an independent-duty exception to the economic loss rule. But the case on which Target relies, *St. Denis v. Dep't of Housing & Urban Dev.*, 900 F.Supp. 1194 (D. Alaska 1995), exhaustively cataloged all relevant caselaw regarding the independent-duty exception to the economic loss rule . . . and determined that Alaska law recognizes negligence claims "only if the breach of duty created a risk of personal injury or property damage." This authority forecloses Plaintiff's Alaska negligence claim, and that claim is dismissed.

b. California

A court applying California law has dismissed negligence claims in a data-breach case under the economic loss rule. *In re Sony Gaming Networks & Customer Data Sec. Breach Litig.* ("Sony II"), 996 F. Supp. 2d 942, 967 (S.D. Cal. 2014). Plaintiffs argue that *Sony II* misapplied the economic loss rule because California law recognizes such claims where there is an independent duty. But *Sony II* is directly on point and Plaintiffs cite no other authority that disagrees with *Sony II*'s statement of the law. Plaintiffs' California negligence claims are dismissed on the basis of the economic loss rule.

c. District of Columbia

There is only one decision in the District of Columbia that addresses the economic loss rule and the parties disagree about its import, *Aguilar v. RP MRP Washington Harbour, LLC*, 98 A.3d 979 (D.C. 2014). *Aguilar* involved workers seeking lost wages caused by the property owner's alleged failure to raise flood walls around the property, allowing the property to flood and forcing the workers' employers to close temporarily or, in one case, permanently. The court first determined that the economic loss rule barred recovery in negligence for "a plaintiff who suffers only pecuniary injury." The court recognized, however, that where a "special relationship" exists that "provide[s] an independent duty of care," the economic loss rule may not apply.

Although the *Aguilar* court affirmed the grant of a motion to dismiss based on the economic loss rule, much of the opinion discussing the "special relationship" exception relied on factual determinations. For example, the court noted that the plaintiffs "were not especially likely to suffer serious economic loss as a result of [defendants'] conduct because too many variables beyond [defendants'] negligence . . . could prove determinative." But this is a factual determination: whether Plaintiffs can establish that, by virtue of giving Target access to their personal financial information, they were "especially likely to suffer serious economic loss as a result of [Target's] negligence" is a question of fact. The application of the economic loss rule to Plaintiff's District of Columbia negligence claims is premature and must await further record development.

d. Georgia

Target cites to a data-breach case in Georgia that it contends forecloses any argument that Georgia's economic loss rule does not bar Plaintiffs' Georgia negligence claims, *Willingham v. Global Payments, Inc.*, No. 1:12cv1157 (N.D. Ga. Feb. 5, 2013). But this opinion is a Magistrate Judge's Report and

Recommendation; it was not adopted or rejected by a District Court Judge because the parties settled the case during the objection period. Thus, unlike California where there is an opinion directly on point, the existence of this R & R does not by itself mean that Georgia's economic loss rule bars Plaintiffs' claims. Plaintiffs argue that Georgia recognizes an independent-duty exception to the economic loss rule.

The court in *Willingham* faced a negligence claim brought by consumers against the credit-card processor, not the merchant. The court rejected the notion that an independent duty might lie between the plaintiffs and the credit-card processor. But that is not the situation here. Plaintiffs and Target have a direct relationship, not an attenuated one.

Plaintiffs cite *Waithe v. Arrowhead Clinic*, Inc., No. CV 409-021, (S.D. Ga. Mar. 7, 2012). In *Waithe*, the plaintiffs alleged negligence against a group of lawyers. On summary judgment, the court noted that Georgia's economic loss rule does not bar a tort claim "where 'an independent duty exists under the law.'" The *Waithe* court found no independent duty in that case because Georgia courts had not recognized the duty on which the *Waithe* plaintiffs relied.

Neither party cites any authority regarding the duty Plaintiffs here allege: the duty to safeguard information. Absent Georgia authority refusing to recognize such an independent duty, Plaintiffs' allegations are sufficient to establish that the economic loss rule does not bar their Georgia negligence claims.

e. Idaho

Under Idaho law, the economic loss rule will bar a negligence claim for pecuniary loss unless there is a special relationship between the parties or "where unique circumstances require a reallocation of the risk." *Aardema v. U.S. Dairy Sys., Inc.*, 147 Idaho 785 (2009). Plaintiffs do not allege that the special-relationship exception applies because in Idaho that exception is "extremely narrow." Plaintiffs argue, instead, that there are unique circumstances here that require a reallocation of the risk.

Target points to a case holding that the "sale and purchase of a particular product does not create the type of 'unique circumstance' required to justify a different allocation of risk." *Millenkamp v. Davisco Foods Int'l, Inc.*, 391 F. Supp. 2d 872, 879 (D. Idaho 2005). But neither party cites to a case with facts close to this case, and thus it is an open question whether the situation here fits within the "unique circumstances" exception to Idaho's economic loss rule. Dismissal of Plaintiffs' Idaho negligence claim is inappropriate at this stage.

f. Illinois

The court in *In re Michaels* faced a data-breach case similar to the instant matter and determined that Illinois's economic loss rule barred the plaintiffs' negligence claims. 830 F. Supp. 2d at 530. Plaintiffs argue that the *In re Michaels* court misapplied Illinois law because Illinois law ostensibly recognizes the independent-duty exception. But *In re Michaels* exhaustively surveyed the Illinois economic loss rule, including the *Congregation of the Passion* case. As the court found, *Congregation of the Passion* merely recognized an exception for professional malpractice cases if the duty breached is independent of contract. The *In re Michaels* court concluded that the only exceptions to Illinois's economic loss rule were (1) when the plaintiff suffered personal injury or property damage; (2) when the damages alleged were caused by an intentional, false representation; or (3) when the damages were caused by a negligent misrepresentation "of a defendant in the business of supplying information for the guidance of others in business transactions." None of these exceptions applies here, and thus Plaintiffs' Illinois negligence claim is barred by the economic loss rule.

g. Iowa

Plaintiffs contend that Iowa recognizes the independent-duty exception and that this exception saves their Iowa negligence claim. But a recent decision by the Iowa Supreme Court forecloses Plaintiffs' argument. *See St. Malachy Roman Catholic Congregation of Geneseo v. Ingram*, 841 N.W.2d 338 (Iowa 2013). In *Ingram*, the Iowa Supreme Court recognized three exceptions to the economic loss rule: professional negligence against attorneys and accountants, negligent misrepresentation claims, and when the duty arises out of a principal-agent relationship. Plaintiffs cite no case establishing any other independent-duty exception. Rather, the case on which Plaintiffs rely merely states that the "damage for which recovery is sought [must] extend beyond the product itself in order for tort principles to apply," and does not hold that an independent duty gives rise to an exception to the economic loss rule. Plaintiffs' Iowa negligence claim is barred by the economic loss rule.

h. Massachusetts

Interpreting Massachusetts law, the court in another data-breach case dismissed the plaintiffs' negligence claim under the economic loss rule. *In re TJX Cos. Retail Sec. Breach Litig.*, 564 F.3d 489, 498-99 (1st Cir. 2009). Plaintiffs contend that *In re TJX* did not consider the existence of the independent-duty exception, but the case they cite for that exception was applying New Hampshire law, not Massachusetts law. *MacDonald v. Old Republic Nat'l Title Ins. Co.*, 882 F. Supp. 2d 236, 246 (D. Mass. 2012). Target argues, without opposition, that Massachusetts recognizes no independent-duty exception. Plaintiffs' Massachusetts negligence claim is dismissed.

i. New Hampshire

As noted above, New Hampshire does recognize an independent-duty exception to the economic loss rule. Target contends that this exception does not apply. *Wyle v. Lees*, 162 N.H. 406, 33 A.3d 1187, 1191 (2011). *Wyle* held that economic loss recovery is permitted when there is a special relationship between the parties or when there is "a negligent misrepresentation made by a defendant who is in the business of supplying information." According to Target, the New Hampshire Supreme Court has limited the special-relationship exception to situations involving either attorneys who draft a will and the intended beneficiaries or insurance investigators and the insured.

But *Plourde* also recognized that other independent duties may take a case out of the economic loss rule, although the court did not apply the independent-duty exception in that case. . . . Thus, the court did not examine the contours of any independent-duty exception to the New Hampshire's economic loss rule.

In the absence of authority as to the application of an independent duty under New Hampshire law, or excluding a situation akin to that here from the application of any independent-duty exception, dismissal of Plaintiffs' New Hampshire negligence claim at this stage is not warranted.

j. New York

The parties seem to agree that New York recognizes an independent-duty exception to the economic loss rule. Target contends that it does not apply here, but cites no case outlining that exception under New York law. Rather, the case on which Target relies, *In re Facebook Inc., IPO Sec. & Derivative Litig.*, 986 F.Supp.2d 428 (S.D.N.Y. 2013) determined that the independent-duty exception could apply if the parties' "relationship [was] so close as to approach that of privity" or if "the defendant has a created a[sic] duty to protect the plaintiff." But that is what Plaintiffs allege here: a quasi-contractual, privity-like relationship with respect to their personal financial information. Dismissal of Plaintiffs' New York negligence claims is not appropriate.

k. Pennsylvania

Finally, Pennsylvania courts have determined in a data-breach case that the economic loss rule bars a negligence claim. *Sovereign Bank v. BJ's Wholesale Club, Inc.*, 533 F.3d 162, 177-78 (3d Cir. 2008). The situation in *Sovereign Bank*, however, is more akin to that in the Financial Institution Cases: as in those cases, Sovereign Bank involved an issuer bank suing a merchant for a data breach. Because of the clear contractual relationship between the parties in *Sovereign Bank*, the application of the economic loss rule to bar the bank's negligence claim was more straightforward than application of the rule is in this case. Moreover, Pennsylvania recognizes a "special relationship" exception in situations involving "confidentiality, the repose of special trust or fiduciary responsibilities." *Valley Forge Convention & Visitors Bureau v. Visitor's Servs., Inc.*, 28 F. Supp. 2d 947, 952 (E.D. Pa. 1998). Plaintiffs' allegations here are that they reposed trust in Target or that Target bore a fiduciary-like responsibility to safeguard their financial information. Plaintiffs have plausibly pled the existence of a special relationship that Pennsylvania courts would recognize as an exception to the economic loss rule. Therefore, Plaintiffs' Pennsylvania negligence claim will not be dismissed.

Conclusion

The economic loss rule in Alaska, California, Illinois, Iowa, and Massachusetts appears to bar Plaintiffs' negligence claims under the laws of those states. Plaintiffs' negligence claims in the remaining states may go forward.

In re **The Home Depot Shareholder Derivative Litigation,** 223 F. Supp. 3d 1317 (N.D. Ga. 2016)

As explained in Chapter 4, courts have set a high bar for shareholders who file derivative lawsuits against company management and board officers after a data breach. This opinion is one of the more recent examples of such an unsuccessful attempt.

November 30, 2016

Opinion by Thomas W. Thrash Jr., District Judge

This is a shareholder derivative action. It is before the Court on the Defendants' Motion to Dismiss. For the reasons set forth below, the Defendants' Motion to Dismiss is GRANTED.

I. Background

This case arises out of the breach of Home Depot's security systems and the theft of their customers' personal financial data (the "Breach") over the course of several months in 2014. Plaintiffs Bennek and Frohman are current Home Depot shareholders, and held shares in Home Depot at the time of the Breach. The nominal Defendant, The Home Depot, Inc. ("Home Depot") is a multinational home improvement retailer that is incorporated in Delaware, with its principal place of business in Georgia.

Included as defendants in the suit are three current and former officers of Home Depot (the "Officers"). Francis Blake was previously Chairman of the Board from January 2007 to February 2015, and served as CEO during that time until November 2014. Matthew Carey is Home Depot's Executive Vice President and Chief Information Officer ("CIO"). Craig Menear served as President of Home Depot's retail division from February to October 2014, and was appointed as CEO, President, and placed on the Board on November 1, 2014. On February 2, 2015, Menear was appointed Chairman of the Board.

Also included as defendants are a number of current and former members of Home Depot's Board of Directors. Home Depot's Board currently consists of twelve members, nine of whom are named as defendants. One of them is Menear, who is also the Company's CEO and President. The remaining eight current directors are Defendants Bousbib, Brenneman, Brown, A. Carey, Codina, Foulkes, Katen, and Vadon, all of whom were Directors when the Breach occurred (collectively, the "Outside Directors"). Defendants Hill and Ackerman are former Directors who were on the Board during the Breach (collectively, the "Former Directors").

On September 2, 2014, Home Depot learned that it may have been the victim of a criminal breach of its payment card data systems. After an investigation, Home Depot confirmed that the Breach had occurred and that hackers had managed to steal the financial data of 56 million customers between April and September of 2014. This followed on the heels of a number of well publicized data breaches that occurred at major retailers like Target and Neiman Marcus the previous year. The hackers used a third-party vendor's user name and password to enter into Home Depot's network. The hackers then gained elevated rights which allowed them to access the rest of Home Depot's network and install a custom version of malware called BlackPOS. A similar version of BlackPOS was used in the Target data breach a few months prior, and essentially allowed the hackers to capture a customer's financial data every time a card was swiped at one of Home Depot's Point of Sale ("POS") terminals (e.g., a cash register). A little over a year after the Breach occurred, Home Depot reported that it had registered a net cost to the Company of $152 million. After all is said and done, the total cost to Home Depot because of the Breach has been estimated to eventually reach nearly $10 billion.

In August of 2015, Bennek filed a derivative complaint against Home Depot, and Frohman's derivative case was later consolidated with Bennek's. The Plaintiffs allege that the Defendants breached their duty of loyalty to Home Depot because the Defendants failed to institute internal controls sufficient to oversee the risks that Home Depot faced in the event of a breach and because they disbanded a Board of Directors committee that was supposed to have oversight of those risks. As a result of their alleged failure to take the risk of a data breach seriously and immediately implement security measures, the Breach occurred. The Plaintiffs also allege that the Defendants wasted corporate assets, and that the Current Directors violated Section 14(a) of the Securities Exchange Act in their 2014 and 2015 proxy filings.

All of the Plaintiffs' charges against the Defendants ultimately relate to what the Defendants knew before the Breach and what they did about that knowledge. According to the Complaint, Home Depot's by-laws authorized the Board to delegate any or all of its powers to committees to the extent allowed by law. The by-laws provided for no procedure to do this, other than referencing resolutions of the Board. The Company's Governance Guidelines, however, said that the roles of committees are defined "by the Company's by-laws and by Committee charters adopted by the Board." When it came to overseeing the company's information technology (IT) and digital security, Home Depot had previously instituted what was called the Infrastructure Committee. The

Infrastructure Committee, however, was dissolved by Home Depot in May 2012.

Home Depot said in its 2012 Proxy Statement that the responsibility for IT and data security which had previously been the domain of the Infrastructure Committee was now being borne by the Audit Committee. However, the Audit Committee's charter was never amended to reflect this change. And according to the Complaint, Home Depot's 2014 and 2015 Proxy Statements, which were issued after the Breach had begun, did not include any indication that the Audit Committee's charter had not been changed to reflect its new duties.

In addition to raising the issue of whether anyone had proper oversight over IT and data security, the Complaint also alleges a number of deficiencies in Home Depot's network security as it stood at the time of the Breach. According to the Complaint, Home Depot's contracts with financial institutions required them to comply with the Payment Card Industry Data Security Standards ("PCI DSS"), which established a minimum level of protection for data security. PCI DSS 2.0, the version of the standards in place at the time of the Breach, required Home Depot to: (1) install and maintain a firewall, (2) protect against malware and regularly update its anti-virus software, (3) encrypt transmission of cardholder data, (4) not store cardholder data beyond the time necessary to authorize a transaction, (5) limit access to payment card data, and (6) to regularly test its data security systems.

On multiple occasions before the Breach, the Board and the Audit Committee were informed by M. Carey that Home Depot was out of compliance with PCI DSS on multiple levels. M. Carey acknowledged that Home Depot was out of compliance, and admitted that Home Depot would likely continue to be out of compliance until February 2015. M. Carey assured the Board that there was a plan in place, and that it was in the process of being implemented. During this time, the Board continued to receive regular updates from M. Carey.

On September 8, 2014, Home Depot acknowledged that there had been a breach of its network. At the time of the Breach, Home Depot's security systems were still "desperately out of date," according to then-CEO, the Defendant Blake. For example, encryption technology had only been installed at twenty-five percent of its stores by the time the Breach was discovered in September 2015. In response, Home Depot accelerated its efforts to increase its security, and was able to install encryption technology on the remaining seventy-five percent of its stores in just six days.

As a result of the harm caused to Home Depot by its delay in responding to threats Home Depot acknowledged as significant, the Plaintiffs filed this derivative suit. The Plaintiffs claim that the Defendants breached their duties of care and loyalty, wasted corporate assets, and violated Section 14(a) of the Securities Exchange Act. The Defendants now move to dismiss the claims against them under Rules 12(b)(6) and 23.1(b)(3) of the Federal Rules of Civil Procedure. . . .

III. Discussion

Rule 23.1 clearly "contemplates both the demand requirement and the possibility that demand may be excused . . . [but] it does not create a demand requirement of any particular dimension."[4] Because the demand doctrine is a matter of substance, the Court looks to the state of incorporation to provide the rule of decision. In this case, Home Depot is incorporated in Delaware; therefore, the Court looks to Delaware's substantive law.

"A cardinal precept of the General Corporation Law of the State of Delaware is that directors, rather than shareholders, manage the business and affairs of the corporation." Shareholder derivative suits restrict this managerial authority. Therefore, as a prerequisite to a shareholder derivative suit, Delaware law requires an aggrieved shareholder to demand that the board take the desired action. This demand requirement "insure[s] that a stockholder exhausts his intracorporate remedies, and . . . provide[s] a safeguard against strike suits."[5]

It is undisputed that no demand was made in this instance. The Plaintiff shareholder thus has the burden of demonstrating that demand is excused because it would have been futile. In situations like this case where the Plaintiffs complain of Board inaction and do not challenge a specific decision of the Board, a finding of demand futility is authorized only where "particularized factual allegations of [the] derivative stockholder complaint create a reasonable doubt that, as of the time the complaint is filed, the board of directors could have properly exercised its independent and disinterested business judgment in responding to a demand."[6] Because the independence of the Board is determined at the time of filing, the Court only need look to the claims against the Current Directors. And further, because the Board acts by will of the majority, the Plaintiffs' Complaint must show that a majority of the Directors were not independent. As such, the Court only need address the Plaintiffs' claims against the Outside Directors (the Defendants Bousbib, Brenneman, Brown, A. Carey, Codina, Foulkes, Katen, and Vadon), who make up a majority of the Board and are all similarly situated, to determine whether the Board of Directors was independent.

Interest is demonstrated where a director "will receive a personal financial benefit from a transaction that is not equally shared by the stockholders," or "where a corporate decision will have a materially detrimental impact on a director, but not on the corporation and the stockholders." Only the former is at issue here.

---

4 Kamen v. Kemper Fin. Servs., Inc., 500 U.S. 90, 96 (1991).

5 Aronson v. Lewis, 473 A.2d 805, 811 (Del. 1984), overruled on other grounds by Brehm v. Eisner, 746 A.2d 244 (Del. 2000).

6 Rales v. Blasband, 634 A.2d 927, 934 (Del. 1993).

Initially, it seems obvious that the Board was interested given that a majority of its members are named in this lawsuit. After all, very few people would choose to sue themselves. However, as this Court previously noted, under Delaware law "derivative action plaintiffs do not ring the futility bell merely by including a majority of the directors as defendants."[7] To do so would eviscerate the demand requirement entirely. Instead, Delaware law requires the Plaintiffs to show director conduct that is "so egregious on its face that board approval cannot meet the test of business judgment, and a substantial likelihood of director liability therefore exists."[8] . . .

Individual and particularized facts for each defendant would be more necessary in cases, for example, where the directors are alleged to be financially interested in a proposed merger. In those cases, to determine whether a majority of the board of directors were interested would require an individual analysis. But in this case, all of the Plaintiffs' claims against the non-officer Current Directors essentially allege that they are liable because of information they received and decisions they took collectively. There is nothing to be gained by addressing each Outside Director individually because they are all similarly situated. As such, the Court now addresses each of the claims against the Outside Directors and takes them together as a group.

A. Duty of Loyalty Claims

The Plaintiffs' primary claim for liability is that the Directors breached their duty of loyalty to the company. In cases such as this one, where the Plaintiffs allege a failure of oversight on the part of the Board, the Plaintiffs must show that the Directors either "knew they were not discharging their fiduciary obligations or that the directors demonstrated a conscious disregard for their responsibilities such as by failing to act in the face of a known duty to act."[9] When added to the general demand futility standard, the Plaintiffs essentially need to show with particularized facts beyond a reasonable doubt that a majority of the Board faced substantial liability because it consciously failed to act in the face of a known duty to act. This is an incredibly high hurdle for the Plaintiffs to overcome, and it is not surprising that they fail to do so.

The Plaintiffs first attempt to clear this hurdle by pointing to the disbanding of the Infrastructure Committee. According to the Complaint, when the Board disbanded the Infrastructure Committee, it failed to amend the Audit Committee's charter to reflect the new responsibilities for data security that had been transferred from the Infrastructure Committee, as required by the Company's Corporate Governance Guidelines. The Plaintiffs argue, therefore,

---

7 In re Coca-Cola Enterprises, Inc. Derivative Litigation, 478 F.Supp.2d 1369, 1374 (N.D. Ga. 2007).

8 Aronson, 473 A.2d at 815.

9 In re Citigroup, 964 A.2d at 123.

that the Board failed to designate anyone with the responsibility to oversee data security, thereby leaving them without a reporting system.

This argument is much too formal. Even if the Board's failure to amend the Audit Committee charter meant that it did not have authority to oversee data security, and the Court doubts that is true, it is irrelevant here. Demand futility is a fact based analysis. Whether or not the Audit Committee had technical authority, both the Committee and the Board believed it did. The Complaint itself details numerous instances where the Audit Committee received regular reports from management on the state of Home Depot's data security, and the Board in turn received briefings from both management and the Audit Committee. Based on those facts alone, there can be no question that the Board was fulfilling its duty of loyalty to ensure that a reasonable system of reporting existed.

The Plaintiffs then argue that the Board "failed to ensure that a plan was in place to immediately remedy the deficiency [in Home Depot's data security], and that the proposed remedy complied with PCI DSS." Importantly, the Plaintiffs repeatedly acknowledge that there was a plan, but that in the Plaintiffs' opinion it moved too slowly. Under Delaware law, however, directors violate their duty of loyalty only "if they knowingly and completely failed to undertake their responsibilities."[10] In other words, as long as the Outside Directors pursued any course of action that was reasonable, they would not have violated their duty of loyalty. The Court suspects that is why the Plaintiffs awkwardly try to reframe their argument to say that the Board "failed to take any action to remediate the problems." But the Plaintiffs cannot escape the facts in their Complaint and their own contradictory arguments. At the end of the day, the Plaintiffs are alleging that the Board's plan was not good enough.

The Plaintiffs may be right, but Delaware courts have held that "[b]ad faith cannot be shown by merely showing that the directors failed to do all they should have done under the circumstances."[11] Rather, they use language like "utterly" and "completely" to describe the failure necessary to violate the duty of loyalty by inaction. The cases cited in the Plaintiffs' Response to the Defendants' Motion to Dismiss work against their argument on this point. In *Abbott Labs.*, the Seventh Circuit found demand excused where the complaint sufficiently alleged that in the face of numerous known violations of law, the directors "took no steps in an effort to prevent or remedy the situation...."[12] In *Pfizer*, the court held that demand was futile because the directors received numerous warnings of illegal marketing practices, but they "chose to disregard

---

10 Lyondell Chemical Co. v. Ryan, 970 A.2d 235, 243-44 (Del. 2009).
11 Wayne Cty. Employees' Ret. Sys. v. Corti, No. CIV.A. 3534-CC, 2009 WL 2219260, at *14 (Del. Ch. July 24, 2009), *aff'd*, 996 A.2d 795 (Del. 2010).
12 In re Abbott Labs. Deriv. S'holders Litig., 325 F.3d 795, 809 (7th Cir. 2003).

it."[13] And in *Veeco Instruments*, the company failed to do anything for more than a year to address deficiencies in its accounting department.[14] Though the board acted in that case, the court found demand excused because the board failed to act until after the harm had occurred.

But in this case, the Complaint acknowledges that the Board acted before the Breach occurred. The Board approved a plan that would have fixed many of Home Depot's security weaknesses and it would be fully implemented by February 2015. With the benefit of hindsight, one can safely say that the implementation of the plan was probably too slow, and that the plan probably would not have fixed all of the problems Home Depot had with its security. But the "Directors' decisions must be reasonable, not perfect." While the Board probably should have done more, "[s]imply alleging that a board incorrectly exercised its business judgment and made a 'wrong' decision in response to red flags . . . is not enough to plead bad faith."[15]

Therefore, the Court finds that the Plaintiffs have failed to show beyond a reasonable doubt that a majority of the Board faced substantial liability because it consciously failed to act in the face of a known duty to act. As such, demand is not excused on the basis of the Plaintiffs' duty of loyalty claims.

B. Corporate Waste

The Plaintiffs also allege that the Board wasted corporate assets. Under Delaware law, corporate waste is "an exchange that is so one sided that no business person of ordinary, sound judgment could conclude that the corporation has received adequate consideration." Because waste claims entail an action on the part of the Board, they are evaluated under the *Aronson* test. To show demand futility under *Aronson*, the Plaintiffs "must provide particularized factual allegations that raise a reasonable doubt that '(1) the directors are disinterested and independent [or] (2) the challenged transaction was otherwise the product of a valid exercise of business judgment.'"[16] The Plaintiffs do not challenge the independence of the Board, but rather their allegations fall under the second prong of *Aronson*.

The Plaintiffs first maintain that the Board's insufficient reaction to the threat posed by the holes in Home Depot's data security caused significant losses to the Company, which they claim is a waste of Home Depot's assets. The problem with the Plaintiffs' argument is that there is no transaction. Corporate waste claims typically involve situations where there has been an exchange of corporate assets for no corporate purpose or for no consideration;

---

13 In re Pfizer Inc. S'holder Deriv. Litig., 722 F.Supp.2d 453, 460 (S.D.N.Y. 2010).

14 Veeco Instruments, Inc. v. Braun, 434 F.Supp.2d 267 (S.D.N.Y. 2006).

15 Melbourne Mun. Firefighters' Pension Trust Fund on Behalf of Qualcomm, Inc. v. Jacobs, C.A. No. 10872-VCMR, 2016 WL 4076369, at *9 (Del. Ch. Aug. 1, 2016).

16 *In re* Citigroup, 964 A.2d at 120.

in effect, waste is a gift. The Plaintiffs cite no case law to suggest anything to the contrary.

Rather, the Plaintiffs' claim is fundamentally a challenge to the Directors' exercise of their business judgment. To paraphrase the Delaware Chancery Court, what the Plaintiffs are asking the Court to conclude from the presence of these "red flags" is that the Directors failed to see the extent of Home Depot's security risk and therefore made a "wrong" business decision by allowing Home Depot to be exposed to the threat of a security breach. With hindsight, it is easy to see that the Board's decision to upgrade Home Depot's security at a leisurely pace was an unfortunate one. But this decision falls squarely within the discretion of the Board and is under the protection of the business judgment rule. . . .

[The Court also concluded that the plaintiffs failed to adequately allege that the Current Director Defendants violated Section 14(a) of the Securities Exchange Act when issuing their proxy statements.]

IV. Conclusion

For the foregoing reasons, the Plaintiffs have failed to show that demand was futile on any of the claims alleged. Because the pleading requirements of Rule 23.1 are more demanding than those under 12(b)(6), the Court need not address the Defendants' 12(b)(6) argument. The Defendants' Motion to Dismiss is GRANTED.

United States v. Rodriguez, 628 F.3d 1258 (11th Cir. 2010)

Chapter 5 discusses the two main approaches that courts take in determining whether an individual has exceeded authorized access to a computer, and violated the Computer Fraud and Abuse Act (CFAA). In this 2010 opinion, the United States Court of Appeals for the Eleventh Circuit set forth an expansive interpretation of "exceeds authorized access," which many other courts have adopted.

December 27, 2010

Opinion by William H. Pryor, Jr., Circuit Judge:

The main issue in this appeal is whether the prying by a former bureaucrat is criminal: that is, whether the defendant violated the Computer Fraud and Abuse Act, which prohibits "intentionally access[ing] a computer without authorization or exceed[ing] authorized access, and thereby obtain[ing] . . . information from any department or agency of the United States." Roberto Rodriguez, a former employee of the Social Security Administration, appeals his conviction for violating the Act on the grounds that he did not exceed his authorized access to his former employer's databases and that he did not use the information to further another crime or to gain financially. The Administration prohibits accessing information on its databases for nonbusiness reasons, and Rodriguez at trial admitted that he accessed information for nonbusiness reasons when he obtained personal identifying information, such as birth dates and home addresses, of 17 persons he knew or their relatives. Rodriguez also appeals his sentence of 12 months of imprisonment on the ground that it is unreasonable. Because the record establishes that Rodriguez exceeded his authorized access and the Act does not require proof that Rodriguez used the information to further another crime or to gain financially, we affirm his conviction. We also conclude that Rodriguez's sentence is reasonable.

I. BACKGROUND

From 1995 to 2009, Roberto Rodriguez worked as a TeleService representative for the Social Security Administration. Rodriguez's duties included answering questions of the general public about social security benefits over the telephone. As a part of his duties, Rodriguez had access to Administration databases that contained sensitive personal information, including any person's social security number, address, date of birth, father's name, mother's maiden name, amount and type of social security benefit received, and annual income.

The Administration established a policy that prohibits an employee from obtaining information from its databases without a business reason. The Administration informed its TeleService employees about its policy through mandatory training sessions, notices posted in the office, and a banner that appeared on every computer screen daily. The Administration also required TeleService employees annually to sign acknowledgment forms after receiving the policies in writing. The Administration warned employees that they faced criminal penalties if they violated policies on unauthorized use of databases. From 2006 to 2008, Rodriguez refused to sign the acknowledgment forms. He asked a supervisor rhetorically, "Why give the government rope to hang me?" To monitor access and prevent unauthorized use, the Administration issued unique personal identification numbers and passwords to each TeleService employee and reviewed usage of the databases.

In August 2008, the Administration flagged Rodriguez's personal identification number for suspicious activity. Administration records established that Rodriguez had accessed the personal records of 17 different individuals for nonbusiness reasons. The Administration informed Rodriguez that it was conducting a criminal investigation into his use of the databases, but Rodriguez continued his unauthorized use. None of the 17 victims knew that Rodriguez had obtained their personal information without authorization until investigators informed them of his actions.

Most of Rodriguez's victims testified at trial. Cecilia Collins was married to Rodriguez from 1985 to 1990. In 2008 and 2009, Rodriguez used the Administration databases to determine how much Collins was earning.

Rodriguez also accessed the personal information of Collins's sister for non-business reasons.

Sally Culver lived with Rodriguez from 2001 to 2005. She testified that she had not spoken with Rodriguez since 2005. Culver testified that on one occasion, when she complained to Rodriguez about pay disparities at her place of work, Rodriguez stated that, if Culver gave him the name, birth date, and approximate age of a coworker, then he could tell her how much that coworker earned. Culver declined Rodriguez's offer and did not provide him the coworker's name. Rodriguez also accessed the personal information of Culver's father for nonbusiness reasons. Rodriguez also told Culver that, if he was ever asked about his unauthorized searches, then he would make up an explanation. In 2008 and 2009, long after Culver and Rodriguez ended their relationship, Rodriguez accessed Culver's personal information 62 times.

Theresa Ivey had worked with Rodriguez at a post office, but Ivey had not spoken to Rodriguez since 1999. Ivey's daughter testified that she met Rodriguez in 1993 when she was a child. In 2008, Rodriguez accessed Ivey's personal information twice and her daughter's personal information 22 times.

Diamselis Rodriguez worked at a restaurant that Rodriguez frequently visited. Rodriguez gave Diamselis a pair of earrings on her birthday. In 2008, Rodriguez accessed Diamselis's personal information 20 times.

Dana Fennell, a professor of sociology from Mississippi, testified that she met Rodriguez at a Unitarian Universalist church study group when she was visiting her parents in Florida. Fennell interviewed Rodriguez for a study on the health effects of religion, but she did not consider him to be a friend. After Fennell returned to her home in Mississippi, she received flowers from Rodriguez on Valentine's Day even though she had not given Rodriguez her address. Rodriguez later arrived at Fennell's doorstep unannounced, and Fennell was surprised and frightened by his presence. On another occasion, Rodriguez mentioned Fennell's father's birthday to Fennell even though she had never mentioned her father to Rodriguez. Rodriguez also told Fennell that he had the ability to listen to the telephone conversations of others. Rodriguez later called Fennell to wish her a happy "half-birthday" although she did not recall telling Rodriguez her date of birth. Rodriguez accessed Fennell's personal information on Administration databases 65 times, and he accessed the personal information of Fennell's mother and father multiple times.

Jessica Fox also met Rodriguez at the church study group. Fox testified that she received a letter from Rodriguez at her home address and was shocked because she had not given Rodriguez her address, she ordinarily receives all her mail at a post office box, and her middle initial was on the envelope although she had not used it since grade school. Rodriguez accessed Fox's personal information 45 times.

Rodriguez accessed the personal information of several other women he met at the church study group. Annemarie Jiovenetta considered Rodriguez to be an acquaintance, and Rodriguez accessed Jiovenetta's personal information 23 times. Joan Ginnell considered Rodriguez to be her friend, and she testified that he seemed romantically interested in her. Rodriguez accessed Ginnell's personal information 30 times. Catherine Schuman avoided Rodriguez after it became apparent that he wanted a romantic relationship with her, and Rodriguez attempted to access her information 29 times. Rodriguez accessed Marianne Silverstein's personal information seven times and Jane Dekovitch's personal information ten times. Nitza Dominguez did not testify at trial, but the government presented evidence that Rodriguez accessed Dominguez's personal information 34 times for nonbusiness reasons.

On April 2, 2009, a grand jury indicted Rodriguez with 17 misdemeanor counts of violating the Computer Fraud and Abuse Act. The indictment charged Rodriguez with "intentionally access[ing] a computer without authorization or exceed[ing] authorized access, and thereby obtain[ing] . . . information from any department or agency of the United States." 18 U.S.C. § 1030(a)(2)(B). Trial commenced on July 27, 2009.

During his opening statement, Rodriguez's attorney conceded that Rodriguez had "access[ed] things that were unauthorized." Rodriguez also testified in his defense and admitted accessing the personal information of the victims. Rodriguez testified that he had accessed the personal information as part of a whistle-blowing operation to test whether his unauthorized use of the databases would trigger the attention of the Administration because he was conducting an investigation into improper denials of disability benefits. Rodriguez admitted that he did not access the victims' records as a part of his duties as a TeleService representative. On July 29, 2009, the jury rejected Rodriguez's argument about his conduct and returned a guilty verdict on all 17 counts.

The presentence investigation report provided a statutory maximum sentence of one year of imprisonment, and a sentencing guidelines range between zero and six months of imprisonment. Rodriguez did not object to the sentencing report. The government sought an upward variance from the guidelines range to 36 months of imprisonment. The government asked the district court to impose the statutory maximum of 12 months on some of the counts and order that the sentences run consecutively. The government argued that the guidelines range did not sufficiently account for the number of victims or the harm they suffered. The government also argued that an upward variance would better reflect the seriousness of the offense and promote respect for the law. At the sentencing hearing, Rodriguez presented more testimony about his discredited whistle-blowing motivation and expressed regret. Rodriguez requested a probationary sentence.

After considering the statutory factors for sentencing, the district court varied upward and sentenced Rodriguez to 12 months of imprisonment and

12 months of supervised release. The district court agreed with the government that the guidelines range did not adequately account for the number of Rodriguez's victims or the harm they suffered. Rodriguez objected to the upward variance. . . .

III. DISCUSSION

Our discussion of this appeal is divided in two parts. We first discuss whether Rodriguez's conduct supports a conviction under section 1030(a)(2)(B). Next, we discuss whether Rodriguez's sentence is reasonable.

A. Rodriguez Exceeded His Authorized Access Under Section 1030(a)(2)(B) When He Accessed Personal Records for Nonbusiness Reasons.

Rodriguez argues that he did not violate section 1030(a)(2)(B) because he accessed only databases that he was authorized to use as a TeleService representative, but his argument ignores both the law and the record. The Computer Fraud and Abuse Act makes it a crime to "intentionally access[ ] a computer without authorization or exceed[ ] authorized access, and thereby obtain[ ] information from any department or agency of the United States." The Act defines the phrase "exceeds authorized access" as "to access a computer with authorization and to use such access to obtain or alter information in the computer that the accesser is not entitled to obtain or alter." The policy of the Administration is that use of databases to obtain personal information is authorized only when done for business reasons. Rodriguez conceded at trial that his access of the victims' personal information was not in furtherance of his duties as a TeleService representative and that "he did access things that were unauthorized." In the light of this record, the plain language of the Act forecloses any argument that Rodriguez did not exceed his authorized access.

Rodriguez contends that the interpretation of the Act by the Ninth Circuit in *LVRC Holdings LLC v. Brekka*, 581 F.3d 1127 (9th Cir. 2009), supports his argument, but Rodriguez's reliance on *Brekka* is misplaced. The Ninth Circuit held that Brekka, an employee of a residential addiction treatment center, had not violated the Act when he emailed documents that he was authorized to obtain to his personal email account. The treatment center argued that Brekka obtained the documents he emailed without authorization because he later used them for his own personal interests. The treatment center had no policy prohibiting employees from emailing company documents to personal email accounts, and there was no dispute that Brekka had been authorized to obtain the documents or to send the emails while he was employed. *Brekka* is distinguishable because the Administration told Rodriguez that he was not authorized to obtain personal information for nonbusiness reasons.

Rodriguez also relies on *United States v. John*, 597 F.3d 263 (5th Cir. 2010), but his reliance on that decision too is misplaced. The Fifth Circuit held that use of information may constitute "exceeding authorized access," if the use is criminal. John, an employee of Citigroup, was authorized to use her employer's computers and to view and print account information. John used the information to incur fraudulent charges. The Fifth Circuit observed that "John was authorized to view and print all of the information that she accessed," but concluded that "authorization" as used in the Act, "may encompass limits placed on the use of information obtained by permitted access to a computer system and data available on that system" if the use is in furtherance of a crime. Rodriguez erroneously argues that he cannot be convicted under the Act because his use of the information was not criminal. The problem with Rodriguez's argument is that his use of information is irrelevant if he obtained the information without authorization or as a result of exceeding authorized access. Rodriguez exceeded his authorized access and violated the Act when he obtained personal information for a nonbusiness reason.

Rodriguez also argues that his conviction cannot stand because he never used the personal information he accessed without authorization to defraud anyone or to gain financially, but this argument is foreclosed by the plain language of the Act. "The starting point for all statutory interpretation is the language of the statute itself[,]" and "we look to the entire statutory context." *United States v. DBB, Inc.*, 180 F.3d 1277, 1281 (11th Cir. 1999). Sections 1030(c)(2)(B)(i) and (ii) of the Act provide a punishment of up to five years of imprisonment if "the offense was committed for purposes of commercial advantage or private financial gain [or if] the offense was committed in furtherance of any criminal or tortious act." The misdemeanor penalty provision of the Act under which Rodriguez was convicted does not contain any language regarding purposes for committing the offense. Rodriguez's argument would eviscerate the distinction between these misdemeanor and felony provisions. That Rodriguez did not use the information to defraud anyone or gain financially is irrelevant.

[The Court also concluded that Rodriguez's sentence was reasonable.]

IV. CONCLUSION

The judgment of the district court is AFFIRMED.

United States v. Nosal, 676 F.3d 854 (9th Cir. 2012) (en banc) (Nosal I)

A little over a year after the Eleventh Circuit issued its opinion in Rodriguez, *the Ninth Circuit, sitting en banc, released this interpretation of the CFAA's "exceeds authorized access" opinion. The opinion, known as "Nosal I" (because the case would return to the Ninth Circuit a few years later), takes a much narrower view of the CFAA's scope, and has been among the most influential CFAA opinions.*

April 10, 2012

Opinion by Alex Kozinski, Chief Judge:

Computers have become an indispensable part of our daily lives. We use them for work; we use them for play. Sometimes we use them for play at work. Many employers have adopted policies prohibiting the use of work computers for nonbusiness purposes. Does an employee who violates such a policy commit a federal crime? How about someone who violates the terms of service of a social networking website? This depends on how broadly we read the Computer Fraud and Abuse Act (CFAA).

FACTS

David Nosal used to work for Korn/Ferry, an executive search firm. Shortly after he left the company, he convinced some of his former colleagues who were still working for Korn/Ferry to help him start a competing business. The employees used their log-in credentials to download source lists, names and contact information from a confidential database on the company's computer, and then transferred that information to Nosal. The employees were authorized to access the database, but Korn/Ferry had a policy that forbade disclosing confidential information.[17] The government indicted Nosal on twenty counts, including trade secret theft, mail fraud, conspiracy and violations of the CFAA. The CFAA counts charged Nosal with violations of 18 U.S.C. § 1030(a)(4), for aiding and abetting the Korn/Ferry employees in "exceed[ing their] authorized access" with intent to defraud.

Nosal filed a motion to dismiss the CFAA counts, arguing that the statute targets only hackers, not individuals who access a computer with authorization but then misuse information they obtain by means of such access. The district court initially rejected Nosal's argument, holding that when a person accesses a computer "knowingly and with the intent to defraud . . . [it] renders the access unauthorized or in excess of authorization." Shortly afterwards, however, we decided *LVRC Holdings LLC v. Brekka*, 581 F.3d 1127 (9th Cir. 2009), which construed narrowly the phrases "without authorization" and "exceeds authorized access" in the CFAA. Nosal filed a motion for reconsideration and a second motion to dismiss.

The district court reversed field and followed *Brekka*'s guidance that "[t]here is simply no way to read [the definition of 'exceeds authorized access'] to incorporate corporate policies governing use of information unless the word alter is interpreted to mean misappropriate," as "[s]uch an interpretation would defy the plain meaning of the word alter, as well as common sense." Accordingly, the district court dismissed counts 2 and 4-7 for failure to state an offense. The government appeals. . . .

---

17 The opening screen of the database also included the warning: "This product is intended to be used by Korn/Ferry employees for work on Korn/Ferry business only."

DISCUSSION

The CFAA defines "exceeds authorized access" as "to access a computer with authorization and to use such access to obtain or alter information in the computer that the accesser is not entitled so to obtain or alter." This language can be read either of two ways: First, as Nosal suggests and the district court held, it could refer to someone who's authorized to access only certain data or files but accesses unauthorized data or files—what is colloquially known as "hacking." For example, assume an employee is permitted to access only product information on the company's computer but accesses customer data: He would "exceed[] authorized access" if he looks at the customer lists. Second, as the government proposes, the language could refer to someone who has unrestricted physical access to a computer, but is limited in the use to which he can put the information. For example, an employee may be authorized to access customer lists in order to do his job but not to send them to a competitor.

The government argues that the statutory text can support only the latter interpretation of "exceeds authorized access." In its opening brief, it focuses on the word "entitled" in the phrase an "accesser is not entitled so to obtain or alter." Pointing to one dictionary definition of "entitle" as "to furnish with a right," the government argues that Korn/Ferry's computer use policy gives employees certain rights, and when the employees violated that policy, they "exceed[ed] authorized access." But "entitled" in the statutory text refers to how an accesser "obtain[s] or alter[s]" the information, whereas the computer use policy uses "entitled" to limit how the information is used after it is obtained. This is a poor fit with the statutory language. An equally or more sensible reading of "entitled" is as a synonym for "authorized."[18] So read, "exceeds authorized access" would refer to data or files on a computer that one is not authorized to access.

In its reply brief and at oral argument, the government focuses on the word "so" in the same phrase. *See* 18 U.S.C. § 1030(e)(6) ("accesser is not entitled so to obtain or alter"). The government reads "so" to mean "in that manner," which it claims must refer to use restrictions. In the government's view, reading the definition narrowly would render "so" superfluous.

The government's interpretation would transform the CFAA from an anti-hacking statute into an expansive misappropriation statute. This places a great deal of weight on a two-letter word that is essentially a conjunction. If Congress meant to expand the scope of criminal liability to everyone who uses a computer in violation of computer use restrictions—which may well include

---

18 *Fowler's* offers these as usage examples: "Everyone is entitled to an opinion" and "We are entitled to make personal choices." "Fowler's Modern English Usage: Entitled," Answers.com, http://www.answers.com/topic/entitle (last visited Mar. 5, 2012).

everyone who uses a computer—we would expect it to use language better suited to that purpose.[19] Under the presumption that Congress acts interstitially, we construe a statute as displacing a substantial portion of the common law only where Congress has clearly indicated its intent to do so.

In any event, the government's "so" argument doesn't work because the word has meaning even if it doesn't refer to use restrictions. Suppose an employer keeps certain information in a separate database that can be viewed on a computer screen, but not copied or downloaded. If an employee circumvents the security measures, copies the information to a thumb drive and walks out of the building with it in his pocket, he would then have obtained access to information in the computer that he is not "entitled so to obtain." Or, let's say an employee is given full access to the information, provided he logs in with his username and password. In an effort to cover his tracks, he uses another employee's login to copy information from the database. Once again, this would be an employee who is authorized to access the information but does so in a manner he was not authorized "so to obtain." Of course, this all assumes that "so" must have a substantive meaning to make sense of the statute. But Congress could just as well have included "so" as a connector or for emphasis.

While the CFAA is susceptible to the government's broad interpretation, we find Nosal's narrower one more plausible. Congress enacted the CFAA in 1984 primarily to address the growing problem of computer hacking, recognizing that, "[i]n intentionally trespassing into someone else's computer files, the offender obtains at the very least information as to how to break into that computer system." S.Rep. No. 99-432, at 9 (1986). The government agrees that the CFAA was concerned with hacking, which is why it also prohibits accessing a computer "without authorization." According to the government, that prohibition applies to hackers, so the "exceeds authorized access" prohibition must apply to people who are authorized to use the computer, but do so for an unauthorized purpose. But it is possible to read both prohibitions as applying to hackers: "[W]ithout authorization" would apply to outside hackers (individuals who have no authorized access to the computer at all) and "exceeds authorized access" would apply to inside hackers (individuals whose initial access to a computer is authorized but who access unauthorized information or files). This is a perfectly plausible construction of the statutory language that maintains the CFAA's

---

19 Congress did just that in the federal trade secrets statute—18 U.S.C. § 1832—where it used the common law terms for misappropriation, including "with intent to convert," "steals," "appropriates" and "takes." *See* 18 U.S.C. § 1832(a). The government also charged Nosal with violating 18 U.S.C. § 1832, and those charges remain pending.

focus on hacking rather than turning it into a sweeping Internet-policing mandate.[20]

The government's construction of the statute would expand its scope far beyond computer hacking to criminalize any unauthorized use of information obtained from a computer. This would make criminals of large groups of people who would have little reason to suspect they are committing a federal crime. While ignorance of the law is no excuse, we can properly be skeptical as to whether Congress, in 1984, meant to criminalize conduct beyond that which is inherently wrongful, such as breaking into a computer.

The government argues that defendants here did have notice that their conduct was wrongful by the fraud and materiality requirements in subsection 1030(a)(4), which punishes whoever:

> knowingly and with intent to defraud, accesses a protected computer without authorization, or exceeds authorized access, and by means of such conduct furthers the intended fraud and obtains anything of value, unless the object of the fraud and the thing obtained consists only of the use of the computer and the value of such use is not more than $5,000 in any 1-year period.

But "exceeds authorized access" is used elsewhere in the CFAA as a basis for criminal culpability without intent to defraud. Subsection 1030(a)(2)(C) requires only that the person who "exceeds authorized access" have "obtain[ed] . . . information from any protected computer." Because "protected computer" is defined as a computer affected by or involved in interstate commerce—effectively all computers with Internet access—the government's interpretation of "exceeds authorized access" makes every violation of a private computer use policy a federal crime.

The government argues that our ruling today would construe "exceeds authorized access" only in subsection 1030(a)(4), and we could give the phrase

---

20 Although the legislative history of the CFAA discusses this anti-hacking purpose, and says nothing about exceeding authorized use of information, the government claims that the legislative history supports its interpretation. It points to an earlier version of the statute, which defined "exceeds authorized access" as "having accessed a computer with authorization, uses the opportunity such access provides for purposes to which such authorization does not extend." Pub. L. No. 99-474, § 2(c), 100 Stat. 1213 (1986). But that language was removed and replaced by the current phrase and definition. And Senators Mathias and Leahy—members of the Senate Judiciary Committee—explained that the purpose of replacing the original broader language was to "remove[] from the sweep of the statute one of the murkier grounds of liability, under which a[n] ... employee's access to computerized data might be legitimate in some circumstances, but criminal in other (not clearly distinguishable) circumstances." S. Rep. No. 99-432, at 21, 1986 U.S.C.C.A.N. 2479 at 2494. Were there any need to rely on legislative history, it would seem to support Nosal's position rather than the government's.

a narrower meaning when we construe other subsections. This is just not so: Once we define the phrase for the purpose of subsection 1030(a)(4), that definition must apply equally to the rest of the statute pursuant to the "standard principle of statutory construction . . . that identical words and phrases within the same statute should normally be given the same meaning." *Powerex Corp. v. Reliant Energy Servs., Inc.*, 551 U.S. 224, 232 (2007). The phrase appears five times in the first seven subsections of the statute, including subsection 1030(a)(2)(C). Giving a different interpretation to each is impossible because Congress provided a single definition of "exceeds authorized access" for all iterations of the statutory phrase. Congress obviously meant "exceeds authorized access" to have the same meaning throughout section 1030. We must therefore consider how the interpretation we adopt will operate wherever in that section the phrase appears.

In the case of the CFAA, the broadest provision is subsection 1030(a)(2)(C), which makes it a crime to exceed authorized access of a computer connected to the Internet without any culpable intent. Were we to adopt the government's proposed interpretation, millions of unsuspecting individuals would find that they are engaging in criminal conduct.

Minds have wandered since the beginning of time and the computer gives employees new ways to procrastinate, by g-chatting with friends, playing games, shopping or watching sports highlights. Such activities are routinely prohibited by many computer-use policies, although employees are seldom disciplined for occasional use of work computers for personal purposes. Nevertheless, under the broad interpretation of the CFAA, such minor dalliances would become federal crimes. While it's unlikely that you'll be prosecuted for watching Reason.TV on your work computer, you could be. Employers wanting to rid themselves of troublesome employees without following proper procedures could threaten to report them to the FBI unless they quit. Ubiquitous, seldom-prosecuted crimes invite arbitrary and discriminatory enforcement.[21]

Employer-employee and company-consumer relationships are traditionally governed by tort and contract law; the government's proposed interpretation of the CFAA allows private parties to manipulate their computer-use and personnel policies so as to turn these relationships into ones policed by the

---

21 This concern persists even if intent to defraud is required. Suppose an employee spends six hours tending his FarmVille stable on his work computer. The employee has full access to his computer and the Internet, but the company has a policy that work computers may be used only for business purposes. The employer should be able to fire the employee, but that's quite different from having him arrested as a federal criminal. Yet, under the government's construction of the statute, the employee "exceeds authorized access" by using the computer for non-work activities. Given that the employee deprives his company of six hours of work a day, an aggressive prosecutor might claim that he's defrauding the company, and thereby violating section 1030(a)(4).

criminal law. Significant notice problems arise if we allow criminal liability to turn on the vagaries of private polices that are lengthy, opaque, subject to change and seldom read. Consider the typical corporate policy that computers can be used only for business purposes. What exactly is a "nonbusiness purpose"? If you use the computer to check the weather report for a business trip? For the company softball game? For your vacation to Hawaii? And if minor personal uses are tolerated, how can an employee be on notice of what constitutes a violation sufficient to trigger criminal liability?

Basing criminal liability on violations of private computer use polices can transform whole categories of otherwise innocuous behavior into federal crimes simply because a computer is involved. Employees who call family members from their work phones will become criminals if they send an email instead. Employees can sneak in the sports section of the *New York Times* to read at work, but they'd better not visit ESPN.com. And sudoku enthusiasts should stick to the printed puzzles, because visiting www.dailysudoku.com from their work computers might give them more than enough time to hone their sudoku skills behind bars.

The effect this broad construction of the CFAA has on workplace conduct pales by comparison with its effect on everyone else who uses a computer, smart-phone, iPad, Kindle, Nook, X-box, Blu-Ray player or any other Internet-enabled device. The Internet is a means for communicating via computers: Whenever we access a web page, commence a download, post a message on somebody's Facebook wall, shop on Amazon, bid on eBay, publish a blog, rate a movie on IMDb, read www.NYT. com, watch YouTube and do the thousands of other things we routinely do online, we are using one computer to send commands to other computers at remote locations. Our access to those remote computers is governed by a series of private agreements and policies that most people are only dimly aware of and virtually no one reads or understands.

For example, it's not widely known that, up until very recently, Google forbade minors from using its services. Adopting the government's interpretation would turn vast numbers of teens and pre-teens into juvenile delinquents—and their parents and teachers into delinquency contributors. Similarly, Facebook makes it a violation of the terms of service to let anyone log into your account. Yet it's very common for people to let close friends and relatives check their email or access their online accounts. Some may be aware that, if discovered, they may suffer a rebuke from the ISP or a loss of access, but few imagine they might be marched off to federal prison for doing so.

Or consider the numerous dating websites whose terms of use prohibit inaccurate or misleading information. Or eBay and Craigslist, where it's a violation of the terms of use to post items in an inappropriate category. Under the government's proposed interpretation of the CFAA, posting for sale an item prohibited by Craigslist's policy, or describing yourself as "tall, dark and handsome," when you're actually short and homely, will earn you a handsome orange jumpsuit.

Not only are the terms of service vague and generally unknown—unless you look real hard at the small print at the bottom of a webpage—but website owners retain the right to change the terms at any time and without notice. . . . Accordingly, behavior that wasn't criminal yesterday can become criminal today without an act of Congress, and without any notice whatsoever.

The government assures us that, whatever the scope of the CFAA, it won't prosecute minor violations. But we shouldn't have to live at the mercy of our local prosecutor. . . . And it's not clear we can trust the government when a tempting target comes along. Take the case of the mom who posed as a 17-year-old boy and cyber-bullied her daughter's classmate. The Justice Department prosecuted her under 18 U.S.C. § 1030(a)(2)(C) for violating MySpace's terms of service, which prohibited lying about identifying information, including age. See *United States v. Drew*, 259 F.R.D. 449 (C.D. Cal. 2009). Lying on social media websites is common: People shave years off their age, add inches to their height and drop pounds from their weight. The difference between puffery and prosecution may depend on whether you happen to be someone an AUSA has reason to go after.

In *United States v. Kozminski*, 487 U.S. 931 (1988), the Supreme Court refused to adopt the government's broad interpretation of a statute because it would "criminalize a broad range of day-to-day activity." Applying the rule of lenity, the Court warned that the broader statutory interpretation would "delegate to prosecutors and juries the inherently legislative task of determining what type of . . . activities are so morally reprehensible that they should be punished as crimes" and would "subject individuals to the risk of arbitrary or discriminatory prosecution and conviction." By giving that much power to prosecutors, we're inviting discriminatory and arbitrary enforcement.

We remain unpersuaded by the decisions of our sister circuits that interpret the CFAA broadly to cover violations of corporate computer use restrictions or violations of a duty of loyalty. See *United States v. Rodriguez*, 628 F.3d 1258 (11th Cir. 2010); *United States v. John*, 597 F.3d 263 (5th Cir. 2010); *Int'l Airport Ctrs., LLC v. Citrin*, 440 F.3d 418 (7th Cir. 2006). These courts looked only at the culpable behavior of the defendants before them, and failed to consider the effect on millions of ordinary citizens caused by the statute's unitary definition of "exceeds authorized access." They therefore failed to apply the long-standing principle that we must construe ambiguous criminal statutes narrowly so as to avoid "making criminal law in Congress's stead." *United States v. Santos*, 553 U.S. 507, 514 (2008).

We therefore respectfully decline to follow our sister circuits and urge them to reconsider instead. For our part, we continue to follow in the path blazed by *Brekka*, and the growing number of courts that have reached the same conclusion. These courts recognize that the plain language of the CFAA "target[s] the unauthorized procurement or alteration of information, not its misuse or misappropriation." *Shamrock Foods Co. v. Gast*, 535 F. Supp. 2d 962, 965 (D.Ariz. 2008). . . .

CONCLUSION

We need not decide today whether Congress could base criminal liability on violations of a company or website's computer use restrictions. Instead, we hold that the phrase "exceeds authorized access" in the CFAA does not extend to violations of use restrictions. If Congress wants to incorporate misappropriation liability into the CFAA, it must speak more clearly. The rule of lenity requires "penal laws . . . to be construed strictly." *United States v. Wiltberger*, 18 U.S. (5 Wheat.) 76, 95 (1820). . . .

This narrower interpretation is also a more sensible reading of the text and legislative history of a statute whose general purpose is to punish hacking—the circumvention of technological access barriers—not misappropriation of trade secrets—a subject Congress has dealt with elsewhere. Therefore, we hold that "exceeds authorized access" in the CFAA is limited to violations of restrictions on access to information, and not restrictions on its use.

Because Nosal's accomplices had permission to access the company database and obtain the information contained within, the government's charges fail to meet the element of "without authorization, or exceeds authorized access" under 18 U.S.C. § 1030(a)(4). Accordingly, we affirm the judgment of the district court dismissing counts 2 and 4-7 for failure to state an offense. The government may, of course, prosecute Nosal on the remaining counts of the indictment.

AFFIRMED.

Dissent by Judge Barry Silverman, Circuit Judge:

This case has nothing to do with playing sudoku, checking email, fibbing on dating sites, or any of the other activities that the majority rightly values. It has everything to do with stealing an employer's valuable information to set up a competing business with the purloined data, siphoned away from the victim, knowing such access and use were prohibited in the defendants' employment contracts. The indictment here charged that Nosal and his co-conspirators knowingly exceeded the access to a protected company computer they were given by an executive search firm that employed them; that they did so with the intent to defraud; and further, that they stole the victim's valuable proprietary information by means of that fraudulent conduct in order to profit from using it. In ridiculing scenarios not remotely presented by this case, the majority does a good job of knocking down straw men—far-fetched hypotheticals involving neither theft nor intentional fraudulent conduct, but innocuous violations of office policy.

The majority also takes a plainly written statute and parses it in a hyper-complicated way that distorts the obvious intent of Congress. No other circuit that has considered this statute finds the problems that the majority does.

18 U.S.C. § 1030(a)(4) is quite clear. It states, in relevant part:

> (a) Whoever—
> (4) knowingly and with intent to defraud, accesses a protected computer without authorization, or exceeds authorized access, and by means of such conduct furthers the intended fraud and obtains anything of value . . .
> shall be punished . . . .

Thus, it is perfectly clear that a person with both the requisite mens rea and the specific intent to defraud—but only such persons—can violate this subsection in one of two ways: first, by accessing a computer without authorization, or second, by exceeding authorized access. 18 U.S.C. § 1030(e)(6) defines "exceeds authorized access" as "to access a computer with authorization and to use such access to obtain or alter information in the computer that the accesser is not entitled so to obtain or alter." . . .

In *Brekka*, we explained that a person "exceeds authorized access" when that person has permission to access a computer but accesses information on the computer that the person is not entitled to access. In that case, an employee allegedly emailed an employer's proprietary documents to his personal computer to use in a competing business. We held that one does not exceed authorized access simply by "breach[ing] a state law duty of loyalty to an employer" and that, because the employee did not breach a contract with his employer, he could not be liable under the Computer Fraud and Abuse Act.

This is not an esoteric concept. A bank teller is entitled to access a bank's money for legitimate banking purposes, but not to take the bank's money for himself. A new car buyer may be entitled to take a vehicle around the block on a test drive. But the buyer would not be entitled—he would "exceed his authority"—to take the vehicle to Mexico on a drug run. A person of ordinary intelligence understands that he may be totally prohibited from doing something altogether, or authorized to do something but prohibited from going beyond what is authorized. This is no doubt why the statute covers not only "unauthorized access," but also "exceed[ing] authorized access." The statute contemplates both means of committing the theft.

The majority holds that a person "exceeds authorized access" only when that person has permission to access a computer generally, but is completely prohibited from accessing a different portion of the computer (or different information on the computer). The majority's interpretation conflicts with the plain language of the statute. Furthermore, none of the circuits that have analyzed the meaning of "exceeds authorized access" as used in the Computer Fraud and

Abuse Act read the statute the way the majority does. Both the Fifth and Eleventh Circuits have explicitly held that employees who knowingly violate clear company computer restrictions agreements "exceed authorized access" under the CFAA.

In *United States v. John*, the Fifth Circuit held that an employee of Citigroup exceeded her authorized access in violation of § 1030(a)(2) when she accessed confidential customer information in violation of her employer's computer use restrictions and used that information to commit fraud. As the Fifth Circuit noted in John, "an employer may 'authorize' employees to utilize computers for any lawful purpose but not for unlawful purposes and only in furtherance of the employer's business. An employee would 'exceed[] authorized access' if he or she used that access to obtain or steal information as part of a criminal scheme." At the very least, when an employee "knows that the purpose for which she is accessing information in a computer is both in violation of an employer's policies and is part of [a criminally fraudulent] scheme, it would be 'proper' to conclude that such conduct 'exceeds authorized access.'"

Similarly, the Eleventh Circuit held in *United States v. Rodriguez* that an employee of the Social Security Administration exceeded his authorized access under § 1030(a)(2) when he obtained personal information about former girl-friends and potential paramours and used that information to send the women flowers or to show up at their homes. The court rejected Rodriguez's argument that unlike the defendant in John, his use was "not criminal." The court held: "The problem with Rodriguez's argument is that his use of information is irrel-evant if he obtained the information without authorization or as a result of exceeding authorized access." . . .

The indictment here alleges that Nosal and his coconspirators knowingly exceeded the authority that they had to access their employer's computer, and that they did so with the intent to defraud and to steal trade secrets and propri-etary information from the company's database for Nosal's competing busi-ness. It is alleged that at the time the employee coconspirators accessed the database they knew they only were allowed to use the database for a legitimate business purpose because the co-conspirators allegedly signed an agreement which restricted the use and disclosure of information on the database except for legitimate Korn/Ferry business. Moreover, it is alleged that before using a unique username and password to log on to the Korn/Ferry computer and database, the employees were notified that the information stored on those computers were the property of Korn/Ferry and that to access the information without relevant authority could lead to disciplinary action and criminal pros-ecution. Therefore, it is alleged, that when Nosal's co-conspirators accessed the database to obtain Korn/Ferry's secret source lists, names, and contact infor-mation with the intent to defraud Korn/Ferry by setting up a competing com-pany to take business away using the stolen data, they "exceed[ed their] authorized access" to a computer with an intent to defraud Korn/Ferry and therefore violated 18 U.S.C. § 1030(a)(4). If true, these allegations adequately state a crime under a commonsense reading of this particular subsection.

Furthermore, it does not advance the ball to consider, as the majority does, the parade of horribles that might occur under different subsections of the CFAA, such as subsection (a)(2)(C), which does not have the scienter or specific intent to defraud requirements that subsection (a)(4) has. . . . Other sections of the CFAA may or may not be unconstitutionally vague or pose other problems. We need to wait for an actual case or controversy to frame these issues, rather than posit a laundry list of wacky hypotheticals. I express no opinion on the validity or application of other subsections of 18 U.S.C. § 1030, other than § 1030(a)(4), and with all due respect, neither should the majority.

The majority's opinion is driven out of a well-meaning but ultimately misguided concern that if employment agreements or internet terms of service violations could subject someone to criminal liability, all internet users will suddenly become criminals overnight. I fail to see how anyone can seriously conclude that reading ESPN.com in contravention of office policy could come within the ambit of 18 U.S.C. § 1030(a)(4), a statute explicitly requiring an intent to defraud, the obtaining of something of value by means of that fraud, while doing so "knowingly." And even if an imaginative judge can conjure up far-fetched hypotheticals producing federal prison terms for accessing word puzzles, jokes, and sports scores while at work, well, . . . that is what an as-applied challenge is for. Meantime, back to this case, 18 U.S.C. § 1030(a)(4) clearly is aimed at, and limited to, knowing and intentional fraud. Because the indictment adequately states the elements of a valid crime, the district court erred in dismissing the charges.

I respectfully dissent.

United States v. Nosal, 844 F.3d 1024 (9th Cir. 2016) ("Nosal II")

After the Ninth Circuit ruled in favor of Nosal, the case went back to the district court and once again was appealed to the Ninth Circuit. This time, the court was asked to interpret the scope of the other basis for CFAA claims: accessing computers "without authorization." This time, the Ninth Circuit would take a less defendant-friendly approach to interpreting the scope of the CFAA.

Opinion by M. Margaret McKeown, Circuit Judge:

This is the second time we consider the scope of the Computer Fraud and Abuse Act ("CFAA"), 18 U.S.C. § 1030, with respect to David Nosal. The CFAA imposes criminal penalties on whoever "knowingly and with intent to defraud, accesses a protected computer without authorization, or exceeds authorized access, and by means of such conduct furthers the intended fraud and obtains anything of value."

Only the first prong of the section is before us in this appeal: "knowingly and with intent to defraud" accessing a computer "without authorization."

Embracing our earlier precedent and joining our sister circuits, we conclude that "without authorization" is an unambiguous, non-technical term that, given its plain and ordinary meaning, means accessing a protected computer without permission. Further, we have held that authorization is not pegged to website terms and conditions. This definition has a simple corollary: once authorization to access a computer has been affirmatively revoked, the user cannot sidestep the statute by going through the back door and accessing the computer through a third party. Unequivocal revocation of computer access closes both the front door and the back door. This provision, coupled with the requirement that access be "knowingly and with intent to defraud," means that the statute will not sweep in innocent conduct, such as family password sharing.

Nosal worked at the executive search firm Korn/Ferry International when he decided to launch a competitor along with a group of co-workers. Before leaving Korn/Ferry, Nosal's colleagues began downloading confidential information from a Korn/Ferry database to use at their new enterprise. Although they were authorized to access the database as current Korn/Ferry employees, their downloads on behalf of Nosal violated Korn/Ferry's confidentiality and computer use policies. In 2012, we addressed whether those employees "exceed[ed] authorized access" with intent to defraud under the CFAA. *United States v. Nosal (Nosal I)*, 676 F.3d 854 (9th Cir. 2012) (en banc). Distinguishing between access restrictions and use restrictions, we concluded that the "exceeds authorized access" prong of § 1030(a)(4) of the CFAA "does not extend to violations of [a company's] use restrictions." We affirmed the district court's dismissal of the five CFAA counts related to Nosal's aiding and abetting misuse of data accessed by his co-workers with their own passwords.

The remaining counts relate to statutory provisions that were not at issue in *Nosal I*: access to a protected computer "without authorization" under the CFAA and trade secret theft under the Economic Espionage Act ("EEA"), 18 U.S.C. § 1831 *et seq.* When Nosal left Korn/Ferry, the company revoked his computer access credentials, even though he remained for a time as a contractor. The company took the same precaution upon the departure of his accomplices, Becky Christian and Mark Jacobson. Nonetheless, they continued to access the database using the credentials of Nosal's former executive assistant, Jacqueline Froehlich-L'Heureaux ("FH"), who remained at Korn/Ferry at Nosal's request. The question we consider is whether the jury properly convicted Nosal of conspiracy to violate the "without authorization" provision of the CFAA for unauthorized access to, and downloads from, his former employer's database called Searcher.[22] Put simply, we are asked to decide whether the

---

22 As in *Nosal I*, Nosal did not himself access and download information from Korn/Ferry's database. Nosal was convicted of three substantive CFAA counts on either an aiding and abetting or conspiracy theory. Under either, Nosal is liable for the conduct of Christian and Jacobson.

"without authorization" prohibition of the CFAA extends to a former employee whose computer access credentials have been rescinded but who, disregarding the revocation, accesses the computer by other means.

We directly answered this question in *LVRC Holdings LLC v. Brekka*, 581 F.3d 1127 (9th Cir. 2009), and reiterate our holding here: "[A] person uses a computer 'without authorization' under [the CFAA] . . . when the employer has rescinded permission to access the computer and the defendant uses the computer anyway." This straightforward principle embodies the common sense, ordinary meaning of the "without authorization" prohibition.

Nosal and various amici spin hypotheticals about the dire consequences of criminalizing password sharing. But these warnings miss the mark in this case. This appeal is not about password sharing. Nor is it about violating a company's internal computer-use policies. The conduct at issue is that of Nosal and his co-conspirators, which is covered by the plain language of the statute. Nosal is charged with conspiring with former Korn/Ferry employees whose user accounts had been terminated, but who nonetheless accessed trade secrets in a proprietary database through the back door when the front door had been firmly closed. Nosal knowingly and with intent to defraud Korn/Ferry blatantly circumvented the affirmative revocation of his computer system access. This access falls squarely within the CFAA's prohibition on "knowingly and with intent to defraud" accessing a computer "without authorization," and thus we affirm Nosal's conviction for violations of § 1030(a)(4) of the CFAA.

The dissent mistakenly focuses on FH's authority, sidestepping the authorization question for Christian and Jacobson. To begin, FH had no authority from Korn/Ferry to provide her password to former employees whose computer access had been revoked. Also, in collapsing the distinction between FH's authorization and that of Christian and Jacobson, the dissent would render meaningless the concept of authorization. And, pertinent here, it would remove from the scope of the CFAA any hacking conspiracy with an inside person. That surely was not Congress's intent. . . .

BACKGROUND

I. FACTUAL BACKGROUND

Nosal was a high-level regional director at the global executive search firm Korn/Ferry International. Korn/Ferry's bread and butter was identifying and recommending potential candidates for corporate positions. In 2004, after being passed over for a promotion, Nosal announced his intention to leave Korn/Ferry. Negotiations ensued and Nosal agreed to stay on for an additional year as a contractor to finish a handful of open searches, subject to a blanket non-competition agreement. As he put it, Korn/Ferry was giving him "a lot of money" to "stay out of the market."

During this interim period, Nosal was very busy, secretly launching his own search firm along with other Korn/Ferry employees, including Christian, Jacobson and FH. As of December 8, 2004, Korn/Ferry revoked Nosal's access to its computers, although it permitted him to ask Korn/Ferry employees for research help on his remaining open assignments. In January 2005, Christian left Korn/Ferry and, under instructions from Nosal, set up an executive search firm—Christian & Associates—from which Nosal retained 80% of fees. Jacobson followed her a few months later. As Nosal, Christian and Jacobson began work for clients, Nosal used the name "David Nelson" to mask his identity when interviewing candidates.

The start-up company was missing Korn/Ferry's core asset: "Searcher," an internal database of information on over one million executives, including contact information, employment history, salaries, biographies and resumes, all compiled since 1995. Searcher was central to Korn/Ferry's work for clients. When launching a new search to fill an open executive position, Korn/Ferry teams started by compiling a "source list" of potential candidates. In constructing the list, the employees would run queries in Searcher to generate a list of candidates. To speed up the process, employees could look at old source lists in Searcher to see how a search for a similar position was constructed, or to identify suitable candidates. The resulting source list could include hundreds of names, but then was narrowed to a short list of candidates presented to the client. Korn/Ferry considered these source lists proprietary.

Searcher included data from a number of public and quasi-public sources like LinkedIn, corporate filings and Internet searches, and also included internal, non-public sources, such as personal connections, unsolicited resumes sent to Korn/Ferry and data inputted directly by candidates via Korn/Ferry's website. The data was coded upon entry; as a result, employees could run targeted searches for candidates by criteria such as age, industry, experience or other data points. However, once the information became part of the Searcher system, it was integrated with other data and there was no way to identify the source of the data.

Searcher was hosted on the company's internal computer network and was considered confidential and for use only in Korn/Ferry business. Korn/Ferry issued each employee a unique username and password to its computer system; no separate password was required to access Searcher. Password sharing was prohibited by a confidentiality agreement that Korn/Ferry required each new employee to sign. When a user requested a custom report in Searcher, Searcher displayed a message which stated: "This product is intended to be used by Korn/Ferry employees for work on Korn/Ferry business only."

Nosal and his compatriots downloaded information and source lists from Searcher in preparation to launch the new competitor. Before leaving Korn/

Ferry, they used their own usernames and passwords, compiling proprietary Korn/Ferry data in violation of Korn/Ferry's computer use policy. Those efforts were encompassed in the CFAA accounts appealed in *Nosal I*.

After Nosal became a contractor and Christian and Jacobson left Korn/Ferry, Korn/Ferry revoked each of their credentials to access Korn/Ferry's computer system. Not to be deterred, on three occasions Christian and Jacobson borrowed access credentials from FH, who stayed on at Korn/Ferry at Nosal's request. In April 2005, Nosal instructed Christian to obtain some source lists from Searcher to expedite their work for a new client. Thinking it would be difficult to explain the request to FH, Christian asked to borrow FH's access credentials, which Christian then used to log in to Korn/Ferry's computer system and run queries in Searcher. Christian sent the results of her searches to Nosal. In July 2005, Christian again logged in as FH to generate a custom report and search for information on three individuals. Later in July, Jacobson also logged in as FH, to download information on 2,400 executives. None of these searches related to any open searches that fell under Nosal's independent contractor agreement.

In March 2005, Korn/Ferry received an email from an unidentified person advising that Nosal was conducting his own business in violation of his non-compete agreement. The company launched an investigation and, in July 2005, contacted government authorities.

II. PROCEDURAL BACKGROUND

In the first indictment, Nosal was charged with twenty criminal counts, including eight counts under the CFAA, two trade secrets counts under the Economic Espionage Act and one conspiracy count. Five of the eight CFAA counts were based on allegations that FH and Christian downloaded material from Searcher using their own credentials while employed by Korn/Ferry in violation of company policies. The district court dismissed these counts, citing our decision in *Brekka*. That dismissal was affirmed by the en banc court in *Nosal I*, and the case was remanded for trial on the remaining counts.

The government filed a second superseding indictment in February 2013 with three CFAA counts, two trade secrets counts and one conspiracy count. Nosal's remaining CFAA counts were based on the three occasions when Christian and Jacobson accessed Korn/Ferry's system for their new clients using FH's login credentials. The district court denied Nosal's motion to dismiss the three remaining CFAA counts, rejecting the argument that *Nosal I* limited the statute's applicability "to hacking crimes where the defendant circumvented technological barriers to access a computer." Alternatively, the court held that "the indictment sufficiently allege[d] such circumvention." A jury convicted Nosal on all counts. The district court sentenced Nosal to one year and one day in prison, three years of supervised release, a \$60,000 fine, a \$600 special assessment and approximately \$828,000 in restitution to Korn/Ferry.

ANALYSIS

I. CONVICTIONS UNDER THE COMPUTER FRAUD AND ABUSE ACT

[The court first recited much of the legislative history of the CFAA discussed in Chapter 5 of this book.]

B. Meaning of "Authorization" Under the CFAA

The interpretive fireworks under § 1030(a)(4) of the CFAA have been reserved for its second prong, the meaning of "exceeds authorized access." Not surprisingly, there has been no division among the circuits on the straightforward "without authorization" prong of this section. We begin with the two Ninth Circuit cases that bind our interpretation of "without authorization"—*Brekka* and *Nosal I*—and then move on to address the cases from our sister circuits that are in accord with *Brekka*, agreeing that "without authorization" is an unambiguous term that should be given its ordinary meaning.

Brekka involved a former employee in circumstances remarkably similar to Nosal: he wanted to compete using confidential data from his former company. Christopher Brekka worked as an internet marketer with LVRC Holdings, LLC ("LVRC"), a residential addiction treatment center. LVRC assigned him a computer and gave him access credentials to a third-party website that tracked traffic and other information for LVRC's website. When negotiations to become part owner of LVRC broke down, Brekka left the company. LVRC sued him, claiming that he violated the CFAA by emailing certain confidential company documents to his personal email account while an employee and also by continuing to access LVRC's account on the external website after he left the company.

In *Brekka* we analyzed both the "without authorization" and "exceeds authorization" provisions of the statute under §§ 1030(a)(2) and (4). Because the CFAA does not define the term "authorization," we looked to the ordinary, contemporaneous meaning of the term: "'permission or power granted by an authority.'" In determining whether an employee has authorization, we stated that, consistent with "the plain language of the statute . . . 'authorization' [to use an employer's computer] depends on actions taken by the employer." We concluded that because Brekka had permission to use his employer's computer, "[t]he most straightforward interpretation of §§ 1030(a)(2) and (4) is that Brekka had authorization to use the computer" while an employee.

Brekka's access after LVRC terminated his employment presented a starkly different situation: "There is no dispute that if Brekka accessed LVRC's information on the [traffic monitoring] website after he left the company . . . , Brekka would have accessed a protected computer 'without authorization' for purposes of the CFAA."[23] Stated differently, we held that "a person uses a computer 'without authorization' under §§ 1030(a)(2) and (4)... when the employer has rescinded permission to access the computer and the defendant uses the computer anyway." In Brekka's case, there was no genuine issue of material fact as to whether Brekka actually accessed the website, and thus we affirmed the district court's grant of summary judgment.

Not surprisingly, in *Nosal I* as in this appeal, both the government and Nosal cited *Brekka* extensively. The focus of Nosal's first appeal was whether the CFAA could be interpreted "broadly to cover violations of corporate computer use restrictions or violations of a duty of loyalty." We unequivocally said "no": "For our part, we continue to follow in the path blazed by *Brekka* and the growing number of courts that have reached the same conclusion. These courts recognize that the plain language of the CFAA 'target[s] the unauthorized procurement or alteration of information, not its misuse or misappropriation.'" In line with *Brekka*, we stated that "'[w]ithout authorization' would apply to outside hackers (individuals who have no authorized access to the computer at all) and 'exceeds authorization access' would apply to inside hackers (individuals whose initial access to a computer is authorized but who access unauthorized information or files)." Because Nosal's accomplices had authority to access the company computers, we affirmed the district court's dismissal of the CFAA counts related to the period when the accomplices were still employed at Korn/Ferry.

In *Nosal I*, authorization was not in doubt. The employees who accessed the Korn/Ferry computers unquestionably had authorization from the company to access the system; the question was whether they exceeded it. What *Nosal I* did not address was whether Nosal's access to Korn/Ferry computers after both Nosal and his coconspirators had terminated their employment and Korn/Ferry revoked their permission to access the computers was "without authorization." *Brekka* is squarely on point on that issue: Nosal and his co-conspirators acted "without authorization" when they continued to access Searcher by other means after Korn/Ferry rescinded permission to access its computer system. As *Nosal I* made clear, the CFAA was not intended to cover unauthorized use of information. Such use is not at issue here. Rather, under § 1030(a)(4), Nosal is charged with unauthorized access—getting into the computer after categorically being barred from entry.

The text of the CFAA confirms *Brekka*'s approach. Employing classic statutory interpretation, we consider the plain and ordinary meaning of the words "without authorization." Under our analysis in *Brekka*, "authorization" means

---

23 Brekka's authorization terminated when his employment terminated, not because his password expired. Expired passwords do not necessarily mean that authorization terminates: authorized account-holders often let their passwords lapse before updating the password or contacting the company's technical support team for help, but expiration of a password doesn't necessarily mean that account authorization has terminated.

"'permission or power granted by an authority.'" Other sources employ similar definitions. Black's Law Dictionary defines "authorization" as "[o]fficial permission to do something; sanction or warrant." The Oxford English Dictionary defines it as "the action of authorizing," which means to "give official permission for or approval to." That common sense meaning is not foreign to Congress or the courts: the terms "authorize," "authorized" or "authorization" are used without definition over 400 times in Title 18 of the United States Code. We conclude that given its ordinary meaning, access "without authorization" under the CFAA is not ambiguous.

That straightforward meaning is also unambiguous as applied to the facts of this case. Nosal and his co-conspirators did exactly what *Brekka* prohibits—a conclusion that is not affected by the co-conspirators' use of FH's legitimate access credentials. Implicit in the definition of authorization is the notion that someone, including an entity, can grant or revoke that permission. Here, that entity was Korn/Ferry, and FH had no mantle or authority to override Korn/Ferry's authority to control access to its computers and confidential information by giving permission to former employees whose access had been categorically revoked by the company.[24] Korn/Ferry owned and controlled access to its computers, including the Searcher database, and it retained exclusive discretion to issue or revoke access to the database. By revoking Nosal's login credentials on December 8, 2004, Korn/Ferry unequivocally conveyed to Nosal that he was an "outsider" who was no longer authorized to access Korn/Ferry computers and confidential information, including Searcher.[25] Korn/Ferry also rescinded Christian and Jacobson's credentials after they left, at which point the three former employees were no longer "insiders" accessing company information. Rather, they had become "outsiders" with no authorization to access Korn/Ferry's computer system. One can certainly pose hypotheticals in which a less stark revocation is followed by more sympathetic access through an authorized third party. But the facts before us—in which Nosal received particularized notice of his revoked access following a prolonged negotiation—present no such difficulties, which can be reserved for another day.

Our analysis is consistent with that of our sister circuits, which have also determined that the term "without authorization" is unambiguous. Although

---

24 The dissent rests its argument on the fact that Brekka had "no possible source of authorization." The same is true here—Nosal had "no possible source of authorization" since the company revoked his authorization and, while FH might have been wrangled into giving out her password, she and the others knew that she had no authority to control system access.

25 Nosal argues that he cannot be held liable because, as a contractor, he was entitled to access information from Korn/Ferry's database. Nosal misconstrues his authorization following his departure from Korn/Ferry: he was entitled only to information related to his open searches, and being entitled to receive information does not equate to permission to access the database. Further, Nosal's liability as a co-conspirator turns on whether Christian and Jacobson acted "without authorization."

the meaning of "exceeds authorized access" in the CFAA has been subject to much debate among the federal courts, the definition of "without authorization" has not engendered dispute. Indeed, Nosal provides no contrary authority that a former employee whose computer access has been revoked can access his former employer's computer system and be deemed to act with authorization. . . .

In the face of multiple circuits that agree with our plain meaning construction of the statute, the dissent would have us ignore common sense and turn the statute inside out. Indeed, the dissent frames the question upside down in assuming that permission from FH is at issue. Under this approach, ignoring reality and practice, an employee could undermine the company's ability to control access to its own computers by willy nilly giving out passwords to anyone outside the company—former employees whose access had been revoked, competitors, industrious hackers or bank robbers who find it less risky and more convenient to access accounts via the Internet rather than through armed robbery.

Our conclusion does nothing to expand the scope of violations under the CFAA beyond *Brekka*; nor does it rest on the grace of prosecutorial discretion. We are mindful of the examples noted in *Nosal I*—and reiterated by Nosal and various amici—that ill-defined terms may capture arguably innocuous conduct, such as password sharing among friends and family, inadvertently "mak[ing] criminals of large groups of people who would have little reason to suspect they are committing a federal crime." *Nosal I*, 676 F.3d at 859. But these concerns are ill-founded because § 1030(a)(4) requires access be "knowingly and with intent to defraud" and further, we have held that violating use restrictions, like a website's terms of use, is insufficient without more to form the basis for liability under the CFAA. The circumstance here—former employees whose computer access was categorically revoked and who surreptitiously accessed data owned by their former employer—bears little resemblance to asking a spouse to log in to an email account to print a boarding pass. The charges at issue in this appeal do not stem from the ambiguous language of *Nosal I*—"exceeds authorized access"—or even an ambiguous application of the phrase "without authorization," but instead relate to the straightforward application of a common, unambiguous term to the facts and context at issue.

The *Brekka* analysis of the specific phrase "without authorization"—which is consistent with our sister circuits—remains controlling and persuasive. We therefore hold that Nosal, a former employee whose computer access credentials were affirmatively revoked by Korn/Ferry acted "without authorization" in violation of the CFAA when he or his former employee co-conspirators used the login credentials of a current employee to gain access to confidential computer data owned by the former employer and to circumvent Korn/Ferry's revocation of access.

C. Jury Instruction on "Without Authorization"

With respect to the meaning of "without authorization," the district court instructed the jury as follows:

> Whether a person is authorized to access the computers in this case depends on the actions taken by Korn/Ferry to grant or deny permission to that person to use the computer. A person uses a computer "without authorization" when the person has not received permission from Korn/Ferry to use the computer for any purpose (such as when a hacker accesses the computer without any permission), or when Korn/Ferry has rescinded permission to use the computer and the person uses the computer anyway.

The instruction is derived directly from our decision in *Brekka* and is a fair and accurate characterization of the plain meaning of "without authorization." Although the term "without authorization" is unambiguous, it does not mean that the facts don't matter; the source and scope of authorization may well be at issue. Here, it was not disputed that Korn/Ferry was the source of permission to grant authorization. The jury instruction left to the jury to determine whether such permission was given.

Nosal challenges the instruction on the basis that the CFAA only criminalizes access where the party circumvents a technological access barrier. Not only is such a requirement missing from the statutory language, but it would make little sense because some § 1030 offenses do not require access to a computer at all. For example, § (a)(6) imposes penalties for trafficking in passwords "through which a computer can be accessed without authorization . . . ."

In any event, Nosal's argument misses the mark on the technological access point. Even if he were correct, any instructional error was without consequence in light of the evidence. The password system adopted by Korn/Ferry is unquestionably a technological barrier designed to keep out those "without authorization." Had a thief stolen an employee's password and then used it to rifle through Searcher, without doubt, access would have been without authorization.

The same principle holds true here. A password requirement is designed to be a technological access barrier. . . .

Dissent by Stephen Reinhardt, Circuit Judge:

This case is about password sharing. People frequently share their passwords, notwithstanding the fact that websites and employers have policies prohibiting it. In my view, the Computer Fraud and Abuse Act ("CFAA") does not make the millions of people who engage in this ubiquitous, useful, and generally harmless conduct into unwitting federal criminals. Whatever other liability, criminal or civil, Nosal may have incurred in his improper attempt to compete with his former employer, he has not violated the CFAA.

The first time this case came before us we examined whether Nosal's former colleagues acted "without authorization, or exceed[ed] authorized access" when they downloaded information from Searcher while still employed at Korn/Ferry and shared it with Nosal in violation of the firm's policies. We said "no," rejecting the approach of a few other circuits which had interpreted the CFAA looking "only at the culpable behavior of the defendants before them, and fail[ing] to consider the effect on millions of ordinary citizens." In doing so, we stated that they turned the CFAA into a "sweeping Internet-policing mandate," instead of maintaining its "focus on hacking." We emphatically refused to turn violations of use restrictions imposed by employers or websites into crimes under the CFAA, declining to put so many citizens "at the mercy of [their] local prosecutor." Since then, both circuits to rule on the point have agreed with our interpretation. See *United States v. Valle*, 807 F.3d 508, 526-28 (2d Cir. 2015); *WEC Carolina Energy Sols. LLC v. Miller*, 687 F.3d 199, 204 (4th Cir. 2012).

Today, addressing only slightly different conduct, the majority repudiates important parts of *Nosal I*, jeopardizing most password sharing. It loses sight of the anti-hacking purpose of the CFAA, and despite our warning, threatens to criminalize all sorts of innocuous conduct engaged in daily by ordinary citizens.

At issue are three incidents of password sharing. On these occasions while FH was still employed at Korn/Ferry, she gave her password to Jacobson or Christian, who had left the company. Her former colleagues then used her password to download information from Searcher. FH was authorized to access Searcher, but she did not download the information herself because it was easier to let Jacobson or Christian do it than to have them explain to her how to find it. It would not have been a violation of the CFAA if they had simply given FH step-by-step directions, which she then followed. Thus the question is whether because Jacobson and Christian instead used FH's password with her permission, they are criminally liable for access "without authorization" under the Act.[26]

The majority finds the answer is "yes," but in doing so commits the same error as the circuits whose views we rejected in *Nosal I*. My colleagues claim that they do not have to address the effect of their decision on the wider population because Nosal's infelicitous conduct "bears little resemblance" to everyday password sharing. Notably this is the exact argument the dissent made in *Nosal I*: "This case has nothing to do with playing sudoku, checking email, [or] fibbing on dating sites. . . . The role of the courts is neither to issue advisory opinions nor to declare rights in hypothetical cases."

---

26 Nosal was charged as criminally culpable for Jacobson's and Christian's alleged violations under a theory of either aiding and abetting or conspiracy.

We, of course, rejected the dissent's argument in *Nosal I*. We did so because we recognized that the government's theory made all violations of use restrictions criminal under the CFAA, whether the violation was innocuous, like checking your personal email at work, or more objectionable like that at issue here. Because the statute was susceptible to a narrower interpretation, we rejected the government's broader reading under which "millions of unsuspecting individuals would find that they are engaging in criminal conduct." The same is true here. The majority does not provide, nor do I see, a workable line which separates the consensual password sharing in this case from the consensual password sharing of millions of legitimate account holders, which may also be contrary to the policies of system owners. There simply is no limiting principle in the majority's world of lawful and unlawful password sharing.

Therefore, despite the majority's attempt to construe *Nosal I* as only applicable to "exceeds authorized access," the case's central lesson that the CFAA should not be interpreted to criminalize the ordinary conduct of millions of citizens applies equally strongly here. Accordingly, I would hold that consensual password sharing is not the kind of "hacking" covered by the CFAA. That is the case whether or not the voluntary password sharing is with a former employee and whether or not the former employee's own password had expired or been terminated. . . .

"There is no doubt that this case is distasteful; it may be far worse than that." *McDonnell v. United States*, 136 S. Ct. 2355 (2016). As the Supreme Court said in *McDonnell*, "our concern is not with tawdry tales of Ferraris, Rolexes, and ball gowns. It is instead with the broader legal implications of the Government's boundless interpretation" of a federal statute. Here, our concern is not with tawdry tales of corporate thievery and executive searches gone wrong. "It is instead with the broader legal implications of the Government's boundless interpretation" of the CFAA. Nosal may have incurred substantial civil liability, and may even be subject to criminal prosecution, but I do not believe he has violated the CFAA, properly construed. I respectfully dissent.

International Airport Centers v. Citrin, 440 F.3d 418 (7th Cir. 2006)

As discussed in Chapter 5, Section (a)(5) of the CFAA applies to three different acts that cause damage to a computer. In 2006, Judge Posner succinctly explained the differences between these CFAA prongs. Note that the case was decided before amendments to the CFAA that changed the wording and section numbering of some of the relevant CFAA provisions.

March 8, 2006

Opinion by Richard Posner, Circuit Judge:

This appeal from the dismissal of the plaintiffs' suit for failure to state a claim mainly requires us to interpret the word "transmission" in a key provision of the Computer Fraud and Abuse Act, 18 U.S.C. § 1030. The complaint alleges the following facts, which for purposes of deciding the appeal we must take as true. The defendant, Citrin, was employed by the plaintiffs—affiliated companies engaged in the real estate business that we'll treat as one to simplify the opinion, and call "IAC"—to identify properties that IAC might want to acquire, and to assist in any ensuing acquisition. IAC lent Citrin a laptop to use to record data that he collected in the course of his work in identifying potential acquisition targets.

Citrin decided to quit IAC and go into business for himself, in breach of his employment contract. Before returning the laptop to IAC, he deleted all the data in it—not only the data that he had collected but also data that would have revealed to IAC improper conduct in which he had engaged before he decided to quit. Ordinarily, pressing the "delete" key on a computer (or using a mouse click to delete) does not affect the data sought to be deleted; it merely removes the index entry and pointers to the data file so that the file appears no longer to be there, and the space allocated to that file is made available for future write commands. Such "deleted" files are easily recoverable. But Citrin loaded into the laptop a secure-erasure program, designed, by writing over the deleted files, to prevent their recovery. . . . IAC had no copies of the files that Citrin erased.

The provision of the Computer Fraud and Abuse Act on which IAC relies provides that whoever "knowingly causes the transmission of a program, information, code, or command, and as a result of such conduct, intentionally causes damage without authorization, to a protected computer [a defined term that includes the laptop that Citrin used]," violates the Act. 18 U.S.C. § 1030(a)(5)(A) (i). Citrin argues that merely erasing a file from a computer is not a "transmission." Pressing a delete or erase key in fact transmits a command, but it might be stretching the statute too far (especially since it provides criminal as well as civil sanctions for its violation) to consider any typing on a computer keyboard to be a form of "transmission" just because it transmits a command to the computer.

There is more here, however: the transmission of the secure-erasure program to the computer. We do not know whether the program was downloaded from the Internet or copied from a floppy disk (or the equivalent of a floppy disk, such as a CD) inserted into a disk drive that was either inside the computer or attached to it by a wire. Oddly, the complaint doesn't say; maybe IAC doesn't know—maybe all it knows is that when it got the computer back, the files in it had been erased. But we don't see what difference the precise mode of transmission can make. In either the Internet download or the disk insertion, a program intended to cause damage (not to the physical computer, of course, but to its files—but "damage" includes "any impairment to the integrity or availability of data, a program, a system, or information," 18 U.S.C. § 1030(e)(8)) is transmitted to the computer electronically. The only difference, so far as the mechanics of transmission are concerned, is that the disk is inserted manually before the program on it is transmitted electronically to the computer. The difference vanishes if the disk drive into which the disk is inserted is an external drive, connected to the computer by a wire, just as the computer is connected to the Internet by a telephone cable or a broadband cable or wirelessly.

There is the following contextual difference between the two modes of transmission, however: transmission via disk requires that the malefactor have physical access to the computer. By using the Internet, Citrin might have erased the laptop's files from afar by transmitting a virus. Such long-distance attacks can be more difficult to detect and thus to deter or punish than ones that can have been made only by someone with physical access, usually an employee. The inside attack, however, while easier to detect may also be easier to accomplish. Congress was concerned with both types of attack: attacks by virus and worm writers, on the one hand, which come mainly from the outside, and attacks by disgruntled programmers who decide to trash the employer's data system on the way out (or threaten to do so in order to extort payments), on the other. If the statute is to reach the disgruntled programmer, which Congress intended by providing that whoever "intentionally accesses a protected computer without authorization, and as a result of such conduct, recklessly causes damage" violates the Act, 18 U.S.C. § 1030(a)(5)(A)(ii), it can't make any difference that the destructive program comes on a physical medium, such as a floppy disk or CD.

Citrin violated that subsection too. For his authorization to access the laptop terminated when, having already engaged in misconduct and decided to quit IAC in violation of his employment contract, he resolved to destroy files that incriminated himself and other files that were also the property of his employer, in violation of the duty of loyalty that agency law imposes on an employee. . . .

Muddying the picture some, the Computer Fraud and Abuse Act distinguishes between "without authorization" and "exceeding authorized access," 18 U.S.C. §§ 1030(a)(1), (2), (4), and, while making both punishable, defines the latter as "access[ing] a computer with authorization and . . . us[ing] such access to obtain or alter information in the computer that the accesser is not entitled so to obtain or alter." § 1030(e)(6). That might seem the more apt description of what Citrin did.

The difference between "without authorization" and "exceeding authorized access" is paper thin, but not quite invisible. In *EF Cultural Travel BV v. Explorica, Inc.*, 274 F.3d 577, 583-84 (1st Cir. 2001), for example, the former employee of a travel agent, in violation of his confidentiality agreement with his former employer, used confidential information that he had obtained as an employee to create a program that enabled his new travel company to obtain information from his former employer's website that he could not have obtained as efficiently without the use of that confidential information. The website was open to the public, so he was authorized to use it, but he exceeded his authorization by using confidential information to obtain better access than other members of the public.

Our case is different. Citrin's breach of his duty of loyalty terminated his agency relationship (more precisely, terminated any rights he might have claimed as IAC's agent—he could not by unilaterally terminating any duties he owed his principal gain an advantage!) and with it his authority to access the laptop, because the only basis of his authority had been that relationship. "Violating the duty of loyalty, or failing to disclose adverse interests, voids the agency relationship." *State v. DiGiulio*, 172 Ariz. 156 (App.1992). "Unless otherwise agreed, the authority of the agent terminates if, without knowledge of the principal, he acquires adverse interests or if he is otherwise guilty of a serious breach of loyalty to the principal." . . .

Citrin points out that his employment contract authorized him to "return or destroy" data in the laptop when he ceased being employed by IAC. But it is unlikely, to say the least, that the provision was intended to authorize him to destroy data that he knew the company had no duplicates of and would have wanted to have—if only to nail Citrin for misconduct. The purpose of the provision may have been to avoid overloading the company with returned data of no further value, which the employee should simply have deleted. More likely the purpose was simply to remind Citrin that he was not to disseminate confidential data after he left the company's employ—the provision authorizing him to return or destroy data in the laptop was limited to "Confidential" information. There may be a dispute over whether the incriminating files that Citrin destroyed contained "confidential" data, but that issue cannot be resolved on this appeal.

The judgment is reversed with directions to reinstate the suit, including the supplemental claims that the judge dismissed because he was dismissing IAC's federal claim.

Katz v. United States, 389 U.S. 347 (1967)

Although not a cybersecurity-related opinion, as it was issued in 1967, this Supreme Court opinion would set the framework for all later Fourth Amendment cases involving government surveillance. The opinion—and, in particular, Justice Harlan's concurrence—shaped the "reasonable expectation of privacy" analysis on which much of the first part of Chapter 7 is based.

December 18, 1967

Majority Opinion by Justice Potter Stewart:

The petitioner was convicted in the District Court for the Southern District of California under an eight-count indictment charging him with transmitting wagering information by telephone from Los Angeles to Miami and Boston, in violation of a federal statute. At trial the Government was permitted, over the petitioner's objection, to introduce evidence of the petitioner's end of telephone conversations, overheard by FBI agents who had attached an electronic listening and recording device to the outside of the public telephone booth from which he had placed his calls. In affirming his conviction, the Court of Appeals rejected the contention that the recordings had been obtained in violation of the Fourth Amendment, because "[t]here was no physical entrance into the area occupied by [the petitioner]." We granted certiorari in order to consider the constitutional questions thus presented.

The petitioner has phrased those questions as follows:

> A. Whether a public telephone booth is a constitutionally protected area so that evidence obtained by attaching an electronic listening recording device to the top of such a booth is obtained in violation of the right to privacy of the user of the booth.
> B. Whether physical penetration of a constitutionally protected area is necessary before a search and seizure can be said to be violative of the Fourth Amendment to the United States Constitution.

We decline to adopt this formulation of the issues. In the first place, the correct solution of Fourth Amendment problems is not necessarily promoted by incantation of the phrase "constitutionally protected area." Secondly, the Fourth Amendment cannot be translated into a general constitutional "right to privacy." That Amendment protects individual privacy against certain kinds of governmental intrusion, but its protections go further, and often have nothing to do with privacy at all. Other provisions of the Constitution protect personal privacy from other forms of governmental invasion. But the protection of a person's general right to privacy— his right to be let alone by other people—is, like the protection of his property and of his very life, left largely to the law of the individual States.

Because of the misleading way the issues have been formulated, the parties have attached great significance to the characterization of the telephone booth from which the petitioner placed his calls. The petitioner has strenuously argued that the booth was a "constitutionally protected area." The Government has maintained with equal vigor that it was not. But this effort to decide whether or not a given "area," viewed in the abstract, is "constitutionally protected" deflects attention from the problem presented by this case. For the Fourth Amendment protects people, not places. What a person knowingly exposes to the public, even in his own home or office, is not a subject of Fourth Amendment protection. But what he seeks to preserve as private, even in an area accessible to the public, may be constitutionally protected.

The Government stresses the fact that the telephone booth from which the petitioner made his calls was constructed partly of glass, so that he was as visible after he entered it as he would have been if he had remained outside. But what he sought to exclude when he entered the booth was not the intruding eye—it was the uninvited ear. He did not shed his right to do so simply because he made his calls from a place where he might be seen. No less than an individual in a business office, in a friend's apartment, or in a taxicab, a person in a telephone booth may rely upon the protection of the Fourth Amendment. One who occupies it, shuts the door behind him, and pays the toll that permits him to place a call is surely entitled to assume that the words he utters into the mouthpiece will not be broadcast to the world. To read the Constitution more narrowly is to ignore the vital role that the public telephone has come to play in private communication.

The Government contends, however, that the activities of its agents in this case should not be tested by Fourth Amendment requirements, for the surveillance technique they employed involved no physical penetration of the telephone booth from which the petitioner placed his calls. It is true that the absence of such penetration was at one time thought to foreclose further Fourth Amendment inquiry, *Olmstead v. United States*, 277 U.S. 438, 457, 464, 466; *Goldman v. United States*, 316 U.S. 129, 134-136, for that Amendment was thought to limit only searches and seizures of tangible property. But "[t]he premise that property interests control the right of the Government to search and seize has been discredited." *Warden v. Hayden*, 387 U.S. 294, 304. Thus, although a closely divided Court supposed in *Olmstead* that surveillance without any trespass and without the seizure of any material object fell outside the ambit of the Constitution, we have since departed from the narrow view on which that decision rested. Indeed, we have expressly held that the Fourth Amendment governs not only the seizure of tangible items, but extends as well to the recording of oral statements, over-heard without any "technical trespass under . . . local property law." *Silverman v. United States*, 365 U.S. 505, 511. Once this much is acknowledged, and once it is recognized that the Fourth Amendment protects people— and not simply "areas"—against unreasonable searches and seizures, it becomes clear that the reach of that Amendment cannot turn upon the presence or absence of a physical intrusion into any given enclosure.

We conclude that the underpinnings of *Olmstead* and *Goldman* have been so eroded by our subsequent decisions that the "trespass" doctrine there enunciated can no longer be regarded as controlling. The Government's activities in electronically listening to and recording the petitioner's words violated the privacy upon which he justifiably relied while using the telephone booth and thus constituted a "search and seizure" within the meaning of the Fourth Amendment. The fact that the electronic device employed to achieve that end did not happen to penetrate the wall of the booth can have no constitutional significance.

The question remaining for decision, then, is whether the search and seizure conducted in this case complied with constitutional standards. In that regard, the Government's position is that its agents acted in an entirely defensible manner: They did not begin their electronic surveillance until investigation of the petitioner's activities had established a strong probability that he was using the telephone in question to transmit gambling information to persons in other States, in violation of federal law. Moreover, the surveillance was limited, both in scope and in duration, to the specific purpose of establishing the contents of the petitioner's unlawful telephonic communications. The agents confined their surveillance to the brief periods during which he used the telephone booth, and they took great care to overhear only the conversations of the petitioner himself.

Accepting this account of the Government's actions as accurate, it is clear that this surveillance was so narrowly circumscribed that a duly authorized magistrate, properly notified of the need for such investigation, specifically informed of the basis on which it was to proceed, and clearly apprised of the precise intrusion it would entail, could constitutionally have authorized, with appropriate safeguards, the very limited search and seizure that the Government asserts in fact took place. Only last Term we sustained the validity of such an authorization, holding that, under sufficiently "precise and discriminate circumstances," a federal court may empower government agents to employ a concealed electronic device "for the narrow and particularized purpose of ascertaining the truth of the . . . allegations" of a "detailed factual affidavit alleging the commission of a specific criminal offense." *Osborn v. United States*, 385 U.S. 323, 329-330. Discussing that holding, the Court in *Berger v. New York*, 388 U.S. 41, said that "the order authorizing the use of the electronic device" in *Osborn* "afforded similar protections to those . . . of conventional warrants authorizing the seizure of tangible evidence." Through those protections, "no greater invasion of privacy was permitted than was necessary under the circumstances." Here, too, a similar judicial order could have accommodated "the legitimate needs of law enforcement" by authorizing the carefully limited use of electronic surveillance.

The Government urges that, because its agents relied upon the decisions in *Olmstead* and *Goldman*, and because they did no more here than they might properly have done with prior judicial sanction, we should retroactively validate their conduct. That we cannot do. It is apparent that the agents in this case acted with restraint. Yet the inescapable fact is that this restraint was imposed by the agents themselves, not by a judicial officer. They were not required, before commencing the search, to present their estimate of probable cause for detached scrutiny by a neutral magistrate. They were not compelled, during the conduct of the search itself, to observe precise limits established in advance by a specific court order. Nor were they directed, after the search had been completed, to notify the authorizing magistrate in detail of all that had been seized. In the absence of such safeguards, this Court has never sustained a search upon the sole ground that officers reasonably expected to find evidence of a particular crime and voluntarily confined their activities to the least intrusive means consistent with that end. Searches conducted without warrants have been held unlawful "notwithstanding facts unquestionably showing probable cause," *Agnello v. United States*, 269 U.S. 20, 33, for the Constitution requires "that the deliberate, impartial judgment of a judicial officer . . . be interposed between the citizen and the police . . . ." *Wong Sun v. United States*, 371 U.S. 471, 481-482. . . .

It is difficult to imagine how any of those exceptions could ever apply to the sort of search and seizure involved in this case. Even electronic surveillance substantially contemporaneous with an individual's arrest could hardly be deemed an "incident" of that arrest. Nor could the use of electronic surveillance without prior authorization be justified on grounds of "hot pursuit." And, of course, the very nature of electronic surveillance precludes its use pursuant to the suspect's consent.

The Government does not question these basic principles. Rather, it urges the creation of a new exception to cover this case.[27] It argues that surveillance of a telephone booth should be exempted from the usual requirement of advance authorization by a magistrate upon a showing of probable cause. We cannot agree. Omission of such authorization

> bypasses the safeguards provided by an objective predetermination of probable cause, and substitutes instead the far less reliable procedure of an after-the-event justification for the . . . search, too likely to be subtly influenced by the familiar shortcomings of hindsight judgment.

Beck v. Ohio, 379 U.S. 89, 96. And bypassing a neutral predetermination of the scope of a search leaves individuals secure from Fourth Amendment violations "only in the discretion of the police."

These considerations do not vanish when the search in question is transferred from the setting of a home, an office, or a hotel room to that of a telephone booth. Wherever a man may be, he is entitled to know that he will remain free from unreasonable searches and seizures. The government agents here ignored "the procedure of antecedent justification . . . that is central to the Fourth Amendment," a procedure that we hold to be a constitutional precondition of the kind of electronic surveillance involved in this case. Because the surveillance here failed to meet that condition, and because it led to the petitioner's conviction, the judgment must be reversed.

It is so ordered.

Concurring Opinion by Justice William O. Douglas:

---

27 Whether safeguards other than prior authorization by a magistrate would satisfy the Fourth Amendment in a situation involving the national security is a question not presented by this case.

While I join the opinion of the Court, I feel compelled to reply to the separate concurring opinion of my Brother White, which I view as a wholly unwarranted green light for the Executive Branch to resort to electronic eavesdropping without a warrant in cases which the Executive Branch itself labels "national security" matters.

Neither the President nor the Attorney General is a magistrate. In matters where they believe national security may be involved they are not detached, disinterested, and neutral as a court or magistrate must be. Under the separation of powers created by the Constitution, the Executive Branch is not supposed to be neutral and disinterested. Rather it should vigorously investigate and prevent breaches of national security and prosecute those who violate the pertinent federal laws. The President and Attorney General are properly interested parties, cast in the role of adversary, in national security cases. They may even be the intended victims of subversive action. Since spies and saboteurs are as entitled to the protection of the Fourth Amendment as suspected gamblers like petitioner, I cannot agree that where spies and saboteurs are involved adequate protection of Fourth Amendment rights is assured when the President and Attorney General assume both the position of adversary-and-prosecutor and disinterested, neutral magistrate.

There is, so far as I understand constitutional history, no distinction under the Fourth Amendment between types of crimes. Article III, § 3, gives "treason" a very narrow definition and puts restrictions on its proof. But the Fourth Amendment draws no lines between various substantive offenses. The arrests in cases of "hot pursuit" and the arrests on visible or other evidence of probable cause cut across the board and are not peculiar to any kind of crime.

I would respect the present lines of distinction and not improvise because a particular crime seems particularly heinous. When the Framers took that step, as they did with treason, the worst crime of all, they made their purpose manifest.

Concurring Opinion by Justice John Marshall Harlan:

I join the opinion of the Court, which I read to hold only (a) that an enclosed telephone booth is an area where, like a home, *Weeks v. United States*, 232 U.S. 383, and unlike a field, *Hester v. United States*, 265 U.S. 57, a person has a constitutionally protected reasonable expectation of privacy; (b) that electronic as well as physical intrusion into a place that is in this sense private may constitute a violation of the Fourth Amendment; and (c) that the invasion of a constitutionally protected area by federal authorities is, as the Court has long held, presumptively unreasonable in the absence of a search warrant.

As the Court's opinion states, "the Fourth Amendment protects people, not places." The question, however, is what protection it affords to those people. Generally, as here, the answer to that question requires reference to a "place." My understanding of the rule that has emerged from prior decisions is that there is a twofold requirement, first that a person have exhibited an actual (subjective) expectation of privacy and, second, that the expectation be one that society is prepared to recognize as "reasonable." Thus a man's home is, for most purposes, a place where he expects privacy, but objects, activities, or statements that he exposes to the "plain view" of outsiders are not "protected" because no intention to keep them to himself has been exhibited. On the other hand, conversations in the open would not be protected against being overheard, for the expectation of privacy under the circumstances would be unreasonable.

The critical fact in this case is that "[o]ne who occupies it, [a telephone booth] shuts the door behind him, and pays the toll that permits him to place a call is surely entitled to assume" that his conversation is not being intercepted. The point is not that the booth is "accessible to the public" at other times, but that it is a temporarily private place whose momentary occupants' expectations of freedom from intrusion are recognized as reasonable.

In *Silverman v. United States*, 365 U.S. 505, we held that eavesdropping accomplished by means of an electronic device that penetrated the premises occupied by petitioner was a violation of the Fourth Amendment. That case established that interception of conversations reasonably intended to be private could constitute a "search and seizure," and that the examination or taking of physical property was not required. This view of the Fourth Amendment was followed in *Wong Sun v. United States*, 371 U.S. 471, at 485, and *Berger v. New York*, 388 U.S. 41, at 51. In *Silverman* we found it unnecessary to re-examine *Goldman v. United States*, 316 U.S. 129, which had held that electronic surveillance accomplished without the physical penetration of petitioner's premises by a tangible object did not violate the Fourth Amendment. This case requires us to reconsider *Goldman*, and I agree that it should now be overruled. Its limitation on Fourth Amendment protection is, in the present day, bad physics as well as bad law, for reasonable expectations of privacy may be defeated by electronic as well as physical invasion.

Finally, I do not read the Court's opinion to declare that no interception of a conversation one-half of which occurs in a public telephone booth can be reasonable in the absence of a warrant. As elsewhere under the Fourth Amendment, warrants are the general rule, to which the legitimate needs of law enforcement may demand specific exceptions. It will be time enough to consider any such exceptions when an appropriate occasion presents itself, and I agree with the Court that this is not one.

Concurring Opinion by Justice Byron White:

I agree that the official surveillance of petitioner's telephone conversations in a public booth must be subjected to the test of reasonableness under the Fourth Amendment and that on the record now before us the particular surveillance undertaken was unreasonable absent a warrant properly authorizing it. This application of the Fourth Amendment need not interfere with legitimate needs of law enforcement.

In joining the Court's opinion, I note the Court's acknowledgment that there are circumstances in which it is reasonable to search without a warrant. In this connection, in footnote 23 the Court points out that today's decision does not reach national security cases. Wiretapping to protect the security of the Nation has been authorized by successive Presidents. The present Administration would apparently save national security cases from restrictions against wiretapping. We should not require the warrant procedure and the magistrate's judgment if the President of the United States or his chief legal officer, the Attorney General, has considered the requirements of national security and authorized electronic surveillance as reasonable.

Dissent by Justice Hugo Black:

If I could agree with the Court that eavesdropping carried on by electronic means (equivalent to wiretapping) constitutes a "search" or "seizure," I would be happy to join the Court's opinion. For on that premise my Brother Stewart sets out methods in accord with the Fourth Amendment to guide States in the enactment and enforcement of laws passed to regulate wiretapping by government. In this respect today's opinion differs sharply from *Berger v. New York*, 388 U.S. 41, decided last Term, which held void on its face a New York statute authorizing wiretapping on warrants issued by magistrates on showings of probable cause. The *Berger* case also set up what appeared to be insuperable obstacles to the valid passage of such wiretapping laws by States. The Court's opinion in this case, however, removes the doubts about state power in this field and abates to a large extent the confusion and near-paralyzing effect of the *Berger* holding. Notwithstanding these good efforts of the Court, I am still unable to agree with its interpretation of the Fourth Amendment.

My basic objection is twofold: (1) I do not believe that the words of the Amendment will bear the meaning given them by today's decision, and (2) I do not believe that it is the proper role of this Court to rewrite the Amendment in order "to bring it into harmony with the times" and thus reach a result that many people believe to be desirable.

While I realize that an argument based on the meaning of words lacks the scope, and no doubt the appeal, of broad policy discussions and philosophical discourses on such nebulous subjects as privacy, for me the language of the Amendment is the crucial place to look in construing a written document such as our Constitution. The Fourth Amendment says that

> The right of the people to be secure in their persons, houses, papers, and effects, against unreasonable searches and seizures, shall not be violated, and no Warrants shall issue, but upon probable cause, supported by Oath or affirmation, and particularly describing the place to be searched, and the persons or things to be seized.

The first clause protects "persons, houses, papers, and effects, against unreasonable searches and seizures . . . ." These words connote the idea of tangible things with size, form, and weight, things capable of being searched, seized, or both. The second clause of the Amendment still further establishes its Framers' purpose to limit its protection to tangible things by providing that no warrants shall issue but those "particularly describing the place to be searched, and the persons or things to be seized." A conversation overheard by eavesdropping, whether by plain snooping or wiretapping, is not tangible and, under the normally accepted meanings of the words, can neither be searched nor seized. In addition the language of the second clause indicates that the Amendment refers not only to something tangible so it can be seized but to something already in existence so it can be described. Yet the Court's interpretation would have the Amendment apply to overhearing future conversations which by their very nature are nonexistent until they take place. How can one "describe" a future conversation, and, if one cannot, how can a magistrate issue a warrant to eavesdrop one in the future? It is argued that information showing what is expected to be said is sufficient to limit the boundaries of what later can be admitted into evidence; but does such general information really meet the specific language of the Amendment which says "particularly describing"? Rather than using language in a completely artificial way, I must conclude that the Fourth Amendment simply does not apply to eavesdropping.

Tapping telephone wires, of course, was an unknown possibility at the time the Fourth Amendment was adopted. But eavesdropping (and wiretapping is nothing more than eavesdropping by telephone) was, as even the majority opinion in *Berger*, recognized, "an ancient practice which at common law was condemned as a nuisance." In those days the eavesdropper listened by naked ear under the eaves of houses or their windows, or beyond their walls seeking out private discourse. There can be no doubt that the Framers were aware of this practice, and if they had desired to outlaw or restrict the use of evidence obtained by eavesdropping, I believe that they would have used the appropriate language to do so in the Fourth Amendment. They certainly would not have left such a task to the ingenuity of language-stretching judges. No one, it seems to me, can read the debates on the Bill of Rights without reaching the conclusion that its Framers and critics well knew the meaning of the words they used, what they would be understood to mean by others, their scope and their limitations. Under these circumstances it strikes me as a charge against their scholarship, their common sense and their candor to give to the Fourth Amendment's language the eavesdropping meaning the Court imputes to it today.

I do not deny that common sense requires and that this Court often has said that the Bill of Rights' safeguards should be given a liberal construction. This principle, however, does not justify construing the search and seizure amendment as applying to eavesdropping or the "seizure" of conversations. The

Fourth Amendment was aimed directly at the abhorred practice of breaking in, ransacking and searching homes and other buildings and seizing people's personal belongings without warrants issued by magistrates. The Amendment deserves, and this Court has given it, a liberal construction in order to protect against warrantless searches of buildings and seizures of tangible personal effects. But until today this Court has refused to say that eavesdropping comes within the ambit of Fourth Amendment restrictions.

So far I have attempted to state why I think the words of the Fourth Amendment prevent its application to eavesdropping. It is important now to show that this has been the traditional view of the Amendment's scope since its adoption and that the Court's decision in this case, along with its amorphous holding in *Berger* last Term, marks the first real departure from that view.

The first case to reach this Court which actually involved a clear-cut test of the Fourth Amendment's applicability to eavesdropping through a wiretap was, of course, *Olmstead*. In holding that the interception of private telephone conversations by means of wiretapping was not a violation of the Fourth Amendment, this Court, speaking through Mr. Chief Justice Taft, examined the language of the Amendment and found, just as I do now, that the words could not be stretched to encompass overheard conversations:

> The Amendment itself shows that the search is to be of material things—the person, the house, his papers or his effects. The description of the warrant necessary to make the proceeding lawful, is that it must specify the place to be searched and the person or things to be seized. . . .
>
> Justice Bradley in the *Boyd* case and Justice Clark[e] in the *Gouled* case said that the Fifth Amendment and the Fourth Amendment were to be liberally construed to effect the purpose of the framers of the Constitution in the interest of liberty. But that can not justify enlargement of the language employed beyond the possible practical meaning of houses, persons, papers, and effects, or so to apply the words search and seizure as to forbid hearing or sight.

277 U.S. at 464-465.

Goldman v. United States, 316 U.S. 129, is an even clearer example of this Court's traditional refusal to consider eavesdropping as being covered by the Fourth Amendment. There federal agents used a detectaphone, which was placed on the wall of an adjoining room, to listen to the conversation of a defendant carried on in his private office and intended to be confined within the four walls of the room. This Court, referring to *Olmstead*, found no Fourth Amendment violation.

It should be noted that the Court in *Olmstead* based its decision squarely on the fact that wiretapping or eavesdropping does not violate the Fourth Amendment. As shown, *supra,* in the cited quotation from the case, the Court went to great pains to examine the actual language of the Amendment and found that the words used simply could not be stretched to cover eavesdropping. That there was no trespass was not the determinative factor, and indeed the Court in citing *Hester v. United States,* indicated that even where there was a trespass the Fourth Amendment does not automatically apply to evidence obtained by "hearing or sight." The *Olmstead* majority characterized *Hester* as holding "that the testimony of two officers of the law who trespassed on the defendant's land, concealed themselves one hundred yards away from his house and saw him come out and hand a bottle of whiskey to another, was not inadmissible. While there was a trespass, there was no search of person, house, papers or effects." Thus the clear holding of the *Olmstead* and *Goldman* cases, undiluted by any question of trespass, is that eavesdropping, in both its original and modern forms, is not violative of the Fourth Amendment.

While my reading of the *Olmstead* and *Goldman* cases convinces me that they were decided on the basis of the inapplicability of the wording of the Fourth Amendment to eavesdropping, and not on any trespass basis, this is not to say that unauthorized intrusion has not played an important role in search and seizure cases. This Court has adopted an exclusionary rule to bar evidence obtained by means of such intrusions. As I made clear in my dissenting opinion in *Berger v. New York,* I continue to believe that this exclusionary rule, formulated in *Weeks v. United States,* rests on the "supervisory power" of this Court over other federal courts and is not rooted in the Fourth Amendment. This rule has caused the Court to refuse to accept evidence where there has been such an intrusion regardless of whether there has been a search or seizure in violation of the Fourth Amendment. As this Court said in *Lopez v. United States,* "The Court has in the past sustained instances of 'electronic eavesdropping' against constitutional challenge, when devices have been used to enable government agents to overhear conversations which would have been beyond the reach of the human ear. It has been insisted only that the electronic device not be planted by an unlawful physical invasion of a constitutionally protected area." . . .

Since I see no way in which the words of the Fourth Amendment can be construed to apply to eavesdropping, that closes the matter for me. In interpreting the Bill of Rights, I willingly go as far as a liberal construction of the language takes me, but I simply cannot in good conscience give a meaning to words which they have never before been thought to have and which they certainly do not have in common ordinary usage. I will not distort the words of the Amendment in order to "keep the Constitution up to date" or "to bring it into harmony with the times." It was never meant that this Court have such power, which in effect would make us a continuously functioning constitutional convention.

With this decision the Court has completed, I hope, its rewriting of the Fourth Amendment, which started only recently when the Court began referring incessantly to the Fourth Amendment not so much as a law against unreasonable searches and seizures as one to protect an individual's privacy. By clever word juggling the Court finds it plausible to argue that language aimed specifically at searches and seizures of things that can be searched and seized may, to protect privacy, be applied to eavesdropped evidence of conversations that can neither be searched nor seized. Few things happen to an individual that do not affect his privacy in one way or another. Thus, by arbitrarily substituting the Court's language, designed to protect privacy, for the Constitution's language, designed to protect against unreasonable searches and seizures, the Court has made the Fourth Amendment its vehicle for holding all laws violative of the Constitution which offend the Court's broadest concept of privacy. As I said in *Griswold v. Connecticut*, "The Court talks about a constitutional 'right of privacy' as though there is some constitutional provision or provisions forbidding any law ever to be passed which might abridge the 'privacy' of individuals. But there is not." I made clear in that dissent my fear of the dangers involved when this Court uses the "broad, abstract and ambiguous concept" of "privacy" as a "comprehensive substitute for the Fourth Amendment's guarantee against 'unreasonable searches and seizures.'"

The Fourth Amendment protects privacy only to the extent that it prohibits unreasonable searches and seizures of "persons, houses, papers, and effects." No general right is created by the Amendment so as to give this Court the unlimited power to hold unconstitutional everything which affects privacy. Certainly the Framers, well acquainted as they were with the excesses of governmental power, did not intend to grant this Court such omnipotent lawmaking authority as that. The history of governments proves that it is dangerous to freedom to repose such powers in courts.

Smith v. Maryland, 442 U.S. 735 (1979)

The Supreme Court recognized an important exception to the privacy rights protected by its Fourth Amendment rules. The Third Party Doctrine holds that individuals do not have a reasonable expectation of privacy in information that already had been provided to third parties. As third parties such as telecommunications companies and banks increasingly gained access to individuals' information, the Third Party Doctrine would create important questions for cyber surveillance.

June 20, 1979

Majority Opinion by Justice Harry Blackmun:

This case presents the question whether the installation and use of a pen register[28] constitutes a "search" within the meaning of the Fourth Amendment, made applicable to the States through the Fourteenth Amendment. *Mapp v. Ohio.*

On March 5, 1976, in Baltimore, Md., Patricia McDonough was robbed. She gave the police a description of the robber and of a 1975 Monte Carlo automobile she had observed near the scene of the crime. After the robbery, McDonough began receiving threatening and obscene phone calls from a man identifying himself as the robber. On one occasion, the caller asked that she step out on her front porch; she did so, and saw the 1975 Monte Carlo she had earlier described to police moving slowly past her home. On March 16, police spotted a man who met McDonough's description driving a 1975 Monte Carlo in her neighborhood. By tracing the license plate number, police learned that the car was registered in the name of petitioner, Michael Lee Smith.

The next day, the telephone company, at police request, installed a pen register at its central offices to record the numbers dialed from the telephone at petitioner's home. The police did not get a warrant or court order before having the pen register installed. The register revealed that on March 17 a call was placed from petitioner's home to McDonough's phone. On the basis of this and other evidence, the police obtained a warrant to search petitioner's residence. The search revealed that a page in petitioner's phone book was turned down to the name and number of Patricia McDonough; the phone book was seized. Petitioner was arrested, and a six-man lineup was held on March 19. McDonough identified petitioner as the man who had robbed her.

Petitioner was indicted in the Criminal Court of Baltimore for robbery. By pretrial motion, he sought to suppress "all fruits derived from the pen register" on the ground that the police had failed to secure a warrant prior to its installation. The trial court denied the suppression motion, holding that the warrantless installation of the pen register did not violate the Fourth Amendment. Petitioner then waived a jury, and the case was submitted to the court on an agreed statement of facts. The pen register tape (evidencing the fact that a phone call had been made from petitioner's phone to McDonough's phone) and the phone book seized in the search of petitioner's residence were admitted into evidence against him. Petitioner was convicted, and was sentenced to six years. He appealed to the Maryland Court

---

28 "A pen register is a mechanical device that records the numbers dialed on a telephone by monitoring the electrical impulses caused when the dial on the telephone is released. It does not overhear oral communications and does not indicate whether calls are actually completed." *United States v. New York Tel. Co.*, 434 U.S. 159, 161 n. 1 (1977). A pen register is "usually installed at a central telephone facility [and] records on a paper tape all numbers dialed from [the] line" to which it is attached. *United States v. Giordano*, 416 U.S. 505, 549 n. 1 (1974) (opinion concurring in part and dissenting in part).

of Special Appeals, but the Court of Appeals of Maryland issued a writ of certiorari to the intermediate court in advance of its decision in order to consider whether the pen register evidence had been properly admitted at petitioner's trial.

The Court of Appeals affirmed the judgment of conviction, holding that "there is no constitutionally protected reasonable expectation of privacy in the numbers dialed into a telephone system and hence no search within the fourth amendment is implicated by the use of a pen register installed at the central offices of the telephone company." Because there was no "search," the court concluded, no warrant was needed. Three judges dissented, expressing the view that individuals do have a legitimate expectation of privacy regarding the phone numbers they dial from their homes; that the installation of a pen register thus constitutes a "search"; and that, in the absence of exigent circumstances, the failure of police to secure a warrant mandated that the pen register evidence here be excluded. Certiorari was granted in order to resolve indications of conflict in the decided cases as to the restrictions imposed by the Fourth Amendment on the use of pen registers.

II

A

[The Court briefly reviewed the doctrine that it established in *Katz*.]

B

In applying the *Katz* analysis to this case, it is important to begin by specifying precisely the nature of the state activity that is challenged. The activity here took the form of installing and using a pen register. Since the pen register was installed on telephone company property at the telephone company's central offices, petitioner obviously cannot claim that his "property'" was invaded or that police intruded into a "constitutionally protected area." Petitioner's claim, rather, is that, notwithstanding the absence of a trespass, the State, as did the Government in *Katz*, infringed a "legitimate expectation of privacy" that petitioner held. Yet a pen register differs significantly from the listening device employed in *Katz*, for pen registers do not acquire the contents of communications. This Court recently noted:

> Indeed, a law enforcement official could not even determine from the use of a pen register whether a communication existed. These devices do not hear sound. They disclose only the telephone numbers that have been dialed—a means of establishing communication. Neither the purport of any communication between the caller and the recipient of the call, their identities, nor whether the call was even completed is disclosed by pen registers.

United States v. New York Tel. Co., 434 U.S. 159, 167 (1977).

Given a pen register's limited capabilities, therefore, petitioner's argument that its installation and use constituted a "search" necessarily rests upon a claim that he had a "legitimate expectation of privacy" regarding the numbers he dialed on his phone.

This claim must be rejected. First, we doubt that people in general entertain any actual expectation of privacy in the numbers they dial. All telephone users realize that they must "convey" phone numbers to the telephone company, since it is through telephone company switching equipment that their calls are completed. All subscribers realize, moreover, that the phone company has facilities for making permanent records of the numbers they dial, for they see a list of their long-distance (toll) calls on their monthly bills. In fact, pen registers and similar devices are routinely used by telephone companies "for the purposes of checking billing operations, detecting fraud, and preventing violations of law." *United States v. New York Tel. Co.*, 434 U.S., at 174-175. Electronic equipment is used not only to keep billing records of toll calls, but also "to keep a record of all calls dialed from a telephone which is subject to a special rate structure." *Hodge v. Mountain States Tel. & Tel. Co.*, 555 F.2d 254, 266 (9th Cir. 1977) (concurring opinion). Pen registers are regularly employed "to determine whether a home phone is being used to conduct a business, to check for a defective dial, or to check for overbilling." Although most people may be oblivious to a pen register's esoteric functions, they presumably have some awareness of one common use: to aid in the identification of persons making annoying or obscene calls. Most phone books tell subscribers, on a page entitled "Consumer Information," that the company "can frequently help in identifying to the authorities the origin of unwelcome and troublesome calls." Telephone users, in sum, typically know that they must convey numerical information to the phone company; that the phone company has facilities for recording this information; and that the phone company does in fact record this information for a variety of legitimate business purposes. Although subjective expectations cannot be scientifically gauged, it is too much to believe that telephone subscribers, under these circumstances, harbor any general expectation that the numbers they dial will remain secret.

Petitioner argues, however, that, whatever the expectations of telephone users in general, he demonstrated an expectation of privacy by his own conduct here, since he "us[ed] the telephone in his house to the exclusion of all others." But the site of the call is immaterial for purposes of analysis in this case. Although petitioner's conduct may have been calculated to keep the contents of his conversation private, his conduct was not and could not have been calculated to preserve the privacy of the number he dialed. Regardless of his location, petitioner had to convey that number to the telephone company in precisely the same way if he wished to complete his call. The fact that he dialed the number on his home phone rather than on some other phone could make no conceivable difference, nor could any subscriber rationally think that it would.

Second, even if petitioner did harbor some subjective expectation that the phone numbers he dialed would remain private, this expectation is not "one that society is prepared to recognize as 'reasonable.'" *Katz v. United States*, 389 U.S., at 361. This Court consistently has held that a person has no legitimate expectation of privacy in information he voluntarily turns over to third parties. *E.g.*, *United States v. Miller*, 425 U.S., at 442-444. . . . In *Miller*, for example, the Court held that a bank depositor has no "legitimate 'expectation of privacy'" in financial information "voluntarily conveyed to . . . banks and exposed to their employees in the ordinary course of business." 425 U.S., at 442. The Court explained:

> The depositor takes the risk, in revealing his affairs to another, that the information will be conveyed by that person to the Government. . . . This Court has held repeatedly that the Fourth Amendment does not prohibit the obtaining of information revealed to a third party and conveyed by him to Government authorities, even if the information is revealed on the assumption that it will be used only for a limited purpose and the confidence placed in the third party will not be betrayed.

Id., at 443.

Because the depositor "assumed the risk" of disclosure, the Court held that it would be unreasonable for him to expect his financial records to remain private.

This analysis dictates that petitioner can claim no legitimate expectation of privacy here. When he used his phone, petitioner voluntarily conveyed numerical information to the telephone company and "exposed" that information to its equipment in the ordinary course of business. In so doing, petitioner assumed the risk that the company would reveal to police the numbers he dialed. The switching equipment that processed those numbers is merely the modern counterpart of the operator who, in an earlier day, personally completed calls for the subscriber. Petitioner concedes that if he had placed his calls through an operator, he could claim no legitimate expectation of privacy. We are not inclined to hold that a different constitutional result is required because the telephone company has decided to automate.

Petitioner argues, however, that automatic switching equipment differs from a live operator in one pertinent respect. An operator, in theory at least, is capable of remembering every number that is conveyed to him by callers. Electronic equipment, by contrast, can "remember" only those numbers it is programmed to record, and telephone companies, in view of their present billing practices, usually do not record local calls. Since petitioner, in calling McDonough, was making a local call, his expectation of privacy as to her number, on this theory, would be "legitimate."

This argument does not withstand scrutiny. The fortuity of whether or not the phone company in fact elects to make a quasi-permanent record of a particular number dialed does not, in our view, make any constitutional difference. Regardless of the phone company's election, petitioner voluntarily conveyed to it information that it had facilities for recording and that it was free to record. In these circumstances, petitioner assumed the risk that the information would be divulged to police. Under petitioner's theory, Fourth Amendment protection would exist, or not, depending on how the telephone company chose to define local-dialing zones, and depending on how it chose to bill its customers for local calls. Calls placed across town, or dialed directly, would be protected; calls placed across the river, or dialed with operator assistance, might not be. We are not inclined to make a crazy quilt of the Fourth Amendment, especially in circumstances where (as here) the pattern of protection would be dictated by billing practices of a private corporation.

We therefore conclude that petitioner in all probability entertained no actual expectation of privacy in the phone numbers he dialed, and that, even if he did, his expectation was not "legitimate." The installation and use of a pen register, consequently, was not a "search," and no warrant was required.

It is so ordered.

Dissenting Opinion by Justice Potter Stewart:

I am not persuaded that the numbers dialed from a private telephone fall outside the constitutional protection of the Fourth and Fourteenth Amendments.

In *Katz v. United States*, the Court acknowledged the "vital role that the public telephone has come to play in private communication[s]." The role played by a private telephone is even more vital, and since *Katz* it has been abundantly clear that telephone conversations carried on by people in their homes or offices are fully protected by the Fourth and Fourteenth Amendments. As the Court said in *United States v. United States District Court*, "the broad and unsuspected governmental incursions into conversational privacy which electronic surveillance entails necessitate the application of Fourth Amendment safeguards."

Nevertheless, the Court today says that those safeguards do not extend to the numbers dialed from a private telephone, apparently because when a caller dials a number the digits may be recorded by the telephone company for billing purposes. But that observation no more than describes the basic nature of telephone calls. A telephone call simply cannot be made without the use of telephone company property and without payment to the company for the service. The telephone conversation itself must be electronically transmitted by telephone company equipment, and may be recorded or overheard by the use of other company equipment. Yet we have squarely held that the user of even a public telephone is entitled "to assume that the words he utters into the mouthpiece will not be broadcast to the world." *Katz v. United States.*

The central question in this case is whether a person who makes telephone calls from his home is entitled to make a similar assumption about the numbers he dials. What the telephone company does or might do with those numbers is no more relevant to this inquiry than it would be in a case involving the conversation itself. It is simply not enough to say, after *Katz*, that there is no legitimate expectation of privacy in the numbers dialed because the caller assumes the risk that the telephone company will disclose them to the police.

I think that the numbers dialed from a private telephone— like the conversations that occur during a call—are within the constitutional protection recognized in *Katz*. It seems clear to me that information obtained by pen register surveillance of a private telephone is information in which the telephone subscriber has a legitimate expectation of privacy. The information captured by such surveillance emanates from private conduct within a person's home or office—locations that without question are entitled to Fourth and Fourteenth Amendment protection. Further, that information is an integral part of the telephonic communication that under *Katz* is entitled to constitutional protection, whether or not it is captured by a trespass into such an area.

The numbers dialed from a private telephone—although certainly more prosaic than the conversation itself—are not without "content." Most private telephone subscribers may have their own numbers listed in a publicly distributed directory, but I doubt there are any who would be happy to have broadcast to the world a list of the local or long distance numbers they have called. This is not because such a list might in some sense be incriminating, but because it easily could reveal the identities of the persons and the places called, and thus reveal the most intimate details of a person's life.

I respectfully dissent.

Dissenting Opinion by Justice Thurgood Marshall:

The Court concludes that because individuals have no actual or legitimate expectation of privacy in information they voluntarily relinquish to telephone companies, the use of pen registers by government agents is immune from Fourth Amendment scrutiny. Since I remain convinced that constitutional protections are not abrogated whenever a person apprises another of facts valuable in criminal investigations, I respectfully dissent.

Applying the standards set forth in *Katz v. United States* (Harlan, J., concurring), the Court first determines that telephone subscribers have no subjective expectations of privacy concerning the numbers they dial. To reach this conclusion, the Court posits that individuals somehow infer from the long-distance listings on their phone bills, and from the cryptic assurances of "help" in tracing obscene calls included in "most" phone books, that pen registers are regularly used for recording local calls. But even assuming, as I do not, that individuals "typically know" that a phone company monitors calls for internal reasons, it does not follow that they expect this information to be made available to the public in general or the government in particular. Privacy is not a discrete commodity, possessed absolutely or not at all. Those who disclose certain facts to a bank or phone company for a limited business purpose need not assume that this information will be released to other persons for other purposes.

The crux of the Court's holding, however, is that whatever expectation of privacy petitioner may in fact have entertained regarding his calls, it is not one "society is prepared to recognize as 'reasonable.'" In so ruling, the Court determines that individuals who convey information to third parties have "assumed the risk" of disclosure to the government. This analysis is misconceived in two critical respects.

Implicit in the concept of assumption of risk is some notion of choice. At least in the third-party consensual surveillance cases, which first incorporated risk analysis into Fourth Amendment doctrine, the defendant presumably had exercised some discretion in deciding who should enjoy his confidential communications. . . . By contrast here, unless a person is prepared to forgo use of what for many has become a personal or professional necessity, he cannot help but accept the risk of surveillance. It is idle to speak of "assuming" risks in contexts where, as a practical matter, individuals have no realistic alternative.

More fundamentally, to make risk analysis dispositive in assessing the reasonableness of privacy expectations would allow the government to define the scope of Fourth Amendment protections. For example, law enforcement officials, simply by announcing their intent to monitor the content of random samples of first-class mail or private phone conversations, could put the public on notice of the risks they would thereafter assume in such communications. Yet, although acknowledging this implication of its analysis, the Court is willing to concede only that, in some circumstances, a further "normative inquiry would be proper." No meaningful effort is made to explain what those circumstances might be, or why this case is not among them.

In my view, whether privacy expectations are legitimate within the meaning of *Katz* depends not on the risks an individual can be presumed to accept when imparting information to third parties, but on the risks he should be forced to assume in a free and open society. By its terms, the constitutional prohibition of unreasonable searches and seizures assigns to the judiciary some prescriptive responsibility. As Mr. Justice Harlan, who formulated the standard the Court applies today, himself recognized: "[s]ince it is the task of the law to form and project, as well as mirror and reflect, we should not . . . merely recite . . . risks without examining the desirability of saddling them upon society." *United States v. White, supra,* at 786 (dissenting opinion). In making this assessment, courts must evaluate the "intrinsic character" of investigative practices with reference to the basic values underlying the Fourth Amendment. And for those "extensive intrusions that significantly jeopardize [individuals'] sense of security ... , more than self-restraint by law enforcement officials is required." *United States v. White* (Harlan, J., dissenting).

The use of pen registers, I believe, constitutes such an extensive intrusion. To hold otherwise ignores the vital role telephonic communication plays in our personal and professional relationships, as well as the First and Fourth Amendment interests implicated by unfettered official surveillance. Privacy in placing calls is of value not only to those engaged in criminal activity. The prospect of unregulated governmental monitoring will undoubtedly prove disturbing even to those with nothing illicit to hide. Many individuals, including members of unpopular political organizations or journalists with confidential sources, may legitimately wish to avoid disclosure of their personal contacts. Permitting governmental access to telephone records on less than probable cause may thus impede certain forms of political affiliation and journalistic endeavor that are the hallmark of a truly free society. Particularly given the Government's previous reliance on warrantless telephonic surveillance to trace reporters' sources and monitor protected political activity, I am unwilling to insulate use of pen registers from independent judicial review.

Just as one who enters a public telephone booth is "entitled to assume that the words he utters into the mouthpiece will not be broadcast to the world," *Katz v. United States*, so too, he should be entitled to assume that the numbers he dials in the privacy of his home will be recorded, if at all, solely for the phone company's business purposes. Accordingly, I would require law enforcement officials to obtain a warrant before they enlist telephone companies to secure information otherwise beyond the government's reach.

Carpenter v. United States, 138 S. Ct. 2206 (2018)

Chapter 7 describes the increased difficulties that courts have experienced when applying the Fourth Amendment's principles regarding searches and seizures to new technologies that gather large amounts of data, such as email and cell-site location. These issues came to a head in the Supreme Court in 2018, when it issued its opinion in Carpenter v. United States, *requiring a warrant supported by probable cause for cell-site location information. Chief Justice Roberts's opinion provides an excellent overview of the evolution of the Fourth Amendment amid new technology. In addition to the Chief Justice's majority opinion, four Justices individually wrote dissents, which are addressed in the majority opinion but not included in this excerpt, as the majority and four dissenting opinions totaled 119 pages.*

June 22, 2018

Majority opinion by Chief Justice John Roberts:

This case presents the question whether the Government conducts a search under the Fourth Amendment when it accesses historical cell phone records that provide a comprehensive chronicle of the user's past movements.

I

A.

There are 396 million cell phone service accounts in the United States—for a Nation of 326 million people. Cell phones perform their wide and growing variety of functions by connecting to a set of radio antennas called "cell sites." Although cell sites are usually mounted on a tower, they can also be found on light posts, flagpoles, church steeples, or the sides of buildings. Cell sites typically have several directional antennas that divide the covered area into sectors.

Cell phones continuously scan their environment looking for the best signal, which generally comes from the closest cell site. Most modern devices, such as smartphones, tap into the wireless network several times a minute whenever their signal is on, even if the owner is not using one of the phone's features. Each time the phone connects to a cell site, it generates a time-stamped record known as cell-site location information (CSLI). The precision of this information depends on the size of the geographic area covered by the cell site. The greater the concentration of cell sites, the smaller the coverage area. As data usage from cell phones has increased, wireless carriers have installed more cell sites to handle the traffic. That has led to increasingly compact coverage areas, especially in urban areas.

Wireless carriers collect and store CSLI for their own business purposes, including finding weak spots in their network and applying "roaming" charges when another carrier routes data through their cell sites. In addition, wireless carriers often sell aggregated location records to data brokers, without individual identifying information of the sort at issue here. While carriers have long retained CSLI for the start and end of incoming calls, in recent years phone companies have also collected location information from the transmission of text messages and routine data connections. Accordingly, modern cell phones generate increasingly vast amounts of increasingly precise CSLI.

B.

In 2011, police officers arrested four men suspected of robbing a series of Radio Shack and (ironically enough) T-Mobile stores in Detroit. One of the men confessed that, over the previous four months, the group (along with a rotating cast of getaway drivers and lookouts) had robbed nine different stores in Michigan and Ohio. The suspect identified 15 accomplices who had participated in the heists and gave the FBI some of their cell phone numbers; the FBI then reviewed his call records to identify additional numbers that he had called around the time of the robberies.

Based on that information, the prosecutors applied for court orders under the Stored Communications Act to obtain cell phone records for petitioner

Timothy Carpenter and several other suspects. That statute, as amended in 1994, permits the Government to compel the disclosure of certain telecommunications records when it "offers specific and articulable facts showing that there are reasonable grounds to believe" that the records sought "are relevant and material to an ongoing criminal investigation." 18 U.S.C. § 2703(d). Federal Magistrate Judges issued two orders directing Carpenter's wireless carriers— MetroPCS and Sprint—to disclose "cell/site sector [information] for [Carpenter's] telephone[ ] at call origination and at call termination for incoming and outgoing calls" during the four-month period when the string of robberies occurred. The first order sought 152 days of cell-site records from MetroPCS, which produced records spanning 127 days. The second order requested seven days of CSLI from Sprint, which produced two days of records covering the period when Carpenter's phone was "roaming" in northeastern Ohio. Altogether the Government obtained 12,898 location points cataloging Carpenter's movements—an average of 101 data points per day.

Carpenter was charged with six counts of robbery and an additional six counts of carrying a firearm during a federal crime of violence. Prior to trial, Carpenter moved to suppress the cell-site data provided by the wireless carriers. He argued that the Government's seizure of the records violated the Fourth Amendment because they had been obtained without a warrant supported by probable cause. The District Court denied the motion.

At trial, seven of Carpenter's confederates pegged him as the leader of the operation. In addition, FBI agent Christopher Hess offered expert testimony about the cell-site data. Hess explained that each time a cell phone taps into the wireless network, the carrier logs a time-stamped record of the cell site and particular sector that were used. With this information, Hess produced maps that placed Carpenter's phone near four of the charged robberies. In the Government's view, the location records clinched the case: They confirmed that Carpenter was "right where the . . . robbery was at the exact time of the robbery." Carpenter was convicted on all but one of the firearm counts and sentenced to more than 100 years in prison.

The Court of Appeals for the Sixth Circuit affirmed. The court held that Carpenter lacked a reasonable expectation of privacy in the location information collected by the FBI because he had shared that information with his wireless carriers. Given that cell phone users voluntarily convey cell-site data to their carriers as "a means of establishing communication," the court concluded that the resulting business records are not entitled to Fourth Amendment protection.

We granted certiorari.

II

A.

The Fourth Amendment protects "[t]he right of the people to be secure in their persons, houses, papers, and effects, against unreasonable searches and seizures." The "basic purpose of this Amendment," our cases have recognized, "is to safeguard the privacy and security of individuals against arbitrary invasions by governmental officials." *Camara v. Municipal Court of City and County of San Francisco* (1967). The Founding generation crafted the Fourth Amendment as a "response to the reviled 'general warrants' and 'writs of assistance' of the colonial era, which allowed British officers to rummage through homes in an unrestrained search for evidence of criminal activity." *Riley v. California* (2014). In fact, as John Adams recalled, the patriot James Otis's 1761 speech condemning writs of assistance was "the first act of opposition to the arbitrary claims of Great Britain" and helped spark the Revolution itself.

For much of our history, Fourth Amendment search doctrine was "tied to common-law trespass" and focused on whether the Government "obtains information by physically intruding on a constitutionally protected area." *United States v. Jones* (2012). More recently, the Court has recognized that "property rights are not the sole measure of Fourth Amendment violations." In *Katz v. United States* (1967), we established that "the Fourth Amendment protects people, not places," and expanded our conception of the Amendment to protect certain expectations of privacy as well. When an individual "seeks to preserve something as private," and his expectation of privacy is "one that society is prepared to recognize as reasonable," we have held that official intrusion into that private sphere generally qualifies as a search and requires a warrant supported by probable cause.

Although no single rubric definitively resolves which expectations of privacy are entitled to protection, the analysis is informed by historical understandings "of what was deemed an unreasonable search and seizure when [the Fourth Amendment] was adopted." On this score, our cases have recognized some basic guideposts. First, that the Amendment seeks to secure "the privacies of life" against "arbitrary power." . . .

We have kept this attention to Founding-era understandings in mind when applying the Fourth Amendment to innovations in surveillance tools. As technology has enhanced the Government's capacity to encroach upon areas normally guarded from inquisitive eyes, this Court has sought to "assure[ ] preservation of that degree of privacy against government that existed when the Fourth Amendment was adopted." *Kyllo v. United States* (2001). For that reason, we rejected in *Kyllo* a "mechanical interpretation" of the Fourth Amendment and held that use of a thermal imager to detect heat radiating from the side of the defendant's home was a search. Because any other conclusion would leave homeowners "at the mercy of advancing technology," we determined that the Government—absent a warrant—could not capitalize on such new sense-enhancing technology to explore what was happening within the home.

Likewise in *Riley*, the Court recognized the "immense storage capacity" of modern cell phones in holding that police officers must generally obtain a warrant before searching the contents of a phone. We explained that while the general rule allowing warrantless searches incident to arrest "strikes the appropriate balance in the context of physical objects, neither of its rationales has much force with respect to" the vast store of sensitive information on a cell phone.

B.

The case before us involves the Government's acquisition of wireless carrier cell-site records revealing the location of Carpenter's cell phone whenever it made or received calls. This sort of digital data—personal location information maintained by a third party—does not fit neatly under existing precedents. Instead, requests for cell-site records lie at the intersection of two lines of cases, both of which inform our understanding of the privacy interests at stake.

The first set of cases addresses a person's expectation of privacy in his physical location and movements. In *United States v. Knotts* (1983), we considered the Government's use of a "beeper" to aid in tracking a vehicle through traffic. Police officers in that case planted a beeper in a container of chloroform before it was purchased by one of Knotts's co-conspirators. The officers (with intermittent aerial assistance) then followed the automobile carrying the container from Minneapolis to Knotts's cabin in Wisconsin, relying on the beeper's signal to help keep the vehicle in view. The Court concluded that the "augment[ed]" visual surveillance did not constitute a search because "[a] person traveling in an automobile on public thoroughfares has no reasonable expectation of privacy in his movements from one place to another." Since the movements of the vehicle and its final destination had been "voluntarily conveyed to anyone who wanted to look," Knotts could not assert a privacy interest in the information obtained.

This Court in *Knotts*, however, was careful to distinguish between the rudimentary tracking facilitated by the beeper and more sweeping modes of surveillance. The Court emphasized the "limited use which the government made of the signals from this particular beeper" during a discrete "automotive journey." Significantly, the Court reserved the question whether "different constitutional principles may be applicable" if "twenty-four hour surveillance of any citizen of this country [were] possible."

Three decades later, the Court considered more sophisticated surveillance of the sort envisioned in *Knotts* and found that different principles did indeed apply. In *United States v. Jones*, FBI agents installed a GPS tracking device on

Jones's vehicle and remotely monitored the vehicle's movements for 28 days. The Court decided the case based on the Government's physical trespass of the vehicle. At the same time, five Justices agreed that related privacy concerns would be raised by, for example, "surreptitiously activating a stolen vehicle detection system" in Jones's car to track Jones himself, or conducting GPS tracking of his cell phone. Since GPS monitoring of a vehicle tracks "every movement" a person makes in that vehicle, the concurring Justices concluded that "longer term GPS monitoring in investigations of most offenses impinges on expectations of privacy"—regardless whether those movements were disclosed to the public at large.

In a second set of decisions, the Court has drawn a line between what a person keeps to himself and what he shares with others. We have previously held that "a person has no legitimate expectation of privacy in information he voluntarily turns over to third parties." *Smith v. Maryland.* That remains true "even if the information is revealed on the assumption that it will be used only for a limited purpose." *United States v. Miller*, 425 U.S. 435, 443 (1976). As a result, the Government is typically free to obtain such information from the recipient without triggering Fourth Amendment protections.

This third-party doctrine largely traces its roots to *Miller*. While investigating Miller for tax evasion, the Government subpoenaed his banks, seeking several months of canceled checks, deposit slips, and monthly statements. The Court rejected a Fourth Amendment challenge to the records collection. For one, Miller could "assert neither ownership nor possession" of the documents; they were "business records of the banks." For another, the nature of those records confirmed Miller's limited expectation of privacy, because the checks were "not confidential communications but negotiable instruments to be used in commercial transactions," and the bank statements contained information "exposed to [bank] employees in the ordinary course of business." The Court thus concluded that Miller had "take[n] the risk, in revealing his affairs to another, that the information [would] be conveyed by that person to the Government."

Three years later, *Smith* applied the same principles in the context of information conveyed to a telephone company. The Court ruled that the Government's use of a pen register—a device that recorded the outgoing phone numbers dialed on a landline telephone—was not a search. Noting the pen register's "limited capabilities," the Court "doubt[ed] that people in general entertain any actual expectation of privacy in the numbers they dial." Telephone subscribers know, after all, that the numbers are used by the telephone company "for a variety of legitimate business purposes," including routing calls. And at any rate, the Court explained, such an expectation "is not one that society is prepared to recognize as reasonable." When Smith placed a call, he "voluntarily conveyed" the dialed numbers to the phone company by "expos[ing] that information to its equipment in the ordinary course of business." Once again, we held that the defendant "assumed the risk" that the company's records "would be divulged to police."

III

The question we confront today is how to apply the Fourth Amendment to a new phenomenon: the ability to chronicle a person's past movements through the record of his cell phone signals. Such tracking partakes of many of the qualities of the GPS monitoring we considered in *Jones*. Much like GPS tracking of a vehicle, cell phone location information is detailed, encyclopedic, and effortlessly compiled.

At the same time, the fact that the individual continuously reveals his location to his wireless carrier implicates the third-party principle of *Smith* and *Miller*. But while the third-party doctrine applies to telephone numbers and bank records, it is not clear whether its logic extends to the qualitatively different category of cell-site records. After all, when Smith was decided in 1979, few could have imagined a society in which a phone goes wherever its owner goes, conveying to the wireless carrier not just dialed digits, but a detailed and comprehensive record of the person's movements.

We decline to extend *Smith* and *Miller* to cover these novel circumstances. Given the unique nature of cell phone location records, the fact that the information is held by a third party does not by itself overcome the user's claim to Fourth Amendment protection. Whether the Government employs its own surveillance technology as in *Jones* or leverages the technology of a wireless carrier, we hold that an individual maintains a legitimate expectation of privacy in the record of his physical movements as captured through CSLI. The location information obtained from Carpenter's wireless carriers was the product of a search.

A

A person does not surrender all Fourth Amendment protection by venturing into the public sphere. To the contrary, "what [one] seeks to preserve as private, even in an area accessible to the public, may be constitutionally protected." *Katz*. A majority of this Court has already recognized that individuals have a reasonable expectation of privacy in the whole of their physical movements. Prior to the digital age, law enforcement might have pursued a suspect for a brief stretch, but doing so "for any extended period of time was difficult and costly and therefore rarely undertaken." For that reason, "society's expectation has been that law enforcement agents and others would not—and indeed, in the main, simply could not—secretly monitor and catalogue every single movement of an individual's car for a very long period."

Allowing government access to cell-site records contravenes that expectation. Although such records are generated for commercial purposes, that distinction does not negate Carpenter's anticipation of privacy in his physical location. Mapping a cell phone's location over the course of 127 days provides an all-encompassing record of the holder's whereabouts. As with GPS information, the time-stamped data provides an intimate window into a person's life, revealing not only his particular movements, but through them his "familial, political, professional, religious, and sexual associations." These location records "hold for many Americans the 'privacies of life.'" And like GPS monitoring, cell phone tracking is remarkably easy, cheap, and efficient compared to traditional investigative tools. With just the click of a button, the Government can access each carrier's deep repository of historical location information at practically no expense.

In fact, historical cell-site records present even greater privacy concerns than the GPS monitoring of a vehicle we considered in *Jones*. Unlike the bugged container in *Knotts* or the car in *Jones*, a cell phone—almost a "feature of human anatomy,"—tracks nearly exactly the movements of its owner. While individuals regularly leave their vehicles, they compulsively carry cell phones with them all the time. A cell phone faithfully follows its owner beyond public thoroughfares and into private residences, doctor's offices, political headquarters, and other potentially revealing locales. . . . Accordingly, when the Government tracks the location of a cell phone it achieves near perfect surveillance, as if it had attached an ankle monitor to the phone's user.

Moreover, the retrospective quality of the data here gives police access to a category of information otherwise unknowable. In the past, attempts to reconstruct a person's movements were limited by a dearth of records and the frailties of recollection. With access to CSLI, the Government can now travel back in time to retrace a person's whereabouts, subject only to the retention polices of the wireless carriers, which currently maintain records for up to five years. Critically, because location information is continually logged for all of the 400 million devices in the United States—not just those belonging to persons who might happen to come under investigation—this newfound tracking capacity runs against everyone. Unlike with the GPS device in *Jones*, police need not even know in advance whether they want to follow a particular individual, or when.

Whoever the suspect turns out to be, he has effectively been tailed every moment of every day for five years, and the police may—in the Government's view—call upon the results of that surveillance without regard to the constraints of the Fourth Amendment. Only the few without cell phones could escape this tireless and absolute surveillance.

The Government and Justice Kennedy contend, however, that the collection of CSLI should be permitted because the data is less precise than GPS information. Not to worry, they maintain, because the location records did "not on their own suffice to place [Carpenter] at the crime scene"; they placed him within a wedge-shaped sector ranging from one-eighth to four square miles. Yet the Court has already rejected the proposition that "inference insulates a search." From the 127 days of location data it received, the Government could, in combination with other information, deduce a detailed log of Carpenter's movements, including when he was at the site of the robberies. And the Government thought the CSLI accurate enough to highlight it during the closing argument of his trial.

At any rate, the rule the Court adopts "must take account of more sophisticated systems that are already in use or in development." While the records in this case reflect the state of technology at the start of the decade, the accuracy of CSLI is rapidly approaching GPS-level precision. As the number of cell sites has proliferated, the geographic area covered by each cell sector has shrunk, particularly in urban areas. In addition, with new technology measuring the time and angle of signals hitting their towers, wireless carriers already have the capability to pinpoint a phone's location within 50 meters.

Accordingly, when the Government accessed CSLI from the wireless carriers, it invaded Carpenter's reasonable expectation of privacy in the whole of his physical movements.

B

The Government's primary contention to the contrary is that the third-party doctrine governs this case. In its view, cell-site records are fair game because they are "business records" created and maintained by the wireless carriers. The Government (along with Justice Kennedy) recognizes that this case features new technology, but asserts that the legal question nonetheless turns on a garden-variety request for information from a third-party witness.

The Government's position fails to contend with the seismic shifts in digital technology that made possible the tracking of not only Carpenter's location but also everyone else's, not for a short period but for years and years. Sprint Corporation and its competitors are not your typical witnesses. Unlike the nosy neighbor who keeps an eye on comings and goings, they are ever alert, and their memory is nearly infallible. There is a world of difference between the limited types of personal information addressed in *Smith* and *Miller* and the exhaustive chronicle of location information casually collected by wireless carriers today. The Government thus is not asking for a straightforward application of the third-party doctrine, but instead a significant extension of it to a distinct category of information.

The third-party doctrine partly stems from the notion that an individual has a reduced expectation of privacy in information knowingly shared with another. But the fact of "diminished privacy interests does not mean that the Fourth Amendment falls out of the picture entirely." *Smith* and *Miller*, after all, did not rely solely on the act of sharing. Instead, they considered "the nature of the particular documents sought" to determine whether "there is a legitimate 'expectation of privacy' concerning their contents." *Smith* pointed out the limited capabilities of a pen register; as explained in *Riley*, telephone call logs reveal little in the way of "identifying information." *Miller* likewise noted that checks were "not confidential communications but negotiable instruments to be used in commercial transactions." In mechanically applying the third-party doctrine to this case, the Government fails to appreciate that there are no comparable limitations on the revealing nature of CSLI.

The Court has in fact already shown special solicitude for location information in the third-party context. In *Knotts*, the Court relied on *Smith* to hold that an individual has no reasonable expectation of privacy in public movements that he "voluntarily conveyed to anyone who wanted to look." But when confronted with more pervasive tracking [in *Jones*], five Justices agreed that longer term GPS monitoring of even a vehicle traveling on public streets constitutes a search. . . . Yet this case is not about "using a phone" or a person's movement at a particular time. It is about a detailed chronicle of a person's physical presence compiled every day, every moment, over several years. Such a chronicle implicates privacy concerns far beyond those considered in *Smith* and *Miller*.

Neither does the second rationale underlying the third-party doctrine—voluntary exposure—hold up when it comes to CSLI. Cell phone location information is not truly "shared" as one normally understands the term. In the first place, cell phones and the services they provide are "such a pervasive and insistent part of daily life" that carrying one is indispensable to participation in modern society. *Riley*. Second, a cell phone logs a cell-site record by dint of its operation, without any affirmative act on the part of the user beyond powering up. Virtually any activity on the phone generates CSLI, including incoming calls, texts, or e-mails and countless other data connections that a phone automatically makes when checking for news, weather, or social media updates. Apart from disconnecting the phone from the network, there is no way to avoid leaving behind a trail of location data. As a result, in no meaningful sense does the user voluntarily "assume[] the risk" of turning over a comprehensive dossier of his physical movements.

We therefore decline to extend *Smith* and *Miller* to the collection of CSLI. Given the unique nature of cell phone location information, the fact that the Government obtained the information from a third party does not overcome Carpenter's claim to Fourth Amendment protection. The Government's acquisition of the cell-site records was a search within the meaning of the Fourth Amendment.

***

Our decision today is a narrow one. We do not express a view on matters not before us: real-time CSLI or "tower dumps" (a download of information on all the devices that connected to a particular cell site during a particular interval). We do not disturb the application of *Smith* and *Miller* or call into question conventional surveillance techniques and tools, such as security cameras. Nor do we address other business records that might incidentally reveal location information. Further, our opinion does not consider other collection techniques involving foreign affairs or national security. As Justice Frankfurter noted when considering new innovations in airplanes and radios, the Court must tread carefully in such cases, to ensure that we do not "embarrass the future."

IV

Having found that the acquisition of Carpenter's CSLI was a search, we also conclude that the Government must generally obtain a warrant supported by probable cause before acquiring such records. Although the "ultimate measure of the constitutionality of a governmental search is 'reasonableness,'" our cases establish that warrantless searches are typically unreasonable where "a search is undertaken by law enforcement officials to discover evidence of criminal wrongdoing." Thus, "[i]n the absence of a warrant, a search is reasonable only if it falls within a specific exception to the warrant requirement."

The Government acquired the cell-site records pursuant to a court order issued under the Stored Communications Act, which required the Government to show "reasonable grounds" for believing that the records were "relevant and material to an ongoing investigation." 18 U.S.C. § 2703(d). That showing falls well short of the probable cause required for a warrant. The Court usually requires "some quantum of individualized suspicion" before a search or seizure may take place. Under the standard in the Stored Communications Act, however, law enforcement need only show that the cell-site evidence might be pertinent to an ongoing investigation—a "gigantic" departure from the probable cause rule, as the Government explained below. Consequently, an order issued under Section 2703(d) of the Act is not a permissible mechanism for accessing historical cell-site records. Before compelling a wireless carrier to turn over a subscriber's CSLI, the Government's obligation is a familiar one—get a warrant.

Justice Alito contends that the warrant requirement simply does not apply when the Government acquires records using compulsory process. Unlike an actual search, he says, subpoenas for documents do not involve the direct taking of evidence; they are at most a "constructive search" conducted by the target of the subpoena. Given this lesser intrusion on personal privacy, Justice Alito argues that the compulsory production of records is not held to the same probable cause standard. In his view, this Court's precedents set forth a categorical rule—separate and distinct from the third-party doctrine—subjecting subpoenas to lenient scrutiny without regard to the suspect's expectation of privacy in the records.

But this Court has never held that the Government may subpoena third parties for records in which the suspect has a reasonable expectation of privacy. Almost all of the examples Justice Alito cites contemplated requests for evidence implicating diminished privacy interests or for a corporation's own books. The lone exception, of course, is *Miller*, where the Court's analysis of the third-party subpoena merged with the application of the third-party doctrine.

Justice Alito overlooks the critical issue. At some point, the dissent should recognize that CSLI is an entirely different species of business record—something that implicates basic Fourth Amendment concerns about arbitrary government power much more directly than corporate tax or payroll ledgers. When confronting new concerns wrought by digital technology, this Court has been careful not to uncritically extend existing precedents.

If the choice to proceed by subpoena provided a categorical limitation on Fourth Amendment protection, no type of record would ever be protected by the warrant requirement. Under Justice Alito's view, private letters, digital contents of a cell phone—any personal information reduced to document form, in fact—may be collected by subpoena for no reason other than "official curiosity." Justice Kennedy declines to adopt the radical implications of this theory, leaving open the question whether the warrant requirement applies "when the Government obtains the modern-day equivalents of an individual's own 'papers' or 'effects,' even when those papers or effects are held by a third party." (citing *United States v. Warshak*, 631 F.3d 266, 283-288 (6th Cir. 2010)). That would be a sensible exception, because it would prevent the subpoena doctrine from overcoming any reasonable expectation of privacy. If the third-party doctrine does not apply to the "modern-day equivalents of an individual's own 'papers' or 'effects,'" then the clear implication is that the documents should receive full Fourth Amendment protection. We simply think that such protection should extend as well to a detailed log of a person's movements over several years.

This is certainly not to say that all orders compelling the production of documents will require a showing of probable cause. The Government will be able to use subpoenas to acquire records in the overwhelming majority of investigations. We hold only that a warrant is required in the rare case where the suspect has a legitimate privacy interest in records held by a third party.

Further, even though the Government will generally need a warrant to access CSLI, case-specific exceptions may support a warrantless search of an individual's cell-site records under certain circumstances. "One well-recognized exception applies when 'the exigencies of the situation' make the needs of law enforcement so compelling that [a] warrantless search is objectively reasonable under the Fourth Amendment." *Kentucky v. King*, 563 U.S. 452, 460 (2011). Such exigencies include the need to pursue a fleeing suspect, protect individuals who are threatened with imminent harm, or prevent the imminent destruction of evidence.

As a result, if law enforcement is confronted with an urgent situation, such fact-specific threats will likely justify the warrantless collection of CSLI. Lower courts, for instance, have approved warrantless searches related to bomb threats, active shootings, and child abductions. Our decision today does not call into doubt warrantless access to CSLI in such circumstances. While police must get a warrant when collecting CSLI to assist in the mine-run criminal investigation, the rule we set forth does not limit their ability to respond to an ongoing emergency.

***

As Justice Brandeis explained in his famous dissent, the Court is obligated—as "[s]ubtler and more far-reaching means of invading privacy have become available to the Government"—to ensure that the "progress of science" does not erode Fourth Amendment protections. *Olmstead v. United States*, 277 U.S. 438, 473-474 (1928). Here the progress of science has afforded law enforcement a powerful new tool to carry out its important responsibilities. At the same time, this tool risks Government encroachment of the sort the Framers, "after consulting the lessons of history," drafted the Fourth Amendment to prevent.

We decline to grant the state unrestricted access to a wireless carrier's database of physical location information. In light of the deeply revealing nature of CSLI, its depth, breadth, and comprehensive reach, and the inescapable and automatic nature of its collection, the fact that such information is gathered by a third party does not make it any less deserving of Fourth Amendment protection. The Government's acquisition of the cell-site records here was a search under that Amendment.

The judgment of the Court of Appeals is reversed, and the case is remanded for further proceedings consistent with this opinion.

It is so ordered.

United States v. Keith, 980 F. Supp. 2d 33 (D. Mass. 2013)

In 2013, a federal district judge in Massachusetts dealt a significant setback to an established system that the government has used to investigate and prosecute child pornography cases.

November 5, 2013

Opinion by George A. O'Toole, Jr., District Judge

The defendant, David Keith, is charged with distribution of child pornography in violation of 18 U.S.C. § 2252(a)(2) and possessing and accessing child pornography in violation of 18 U.S.C. § 2252(a)(4)(B). He has moved to suppress physical evidence and statements obtained as the result of a search of his residence by the Massachusetts State Police pursuant to a warrant.

The application for the warrant relied on two distinct sources of information for a showing of probable cause. First, in December 2009, the National Center for Missing and Exploited Children ("NCMEC") made available to the Massachusetts State Police a "CyberTipline" report indicating that a computer that eventually was linked to the defendant's residence was likely the source of an emailed file that contained what appeared to be child pornography meeting the federal criminal definition. Second, on July 29, 2010, employees of a Staples store in New Hampshire notified local police that a laptop computer left for repair contained files with filenames apparently describing child pornography. The work order for the Staples laptop listed the defendant's name and his residential address in Haverhill, Massachusetts. When later questioned by the police in New Hampshire, the defendant admitted both that the Staples laptop was his and that he had seen and downloaded files depicting images of children as young as eight years old engaging in sexual activity. The New Hampshire police ultimately shared with the Massachusetts State Police information they had gathered in their investigation, including some evidence from a warranted search of the laptop. Relying on both the NCMEC CyberTipline report and the information from the New Hampshire police, the Massachusetts State Police applied for and obtained a search warrant for the defendant's residence, which was executed on September 17, 2010. The search yielded incriminating information, and the defendant also made incriminating admissions after having been advised of his Miranda rights.

I. The CyberTipline Report

The following factual findings are based on the parties' written submissions and testimony given at an evidentiary hearing.

America Online ("AOL"), which may be described variously as an electronic service provider ("ESP") and an internet service provider ("ISP"), provides an email service for subscribers. To prevent its communications network from serving as a conduit for illicit activity, AOL systematically attempts to identify suspected child pornography that may be sent through its facilities. It uses an Image Detection and Filtering Process ("IDFP") of its own devise which compares files embedded in or attached to transmitted emails against a database containing what is essentially a catalog of files that have previously been identified as containing child pornography.

Commonly, AOL may be alerted that an image or video file being transmitted through its facilities likely contains child pornography by a complaint from a customer. When AOL receives such a complaint, an employee called a "graphic review analyst" opens and looks at the image or video file and forms an opinion whether what is depicted likely meets the federal criminal definition of child pornography. If the employee concludes that the file contains child pornography, a hash value of the file is generated automatically by operation of an algorithm designed for that purpose. A hash value is an alphanumeric sequence that is unique to a specific digital file. Any identical copy of the file will have exactly the same hash value as the original, but any alteration of the file, including even a change of one or two pixels, would result in a different hash value. Consequently, once a file has been "hashed," a suspected copy can be determined to be identical to the original file if it has the same hash value as the original, and not to be identical if it has a different hash value.

AOL maintains a "flat file" database of hash values of files that AOL has at some time concluded contain child pornography. It does not maintain the actual files themselves; once a file is determined to contain child pornography, it is deleted from AOL's system. When AOL detects a file passing through its network that has the same hash value as one in the flat file database, AOL reports that fact to NCMEC via the latter's CyberTipline. By statute, an ESP or ISP such as AOL has a duty to report to NCMEC any apparent child pornography it discovers "as soon as reasonably possible." 18 U.S.C. § 2258A(a)(1). The CyperTipline report transmits the intercepted file to NCMEC, but no AOL employee opens or views the file. AOL's decision to report a file to NCMEC is made solely on the basis of the match of the hash value of the file to a stored hash value.

A CyberTipline report is typically created by direct upload to NCMEC's server through a facility made available by NCMEC to an ESP such as AOL specifically for that purpose. After a report is received, a NCMEC analyst opens and views the file to determine whether its content meets the federal criminal definition of child pornography. If it is determined that the file contains child pornography, the NCMEC analyst queries the email sender's internet protocol ("IP") address using conventional "open source" search engines to try to identify the sender's geographic location, as well as the ISP through which the sender accesses the internet. When the general geographic location and the relevant ISP for the computer of interest have been determined, the NCMEC analyst adds the report containing the file to a database that is accessible only to law enforcement agencies in the identified geographic location via a virtual private network ("VPN") that is dedicated to that use.

In this case, AOL identified a suspect file in an email sent on November 26, 2009. The following day, AOL uploaded a CyberTipline report that contained the file to NCMEC's server. In accordance with its practice, no AOL employee opened or viewed the file before it was forwarded to NCMEC. Rather, it was forwarded solely because its hash value matched a hash value in AOL's flat file database. Nothing is known about how the file came to be originally hashed and added to the flat file database, except that it was AOL's practice to hash and add to the database either the hash value of any file that was identified by one of its graphic file analysts as containing child pornography or a hash value similarly generated by a different ESP or ISP and shared with AOL.

After the file was received at NCMEC, an analyst opened and examined the image file, determined that it met the criteria for classification as child pornography, investigated the IP address from which the offending email originated, and determined that the IP address was located within Massachusetts. NCMEC then created the CyberTipline report and made it accessible to law enforcement personnel in Massachusetts through the dedicated VPN, along with information about the email sender's IP address and ISP. Subsequently subpoenaed records from the ISP associated the IP address with a computer at the defendant's residential address in Haverhill, Massachusetts. The Massachusetts State Police also independently matched the IP address to the defendant's address.

II. NCMEC and Its CyberTipline

According to a statement on its website, NCMEC

> was established in 1984 as a private, nonprofit 501(c)(3) organization. NCMEC works in partnership with the U.S. Department of Justice to help law enforcement find missing children, eliminate child sexual exploitation and prevent child victimization.

The "partnership" is reflected in an explicit statutory finding by the United States Congress:

> The Congress finds that—
>
> . . .
>
> (8) the Office of Juvenile Justice and Delinquency Prevention administers programs under this chapter through the Child Protection Division, including programs which prevent or address offenses committed against vulnerable children and which support missing children's organizations; and
> (9) a key component of such programs is the National Center for Missing and Exploited Children, which—
> (A) serves as a national resource center and clearinghouse;
> (B) works in partnership with the Department of Justice, the Federal Bureau of Investigation, the United States Marshals Service, the Department of the Treasury, the Department of State, the Bureau of Immigration and Customs Enforcement, the United States Secret Service, the United States Postal Inspection Service, and many other agencies in the effort to find missing children and prevent child victimization; and
> (C) operates a national network, linking the Center online with each of the missing children clearinghouses operated by the 50 States, the District of Columbia, and Puerto Rico, as well as with international organizations, including Scotland Yard in the United Kingdom, the Royal Canadian Mounted Police, INTERPOL headquarters in Lyon, France, and others, which enable the Center to transmit images and information regarding missing and exploited children to law enforcement across the United States and around the world instantly.

42 U.S.C. § 5771. To support this work of the Center, Congress has mandated funding for the Center by means of annual grants administered through the Office of Juvenile Justice and Delinquency Prevention of the Department of Justice. One of the purposes of the annual grant is specifically to support NCMEC's CyberTipline:

> The Administrator shall annually make a grant to the Center, which shall be used to— ...
> (P) operate a cyber tipline to provide online users and electronic service providers an effective means of reporting Internet-related child sexual exploitation in the areas of—
> (i) possession, manufacture, and distribution of child pornography; and subsequently to transmit such reports, including relevant images and information, to the appropriate international, Federal, State or local law enforcement agency for investigation ... .

Id. § 5773(b)(1). As noted above, the CyberTipline is supported by the statutory mandate that any ESP that discovers what appears to be child pornography must report that fact and its surrounding circumstances to the CyberTipline. 18 U.S.C. § 2258A(a). A knowing failure by an ESP to make such a report is punishable by a fine. When it receives such a report via the CyberTipline, NCMEC must forward it to an appropriate federal law enforcement agency, and is authorized to do likewise with respect to state law enforcement agencies.

According to NCMEC's annual report, for the year ending December 31, 2012, NCMEC received government contracts and grants slightly in excess of $36 million, approximately 70% of its total revenue for the year from all sources. It also receives annual donations from private citizens. For 2012, private contributions were approximately $7.7 million, a little over 15% of total revenue from all sources.

In addition to the CyberTipline, NCMEC also administers a number of other programs relating to missing and exploited children which are not directly relevant to the issues presented in this case.

III. Expectation of Privacy in the Contents of Emails

The defendant attacks the inspections of his intercepted email by both AOL and NCMEC respectively as violations of his right "to be secure in [his] . . . papers[] and effects, against unreasonable searches and seizures" guaranteed by the Fourth Amendment. A "search" for purposes of the Fourth Amendment occurs when there has been a governmental intrusion into a place or thing as to which a person has a reasonable expectation of privacy. Put another way, the inquiry is whether the defendant had a subjective expectation of privacy in the place or thing that society recognizes as reasonable.

Email has become one of the most common forms of communication, but courts have yet to come to a consensus regarding whether and to what extent a sender has, for Fourth Amendment purposes, a reasonable expectation of privacy in email committed to the custody of an ISP. . . . There are some perhaps useful analogs from other methods of transmitting communications. So, for example, while there is not a reasonable expectation of privacy in the matter on the outside of a mailed envelope, there is as to the letter sealed inside, and while there is not a reasonable expectation of privacy in the numbers dialed from a telephone, there is as to the conversation itself. Following the principles at work in these and similar cases, one might conclude that a sender of emails has a reasonable expectation of privacy in some aspects of the email, such as the contents of the message including embedded or attached files, but not in other aspects, such as the address header and various metadata.

In any event, the government has not taken the position that the defendant lacked a legitimate privacy interest in the contents of the emailed file, and so it is assumed for present purposes that he had such an interest. That being so, any governmental invasion of that privacy interest would be a "search" for Fourth Amendment purposes.

IV. Private or Governmental Search?

"The Fourth Amendment's protection against unreasonable searches and seizures applies only to government action and not to a search or seizure, even an unreasonable one, effected by a private individual not acting as an agent of the government." *United States v. Silva*, 554 F.3d 13, 18 (1st Cir. 2009). The defendant argues that neither AOL nor NCMEC was acting as a private party in screening and examining the email file because each was acting under a statutory duty or compulsion and thus must be considered to have been effectively a government agent. Therefore, he contends, their searches are to be regarded as having been conducted by the government for purposes of enforcing the criminal law and thus were subject to the requirements of the Fourth Amendment.

Under First Circuit precedent, whether a private party is acting effectively as an agent of the government in conducting a search is evaluated against three principal factors: (1) "the extent of the government's role in instigating or participating in the search"; (2) "[the government's] intent and the degree of control it exercises over the search and the private party"; and (3) "the extent to which the private party aims primarily to help the government or to serve its own interests." *Silva*.

AOL's comparison of the hash value of the file transmitted from the defendant's computer with its database of stored hash values of files thought to contain child pornography was not a search conducted by or on behalf of the government. None of the so-called "*Silva* factors" are present. Contrary to the defendant's suggestion, AOL is not required by law to monitor email traffic for possible child pornography, but only to report it when it is found. The government exercises no control over AOL's monitoring of its network. Most importantly, the evidence considered on the present motion established, and I find, that AOL is motivated by its own wholly private interests in seeking to detect and deter the transmission of child pornography through its network facilities. An AOL representative testified at the evidentiary hearing held on the present motion that AOL had an important business reason for its IDFP filtering process:

> We found that, again, providing a safer, more family-friendly environment for our users sustains our ability to keep our members. We've noticed when members call and say, "I want to discontinue my AOL service," we usually ask them why. And there are many reasons why somebody may want to leave, but one of these that we're routinely concerned about is objectionable content sent to them through our servers by other members or other Internet users. So they end up leaving AOL because of this bad content. So as a business, we would like to actually keep the members who complain about it and have a countermeasure against those who do it.

This legitimate business interest is distinct from the government's interest in prosecuting crime, and the *Silva* factors are not met. . . .

On the other hand, NCMEC's examination of the file uploaded by AOL to the NCMEC CyberTipline was a search conducted for the sole purpose of assisting the prosecution of child pornography crimes. NCMEC's goal in operating the CyberTipline is a worthy and laudable one, but it is one that it pursues in "partnership," 42 U.S.C. § 5771(9)(B), with the government. Unlike AOL, which monitors its email traffic to serve its own business interest, NCMEC's operation of the CyberTipline is intended to, and does, serve the public interest in crime prevention and prosecution, rather than a private interest.

The *Silva* factors are satisfied. Through congressional authorization and funding of the CyberTipline, the government "instigat[es]" such searches. A statutory provision requires NCMEC to report discovered child pornography to federal law enforcement, and another encourages similar reporting to state and foreign law enforcement agencies. This requirement addresses the "control" factor identified by the First Circuit. Finally, the CyberTipline serves no private purpose for NCMEC separate from assisting law enforcement, the third *Silva* factor.

While not directly addressing the question presented here, the First Circuit has noted that NCMEC reviews suspected files and "conducts an online search regarding the provided suspect information . . . aimed at identifying the appropriate law enforcement agency with jurisdiction to investigate the suspected child pornography activity." *Cameron*, 699 F.3d at 633. The court further observed that "[a]lthough NCMEC is not officially a government entity, it receives a grant from the government, and one of the uses to which NCMEC puts this grant money is to operate the CyberTipline and forward reports of child pornography to law enforcement." The "partnership" between NCMEC and law enforcement with respect to the operation of the CyberTipline is not just rhetorical but real. Members of law enforcement serve on various NCMEC boards, and U.S. Marshals and other law enforcement personnel provide on-site support and referral assistance for NCMEC's Exploited Child Division. As noted above, NCMEC makes the results of its examination of suspected files available exclusively to federal and state law enforcement officials by means of a dedicated VPN, accessible only to law enforcement personnel. It is clear that NCMEC's CyberTipline is, and is intended by Congress to be, an integral part of the governmental effort to detect and prosecute child pornography crimes. . . .

If AOL had sent the file directly to the FBI or the State Police instead of to NCMEC's CyberTipline, it could not seriously be contended that the law enforcement agency could open and inspect the contents of the file without regard to the Fourth Amendment's warrant requirement. *See Walter v. United States*, 447 U.S. 649 (1980). In *Walter*, a package containing boxes of film was mistakenly delivered to a private company. The company's employees opened the package and saw that the individual boxes bore outside labeling suggesting that they contained obscene material. They notified FBI agents, who took custody of the boxes, opened them, and viewed the films, confirming what the outside labeling suggested. The Court held that the opening and viewing of the films by the FBI was an expansion of the private search that required a warrant. Although the media in which criminally obscene material was stored are different in *Walter* and this case, the pattern is the same. A label (here, hash value) that is examined without opening the film or file suggested the nature of the contents. For that reason, concerned private parties provided the film or file to the government without first reviewing the contents themselves. Government personnel then examined the contents of the film or file by opening and viewing it. *Walter* holds that the examination should not have been done without due compliance with the warrant requirement imposed by the Fourth Amendment. The only possibly significant difference between the circumstances in *Walter* and here is that instead of a direct employee of the FBI or State Police performing the examination, an outside contractor performed the examination for the benefit of the law enforcement agency. There is nothing wrong with the government outsourcing part of its investigative work to a private cooperating partner, but doing so does not avoid the obligation to abide by the requirements of the Fourth Amendment.

The government weakly argues that a NCMEC analyst's viewing of the contents of the file was not an expansion of AOL's private search, citing

United States v. Jacobsen, 466 U.S. 109 (1984). In that case, FedEx employees opened a damaged box for private, non-governmental reasons, discovered what appeared to be cocaine, and contacted the Drug Enforcement Administration. The FedEx employees put the contents back in the box. When DEA agents arrived, they reopened the package and removed the cocaine. In these circumstances, the Supreme Court held there had been no separate search by the police to which the Fourth Amendment applied. An argument that *Jacobsen* is factually similar to this case is untenable in light of the testimony given at the evidentiary hearing. It is indisputable that AOL forwarded the suspect file only because its hash value matched a stored hash value, not because some AOL employee had opened the file and viewed the contents. The NCMEC analyst expanded the review by opening the file and viewing (and evaluating) its contents. *Walter*, and not *Jacobsen*, is the better analog.

In this regard it is worth noting that matching the hash value of a file to a stored hash value is not the virtual equivalent of viewing the contents of the file. What the match says is that the two files are identical; it does not itself convey any information about the contents of the file. It does say that the suspect file is identical to a file that someone, sometime, identified as containing child pornography, but the provenance of that designation is unknown. So a match alone indicts a file as contraband but cannot alone convict it. That is surely why a CyberTipline analyst opens the file to view it, because the actual viewing of the contents provides information additional to the information provided by the hash match. This is unlike what the Court found the case to be in *Jacobsen*, where the subsequent DEA search provided no more information than had already been exposed by the initial FedEx search. *Jacobsen* is inapposite.

[The Court proceeded to deny Keith's motion to suppress, concluding that the warrant was sufficiently supported by evidence found on Keith's laptop.]

United States v. Warshak, 631 F.3d 266 (6th Cir. 2010)

This opinion is the first comprehensive federal appellate court ruling as to the scope of Fourth Amendment protections for stored email. The lengthy opinion considered a number of issues involved in this complex criminal case; this excerpt only includes the analysis of the Fourth Amendment challenge in the majority and concurring opinions.

December 14, 2010

Opinion by Danny Julian Boggs, Circuit Judge

Berkeley Premium Nutraceuticals, Inc., was an incredibly profitable company that served as the distributor of Enzyte, an herbal supplement purported to enhance male sexual performance. In this appeal, defendants Steven Warshak ("Warshak"), Harriet Warshak ("Harriet"), and TCI Media, Inc.

("TCI"), challenge their convictions stemming from a massive scheme to defraud Berkeley's customers. Warshak and Harriet also challenge their sentences, as well as two forfeiture judgments. . . .

In September 2006, a grand jury sitting in the Southern District of Ohio returned a 112-count indictment charging Warshak, Harriet, TCI, and several others with various crimes related to Berkeley's business. Warshak was charged with conspiracy to commit mail, wire, and bank fraud (Count 1); mail fraud (Counts 2-13); making false statements to banks (Counts 14, 16-22, 24-26, 28); bank fraud (Counts 15, 23, 27); conspiracy to commit and attempt to commit access-device fraud (Count 29); conspiracy to commit money laundering (Count 34); money laundering (Counts 32-98, 102-106, 108); conspiracy to commit misbranding (Count 109); misbranding (Count 110); and, lastly, conspiracy to obstruct a Federal Trade Commission ("FTC") proceeding (Count 112). Harriet was charged with conspiracy to commit mail, wire, and bank fraud (Count 1); bank fraud (Count 27); making false statements to a bank (Count 28); conspiracy to commit money laundering (Counts 30-31); and money laundering (Counts 99-101, 107). TCI was charged with money laundering (Counts 57-58, 60-73, 79, 83, 91-93).

Before trial, numerous motions were filed. First, Warshak moved to exclude thousands of emails that the government obtained from his Internet Service Providers. That motion was denied. Warshak also moved to bar the government from using any evidence "derived through improper access to privileged attorney-client communications." . . .

Over fifteen months later, in January 2008, the case proceeded to trial. Approximately six weeks later, the trial ended and the defendants were convicted of the majority of the charges. Warshak was acquitted of Counts 14-22, 24-26, and 28, which charged him with making false statements to banks, and he was also acquitted of Counts 109-110, which charged him with misbranding offenses. Harriet was acquitted of Count 28, which alleged that she made false statements to a bank. She was convicted on Counts 27, 30-31, 99-101, and 107. . . .

On August 27, 2008, the defendants were sentenced. Warshak received a sentence of 25 years of imprisonment. He was also ordered to pay a fine of $93,000 and a special assessment of $9,300. In addition, he was ordered to surrender $459,540,000 in proceeds-money-judgment forfeiture and $44,876,781.68 in money-laundering-judgment forfeiture. Harriet was sentenced to 24 months of imprisonment, ordered to pay a special assessment of $800, and held jointly and severally liable for the forfeiture judgments. TCI was sentenced to five years of probation and ordered to pay a fine of $160,000 and a special assessment of $6,400.

Following a series of unsuccessful post-trial motions, the defendants timely appealed.

II. ANALYSIS

A. The Search & Seizure of Warshak's Emails

Warshak argues that the government's warrantless, ex parte seizure of approximately 27,000 of his private emails constituted a violation of the Fourth Amendment's prohibition on unreasonable searches and seizures.[29] The government counters that, even if government agents violated the Fourth Amendment in obtaining the emails, they relied in good faith on the Stored Communications Act ("SCA"), a statute that allows the government to obtain certain electronic communications without procuring a warrant. The government also argues that any hypothetical Fourth Amendment violation was harmless. We find that the government did violate Warshak's Fourth Amendment rights by compelling his Internet Service Provider ("ISP") to turn over the contents of his emails. However, we agree that agents relied on the SCA in good faith, and therefore hold that reversal is unwarranted.

1. The Stored Communications Act

The Stored Communications Act ("SCA") "permits a 'governmental entity' to compel a service provider to disclose the contents of [electronic] communications in certain circumstances." *Warshak II*, 532 F.3d at 523. As this court explained in *Warshak II*:

> Three relevant definitions bear on the meaning of the compelled-disclosure provisions of the Act. "[E]lectronic communication service[s]" permit "users . . . to send or receive wire or electronic communications," [18 U.S.C.] § 2510(15), a definition that covers basic e-mail services, *see* Patricia L. Bellia et al., CYBERLAW: PROBLEMS OF POLICY AND JURISPRUDENCE IN THE INFORMATION AGE 584 (2d ed. 2004). "[E]lectronic storage" is "any temporary, intermediate storage of a wire or electronic communication . . . and . . . any storage of such communication by an electronic communication service for purposes of backup protection of such communication." 18 U.S.C. § 2510(17). "[R]emote computing service[s]" provide "computer storage or processing services" to customers, id. § 2711(2), and are designed for longer-term storage, *see* Orin S. Kerr, *A User's Guide to the Stored Communications*

---

29 This is not the first time Warshak has raised this argument. In *Warshak v. United States*, 490 F.3d 455 (6th Cir.2007) ("Warshak I"), a panel of this court determined that Warshak did indeed have a privacy interest in the contents of his emails. That decision was vacated on ripeness grounds. See *Warshak v. United States*, 532 F.3d 521 (6th Cir.2008) (en banc) ("Warshak II"). In the present case, Warshak's claim is ripe for review.

Act, and a Legislator's Guide to Amending It, 72 GEO. WASH. L.
REV. 1208, 1216 (2004).

The compelled-disclosure provisions give different levels of
privacy protection based on whether the e-mail is held with an
electronic communication service or a remote computing service
and based on how long the e-mail has been in electronic storage.
The government may obtain the contents of e-mails that are "in
electronic storage" with an electronic communication service for
180 days or less "only pursuant to a warrant." 18 U.S.C. § 2703(a).
The government has three options for obtaining communications
stored with a remote computing service and communications
that have been in electronic storage with an electronic service
provider for more than 180 days: (1) obtain a warrant; (2) use an
administrative subpoena; or (3) obtain a court order under §
2703(d). *Id.* § 2703(a), (b).

532 F.3d at 523-24 (some alterations in original).

2. *Factual Background*

Email was a critical form of communication among Berkeley personnel. As a
consequence, Warshak had a number of email accounts with various ISPs,
including an account with NuVox Communications. In October 2004, the
government formally requested that NuVox prospectively preserve the contents of any emails to or from Warshak's email account. The request was made
pursuant to 18 U.S.C. § 2703(f) and it instructed NuVox to preserve all future
messages.[30] NuVox acceded to the government's request and began preserving
copies of Warshak's incoming and outgoing emails—copies that would not
have existed absent the prospective preservation request. Per the government's instructions, Warshak was not informed that his messages were being
archived.

In January 2005, the government obtained a subpoena under § 2703(b)
and compelled NuVox to turn over the emails that it had begun preserving
the previous year. In May 2005, the government served NuVox with an ex
parte court order under § 2703(d) that required NuVox to surrender any
additional email messages in Warshak's account. In all, the government
compelled NuVox to reveal the contents of approximately 27,000 emails.
Warshak did not receive notice of either the subpoena or the order until
May 2006.

---

30 Warshak appears to have accessed emails from his NuVox account via POP, or "Post Office
Protocol." When POP is utilized, emails are downloaded to the user's personal computer and
generally deleted from the ISP's server.

3. The Fourth Amendment

The Fourth Amendment provides that "[t]he right of the people to be secure in their persons, houses, papers, and effects, against unreasonable searches and seizures, shall not be violated, and no Warrants shall issue, but upon probable cause... ." U.S. CONST. amend. IV. The fundamental purpose of the Fourth Amendment "is to safeguard the privacy and security of individuals against arbitrary invasions by government officials." *Camara v. Mun. Ct.*, 387 U.S. 523, 528 (1967) . . . .

Not all government actions are invasive enough to implicate the Fourth Amendment . . . . A "search" occurs when the government infringes upon "an expectation of privacy that society is prepared to consider reasonable." *United States v. Jacobsen*, 466 U.S. 109, 113 (1984). This standard breaks down into two discrete inquiries: "first, has the [target of the investigation] manifested a subjective expectation of privacy in the object of the challenged search? Second, is society willing to recognize that expectation as reasonable?" *California v. Ciraolo*, 476 U.S. 207, 211 (1986).

Turning first to the subjective component of the test, we find that Warshak plainly manifested an expectation that his emails would be shielded from outside scrutiny. As he notes in his brief, his "entire business and personal life was contained within the . . . emails seized." Given the often sensitive and sometimes damning substance of his emails,[31] we think it highly unlikely that Warshak expected them to be made public, for people seldom unfurl their dirty laundry in plain view. . . .Therefore, we conclude that Warshak had a subjective expectation of privacy in the contents of his emails.

The next question is whether society is prepared to recognize that expectation as reasonable. This question is one of grave import and enduring consequence, given the prominent role that email has assumed in modern communication. Since the advent of email, the telephone call and the letter have waned in importance, and an explosion of Internet-based communication has taken place. People are now able to send sensitive and intimate information, instantaneously, to friends, family, and colleagues half a world away. Lovers exchange sweet nothings, and businessmen swap ambitious plans, all with the click of a mouse button. Commerce has also taken hold in email. Online purchases are often documented in email accounts, and email is frequently used to remind patients and clients of imminent appointments. In short, "account" is an apt word for the conglomeration of stored messages that comprises an email account, as it provides an account of its owner's life. By obtaining access to someone's email, government agents gain the ability to peer deeply into his activities. Much hinges, therefore, on whether the government

---

31 In a number of the NuVox emails, Warshak discussed the creation of trusts for his children, as well as the possibility that his financial dealings would mislead FTC investigators.

is permitted to request that a commercial ISP turn over the contents of a subscriber's emails without triggering the machinery of the Fourth Amendment.

In confronting this question, we take note of two bedrock principles. First, the very fact that information is being passed through a communications network is a paramount Fourth Amendment consideration. . . . Second, the Fourth Amendment must keep pace with the inexorable march of technological progress, or its guarantees will wither and perish. . . .

With those principles in mind, we begin our analysis by considering the manner in which the Fourth Amendment protects traditional forms of communication. In *Katz*, the Supreme Court was asked to determine how the Fourth Amendment applied in the context of the telephone. There, government agents had affixed an electronic listening device to the exterior of a public phone booth, and had used the device to intercept and record several phone conversations. *See* 389 U.S. at 348. The Supreme Court held that this constituted a search under the Fourth Amendment, notwithstanding the fact that the telephone company had the capacity to monitor and record the calls. In the eyes of the Court, the caller was "surely entitled to assume that the words he utter[ed] into the mouthpiece w[ould] not be broadcast to the world." *Katz*, 389 U.S. at 352. The Court's holding in *Katz* has since come to stand for the broad proposition that, in many contexts, the government infringes a reasonable expectation of privacy when it surreptitiously intercepts a telephone call through electronic means. . . .

Letters receive similar protection. . . . While a letter is in the mail, the police may not intercept it and examine its contents unless they first obtain a warrant based on probable cause. This is true despite the fact that sealed letters are handed over to perhaps dozens of mail carriers, any one of whom could tear open the thin paper envelopes that separate the private words from the world outside. Put another way, trusting a letter to an intermediary does not necessarily defeat a reasonable expectation that the letter will remain private. . . .

Given the fundamental similarities between email and traditional forms of communication, it would defy common sense to afford emails lesser Fourth Amendment protection. . . . Email is the technological scion of tangible mail, and it plays an indispensable part in the Information Age. Over the last decade, email has become "so pervasive that some persons may consider [it] to be [an] essential means or necessary instrument[] for self-expression, even self-identification." *City of Ontario v. Quon*, 130 S. Ct. 2619, 2630 (2010). It follows that email requires strong protection under the Fourth Amendment; otherwise, the Fourth Amendment would prove an ineffective guardian of private communication, an essential purpose it has long been recognized to serve. . . . As some forms of communication begin to diminish, the Fourth Amendment must recognize and protect nascent ones that arise. . . .

If we accept that an email is analogous to a letter or a phone call, it is manifest that agents of the government cannot compel a commercial ISP to turn over the contents of an email without triggering the Fourth Amendment. An ISP is the intermediary that makes email communication possible. Emails must pass through an ISP's servers to reach their intended recipient. Thus, the ISP is the functional equivalent of a post office or a telephone company. As we have discussed above, the police may not storm the post office and intercept a letter, and they are likewise forbidden from using the phone system to make a clandestine recording of a telephone call—unless they get a warrant, that is. It only stands to reason that, if government agents compel an ISP to surrender the contents of a subscriber's emails, those agents have thereby conducted a Fourth Amendment search, which necessitates compliance with the warrant requirement absent some exception.

In *Warshak I*, the government argued that this conclusion was improper, pointing to the fact that NuVox contractually reserved the right to access Warshak's emails for certain purposes. While we acknowledge that a subscriber agreement might, in some cases, be sweeping enough to defeat a reasonable expectation of privacy in the contents of an email account, we doubt that will be the case in most situations, and it is certainly not the case here.

As an initial matter, it must be observed that the mere ability of a third-party intermediary to access the contents of a communication cannot be sufficient to extinguish a reasonable expectation of privacy. In *Katz*, the Supreme Court found it reasonable to expect privacy during a telephone call despite the ability of an operator to listen in. Similarly, the ability of a rogue mail handler to rip open a letter does not make it unreasonable to assume that sealed mail will remain private on its journey across the country. Therefore, the threat or possibility of access is not decisive when it comes to the reasonableness of an expectation of privacy.

Nor is the right of access. As the Electronic Frontier Foundation points out in its amicus brief, at the time Katz was decided, telephone companies had a right to monitor calls in certain situations. Specifically, telephone companies could listen in when reasonably necessary to "protect themselves and their properties against the improper and illegal use of their facilities." *Bubis v. United States*, 384 F.2d 643, 648 (9th Cir. 1967). In this case, the NuVox subscriber agreement tracks that language, indicating that "NuVox may access and use individual Subscriber information in the operation of the Service and as necessary to protect the Service." Thus, under *Katz*, the degree of access granted to NuVox does not diminish the reasonableness of Warshak's trust in the privacy of his emails.

Our conclusion finds additional support in the application of Fourth Amendment doctrine to rented space. Hotel guests, for example, have a reasonable expectation of privacy in their rooms. This is so even though maids routinely enter hotel rooms to replace the towels and tidy the furniture. Similarly, tenants have a legitimate expectation of privacy in their apartments. That expectation persists, regardless of the incursions of handymen to fix leaky faucets. Consequently, we are convinced that some degree of routine access is hardly dispositive with respect to the privacy question.

Again, however, we are unwilling to hold that a subscriber agreement will never be broad enough to snuff out a reasonable expectation of privacy. As the panel noted in *Warshak I*, if the ISP expresses an intention to "audit, inspect, and monitor" its subscriber's emails, that might be enough to render an expectation of privacy unreasonable. But where, as here, there is no such statement, the ISP's "control over the [emails] and ability to access them under certain limited circumstances will not be enough to overcome an expectation of privacy."

We recognize that our conclusion may be attacked in light of the Supreme Court's decision in *United States v. Miller*, 425 U.S. 435 (1976). In *Miller*, the Supreme Court held that a bank depositor does not have a reasonable expectation of privacy in the contents of bank records, checks, and deposit slips. The Court's holding in *Miller* was based on the fact that bank documents, "including financial statements and deposit slips, contain only information voluntarily conveyed to the banks and exposed to their employees in the ordinary course of business." . . .

But *Miller* is distinguishable. First, *Miller* involved simple business records, as opposed to the potentially unlimited variety of "confidential communications" at issue here. Second, the bank depositor in *Miller* conveyed information to the bank so that the bank could put the information to use "in the ordinary course of business." By contrast, Warshak received his emails through NuVox. NuVox was an intermediary, not the intended recipient of the emails. Thus, *Miller* is not controlling.

Accordingly, we hold that a subscriber enjoys a reasonable expectation of privacy in the contents of emails "that are stored with, or sent or received through, a commercial ISP." The government may not compel a commercial ISP to turn over the contents of a subscriber's emails without first obtaining a warrant based on probable cause. Therefore, because they did not obtain a warrant, the government agents violated the Fourth Amendment when they obtained the contents of Warshak's emails. Moreover, to the extent that the SCA purports to permit the government to obtain such emails warrantlessly, the SCA is unconstitutional.

4. Good-Faith Reliance

Even though the government's search of Warshak's emails violated the Fourth Amendment, the emails are not subject to the exclusionary remedy if the officers relied in good faith on the SCA to obtain them. In *Illinois v. Krull*, 480 U.S. 340 (1987), the Supreme Court noted that the exclusionary rule's purpose of deterring law enforcement officers from engaging in unconstitutional conduct would not be furthered by holding officers accountable for mistakes of the legislature. Thus, even if a statute is later found to be unconstitutional, an officer "cannot be expected to question the judgment of the legislature." However, an officer cannot "be said to have acted in good-faith reliance upon a statute if its provisions are such that a reasonable officer should have known that the statute was unconstitutional."

Naturally, Warshak argues that the provisions of the SCA at issue in this case were plainly unconstitutional. He argues that any reasonable law enforcement officer would have understood that a warrant based on probable cause would be required to compel the production of private emails. In making this argument, he leans heavily on *Warshak I*, which opined that the SCA permits agents to engage in searches "that clearly do not comport with the Fourth Amendment."

However, we disagree that the SCA is so conspicuously unconstitutional as to preclude good-faith reliance. As we noted in *Warshak II*, "[t]he Stored Communications Act has been in existence since 1986 and to our knowledge has not been the subject of any successful Fourth Amendment challenges, in any context, whether to § 2703(d) or to any other provision." Furthermore, given the complicated thicket of issues that we were required to navigate when passing on the constitutionality of the SCA, it was not plain or obvious that the SCA was unconstitutional, and it was therefore reasonable for the government to rely upon the SCA in seeking to obtain the contents of Warshak's emails.

But the good-faith reliance inquiry does not end with the facial validity of the statute at issue. In *Krull*, the Supreme Court hinted that the good-faith exception does not apply if the government acted "outside the scope of the statute" on which it purported to rely. It should be noted that this portion of the *Krull* Court's opinion was merely dicta, and it appears that we have yet to pass on the question. However, it seems evident that an officer's failure to adhere to the boundaries of a given statute should preclude him from relying upon it in the face of a constitutional challenge. Once the officer steps outside the scope of an unconstitutional statute, the mistake is no longer the legislature's, but the officer's. Therefore, use of the exclusionary rule is once again efficacious in deterring officers from engaging in conduct that violates the Constitution.

Warshak argues that the government violated several provisions of the SCA and should therefore be precluded from arguing good-faith reliance. First, Warshak argues that the government violated the SCA's notice provisions. Under § 2703(b)(1)(B), the government must provide notice to an account holder if it seeks to compel the disclosure of his emails through either a § 2703(b) subpoena or a § 2703(d) order. However, § 2705 permits the government to delay notification in certain situations. The initial period of delay is 90 days, but the government may seek to extend that period in 90-day increments. In this case, the government issued both a § 2703(b) subpoena and a § 2703(d) order to NuVox, seeking disclosure of Warshak's emails. At the time, the government made the requisite showing that notice should be delayed. However, the government did not seek to renew the period of delay. In all, the government failed to inform Warshak of either the subpoena or the order for over a year.

Conceding that it violated the notice provisions, the government argues that such violations are irrelevant to the issue of whether it reasonably relied on the SCA in obtaining the contents of Warshak's emails. We agree. As the government notes, the violations occurred after the emails had been obtained. Thus, the mistakes at issue had no bearing on the constitutional violations. Because the exclusionary rule was designed to deter constitutional violations, we decline to invoke it in this situation.

But Warshak does not hang his hat exclusively on the government's violations of the SCA's notice provisions. He also argues that the government exceeded its authority under another SCA provision—§ 2703(f)—by requesting NuVox to engage in prospective preservation of his future emails. Under § 2703(f), "[a] provider of wire or electronic communication services or a remote computing service, upon the request of a governmental entity, shall take all necessary steps to preserve records and other evidence in its possession pending the issuance of a court order or other process." Warshak argues that this statute permits only retrospective preservation—in other words, preservation of emails already in existence. . . .

Ultimately, however, this statutory violation, whether it occurred or not, is irrelevant to the issue of good-faith reliance. The question here is whether the government relied in good faith on § 2703(b) and § 2703(d) to obtain copies of Warshak's emails. True, the government might not have been able to gain access to the emails without the prospective preservation request, as it was NuVox's practice to delete all emails once they were downloaded to the account holder's computer. Thus, in a sense, the government's use of § 2703(f) was a but-for cause of the constitutional violation. But the actual violation at issue was obtaining the emails, and the government did not rely on § 2703(f) specifically to do that. Instead, the government relied on § 2703(b) and § 2703(d). The proper inquiry, therefore, is whether the government violated either of those provisions, and the preservation request is of no consequence to that inquiry.

Warshak's next argument is that the government violated § 2703(d) by failing to provide any particularized factual basis when seeking an order for disclosure. Under § 2703(d), such an order "shall issue only if the governmental entity offers specific and articulable facts showing that there are reasonable grounds to believe that the contents of a wire or electronic communication . . . are relevant and material to an ongoing criminal investigation."

To the extent that he is arguing that the government's application was insufficient, Warshak is wrong. The government's application indicated that it was "investigating a complex, large-scale mail and wire fraud operation based in Cincinnati, Ohio." The application also indicated that "interviews of current and former employees of the target company suggest that electronic mail is a vital communication tool that has been used to perpetuate the fraudulent conduct." Additionally, the application observed that "various sources [have verified] that NuVox provides electronic communications services to certain individual(s) [under] investigation." In light of these statements, it is clear that the application was, in fact, supported by specific and articulable facts, especially given the diminished standard that applies to § 2703(d) applications. . . .

Finally, Warshak argues that a finding of good-faith reliance is improper because the government presented the magistrate with an erroneous definition of the term "electronic storage." As noted above, if an email is in electronic storage for less than 180 days, the government may not compel its disclosure without a warrant. In applying for the subpoena and the order that eventually resulted in the disclosure of Warshak's NuVox emails, the government suggested to the magistrate that an email is not in electronic storage if it has already been "accessed, viewed, or downloaded." Warshak argues that this definition of electronic storage does not comport with the Ninth Circuit's decision in *Theofel v. Farey-Jones*, 359 F.3d 1066, 1071 (9th Cir. 2004), which held that "prior access is irrelevant to whether the [emails] at issue were in electronic storage." Warshak further argues that, because the government failed to mention the Ninth Circuit's definition, it "usurped the court's function to determine whether an email . . . [is] in 'electronic storage[.]'"

As an initial matter, it is manifest that the decisions of the Ninth Circuit are not binding on courts in this circuit. It therefore cannot be said that the government somehow violated § 2703 by failing to cite an out-of-circuit decision that it thought to be wrongly decided. Incidentally, the government is not alone in thinking that the Ninth Circuit's definition of electronic storage is incorrect. . . . Furthermore, it does a disservice to the magistrate judge to suggest that the government usurped the role of the court. The government's application did include a proposed definition of the term "electronic storage." That does not mean, however, that the magistrate judge unhesitatingly received that definition, and, as the government notes, the magistrate "presumably [had] the opportunity to consider and review relevant precedent."

Consequently, we find that, although the government violated the Fourth Amendment, the exclusionary rule does not apply, as the government relied in good faith on § 2703(b) and § 2703(d) to access the contents of Warshak's emails . . . .

Concurring Opinion by Damon Keith, Circuit Judge

Although I concur in the result the majority reaches, I write separately to provide clarification concerning whether Warshak's emails, obtained in violation of the Fourth Amendment, should have been excluded from trial under the exclusionary rule.

I.

The Fourth Amendment guarantees "[t]he right of the people to be secure in their persons, houses, papers, and effects, against unreasonable searches and seizures" without warrants issued based upon probable cause. The exclusionary rule is a "remedy designed to safeguard Fourth Amendment rights generally through its deterrent effect. . . ." *United States v. Leon*, 468 U.S. 897, 906, (1984). Where evidence is collected in violation of an individual's reasonable expectation of privacy, it is subject to the exclusionary rule and will generally be suppressed at trial to deter further police misconduct in the future. However, where an officer acts in objectively reasonable reliance upon a statute that is later found unconstitutional, exclusion of the evidence would not deter future police misconduct. . . .

Here, we are presented with a unique situation. As the majority notes, because the government requested a secret subpoena to confiscate Warshak's personal emails without his knowledge pursuant to § 2703(b) and (d) of the Stored Communications Act ("SCA"), there is no need to exclude the evidence. The officers took these actions in good faith reliance upon these statutes. They requested the emails from NuVox via a § 2703(b) subpoena and a § 2703(d) order. Though the government failed to give notice within ninety days after the initial request, it did so only after the emails had been obtained and after an initial showing that notice should be delayed. While we today declare these statutes unconstitutional insofar as they permit the government to obtain such emails without a warrant, it does not follow that the evidence should have been excluded from Warshak's trial. Such an exclusion would not have a substantial deterrent effect on future Fourth Amendment violations enacted by the legislature. . . . Therefore, the majority rightfully affirms the district court's refusal to suppress Warshak's emails. With this I agree.

However, there is a further wrongdoing that troubles me today. Specifically, the government's request that NuVox preserve Warshak's stored and future email communications without Warshak's knowledge and without a warrant pursuant to § 2703(f). Under § 2703(f), "[a] provider of wire or electronic communication services or a remote computing service, upon the request of a governmental entity, shall take all necessary steps to preserve records and other evidence in its possession pending the issuance of a court order or other process." This subsection was added to the SCA in 1996 in an effort to supplement law enforcement resources and security. While added in a completely different context from the creation of the statute, it is worthwhile to review the purpose of the statute as a whole when considering the meaning of this subsection.

Section 2703, as part of the Electronic Communications Privacy Act ("ECPA"), was enacted in 1986 as part of Congress's effort to maintain "a fair balance between the privacy expectations of American citizens and the legitimate needs of law enforcement agencies." S. Rep. 99-541, at 4. Moreover, the advent of the ECPA was precipitated by concerns about advancements in technology and the desire to protect personal and business information which individuals can no longer "lock away" with ease. The plain language of § 2703(f) permits only the preservation of emails in the service provider's possession at the time of the request, not the preservation of future emails. Moreover, the Department of Justice, along with some theorists, emphasize that these requests "have no prospective effect." . . . I find this statutory interpretation persuasive.

Following NuVox's policy, the provider would have destroyed Warshak's old emails but for the government's request that they maintain all current and prospective emails for almost a year without Warshak's knowledge. In practice, the government used the statute as a means to monitor Warshak after the investigation started without his knowledge and without a warrant. Such a practice is no more than back-door wiretapping. I doubt that such actions, if contested directly in court, would withstand the muster of the Fourth Amendment. Email, much like telephone, provides individuals with a means to communicate in private. . . . The government cannot use email collection as a means to monitor citizens without a warrant anymore than they can tap a telephone line to monitor citizens without a warrant. The purpose of § 2703, along with the Stored Communications Act as a whole, is to maintain the boundaries between a citizen's reasonable expectation of privacy and crime prevention in light of quickly advancing technology. To interpret § 2703(f) as having both a retroactive and prospective effect would be contrary to the purpose of the statute as a whole.

While it was not the issue in today's decision, a policy whereby the government requests emails prospectively without a warrant deeply concerns me. I am furthermore troubled by the majority's willingness to disregard the current reading of § 2703(f) without concern for future analysis of this statute. Nevertheless, because the government's violation of the Fourth Amendment stems from the order and/or subpoena to obtain Warshak's email communications pursuant to § 2703(b) and (d), the government acted in good faith upon the statute. The fact that their policy likely exceeded the parameters of § 2703(f) is irrelevant to this analysis as they did not rely upon § 2703 as a whole in requesting the secret subpoena and order to obtain these emails. Accordingly, the majority was correct in holding that the evidence falls within the good faith exception to the exclusionary rule.

Index

Cybersecurity Law, Second Edition. Jeff Kosseff.
© 2020 John Wiley & Sons, Inc. Published 2020 by John Wiley & Sons, Inc.
Companion Website: www.wiley.com/go/kosseff/cybersecurity2e